# Greenberg's
### GUIDES

# LIONEL® TRAINS
## POCKET PRICE GUIDE

Edited by Roger Carp

KALMBACH BOOKS

**Kalmbach Books**
21027 Crossroads Circle
Waukesha, Wisconsin 53186
www.kalmbach.com/books

Published in 2010
Thirty-first Edition

Manufactured in the United States of America

ISBN: 978-0-89778-539-6

Front cover photo: Model 2360 Pennsylvania GG1 electric
locomotive cataloged in 1956-58 and 1961-63, provided by
Joe Algozzini

Back cover photo: Model 3619 helicopter reconnaissance car
cataloged in 1962-64

We constantly strive to improve Greenberg's Pocket Price Guides
you find missing items or detect misinformation, please contact
Send your comments, new information, or corrections via e-ma
to books@kalmbach.com or by mail to Lionel Pocket Price Guic
Editor at the address above.

# Railroad names

| | |
|---|---|
| LV | Lehigh Valley |
| 'ID&W | Minnesota, Dakota & Western |
| MKT | Missouri-Kansas-Texas |
| N&S | Minneapolis, Northfield & Southern |
| MP | Missouri Pacific |
| MPA | Maryland & Pennsylvania |
| MILW | Milwaukee Road |
| M&StL | Minneapolis & St. Louis |
| NC&StL | Nashville, Chattanooga & St. Louis |
| NdeM | Nacionales de Mexico Railway |
| NH | New Haven |
| NKP | Nickel Plate Road |
| NP | Northern Pacific |
| NS | Norfolk Southern |
| N&W | Norfolk & Western |
| NYC | New York Central |
| NYNH&H | New York, New Haven & Hartford |
| NYO&W | New York, Ontario & Western |
| PC | Penn Central |
| P&E | Peoria & Eastern |
| P&LE | Pittsburgh & Lake Erie |
| PRR | Pennsylvania Railroad |
| RF&P | Richmond, Fredericksburg & Potomac |
| RI | Rock Island |
| SMARRCO | San Manuel Arizona Railroad Company |
| SP | Southern Pacific |
| SP&S | Spokane, Portland & Seattle |
| TA&G | Tennessee, Alabama & Georgia |
| TH&B | Toronto, Hamilton & Buffalo |
| T&P | Texas & Pacific |
| TP&W | Toledo, Peoria & Western |
| UP | Union Pacific |
| V&TRR | Virginia & Truckee Railroad |
| W&ARR | Western & Atlantic Railroad |
| WM | Western Maryland |
| WP | Western Pacific |

# Build your toy train library

## *Classic Toy Trains* magazine

Captures your imagination and sparks your enthusiasm for toy trains! Issues include reviews of the latest locomotives and accessories, track planning ideas, great photos of the best layouts, and information on collecting.

**9 issues/year**

## Greenberg's *Repair and Operating Manual for Lionel Trains, 1945–1969, 7th Edition*

Offers more than a thousand repair and maintenance tips for Lionel locomotives, operating cars, accessories, transformers, light bulbs, and switches. Provides Lionel technical advice as well as handy techniques submitted by toy train collectors and operators.

**10-8160 • $24.95**

## *Lionel Accessories at Work on Toy Train Layouts*

Add classic accessories to your toy train layout! Lionel's electronic accessory items from the 1940s and 1950s through the present day have been very popular with toy train enthusiasts. Former *Classic Toy Trains* editor Neil Besougloff helps you incorporate these accessories, both originals and modern reproductions, into your layout.

**10-8355 • $17.95**

# CONTENTS

## The latest and greatest guide

Welcome to the latest edition of what hobbyists regard as the most authoritative and trusted price guide for toy trains and accessories manufactured by the company now known as Lionel LLC. Whether you are a longtime Lionel enthusiast or a newcomer to the toy train hobby, you'll find the information needed to identify and evaluate thousands of items made by Lionel between 1901 and 2011. Most of all, you will have at your fingertips the most up-to-date prices for locomotives, freight cars, passenger cars, stations, tunnels, signals, track sections, transformers, and other items.

The *Lionel Pocket Price Guide 1901-2011* contains information on just about every toy train product marketed by Lionel since it brought out its first trains in 1901. Lionel has, with the exception of two years during World War II when federal restrictions prevented it from manufacturing toy trains (1943 and 1944), continued to bring out innovative and entertaining models ever since.

## What is listed and what isn't

Almost every Lionel toy train produced over the years is listed in the pages that follow. The only notable items not included are the boxed train sets (what Lionel referred to as *outfits*) offered just prior to and after World War II. These outfits are omitted because, to be considered complete, they must have all the items, including ancillary ones, that Lionel packed with them. Furthermore, they should be in their original boxes. This level of completeness puts outfits beyond the scope of this pocket guide.

Also left out of this pocket guide are some rare items that have surfaced. These unique pieces include mock-ups of products that were assembled by members of Lionel's Engineering Department. They include models created for company executives to evaluate different paint and lettering schemes. These items, some of which are truly one of a kind, are considered so scarce that values cannot be assigned to them.

Lionel marketed smaller HO scale trains between 1957 and 1966 and from 1974 to 1977. None of these locomotives and cars are included in this price guide nor are Lionel's large scale models.

This edition of the *Lionel Pocket Price Guide* contains information about new additions to the product line as described in Lionel catalogs, press releases, and other sources. Any additions that Lionel makes to its line after this book is printed will be reported in the 2012 edition.

In addition, the *Lionel Pocket Price Guide* provides information about items associated with Lionel yet not mentioned in its catalogs. These uncataloged or promotional items include unique train sets and specially decorated locomotives and cars that Lionel produces for national and regional toy train collecting and operating groups, museums, local railroad clubs, and other customers.

## Models not listed in the guide

As hard as the contributors and editors try to make this guide complete, they occasionally miss something. If you discover a Lionel model that is not listed here, there are a few steps to take.

First, determine whether or not Lionel made it. Somewhere on almost every locomotive, car, and accessory, Lionel placed a mark to identify itself as the manufacturer.

Then, verify that your item was either a part of the cataloged line or a promotional piece offered by a toy train organization, museum, or other group. This process involves finding a reference to it in a Lionel catalog or in paperwork available from the sponsor.

Check that your item is legitimate by asking the opinion of other toy train enthusiasts, including dealers and hobby shop owners. Contact hobbyists with experience and knowledge of Lionel trains.

Once you are sure that you have a legitimate and original item, send a description and a color photograph of it to Kalmbach Publishing Co.

## When to consult this guide

Many readers of the *Lionel Pocket Price Guide* use it after the fact. They already have some trains and accessories and now want to identify and evaluate those items. Maybe someone lucked upon a bridge at a garage sale and wants to know whether it's a 300 Hell Gate or a 314 deck girder type. Somebody else needs to provide his or her insurance agent with a complete list of O gauge locomotives that includes their conditions and current values. This guide contains the information needed to identify that bridge as well as determining present values for that engine roster.

In addition, the *Lionel Pocket Price Guide* can help you think about what to acquire in the future. That's really when the fun begins! You just have to spend some time considering how you want to approach the hobby. Collect, operate, or both? Prewar, postwar, or modern? Particular types of locomotives or cars? Favorite railroads? Promotional items?

Once you have a general idea of how to enjoy this hobby, you can make informed decisions about which trains you want.

| Number | Description | Condition ——— Good | Exc | Cond/$ |
|---|---|---|---|---|
| **2561** | *Vista Valley* Observation Car, *59–61*\* | 130 | 300 | ___ |
| **X6454** | NYC Boxcar, *48* | | | |
| | (A) Brown body | 24 | 52 | ___ |
| | (B) Orange body | 44 | 131 | ___ |
| | (C) Tan body | 21 | 43 | ___ |
| **6475** | Libby's Crushed Pineapple Vat Car, *63 u* | 25 | 75 | ___ |

## Identifying a catalog number

A Lionel catalog number is usually stamped, printed, engraved, or painted on an item. However, some products do not contain a catalog number. In these cases, you can match the product with its catalog number through a comprehensive reference book, such as one of Greenberg's Guide To books, or various websites including www.Lionel.com, where you can find past and current catalogs.

Two-, three-, and four-digit numbers predominated during the prewar and postwar periods. Four- and five-digit numbers have been most common during the modern era.

On the models, catalog numbers often double as road numbers, which were added to locomotives and cars to enhance an item's realism. Sometimes separate road numbers were added. Lionel also placed other numbers on its rolling stock to make it look more realistic. Numbers having a prefix of HT or WT refer to the height and weight of the full-sized prototype on which a car was modeled. A Built date or a New date does not necessarily indicate the actual year Lionel made or cataloged a car.

## Locating an item

Each section is arranged in numerical order by catalog numbers. Items with one or more zeroes as placeholders are listed before numbers without placeholders. For example, a 042 pair of switches is found in front of a 42 electric locomotive.

In the prewar and postwar sections, some items such as transformers and track pieces, are identified by a letter. These products follow the numbered items, and products without numbers are also found at the end of the section.

## Reading an entry

Every entry begins with the product's catalog number assigned by Lionel. (Club and special production cars may have numbers that were assigned by the group.)

A basic description of the model follows. It gives the type of product, lists the name of any railroad identified with it, and includes identifying characteristics, such as color or lettering. If the item has a road number that differs from its catalog number, that number is shown in quotation marks. Abbreviations used in the descriptions, including those of railroad names, are listed at the back of the price guide.

Next, you'll find the year or years during which that item was part of Lionel's cataloged product line. The years are shown in italics. If a year is followed by a *u*, then this item is considered to be uncataloged. It was not part of the cataloged line but was a promotional item that Lionel made or sponsored for an outside business or group.

Some entries show an asterisk (*) after the year, which means that one or more reissues of the item have been made. Lionel reissues of prewar Standard and O gauge trains and accessories appear in Section 4.

Many entries feature variations, each indicated by a separate letter (A, B, and so forth). Variations amount to slight yet noteworthy differences in appearance that distinguish models that otherwise seem identical. These differences can relate to color, lettering, and details that were added or deleted. For items having many variations, an entry may not include every variation.

An entry concludes with an indication of the value of the item for several common conditions.

## Condition

Lionel enthusiasts should be familiar with the condition and grading standards established by the Train Collectors Association, which are used as the basis for evaluating the condition of toy trains and accessories:

**C-10 Mint:** brand new—all original, unused, and unblemished.

**C-9 Factory New:** same condition as Mint but with evidence of factory rubs or slight signs of handling, shipping, and being test run at the factory.

**C-8 Like New:** complete and all original with no rust or no missing parts; may show effects of being displayed or signs of age and may have been run.

**C-7 Excellent:** all original and may have minute scratches and paint nicks; no rust, no missing parts, and no distortion of component parts.

**C-6 Very Good:** has minor scratches, paint nicks, or minor spots of surface rust; is free of dents and may have minor parts replaced.

**C-5 Good:** shows evidence of heavy use and signs of play wear—small dents, scratches, minor paint loss, and minor surface rust.

**C-4** **Fair:** shows evidence of heavy use—scratches and dents, moderate paint loss, missing parts, and surface rust.

**C-3** **Poor:** requires major body repair and is a candidate for restoration; major rust, missing parts, and heavily scratched.

**C-2** **Restoration:** needs to be restored.

**C-1** **Junk:** parts value only.

In this guide, values are listed for prewar and postwar trains in Good (C-5) and Excellent (C-7) conditions. For modern-era trains, including special production and club cars, the values for Excellent (C-7) and Mint (C-10) are shown.

You may also see NRS listed as a value in the guide. NRS (No Reported Sales) refers to an item for which no adequate pricing data is available. Typically, these items are so scarce that only a handful have been reported.

## Determining a model's condition

Look over a model carefully to see whether it has suffered serious damage, including warping and breaking. Then note whether any parts are missing. Feel for dents in metal and cracks in plastic. Check for areas marred by rust, mildew, or chipped paint.

The TCA condition standards will assist you in evaluating your model, such as deciding whether a prewar or postwar model falls below Good or above Excellent.

The assessment of a toy train's value is based on the expectations that it has not been modified and that all parts are present and original to it. Repainting or relettering a model seriously undermines a train's value, regardless of how beat-up and scratched it may have been before undergoing modification. Any model that has been altered should be labeled as a restoration; potential buyers deserve to be informed about how it has been modified, so they do not mistake it for an original.

A model that is missing some parts should be sold as is or have those parts replaced by identical originals. A tank car cataloged in 1935 that needs a brake wheel must have a part from 1935 put on it to be considered a true original. Adding a brake wheel from 1936 undermines the car's legitimacy as much as adding one from 2010 does.

The same rule applies to the ancillary items that came with various models. The value of a flatcar may depend largely on the miniature airplane or rocket packed with it; therefore, having a load that is a genuine original is essential to maintaining the value of that flatcar. Similarly, freight loaders must have whatever cargo came with them (coal, logs, trailers, and so forth). Reproductions should be identified as such.

The *Lionel Pocket Price Guide* has been divided into six major sections. The first three are based on the time period associated with a particular item's manufacture. Spend any amount of time among knowledgeable Lionel hobbyists and you're sure to hear them toss around the terms *prewar*, *postwar*, and *modern*. These general terms refer to the period when a train or other item was described or pictured in a Lionel catalog.

The first two sections use World War II as a dividing point. Prewar fits anything cataloged by Lionel from its initial line in 1901 to 1942, when federal restrictions curtailed toy train production. Postwar fits anything cataloged from 1945 to 1969.

In 1969, the Lionel Corp. leased the rights to manufacture and market its trains to General Mills, an act that effectively concluded the postwar period of Lionel's history. What hobbyists refer to as the modern era now covers 40 years.

Purpose categorizes Sections 4 and 5. A particular item could be a reissue of an older one or an item produced to benefit a club or an organization but was not publicized in Lionel catalogs.

Original product boxes constitute a separate section.

## Section 1: Prewar 1901-1942

Section 1 of the *Lionel Pocket Price Guide* is devoted to the prewar period. The entries cover just about every train, accessory, and transformer associated with Lionel's line during its first 42 years.

The only outfits listed are those of articulated streamlined trains that consist of a powered unit and attached unpowered cars.

In an item's listing, the basic description specifies its gauge (the distance between the inside of the outermost rails). During this time, Lionel catalogued models in four sizes. It is noted in parentheses whether an item is 2⅞-inch, Standard (2⅛ inches), O (1¼ inches), or OO (¾ inches). O gauge models intended to run on tighter 27-inch-diameter track belong to Lionel's O27 gauge line and are identified as such.

Transformers, rheostats, and many accessories were not limited to a single gauge, so their descriptions do not specify a gauge.

## Section 2: Postwar 1945-1969

Section 2 concentrates on the postwar period. Nearly every train and accessory (except outfits) that Lionel cataloged between 1945 and 1969 has its own listing. By this time, Lionel no longer made trains in 2⅞-inch, Standard, or OO gauge. Instead, it offered trains that ran on track that had a diameter of either 31 inches (O gauge) or 27 inches (O27 gauge). However, the entries in this section do not distinguish between O and O27 since only a handful of locomotives and cars could operate solely on the wider curves.

## Section 3: Modern era 1970-2011

Section 3 shows the trains (including outfits), accessories, transformers, and other items that Lionel has cataloged since 1970. The modern era encompasses the products of three companies: Model Products Corp. (MPC, a division of General Mills), 1970-85; Lionel Trains Inc. (LTI), 1986-95; and Lionel LLC (LLC), 1996-2011.

These incarnations of Lionel are responsible for an enormous inventory of trains, transformers, and accessories. Cataloged and uncataloged O gauge items (ranging from the near-scale Standard O to the toy-like O27) can be found within the pages of this section, while reissues of prewar Standard and O gauge items appear in Section 4.

All items in Section 3 are arranged according to their Lionel catalog number (omitting the number 6 used as a prefix). The descriptions of products made during the modern era may include information that relates to where in the product line a particular item belongs. Models derived from MPC designs have been described as *traditional*. Rolling stock whose dimensions and features approach scale realism may be designated as Standard O (abbreviated as std O). Locomotives equipped with TrainMaster Command Control are identified as such, often with the abbreviation CC.

## Section 4: Modern tinplate

Section 4 covers a category of modern-era trains that is referred to as modern tinplate. Here you'll find reissues of Standard and O gauge trains and accessories dating from the prewar period that LTI and LLC brought out for the purpose of satisfying a growing market. Also included in this section are a few Standard gauge trains that Lionel LLC has created, based on new designs.

# Section 5: Club cars and special production

Section 5 gathers the various items, principally locomotives and rolling stock, that Lionel has made or sponsored for different hobby organizations, museums, and businesses since the 1970s. These uncataloged club cars and special production items are arranged according to the groups that offered them for sale. Those groups are listed alphabetically; regional divisions of national organizations follow the parent organization's listing. Within each subordinate section, items are listed in a numerical (not chronological) order, with a basic description similar to that used for cataloged entries.

# Section 6: Boxes

Over the past 20 years, original boxes and other forms of packaging have assumed significance for some collectors. These hobbyists insist that the trains they buy come in the boxes and have the paperwork and ancillary pieces (inserts, instruction sheets, and envelopes) that the manufacturer packed with them before offering them for sale.

Cardboard boxes, inserts, and assorted sheets of paper are more fragile than die-cast metal or plastic trains. They were also deemed to be less important to the children playing with toy trains long ago and so were not treated with the same care. Instruction sheets were lost, and boxes were discarded. As a result, fewer boxes and instruction sheets have survived than have the trains and accessories that went with them. In some cases, the box that a particular locomotive, car, or even outfit came in is now valued above the item itself.

Boxes are evaluated according to standards and conditions established by the Train Collectors Association, similar to those developed for toy trains and accessories:

**P-10 Mint:** Brand new, complete, all original as manufactured, and unused. Flaps appear to never have been opened, and edges are crisp. No tears, fading, or wear marks. Contains original contents and all applicable sealing tape, wrap, and staples.

**P-9 Store New:** Complete, all original, and unused. Box may have merchant additions such as store stamps and price tags. Must have appropriate inner liners.

**P-8 Like New:** Complete and all original. There is evidence of light use and aging. Box may have notations (discrete) added since leaving the manufacturer.

**P-7 Excellent:** Complete and all original. Box shows moderate signs of being opened and closed including edge and corner wear. All flaps must be intact.

**P-6** **Very Good:** Complete and all original. Box shows signs of usage such as minor abrasions, small tears, color changes, and minor soiling. Inner liners may be missing, and inner flaps may require strengthening. The box can still safely store its original contents.

**P-5** **Good:** Box shows substantial wear, and edges may be damaged. Box may have extensive color fading but no evident water damage or cardboard deterioration. Exterior flaps are present, but their connection to the box may require repair. Inner liners may be missing. With care, the box can still store contents. (Any box that has been repaired cannot be graded above P-5.)

**P-4** **Fair:** Box shows heavy damage and may have been repaired. Inner flaps may be missing. Box cannot store its original contents. Water damage may be present.

Values for postwar boxes in this section are shown for Good (P-5) and Excellent (P-7) conditions. Box types include

**Art Deco:** Original postwar box with bold orange and blue design and lettering. Used 1946 and 1947.

**Classic:** More understated design than Art Deco. Was main component box from 1948 through 1958. Can be divided into Early (1948-49), Middle (1949-55), and Late (1956-58) Classic designs, which are marked by minor lettering changes.

**Orange Perforated:** Was a significant change from the Classic design. Solid orange box features white lettering and a tear-out perforated front panel. Used 1959 and 1960.

**Orange Picture:** Instead of a perforated panel, this version of the Orange Perforated box features an illustration of a steam locomotive and F3 diesel on the front. It was used 1961 to 1964.

**Hillside Orange Picture:** Similar to an Orange Picture box, it is labeled with Hillside, N.J., where Lionel's plant was located. It was used in 1965.

**Cellophane:** Used in 1966, this box features a clear cellophane window on the front.

**Hagerstown Checkerboard:** Has a Lionel checkerboard pattern and Hagerstown, Maryland, printed on end flap bottoms. Used in 1968.

**Hillside Checkerboard:** 1969 box is same as Hagerstown Checkerboard but with Hillside, New Jersey, printed on it.

Lionel also used brown corrugated and plain white boxes.

Every user of the *Lionel Pocket Price Guide* wants to know how the values are ascertained. There's nothing mysterious or arbitrary about the process. Over the years, we at Kalmbach Publishing Co. have gained the cooperation of many dealers and hobbyists, some of whom serve on our national review panel. These knowledgeable individuals share information about the trains and accessories they have bought and sold. They report on transactions conducted at meets across the United States, in retail outlets, and at live and online auctions. The editors of this guide study the information and supplement it with data from the publications of hobby groups that relates to buying and selling Lionel trains.

The values presented here are an averaged reflection of prices for items bought and sold across the country over the year prior to the publication of this edition. These values are offered as guidelines and should be viewed as starting points that buyers and sellers can use to begin informed and reasonable negotiations.

In a listing, the value of a steam locomotive includes a tender, even if the tender is not listed in detail. The value of steam locomotives, particularly prewar items, may be affected significantly by the type of tender included.

Values for individual items may differ from what is listed in this price guide due to a few key factors. Where collectible trains are scarce and demand outruns supply, actual values may exceed what is shown. Values may also rise where certain items are especially popular, often because of their road names. And as with all collectibles, national and local economic conditions will impact values, which tend to drop when times are tough and demand falls.

Another factor influencing what a toy train is worth relates to the venue in which it is being sold. Antiques dealers generally ask more for an item than do folks putting it out at a garage sale. Mail-order and retail outlets tend to charge more for trains than do individuals at shows because they need to be compensated for the additional costs generated by operating a store, compiling and distributing price lists, and packing and shipping trains. Of course, the cost of any item can balloon far beyond its listed value when two or more people compete for it at a live or online auction.

## Original packaging

When the first editions of this guide were published, less interest in boxes existed. That has since changed, although the consensus of opinion holds that only items in Like New or better condition require their original packaging to maintain their high level of value. For that reason and because demand for boxes and related paperwork affects only the top echelons of collecting, the values given for items in Good and Excellent condition are not based on the expectation that a box and other associated items are present.

Items that do have their original packaging, especially if it is complete and undamaged, command a premium among collectors of prewar and postwar trains. No hard-and-fast rules can be stated as to how much higher their value is over the same items in Excellent condition. Generally speaking, though, boxed items in Like New condition are valued about 50 percent above the same item without a box.

## Using the values

The values listed should be considered to be what a consumer would pay—more or less—to get a particular item in a specific condition. One collector selling that item to another would probably ask the stated value and expect to get something close to it.

However, someone selling that same item to a person or business that intends to resell it (a train dealer) is unlikely to receive the stated value. Experience shows that sellers get about half the amount. Dealers offer less than the stated value so that they can then raise their asking price in hopes of earning a profit when reselling an item.

Regardless of whether you are buying or selling a toy train, you should proceed with care and acquire as much knowledge as you can. Start by consulting this price guide and then, if possible, learn more about the item that interests you. You can read more about it in one of the comprehensive reference guides on toy trains and ask more experienced hobbyists for their opinion about the item's condition and value.

The chances are pretty good that, if you've made it this far in the price guide, you already have a strong interest in toy trains. Perhaps you discovered your grandfather's Lionel accessories in the family attic and are attempting to determine their value. Maybe you received a Lionel outfit as a child and are trying to piece together what you remember playing with. Or you could be looking for a new hobby.

You've come to the right place! Enjoying toy trains is something that you can do by yourself or with family members and friends.

## Finding a specialty

Reasons to collect and operate Lionel trains and accessories abound. Some hobbyists are motivated by nostalgia. Other enthusiasts have fun restoring beat-up models. Buying and selling trains for a profit drives some others. Once you decide why you like Lionel trains, you can make some decisions about which items you want to collect or operate.

Many hobbyists choose to specialize and profess to having a favorite era of Lionel history. The post-World War II decades, when Lionel trains were the finest and most sophisticated toy a child could receive, boast the largest following among Lionel enthusiasts. Other people, including many who were born long after World War II, vote for prewar trains. Some opt for the beauty and heft of Standard gauge, and others enjoy the colorful, toy-like models that characterized Lionel's O and O27 gauge lines.

The modern era of Lionel production is gaining more supporters, thanks to the tremendous variety of trains manufactured over the past 40 years. You can specialize in modern tinplate (and venture into the prewar period for original versions of these contemporary reissues). You can focus on a particular railroad and fill your train room with Illinois Central, New Haven, or Southern Pacific locomotives and rolling stock. You can acquire only steam locomotives, only boxcars, only freight loaders, or any other "only" that pleases you.

## Finding and buying items

After compiling a list of what you're looking for—or at least have in mind a train or two that you'd love to own—you're ready to join the hunt. The information in this price guide will assist you when attending train meets, visiting hobby shops, and bidding in online auctions.

Some hobbyists report making great finds by combing through boxes at estate and garage sales or by placing ads for old trains in newspapers and magazines. By and large, however, you're less likely to discover an outfit in a private home or the bargain bin of a charitable group. Those sources, once so rich for collectors, are rapidly drying up.

What has jumped in importance for individuals buying and selling toy trains in recent years is the Internet. Rather than spread out their inventory on tables at a meet, people are depending on online auction sites to sell their trains. Buyers benefit because they no longer have to travel to search for the trains they want. Investigations can be conducted from your living room at any hour of the day.

The starting point when you're buying any toy train is to proceed with care and knowledge. If the train is not accessible, gather as much information as you can from pictures and descriptions of what's being offered.

And pose questions about the item. Don't hesitate to ask the seller about a car's condition or a locomotive's performance. (At some train meets, the sponsor sets up a short track for testing locomotives.) Find out whether an outfit that's said to be complete has all its components, including paperwork. Discover whether an item purported to be original has been restored, right down to its couplers, trucks, and load.

Longtime hobbyists prefer to deal with individuals they know and have done business with previously. Newcomers should look to their more experienced friends and associates for guidance here, although most regular dealers conduct business fairly and honestly and so encourage customers to return. When buying from someone online, check the feedback that the seller has been given, so you know whether previous customers believe they have been treated fairly and professionally.

Let's suppose that you have ample information about an item that you want. All your questions have been answered. You're satisfied with its condition and performance. And you understand that it is being sold as-is. What you do next depends on where you are.

If you're attending a train meet or yard sale, you can either pay the ticketed price or, as is the practice, make an offer 10 to 20 percent below it. Some sellers stick firmly to their asking price. Others enjoy the negotiating and recognize that they'll have to make a slight concession to close the deal.

If you're buying a train at a hobby shop, dickering over prices is less common, especially when the item purchased is brand new or in current production.

If you're participating in a live or online auction, be sure you have a firm sense of how much you can reasonably bid. And remember to factor in any shipping, insurance, and miscellaneous costs.

## Caring for your trains

What you do with your Lionel trains and accessories once you acquire them is up to you. Arranging them on open shelving for the world to admire is one choice; putting them on a layout is another. Either way, however, your new prizes will gradually gather dust and maybe a bit of moisture. The lighting you install may affect their finish.

Should you be worried about your trains fading, corroding, or disintegrating? Not really. The metals that Lionel used (sheet as well as die-cast) and the types of plastic have, by and large, stood the test of time. So has the applied lettering and the paints sprayed over the frames and chassis. Lionel trains and accessories are rugged and durable, so the chances of them being damaged under normal conditions are small.

Still, your peace of mind will be made greater if you take some simple precautions when displaying and storing your trains, regardless of their age, materials, and value.

**Temperature:** Maintain your train room at an even and moderate temperature. Install a thermometer to ensure the room stays between 55 and 72 degrees Fahrenheit.

**Humidity:** Have one dehumidifier running at all times in your train room. Use two dehumidifiers if you store your models in a basement, where water vapor can cause metal parts to rust. Buy a hygrometer (available from hardware stores and home improvement centers) to measure the humidity, which should be kept at 50 to 60 percent.

**Cleaning:** Items kept out on shelves or a layout should be cleaned on a regular basis. Use a soft brush or a can of compressed air to remove dust. If a more thorough cleaning is necessary, use warm water and a mild soap (liquid dishwashing detergent works well). Avoid dampening lettering and decals that may be marred by the water. Finish by drying everything carefully with a warm cloth towel or a hair dryer.

**Wrapping:** Items not on display or in operation should be stored with care. Start by drying anything you plan to store with a warm cloth towel. When all the moisture has been removed, wrap sheet metal and plastic items in two or three sheets of acid-free (alkaline) tissue paper. Do not wrap them in newspapers, plastic bubble wrap, or old clothes. Make sure to wrap flatcar loads separately, after removing elastic bands and tie-tapes.

**Labeling:** Once you have finished wrapping an item, add a note to identify it. Write down the catalog or product number, the type of model, and other pertinent data.

**Storing:** Place wrapped and labeled items inside the boxes they came in or in other storage boxes. Cover any staples or metal stabilizers in the boxes that can scratch your trains. Then place one or two packets of silica gel inside each box to reduce moisture, protecting the boxes from mold and mildew and the trains from rust. Store the trains in a cupboard, drawer, or other dark, dry area. Always keep them out of direct sunlight and fluorescent lighting.

## Insuring your trains

The protection you give individual models by cleaning and storing them properly in a climate-controlled environment should be matched by the protection you give your entire collection. Valuable toy trains should be insured against damage or theft.

**Information:** Contact your insurance agent or company and ask about collectible insurance riders or policies. Discuss the coverage and rates available. You can get information that applies specifically to toy train collections from agencies that advertise such policies in toy train magazines and publications put out by toy train collecting groups.

**Inventory:** Regardless of the size and value of your collection, it's smart to keep an up-to-date written inventory, which is required for most insurance policies. In addition, keep track of what you acquire to avoid purchasing duplicates.

Each entry should start with a description of the item, including its manufacturer, type of model, catalog number, year (if known), railroad name, color, original packaging (if relevant), and other important characteristics. Next, evaluate the item's condition. Finally, using this price guide, note the value of the item.

**Photos:** In addition to your written inventory, you may wish to photograph your entire collection or layout. At the very least, take pictures of the most significant and expensive items that you own to supplement the written descriptions. A digital camera works well for creating a visual record of what you have. A video camera can also be used for this task, but be sure to take your time and get sharp, complete photographs of each model.

**Policies:** Blanket policies can be obtained to provide general coverage, but they may limit the amount of protection.

Exclusions characterize just about every collectibles insurance plan. They can include gradual depreciation and deterioration; damage caused by cold, dampness, heat, or insects; dishonesty; and negligence.

Limitations also characterize just about every collectibles insurance plan. They can include newly acquired items, models in transit, and paper-related memorabilia.

Deductibles come with these policies, and the designated amount varies.

Costs of policies can differ, depending on the insurance company or the location where the collection is kept.

## Prewar trains and accessories

Nearly all the Lionel enthusiasts that specialize in prewar trains and accessories consider themselves collectors. Most of them acquire items that they display on shelves or in enclosed showcases. They search for items that share style or design traits or were part of a series of cataloged freight cars. The array of colors that Lionel used to paint its passenger cars fascinates some hobbyists, and they specialize in collecting them.

To be sure, some prewar fans do build layouts, especially around the holidays. Everyone gets a kick out of seeing an antique electric train rumbling around a circle of track. Prewar accessories enhance even the smallest model railroad, and with flashing lights and remote-controlled animation, they delight kids of all ages.

Regardless of the approach you take, here are a few observations about the current market for prewar Lionel trains.

First, the supply of prewar trains in all conditions on the market is increasing because the number of hobbyists who grew up with these trains is decreasing. Collections are hitting the market, and younger enthusiasts are finding great satisfaction in chasing after the colorful, toy-like models that Lionel cataloged more than 68 years ago.

Second, the demand for virtually any prewar Lionel item in Like New or better condition, especially if it has its original packaging, remains high. Perhaps the strongest segment of the current market consists of the scale and near-scale locomotives and rolling stock that Lionel introduced to its O gauge line in the late 1930s and early 1940s.

Also very hot right now are Standard gauge pieces, notably those that were cataloged during the classic era that lasted from the mid-1920s into the early 1930s. Accessories, principally the stations, bridges, tunnels, and railroad structures painted in bright colors, have never lost their appeal, especially for anyone planning a layout.

So how can you make inroads into the prewar market? If you want trains in Good or Excellent condition, you will find supplies—and bargains—to be plentiful. What the high-end collectors ignore may still look great in your train room or, even better, on a layout designed to capture the feel of a department store display from the Depression era.

Another smart move, besides relaxing your standards about condition, is to stray from the main line. Consider buying items other than those attracting the most attention. Small Standard gauge locomotives and passenger cars, lithographed O27 freight cars, and O gauge trains from the 1920s always seem to get short shrift when enthusiasts describe what they dream of owning. Learn more about these items and see how nice they look.

However, if you are determined to own examples of some of the finest prewar trains but have a fairly limited budget for hobby expenses, you need not go home empty-handed. The Modern Tinplate line that LTI and LLC developed featured reissues of outstanding Standard and O gauge trains and accessories. The gorgeous colors, shiny details, and superb motors of these updated versions make them perfect additions, especially for operators.

The Modern Tinplate line enabled hobbyists, younger ones in particular, to experience the joy of seeing prewar trains at their best. Some of these newcomers were then motivated to look for actual prewar pieces to complement their reissues.

Whether with originals or reissues, hobbyists who have a preference for prewar Lionel trains, especially Standard gauge, should find this a good time to specialize in these antiques. The supply appears to be increasing, and demand remains strong. Secondary fields offer bargains for those enthusiasts who enjoy collecting or even restoring old trains.

## Postwar trains and accessories

This is a curious time to be concentrating on postwar Lionel. On the one hand, serious collectors are paying record prices for Like New and Mint items, boxes are escalating in value, and demand for original and complete outfits, top-of-the-line locomotives, and scarce variations continues to rise.

On the other hand, the need that operators once felt to acquire postwar pieces to run on their O gauge layouts has all but vanished. Lionel catalogs continue to display a mind-boggling selection of steam and diesel locomotives and near-scale rolling stock that just gets greater every year.

As a result, folks who want to run trains can choose from models that promise superior performance and outstanding detail. Few enthusiasts can say that the postwar line surpassed what is available today, which is why operators are devouring new catalogs and paying less attention to what was offered 50 years ago.

Anyone who wants Good and even Excellent trains to display or operate will find that all but the most deluxe and exotic models are available in abundant supply and at affordable prices. Collectors with deep pockets and high standards may turn up their noses at common pieces as well as notable ones because those items are graded below Like New or do not come with all their original packaging.

So collectors willing to forgo a box and accept a scratch or paint chip may find items available that they once thought were beyond their aspirations. They may also benefit from the shift of operators away from postwar trains to contemporary ones. Operating cars, especially those models and road names that are considered fairly common, deserve more attention. In contrast, passenger cars continue to dazzle serious collectors, and so their prices have stayed at the same level or have even climbed.

Demand for certain items in the higher grades seems stronger, which means that those same trains and accessories in Good or possibly Excellent condition may be overlooked. For example, many of the items that Lionel cataloged in the late 1940s, particularly those at the upper end, continue to gain strength on the collector market. The same can be said of the less mundane motorized units, in particular, intact examples (most of the top motorized units show up with key parts broken or missing). Original and complete flatcar loads also draw attention, probably because reproductions (marked and unmarked) have inundated the market. Alco diesels and switchers command more interest as collectors search for models they had overlooked.

Now may be a great time to collect or operate postwar trains, provided you're willing to make a few compromises in the appearance, performance, and packaging of the locomotives, cars, and accessories you buy. Most F3 and Train Master diesels are available and so are Berkshire and small Hudson steam locomotives (be sure to get the correct tender). Nearly all the boxcars in the esteemed 6464 series can be found in good quantities through train shows, mail-order dealers, and Internet sites. Accessories also appear plentiful, so you can easily acquire the freight loaders, signals, bridges, and stations needed for a layout or a tabletop display at the holidays.

# Modern trains and accessories

Anyone who wants to assess the history of Lionel and the current state of the toy train hobby need only to observe the pages in this guide. The assorted trains and accessories that Lionel cataloged in the 42 years of the prewar period are covered in 40 pages and the trains of the 25-year postwar period in another 40 pages. But the modern era, covering the past 40 years, requires 200 pages to describe and present values for all the O and O27 items Lionel has produced. There is no doubt that, based on the huge variety of items available, today's toy train lovers are living in a golden age.

Flip through Section 3 and you'll come across models of every major type of steam or diesel locomotive and any kind of freight or passenger car imaginable. Railroads, large and small, prominent and forgotten, are represented.

Increasing numbers of Lionel enthusiasts are jumping on the contemporary bandwagon and buying trains of recent vintage to operate on their layouts. This trend doesn't mean that nobody is collecting modern-era trains. The boxcars and refrigerator cars put out by MPC to advertise brands of cigarettes, beer, and spirits are rising steadily in value. Demand is also growing for similar rolling stock decorated with the names of national fast food chains, candy, and local short lines that burst forth, only to disappear from the scene almost overnight.

While you're paging through the section on modern era trains, don't miss all the models that Lionel has decorated with beloved cartoon characters on them. Every Disney favorite has ridden over Lionel's three-rail track and so have the Simpsons and classic Warner Bros. characters. The recent *Christmas Story*, *Polar Express* and *Hogwarts Express* outfits also capture the attention of collectors of miniature trains, toys, and movie memorabilia.

Returning to the realm of more traditional railroad models, collectors have expanded their rosters of prized diesel locomotives by mixing postwar classics, such as F3s and Train Masters, with the new road names added to modern models. Each year, Lionel brings out numerous exciting new models and replicas of past models as well as producing items under the K-Line brand.

Nonetheless, it is the operators who have found real enjoyment. They have dozens of new locomotives to run and hundreds of cars to couple behind them. Better yet, the performance of these diesels and steamers have an added dimension of sophistication and excitement through Lionel's Legacy and TrainMaster systems of command control. Operators have adopted these great systems and seen how fun it can be to run trains without having to plant themselves at the handles of an ancient ZW transformer and a network of glowing remote-control switch machines.

What is remarkable about the modern era is the number of brand-new accessories that the engineering staff at Lionel has developed. Lionel's growing roster of structure kits and tractor-trailers has also made an impact on the O gauge model railroads that are being constructed. These items have retained their value, and demand for them continues to stay strong.

Additional evidence of the popularity of Lionel trains can be found in Section 5, which focuses on uncataloged club cars and special production items. Every year, more locomotives and cars are being used by groups to promote themselves. Because the size of the production run of these unique items is small, collectors and operators snap them up. If you're looking for bargains or something to spice up your roster, the promotional pieces listed in Section 5 will give you lots of possibilities.

| | | Good | Exc | Cond/$ |
|---|---|---|---|---|
| **001** | 4-6-4 Locomotive (OO), *38–42* | 195 | 395 | ____ |
| **1** | Bild-A-Motor (O), *28–31* | 60 | 140 | ____ |
| **1** | Trolley (std), *06–14* | | | |
| | (A) Cream body, orange band and roof | 1900 | 4750 | ____ |
| | (B) White body, blue band and roof | 1750 | 4750 | ____ |
| | (C) Cream body, blue band and roof | 1300 | 3150 | ____ |
| | (D) Cream body, blue band and roof, Curtis Bay | 2150 | 5550 | ____ |
| | (E) Blue, cream band, blue roof | 1450 | 3150 | ____ |
| **1/111** | Trolley Trailer (std), *06–14* | 1000 | 2700 | ____ |
| **002** | 4-6-4 Locomotive (OO), *39–42* | 160 | 315 | ____ |
| **2** | Bild-A-Motor (std), *28–31* | 100 | 180 | ____ |
| **2** | Trolley (std), *06–16\** | | | |
| | (A) Yellow, red band | 1200 | 2250 | ____ |
| | (B) Red, yellow band | 1200 | 2250 | ____ |
| **2/200** | Trolley Trailer (std), *06–16* | 1000 | 1800 | ____ |
| **003** | 4-6-4 Locomotive (OO), *39–42* | | | |
| | (A) 003W whistling Tender | 190 | 395 | ____ |
| | (B) 003T nonwhistling Tender | 175 | 355 | ____ |
| **3** | Trolley (std), *06–13* | | | |
| | (A) Cream, orange band | 1400 | 3100 | ____ |
| | (B) Cream, dark olive green band | 1400 | 3100 | ____ |
| | (C) Orange, dark olive green band | 1400 | 3100 | ____ |
| | (D) Dark green, cream windows | 1400 | 3100 | ____ |
| | (E) Green, cream windows, Bay Shore | 1650 | 3700 | ____ |
| **3/300** | Trolley Trailer (std), *06–13* | 1500 | 3500 | ____ |
| **004** | 4-6-4 Locomotive (OO), *39–42* | | | |
| | (A) 004W whistling Tender | 210 | 350 | ____ |
| | (B) 004T nonwhistling Tender | 190 | 310 | ____ |
| **4** | Electric Locomotive 0-4-0 (O), *28–32\** | | | |
| | (A) Orange, black frame | 550 | 875 | ____ |
| | (B) Gray, apple green stripe | 580 | 1050 | ____ |
| **4** | Trolley (std), *06–12* | | | |
| | (A) Cream, dark olive green band | 3000 | 4950 | ____ |
| | (B) Green or olive green, cream roof | 3000 | 4950 | ____ |
| **4U** | No. 4 Kit Form (O), *28–29* | 1150 | 1600 | ____ |

| | | Good | Exc | Cond/$ |
|---|---|---|---|---|
| **5** | 0-4-0 Locomotive, no tender, early (std), *06–07* | | | |
| | (A) NYC & HRR | 1000 | 1450 | ____ |
| | (B) Pennsylvania | 1400 | 2300 | ____ |
| | (C) NYC & HRRR (3 Rs) | 1250 | 2050 | ____ |
| | (D) B&O RR | 1500 | 2400 | ____ |
| **5** | 0-4-0 Locomotive, tender, early Special (std), *06–09* | 980 | 1300 | ____ |
| **5** | 0-4-0 Locomotive, no tender, later (std), *10–11* | 750 | 1150 | ____ |
| **5** | 0-4-0 Locomotive, tender, later Special (std), *10–11* | 920 | 1200 | ____ |
| **5/51** | 0-4-0 Locomotive, tender, latest (std), *12–23* | 800 | 1100 | ____ |
| **6** | 4-4-0 Locomotive (std), *06–23* | 860 | 1250 | ____ |
| **6** | 0-4-0 Locomotive Special (std), *08–09* | 2050 | 2950 | ____ |
| **7** | Steam 4-4-0 Locomotive (std), *10–23\** | 1850 | 2300 | ____ |
| **8** | Electric Locomotive 0-4-0 (std), *25–32* | | | |
| | (A) Maroon, brass windows and trim | 235 | 250 | ____ |
| | (B) Olive green or mojave, brass windows | 155 | 205 | ____ |
| | (C) Red, brass or cream windows | 195 | 250 | ____ |
| | (D) Peacock, orange windows | 520 | 750 | ____ |
| **8** | Trolley (std), *08–14\** | | | |
| | (A) Cream, orange band and roof | 3000 | 5400 | ____ |
| | (B) Dark green, cream windows | 3000 | 5400 | ____ |
| **8E** | Electric Locomotive 0-4-0 (std), *26–32* | | | |
| | (A) Mojave, brass windows and trim | 175 | 240 | ____ |
| | (B) Red, brass or cream windows | 150 | 225 | ____ |
| | (C) Peacock, orange windows | 370 | 590 | ____ |
| | (D) Pea green, cream stripe | 465 | 670 | ____ |
| **9** | Electric Locomotive 0-4-0 (std), *29\** | 1200 | 2150 | ____ |
| **9** | Motor Car (std), *09–12* | | NRS | ____ |
| **9** | Trolley (std), *09* | 3000 | 5400 | ____ |
| **9E** | Electric Locomotive (std), *28–35\** | | | |
| | (A) 0-4-0, orange | 700 | 1250 | ____ |
| | (B) 2-4-2, two-tone green | 880 | 1600 | ____ |
| | (C) 2-4-2, gunmetal gray | 860 | 1100 | ____ |
| **10** | Electric Locomotive 0-4-0 (std), *25–29\** | | | |
| **9U** | Electric Locomotive 0-4-0 Kit (std), *28–29* | 1050 | 1750 | ____ |
| | (A) Mojave, brass trim | 150 | 215 | ____ |
| | (B) Gray, brass trim | 125 | 205 | ____ |
| | (C) Peacock, brass inserts | 145 | 205 | ____ |
| | (D) Red, cream stripe | 580 | 880 | ____ |

| | | Good | Exc | Cond/$ |
|---|---|---|---|---|
| **10** | Interurban (std), *10–16* | | | |
| | (A) Maroon | 3000 | 5750 | ____ |
| | (B) Dark olive green | 1200 | 2150 | ____ |
| **10E** | Electric Locomotive 0-4-0 (std), *26–30* | | | |
| | (A) Olive green, black frame | | NRS | ____ |
| | (B) Peacock, dark green or black frame | 295 | 400 | ____ |
| | (C) State brown, dark green frame | 435 | 630 | ____ |
| | (D) Gray, black frame | 165 | 220 | ____ |
| | (E) Red, cream stripe | 620 | 890 | ____ |
| **011** | Switches, pair (O), *33–37* | 17 | 35 | ____ |
| **11** | Flatcar, early (std), *06–08* | 150 | 360 | ____ |
| **11** | Flatcar, later (std), *09–15* | 50 | 90 | ____ |
| **11** | Flatcar, latest (std), *16–18* | 50 | 90 | ____ |
| **11** | Flatcar, Lionel Corp. (std), *18–26* | 50 | 80 | ____ |
| **012** | Switches, pair (O), *27–33* | 21 | 42 | ____ |
| **12** | Gondola, early (std), *06–08* | 150 | 360 | ____ |
| **12** | Gondola, later (std), *09–15* | 50 | 100 | ____ |
| **12** | Gondola, latest (std), *16–18* | 45 | 70 | ____ |
| **12** | Gondola, Lionel Corp. (std), *18–26* | 50 | 70 | ____ |
| **013** | 012 Switches and 439 panel board, *27–33* | 120 | 190 | ____ |
| **13** | Cattle Car, early (std), *06–08* | 300 | 450 | ____ |
| **13** | Cattle Car, later (std), *09–15* | 150 | 225 | ____ |
| **13** | Cattle Car, latest (std), *16–18* | 65 | 115 | ____ |
| **13** | Cattle Car, Lionel Corp. (std), *18–26* | 65 | 115 | ____ |
| **0014** | Boxcar (OO), *38–42* | | | |
| | (A) Yellow, Lionel Lines | 80 | 155 | ____ |
| | (B) Tuscan, Pennsylvania | 50 | 75 | ____ |
| **14** | Boxcar, early (std), *06–08* | 195 | 435 | ____ |
| **14** | Boxcar, later (std), *09–15* | 80 | 105 | ____ |
| **14** | Boxcar, latest (std), *16–18* | 80 | 105 | ____ |
| **14** | Boxcar, Lionel Corp. (std), *18–26* | 80 | 105 | ____ |
| **0015** | Tank Car (OO), *38–42* | | | |
| | (A) Silver, Sun Oil | 40 | 90 | ____ |
| | (B) Black, Shell | 40 | 75 | ____ |
| **15** | Oil Car, early (std), *06–08* | 200 | 360 | ____ |
| **15** | Oil Car, later (std), *09–15* | 75 | 115 | ____ |
| **15** | Oil Car, latest (std), *16–18* | 75 | 115 | ____ |
| **15** | Oil Car, Lionel Corp. (std), *18–26* | 75 | 115 | ____ |
| **0016** | Hopper Car (OO), *38–42* | | | |
| | (A) Gray | 75 | 145 | ____ |
| | (B) Black | 75 | 115 | ____ |

| | | Good | Exc | Cond/$ |
|---|---|---|---|---|
| **16** | Ballast Dump Car, early (std), *06–11* | 400 | 700 | ____ |
| **16** | Ballast Dump Car, later (std), *09–15* | 95 | 175 | ____ |
| **16** | Ballast Dump Car, latest (std), *16–18* | 95 | 175 | ____ |
| **16** | Ballast Dump Car, Lionel Corp. (std), *18–26* | 95 | 175 | ____ |
| **0017** | Caboose (OO), *38–42* | 50 | 90 | ____ |
| **17** | Caboose, early (std), *06–08* | 220 | 440 | ____ |
| **17** | Caboose, later (std), *09–15* | 70 | 135 | ____ |
| **17** | Caboose, latest (std), *16–18* | 75 | 135 | ____ |
| **17** | Caboose, Lionel Corp. (std), *18–26* | 50 | 90 | ____ |
| **18** | Pullman Car (std), *08* | | | |
| | (A) Dark olive green, nonremovable roof | 700 | 2150 | ____ |
| | (B) Dark olive green, removable roof | 105 | 215 | ____ |
| | (C) Yellow-orange, removable roof | 315 | 870 | ____ |
| | (D) Orange, removable roof | 90 | 205 | ____ |
| | (E) Mojave, removable roof | 305 | 890 | ____ |
| **18** | Pullman Car (std), *11–13* | 600 | 900 | ____ |
| **18** | Pullman Car (std), *13–15* | 150 | 270 | ____ |
| **18** | Pullman Car (std), *15–18* | 150 | 270 | ____ |
| **18** | Pullman Car (std), *18–22* | 90 | 155 | ____ |
| **18** | Pullman Car (std), *23–26* | 270 | 530 | ____ |
| **19** | Combine Car (std), *08* | | | |
| | (A) Dark olive green, nonremovable roof | 1100 | 2600 | ____ |
| | (B) Dark olive green, removable roof | 90 | 145 | ____ |
| | (C) Yellow-orange, removable roof | 260 | 430 | ____ |
| | (D) Orange, removable roof | 115 | 205 | ____ |
| | (E) Mojave, removable roof | 305 | 890 | ____ |
| **19** | Combine Car (std), *11–13* | 600 | 900 | ____ |
| **19** | Combine Car (std), *13–15* | 200 | 270 | ____ |
| **19** | Combine Car (std), *15–18* | 200 | 270 | ____ |
| **19** | Combine Car (std), *18–22* | 90 | 155 | ____ |
| **19** | Combine Car (std), *23–26* | 265 | 520 | ____ |
| **020** | 90-degree Crossover (O), *15–42* | 2 | 5 | ____ |
| **020X** | 45-degree Crossover (O), *17–42* | 2 | 9 | ____ |
| **20** | 90-degree Crossover (std), *09–32* | 4 | 10 | ____ |
| **20** | Direct Current Reducer, *06* | | 195 | ____ |
| **20X** | 45-degree Crossover (std), *28–32* | 5 | 10 | ____ |
| **021** | Switches, pair (O), *15–37* | 20 | 48 | ____ |
| **21** | 90-degree Crossover (std), *06* | 10 | 18 | ____ |
| **21** | Switches, pair (std), *15–25* | 40 | 70 | ____ |
| **022** | Remote Control Switches, pair (O), *38–42* | 38 | 70 | ____ |
| **22** | Manual Switches, pair (std), *06–25* | 47 | 75 | ____ |

| | | Good | Exc | Cond/$ |
|---|---|---|---|---|
| **023** | Bumper (O), *15–33* | 15 | 37 | ____ |
| **23** | Bumper (std), *06–23* | 17 | 39 | ____ |
| **0024** | Pennsylvania Boxcar (OO), *39–42* | 45 | 75 | ____ |
| **24** | Railway Station (std), *06* | | NRS | ____ |
| **025** | Bumper (O), *28–42* | 22 | 33 | ____ |
| **0025** | Tank Car (OO), *39–42* | | | |
| | (A) Black, Shell | 40 | 90 | ____ |
| | (B) Silver, Sunoco | 40 | 80 | ____ |
| **25** | Open Station (std), *06* | | NRS | ____ |
| **25** | Bumper (std), *27–42* | 30 | 47 | ____ |
| **26** | Passenger Bridge (std), *06* | | 40 | ____ |
| **0027** | Caboose (OO), *39–42* | 40 | 70 | ____ |
| **27** | Lighting Set, *11–23* | 15 | 41 | ____ |
| **27** | Station (std), *09–12* | | NRS | ____ |
| **28** | Double Station with dome, *09–12* | | NRS | ____ |
| **29** | Day Coach (std), *07–22* | | | |
| | (A) Dark olive green, 9 windows | 1500 | 3000 | ____ |
| | (B) Maroon, 10 windows | 1200 | 1500 | ____ |
| | (C) Dark green, 10 windows | 3000 | 4500 | ____ |
| | (D) Dark olive green, 10 windows | 680 | 1000 | ____ |
| | (E) Dark green, 10 windows | 500 | 900 | ____ |
| **0031** | 2-rail 13" Curve Track (OO), *39–42* | 5 | 10 | ____ |
| **31** | Combine Car (std), *21–25* | | | |
| | (A) Maroon | 70 | 90 | ____ |
| | (B) Orange | 125 | 195 | ____ |
| | (C) Dark olive green | 70 | 90 | ____ |
| | (D) Brown | 75 | 95 | ____ |
| **0032** | 2-rail 12" Straight Track (OO), *39–42* | 10 | 15 | ____ |
| **32** | Mail Car (std), *21–25* | | | |
| | (A) Maroon | 85 | 125 | ____ |
| | (B) Orange | 120 | 185 | ____ |
| | (C) Dark olive green | 65 | 85 | ____ |
| | (D) Brown | 70 | 90 | ____ |
| **32** | Miniature Figures, *09–18* | 93 | 253 | ____ |
| **33** | Electric Locomotive 0-6-0, early (std), *13* | | | |
| | (A) Dark olive green, NYC in oval | 90 | 175 | ____ |
| | (B) Black, NYC | 440 | 950 | ____ |
| | (C) Dark olive green, NYC | 440 | 950 | ____ |
| | (D) Pennsylvania RR | 580 | 1250 | ____ |

| | | Good | Exc | Cond/S |
|---|---|---|---|---|
| **33** | Electric Locomotive 0-4-0, later (std), *13–24* | | | |
| | (A) Dark olive green or black, NYC | 105 | 170 | ____ |
| | (B) Black, lettered C&O | 395 | 720 | ____ |
| | (C) Maroon, red, or peacock | 340 | 620 | ____ |
| **0034** | 2-rail 13" Curve Track, electrical connectors (OO), *39–42* | 10 | 15 | ____ |
| **34** | Electric Locomotive 0-6-0, early (std), *12* | 520 | 860 | ____ |
| **34** | Electric Locomotive 0-4-0 (std), *13* | 200 | 385 | ____ |
| **35** | Pullman Car (std), *12–13* | | | |
| | (A) Dark blue | 470 | 900 | ____ |
| | (B) Dark olive green | 170 | 235 | ____ |
| **35** | Pullman Car (std), *14–16* | | | |
| | (A) Dark olive green, maroon windows | 50 | 70 | ____ |
| | (B) Maroon, green windows | 85 | 105 | ____ |
| | (C) Orange, maroon windows | 135 | 195 | ____ |
| **35** | Pullman Car (std), *15–18* | 50 | 70 | ____ |
| **35** | Pullman Car (std), *18–23* | | | |
| | (A) Dark olive green, maroon windows | 36 | 50 | ____ |
| | (B) Maroon, green windows | 30 | 45 | ____ |
| | (C) Orange, maroon windows | 120 | 210 | ____ |
| | (D) Brown, green windows | 36 | 50 | ____ |
| **35** | Boulevard Street Lamp, 6⅛" high, *40–42* | 25 | 50 | ____ |
| **35** | Pullman Car (std), *24* | 40 | 55 | ____ |
| **35** | Pullman Car (std), *25–26* | 40 | 55 | ____ |
| **36** | Observation Car (std), *12–13* | | | |
| | (A) Dark blue | 315 | 810 | ____ |
| | (B) Dark olive green | 145 | 205 | ____ |
| **36** | Observation Car (std), *14–16* | | | |
| | (A) Dark olive green, maroon windows | 70 | 95 | ____ |
| | (B) Maroon, green windows | 50 | 70 | ____ |
| | (C) Orange, maroon windows | 180 | 290 | ____ |
| | (D) Brown, green windows | 60 | 75 | ____ |
| **36** | Observation Car (std), *15–18* | 60 | 80 | ____ |
| **36** | Observation Car (std), *18–23* | | | |
| | (A) Dark olive green, maroon windows | 40 | 55 | ____ |
| | (B) Maroon, green windows | 40 | 55 | ____ |
| | (C) Orange, maroon windows | 130 | 215 | ____ |
| | (D) Brown, green windows | 40 | 55 | ____ |
| **36** | Observation Car (std), *24* | 40 | 55 | ____ |
| **36** | Observation Car (std), *25–26* | 40 | 55 | ____ |

| | | Good | Exc | Cond/$ |
|---|---|---|---|---|
| **38** | Electric Locomotive 0-4-0 (std), *13–24* | | | |
| | (A) Black | 100 | 135 | ____ |
| | (B) Red | 475 | 680 | ____ |
| | (C) Mojave or pea green | 405 | 540 | ____ |
| | (D) Dark green | 270 | 360 | ____ |
| | (E) Brown | 270 | 315 | ____ |
| | (F) Red, cream trim | 405 | 540 | ____ |
| | (G) Maroon | 170 | 270 | ____ |
| | (H) Gray | 110 | 125 | ____ |
| **41** | Accessory Contactor, *37–42* | 3 | 7 | ____ |
| **042** | Switches, pair (O), *38–42* | 17 | 39 | ____ |
| **42** | Electric Locomotive 0-4-4-0, square hood, early (std), *12\** | 760 | 1650 | ____ |
| **42** | Electric Locomotive 0-4-4-0, round hood, later (std), *13–23* | | | |
| | (A) Black or gray | 300 | 510 | ____ |
| | (B) Maroon | 1250 | 2050 | ____ |
| | (C) Dark gray | 375 | 600 | ____ |
| | (D) Dark green or mojave | 500 | 800 | ____ |
| | (E) Peacock | 1100 | 1800 | ____ |
| | (F) Olive or dark olive green | 750 | 1200 | ____ |
| **043/43** | Bild-A-Motor Gear Set, *29* | | 85 | ____ |
| **0044** | Boxcar (OO), *39–42* | 41 | 80 | ____ |
| **0044K** | Boxcar Kit (OO), *39–42* | 75 | 120 | ____ |
| **0045** | Tank Car (OO), *39–42* | | | |
| | (A) Black, Shell | 40 | 95 | ____ |
| | (B) Silver, Sunoco | 40 | 80 | ____ |
| **0045K** | Tank Car Kit (OO), *39–42* | 75 | 120 | ____ |
| **45N** | Automatic Gateman (std O), *37–42* | 40 | 89 | ____ |
| **0046** | Hopper Car (OO), *39–42* | 50 | 90 | ____ |
| **0046K** | Hopper Car Kit (OO), *39–42* | | | |
| | (A) Southern Pacific | 75 | 135 | ____ |
| | (B) Reading | | NRS | ____ |
| **46** | Crossing Gate, *39–42* | 75 | 120 | ____ |
| **0047** | Caboose (OO), *39–42* | 31 | 60 | ____ |
| **0047K** | Caboose Kit (OO), *39–42* | 75 | 135 | ____ |
| **47** | Crossing Gate, *39–42* | 70 | 140 | ____ |
| **48W** | Whistle Station, *37–42* | 22 | 65 | ____ |
| **49** | Lionel Airport, *37–39* | 160 | 410 | ____ |
| **50** | Airplane, *36–39* | 135 | 320 | ____ |

| | | Good | Exc | Cond/$ |
|---|---|---|---|---|
| **50** | Electric Locomotive 0-4-0 (std), *24* | | | |
| | (A) Dark green or dark gray | 145 | 250 | ____ |
| | (B) Maroon | 315 | 600 | ____ |
| | (C) Mojave | 175 | 345 | ____ |
| **50** | Cardboard Train, Cars, Accessory (O), *43\** | 200 | 360 | ____ |
| **0051** | 7" Curve Track (OO), *39–42* | 5 | 15 | ____ |
| **51** | 0-4-0 Locomotive, late, 8-wheel (std), *12–23* | 800 | 1150 | ____ |
| **51** | Lionel Airport, *36, 38* | 155 | 395 | ____ |
| **0052** | 7" Straight Track (OO), *39–42* | 10 | 15 | ____ |
| **52** | Lamp Post, *33–41* | 44 | 95 | ____ |
| **53** | Electric Locomotive 0-4-4-0, early (std), *12–14* | 1200 | 2450 | ____ |
| **53** | Electric Locomotive 0-4-0, later (std), *15–19* | | | |
| | (A) Maroon | 550 | 950 | ____ |
| | (B) Mojave | 670 | 1350 | ____ |
| | (C) Dark olive green | 560 | 1150 | ____ |
| **53** | Electric Locomotive 0-4-0, latest (std), *20–21* | 200 | 450 | ____ |
| **53** | Electric Locomotive 0-6-6-0, early (std), *11* | | NRS | ____ |
| **53** | Lamp Post, *31–42* | 33 | 49 | ____ |
| **0054** | 7" Curve Track, electrical connectors (OO), *39–42* | 10 | 15 | ____ |
| **54** | Electric Locomotive 0-4-4-0, early (std), *12\** | 2500 | 4050 | ____ |
| **54** | Electric Locomotive 0-4-4-0, late (std), *13–23* | 1800 | 2700 | ____ |
| **54** | Lamp Post, *29–35* | 50 | 67 | ____ |
| **55** | Airplane with stand, *37–39* | 190 | 520 | ____ |
| **56** | Lamp Post, removable lens and cap, *24–42* | 35 | 80 | ____ |
| **57** | Lamp Post with street names, *22–42* | 36 | 85 | ____ |
| **58** | Lamp Post, 7⅜" high, *22–42* | 33 | 48 | ____ |
| **59** | Lamp Post, 8¾" high, *20–36* | 40 | 85 | ____ |
| **060** | Telegraph Post (O), *29–42* | 13 | 23 | ____ |
| **60** | Telegraph Post (std), *20–28* | 13 | 23 | ____ |
| **60** | Electric Locomotive 0-4-0, FAO Schwartz (std), *15 u* | | NRS | ____ |
| **0061** | 7" Curve Track, tubular (OO), *38* | 3 | 8 | ____ |
| **61** | Lamp Post, one globe, *14–36* | 40 | 65 | ____ |
| **61** | Electric Locomotive 0-4-4-0, FAO Schwartz (std), *15 u* | | NRS | ____ |
| **0062** | 7" Straight Track, tubular (OO), *38* | 5 | 10 | ____ |
| **62** | Semaphore, *20–32* | 28 | 50 | ____ |
| **62** | Electric Locomotive 0-4-0, FAO Schwartz (std), *24–32 u* | | NRS | ____ |
| **0063** | Half Curve Track, tubular (OO), *38–42* | 8 | 15 | ____ |
| **63** | Semaphore, *15–21* | 25 | 50 | ____ |

| | | Good | Exc | Cond/$ |
|---|---|---|---|---|
| **63** | Lamp Post, two globes, *33–42* | 135 | 265 | ___ |
| **0064** | 7" Curve Track, tubular, electrical connectors (OO), *38* | 8 | 15 | ___ |
| **64** | Lamp Post, *40–42* | 37 | 70 | ___ |
| **64** | Semaphore, 6¾" high, *15–21* | 30 | 60 | ___ |
| **0065** | Half Straight Track, tubular (OO), *38–42* | 10 | 15 | ___ |
| **65** | Semaphore, one-arm, *15–26* | 30 | 60 | ___ |
| **65** | Whistle Controller, *35* | 5 | 7 | ___ |
| **0066** | 5⅝" Straight Track (OO), *38–42* | 10 | 15 | ___ |
| **66** | Semaphore, two-arm, *15–26* | 35 | 70 | ___ |
| **66** | Whistle Controller, *36–39* | 9 | 10 | ___ |
| **67** | Lamp Post, *15–32* | 85 | 145 | ___ |
| **67** | Whistle Controller, *36–39* | 4 | 8 | ___ |
| **068** | Warning Signal (O), *25–42* | 11 | 19 | ___ |
| **69N** | Electric Warning Signal (std O), *36–42* | 33 | 72 | ___ |
| **0070** | 90-degree Crossing, *38–42* | 5 | 10 | ___ |
| **70** | Outfit: 62 (2), 59 (1), 68 (1), *21–32* | 60 | 130 | ___ |
| **071** | 060 Telegraph Poles, 6 pieces (std), *24–42* | 70 | 160 | ___ |
| **71** | 60 Telegraph Post Set, 6 pieces, *21–31* | 70 | 160 | ___ |
| **0072** | Remote Control Switches, pair (OO), *38–42* | 175 | 288 | ___ |
| **0072L** | Remote Control Switch, left hand (OO), *38–42* | 50 | 95 | ___ |
| **0072R** | Remote Control Switch, right hand (OO) | 50 | 95 | ___ |
| **0074** | Boxcar (OO), *39–42* | 36 | 70 | ___ |
| **0075** | Tank Car (OO), *39–42* | 48 | 90 | ___ |
| **076** | Block Signal (O), *23–28* | 25 | 65 | ___ |
| **76** | Warning Bell and Shack, *39–42* | 65 | 179 | ___ |
| **0077** | Caboose (OO), *39–42* | 34 | 60 | ___ |
| **77/077** | Automatic Crossing Gate, *23–35* | 28 | 49 | ___ |
| **78/078** | Train Signal, *24–32* | 40 | 100 | ___ |
| **79** | Flashing Signal, *28–42* | 120 | 148 | ___ |
| **80/080** | Semaphore, *26–35* | 50 | 120 | ___ |
| **81** | Controlling Rheostat, *27–33* | 2 | 6 | ___ |
| **82/082** | Semaphore, *27–35* | 50 | 120 | ___ |
| **83** | Flashing Traffic Signal, *27–42* | 65 | 195 | ___ |
| **084** | Semaphore, *28–32* | 60 | 100 | ___ |
| **84** | Semaphore, *27–32* | 55 | 85 | ___ |
| **85** | Telegraph Pole (std), *29–42* | 15 | 27 | ___ |
| **86** | Telegraph Poles, 6 pieces, *29–42* | 60 | 120 | ___ |
| **87** | Flashing Crossing Signal, *27–42* | 85 | 300 | ___ |
| **88** | Battery Rheostat, *15–27* | 3 | 9 | ___ |
| **88** | Rheostat Controller, *33–42* | 4 | 8 | ___ |
| **89** | Flagpole, *23–34* | 44 | 75 | ___ |

| | | Good | Exc | Cond/$ |
|---|---|---|---|---|
| **90** | Flagpole, *27–42* | 39 | 95 | ____ |
| **91** | Circuit Breaker, *30–42* | 34 | 48 | ____ |
| **092** | Signal Tower, *23–27* | 83 | 190 | ____ |
| **92** | Floodlight Tower, *31–42** | 150 | 290 | ____ |
| **93** | Water Tower, *31–42* | 60 | 107 | ____ |
| **94** | High Tension Tower, *32–42** | 150 | 290 | ____ |
| **95** | Controlling Rheostat, *34–42* | 2 | 6 | ____ |
| **96** | Coal Elevator, manual, *38–40* | 165 | 220 | ____ |
| **097** | Telegraph Set (O) | 50 | 75 | ____ |
| **97** | Coal Elevator, *38–42* | 125 | 200 | ____ |
| **98** | Coal Bunker, *38–40* | 160 | 318 | ____ |
| **99N** | Train Control Block Signal, *36–42* | 44 | 155 | ____ |
| **100** | Wooden Gondola (2⅞"), *01* | | NRS | ____ |
| **100** | Bridge Approaches, 2 ramps (std), *20–31* | 20 | 36 | ____ |
| **100** | Electric Locomotive (2⅞"), *03–05** | 2900 | 5200 | ____ |
| **100** | Trolley (std), *10–16* | | | |
| | (A) Blue, white windows | 1300 | 2700 | ____ |
| | (B) Blue, cream windows | 1850 | 3600 | ____ |
| | (C) Red, cream windows | 1300 | 2700 | ____ |
| **101** | Bridge, span (104) and 2 approaches (100), *20–31* | 65 | 120 | ____ |
| **101** | Summer Trolley (std), *10–13* | 1300 | 2700 | ____ |
| **102** | Bridge, 2 spans (104) and 2 approaches (100), *20–31* | 70 | 175 | ____ |
| **103** | Bridge (std), *13–16* | 50 | 70 | ____ |
| **103** | Bridge, 3 spans (104) and 2 approaches (100), *20–31* | 60 | 145 | ____ |
| **104** | Bridge Center Span (std), *20–31* | 20 | 45 | ____ |
| **104** | Tunnel, papier mache (std), *09–14* | 50 | 135 | ____ |
| **105** | Bridge (std), *11–14* | 40 | 70 | ____ |
| **105** | Bridge Approaches, 2 ramps (O), *20–31* | 50 | 70 | ____ |
| **106** | Bridge, span (110) and 2 approaches (105), *20–31* | 30 | 65 | ____ |
| **106** | Rheostat, *11–14* | 3 | 9 | ____ |
| **107** | DC Reducer, 110V, *23–32* | | NRS | ____ |
| **108** | Bridge, 2 spans (110) and 2 approaches (105), *20–31* | 50 | 90 | ____ |
| **109** | Bridge, 3 spans, (110) and 2 approaches (105), *20–32* | 50 | 115 | ____ |
| **109** | Tunnel, papier mache (std), *13–14* | 30 | 70 | ____ |
| **110** | Bridge Center Span (O), *20–31* | 12 | 23 | ____ |
| **111** | Box of 50 Bulbs, *20–31* | 55 | 105 | ____ |
| **112** | Gondola, early (std), *10–12* | 225 | 400 | ____ |

| | | Good | Exc | Cond/$ |
|---|---|---|---|---|
| **112** | Gondola, later (std), *12–16* | 40 | 65 | ____ |
| **112** | Gondola, latest (std), *16–18* | 40 | 65 | ____ |
| **112** | Gondola, Lionel Corp. (std), *18–26* | 40 | 65 | ____ |
| **112** | Station, *31–35* | 145 | 270 | ____ |
| **113** | Cattle Car, later (std), *12–16* | 50 | 70 | ____ |
| **113** | Cattle Car, latest (std), *16–18* | 50 | 70 | ____ |
| **113** | Cattle Car, Lionel Corp. (std), *18–26* | 40 | 55 | ____ |
| **113** | Station, *31–34* | 150 | 310 | ____ |
| **114** | Boxcar, later (std), *12–16* | 50 | 90 | ____ |
| **114** | Boxcar, latest (std), *16–18* | 40 | 70 | ____ |
| **114** | Boxcar, Lionel Corp. (std), *18–26* | 40 | 70 | ____ |
| **114** | Station, *31–34* | 530 | 1200 | ____ |
| **115** | Station, *35–42\** | 235 | 368 | ____ |
| **116** | Ballast Car, early and later (std), *10–16* | 85 | 115 | ____ |
| **116** | Ballast Car, latest (std), *16–18* | 65 | 105 | ____ |
| **116** | Ballast Car, Lionel Corp. (std), *18–26* | 55 | 95 | ____ |
| **116** | Station with stop, *35–42\** | 640 | 923 | ____ |
| **117** | Caboose, early (std), *12* | 60 | 70 | ____ |
| **117** | Caboose, later (std), *12–16* | 50 | 70 | ____ |
| **117** | Caboose, latest (std), *16–18* | 50 | 70 | ____ |
| **117** | Caboose, Lionel Corp. (std), *18–26* | 38 | 60 | ____ |
| **117** | Station, *36–42* | 90 | 235 | ____ |
| **118** | Tunnel, metal, 8" long (O), *20–32* | 20 | 55 | ____ |
| **118L** | Tunnel, metal, lighted, 8" long, *27* | 20 | 55 | ____ |
| **119** | Tunnel, metal, 12" long, *20–42* | 22 | 60 | ____ |
| **119L** | Tunnel, metal, lighted, 12" long, *27–33* | 20 | 55 | ____ |
| **120** | Tunnel, metal, 17" long, *22–27* | 27 | 75 | ____ |
| **120L** | Tunnel, metal, lighted, 17" long, *27–42* | 75 | 140 | ____ |
| **121** | Station, lighted (std), *09–16* | | | |
| | (A) 14" x 10" x 9" | | NRS | ____ |
| | (B) 13" x 9" x 13" | 150 | 300 | ____ |
| **121** | Station (std), *20–26* | 75 | 165 | ____ |
| **121X** | Station (std), *17–19* | 110 | 255 | ____ |
| **122** | Station (std), *20–30* | 80 | 190 | ____ |
| **123** | Station (std), *20–23* | 75 | 205 | ____ |
| **123** | Tunnel, paperboard base, 18½" long (O), *33–42* | 105 | 235 | ____ |
| **124** | Lionel City Station, *20–36\** | | | |
| | (A) Tan or gray base, pea green roof | 90 | 200 | ____ |
| | (B) Pea green base, red roof | 200 | 360 | ____ |
| **125** | Lionelville Station, *23–25* | 80 | 185 | ____ |
| **125** | Track Template, *38* | 1 | 5 | ____ |

| | | Good | Exc | Cond/$ |
|---|---|---|---|---|
| **126** | Lionelville Station, *23–36* | 95 | 205 | ___ |
| **127** | Lionel Town Station, *23–36* | 90 | 160 | ___ |
| **128** | 115 Station and 129 Terrace, *35–42\** | 900 | 1900 | ___ |
| **128** | 124 Station and 129 Terrace, *31–34\** | 900 | 1900 | ___ |
| **129** | Terrace, *28–42\** | 600 | 1100 | ___ |
| **130** | Tunnel, 26" long (O), *20–36* | 100 | 450 | ___ |
| **130L** | Tunnel, lighted, 26" long, *27–33* | 150 | 450 | ___ |
| **131** | Corner Display, *24–28* | 125 | 295 | ___ |
| **132** | Corner Grass Plot, *24–28* | 125 | 295 | ___ |
| **133** | Heart-shaped Plot, *24–28* | 125 | 295 | ___ |
| **134** | Lionel City Station with stop, *37–42* | 230 | 445 | ___ |
| **134** | Oval-shaped Plot, *24–28* | 125 | 300 | ___ |
| **135** | Circular Plot, *24–28* | 125 | 295 | ___ |
| **136** | Large Elevation, *24–28* | | NRS | ___ |
| **136** | Lionelville Station with stop, *37–42* | 85 | 180 | ___ |
| **137** | Station with stop, *37–42* | 85 | 135 | ___ |
| **140L** | Tunnel, lighted, 37" long, *27–32* | 460 | 1050 | ___ |
| **150** | Electric Locomotive 0-4-0, early (O), *17* | 90 | 160 | ___ |
| **150** | Electric Locomotive 0-4-0, late (O), *18–25* | | | |
| | (A) Brown, brown or olive windows | 95 | 150 | ___ |
| | (B) Maroon, dark olive windows | 90 | 135 | ___ |
| **152** | Electric Locomotive 0-4-0 (O), *17–27* | | | |
| | (A) Dark green | 90 | 135 | ___ |
| | (B) Gray | 115 | 160 | ___ |
| | (C) Mojave | 340 | 680 | ___ |
| | (D) Peacock | 340 | 680 | ___ |
| **152** | Crossing Gate, *40–42* | 18 | 42 | ___ |
| **153** | Block Signal, *40–42* | 23 | 45 | ___ |
| **153** | Electric Locomotive 0-4-0 (O), *24–25* | | | |
| | (A) Dark green | 100 | 160 | ___ |
| | (B) Gray | 100 | 160 | ___ |
| | (C) Mojave | 100 | 160 | ___ |
| **154** | Electric Locomotive 0-4-0 (O), *17–23* | 100 | 180 | ___ |
| **154** | Highway Signal, *40–42* | | | |
| | (A) Black base | 21 | 49 | ___ |
| | (B) Orange base | 47 | 178 | ___ |
| **155** | Freight Shed, *30–42\** | | | |
| | (A) Cream base, terra cotta floor | 180 | 320 | ___ |
| | (B) Ivory base, red floor | 240 | 400 | ___ |
| **156** | Electric Locomotive 0-4-0 (O), *17–23* | 400 | 720 | ___ |
| **156** | Station Platform, *39–42* | 85 | 133 | ___ |

| | | Good | Exc | Cond/$ |
|---|---|---|---|---|
| **156** | Electric Locomotive 4-4-4 (O), *17–23* | | | |
| | (A) Dark green | 475 | 810 | ____ |
| | (B) Maroon | 540 | 890 | ____ |
| | (C) Olive green | 600 | 1050 | ____ |
| | (D) Gray | 670 | 1200 | ____ |
| **156X** | Electric Locomotive 0-4-0 (O), *23–24* | | | |
| | (A) Maroon | 380 | 495 | ____ |
| | (B) Olive green | 440 | 550 | ____ |
| | (C) Gray | 530 | 710 | ____ |
| | (D) Brown | 470 | 600 | ____ |
| **157** | Hand Truck, *30–32* | 25 | 41 | ____ |
| **158** | Electric Locomotive 0-4-0 (O), *19–23* | | | |
| | (A) Gray or red windows | 75 | 205 | ____ |
| | (B) Black | 95 | 250 | ____ |
| **158** | Station Set: 136 Station and 2 platforms (156), *40–42* | 120 | 280 | ____ |
| **159** | Block Actuator, *40* | 10 | 27 | ____ |
| **161** | Baggage Truck, *30–32** | 42 | 80 | ____ |
| **162** | Dump Truck, *30–32** | 42 | 80 | ____ |
| **163** | Freight Accessory Set: 2 hand trucks (157), baggage truck (161), and dump truck (162), *30–42** | 220 | 360 | ____ |
| **164** | Log Loader, *40–42* | 160 | 225 | ____ |
| **165** | Magnetic Crane, *40–42* | 175 | 285 | ____ |
| **165-22** | Scrap Steel with bag, *40–42* | 50 | 125 | ____ |
| **165-83** | Scrap Steel with bag, *40–42* | | 75 | ____ |
| **166** | Whistle Controller, *40–42* | 3 | 7 | ____ |
| **167** | Whistle Controller, *40–42* | 6 | 23 | ____ |
| **167X** | Whistle Controller (OO), *40–42* | 5 | 14 | ____ |
| **168** | Magic Electrol Controller, *40–42* | | 77 | ____ |
| **169** | Controller, *40–42* | 3 | 8 | ____ |
| **170** | DC Reducer, 220V, *14–38* | 3 | 8 | ____ |
| **171** | DC to AC Inverter, 110V, *36–42* | 3 | 15 | ____ |
| **172** | DC to AC Inverter, 229V, *39–42* | 3 | 7 | ____ |
| **180** | Pullman Car (std), *11–13* | | | |
| | (A) Maroon body and roof | 145 | 205 | ____ |
| | (B) Brown body and roof | 145 | 255 | ____ |
| **180** | Pullman Car (std), *13–15* | 80 | 160 | ____ |
| **180** | Pullman Car (std), *15–18* | 80 | 160 | ____ |
| **180** | Pullman Car (std), *18–22* | 80 | 135 | ____ |

| | | Good | Exc | Cond/$ |
|---|---|---|---|---|
| **181** | Combine Car (std), *11–13* | | | ____ |
| | (A) Maroon, dark olive doors | 145 | 205 | ____ |
| | (B) Brown, dark olive doors | 145 | 205 | ____ |
| | (C) Yellow-orange, orange doors | 350 | 495 | ____ |
| **181** | Combine Car (std), *13–15* | 80 | 160 | ____ |
| **181** | Combine Car (std), *15–18* | 80 | 160 | ____ |
| **181** | Combine Car (std), *18–22* | 80 | 135 | ____ |
| **182** | Observation Car (std), *11–13* | | | |
| | (A) Maroon, dark olive doors | 145 | 205 | ____ |
| | (B) Brown, dark olive doors | 145 | 205 | ____ |
| | (C) Yellow-orange, orange doors | 350 | 495 | ____ |
| **182** | Observation Car (std), *13–15* | 80 | 160 | ____ |
| **182** | Observation Car (std), *15–18* | 80 | 160 | ____ |
| **182** | Observation Car (std), *18–22* | 80 | 135 | ____ |
| **184** | Bungalow, illuminated, *23–32*\* | 65 | 110 | ____ |
| **185** | Bungalow, *23–24* | 50 | 115 | ____ |
| **186** | 184 Bungalows, set of 5, *23–32* | 195 | 610 | ____ |
| **186** | Log Loader Outfit, *40–41* | 130 | 340 | ____ |
| **187** | 185 Bungalows, set of 5, *23–24* | 170 | 590 | ____ |
| **188** | Elevator and Car Set, *38–41* | 115 | 370 | ____ |
| **189** | Villa, illuminated, *23–32*\* | 133 | 225 | ____ |
| **190** | Observation Car (std), *08* | | | |
| | (A) Dark olive green, nonremovable roof | 1150 | 2600 | ____ |
| | (B) Dark olive green, removable roof | 115 | 205 | ____ |
| | (C) Yellow-orange, removable roof | 320 | 620 | ____ |
| | (D) Orange, removable roof | 115 | 205 | ____ |
| | (E) Mojave, removable roof | 345 | 870 | ____ |
| **190** | Observation Car (std), *11–13* | 600 | 900 | ____ |
| **190** | Observation Car (std), *13–15* | 200 | 295 | ____ |
| **190** | Observation Car (std), *15–18* | 200 | 295 | ____ |
| **190** | Observation Car (std), *18–22* | 80 | 135 | ____ |
| **190** | Observation Car (std), *23–26* | 230 | 475 | ____ |
| **191** | Villa, illuminated, *23–32*\* | 123 | 325 | ____ |
| **192** | Illuminated Villa Set: 189, 191, 184 (2), *27–32* | | 800 | ____ |
| **193** | Automatic Accessory Set (O), *27–29* | 150 | 325 | ____ |
| **194** | Automatic Accessory Set (std), *27–29* | 100 | 325 | ____ |
| **195** | Terrace, *27–30* | 350 | 740 | ____ |
| **196** | Accessory Set, *27* | 200 | 335 | ____ |
| **200** | Electric Express (2⅞"), *03–05*\* | 4000 | 6300 | ____ |
| **200** | Trailer, matches No. 2 Trolley (std), *11–16* | | 2400 | ____ |
| **200** | Turntable, *28–33*\* | 85 | 190 | ____ |

| | | Good | Exc | Cond/$ |
|---|---|---:|---:|---|
| **201** | 0-6-0 Locomotive (O), *40–42* | | | |
| | (A) 2201B Tender, bell | 375 | 760 | ____ |
| | (B) 2201T Tender, no bell | 345 | 690 | ____ |
| **202** | Summer Trolley (std), *10–13* | | | |
| | (A) Electric Rapid Transit | 1300 | 2700 | ____ |
| | (B) Preston St. | 3250 | 4500 | ____ |
| **203** | Armored 0-4-0 (O), *17–21* | 1100 | 1800 | ____ |
| **203** | 0-6-0 Locomotive (O), *40–42* | | | |
| | (A) 2203B Tender, bell | 400 | 495 | ____ |
| | (B) 2203T Tender, no bell | 365 | 550 | ____ |
| **204** | 2-4-2 Locomotive (O), *40–42 u* | | | |
| | (A) Black | 55 | 105 | ____ |
| | (B) Gunmetal gray | 80 | 165 | ____ |
| **205** | Merchandise Containers, 3 pieces, *30–38\** | 130 | 320 | ____ |
| **206** | Sack of Coal, *38–42* | 5 | 18 | ____ |
| **208** | Tool Set: 6 assorted tools, *34–42\** | 65 | 150 | ____ |
| **0209** | Barrels, wooden, 6 pieces (O), *34–42* | 8 | 26 | ____ |
| **209** | Barrels, wooden, 4 pieces (std), *34–42* | 10 | 22 | ____ |
| **210** | Switches, pair (std), *26, 34–42* | 42 | 75 | ____ |
| **211** | Flatcar (std), *26–40\** | 125 | 225 | ____ |
| **212** | Gondola (std), *26–40\** | | | |
| | (A) Gray or light green | 100 | 205 | ____ |
| | (B) Maroon | 75 | 135 | ____ |
| **213** | Cattle Car (std), *26–40\** | | | |
| | (A) Mojave, maroon roof | 160 | 365 | ____ |
| | (B) Terra-cotta, pea green roof | 130 | 285 | ____ |
| | (C) Cream, maroon roof | 300 | 650 | ____ |
| **214** | Boxcar (std), *26–40\** | | | |
| | (A) Terra-cotta, green roof | 195 | 323 | ____ |
| | (B) Cream body, orange roof | 150 | 270 | ____ |
| | (C) Yellow, brown roof | 300 | 495 | ____ |
| **214R** | Refrigerator Car (std), *29–40\** | | | |
| | (A) Ivory or white, peacock roof | 325 | 495 | ____ |
| | (B) White, light blue nickel roof | 435 | 790 | ____ |
| **215** | Tank Car (std), *26–40\** | | | |
| | (A) Pea green | 150 | 215 | ____ |
| | (B) Ivory | 220 | 360 | ____ |
| | (C) Aluminum | 315 | 720 | ____ |
| **216** | Hopper Car (std), *26–38\** | | | |
| | (A) Dark green, brass plates | 195 | 335 | ____ |
| | (B) Dark green, nickel plates | 445 | 1100 | ____ |

| | | Good | Exc | Cond/$ |
|---|---|---|---|---|
| **217** | Caboose (std), *26–40\** | | | |
| | (A) Orange, maroon roof | 250 | 510 | ____ |
| | (B) Red, peacock roof | 120 | 235 | ____ |
| | (C) Red body and roof, ivory doors | 150 | 320 | ____ |
| **217** | Lighting Set, *14–23* | | NRS | ____ |
| **218** | Dump Car (std), *26–38\** | 220 | 365 | |
| **219** | Crane Car (std), *26–40\** | | | |
| | (A) Peacock, red boom | 135 | 255 | ____ |
| | (B) Yellow, light green or red boom | 270 | 440 | ____ |
| | (C) Ivory, light green boom | 270 | 480 | ____ |
| **220** | Floodlight Car (std), *31–40\** | | | |
| | (A) Terra-cotta base | 225 | 385 | ____ |
| | (B) Green base | 340 | 485 | ____ |
| **220** | Switches, pair (std), *26\** | 25 | 90 | ____ |
| **222** | Switches, pair (std), *26–32* | 40 | 100 | ____ |
| **223** | Switches, pair (std), *32–42* | 33 | 120 | ____ |
| **224/224E** | 2-6-2 Locomotive (O), *38–42* | | | |
| | (A) Black, die-cast 2224 Tender | 155 | 253 | ____ |
| | (B) Black, plastic 2224 Tender | 110 | 195 | ____ |
| | (C) Gunmetal, die-cast 2224 Tender | 385 | 950 | ____ |
| | (D) Gunmetal, sheet-metal 2689 Tender | 120 | 210 | ____ |
| **225** | 222 Switches and 439 Panel, *29–32* | 115 | 260 | ____ |
| **225/225E** | 2-6-2 Locomotive (O), *38–42* | | | |
| | (A) Black, 2235 or 2245 Tender | 210 | 370 | ____ |
| | (B) Black, 2235 plastic Tender | 185 | 320 | ____ |
| | (C) Gunmetal, 2225 or 2265 Tender | 210 | 360 | ____ |
| | (D) Gunmetal, 2235 die-cast Tender | 285 | 730 | ____ |
| **226/226E** | 2-6-4 Locomotive (O), *38–41* | 275 | 632 | ____ |
| **227** | 0-6-0 Locomotive (O), *39–42* | | | |
| | (A) 2227B Tender, bell | 600 | 1250 | ____ |
| | (B) 2227T Tender, no bell | 600 | 1150 | ____ |
| **228** | 0-6-0 Locomotive (O), *39–42* | | | |
| | (A) 2228B Tender, bell | 600 | 1250 | ____ |
| | (B) 2228T Tender, no bell | 600 | 1150 | ____ |
| **229** | 2-4-2 Locomotive (O), *39–42* | | | |
| | (A) Black or gunmetal, 2689W Tender | 155 | 263 | ____ |
| | (B) Black or gunmetal, 2689T Tender | 120 | 200 | ____ |
| | (C) Black, 2666W whistle Tender | 155 | 280 | ____ |
| | (D) Black, 2666T nonwhistling Tender | 120 | 200 | ____ |
| **230** | 0-6-0 Locomotive (O), *39–42* | 1100 | 2050 | ____ |
| **231** | 0-6-0 Locomotive (O), *39* | 1000 | 1800 | ____ |

| | | Good | Exc | Cond/$ |
|---|---|---|---|---|
| **232** | 0-6-0 Locomotive (O), *40–42* | 1000 | 1800 | ____ |
| **233** | 0-6-0 Locomotive (O), *40–42* | 1000 | 1800 | ____ |
| **238** | 4-4-2 Locomotive (O), *39–40 u* | 430 | 710 | ____ |
| **238E** | 4-4-2 Locomotive (O), *36–38* | | | |
| | (A) 265W or 2225W whistle Tender | 280 | 343 | ____ |
| | (B) 265 or 2225T nonwhistling Tender | 275 | 360 | ____ |
| **248** | Electric Locomotive 0-4-0 (O), *27–32* | 150 | 240 | ____ |
| **249/249E** | 2-4-2 Locomotive (O), *36–39* | | | |
| | (A) Gunmetal, 265T or 265W Tender | 100 | 269 | ____ |
| | (B) Black, 265W Tender | 110 | 210 | ____ |
| **250** | Electric Locomotive 0-4-0, early (O), *26* | 125 | 220 | ____ |
| **250** | Electric Locomotive 0-4-0, late (O), *34* | | | |
| | (A) Yellow-orange body, terra-cotta frame | 145 | 245 | ____ |
| | (B) Terra-cotta body, maroon frame | 160 | 270 | ____ |
| **250E** | 4-4-2 *Hiawatha* Locomotive (O), *35–42\** | 400 | 1100 | ____ |
| **251** | Electric Locomotive 0-4-0 (O), *25–32* | | | |
| | (A) Gray body, red windows | 190 | 340 | ____ |
| | (B) Red body, ivory stripe | 215 | 410 | ____ |
| | (C) Red body, no ivory stripe | 200 | 380 | ____ |
| **251E** | Electric Locomotive 0-4-0 (O), *27–32* | | | |
| | (A) Red body, ivory stripe | 225 | 425 | ____ |
| | (B) Red body, no ivory stripe | 215 | 395 | ____ |
| | (C) Gray, red trim | 195 | 350 | ____ |
| **252** | Electric Locomotive 0-4-0 (O), *26–32* | | | |
| | (A) Peacock or olive green | 95 | 170 | ____ |
| | (B) Terra-cotta or yellow-orange | 125 | 214 | ____ |
| **252E** | Electric Locomotive 0-4-0 (O), *33–35* | | | |
| | (A) Terra-cotta | 145 | 250 | ____ |
| | (B) Yellow-orange | 125 | 205 | ____ |
| **253** | Electric Locomotive 0-4-0 (O), *24–32* | | | |
| | (A) Maroon | 180 | 430 | ____ |
| | (B) Dark green | 105 | 249 | ____ |
| | (C) Mojave | 105 | 235 | ____ |
| | (D) Terra-cotta | 180 | 430 | ____ |
| | (E) Peacock | 95 | 195 | ____ |
| | (F) Red | 210 | 475 | ____ |
| **253E** | Electric Locomotive 0-4-0 (O), *31–36* | | | |
| | (A) Green | 150 | 205 | ____ |
| | (B) Terra-cotta | 190 | 305 | ____ |
| **254** | Electric Locomotive 0-4-0 (O), *24–32* | 240 | 340 | ____ |
| **254E** | Electric Locomotive 0-4-0 (O), *27–34* | 190 | 263 | ____ |

| | | Good | Exc | Cond/$ |
|---|---|---|---|---|
| **255E** | 2-4-2 Locomotive (O), *35–36* | 485 | 1000 | ____ |
| **256** | Electric Locomotive 0-4-4-0 (O), *24–30\** | | | |
| | (A) Rubber-stamped lettering | 470 | 1250 | ____ |
| | (B) no outline around Lionel | 425 | 770 | ____ |
| | (C) Lionel Lines and No. 256 on brass | 450 | 1050 | ____ |
| **257** | 2-4-0 Locomotive (O), *30–35 u* | | | |
| | (A) Black tender | 145 | 300 | ____ |
| | (B) Black crackle-finish tender | 240 | 435 | ____ |
| **258** | 2-4-0 Locomotive, early (O), *30–35 u* | | | |
| | (A) 4-wheel 257 Tender | 85 | 170 | ____ |
| | (B) 8-wheel 258 Tender | 100 | 195 | ____ |
| **258** | 2-4-2 Locomotive, late (O), *41 u* | | | |
| | (A) Black | 60 | 90 | ____ |
| | (B) Gunmetal | 85 | 135 | ____ |
| **259** | 2-4-2 Locomotive (O), *32* | 70 | 135 | ____ |
| **259E** | 2-4-2 Locomotive (O), *33–42* | 80 | 155 | ____ |
| **260E** | 2-4-2 Locomotive (O), *30–35\** | | | |
| | (A) Black body, green or black frame | 385 | 548 | ____ |
| | (B) Dark gunmetal body and frame | 440 | 640 | ____ |
| **261** | 2-4-2 Locomotive (O), *31* | 125 | 210 | ____ |
| **261E** | 2-4-2 Locomotive (O), *35* | 190 | 285 | ____ |
| **262** | 2-4-2 Locomotive (O), *31–32* | 215 | 311 | ____ |
| **262E** | 2-4-2 Locomotive (O), *33–36* | | | |
| | (A) Gloss black, copper and brass trim | 100 | 210 | ____ |
| | (B) Satin black, nickel trim | 125 | 258 | ____ |
| **263E** | 2-4-2 Locomotive (O), *36–39\** | | | |
| | (A) Gunmetal gray | 315 | 610 | ____ |
| | (B) 2-tone blue, from *Blue Comet* | 415 | 950 | ____ |
| **264E** | 2-4-2 Locomotive (O), *35–36* | | | |
| | (A) Red, Red Comet | 150 | 295 | ____ |
| | (B) Black | 220 | 380 | ____ |
| **265E** | 2-4-2 Locomotive (O), *35–40* | | | |
| | (A) Black or gunmetal | 170 | 330 | ____ |
| | (B) Light blue, Blue Streak | 460 | 800 | ____ |
| **267E/W** | Set: 616, 617 (2), 618, *35–41* | | 560 | ____ |
| **270** | Bridge, 10" long (O), *31–42* | 18 | 50 | ____ |
| **270** | Lighting Set, *15–23* | | NRS | ____ |
| **271** | 270 Bridges, set of 2, *31–33, 35–40* | 65 | 150 | ____ |
| **271** | Lighting Set, *15–23* | | NRS | ____ |
| **272** | 270 Bridges, set of 3, *31–33, 35–40* | 60 | 165 | ____ |
| **280** | Bridge, 14" long (std), *31–42* | 50 | 115 | ____ |

| | | Good | Exc | Cond/$ |
|---|---|---|---|---|
| **281** | 280 Bridges, set of 2, *31–33, 35–40* | 90 | 205 | ____ |
| **282** | 280 Bridges, set of 3, *31–33, 35–40* | 105 | 265 | ____ |
| **289E** | 2-4-2 Locomotive (O), *37 u* | 120 | 305 | ____ |
| **300** | Electric Trolley Car (2⅞"), *01–05* | 2000 | 3600 | ____ |
| **300** | Hell Gate Bridge (std), *28–42\** | | | |
| | (A) Cream towers, green truss | 800 | 1350 | ____ |
| | (B) Ivory towers, aluminum truss | 763 | 1600 | ____ |
| **303** | Summer Trolley, *10–13* | 1500 | 3150 | ____ |
| **308** | Signs, set of 5 (O), *40–42* | 26 | 70 | ____ |
| **309** | Electric Trolley Trailer (2⅞"), *01–05* | 2500 | 4050 | ____ |
| **309** | Pullman Car (std), *26–39* | | | |
| | (A) Maroon body and roof, mojave windows | 100 | 160 | ____ |
| | (B) Mojave body and roof, maroon windows | 100 | 160 | ____ |
| | (C) Light brown body, dark brown roof | 120 | 190 | ____ |
| | (D) Medium blue body, dark blue roof | 170 | 280 | ____ |
| | (E) Apple green body, dark green roof | 170 | 280 | ____ |
| | (F) Pale blue body, silver roof | 100 | 185 | ____ |
| | (G) Maroon body, terra-cotta roof | 130 | 195 | ____ |
| **310** | Rails and Ties, complete section (2⅞"), *01–02* | 5 | 14 | ____ |
| **310** | Baggage Car (std), *26–39* | | | |
| | (A) Maroon body and roof, mojave windows | 100 | 160 | ____ |
| | (B) Mojave body and roof, maroon windows | 100 | 160 | ____ |
| | (C) Light brown body, dark brown roof | 115 | 185 | ____ |
| | (D) Medium blue body, dark blue roof | 170 | 280 | ____ |
| | (E) Apple green body, dark green roof | 170 | 280 | ____ |
| | (F) Pale blue body, silver roof | 100 | 175 | ____ |
| **312** | Observation Car (std), *24–39* | | | |
| | (A) Maroon body and roof, mojave windows | 100 | 160 | ____ |
| | (B) Mojave body and roof, maroon windows | 100 | 160 | ____ |
| | (C) Light brown body, dark brown roof | 120 | 185 | ____ |
| | (D) Medium blue body, dark blue roof | 170 | 280 | ____ |
| | (E) Apple green body, dark green roof | 170 | 280 | ____ |
| | (F) Pale blue body, silver roof | 100 | 175 | ____ |
| | (G) Maroon body, terra-cotta roof | 130 | 195 | ____ |
| **313** | Bascule Bridge (O), *40–42* | | | |
| | (A) Silver bridge | 235 | 500 | ____ |
| | (B) Gray bridge | 250 | 590 | ____ |
| **314** | Girder Bridge (O), *40–42* | 17 | 40 | ____ |
| **315** | Trestle Bridge (O), *40–42* | 28 | 80 | ____ |

| | | Good | Exc | Cond/$ |
|---|---|---|---|---|
| **316** | Trestle Bridge (O), *40–42* | 21 | 48 | ____ |
| **318** | Electric Locomotive 0-4-0 (std), *24–32* | | | |
| | (A) Gray, dark gray, or mojave | 150 | 250 | ____ |
| | (B) Pea green | 150 | 250 | ____ |
| | (C) State brown | 250 | 395 | ____ |
| **318E** | Electric Locomotive 0-4-0, *26–35* | | | |
| | (A) Gray, mojave, or pea green | 150 | 250 | ____ |
| | (B) State brown | 275 | 440 | ____ |
| | (C) Black | 550 | 1275 | ____ |
| **319** | Pullman Car (std), *24–27* | 105 | 175 | ____ |
| **320** | Baggage Car (std), *25–27* | 100 | 175 | ____ |
| **320** | Switch and Signal (2⅞"), *02–05* | | NRS | ____ |
| **322** | Observation Car (std), *24–27, 29–30 u* | 100 | 175 | ____ |
| **330** | 90-degree Crossing (2⅞"), *02–05* | | NRS | ____ |
| **332** | Baggage Car (std), *26–33* | | | |
| | (A) Red body and roof, cream doors | 80 | 120 | ____ |
| | (B) Peacock body and roof, orange doors | 75 | 115 | ____ |
| | (C) Gray body and roof, maroon doors | 75 | 115 | ____ |
| | (D) Olive green body and roof, red doors | 90 | 145 | ____ |
| | (E) State brown body, dark brown roof | 190 | 430 | ____ |
| **337** | Pullman Car (std), *25–32* | | | |
| | (A) Red body and roof, cream doors | 95 | 190 | ____ |
| | (B) Mojave body and roof, maroon doors | 95 | 190 | ____ |
| | (C) Olive green body and roof, red doors | 105 | 225 | ____ |
| | (D) Olive green body and roof, maroon doors | 95 | 190 | ____ |
| | (E) Pea green body and roof, cream doors | 210 | 500 | ____ |
| **338** | Observation Car (std), *25–32* | | | |
| | (A) Red body and roof, cream doors | 95 | 190 | ____ |
| | (B) Mojave body and roof, maroon doors | 95 | 190 | ____ |
| | (C) Olive green body and roof, red doors | 105 | 225 | ____ |
| | (D) Olive green body and roof, maroon doors | 95 | 190 | ____ |
| **339** | Pullman Car (std), *25–33* | | | |
| | (A) Peacock body and roof, orange doors | 55 | 88 | ____ |
| | (B) Gray body and roof, maroon doors | 55 | 100 | ____ |
| | (C) State brown body, dark brown roof | 135 | 380 | ____ |
| | (D) Peacock body, dark green roof | 75 | 130 | ____ |
| | (E) Mojave body, maroon roof and doors | 145 | 230 | ____ |
| **340** | Suspension Bridge (2⅞"), *02–05\** | | NRS | ____ |

| | | Good | Exc | Cond/$ |
|---|---|---|---|---|
| **341** | Observation Car (std), *25–33* | | | |
| | (A) Peacock body and roof, orange doors | 50 | 70 | ____ |
| | (B) Gray body and roof, maroon doors | 50 | 70 | ____ |
| | (C) State brown body, dark brown roof | 125 | 157 | ____ |
| | (D) Peacock body, dark green roof | 65 | 95 | ____ |
| | (E) Mojave body, maroon roof and doors | 135 | 165 | ____ |
| **350** | Track Bumper (2⅞"), *02–05* | | 550 | ____ |
| **380** | Elevated Pillars (2⅞"), *04–05** | 30 | 70 | ____ |
| **380** | Electric Locomotive 0-4-0 (std), *23–27* | 310 | 440 | ____ |
| **380E** | Electric Locomotive 0-4-0 (std), *26–29* | | | |
| | (A) Mojave | 445 | 630 | ____ |
| | (B) Maroon | 295 | 400 | ____ |
| | (C) Dark green | 370 | 460 | ____ |
| **381** | Electric Locomotive 4-4-4 (std), *28–29** | 1600 | 2100 | ____ |
| **381E** | Electric Locomotive 4-4-4 (std), *28–36** | | | |
| | (A) State green, apple green subframe | 1500 | 2500 | ____ |
| | (B) State green, red subframe | 1900 | 3250 | ____ |
| **381U** | Electric Locomotive 4-4-4 Kit (std), *28–29* | 1600 | 4100 | ____ |
| **384** | 2-4-0 Locomotive (std), *30–32** | 415 | 730 | ____ |
| **384E** | 2-4-0 Locomotive (std), *30–32** | 425 | 650 | ____ |
| **385E** | 2-4-2 Locomotive (std), *33–39** | 370 | 670 | ____ |
| **390** | 2-4-2 Locomotive (std), *29** | 460 | 820 | ____ |
| **390E** | 2-4-2 Locomotive (std), *29–31** | | | |
| | (A) Black, with or without orange stripe | 460 | 690 | ____ |
| | (B) 2-tone blue, cream-orange stripe | 650 | 1050 | ____ |
| | (C) 2-tone green, orange or green stripe | 990 | 2050 | ____ |
| **392E** | 4-4-2 Locomotive (std), *32–39** | | | |
| | (A) Black, 384 Tender | 750 | 1250 | ____ |
| | (B) Black, large 12-wheel tender | 1050 | 1475 | ____ |
| | (C) Gunmetal gray | 1000 | 1800 | ____ |
| **400** | Express Trail Car (2⅞"), *03–05** | 3500 | 5850 | ____ |
| **400E** | 4-4-4 Locomotive (std), *31–39** | | | |
| | (A) Black | 1400 | 2150 | ____ |
| | (B) Medium blue boiler | 1550 | 2350 | ____ |
| | (C) Black crackle finish | 1550 | 2800 | ____ |
| **402** | Electric Locomotive 0-4-4-0 (std), *23–27* | 365 | 570 | ____ |
| **402E** | Electric Locomotive 0-4-4-0 (std), *26–29* | 345 | 550 | ____ |
| **404** | Summer Trolley (std), *10* | | NRS | ____ |

| | | Good | Exc | Cond/$ |
|---|---|---|---|---|
| **408E** | Electric Locomotive 0-4-4-0 (std), *27–36\** | | | |
| | (A) Apple green or mojave, red pilots | 770 | 980 | ____ |
| | (B) 2-tone brown, brown pilots | 2100 | 2650 | ____ |
| | (C) Dark green, red pilots | 1850 | 3400 | ____ |
| **412** | *California* Pullman Car (std), *29–35\** | | | |
| | (A) Light green body, dark green roof | 590 | 1750 | ____ |
| | (B) Light brown body, dark brown roof | 620 | 2100 | ____ |
| **413** | *Colorado* Pullman Car (std), *29–35\** | | | |
| | (A) Light green body, dark green roof | 590 | 1750 | ____ |
| | (B) Light brown body, dark brown roof | 620 | 2100 | ____ |
| **414** | *Illinois* Pullman Car (std), *29–35\** | | | |
| | (A) Light green body, dark green roof | 590 | 2050 | ____ |
| | (B) Light brown body, dark brown roof | 620 | 2050 | ____ |
| **416** | *New York* Observation Car (std), *29–35\** | | | |
| | (A) Light green body, dark green roof | 590 | 1750 | ____ |
| | (B) Light brown body, dark brown roof | 620 | 2100 | ____ |
| **418** | Pullman Car (std), *23–32\** | 225 | 320 | ____ |
| **419** | Combination (std), *23–32\** | 205 | 280 | ____ |
| **420** | *Faye* Pullman Car (std), *30–40\** | | | |
| | (A) Brass trim | 485 | 900 | ____ |
| | (B) Nickel trim | 500 | 1200 | ____ |
| **421** | *Westphal* Pullman Car (std), *30–40\** | | | |
| | (A) Brass trim | 500 | 900 | ____ |
| | (B) Nickel trim | 500 | 1200 | ____ |
| **422** | *Tempel* Observation Car (std), *30–40\** | | | |
| | (A) Brass trim | 485 | 900 | ____ |
| | (B) Nickel trim | 500 | 1200 | ____ |
| **424** | *Liberty Belle* Pullman Car (std), *31–40\** | | | |
| | (A) Brass trim | 350 | 530 | ____ |
| | (B) Nickel trim | 385 | 650 | ____ |
| **425** | *Stephen Girard* Pullman Car (std), *31–40\** | | | |
| | (A) Brass trim | 350 | 530 | ____ |
| | (B) Nickel trim | 385 | 650 | ____ |
| **426** | *Coral Isle* Observation Car (std), *31–40\** | | | |
| | (A) Brass trim | 350 | 530 | ____ |
| | (B) Nickel trim | 385 | 650 | ____ |
| **428** | Pullman Car (std), *26–30\** | | | |
| | (A) Dark green body and roof | 250 | 385 | ____ |
| | (B) Orange body and roof, apple green windows | 390 | 890 | ____ |

| | | Good | Exc | Cond/$ |
|---|---|---|---|---|
| **429** | Combine Car (std), *26–30\** | | | |
| | (A) Dark green body and roof | 250 | 385 | ____ |
| | (B) Orange body and roof, apple green windows | 390 | 890 | ____ |
| **430** | Observation Car (std), *26–30\** | | | |
| | (A) Dark green body and roof | 250 | 385 | ____ |
| | (B) Orange body and roof, apple green windows | 390 | 890 | ____ |
| **431** | Diner (std), *27–32\** | | | |
| | (A) Mojave body, screw-mounted roof | 350 | 540 | ____ |
| | (B) Mojave body, hinged roof | 465 | 720 | ____ |
| | (C) Dark green body, orange windows | 410 | 720 | ____ |
| | (D) Orange body, apple green windows | 410 | 720 | ____ |
| | (E) Apple green body, red windows | 410 | 720 | ____ |
| **435** | Power Station, *26–38\** | 215 | 400 | ____ |
| **436** | Power Station, *26–37\** | | | |
| | (A) Power Station plate | 135 | 265 | ____ |
| | (B) Edison Service plate | 270 | 610 | ____ |
| **437** | Switch Signal Tower, *26–37\** | 190 | 430 | ____ |
| **438** | Signal Tower, *27–39\** | | | |
| | (A) Mojave base, orange house | 215 | 321 | ____ |
| | (B) Black base, white house | 325 | 640 | ____ |
| | (C) Gray base, ivory house | 325 | 640 | ____ |
| **439** | Panel Board, *28–42\** | 80 | 145 | ____ |
| **440/0440** | Signal Bridge, *32–35\** | 180 | 473 | ____ |
| **440C** | Panel Board, *32–42* | 90 | 145 | ____ |
| **441** | Weighing Station (std), *32–36* | 495 | 1325 | ____ |
| **442** | Landscaped Diner, *38–42* | 198 | 258 | ____ |
| **444** | Roundhouse (std), *32–35\** | 1350 | 2850 | ____ |
| **444-18** | Roundhouse Clip, *33* | | NRS | ____ |
| **450** | Electric Locomotive 0-4-0, Macy's (O), *30 u* | | | |
| | (A) Red, black frame | 295 | 700 | ____ |
| | (B) Apple green, dark green frame | 415 | 880 | ____ |
| **450** | Set: 450, matching 605, 606 (2), *30 u* | 750 | 1800 | ____ |
| **490** | Observation Car (std), *23–32\** | 190 | 255 | ____ |
| **500** | Electric Derrick Car (2⅞"), *03–04\** | 5000 | 6750 | ____ |
| **511** | Flatcar (std), *27–40* | | | |
| | (A) Dark green | 65 | 115 | ____ |
| | (B) Medium green | 75 | 165 | ____ |
| **512** | Gondola (std), *27–39* | | | |
| | (A) Peacock | 38 | 58 | ____ |
| | (B) Light green | 50 | 95 | ____ |

| | | Good | Exc | Cond/$ |
|---|---|---|---|---|
| **513** | Cattle Car (std), *27–38* | | | |
| | (A) Olive green, orange roof | 70 | 165 | ____ |
| | (B) Orange, pea green roof | 60 | 110 | ____ |
| | (C) Cream, maroon roof | 90 | 175 | ____ |
| **514** | Boxcar (std), *29–40* | | | |
| | (A) Cream, orange roof | 90 | 155 | ____ |
| | (B) Yellow, brown roof | 115 | 285 | ____ |
| **514** | Refrigerator Car (std), *27–28* | | | |
| | (A) Ivory or white, peacock roof | 240 | 400 | ____ |
| | (B) Cream, peacock roof | 215 | 340 | ____ |
| | (C) Ivory, peacock roof | 285 | 800 | ____ |
| **514R** | Refrigerator Car (std), *29–40* | | | |
| | (A) Ivory, peacock roof, brass plates | 140 | 190 | ____ |
| | (B) Ivory, light blue roof, nickel plates | 420 | 580 | ____ |
| | (C) White, light blue roof, brass plates | 140 | 180 | ____ |
| **515** | Tank Car (std), *27–40* | | | |
| | (A) Terra-cotta | 90 | 145 | ____ |
| | (B) Light tan | 105 | 185 | ____ |
| | (B) Silver | 90 | 175 | ____ |
| | (D) Orange, red Shell decal | 340 | 690 | ____ |
| **516** | Hopper Car (std), *28–40* | | | |
| | (A) Red | 170 | 240 | ____ |
| | (B) Red, rubber-stamped data | 200 | 300 | ____ |
| | (C) Light red, nickel trim | 200 | 325 | ____ |
| **517** | Caboose (std), *27–40* | | | |
| | (A) Pea green body, red roof | 50 | 100 | ____ |
| | (B) Red body and roof | 105 | 155 | ____ |
| | (C) Red body, black roof, orange windows | 355 | 640 | ____ |
| **520** | Floodlight Car (std), *31–40* | | | |
| | (A) Terra-cotta base | 110 | 210 | ____ |
| | (B) Green base | 110 | 240 | ____ |
| **529** | Pullman Car (O), *26–32* | | | |
| | (A) Olive green body and roof | 25 | 45 | ____ |
| | (B) Terra-cotta body and roof | 25 | 60 | ____ |
| **530** | Observation Car (O), *26–32* | | | |
| | (A) Olive green body and roof | 25 | 45 | ____ |
| | (B) Terra-cotta body and roof | 25 | 63 | ____ |
| **550** | Miniature Figures, boxed (std), *32–36*\* | 175 | 431 | ____ |
| **551** | Engineer (std), *32* | 25 | 45 | ____ |
| **552** | Conductor (std), *32* | 21 | 42 | ____ |
| **553** | Porter with stool (std), *32* | 25 | 50 | ____ |

| | | Good | Exc | Cond/$ |
|---|---|---|---|---|
| **554** | Male Passenger (std), *32* | 25 | 45 | ___ |
| **555** | Female Passenger (std), *32* | 25 | 45 | ___ |
| **556** | Red Cap with suitcase (std), *32* | 25 | 65 | ___ |
| **600** | Derrick Trailer (2⅞"), *03–04*\* | 5000 | 8550 | ___ |
| **600** | Pullman Car, early (O), *15–23* | | | |
| | (A) Dark green | 65 | 170 | ___ |
| | (B) Maroon or brown | 48 | 85 | ___ |
| **600** | Pullman Car, late (O), *33–42* | | | |
| | (A) Light red or gray, red roof | 50 | 90 | ___ |
| | (B) Light blue, aluminum roof | 70 | 120 | ___ |
| **601** | Observation Car, late (O), *33–42* | | | |
| | (A) Light red body and roof | 50 | 90 | ___ |
| | (B) Light gray, red roof | 50 | 90 | ___ |
| | (C) Light blue body, aluminum roof | 70 | 120 | ___ |
| **601** | Pullman Car, early (O), *15–23* | 50 | 70 | ___ |
| **602** | Lionel Lines Baggage Car, late (O), *33–42* | | | |
| | (A) Light red or gray, red roof | 60 | 110 | ___ |
| | (B) Light blue, aluminum roof | 90 | 150 | ___ |
| **602** | NYC Baggage Car (O), *15–23* | 30 | 45 | ___ |
| **602** | Observation Car (O), *22 u* | 30 | 36 | ___ |
| **603** | Pullman Car, early (O), *22 u* | 40 | 70 | ___ |
| **603** | Pullman Car, later (O), *20–25* | 20 | 45 | ___ |
| **603** | Pullman Car, latest (O), *31–36* | | | |
| | (A) Light red body and roof | 45 | 85 | ___ |
| | (B) Red body, black roof | 35 | 60 | ___ |
| | (C) Stephen Girard green body, dark green roof | 35 | 60 | ___ |
| | (D) Maroon body and roof, Macy Special | 60 | 125 | ___ |
| **604** | Observation Car, later (O), *20–25* | 35 | 60 | ___ |
| **604** | Observation Car, latest (O), *31–36* | | | |
| | (A) Light red body and roof | 44 | 85 | ___ |
| | (B) Red body, black roof | 35 | 60 | ___ |
| | (C) Yellow-orange body, terra-cotta roof | 35 | 60 | ___ |
| | (D) Stephen Girard green body, dark green roof | 35 | 60 | ___ |
| | (E) Maroon body and roof | 70 | 150 | ___ |

| | | Good | Exc | Cond/$ |
|---|---|---|---|---|
| **605** | Pullman Car (O), *25–32* | | | |
| | (A) Gray, Lionel Lines | 85 | 170 | ____ |
| | (B) Gray, Illinois Central | 85 | 170 | ____ |
| | (C) Red, Lionel Lines | 170 | 255 | ____ |
| | (D) Red, Illinois Central | 255 | 340 | ____ |
| | (E) Orange, Lionel Lines | 170 | 255 | ____ |
| | (F) Orange, Illinois Central | 300 | 430 | ____ |
| | (G) Olive green, Lionel Lines | 255 | 340 | ____ |
| **606** | Observation Car (O), *25–32* | | | |
| | (A) Gray, Lionel Lines | 130 | 215 | ____ |
| | (B) Gray, Illinois Central | 90 | 170 | ____ |
| | (C) Red, Lionel Lines | 170 | 255 | ____ |
| | (D) Red, Illinois Central | 255 | 340 | ____ |
| | (E) Orange, Lionel Lines | 170 | 255 | ____ |
| | (F) Orange, Illinois Central | 170 | 255 | ____ |
| | (G) Olive green, Lionel Lines | 255 | 340 | ____ |
| **607** | Pullman Car (O), *26–27* | | | |
| | (A) Peacock, Lionel Lines | 50 | 70 | ____ |
| | (B) Peacock, Illinois Central | 75 | 115 | ____ |
| | (C) 2-tone green, Lionel Lines | 50 | 75 | ____ |
| | (D) Red, Lionel Lines | 75 | 110 | ____ |
| **608** | Observation Car (O), *26–37* | | | |
| | (A) Peacock, Lionel Lines | 50 | 70 | ____ |
| | (B) Peacock, Illinois Central | 75 | 115 | ____ |
| | (C) 2-tone green, Lionel Lines | 50 | 75 | ____ |
| | (D) Red, Lionel Lines | 75 | 110 | ____ |
| **609** | Pullman Car (O), *37* | 60 | 85 | ____ |
| **610** | Pullman Car, early (O), *15–25* | | | |
| | (A) Dark green body and roof | 50 | 65 | ____ |
| | (B) Maroon body and roof | 60 | 95 | ____ |
| | (C) Mojave body and roof | 60 | 95 | ____ |
| **610** | Pullman Car, late (O), *26–30* | | | |
| | (A) Olive green body and roof | 65 | 80 | ____ |
| | (B) Mojave body and roof | 55 | 80 | ____ |
| | (C) Terra-cotta body, maroon roof | 100 | 155 | ____ |
| | (D) Pea green body and roof | 70 | 115 | ____ |
| | (E) Light blue body, aluminum roof | 130 | 260 | ____ |
| | (F) Light red body, aluminum-painted roof | 100 | 155 | ____ |
| **611** | Observation Car (O), *37* | 55 | 90 | ____ |

| | | Good | Exc | Cond/$ |
|---|---|---|---|---|
| **612** | Observation Car, early (O), *15–25* | | | |
| | (A) Dark green body and roof | 50 | 60 | ____ |
| | (B) Maroon body and roof | 70 | 90 | ____ |
| | (C) Mojave body and roof | 70 | 90 | ____ |
| **612** | Observation Car, late (O), *26–30* | | | |
| | (A) Olive green body and roof | 55 | 80 | ____ |
| | (B) Mojave body and roof | 55 | 80 | ____ |
| | (C) Terra-cotta body, maroon roof | 100 | 155 | ____ |
| | (D) Pea green body and roof | 70 | 115 | ____ |
| | (E) Light blue body, aluminum roof | 130 | 260 | ____ |
| | (F) Light red body, aluminum-painted roof | 100 | 155 | ____ |
| **613** | Pullman Car (O), *31–40*\* | | | |
| | (A) Terra-cotta body, maroon/terra-cotta roof | 85 | 195 | ____ |
| | (B) Light red body, light red/aluminum roof | 175 | 350 | ____ |
| | (C) Blue, two-tone blue roof | 115 | 225 | ____ |
| **614** | Observation Car (O), *31–40*\* | | | |
| | (A) Terra-cotta body, maroon/terra-cotta roof | 100 | 190 | ____ |
| | (B) Light red body, light red/aluminum roof | 175 | 350 | ____ |
| | (C) Blue, two-tone blue roof | 115 | 225 | ____ |
| **615** | Baggage Car (O), *33–40*\* | 150 | 260 | ____ |
| **616E/W** | Diesel only (O), *35–41* | 90 | 215 | ____ |
| **616E/W** | Set: 616, 617 (2), 618 | 310 | 570 | ____ |
| **617** | Coach (O), *35–41* | | | |
| | (A) Blue and white | 55 | 85 | ____ |
| | (B) Chrome, gunmetal skirts | 55 | 85 | ____ |
| | (C) Chrome, chrome skirts | 55 | 85 | ____ |
| | (D) Silver-painted | 55 | 85 | ____ |
| **618** | Observation Car (O), *35–41* | | | |
| | (A) Blue and white | 55 | 85 | ____ |
| | (B) Chrome, gunmetal skirts | 55 | 85 | ____ |
| | (C) Chrome, chrome skirts | 55 | 85 | ____ |
| | (D) Silver-painted | 55 | 85 | ____ |
| **619** | Combine Car (O), *36–38* | | | |
| | (A) Blue, white windows band | 100 | 205 | ____ |
| | (B) Chrome, chrome skirts | 100 | 205 | ____ |
| **620** | Floodlight Car (O), *37–42* | 50 | 85 | ____ |
| **629** | Pullman Car (O), *24–32* | | | |
| | (A) Dark green body and roof | 30 | 40 | ____ |
| | (B) Orange body and roof | 30 | 40 | ____ |
| | (C) Red body and roof | 20 | 32 | ____ |
| | (D) Light red body and roof | 40 | 55 | ____ |

| | | Good | Exc | Cond/$ |
|---|---|---|---|---|
| **630** | Observation Car, *24–32* | | | |
| | (A) Dark green body and roof | 30 | 40 | ____ |
| | (B) Orange body and roof | 30 | 40 | ____ |
| | (C) Red body and roof | 20 | 32 | ____ |
| | (D) Light red body and roof | 40 | 55 | ____ |
| **636W** | Diesel only (O), *36–39* | 90 | 175 | ____ |
| **636W** | Set: 636W, 637 (2), 638, *36–39* | 375 | 640 | ____ |
| **637** | Coach (O), *36–39* | 70 | 105 | ____ |
| **638** | Observation Car (O), *36–39* | 70 | 105 | ____ |
| **651** | Flatcar (O), *35–40* | 28 | 55 | ____ |
| **652** | Gondola (O), *35–40* | 28 | 55 | ____ |
| **653** | Hopper Car (O), *34–40* | 35 | 65 | ____ |
| **654** | Tank Car (O), *34–42* | | | |
| | (A) Orange or aluminum | 38 | 60 | ____ |
| | (B) Gray | 42 | 75 | ____ |
| **655** | Boxcar (O), *34–42* | | | |
| | (A) Cream, maroon roof | 35 | 60 | ____ |
| | (B) Cream, tuscan roof | 47 | 75 | ____ |
| **656** | Cattle Car (O), *35–40* | | | |
| | (A) Light gray, vermilion roof | 40 | 100 | ____ |
| | (B) Burnt orange, tuscan roof | 70 | 125 | ____ |
| **657** | Caboose (O), *34–42* | | | |
| | (A) Red body and roof | 20 | 34 | ____ |
| | (B) Red body, tuscan roof | 25 | 42 | ____ |
| **659** | Dump Car (O), *35–42* | 40 | 75 | ____ |
| **700** | Electric Locomotive 0-4-0 (O), *15–16* | 360 | 690 | ____ |
| **700E** | 4-6-4 NYC Hudson "5344," scale (O), *37–42*\* | 1400 | 2950 | ____ |
| **700K** | 4-6-4 Locomotive, unbuilt gray primer (O), *38–42* | 4400 | 5950 | ____ |
| **701** | 0-6-0 PRR Locomotive "8976," *41* | | 2350 | ____ |
| **701** | Electric Locomotive 0-4-0 (O), *15–16* | 390 | 660 | ____ |
| **702** | Baggage Car (O), *17–21* | 115 | 305 | ____ |
| **703** | Electric Locomotive 4-4-4 (O), *15–16* | 1400 | 2350 | ____ |
| **706** | Electric Locomotive 0-4-0 (O), *15–16* | 375 | 630 | ____ |
| **708** | 0-6-0 PRR Locomotive "8976" (O), *39–42*\* | 1450 | 2850 | ____ |
| **710** | Pullman Car (O), *24–34* | | | |
| | (A) Red, Lionel Lines | 200 | 300 | ____ |
| | (B) Orange, Lionel Lines | 150 | 225 | ____ |
| | (C) Orange, New York Central | 175 | 225 | ____ |
| | (D) Orange, Illinois Central | 300 | 450 | ____ |
| | (E) 2-tone blue, Lionel Lines | 300 | 415 | ____ |
| | (F) Orange, New York Central | 200 | 260 | ____ |

| | | Good | Exc | Cond/$ |
|---|---|---|---|---|
| **711** | Remote Control Switches, pair (O72), *35–42* | 80 | 150 | ____ |
| **712** | Observation Car (O), *24–34* | | | |
| | (A) Red, Lionel Lines | 185 | 355 | ____ |
| | (B) Orange, Lionel Lines | 140 | 265 | ____ |
| | (C) Orange, New York Central | 168 | 310 | ____ |
| | (D) Orange, Illinois Central | 280 | 530 | ____ |
| | (E) 2-tone blue, Lionel Lines | 280 | 485 | ____ |
| **714** | Boxcar (O), *40–42\** | 350 | 610 | ____ |
| **714K** | Boxcar, unbuilt (O), *40–42* | | 480 | ____ |
| **715** | Tank Car (O), *40–42\** | | | |
| | (A) SEPS 8124 decal | 340 | 610 | ____ |
| | (B) SUNX 715 decal | 435 | 880 | ____ |
| **715K** | Tank Car, unbuilt (O), *40–42* | | 530 | ____ |
| **716** | Hopper Car (O), *40–42\** | 310 | 392 | ____ |
| **716K** | Hopper Car, unbuilt (O), *40–42* | | 730 | ____ |
| **717** | Caboose (O), *40–42\** | 340 | 510 | ____ |
| **717K** | Caboose, unbuilt (O), *40–42* | | 590 | ____ |
| **720** | 90-degree Crossing (O72), *35–42* | 21 | 40 | ____ |
| **721** | Manual Switches, pair (O72), *35–42* | 50 | 105 | ____ |
| **730** | 90-degree Crossing (O72), *35–42* | 20 | 36 | ____ |
| **731** | Remote Control Switches, pair, T-rail (O72), *35–42* | 80 | 135 | ____ |
| **751E/W** | Set: 752, 753 (2), 754 (O), *34–41\** | 640 | 1050 | ____ |
| **752E** | Diesel only (O), *34–41\** | | | |
| | (A) Yellow and brown | 190 | 355 | ____ |
| | (B) Aluminum | 180 | 340 | ____ |
| **753** | Coach (O), *36–41* | | | |
| | (A) Yellow and brown | 100 | 185 | ____ |
| | (B) Aluminum | 95 | 180 | ____ |
| **754** | Observation Car (O), *36–41* | | | |
| | (A) Yellow and brown | 100 | 185 | ____ |
| | (B) Aluminum | 95 | 180 | ____ |
| **760** | Curved Track, 16 pieces, (O72), *35–42* | 37 | 70 | ____ |
| **761** | Curved Track (O72), *34–42* | 1 | 2 | ____ |
| **762** | Straight Track (O72), *34–42* | 1 | 2 | ____ |
| **762S** | Insulated Straight Track (O72), *34–42* | 2 | 5 | ____ |
| **763E** | 4-6-4 Locomotive (O), *37–42* | | | |
| | (A) Gunmetal, 263 or 2263W Tender | 1200 | 2650 | ____ |
| | (B) Gunmetal, 2226X or 2226WX Tender | 1350 | 2950 | ____ |
| | (C) Black, 2226WX Tender | 1200 | 2650 | ____ |
| **771** | Curved Track, T-rail (O72), *35–42* | 3 | 10 | ____ |
| **772** | Straight Track, T-rail (O72), *35–42* | 4 | 12 | ____ |

| | | Good | Exc | Cond/$ |
|---|---|---|---|---|
| 773 | Fishplate Set, 50 plates (072), *36–42* | 25 | 32 | ____ |
| 782 | *Hiawatha* Combine Car (O), *35–41*\* | 230 | 380 | ____ |
| 783 | *Hiawatha* Coach (O), *35–41*\* | 140 | 290 | ____ |
| 784 | *Hiawatha* Observation Car (O), *35–41*\* | 205 | 445 | ____ |
| 792 | *Rail Chief* Combine Car (O), *37–41*\* | 215 | 580 | ____ |
| 793 | *Rail Chief* Coach (O), *37–41*\* | 290 | 800 | ____ |
| 794 | *Rail Chief* Observation Car (O), *37–41*\* | 250 | 800 | ____ |
| 800 | Boxcar (2⅞"), *04–05*\* | 2500 | 4050 | ____ |
| 800 | Boxcar (O), *15–26* | | | |
| | (A) Light orange body, brown-maroon roof | 45 | 70 | ____ |
| | (B) Orange body and roof, PRR | 30 | 43 | ____ |
| 801 | Caboose (O), *15–26* | 36 | 46 | ____ |
| 802 | Stock Car (O), *15–26* | 43 | 60 | ____ |
| 803 | Hopper Car, early (O), *23–28* | 28 | 55 | ____ |
| 803 | Hopper Car, late (O), *29–34* | 39 | 55 | ____ |
| 804 | Tank Car (O), *23–28* | 22 | 45 | ____ |
| 805 | Boxcar (O), *27–34* | | | |
| | (A) Pea green, terra-cotta roof | 35 | 55 | ____ |
| | (B) Pea green, maroon roof | 44 | 115 | ____ |
| | (C) Orange, maroon roof | 44 | 95 | ____ |
| 806 | Stock Car (O), *27–34* | | | |
| | (A) Pea green, terra-cotta roof | 42 | 75 | ____ |
| | (B) Orange, various color roofs | 35 | 50 | ____ |
| 807 | Caboose (O), *27–40* | | | |
| | (A) Peacock body, dark green roof | 20 | 35 | ____ |
| | (B) Red body, peacock roof | 20 | 38 | ____ |
| | (C) Light red body and roof | 23 | 40 | ____ |
| 809 | Dump Car (O), *31–41* | | | |
| | (A) Orange bin | 40 | 70 | ____ |
| | (B) Green bin | 40 | 85 | ____ |
| 810 | Crane Car (O), *30–42* | | | |
| | (A) Terra-cotta cab, maroon roof | 170 | 270 | ____ |
| | (B) Cream cab, vermilion roof | 130 | 205 | ____ |
| 811 | Flatcar (O), *26–40* | | | |
| | (A) Maroon | 40 | 70 | ____ |
| | (B) Aluminum | 47 | 100 | ____ |
| 812 | Gondola (O), *26–42* | 44 | 83 | ____ |
| 812T | Tool Set: pick, shovel, spade, *30–41* | 40 | 95 | ____ |

| | | Good | Exc | Cond/$ |
|---|---|---|---|---|
| **813** | Stock Car (O), *26–42* | | | |
| | (A) Orange body, pea green roof | 65 | 145 | ____ |
| | (B) Orange body, maroon roof | 55 | 135 | ____ |
| | (C) Cream body, maroon roof | 100 | 225 | ____ |
| | (D) Tuscan body and roof | | 1600 | ____ |
| **814** | Boxcar (O), *26–42* | | | |
| | (A) Cream, orange roof | 46 | 105 | ____ |
| | (B) Cream, maroon roof | 115 | 140 | ____ |
| | (C) Yellow, brown roof | 110 | 120 | ____ |
| **814R** | Refrigerator Car (O), *29–42* | | | |
| | (A) Ivory, peacock roof | 100 | 198 | ____ |
| | (B) White, light blue roof | 120 | 265 | ____ |
| | (C) Flat white, brown roof | 600 | 900 | ____ |
| **815** | Tank Car (O), *26–42* | | | |
| | (A) Pea green, maroon frame | 250 | 510 | ____ |
| | (B) Pea green, black frame | 70 | 155 | ____ |
| | (C) Aluminum, black frame | 50 | 115 | ____ |
| | (D) Orange-yellow, black frame | 150 | 255 | ____ |
| **816** | Hopper Car (O), *27–42* | | | |
| | (A) Olive green | 85 | 155 | ____ |
| | (B) Red body | 65 | 115 | ____ |
| | (C) Black body | 370 | 680 | ____ |
| **817** | Caboose (O), *26–42* | | | |
| | (A) Peacock body, dark green roof | 45 | 70 | ____ |
| | (B) Red body, peacock roof | 45 | 80 | ____ |
| | (C) Light red body and roof | 45 | 80 | ____ |
| **820** | Boxcar (O), *15–26* | | | |
| | (A) Orange, Illinois Central | 38 | 80 | ____ |
| | (B) Orange, Union Pacific | 48 | 105 | ____ |
| **820** | Floodlight Car (O), *31–42* | | | |
| | (A) Terra-cotta | 100 | 180 | ____ |
| | (B) Green | 100 | 175 | ____ |
| | (C) Light green | 105 | 180 | ____ |
| **821** | Stock Car (O), *15–16, 25–26* | 45 | 85 | ____ |
| **822** | Caboose (O), *15–26* | 35 | 65 | ____ |
| **831** | Flatcar (O), *27–34* | 24 | 43 | ____ |
| **840** | Industrial Power Station, *28–40*\* | 1200 | 3050 | ____ |
| **900** | Ammunition Car (O), *17–21* | 120 | 340 | ____ |
| **900** | Box Trail Car (2⅞"), *04–05*\* | 2000 | 3600 | ____ |
| **901** | Gondola (O), *19–27* | 25 | 49 | ____ |
| **902** | Gondola (O), *27–34* | 29 | 45 | ____ |

| | | Good | Exc | Cond/$ |
|---|---|---|---|---|
| **910** | Grove of Trees, *32–42* | 70 | 155 | ____ |
| **911** | Country Estate, *32–42* | 195 | 410 | ____ |
| **912** | Suburban Home | 300 | 620 | ____ |
| **913** | Landscaped Bungalow, *40–42* | 140 | 285 | ____ |
| **914** | Park Landscape, *32–35* | 90 | 205 | ____ |
| **915** | Tunnel, 65" or 60" long, *32–33, 35* | 160 | 435 | ____ |
| **916** | Tunnel, 29¼" long, *35* | 95 | 180 | ____ |
| **917** | Scenic Hillside, 34" x 15", *32–36* | 90 | 205 | ____ |
| **918** | Scenic Hillside, 30" x 10", *32–36* | 90 | 205 | ____ |
| **919** | Park Grass, cloth bag, *32–42* | 8 | 17 | ____ |
| **920** | Village, *32–33* | 600 | 1600 | ____ |
| **921** | Scenic Park, 3 pieces, *32–33* | 980 | 2600 | ____ |
| **921C** | Park Center, *32–33* | 400 | 1050 | ____ |
| **922** | Terrace, *32–36* | 90 | 175 | ____ |
| **923** | Tunnel, 40¼" long, *33–42* | 90 | 225 | ____ |
| **924** | Tunnel, 30" long (072), *35–42* | 50 | 135 | ____ |
| **925** | Lubricant, *35–42* | 1 | 2 | ____ |
| **927** | Flag Plot, *37–42* | 70 | 135 | ____ |
| **1000** | Passenger Car (2⅞"), *05** | 4500 | 6750 | ____ |
| **1000** | Trolley Trailer (std), *10–16* | 1400 | 2250 | ____ |
| **1010** | Electric Locomotive 0-4-0, Winner Lines (O), *31–32* | 90 | 160 | ____ |
| **1010** | Interurban Trailer (std), *10–16* | 1000 | 1800 | ____ |
| **1011** | Pullman Car, Winner Lines (O), *31–32* | 55 | 75 | ____ |
| **1012** | Station, *32* | 50 | 70 | ____ |
| **1015** | 0-4-0 Locomotive (O), *31–32* | 100 | 205 | ____ |
| **1017** | Winner Station, *33* | 25 | 70 | ____ |
| **1019** | Observation Car (O), *31–32* | 50 | 70 | ____ |
| **1020** | Baggage Car (O), *31–32* | 65 | 110 | ____ |
| **1021** | 90-degree Crossover (027), *32–42* | 1 | 4 | ____ |
| **1022** | Tunnel, 18¾" long (O), *35–42* | 15 | 32 | ____ |
| **1023** | Tunnel, 19" long, *34–42* | 20 | 41 | ____ |
| **1024** | Switches, pair (027), *37–42* | 4 | 15 | ____ |
| **1025** | Bumper (027), *40–42* | 14 | 25 | ____ |
| **1027** | Transformer Station, *34* | 50 | 115 | ____ |
| **1028** | Transformer, 40 watts, *39* | 3 | 11 | ____ |
| **1029** | Transformer, 25 watts, *36* | 6 | 18 | ____ |
| **1030** | Electric Locomotive 0-4-0 (O), *32* | 75 | 135 | ____ |
| **1030** | Transformer, 40 watts, *35–38* | 6 | 23 | ____ |
| **1035** | 0-4-0 Locomotive (O), *32* | 75 | 115 | ____ |
| **1037** | Transformer, 40 watts, *40–42* | 7 | 23 | ____ |
| **1038** | Transformer, 30 watts, *40* | 2 | 4 | ____ |

| | | Good | Exc | Cond/$ |
|---|---|---|---|---|
| **1039** | Transformer, 35 watts, *37–40* | 7 | 18 | ____ |
| **1040** | Transformer, 60 watts, *37–39* | 12 | 27 | ____ |
| **1041** | Transformer, 60 watts, *39–42* | 13 | 30 | ____ |
| **1045** | Watchman, *38–42* | 30 | 65 | ____ |
| **1050** | Passenger Car Trailer (2⅞"), *05\** | 5000 | 7200 | ____ |
| **1100** | Summer Trolley Trailer (std), *10–13* | | NRS | ____ |
| **1100** | Mickey Mouse Handcar, *35–37\** | | | |
| | (A) Red base | 405 | 640 | ____ |
| | (B) Apple green base, orange shoes | 500 | 880 | ____ |
| | (C) Orange base | 600 | 1225 | ____ |
| **1103** | Peter Rabbit Handcar (O), *35–37\** | 330 | 820 | ____ |
| **1105** | Santa Claus Handcar (O), *35–35\** | | | |
| | (A) Red base | 660 | 1050 | ____ |
| | (B) Green base | 720 | 1200 | ____ |
| **1107** | Transformer Station, *33* | 25 | 70 | ____ |
| **1107** | Donald Duck Handcar (O), *36–37\** | | | |
| | (A) White dog house, red roof | 475 | 1200 | ____ |
| | (B) White dog house, green roof | 450 | 1100 | ____ |
| | (C) Orange dog house, green roof | 640 | 1850 | ____ |
| **1121** | Switches, pair (O27), *37–42* | 15 | 34 | ____ |
| **1506L** | 0-4-0 Locomotive (O), *33–34* | 95 | 125 | ____ |
| **1506M** | 0-4-0 Locomotive (O), *35* | 250 | 430 | ____ |
| **1508** | 0-4-0 Commodore Vanderbilt with 1509 Mickey Mouse stoker Tender, *35* | 420 | 690 | ____ |
| **1511** | 0-4-0 Locomotive (O), *36–37* | 110 | 160 | ____ |
| **1512** | Gondola (O), *31–33, 36–37* | 29 | 47 | ____ |
| **1514** | Boxcar (O), *31–37* | 23 | 41 | ____ |
| **1515** | Tank Car (O), *33–37* | 25 | 41 | ____ |
| **1517** | Caboose (O), *31–37* | 25 | 41 | ____ |
| **1518** | Mickey Mouse Circus Dining Car (O), *35* | 120 | 260 | ____ |
| **1519** | Mickey Mouse Band Car (O), *35* | 120 | 260 | ____ |
| **1520** | Mickey Mouse Circus Car (O), *35* | 120 | 260 | ____ |
| **1536** | Mickey Mouse Circus Set: 1508, 1509, 1518, 1519, 1520, *35* | 770 | 1350 | ____ |
| **1550** | Switches, for windup trains, pair, *33–37* | 2 | 5 | ____ |
| **1555** | 90-degree Crossover, for windup trains, *33–37* | 1 | 2 | ____ |
| **1560** | Station, *33–37* | 15 | 34 | ____ |
| **1569** | Accessory Set, 8 pieces, *33–37* | 35 | 70 | ____ |
| **1588** | 0-4-0 Locomotive (O), *36–37* | 150 | 250 | ____ |
| **1630** | Pullman Car (O), *38–42* | | | |
| | (A) Aluminum windows | 35 | 70 | ____ |
| | (B) Light gray windows | 47 | 80 | ____ |

| | | Good | Exc | Cond/$ |
|---|---|---|---|---|
| **1631** | Observation Car (O), *38–42* | | | |
| | (A) Aluminum windows | 35 | 70 | ____ |
| | (B) Light gray windows | 47 | 80 | ____ |
| **1651E** | Electric Locomotive 0-4-0 (O), *33* | 130 | 240 | ____ |
| **1661E** | 2-4-0 Locomotive (O), *33* | 75 | 160 | ____ |
| **1662** | 0-4-0 Locomotive (O27), *40–42* | 275 | 420 | ____ |
| **1663** | 0-4-0 Locomotive (O27), *40–42* | 200 | 385 | ____ |
| **1664/E** | 2-4-2 Locomotive (O27), *38–42* | | | |
| | (A) Gunmetal | 60 | 100 | ____ |
| | (B) Black | 60 | 95 | ____ |
| **1666/E** | 2-6-2 Locomotive (O27), *38–42* | | | |
| | (A) Gunmetal | 115 | 170 | ____ |
| | (B) Black | 95 | 145 | ____ |
| **1668/E** | 2-6-2 Locomotive (O27), *37–41* | | | |
| | (A) Gunmetal | 75 | 115 | ____ |
| | (B) Black | 75 | 130 | ____ |
| **1673** | Coach (O), *36–37* | | | |
| | (A) Aluminum windows | 35 | 75 | ____ |
| | (B) Light gray windows | 47 | 90 | ____ |
| **1674** | Pullman Car (O), *36–37* | 35 | 75 | ____ |
| **1675** | Observation Car (O), *36–37* | 30 | 70 | ____ |
| **1677** | Gondola (O), *33–35, 39–42* | | | |
| | (A) Light blue, Ives | 40 | 60 | ____ |
| | (B) Blue or red, Lionel | 21 | 37 | ____ |
| **1679** | Boxcar (O), *33–42* | | | |
| | (A) Cream, Ives | 23 | 38 | ____ |
| | (B) Cream, Lionel | 23 | 38 | ____ |
| | (C) Cream or yellow, Baby Ruth | 19 | 38 | ____ |
| **1680** | Tank Car (O), *33–42* | | | |
| | (A) Aluminum, Ives Tank Lines | 80 | 95 | ____ |
| | (B) Aluminum, no Ives lettering | 19 | 34 | ____ |
| | (C) Orange, Shell Oil | 15 | 29 | ____ |
| **1681** | 2-4-0 Locomotive (O), *34–35* | | | |
| | (A) Black, red frame | 55 | 120 | ____ |
| | (B) Red, red frame | 110 | 145 | ____ |
| **1681E** | 2-4-0 Locomotive (O), *34–35* | | | |
| | (A) Black, red frame | 65 | 130 | ____ |
| | (B) Red, red frame | 130 | 165 | ____ |
| **1682** | Caboose (O), *33–42* | | | |
| | (A) Vermilion, Ives | 34 | 70 | ____ |
| | (B) Red or tuscan, Lionel | 17 | 40 | ____ |

| | | Good | Exc | Cond/$ |
|---|---|---|---|---|
| **1684** | 2-4-2 Locomotive (027), *41–42* | | | |
| | (A) Black | 45 | 70 | ____ |
| | (A) Gunmetal | 45 | 70 | ____ |
| **1685** | Coach (O), *33–37 u* | | | |
| | (A) Gray, maroon roof | 240 | 495 | ____ |
| | (B) Red, maroon roof | 170 | 335 | ____ |
| | (C) Blue, silver roof | 170 | 315 | ____ |
| **1686** | Baggage Car (O), *33–37 u* | | | |
| | (A) Gray, maroon roof | 240 | 495 | ____ |
| | (B) Red, maroon roof | 170 | 335 | ____ |
| | (C) Blue, silver roof | 170 | 315 | ____ |
| **1687** | Observation Car (O), *33–37 u* | | | |
| | (A) Gray, maroon roof | 170 | 315 | ____ |
| | (B) Red, maroon roof | 180 | 315 | ____ |
| | (C) Blue, silver roof | 170 | 315 | ____ |
| **1688/E** | 2-4-2 Locomotive (027), *36–46* | 50 | 95 | ____ |
| **1689E** | 2-4-2 Locomotive (027), *36–37* | | | |
| | (A) Gunmetal | 75 | 115 | ____ |
| | (B) Black | 60 | 100 | ____ |
| **1690** | Pullman Car (O), *33–40* | 35 | 60 | ____ |
| **1691** | Observation Car (O), *33–40* | 35 | 60 | ____ |
| **1692** | Pullman Car (027), *39 u* | 45 | 70 | ____ |
| **1693** | Observation Car (027), *39 u* | 45 | 70 | ____ |
| **1700E** | Diesel, power unit only (027), *35–37* | 45 | 70 | ____ |
| **1700E** | Set: 1700, 1701 (2), 1702, *35–37 u* | | | |
| | (A) Aluminum and light red | 140 | 250 | ____ |
| | (B) Chrome and light red | 140 | 250 | ____ |
| | (C) Orange and gray | 155 | 285 | ____ |
| **1701** | Coach (027), *35–37* | | | |
| | (A) Chrome sides and roof | 20 | 46 | ____ |
| | (B) Silver sides and roof | 30 | 55 | ____ |
| | (C) Orange and gray | 75 | 150 | ____ |
| **1702** | Observation Car (027), *35–37* | | | |
| | (A) Chrome sides and roof | 20 | 46 | ____ |
| | (B) Silver sides and roof | 30 | 55 | ____ |
| | (C) Orange and gray | 75 | 150 | ____ |
| **1703** | Observation Car, hooked coupler, *35–37 u* | 49 | 110 | ____ |
| **1717** | Gondola (O), *33–40 u* | 30 | 48 | ____ |
| **1717X** | Gondola (O), *40 u* | 27 | 48 | ____ |
| **1719** | Boxcar (O), *33–40 u* | 30 | 50 | ____ |
| **1719X** | Boxcar (O), *41–42 u* | 30 | 50 | ____ |

| | | Good | Exc | Cond/$ |
|---|---|---|---|---|
| **1722** | Caboose (O), *33–42 u* | 25 | 50 | ____ |
| **1722X** | Caboose (O), *39–40 u* | 26 | 41 | ____ |
| **1766** | Pullman Car (std), *34–40*\* | | | |
| | (A) Terra-cotta, maroon roof, brass trim | 300 | 650 | ____ |
| | (B) Red, maroon roof, nickel trim | 300 | 540 | ____ |
| **1767** | Baggage Car (std), *34–40*\* | | | |
| | (A) Terra-cotta, maroon roof, brass trim | 295 | 850 | ____ |
| | (B) Red, maroon roof, nickel trim | 295 | 700 | ____ |
| **1768** | Observation Car (std), *34–40*\* | | | |
| | (A) Terra-cotta, maroon roof, brass trim | 300 | 650 | ____ |
| | (B) Red, maroon roof, nickel trim | 300 | 540 | ____ |
| **1811** | Pullman Car (O), *33–37* | 32 | 70 | ____ |
| **1812** | Observation Car (O), *33–37* | 30 | 65 | ____ |
| **1813** | Baggage Car (O), *33–37* | 60 | 135 | ____ |
| **1816/W** | Diesel (O), *35–37* | 100 | 240 | ____ |
| **1817** | Coach (O), *35–37* | 22 | 50 | ____ |
| **1818** | Observation Car (O), *35–37* | 22 | 50 | ____ |
| **1835E** | 2-4-2 Locomotive (std), *34–39* | 470 | 730 | ____ |
| **1910** | Electric Locomotive 0-6-0, early (std), *10–11* | 920 | 1550 | ____ |
| **1910** | Electric Locomotive 0-6-0, late (std), *12* | 550 | 1350 | ____ |
| **1910** | Pullman Car (std), *09–10 u* | 860 | 1800 | ____ |
| **1911** | Electric Locomotive 0-4-0, early (std), *10–12* | 860 | 1700 | ____ |
| **1911** | Electric Locomotive 0-4-0, late (std), *13* | 700 | 1100 | ____ |
| **1911** | Electric Locomotive 0-4-4-0 Special (std), *11–12* | 860 | 2500 | ____ |
| **1912** | Electric Locomotive 0-4-4-0 (std), *10–12*\* | | | |
| | (A) New York, New Haven & Hartford | 1550 | 3200 | ____ |
| | (B) New York Central Lines | 1300 | 2700 | ____ |
| **1912** | Electric Locomotive 0-4-4-0 Special (std), *11*\* | 2500 | 4500 | ____ |
| **2200** | Summer Trolley Trailer (std), *10–13* | 1100 | 2250 | ____ |
| **2600** | Pullman Car (O), *38–42* | 80 | 155 | ____ |
| **2601** | Observation Car (O), *38–42* | 60 | 115 | ____ |
| **2602** | Baggage Car (O), *38–42* | 90 | 185 | ____ |
| **2613** | Pullman Car (O), *38–42*\* | | | |
| | (A) Blue, 2-tone blue roof | 100 | 270 | ____ |
| | (B) State green, 2-tone green roof | 200 | 440 | ____ |
| **2614** | Observation Car (O), *38–42*\* | | | |
| | (A) Blue, 2-tone blue roof | 100 | 270 | ____ |
| | (B) State green, 2-tone green roof | 200 | 440 | ____ |
| **2615** | Baggage Car (O), *38–42*\* | | | |
| | (A) Blue, 2-tone blue roof | 115 | 270 | ____ |
| | (B) State green, 2-tone green roof | 200 | 420 | ____ |

| | | Good | Exc | Cond/$ |
|---|---|---|---|---|
| **2620** | Floodlight Car (O), *38–42* | 65 | 100 | ____ |
| **2623** | Pullman Car (O), *41–42* | | | |
| | (A) *Irvington* | 175 | 335 | ____ |
| | (B) *Manhattan* | 165 | 310 | ____ |
| **2624** | Pullman Car (O), *41–42* | 750 | 1700 | ____ |
| **2630** | Pullman Car (O), *38–42* | 30 | 70 | ____ |
| **2631** | Observation Car (O), *38–42* | 30 | 70 | ____ |
| **2640** | Pullman Car, illuminated (O), *38–42* | | | |
| | (A) Light blue, aluminum roof | 30 | 70 | ____ |
| | (B) State green, dark green roof | 28 | 70 | ____ |
| **2641** | Observation Car, illuminated (O), *38–42* | | | |
| | (A) Light blue, aluminum roof | 30 | 70 | ____ |
| | (B) State green, dark green roof | 28 | 70 | ____ |
| **2642** | Pullman Car (O), *41–42* | 32 | 70 | ____ |
| **2643** | Observation Car (O), *41–42* | 30 | 65 | ____ |
| **2651** | Flatcar (O), *38–42* | 30 | 50 | ____ |
| **2652** | Gondola (O), *38–41* | 26 | 55 | ____ |
| **2653** | Hopper Car (O), *38–42* | | | |
| | (A) Stephen Girard green | 38 | 70 | ____ |
| | (B) Black | 60 | 132 | ____ |
| **2654** | Tank Car (O), *38–42* | | | |
| | (A) Aluminum, Sunoco | 35 | 60 | ____ |
| | (B) Orange, Shell | 35 | 60 | ____ |
| | (C) Light gray, Sunoco | 41 | 70 | ____ |
| **2655** | Boxcar (O), *38–42* | | | |
| | (A) Cream, maroon roof | 35 | 65 | ____ |
| | (B) Cream, tuscan roof | 38 | 75 | ____ |
| **2656** | Stock Car (O), *38–41* | | | |
| | (A) Light gray, red roof | 45 | 75 | ____ |
| | (B) Burnt orange, tuscan roof | 75 | 115 | ____ |
| **2657** | Caboose (O), *40–41* | 31 | 45 | ____ |
| **2657X** | Caboose (O), *40–41* | 25 | 41 | ____ |
| **2659** | Dump Car (O), *38–41* | 40 | 70 | ____ |
| **2660** | Crane (O), *38–42* | 85 | 115 | ____ |
| **2672** | Caboose (O27), *41–42* | 22 | 35 | ____ |
| **2677** | Gondola (O27), *39–41* | 26 | 37 | ____ |
| **2679** | Boxcar (O27), *38–42* | 26 | 29 | ____ |
| **2680** | Tank Car (O27), *38–42* | | | |
| | (A) Aluminum, Sunoco | 15 | 41 | ____ |
| | (B) Orange, Shell | 15 | 41 | ____ |
| **2682** | Caboose (O27), *38–42* | 18 | 32 | ____ |

| | | Good | Exc | Cond/$ |
|---|---|---|---|---|
| 2682X | Caboose (027), *38–42* | 22 | 35 | ____ |
| 2717 | Gondola (O), *38–42 u* | 21 | 41 | ____ |
| 2719 | Boxcar (O), *38–42 u* | 29 | 50 | ____ |
| 2722 | Caboose (O), *38–42 u* | 25 | 50 | ____ |
| 2755 | Tank Car (O), *41–42* | 65 | 128 | ____ |
| 2757 | Caboose (O), *41–42* | 26 | 44 | ____ |
| 2757X | Caboose (O), *41–42* | 25 | 36 | ____ |
| 2758 | Automobile Boxcar (O), *41–42* | 38 | 60 | ____ |
| 2810 | Crane Car (O), *38–42* | 145 | 205 | ____ |
| 2811 | Flatcar (O), *38–42* | 65 | 95 | ____ |
| 2812 | Gondola (O), *38–42* | | | |
| | (A) Green | 42 | 83 | ____ |
| | (B) Dark orange | 44 | 95 | ____ |
| 2813 | Stock Car (O), *38–42* | 120 | 223 | ____ |
| 2814 | Boxcar (O), *38–42* | | | |
| | (A) Cream, maroon roof | 85 | 198 | ____ |
| | (B) Orange, brown roof | 85 | 205 | ____ |
| 2814R | Refrigerator Car (O), *38–42* | | | |
| | (A) White, light blue roof, nickel plates | 150 | 258 | ____ |
| | (B) White, brown roof, no plates | 375 | 660 | ____ |
| 2815 | Tank Car (O), *38–42* | | | |
| | (A) Aluminum | 85 | 165 | ____ |
| | (B) Orange | 135 | 250 | ____ |
| 2816 | Hopper Car (O), *35–42* | | | |
| | (A) Red | 100 | 190 | ____ |
| | (B) Black | 110 | 220 | ____ |
| 2817 | Caboose (O), *36–42* | | | |
| | (A) Light red body and roof | 90 | 145 | ____ |
| | (B) Flat red body, tuscan roof | 140 | 225 | ____ |
| 2820 | Floodlight Car (O), *38–42* | | | |
| | (A) Stamped nickel searchlights | 110 | 205 | ____ |
| | (B) Gray die-cast searchlights | 120 | 260 | ____ |
| 2954 | Boxcar (O), *40–42*\* | 145 | 349 | ____ |
| 2955 | Sunoco Tank Car (O), *40–42*\* | | | |
| | (A) Shell decal | 225 | 498 | ____ |
| | (B) Sunoco decal | 340 | 690 | ____ |
| 2956 | Hopper Car (O), *40–42*\* | 160 | 400 | ____ |
| 2957 | Caboose (O), *40–42*\* | 145 | 313 | ____ |
| 3300 | Summer Trolley Trailer (std), *10–13* | 1400 | 2250 | ____ |
| 3651 | Operating Lumber Car (O), *39–42* | 24 | 55 | ____ |
| 3652 | Operating Gondola (O), *39–42* | 36 | 85 | ____ |

| | | Good | Exc | Cond/S |
|---|---|---|---|---|
| **3659** | Operating Dump Car (O), *39–42* | 26 | 32 | ___ |
| **3811** | Operating Lumber Car (O), *39–42* | 33 | 77 | ___ |
| **3814** | Operating Merchandise Car (O), *39–42* | 125 | 245 | ___ |
| **3859** | Operating Dump Car (O), *38–42* | 44 | 100 | ___ |
| **17255** | Chevy DD Boxcar "9200" (std O), *99* | | 38 | ___ |

## Other Transformers and Motors

| | | Good | Exc | Cond/S |
|---|---|---|---|---|
| **A** | Miniature Motor, *04* | 50 | 95 | ___ |
| **A** | Transformer, 40, 60 watts, *21–37* | 8 | 25 | ___ |
| **B** | New Departure Motor, *06–16* | 75 | 135 | ___ |
| **B** | Transformer, 50, 75 watts, *16–38* | 6 | 24 | ___ |
| **C** | New Departure Motor, *06–16* | 100 | 180 | ___ |
| **D** | New Departure Motor, *06–14* | 100 | 180 | ___ |
| **E** | New Departure Motor, *06–14* | 100 | 180 | ___ |
| **F** | New Departure Motor, *06–14* | 100 | 180 | ___ |
| **G** | Fan Motor, battery-operated, *06–14* | 100 | 180 | ___ |
| **K** | Transformer, 150, 200 watts, *13–38* | 19 | 95 | ___ |
| **L** | Transformer, 50, 75 watts, *13–16, 33–38* | 8 | 24 | ___ |
| **M** | Peerless Motor, battery-operated, *15–20* | 30 | 80 | ___ |
| **N** | Transformer, 50 watts, *41–42* | 7 | 23 | ___ |
| **Q** | Transformer, 50 watts, *14–15* | 13 | 32 | ___ |
| **Q** | Transformer, 75 watts, *38–42* | 15 | 40 | ___ |
| **R** | Peerless Motor, battery-operated, reversing, *15–20* | 30 | 75 | ___ |
| **R** | Transformer, 100 watts, *38–42* | 27 | 60 | ___ |
| **S** | Transformer, 50 watts, *14–17* | 18 | 37 | ___ |
| **T** | Transformer, 75, 100, 150 watts, *14–28* | 10 | 28 | ___ |
| **U** | Transformer, Aladdin, *32–33* | 6 | 16 | ___ |
| **V** | Transformer, 150 watts, *39–42* | 55 | 95 | ___ |
| **W** | Transformer, 75 watts, *32–33* | 7 | 37 | ___ |
| **Y** | Peerless Motor, battery-operated, 3-speed, *15–20* | 40 | 80 | ___ |
| **Z** | Transformer, 250 watts, *39–42* | 118 | 170 | ___ |

### Track, Lockons, and Contactors

| | Good | Exc | Cond/$ |
|---|---|---|---|
| O Straight | | 1 | ____ |
| O Curve | | 1 | ____ |
| 072 Straight | 1 | 2 | ____ |
| 072 Curve | 1 | 2 | ____ |
| 027 Straight | | 1 | ____ |
| 027 Curve | | 1 | ____ |
| Standard Straight | 1 | 3 | ____ |
| Standard Curve | 1 | 2 | ____ |
| Standard Insulated Straight, *33–42* | 2 | 4 | ____ |
| Standard Insulated Curve, *33–42* | 1 | 2 | ____ |
| O Gauge Lockon | | 1 | ____ |
| Standard Gauge Lockon | | 1 | ____ |
| UTC Lockon | | 1 | ____ |
| 145C Contactor | 3 | 10 | ____ |
| 153C Contactor | 3 | 7 | ____ |
| Track Clips, dozen (O), *37* | 4 | 12 | ____ |

| | | Good | Exc | Cond/$ |
|---|---|---|---|---|
| **011-11** | Fiber Pins, dozen (O), *46–50* | 1 | 3 | ___ |
| **011-43** | Insulating Pins, dozen (O), *61* | 1 | 2 | ___ |
| **020** | 90-degree Crossover (O), *45–61* | 8 | 11 | ___ |
| **020X** | 45-degree Crossover (O), *46–59* | 7 | 10 | ___ |
| **022** | Remote Control Switches, pair (O), *45–69* | 34 | 46 | ___ |
| **022-500** | Adapter Set (O), *57–61* | 1 | 6 | ___ |
| **022A** | Remote Control Switches, pair (O), *47* | 32 | 165 | ___ |
| **25** | Bumper (O), *46–47* | 8 | 22 | ___ |
| **26** | Bumper, *48–50* | | | |
| | (A) Red, *49–50* | 5 | 20 | ___ |
| | (B) Gray, *48* | 20 | 66 | ___ |
| **027C-1** | Track Clips, box of 12 (O27), *47, 49* | 2 | 9 | ___ |
| **027C-1** | Track Clips, box of 50 (O27) | | 150 | ___ |
| **30** | Water Tower, *47–50* | 49 | 104 | ___ |
| **31** | Curved Track (Super O), *57–66* | 1 | 2 | ___ |
| **31-7** | Power Blade Connection, dozen (Super O), *57–60* | | 1 | ___ |
| **31-15** | Ground Rail Pin, dozen (Super O), *57–66* | | 2 | ___ |
| **31-45** | Power Blade Connection, dozen (Super O), *61–66* | | 2 | ___ |
| **32** | Straight Track (Super O), *57–66* | 1 | 3 | ___ |
| **32-10** | Insulating Pin, dozen (Super O), *57–60* | | 5 | ___ |
| **32-20** | Power Blade Insulator, dozen (Super O), *57–60* | | 3 | ___ |
| **32-25** | Insulating Pin (Super O), *57–61* | | 1 | ___ |
| **32-30** | Ground Pin (Super O), *57–61* | | 1 | ___ |
| **32-31** | Power Pin (Super O), *57–61* | | 1 | ___ |
| **32-32** | Insulating Pin (Super O), *57–61* | | 1 | ___ |
| **32-33** | Ground Pin (Super O), *57–61* | | 1 | ___ |
| **32-34** | Power Pin (Super O), *57–61* | | 1 | ___ |
| **32-45** | Power Blade Insulators, dozen (Super O), *61–66* | 1 | 6 | ___ |
| **32-55** | Insulating Pins, dozen (Super O), *61–66* | 1 | 6 | ___ |
| **33** | Half Curved Track (Super O), *57–66* | 1 | 3 | ___ |
| **34** | Half Straight Track (Super O), *57–66* | 1 | 3 | ___ |
| **35** | Boulevard Lamp, *45–49* | 15 | 40 | ___ |
| **36** | Operating Car Remote Control Set (Super O), *57–66* | 11 | 16 | ___ |
| **37** | Uncoupling Track Set (Super O), *57–66* | 7 | 12 | ___ |
| **38** | Accessory Adapter Tracks, pair (Super O), *57–61* | 6 | 13 | ___ |
| **38** | Operating Water Tower, *46–47* | 160 | 338 | ___ |
| **39** | Operating Set (Super O), *57* | 4 | 8 | ___ |
| **39-5** | Operating Set (Super O), *57–58* | 4 | 8 | ___ |
| **39-6** | Operating Set (Super O), *57–58* | 4 | 25 | ___ |
| **39-15** | Operating Set with blade (Super O), *57–58* | 4 | 8 | ___ |

| | | Good | Exc | Cond/$ |
|---|---|---|---|---|
| **39-20** | Operating Set (Super 0), *57–58* | 4 | 8 | ___ |
| **39-25** | Operating Set (Super 0), *61–66* | 4 | 21 | ___ |
| **39-35** | Operating Set (Super 0), *59* | 4 | 20 | ___ |
| **40** | Hookup Wire, *50–51, 53–63* | | | |
| | (A) Single reel, orange or gray | 7 | 55 | ___ |
| | (B) 8 sealed reels in dealer box | 125 | 500 | ___ |
| **40-25** | Conductor Wire with envelope, *56–59* | 11 | 54 | ___ |
| **40-50** | Cable Reel with envelope, *60–61* | 10 | 53 | ___ |
| **41** | Contactor (Super 0) | 1 | 2 | ___ |
| **41** | U.S. Army Switcher, *55–57* | | | |
| | (A) Unpainted black body | 56 | 113 | ___ |
| | (B) Black-painted body | 250 | 650 | ___ |
| **042/42** | Manual Switches, pair (0), *46–59* | 16 | 39 | ___ |
| **42** | Picatinny Arsenal Switcher, *57* | 113 | 330 | ___ |
| **43** | Power Track (Super 0), *59–66* | 4 | 10 | ___ |
| **44** | U.S. Army Mobile Launcher, *59–62* | 103 | 190 | ___ |
| **44-80** | Missiles, *59–60* | 11 | 26 | ___ |
| **45** | U.S. Marines Mobile Launcher, *60–62* | 133 | 313 | ___ |
| **45** | Automatic Gateman, *46–49* | 24 | 48 | ___ |
| **45N** | Automatic Gateman, *45* | 33 | 50 | ___ |
| **48** | Insulated Straight Track (Super 0), *57–66* | 4 | 10 | ___ |
| **49** | Insulated Curved Track (Super 0), *57–66* | 4 | 10 | ___ |
| **50** | Section Gang Car, *54–64* | | | |
| | (A) Gray bumpers, rotating blue man and fixed olive men, center horn, *54* | 269 | 650 | ___ |
| | (B) Blue bumpers, rotating olive man and fixed blue men, center horn | 34 | 72 | ___ |
| | (C) Blue bumpers, rotating olive man and fixed blue men, off-center horn | 40 | 63 | ___ |
| **51** | Navy Yard Switcher, *56–57* | 75 | 208 | ___ |
| **52** | Fire Car, *58–61* | 103 | 166 | ___ |
| **53** | Rio Grande Snowplow, *57–60* | | | |
| | (A) Backwards "a" in Rio Grande | 120 | 265 | ___ |
| | (B) Correctly printed "a" | 248 | 738 | ___ |
| **54** | Ballast Tamper, *58–61, 66, 68–69* | 105 | 175 | ___ |
| **55** | PRR Tie-Jector Car, *57–61* | 100 | 183 | ___ |
| **55-150** | Ties, 24 pieces, *57–60* | 9 | 35 | ___ |
| **56** | Lamp Post, *46–49* | 27 | 58 | ___ |
| **56** | M&StL Mine Transport, *58* | 245 | 470 | ___ |
| **57** | AEC Switcher, *59–60* | 395 | 645 | ___ |
| **58** | GN Snowplow, *59–61* | 235 | 425 | ___ |
| **58** | Lamp Post, *46–50* | 20 | 58 | ___ |
| **59** | Minuteman Switcher, *62–63* | 240 | 505 | ___ |
| **60** | Lionelville Rapid Transit Trolley, *55–58* | 80 | 113 | ___ |

| | | Good | Exc | Cond/$ |
|---|---|---|---|---|
| **61** | Ground Lockon (Super O), *57–66* | | 1 | ____ |
| **61-25** | Super O Ground clips, dozen, with dealer envelope | 5 | 20 | ____ |
| **62** | Power Lockon (Super O), *57–66* | | 1 | ____ |
| **64** | Street Lamp, *45–49* | 29 | 53 | ____ |
| **65** | Handcar, *62–66* | 113 | 272 | ____ |
| **68** | Executive Inspection Car, *58–61* | 128 | 230 | ____ |
| **69** | Maintenance Car, *60–62* | 85 | 236 | ____ |
| **70** | Yard Light, *49–50* | 20 | 43 | ____ |
| **71** | Lamp Post, *49–59* | 10 | 17 | ____ |
| **75** | Goose Neck Lamps, set of 2, *61–63* | 12 | 21 | ____ |
| **76** | Boulevard Street Lamps, set of 3, *59–66, 68–69* | 16 | 35 | ____ |
| **80** | Controller | 11 | 20 | ____ |
| **88** | Controller, *46–60* | 4 | 10 | ____ |
| **89** | Flagpole, *56–58* | 17 | 47 | ____ |
| **90** | Controller, *55–66* | 4 | 11 | ____ |
| **91** | Circuit Breaker, *57–60* | 13 | 33 | ____ |
| **92** | Circuit Breaker, *59–66, 68–69* | 8 | 20 | ____ |
| **93** | Water Tower, *46–49* | 22 | 60 | ____ |
| **96C** | Controller, *45–54* | 3 | 10 | ____ |
| **97** | Coal Elevator, *46–50* | 83 | 170 | ____ |
| **100** | Multivolt DC/AC Transformer, *58–66* | | 70 | ____ |
| **108** | Trestle Set, 12 black piers | 25 | 36 | ____ |
| **109** | Partial Trestle Set, *61* | | 30 | ____ |
| **110** | Graduated Trestle Set, 22 or 24 piers, *55–69* | 12 | 23 | ____ |
| **111** | Elevated Trestle Set, 10 A piers, *56–69* | 7 | 16 | ____ |
| **111-100** | Elevated Trestle Piers, set of 2, *60–63* | 13 | 56 | ____ |
| **112** | Remote Control Switches, pair (Super O), *57–66* | 75 | 108 | ____ |
| **114** | Newsstand with horn, *57–59* | 32 | 88 | ____ |
| **115** | Passenger Station, *46–49* | 158 | 354 | ____ |
| **118** | Newsstand with whistle, *57–58* | 36 | 97 | ____ |
| **119** | Landscaped Tunnel, *57–58* | | NRS | ____ |
| **120** | 90-degree Crossing (Super O), *57–66* | 7 | 11 | ____ |
| **121** | Landscaped Tunnel, *59–66* | | NRS | ____ |
| **122** | Lamp Assortment, *48–52* | | 183 | ____ |
| **123** | Lamp Assortment, *55–59* | 85 | 185 | ____ |
| **123-60** | Lamp Assortment, *60–63* | | 163 | ____ |
| **125** | Whistle Shack, *50–55* | | | |
| | (A) Gray base | 10 | 40 | ____ |
| | (B) Green base | 15 | 50 | ____ |
| **128** | Animated Newsstand, *57–60* | 70 | 131 | ____ |
| **130** | 60-degree Crossing (Super O), *57–66* | 7 | 13 | ____ |
| **131** | Curved Tunnel, *59–66* | | NRS | ____ |

| | | Good | Exc | Cond/$ |
|---|---|---|---|---|
| 132 | Passenger Station, *49–55* | 48 | 77 | ____ |
| 133 | Passenger Station, *57, 61–62, 66* | 32 | 70 | ____ |
| 137 | Passenger Station, *46* | 87 | 180 | ____ |
| 138 | Water Tower, *53–57* | 43 | 82 | ____ |
| 140 | Automatic Banjo Signal, *54–66* | 16 | 37 | ____ |
| 142 | Manual Switches, pair (Super O), *57–66* | 32 | 59 | ____ |
| 145 | Automatic Gateman, *50–66* | 31 | 51 | ____ |
| 145C | Contactor, *50–60* | 3 | 12 | ____ |
| 147 | Whistle Controller, *61–66* | 1 | 4 | ____ |
| 148 | Dwarf Trackside Signal, *57–60* | 24 | 58 | ____ |
| 148-100 | Controller (SPDT switch), *57–60* | 7 | 15 | ____ |
| 150 | Telegraph Pole Set, *47–50* | 38 | 68 | ____ |
| 151 | Automatic Semaphore, *47–69* | | | |
| | (A) Green base, yellow blade, *47* | 30 | 76 | ____ |
| | (B) Black base, yellow blade, *47* | 19 | 35 | ____ |
| | (C) Black base, red blade, *47* | 168 | 375 | ____ |
| | (D) Green base, yellow blade with raised lenses | 25 | 83 | ____ |
| 152 | Automatic Crossing Gate, *45–49* | 12 | 29 | ____ |
| 153 | Automatic Block Control Signal, *45–59* | 18 | 29 | ____ |
| 153C | Contactor | 3 | 9 | ____ |
| 154 | Automatic Highway Signal, *45–69* | 16 | 30 | ____ |
| 155 | Blinking Light Signal with bell, *55–57* | 32 | 37 | ____ |
| 156 | Station Platform, *46–49* | 45 | 94 | ____ |
| 157 | Station Platform, *52–59* | 12 | 60 | ____ |
| | (A) Maroon base | 20 | 60 | ____ |
| | (B) Red base | 25 | 80 | ____ |
| 160 | Unloading Bin, *52–57* | | | |
| | (A) Plastic | 1 | 5 | ____ |
| | (B) Metal | 19 | 73 | ____ |
| 161 | Mail Pickup Set, *61–63* | 34 | 85 | ____ |
| 163 | Single Target Block Signal, *61–69* | 17 | 30 | ____ |
| 164 | Log Loader, *46–50* | 98 | 178 | ____ |
| 167 | Whistle Controller, *45–46* | 5 | 15 | ____ |
| 175 | Rocket Launcher, *58–60* | 85 | 185 | ____ |
| 175-50 | Extra Rocket, *59–60* | 10 | 27 | ____ |
| 182 | Magnetic Crane, *46–49* | 148 | 267 | ____ |
| 182-22 | Steel Scrap with bag, *46–49* | 50 | 125 | ____ |
| 192 | Operating Control Tower, *59–60* | 110 | 255 | ____ |
| 193 | Industrial Water Tower, *53–55* | | | |
| | (A) Red | 70 | 95 | ____ |
| | (B) Black, *53* | 100 | 160 | ____ |
| 195 | Floodlight Tower, *57–69* | | | |
| | (A) Medium tan base, rubber-stamped lettering | 25 | 80 | ____ |
| | (B) All other variations | 24 | 60 | ____ |

| | | Good | Exc | Cond/$ |
|---|---|---|---|---|
| **195-75** | Floodlight Extension, 8-bulb (with box), *58–60* | 18 | 81 | ___ |
| **196** | Smoke Pellets, *46–47* | 50 | 87 | ___ |
| **197** | Rotating Radar Antenna, *57–59* | 50 | 105 | ___ |
| **199** | Microwave Relay Tower, *58–59* | 28 | 65 | ___ |
| **202** | UP Alco Diesel A Unit, *57* | 42 | 94 | ___ |
| **204** | Santa Fe Alco Diesel AA Units, *57* | 92 | 254 | ___ |
| **205** | Missouri Pacific Alco Diesel AA Units, *57–58* | | | |
| | (A) Plastic pilot bar | 43 | 133 | ___ |
| | (B) Metal pilot bar | 75 | 250 | ___ |
| **206** | Artificial Coal, large bag, *46–68* | 5 | 18 | ___ |
| **207** | Artificial Coal, small bag, *46–48* | 4 | 14 | ___ |
| **208** | Santa Fe Alco Diesel AA Units, *58–59* | 87 | 246 | ___ |
| **209** | New Haven Alco Diesel AA Units, *58* | 323 | 930 | ___ |
| **209** | Wooden Barrels, set of 6, *46–50* | 10 | 23 | ___ |
| **210** | *Texas Special* Alco Diesel AA Units, *58* | 59 | 166 | ___ |
| **211** | *Texas Special* Alco Diesel AA Units, *62–66* | 65 | 150 | ___ |
| **212** | Santa Fe Alco Diesel AA Units, *64–66* | 80 | 155 | ___ |
| **212** | USMC Alco Diesel A Unit, *58–59* | 80 | 175 | ___ |
| **212T** | USMC Diesel Dummy A Unit, *58 u* | 350 | 918 | ___ |
| **213** | M&StL Alco Diesel AA Units, *64* | 70 | 228 | ___ |
| **214** | Plate Girder Bridge, *53–69* | 8 | 23 | ___ |
| **215** | Santa Fe Alco Diesel Units, *65 u* | | | |
| | (A) AB Units | 85 | 165 | ___ |
| | (B) AA Units | 80 | 160 | ___ |
| **216** | Burlington Alco Diesel A Unit, *58* | 115 | 350 | ___ |
| **216** | M&StL Alco Diesel AA Units, *64 u* | 70 | 200 | ___ |
| **217** | B&M Alco Diesel AB Units, *59* | 98 | 239 | ___ |
| **218** | Santa Fe Alco Diesel Units, *59–63* | | | |
| | (A) AA Units | 70 | 165 | ___ |
| | (B) AB Units | 70 | 165 | ___ |
| | (C) AA Units, solid nose decal | 84 | 299 | ___ |
| **219** | Missouri Pacific Alco Diesel AA Units, *59 u* | 80 | 205 | ___ |
| **220** | Santa Fe Alco Diesel Units, *60–61* | | | |
| | (A) A Unit | 65 | 113 | ___ |
| | (B) AA Units | 90 | 183 | ___ |
| **221** | 2-6-4 Locomotive, 221T or 221W Tender, *46–47* | | | |
| | (A) Gray body, black drivers | 80 | 194 | ___ |
| | (B) Black body, nickel-rimmed black drivers, *47* | 80 | 183 | ___ |
| | (C) Gray body, cast-aluminum drivers, *46* | 116 | 300 | ___ |
| **221** | Rio Grande Alco Diesel A Unit, *63–64* | 37 | 79 | ___ |
| **221** | Santa Fe Alco Diesel A Unit, *63–64 u* | 217 | 609 | ___ |
| **221** | U.S. Marine Corps Alco Diesel A Unit, *63–64 u* | 198 | 550 | ___ |
| **222** | Rio Grande Alco Diesel A Unit, *62* | 25 | 60 | ___ |
| **223** | Santa Fe Alco Diesel AB Units, *63* | 100 | 273 | ___ |

| | | Good | Exc | Cond/$ |
|---|---|---|---|---|
| **224** | 2-6-2 Locomotive, 2466T or 2466W Tender, *45–46* | 95 | 169 | ___ |
| **224** | U.S. Navy Alco Diesel AB Units, *60* | 138 | 317 | ___ |
| **225** | C&O Alco Diesel A Unit, *60* | 65 | 118 | ___ |
| **226** | B&M Alco Diesel AB Units, *60 u* | 85 | 193 | ___ |
| **227** | CN Alco Diesel A Unit, *60 u* | 85 | 155 | ___ |
| **228** | CN Alco Diesel A Unit, *61 u* | 80 | 145 | ___ |
| **229** | M&StL Alco Diesel Units, *61–62* | | | |
| | (A) A Unit, *61* | 65 | 110 | ___ |
| | (B) AB Units, *62* | 95 | 213 | ___ |
| **230** | C&O Alco Diesel A Unit, *61* | | | |
| | (A) With red stripe | 100 | 135 | ___ |
| | (B) Without red stripe | 125 | 400 | ___ |
| **232** | New Haven Alco Diesel A Unit, *62* | 60 | 153 | ___ |
| **233** | 2-4-2 Scout Locomotive, 233W Tender, *61–62* | 43 | 80 | ___ |
| **235** | 2-4-2 Scout Locomotive, 1130T or 1060T Tender, *60 u* | 94 | 283 | ___ |
| **236** | 2-4-2 Scout Locomotive, 1130T or 1050T Tender, *61–62* | | | |
| | (A) 1050T slope-back Tender | 18 | 41 | ___ |
| | (B) 1130T Tender | 18 | 41 | ___ |
| **237** | 2-4-2 Scout Locomotive, *63–66* | | | |
| | (A) 1060T Tender | 25 | 55 | ___ |
| | (B) 234W Tender | 45 | 90 | ___ |
| **238** | 2-4-2 Scout Locomotive, 234W Tender, *63–64* | 55 | 173 | ___ |
| **239** | 2-4-2 Scout Locomotive, 234W Tender, *65–66* | 55 | 90 | ___ |
| **240** | 2-4-2 Scout Locomotive, 242T Tender, *64 u* | 95 | 272 | ___ |
| **241** | 2-4-2 Scout Locomotive, 234W Tender, *65 u* | 70 | 135 | ___ |
| **242** | 2-4-2 Scout Locomotive, 1060T or 1062T Tender, *62–66* | 23 | 48 | ___ |
| **243** | 2-4-2 Scout Locomotive, 243W Tender, *60* | 38 | 92 | ___ |
| **244** | 2-4-2 Scout Locomotive, 244T or 1130T Tender, *60–61* | 28 | 42 | ___ |
| **245** | 2-4-2 Scout Locomotive, 1130T Tender, *59 u* | 13 | 98 | ___ |
| **246** | 2-4-2 Scout Locomotive, 244T or 1130T Tender, *59–61* | 22 | 38 | ___ |
| **247** | 2-4-2 Scout Locomotive, 247T Tender, *59* | 27 | 47 | ___ |
| **248** | 2-4-2 Scout Locomotive, 1130T Tender, *58* | 34 | 157 | ___ |
| **249** | 2-4-2 Scout Locomotive, 250T Tender, *58* | 22 | 50 | ___ |
| **250** | 2-4-2 Scout Locomotive, 250T Tender, *57* | 22 | 52 | ___ |
| **251** | 2-4-2 Scout Locomotive, *66 u* | | | |
| | (A) 1062T slope-back Tender | 118 | 278 | ___ |
| | (B) 250T-type Tender | 117 | 277 | ___ |
| **252** | Crossing Gate, *50–62* | 23 | 28 | ___ |

| | | Good | Exc | Cond/ |
|---|---|---|---|---|
| **253** | Block Control Signal, *56–59* | 17 | 28 | ___ |
| **256** | Illuminated Freight Station, *50–53* | | | |
| | (A) Standard | 25 | 40 | ___ |
| | (B) Light green roof | 50 | 150 | ___ |
| **257** | Freight Station with diesel horn, *56–57* | | | |
| | (A) Maroon base | 25 | 100 | ___ |
| | (B) Brown base | 30 | 120 | ___ |
| | (C) Maroon or brown base, light green roof | 70 | 280 | ___ |
| **260** | Bumper, *51–69* | | | |
| | (A) Die-cast | 9 | 19 | ___ |
| | (B) Black plastic | 22 | 45 | ___ |
| **262** | Highway Crossing Gate, *62–69* | 19 | 58 | ___ |
| **264** | Operating Forklift Platform, *57–60* | 165 | 324 | ___ |
| **270** | Metal Bridge (O), *46* | 19 | 58 | ___ |
| **282** | Gantry Crane, *54–57* | 100 | 158 | ___ |
| **282R** | Gantry Crane, *56–57* | 110 | 185 | ___ |
| **299** | Code Transmitter Beacon Set, *61–63* | 85 | 208 | ___ |
| **308** | Railroad Sign Set, die-cast, *45–49* | 28 | 50 | ___ |
| **309** | Yard Sign Set, plastic, *50–59* | 14 | 28 | ___ |
| **310** | Billboard Set, *50–68* | 15 | 21 | ___ |
| **313** | Bascule Bridge, *46–49* | 198 | 455 | ___ |
| **313-82** | Fiber Pins, dozen, *46–60* | 1 | 2 | ___ |
| **313-121** | Fiber Pins, dozen, *61* | 1 | 2 | ___ |
| **314** | Scale Model Girder Bridge, *45–50* | 13 | 43 | ___ |
| **315** | Trestle Bridge, *46–48* | 60 | 120 | ___ |
| **316** | Trestle Bridge, *49* | 17 | 39 | ___ |
| **317** | Trestle Bridge, *50–56* | 20 | 39 | ___ |
| **321** | Trestle Bridge, *58–64* | 13 | 37 | ___ |
| **332** | Arch-Under Trestle Bridge, *59–66* | 19 | 39 | ___ |
| **334** | Operating Dispatching Board, *57–60* | 150 | 325 | ___ |
| **342** | Culvert Loader, *56–58* | 125 | 355 | ___ |
| **345** | Culvert Unloader, *57–59* | 185 | 350 | ___ |
| **346** | Culvert Unloader, manual, *65 u* | 60 | 155 | ___ |
| **347** | Cannon Firing Range Set, *64 u* | 170 | 520 | ___ |
| **348** | Culvert Unloader, manual, *66–69* | 80 | 190 | ___ |
| **350** | Engine Transfer Table, *57–60* | 215 | 368 | ___ |
| **350-50** | Transfer Table Extension, *57–60* | 105 | 250 | ___ |
| **352** | Ice Depot with 6352 Ice Car, *55–57* | 80 | 194 | ___ |
| **353** | Trackside Control Signal, *60–61* | 14 | 35 | ___ |
| **356** | Operating Freight Station, *52–57* | | | |
| | (A) Dark green roof, *52–57* | 50 | 95 | ___ |
| | (B) Light green roof, *57* | 82 | 265 | ___ |

| | | Good | Exc | Cond/$ |
|---|---|---|---|---|
| **362** | Barrel Loader, *52–57* | | | |
| | (A) Gold lettering | 20 | 90 | ____ |
| | (B) Red lettering | 125 | 500 | ____ |
| **362-78** | Wooden Barrels, 6 pieces, *52–57* | | | |
| | (A) Brown | 7 | 23 | ____ |
| | (B) Red | 120 | 330 | ____ |
| **364** | Conveyor Lumber Loader, *48–57* | 55 | 89 | ____ |
| **364C** | On/Off Switch, *48–64* | 3 | 10 | ____ |
| **365** | Dispatching Station, *58–59* | 75 | 130 | ____ |
| **375** | Turntable, *62–64* | 160 | 300 | ____ |
| **390C** | Switch, double-pole, double-throw, *60–64* | 9 | 17 | ____ |
| **394** | Rotary Beacon, *49–53* | | | |
| | (A) Steel tower, red platform | 10 | 40 | ____ |
| | (B) Steel tower, green platform | 25 | 80 | ____ |
| | (C) Aluminum tower, platform, and base | 10 | 40 | ____ |
| | (D) Aluminum tower, red steel base | 20 | 80 | ____ |
| | (E) Steel tower, red platform, stick-on nameplate | 20 | 80 | ____ |
| **395** | Floodlight Tower, *49–56* | | | |
| | (A) Light green, silver, or unpainted aluminum | 15 | 65 | ____ |
| | (B) Red or yellow | 25 | 100 | ____ |
| | (C) Dark green | 138 | 525 | ____ |
| **397** | Operating Coal Loader, *48–57* | | | |
| | (A) Yellow generator, *48* | 143 | 390 | ____ |
| | (B) Blue generator, *49–57* | 59 | 109 | ____ |
| **400** | B&O Passenger Rail Diesel Car, *56–58* | 160 | 205 | ____ |
| **404** | B&O Baggage-Mail Rail Diesel Car, *57–58* | 175 | 330 | ____ |
| **410** | Billboard Blinker, *56–58* | 33 | 55 | ____ |
| **413** | Countdown Control Panel, *62* | 44 | 80 | ____ |
| **415** | Diesel Fueling Station, *55–57* | 75 | 105 | ____ |
| **419** | Heliport Control Tower, *62* | 175 | 410 | ____ |
| **443** | Missile Launching Platform with ammo dump, *60–62* | 17 | 41 | ____ |
| **445** | Switch Tower, lighted, *52–57* | 36 | 62 | ____ |
| **448** | Missile Firing Range Set, *61–63* | 80 | 175 | ____ |
| **450** | Operating Signal Bridge, *52–58* | 29 | 49 | ____ |
| **450L** | Signal Light Head, *52–58* | 19 | 48 | ____ |
| **452** | Overhead Gantry Signal, *61–63* | 75 | 145 | ____ |
| **455** | Operating Oil Derrick, *50–54* | 75 | 152 | ____ |
| **456** | Coal Ramp with 3456 Hopper, *50–55* | 101 | 173 | ____ |
| **460** | Piggyback Transportation Set, *55–57* | | | |
| | (A) Metal stick-on signs on lift truck | 65 | 135 | ____ |
| | (B) Rubber-stamped lettering on lift truck | 75 | 185 | ____ |
| **460P** | Piggyback Platform, *55–57* | 22 | 65 | ____ |

| | | Good | Exc | Cond/$ |
|---|---|---|---|---|
| **461** | Platform with truck and trailer, *66* | 65 | 160 | ____ |
| **462** | Derrick Platform Set, *61–62* | 200 | 325 | ____ |
| **464** | Lumber Mill, *56–60* | 85 | 170 | ____ |
| **465** | Sound Dispatching Station, *56–57* | 60 | 110 | ____ |
| **470** | Missile Launching Platform with target car, *59–62* | 75 | 75 | ____ |
| **479-1** | Truck for 6362 Truck Car with envelope, *55–56* | 18 | 105 | ____ |
| **480-25** | Conversion Magnetic Coupler, *50–60* | 1 | 5 | ____ |
| **480-32** | Conversion Magnetic Coupler, *61–69* | 1 | 5 | ____ |
| **494** | Rotary Beacon, *54–66* | 32 | 48 | ____ |
| **497** | Coaling Station, *53–58* | 80 | 190 | ____ |
| **520** | LL Boxcab Electric Locomotive, *56–57* | | | |
| | (A) Black pantograph | 30 | 85 | ____ |
| | (B) Copper-colored pantograph | 40 | 133 | ____ |
| **600** | MKT NW2 Switcher, *55* | | | |
| | (A) Black frame, black end rails | 80 | 140 | ____ |
| | (B) Gray frame, yellow or black end rails | 220 | 360 | ____ |
| **601** | Seaboard NW2 Switcher, *56* | 110 | 222 | ____ |
| **602** | Seaboard NW2 Switcher, *57–58* | 115 | 180 | ____ |
| **610** | Erie NW2 Switcher, *55* | | | |
| | (A) Black frame | 85 | 145 | ____ |
| | (B) Yellow frame | 285 | 620 | ____ |
| | (C) Replacement body with nameplates | 125 | 285 | ____ |
| **611** | Jersey Central NW2 Switcher, *57–58* | 90 | 155 | ____ |
| **613** | UP NW2 Switcher, *58* | 130 | 322 | ____ |
| **614** | Alaska NW2 Switcher, *59–60* | | | |
| | (A) Plastic bell, no brake | 115 | 175 | ____ |
| | (B) No bell, yellow brake | 135 | 243 | ____ |
| | (C) "Built by Lionel" outlined in yellow near nose | 225 | 390 | ____ |
| **616** | Santa Fe NW2 Switcher, *61–62* | | | |
| | (A) Open E-unit slot and bell/horn slots | 125 | 190 | ____ |
| | (B) Plugged E-unit slot and open bell/horn slots | 100 | 375 | ____ |
| | (C) Plugged E-unit slot and bell/horn slots | 100 | 350 | ____ |
| **617** | Santa Fe NW2 Switcher, *63* | 135 | 420 | ____ |
| **621** | Jersey Central NW2 Switcher, *56–57* | 75 | 180 | ____ |
| **622** | Santa Fe NW2 Switcher, *49–50* | | | |
| | (A) Large GM decal on cab | 163 | 332 | ____ |
| | (B) Small GM decal on side | 148 | 283 | ____ |
| **623** | Santa Fe NW2 Switcher, *52–54* | 138 | 191 | ____ |
| **624** | C&O NW2 Switcher, *52–54* | 119 | 198 | ____ |
| **625** | LV GE 44-ton Switcher, *57–58* | 80 | 123 | ____ |
| **626** | B&O GE 44-ton Switcher, *56–57, 59* | 110 | 313 | ____ |
| **627** | LV GE 44-ton Switcher, *56–57* | 70 | 113 | ____ |

| | | Good | Exc | Cond/$ |
|---|---|---|---|---|
| **628** | NP GE 44-ton Switcher, *56–57* | 108 | 133 | ____ |
| **629** | Burlington GE 44-ton Switcher, *56* | 149 | 348 | ____ |
| **633** | Santa Fe NW2 Switcher, *62* | 110 | 163 | ____ |
| **634** | Santa Fe NW2 Switcher, *63, 65–66* | | | |
| | (A) Safety stripes | 85 | 165 | ____ |
| | (B) No safety stripes | 50 | 110 | ____ |
| **635** | UP NW2 Switcher, *65 u* | 70 | 120 | ____ |
| **637** | 2-6-4 Locomotive, 2046 736W Tender, *59–63* | | | |
| | (A) 2046W Lionel Lines Tender | 55 | 158 | ____ |
| | (B) 736W Pennsylvania Tender | 70 | 178 | ____ |
| **638-2361** | Van Camp's Pork & Beans Boxcar, *62 u* | 21 | 38 | ____ |
| **645** | Union Pacific NW2 Switcher, *69* | 60 | 148 | ____ |
| **646** | 4-6-4 Locomotive, 2046W Tender, *54–58* | 111 | 229 | ____ |
| **665** | 4-6-4 Locomotive, 2046W, 6026W, or 736W Tender, *54–59, 66* | 113 | 260 | ____ |
| **671** | 6-8-6 Steam Turbine Locomotive, *46–49* | | | |
| | (A) 671W Tender | 100 | 204 | ____ |
| | (B) 2671W Tender | 149 | 380 | ____ |
| **671-75** | Smoke Lamp, 12 volt, *46* | 10 | 20 | ____ |
| **671R** | 6-8-6 Steam Turbine Locomotive, 4424W or 4671 Tender, *46–49* | 130 | 280 | ____ |
| **671RR** | 6-8-6 Steam Turbine Locomotive, 2046W-50 Tender, *52* | 120 | 228 | ____ |
| **671S** | Smoke Conversion Kit | 20 | 63 | ____ |
| **675** | 2-6-2 Locomotive, 2466WX or 6466WX Tender, *47–49* | 90 | 170 | ____ |
| **675** | 2-6-4 Locomotive, 2046W Tender, *52* | 61 | 192 | ____ |
| **681** | 6-8-6 Locomotive, 2046W-50 or 2671W Tender, *50–51, 53* | 132 | 223 | ____ |
| **682** | 6-8-6 Steam Turbine Locomotive, 2046W-50 Tender, *54–55* | 237 | 379 | ____ |
| **685** | 4-6-4 Hudson Locomotive, 6026W Tender, *53* | 95 | 263 | ____ |
| **703-10** | Smoke Lamp, 18 volt, *46* | 7 | 24 | ____ |
| **726** | 2-8-4 Berkshire, *47–49* | | | |
| | (A) 2426W Tender, smoke lamp, *46* | 203 | 545 | ____ |
| | (B) 2426W Tender, *47–49* | 235 | 423 | ____ |
| **726RR** | 2-8-4 Berkshire Locomotive, 2046W Tender, *52* | 177 | 310 | ____ |
| **726S** | Smoke Conversion Kit | 53 | 253 | ____ |
| **736** | 2-8-4 Berkshire Locomotive, 2671WX, 2046W, or 736W Tender, *50–66* | 136 | 296 | ____ |
| **746** | N&W 4-8-4 Class J Northern, *57–60* | | | |
| | (A) Tender with long stripe | 534 | 1048 | ____ |
| | (B) Tender with short stripe | 439 | 811 | ____ |
| **760** | Curved Track, 16 sections (O72), *54–57* | 22 | 45 | ____ |

| | | Good | Exc | Cond/$ |
|---|---|---|---|---|
| **773** | 4-6-4 Hudson Locomotive, 2426W Tender, *50* | 785 | 1603 | ____ |
| **773** | 4-6-4 Hudson Locomotive, *64–66* | | | |
| | (A) 773W NYC Tender | 573 | 1063 | ____ |
| | (B) 736W PRR Tender | 458 | 820 | ____ |
| **902** | Elevated Trestle Set, *60* | | 125 | ____ |
| **909** | Smoke Fluid, *57–66, 68–69* | | 7 | ____ |
| **919** | Artificial Grass, *46–64* | | 18 | ____ |
| **920** | Scenic Display Set, *57–58* | 55 | 95 | ____ |
| **920-2** | Tunnel Portals, pair, *58–59* | 29 | 50 | ____ |
| **920-3** | Green Grass, *57* | | 11 | ____ |
| **920-4** | Yellow Grass, *57* | | 11 | ____ |
| **920-5** | Artificial Rock, *57–58* | 3 | 7 | ____ |
| **920-8** | Dyed Lichen, *57–58* | 1 | 11 | ____ |
| **925** | Lubricant, large tube, *46–69* | 1 | 6 | ____ |
| **926** | Lubricant, small tube, *55* | 1 | 2 | ____ |
| **926-5** | Instruction Booklet, *46–48* | 1 | 5 | ____ |
| **927** | Lubricating Kit, *50–59* | 11 | 23 | ____ |
| **928** | Maintenance and Lubricating Kit, *60–63* | 28 | 70 | ____ |
| **943** | Ammo Dump, *59–61* | 28 | 47 | ____ |
| **950** | U.S. Railroad Map, *58–66* | 22 | 50 | ____ |
| **951** | Farm Set, 13 pieces, *58* | 23 | 65 | ____ |
| **952** | Figure Set, 30 pieces, *58* | 25 | 55 | ____ |
| **953** | Figure Set, 32 pieces, *59–62* | 29 | 70 | ____ |
| **954** | Swimming Pool and Playground Set, 30 pieces, *59* | 27 | 65 | ____ |
| **955** | Highway Set, 22 pieces, *58* | 24 | 60 | ____ |
| **956** | Stockyard Set, 18 pieces, *59* | 22 | 48 | ____ |
| **957** | Farm Building and Animal Set, 35 pieces, *58* | 33 | 75 | ____ |
| **958** | Vehicle Set, 24 pieces, *58* | 17 | 55 | ____ |
| **959** | Barn Set, 23 pieces, *58* | 21 | 50 | ____ |
| **960** | Barnyard Set, 29 pieces, *59–61* | 16 | 45 | ____ |
| **961** | School Set, 36 pieces, *59* | 17 | 55 | ____ |
| **962** | Turnpike Set, 24 pieces, *58* | 33 | 85 | ____ |
| **963** | Frontier Set, 18 pieces, *59–60* | 32 | 90 | ____ |
| **963-100** | Frontier Set, 18 pieces, *60* | 115 | 215 | ____ |
| **964** | Factory Site Set, 18 pieces, *59* | 21 | 55 | ____ |
| **965** | Farm Set, 36 pieces, *59* | 23 | 63 | ____ |
| **966** | Firehouse Set, 45 pieces, *58* | 21 | 55 | ____ |
| **967** | Post Office Set, 25 pieces, *58* | 21 | 55 | ____ |
| **968** | TV Transmitter Set, 28 pieces, *58* | 16 | 48 | ____ |
| **969** | Construction Set, 23 pieces, *60* | 23 | 70 | ____ |
| **970** | Ticket Booth, *58–60* | 50 | 145 | ____ |
| **971** | Lichen, *60–64* | 36 | 97 | ____ |
| **972** | Landscape Tree Assortment, *61–64* | 10 | 17 | ____ |

| | | Good | Exc | Cond/$ |
|---|---|---|---|---|
| **973** | Complete Landscaping Set, *60–64* | 14 | 34 | ____ |
| **974** | Scenery Set, *58* | 29 | 509 | ____ |
| **980** | Ranch Set, 14 pieces, *60* | 22 | 75 | ____ |
| **981** | Freight Yard Set, 10 pieces, *60* | 16 | 55 | ____ |
| **982** | Suburban Split Level Set, 18 pieces, *60* | 16 | 47 | ____ |
| **983** | Farm Set, 7 pieces, *60–61* | 16 | 55 | ____ |
| **984** | Railroad Set, 22 pieces, *61–62* | 16 | 55 | ____ |
| **985** | Freight Area Set, 32 pieces, *61* | 18 | 55 | ____ |
| **986** | Farm Set, 20 pieces, *62* | 28 | 50 | ____ |
| **987** | Town Set, 24 pieces, *62* | 28 | 50 | ____ |
| **988** | Railroad Structure Set, 16 pieces, *62* | 28 | 50 | ____ |
| **1001** | 2-4-2 Scout Locomotive, plastic body, 1001T Tender, *48* | | | |
| | (A) Silver rubber-stamped cab number | 35 | 140 | ____ |
| | (B) White heat-stamped cab number | 22 | 41 | ____ |
| **1002** | Gondola, *48–52* | | | |
| | (A) Black, white lettering | 5 | 9 | ____ |
| | (B) Blue, white lettering | 5 | 11 | ____ |
| | (C) Silver, black lettering | 84 | 352 | ____ |
| | (D) Yellow, black lettering | 76 | 349 | ____ |
| | (E) Red, white lettering | 76 | 356 | ____ |
| | (F) Light blue, black lettering | | NRS | ____ |
| **X1004** | PRR Baby Ruth Boxcar, *48–52* | 6 | 14 | ____ |
| **1005** | Sunoco 1-D Tank Car, *48–50* | 8 | 13 | ____ |
| **1007** | LL SP-type Caboose, *48–52* | | | |
| | (A) Red body | 5 | 13 | ____ |
| | (B) Red body, raised board on catwalk | 17 | 55 | ____ |
| | (C) Tuscan body | 275 | 1100 | ____ |
| **1008** | Uncoupling Unit (027), *57–62* | | 1 | ____ |
| **1008-50** | Uncoupling Track Section (027), *57–62* | | 1 | ____ |
| **1010** | Transformer, 35 watts, *61–66* | 8 | 21 | ____ |
| **1011** | Transformer, 25 watts, *48–49* | 8 | 18 | ____ |
| **1012** | Transformer, 35 watts, *50–54* | 7 | 15 | ____ |
| **1013** | Curved Track (027), *45–69* | | 1 | ____ |
| **1013-17** | Steel Pins, dozen (027), *46–60* | | 1 | ____ |
| **1013-42** | Steel Pins, dozen (027), *61–68* | | 2 | ____ |
| **1014** | Transformer, 40 watts, *55* | 13 | 22 | ____ |
| **1015** | Transformer, 45 watts, *56–60* | 8 | 31 | ____ |
| **1016** | Transformer, 35 watts, *59–60* | 7 | 24 | ____ |
| **1018** | Half Straight Track (027), *55–69* | | 1 | ____ |
| **1018** | Straight Track (027), *45–69* | | 1 | ____ |
| **1019** | Remote Control Track Set (027), *46–48* | 2 | 19 | ____ |
| **1020** | 90-degree Crossing (027), *55–69* | 3 | 6 | ____ |
| **1021** | 90-degree Crossing (027), *45–54* | 2 | 5 | ____ |

| | | Good | Exc | Cond/$ |
|---|---|---|---|---|
| **1022** | Manual Switches, pair (027), *53–69* | 9 | 17 | ____ |
| **1023** | 45-degree Crossing (027), *56–69* | 2 | 5 | ____ |
| **1024** | Manual Switches, pair (027), *46–52* | 7 | 15 | ____ |
| **1025** | Illuminated Bumper (027), *46–47* | 13 | 15 | ____ |
| **1025** | Transformer, 45 watts, *61–69* | 13 | 27 | ____ |
| **1026** | Transformer, 25 watts, *61–64* | 5 | 14 | ____ |
| **1032** | Transformer, 75 watts, *48* | 18 | 39 | ____ |
| **1033** | Transformer, 90 watts, *48–56* | 21 | 45 | ____ |
| **1034** | Transformer, 75 watts, *48–54* | 19 | 28 | ____ |
| **1035** | Transformer, 60 watts, *47* | 22 | 41 | ____ |
| **1037** | Transformer, 40 watts, *46–47* | 10 | 25 | ____ |
| **1041** | Transformer, 60 watts, *45–46* | 20 | 28 | ____ |
| **1042** | Transformer, 75 watts, *47–48* | 22 | 44 | ____ |
| **1043** | Transformer, 50 watts, *53–57* | 13 | 27 | ____ |
| **1043-500** | Transformer, 60 watts, ivory, *57–58* | 55 | 110 | ____ |
| **1044** | Transformer, 90 watts, *57–69* | 34 | 60 | ____ |
| **1045** | Operating Watchman, *46–50* | 16 | 47 | ____ |
| **1047** | Operating Switchman, *59–61* | 40 | 145 | ____ |
| **1050** | 0-4-0 Scout Locomotive, 1050T Tender, *59 u* | 73 | 293 | ____ |
| **1053** | Transformer, 60 watts, *56–60* | 19 | 45 | ____ |
| **1055** | *Texas Special* Alco Diesel A Unit, *59–60* | 35 | 78 | ____ |
| **1060** | 2-4-2 Locomotive, 1050T or 1060T Tender, *60–62* | 10 | 29 | ____ |
| **1061** | 0-4-0 or 2-4-2 Scout Locomotive, 1061T Tender, *64, 69* | | | |
| | (A) Slope-back Lionel Lines tender | 14 | 33 | ____ |
| | (B) Paper number labels | 50 | 325 | ____ |
| | (C) No number stamped on cab | 39 | 135 | ____ |
| **1062** | 0-4-0 or 2-4-2 Scout Locomotive, *63–64* | | | |
| | (A) Streamlined Southern Pacific Tender | 10 | 40 | ____ |
| | (B) Other tenders | 10 | 27 | ____ |
| **1063** | Transformer, 75 watts, *60–64* | 16 | 45 | ____ |
| **1065** | Union Pacific Alco Diesel A Unit, *61* | 27 | 70 | ____ |
| **1066** | Union Pacific Alco Diesel A Unit, *64 u* | 35 | 80 | ____ |
| **1073** | Transformer, 60 watts, *61–66* | 19 | 50 | ____ |
| **1101** | Transformer, 25 watts, *48* | 8 | 14 | ____ |
| **1101** | 2-4-2 Scout Locomotive, 1001T Tender, *48 u* | | | |
| | (A) Cab correctly marked "1101" | 20 | 38 | ____ |
| | (B) Cab marked "1001" | 275 | 540 | ____ |
| **1110** | 2-4-2 Locomotive, 1001T Tender, *49, 51–52* | 17 | 24 | ____ |
| **1120** | 2-4-2 Scout Locomotive, 1001T Tender, *50* | 19 | 35 | ____ |
| **1121** | Remote Control Switches, pair (027), *46–51* | 14 | 23 | ____ |
| **1122** | Remote Control Switches, pair (027), *52–53* | 10 | 24 | ____ |
| **1122-34** | Remote Control Switches, pair, *52–53* | 14 | 34 | ____ |

| | | Good | Exc | Cond/S |
|---|---|---|---|---|
| **1122-500** | Gauge Adapter (027), *57–66* | | 5 | ___ |
| **1122E** | Remote Control Switches, pair (027), *53–69* | 13 | 28 | ___ |
| **1130** | 2-4-2 Locomotive, 6066T or 1130T Tender, *53–54* | | | |
| | (A) Plastic body | 20 | 36 | ___ |
| | (B) Die-cast body | 48 | 110 | ___ |
| **1130T** | Tender ( painted shell only) | 30 | 100 | ___ |
| **1144** | Transformer, 75 watts, *61–66* | 5 | 25 | ___ |
| **1232** | Transformer, 75 watts, made for export, *48* | 20 | 80 | ___ |
| **1615** | 0-4-0 Locomotive, 1615T Tender, *55–57* | 45 | 150 | ___ |
| | (A) No grab irons | 97 | 175 | ___ |
| | (B) Grab irons on locomotive and tender | 168 | 360 | ___ |
| **1625** | 0-4-0 Locomotive, 1625T Tender, *58* | 130 | 363 | ___ |
| **1640-100** | Presidential Kit, *60* | 75 | 225 | ___ |
| **1654** | 2-4-2 Locomotive, 1654W Tender, *46–47* | 33 | 70 | ___ |
| **1655** | 2-4-2 Locomotive, 6654W Tender, *48–49* | 35 | 70 | ___ |
| **1656** | 0-4-0 Locomotive, 6403B Tender, *48–49* | 130 | 217 | ___ |
| **1665** | 0-4-0 Locomotive, 2403B Tender, *46* | 190 | 370 | ___ |
| **1666** | 2-6-2 Locomotive, 2466W or 2466WX Tender, *46–47* | 56 | 129 | ___ |
| **1862** | 4-4-0 Civil War *General*, 1862T Tender, *59–62* | | | |
| | (A) Gray smokestack | 85 | 205 | ___ |
| | (B) Black smokestack | 90 | 205 | ___ |
| **1865** | Western & Atlantic Coach, *59–62* | 28 | 55 | ___ |
| **1866** | Western & Atlantic Mail-Baggage Car, *59–62* | 33 | 59 | ___ |
| **1872** | 4-4-0 Civil War *General*, 1872T Tender, *59–62* | 95 | 360 | ___ |
| **1875** | Western & Atlantic Coach, *59–62* | 165 | 397 | ___ |
| **1875W** | Western & Atlantic Coach, whistle, *59–62* | 59 | 207 | ___ |
| **1876** | Western & Atlantic Baggage Car, *59–62* | 28 | 88 | ___ |
| **1877** | Flatcar with fence and horses, *59–62* | 45 | 108 | ___ |
| **1882** | 4-4-0 Civil War *General*, 1882T Tender, *60 u* | 250 | 500 | ___ |
| **1885** | Western & Atlantic Coach, *60 u* | 100 | 305 | ___ |
| **1887** | Flatcar with fences and horses, *60 u* | 87 | 192 | ___ |
| **2001** | Track Make-up Kit (027), *63* | | NRS | ___ |
| **2002** | Track Make-up Kit (027), *63* | | NRS | ___ |
| **2003** | Track Make-up Kit (027), *63* | | NRS | ___ |
| **2016** | 2-6-4 Locomotive, 6026W Tender, *55–56* | 49 | 100 | ___ |
| **2018** | 2-6-4 Locomotive, *56–59, 61* | | | |
| | (A) 6026T Tender | 40 | 70 | ___ |
| | (B) 6026W Tender | 60 | 115 | ___ |
| | (C) 1130T Tender | 43 | 75 | ___ |

| | | Good | Exc | Cond/$ |
|---|---|---|---|---|
| **2020** | 6-8-6 Steam Turbine Locomotive, 2020W or 6020W Tender, *47–49* | 108 | 194 | ____ |
| **2020** | 6-8-6 Steam Turbine Locomotive, 2020W or 2466WX Tender, smoke lamp, *46* | 155 | 216 | ____ |
| **2023** | Union Pacific Alco Diesel AA Units, *50–51* | | | |
| | (A) Yellow body | 140 | 343 | ____ |
| | (B) Gray nose and side frames | 763 | 2100 | ____ |
| | (C) Silver body | 135 | 282 | ____ |
| **2024** | C&O Alco Diesel A Unit, *69* | 34 | 75 | ____ |
| **2025** | 2-6-2 Locomotive, 2466WX or 6466WX Tender, *47–49* | 80 | 161 | ____ |
| **2025** | 2-6-4 Locomotive, 6466W Tender, *52* | 75 | 158 | ____ |
| **2026** | 2-6-2 Locomotive, 6466WX Tender, *48–49* | 67 | 120 | ____ |
| **2026** | 2-6-4 Locomotive, 6466W, 6466T, or 6066T Tender, *51–53* | 40 | 99 | ____ |
| **2028** | Pennsylvania GP7 Diesel, *55* | | | |
| | (A) Gold lettering | 165 | 250 | ____ |
| | (B) Yellow lettering | 140 | 309 | ____ |
| | (C) Tan frame | 275 | 540 | ____ |
| **2029** | 2-6-4 Locomotive, *64–69* | | | |
| | (A) 234W Lionel Lines Tender | 70 | 115 | ____ |
| | (B) LL Tender with "Hagerstown" on bottom | 90 | 135 | ____ |
| | (C) 234W Pennsylvania Tender | 255 | 325 | ____ |
| **2031** | Rock Island Alco Diesel AA Units, *52–54* | 154 | 310 | ____ |
| **2032** | Erie Alco Diesel AA Units, *52–54* | 140 | 207 | ____ |
| **2033** | Union Pacific Alco Diesel AA Units, *52–54* | 150 | 273 | ____ |
| **2034** | 2-4-2 Scout Locomotive, 6066T Tender, *52* | 34 | 65 | ____ |
| **2035** | 2-6-4 Locomotive, 6466W Tender, *50–51* | 65 | 174 | ____ |
| **2036** | 2-6-4 Locomotive, 6466W Tender, *50* | 58 | 115 | ____ |
| **2037** | 2-6-4 Locomotive, *54–55, 57–63* | | | |
| | (A) 6026T or 1130T nonwhistle Tender | 45 | 80 | ____ |
| | (B) 6026W, 233W, or 234W whistle Tender | 63 | 155 | ____ |
| **2037-500** | 2-6-4 Locomotive, pink, 1130T-500 Tender, *57–58* | 248 | 635 | ____ |
| **2041** | Rock Island Alco Diesel AA Units, *69* | 70 | 135 | ____ |
| **2046** | 4-6-4 Locomotive, 2046W Tender, *50–51, 53* | 134 | 205 | ____ |
| **2055** | 4-6-4 Locomotive, 2046W or 6026W Tender, *53–55* | 103 | 186 | ____ |
| **2056** | 4-6-4 Locomotive, 2046W Tender, *52* | 99 | 190 | ____ |
| **2065** | 4-6-4 Locomotive, 2046W or 6026W Tender, *54–56* | 103 | 184 | ____ |
| **2240** | Wabash F3 AB Units, *56* | 380 | 725 | ____ |
| **2242** | New Haven F3 AB Units, *58–59* | 425 | 770 | ____ |

| | | Good | Exc | Cond/S |
|---|---|---|---|---|
| **2243** | Santa Fe F3 AB Units, *55–57* | | | |
| | (A) Gray body mold, raised molded cab door ladder | 150 | 400 | ____ |
| | (B) Typical molded cab door ladder | 100 | 325 | ____ |
| **2243C** | Santa Fe F3 B Unit, *55–57* | 100 | 223 | ____ |
| **2245** | *Texas Special* F3 AB Units, *54–55* | | | |
| | (A) B Unit with portholes, *54* | 275 | 550 | ____ |
| | (B) B Unit without portholes, *55* | 400 | 835 | ____ |
| **2257** | SP-type caboose, *47* | | | |
| | (A) Red body, no smokestack | 7 | 13 | ____ |
| | (B) Tuscan body and smokestack | 55 | 295 | ____ |
| | (C) Red body and smokestack | 75 | 485 | ____ |
| **2321** | Lackawanna FM Train Master Diesel, *54–56* | | | |
| | (A) Gray roof | 198 | 427 | ____ |
| | (B) Maroon roof | 315 | 571 | ____ |
| **2322** | Virginian FM Train Master Diesel, *65–66* | | | |
| | (A) Unpainted blue body, yellow stripes | 315 | 605 | ____ |
| | (B) Blue or black body, painted blue and yellow stripes | 375 | 735 | ____ |
| **2328** | Burlington GP7 Diesel, *55–56* | 225 | 244 | ____ |
| **2329** | Virginian GE E-33 or EL-C Electric Locomotive, *58–59* | 263 | 610 | ____ |
| **2330** | Pennsylvania GG1 Electric Locomotive, green, *50* | 500 | 890 | ____ |
| **2331** | Virginian FM Train Master Diesel, *55–58* | | | |
| | (A) Black and yellow stripes, gray mold, *55* | 550 | 990 | ____ |
| | (B) Yellow stripes, blue mold, *56–58* | 310 | 693 | ____ |
| | (C) Blue and yellow stripes, gray mold | 680 | 1250 | ____ |
| **2332** | Pennsylvania GG1 Electric Locomotive, *47–49* | | | |
| | (A) Black | 865 | 1213 | ____ |
| | (B) Dark green | 258 | 443 | ____ |
| **2333** | NYC F3 Diesel AA Units, *48–49* | | | |
| | (A) Rubber-stamped lettering | 264 | 621 | ____ |
| | (B) Heat-stamped lettering | 247 | 509 | ____ |
| **2333** | Santa Fe F3 Diesel AA Units, *48–49* | 168 | 342 | ____ |
| **2337** | Wabash GP7 Diesel, *58* | 140 | 330 | ____ |
| **2338** | Milwaukee Road GP7 Diesel, *55–56* | | | |
| | (A) Orange band around shell | 434 | 1146 | ____ |
| | (B) Interrupted orange band | 98 | 259 | ____ |
| **2339** | Wabash GP7 Diesel, *57* | 150 | 285 | ____ |
| **2340** | Pennsylvania GG1 Electric Locomotive, *55* | | | |
| | (A) Tuscan | 545 | 1100 | ____ |
| | (B) Dark green | 453 | 885 | ____ |

| | | Good | Exc | Cond/$ |
|---|---|---|---|---|
| **2341** | Jersey Central FM Train Master Diesel, *56* | | | |
| | (A) High-gloss orange | 1000 | 1625 | ___ |
| | (B) Dull orange | 850 | 1450 | ___ |
| **2343** | Santa Fe F3 Diesel AA Units, *50–52* | 170 | 322 | ___ |
| **2343C** | Santa Fe F3 B Unit, *50–55* | | | |
| | (A) Screen roof vents | 113 | 223 | ___ |
| | (B) Louver roof vents | 108 | 223 | ___ |
| **2344** | NYC F3 Diesel AA Units, *50–52* | 190 | 463 | ___ |
| **2344C** | NYC F3 B Unit, *50–55* | 115 | 315 | ___ |
| **2345** | Western Pacific F3 Diesel AA Units, *52* | 535 | 699 | ___ |
| **2346** | B&M GP9 Diesel, *65–66* | 168 | 365 | ___ |
| **2347** | C&O GP7 Diesel, *65 u* | 1400 | 4050 | ___ |
| **2348** | M&StL GP9 Diesel, *58–59* | 160 | 390 | ___ |
| **2349** | Northern Pacific GP9 Diesel, *59–60* | 205 | 435 | ___ |
| **2350** | New Haven EP-5 Electric Locomotive, *56–58* | | | |
| | (A) Painted nose trim, white N and orange H | 370 | 680 | ___ |
| | (B) Decaled nose trim, white N and orange H | 210 | 380 | ___ |
| | (C) Painted nose trim, orange N and black H | 900 | 1550 | ___ |
| | (D) Decaled nose trim, orange N and black H | 510 | 910 | ___ |
| | (E) Orange and white stripes go through doorjambs | 395 | 750 | ___ |
| **2351** | Milwaukee Road EP-5 Electric Locomotive, *57–58* | 185 | 583 | ___ |
| **2352** | Pennsylvania EP-5 Electric Locomotive, *58–59* | | | |
| | (A) Tuscan body | 225 | 700 | ___ |
| | (B) Chocolate brown body | 220 | 480 | ___ |
| **2353** | Santa Fe F3 Diesel AA Units, *53–55* | 267 | 523 | ___ |
| **2354** | NYC F3 Diesel AA Units, *53–55* | 290 | 680 | ___ |
| **2355** | Western Pacific F3 Diesel AA Units, *53* | 673 | 1007 | ___ |
| **2356** | Southern F3 Diesel AA Units, *54–56* | 409 | 775 | ___ |
| **2356C** | Southern F3 B Unit, *54–56* | 181 | 328 | ___ |
| **2357** | SP-type Caboose, *47–48* | | | |
| | (A) Red body and smokestack | 160 | 580 | ___ |
| | (B) Tuscan body and smokestack | 15 | 32 | ___ |
| | (C) Tile red, no smokestack, "6357" stamped on bottom | 49 | 299 | ___ |
| **2358** | Great Northern EP-5 Electric Locomotive, *59–60* | 400 | 910 | ___ |
| **2359** | Boston & Maine GP9 Diesel, *61–62* | 170 | 351 | ___ |
| **2360** | Pennsylvania GG1 Electric Locomotive, *56–58, 61–63* | | | |
| | (A) Tuscan, 5 gold stripes | 575 | 1200 | ___ |
| | (B) Dark green, 5 gold stripes | 463 | 1095 | ___ |
| | (C) Tuscan, gold stripe, heat-stamped letters | 470 | 865 | ___ |
| | (D) Tuscan, gold stripe, decaled lettering | 455 | 760 | ___ |

| | | Good | Exc | Cond/$ |
|---|---|---|---|---|
| **2363** | Illinois Central F3 Diesel AB Units, *55–56* | | | |
| | (A) Black lettering | 435 | 960 | \_\_\_\_ |
| | (B) Brown lettering | 450 | 1090 | \_\_\_\_ |
| **2365** | C&O GP7 Diesel, *62–63* | 110 | 241 | \_\_\_\_ |
| **2367** | Wabash F3 Diesel AB Units, *55* | 350 | 620 | \_\_\_\_ |
| **2368** | B&O F3 Diesel AB Units, *56* | 600 | 1613 | \_\_\_\_ |
| **2373** | CP F3 Diesel AA Units, *57* | 1125 | 2200 | \_\_\_\_ |
| **2378** | Milwaukee Road F3 Diesel AB Units, *56* | | | |
| | (A) Yellow roof line stripes | 900 | 1578 | \_\_\_\_ |
| | (B) No roof line stripes | 740 | 1269 | \_\_\_\_ |
| **2379** | Rio Grande F3 Diesel AB Units, *57–58* | 439 | 779 | \_\_\_\_ |
| **2383** | Santa Fe F3 Diesel AA Units, *58–66* | 243 | 417 | \_\_\_\_ |
| **2400** | *Maplewood* Pullman Car, green, *48–49* | 73 | 166 | \_\_\_\_ |
| **2401** | *Hillside* Observation Car, green, *48–49* | 74 | 132 | \_\_\_\_ |
| **2402** | *Chatham* Pullman Car, green, *48–49* | 70 | 159 | \_\_\_\_ |
| **2404** | Santa Fe Vista Dome Car, *64–65* | 29 | 75 | \_\_\_\_ |
| **2405** | Santa Fe Pullman Car, *64–65* | 29 | 65 | \_\_\_\_ |
| **2406** | Santa Fe Observation Car, *64–65* | 28 | 60 | \_\_\_\_ |
| **2408** | Santa Fe Vista Dome Car, *66* | 41 | 85 | \_\_\_\_ |
| **2409** | Santa Fe Pullman Car, *66* | 38 | 75 | \_\_\_\_ |
| **2410** | Santa Fe Observation Car, *66* | 34 | 70 | \_\_\_\_ |
| **2411** | Lionel Lines Flatcar, *46–48* | | | |
| | (A) with pipes, *46* | 50 | 90 | \_\_\_\_ |
| | (B) with logs, *47–48* | 16 | 36 | \_\_\_\_ |
| **2412** | Santa Fe Vista Dome Car, *59–63* | 33 | 95 | \_\_\_\_ |
| **2414** | Santa Fe Pullman Car, *59–63* | 30 | 115 | \_\_\_\_ |
| **2416** | Santa Fe Observation Car, *59–63* | 27 | 80 | \_\_\_\_ |
| **2419** | DL&W Work Caboose, *46–47* | 25 | 65 | \_\_\_\_ |
| **2420** | DL&W Work Caboose with searchlight, *46–48* | | | |
| | (A) Light or dark gray, heat-stamped lettering | 58 | 154 | \_\_\_\_ |
| | (B) Light or dark gray, rubber-stamped lettering | 65 | 246 | \_\_\_\_ |
| **2421** | *Maplewood* Pullman Car, *50–53* | | | |
| | (A) Gray roof | 40 | 80 | \_\_\_\_ |
| | (B) Silver roof | 34 | 73 | \_\_\_\_ |
| **2422** | *Chatham* Pullman Car, *50–53* | | | |
| | (A) Gray roof | 39 | 73 | \_\_\_\_ |
| | (B) Silver roof | 33 | 67 | \_\_\_\_ |
| **2423** | *Hillside* Observation Car, *50–53* | | | |
| | (A) Gray roof | 40 | 70 | \_\_\_\_ |
| | (B) Silver roof | 38 | 62 | \_\_\_\_ |
| **2429** | *Livingston* Pullman Car, *52–53* | | | |
| | (A) Gray roof | 49 | 118 | \_\_\_\_ |
| | (B) Aluminum roof, no stripe | 49 | 126 | \_\_\_\_ |
| **2430** | Pullman Car, blue, *46–47* | 29 | 78 | \_\_\_\_ |

| | | Good | Exc | Cond/$ |
|---|---|---|---|---|
| **2431** | Observation Car, blue, *46–47* | 31 | 85 | ____ |
| **2432** | *Clifton* Vista Dome Car, *54–58* | 46 | 95 | ____ |
| **2434** | *Newark* Pullman Car, *54–58* | 32 | 82 | ____ |
| **2435** | *Elizabeth* Pullman Car, *54–58* | 45 | 109 | ____ |
| **2436** | *Mooseheart* Observation Car, *57–58* | 30 | 85 | ____ |
| **2436** | *Summit* Observation Car, *54–56* | 33 | 62 | ____ |
| **2440** | Pullman Car, green, *46–47* | 31 | 76 | ____ |
| **2441** | Observation Car, green, *46–47* | 25 | 55 | ____ |
| **2442** | *Clifton* Vista Dome Car, *56* | 63 | 117 | ____ |
| **2442** | Pullman Car, brown, *46–48* | | | |
| | (A) Silver lettering | 26 | 78 | ____ |
| | (B) White lettering | 25 | 61 | ____ |
| **2443** | Observation Car, brown, *46–48* | | | |
| | (A) Silver lettering | 23 | 75 | ____ |
| | (B) White lettering | 25 | 65 | ____ |
| **2444** | *Newark* Pullman Car, *56* | 55 | 123 | ____ |
| **2445** | *Elizabeth* Pullman Car, *56* | 189 | 348 | ____ |
| **2446** | *Summit* Observation Car, *56* | 55 | 165 | ____ |
| **2452** | Pennsylvania Gondola, *45–47* | 10 | 21 | ____ |
| **2452X** | Pennsylvania Gondola, *46–47* | 7 | 23 | ____ |
| **X2454** | Baby Ruth Boxcar, PRR logo, *46–47* | 13 | 30 | ____ |
| **X2454** | Pennsylvania Boxcar, *46* | | | |
| | (A) Brown door | 87 | 163 | ____ |
| | (B) Orange door | 122 | 235 | ____ |
| **2456** | Lehigh Valley Hopper, *48* | 11 | 25 | ____ |
| **2457** | PRR N5-type Caboose "477618," tintype, *45–47* | | | |
| | (A) Red, white lettering | 17 | 44 | ____ |
| | (B) Brown, white lettering | 101 | 371 | ____ |
| **X2458** | PRR Automobile Boxcar, *46–48* | 19 | 50 | ____ |
| **2460** | Bucyrus Erie Crane Car, 12-wheel, *46–50* | | | |
| | (A) Gray cab | 93 | 270 | ____ |
| | (B) Black cab | 35 | 100 | ____ |
| **2461** | Transformer Car, die-cast, *47–48* | | | |
| | (A) Red transformer | 47 | 95 | ____ |
| | (B) Black transformer | 30 | 78 | ____ |
| **2465** | Sunoco 2-D Tank Car, *46–48* | | | |
| | (A) "Gas, Sunoco, and Oils" in diamond | 34 | 75 | ____ |
| | (B) "Sunoco" in diamond | 10 | 18 | ____ |
| | (C) "Sunoco" extends beyond diamond | 10 | 17 | ____ |
| **2472** | PRR N5-type Caboose, tintype, *46–47* | 12 | 23 | ____ |
| **2481** | *Plainfield* Pullman Car, yellow, *50* | 113 | 277 | ____ |
| **2482** | *Westfield* Pullman Car, yellow, *50* | 112 | 274 | ____ |
| **2483** | *Livingston* Observation Car, yellow, *50* | 92 | 240 | ____ |
| **2521** | *President McKinley* Observation Car, *62–66* | 85 | 128 | ____ |

| | | Good | Exc | Cond/$ |
|---|---|---|---|---|
| **2522** | *President Harrison* Vista Dome Car, *62–66* | 80 | 135 | ____ |
| **2523** | *President Garfield* Pullman Car, *62–66* | 70 | 145 | ____ |
| **2530** | REA Baggage Car, *54–60* | | | |
| | (A) Large doors | 226 | 499 | ____ |
| | (B) Small doors | 93 | 182 | ____ |
| **2531** | *Silver Dawn* Observation Car, *52–60* | 80 | 155 | ____ |
| **2532** | *Silver Range* Vista Dome Car, *52–60* | 75 | 133 | ____ |
| **2533** | *Silver Cloud* Pullman Car, *52–59* | 55 | 95 | ____ |
| **2534** | *Silver Bluff* Pullman Car, *52–59* | 63 | 122 | ____ |
| **2541** | *Alexander Hamilton* Observation Car, *55–56** | 85 | 260 | ____ |
| **2542** | *Betsy Ross* Vista Dome Car, *55–56** | 85 | 195 | ____ |
| **2543** | *William Penn* Pullman Car, *55–56** | 70 | 140 | ____ |
| **2544** | *Molly Pitcher* Pullman Car, *55–56** | 85 | 200 | ____ |
| **2550** | B&O Baggage-Mail Rail Diesel Car, *57–58* | 245 | 610 | ____ |
| **2551** | *Banff Park* Observation Car, *57** | 143 | 269 | ____ |
| **2552** | *Skyline 500* Vista Dome Car, *57** | 130 | 247 | ____ |
| **2553** | *Blair Manor* Pullman Car, *57** | 235 | 453 | ____ |
| **2554** | *Craig Manor* Pullman Car, *57** | 220 | 450 | ____ |
| **2555** | Sunoco 1-D Tank Car, *46–48* | 26 | 58 | ____ |
| **2559** | B&O Passenger Rail Diesel Car, *57–58* | 155 | 345 | ____ |
| **2560** | Lionel Lines Crane Car, 8-wheel, *46–47* | | | |
| | (A) Black boom | 25 | 67 | ____ |
| | (B) Brown boom | 24 | 66 | ____ |
| | (C) Green boom | 27 | 80 | ____ |
| | (D) Black boom from 2460 crane, *47* | 24 | 60 | ____ |
| **2561** | *Vista Valley* Observation Car, *59–61** | 130 | 300 | ____ |
| **2562** | *Regal Pass* Vista Dome Car, *59–61** | 145 | 340 | ____ |
| **2563** | *Indian Falls* Pullman Car, *59–61** | 145 | 340 | ____ |
| **2625** | *Irvington* Pullman Car, *46–50** | | | |
| | (A) No silhouettes | 70 | 172 | ____ |
| | (B) Silhouettes | 112 | 262 | ____ |
| **2625** | *Madison* Pullman Car, *46–47** | 108 | 215 | ____ |
| **2625** | *Manhattan* Pullman Car, *46–47** | 85 | 172 | ____ |
| **2627** | *Madison* Pullman Car, *48–50** | | | |
| | (A) No silhouettes | 84 | 167 | ____ |
| | (B) Silhouettes | 95 | 232 | ____ |
| **2628** | *Manhattan* Pullman Car, *48–50** | | | |
| | (A) No silhouettes | 77 | 166 | ____ |
| | (B) Silhouettes | 125 | 275 | ____ |
| **2755** | Sunoco 1-D Tank Car, *45* | 70 | 115 | ____ |
| **X2758** | PRR Automobile Boxcar, *45–46* | 28 | 78 | ____ |

| | | Good | Exc | Cond/$ |
|---|---|---|---|---|
| **2855** | Sunoco 1-D Tank Car, *46–47* | | | |
| | (A) Black | 69 | 215 | ___ |
| | (B) Black, decal without "Gas" and "Oils" | 65 | 253 | ___ |
| | (C) Gray | 51 | 180 | ___ |
| **3309** | Turbo Missile Launch Car, red body, *63–64* | 23 | 50 | ___ |
| **3309-50** | Turbo Missile Launch Car, olive body, *63–64* | 157 | 612 | ___ |
| **3330** | Flatcar with submarine kit, *60–62* | 36 | 108 | ___ |
| **3330-100** | Operating Submarine Kit, *60–61* | 111 | 364 | ___ |
| **3349** | Turbo Missile Launch Car, *62–65* | | | |
| | (A) Red body | 23 | 47 | ___ |
| | (B) Olive drab body | 125 | 548 | ___ |
| **3356** | Operating Horse Car and Corral Set, *56–60, 64–66* | 63 | 117 | ___ |
| **3356** | Operating Horse Car only, *56–60, 64–66* | | | |
| | (A) Built date, bar-end trucks, *56–60* | 47 | 71 | ___ |
| | (B) No built date, AAR trucks, *64–66* | 50 | 153 | ___ |
| **3356-100** | Black Horses, 9 pieces, *56–59* | 10 | 40 | ___ |
| **3356-150** | Horse Car Corral, *57–60* | 30 | 75 | ___ |
| **3357** | Hydraulic Maintenance Car, *62–64* | 34 | 80 | ___ |
| **3359** | Lionel Lines Twin-bin Coal Dump Car, *55–58* | 20 | 42 | ___ |
| **3360** | Operating Burro Crane, self-propelled, *56–57* | 150 | 223 | ___ |
| **3361** | Operating Log Dump Car, *55–58* | 23 | 38 | ___ |
| **3362** | Helium Tank Unloading Car, *61–63, 69* | 17 | 42 | ___ |
| **3362/64** | Operating Dump Car with 2 helium tanks, *65–66, 68* | 20 | 75 | ___ |
| **3364** | Operating Dump Car with 3 logs, *65–66, 68* | 15 | 32 | ___ |
| **3366** | Circus Car Corral Set, *59–62* | 103 | 242 | ___ |
| **3366** | Circus Car only, *59–62* | 90 | 170 | ___ |
| **3366-100** | White Horses, 9 pieces, *59–62* | 48 | 83 | ___ |
| **3370** | W&A Outlaw Car, *61–64* | 30 | 75 | ___ |
| **3376** | Bronx Zoo Car, *60–66, 69* | | | |
| | (A) Blue, white lettering | 20 | 50 | ___ |
| | (B) Green, yellow lettering | 35 | 83 | ___ |
| | (C) Blue, yellow lettering | 94 | 293 | ___ |
| **3386** | Bronx Zoo Car, *60* | 29 | 65 | ___ |
| **3409** | Helicopter Car, *61* | 46 | 100 | ___ |
| **3410** | Helicopter Car, *61–63* | | | |
| | (A) 2 operating couplers, gray Navy helicopter | 20 | 85 | ___ |
| | (B) Single operating coupler, yellow helicopter, *63* | 50 | 200 | ___ |
| **3413** | Mercury Capsule Car, *62–64* | 75 | 120 | ___ |
| **3419** | Helicopter Car, *59–65* | 55 | 81 | ___ |
| **3424** | Wabash Operating Boxcar, *56–58* | 38 | 54 | ___ |
| **3424-100** | Low Bridge Signal Set, *56–58* | 18 | 70 | ___ |
| **3428** | U.S. Mail Operating Boxcar, *59–60* | 49 | 111 | ___ |

| 3429 | USMC Helicopter Car, *60* | | | |
|---|---|---|---|---|
| | (A) USMC helicopter | 210 | 464 | ____ |
| | (B) Navy helicopter | 50 | 205 | ____ |
| 3434 | Poultry Dispatch Car, *59–60, 64–66* | 60 | 110 | ____ |
| 3435 | Traveling Aquarium Car, *59–62* | | | |
| | (A) Gold lettering, tank designations, and circle around L | 428 | 940 | ____ |
| | (B) Gold lettering, tank designations, no circle around L | 280 | 770 | ____ |
| | (C) Gold lettering, no tank designations, no circle around L | 140 | 267 | ____ |
| | (D) Yellow lettering, no tank designations, no circle around L | 100 | 168 | ____ |
| 3444 | Erie Operating Gondola, *57–59* | 50 | 66 | ____ |
| 3451 | Operating Log Dump Car, *46–48* | 19 | 44 | ____ |
| 3454 | PRR Operating Merchandise Car, *46–47* | | | |
| | (A) Red lettering | | NRS | ____ |
| | (B) Blue lettering | 39 | 83 | ____ |
| 3456 | N&W Operating Hopper Car, *50–55* | 17 | 63 | ____ |
| 3459 | LL Operating Coal Dump Car, *46–48* | | | |
| | (A) Aluminum bin | 98 | 298 | ____ |
| | (B) Black bin | 25 | 50 | ____ |
| | (C) Green bin | 30 | 95 | ____ |
| 3460 | Flatcar with trailers, *55–57* | 29 | 75 | ____ |
| 3461 | LL Operating Log Car, *49–55* | | | |
| | (A) Black car | 22 | 38 | ____ |
| | (B) Green car | 27 | 63 | ____ |
| 3462 | Automatic Milk Car, *47–48* | | | |
| | (A) Flat white or cream | 21 | 69 | ____ |
| | (B) Glossy cream | 100 | 332 | ____ |
| 3462-70 | Magnetic Milk Cans, *52–59* | 12 | 22 | ____ |
| 3462P | Milk Car Platform, *47–48* | 8 | 15 | ____ |
| X3464 | ATSF Operating Boxcar, *49–52* | 13 | 23 | ____ |
| X3464 | NYC Operating Boxcar, *49–52* | 11 | 30 | ____ |
| 3469 | LL Operating Coal Dump Car, *49–55* | 20 | 42 | ____ |
| 3470 | Target Launching Car, *62–64* | | | |
| | (A) Dark blue car | 30 | 70 | ____ |
| | (B) Light blue car | 70 | 167 | ____ |
| 3472 | Automatic Milk Car, *49–53* | 24 | 75 | ____ |
| 3474 | Western Pacific Operating Boxcar, *52–53* | 29 | 76 | ____ |
| 3482 | Automatic Milk Car, *54–55* | | | |
| | (A) "RT3472" on right | 38 | 119 | ____ |
| | (B) "RT3482" on right | 28 | 80 | ____ |
| 3484 | Pennsylvania Operating Boxcar, *53* | 15 | 50 | ____ |

| | | Good | Exc | Cond/$ |
|---|---|---|---|---|
| **3484-25** | ATSF Operating Boxcar, *54* | | | |
| | (A) White lettering | 33 | 90 | ____ |
| | (B) Black lettering | 321 | 1060 | ____ |
| **3494-1** | NYC Operating Boxcar, *55* | 55 | 130 | ____ |
| **3494-150** | MP Operating Boxcar, *56* | 65 | 140 | ____ |
| **3494-275** | State of Maine Operating Boxcar, *56–58* | | | |
| | (A) "3494275" on side | 60 | 110 | ____ |
| | (B) No number on side | 60 | 275 | ____ |
| **3494-550** | Monon Operating Boxcar, *57–58* | 135 | 440 | ____ |
| **3494-625** | Soo Operating Boxcar, *57–58* | 150 | 490 | ____ |
| **3509** | Satellite Launching Car, *61* | | | |
| | (A) Chrome satellite cover | 10 | 55 | ____ |
| | (B) Gray satellite cover | 50 | 200 | ____ |
| **3510** | Satellite Launching Car, *62* | 40 | 145 | ____ |
| **3512** | Fireman and Ladder Car, *59–61* | | | |
| | (A) Black extension ladder | 58 | 138 | ____ |
| | (B) Silver extension ladder | 85 | 230 | ____ |
| **3519** | Satellite Launching Car, *61–64* | 22 | 53 | ____ |
| **3520** | Searchlight Car, *52–53* | | | |
| | (A) Serif lettering | 35 | 98 | ____ |
| | (B) Sans serif lettering | 20 | 44 | ____ |
| **3530** | GM Generator Car, *56–58* | | | |
| | (A) Blue fuel tank | 60 | 125 | ____ |
| | (B) Black fuel tank | 65 | 140 | ____ |
| | (C) 3530 underscored | 500 | 2000 | ____ |
| **3530-50** | Searchlight with pole and base, *56–56* | 20 | 65 | ____ |
| **3535** | Security Car with searchlight, *60–61* | 41 | 100 | ____ |
| **3540** | Operating Radar Car, *59–60* | 42 | 142 | ____ |
| **3545** | Operating TV Monitor Car, *61–62* | 55 | 165 | ____ |
| **3559** | Operating Coal Dump Car, *46–48* | 23 | 38 | ____ |
| **3562-1** | ATSF Operating Barrel Car, *54* | | | |
| | (A) Black, black unloading trough | 75 | 185 | ____ |
| | (B) Black, yellow unloading trough | 75 | 193 | ____ |
| | (C) Gray, red lettering | 800 | 2750 | ____ |
| **3562-25** | ATSF Operating Barrel Car, gray, *54* | | | |
| | (A) Red lettering | 165 | 563 | ____ |
| | (B) Blue lettering | 22 | 55 | ____ |
| **3562-50** | ATSF Operating Barrel Car, yellow, *55–56* | | | |
| | (A) Painted | 45 | 134 | ____ |
| | (B) Unpainted | 20 | 59 | ____ |
| **3562-75** | ATSF Operating Barrel Car, orange, *57–58* | 40 | 88 | ____ |
| **3619** | Helicopter Reconnaissance Car, *62–64* | | | |
| | (A) Light yellow | 33 | 108 | ____ |
| | (B) Dark yellow | 40 | 153 | ____ |

| | | Good | Exc | Cond/$ |
|---|---|---|---|---|
| **3620** | Searchlight Car, *54–56* | | | |
| | (A) Gray searchlight, orange generator | 21 | 44 | ____ |
| | (B) Orange searchlight, orange generator | 55 | 108 | ____ |
| **3650** | Extension Searchlight Car, *56–59* | | | |
| | (A) Light gray | 42 | 78 | ____ |
| | (B) Dark gray | 70 | 145 | ____ |
| | (C) Olive gray | | 250 | ____ |
| **3656** | Armour Operating Cattle Car, *49–55* | | | |
| | (A) Black letters, Armour sticker | 64 | 209 | ____ |
| | (B) White letters, Armour sticker | 29 | 74 | ____ |
| | (C) Black letters, no Armour sticker | 63 | 184 | ____ |
| | (D) White letters, no Armour sticker | 26 | 70 | ____ |
| | (E) White letters, open coil below frame | 38 | 95 | ____ |
| | (F) Black letters, open coil below frame | 90 | 300 | ____ |
| **3656** | Stockyard with cattle | 24 | 80 | ____ |
| **3656-34** | Cattle, black, 9 pieces, *49–58* | | | |
| | (A) Rounded ridge on base, *49* | | 110 | ____ |
| | (B) Plain base | | 20 | ____ |
| **3662** | Automatic Milk Car, *55–60, 64–66* | 36 | 70 | ____ |
| **3665** | Minuteman Operating Car, *61–64* | | | |
| | (A) Medium blue roof | 68 | 178 | ____ |
| | (B) Dark blue roof | 55 | 115 | ____ |
| **3666** | Minuteman Boxcar with missile, *64 u* | 165 | 507 | ____ |
| **3672** | Bosco Operating Milk Car, *59–60* | | | |
| | (A) Unpainted yellow | 85 | 220 | ____ |
| | (B) Painted yellow | 115 | 315 | ____ |
| **3820** | USMC Operating Submarine Car, *60–62* | 88 | 215 | ____ |
| **3830** | Operating Submarine Car, *60–63* | 40 | 118 | ____ |
| **3854** | Automatic Merchandise Car, *46–47* | 293 | 456 | ____ |
| **3927** | Lionel Lines Track Cleaning Car, *56–60* | 50 | 70 | ____ |
| **3927-50** | Track Wiping Cylinders, 25 pieces, *57–60* | 6 | 30 | ____ |
| **3927-75** | Track-Clean Detergent, can, *56–69* | 2 | 13 | ____ |
| **4357** | SP-type Caboose, electronic, die-cast stack, *48–49* | | | |
| | (A) Die-cast metal smokestack | 50 | 200 | ____ |
| | (B) Matching plastic smokestack | 100 | 350 | ____ |
| | (C) Matching plastic smokestack, raised board on catwalk | 100 | 350 | ____ |
| **4452** | PRR Gondola, electronic, *46–49* | 43 | 98 | ____ |
| **4454** | Baby Ruth PRR Boxcar, electronic, *46–49* | 60 | 180 | ____ |
| **4457** | PRR N5-type Caboose, tintype, electronic, *46–47* | 45 | 150 | ____ |
| **5159** | Maintenance Kit, *63–65* | 28 | 80 | ____ |
| **5159-50** | Maintenance and Lube Kit, *66–69* | 28 | 80 | ____ |
| **5160** | Viewing Stand, *63* | 50 | 130 | ____ |

| | | Good | Exc | Cond/$ |
|---|---|---|---|---|
| **5459** | LL Coal Dump Car, electronic, *46–49* | 49 | 125 | ___ |
| **6002** | NYC Gondola, *50* | 5 | 13 | ___ |
| **X6004** | Baby Ruth PRR Boxcar, *50* | 4 | 7 | ___ |
| **6007** | Lionel Lines SP-type Caboose, *50* | 3 | 8 | ___ |
| **6009** | Remote Control Uncoupling Track, *53–54* | 1 | 6 | ___ |
| **6012** | Gondola, *51–56* | 2 | 7 | ___ |
| **6014** | Airex Boxcar, *60 u* | 26 | 43 | ___ |
| **6014** | Bosco PRR Boxcar, *58* | | | |
| | (A) White body | 35 | 50 | ___ |
| | (B) Red body | 4 | 7 | ___ |
| | (C) Orange body | 4 | 7 | ___ |
| **6014** | Chun King Boxcar, *57 u* | 60 | 143 | ___ |
| **6014** | Frisco Boxcar, *57, 63–69* | | | |
| | (A) White body | 5 | 12 | ___ |
| | (B) Red body | 4 | 7 | ___ |
| | (C) White body, coin slot | 25 | 45 | ___ |
| | (D) Orange body, *57* | 20 | 80 | ___ |
| | (E) Orange body, *69* | 22 | 39 | ___ |
| **X6014** | Baby Ruth PRR Boxcar, *51–56* | | | |
| | (A) White body | 5 | 9 | ___ |
| | (B) Red body | 10 | 26 | ___ |
| **6014-150** | Wix Boxcar, *59 u* | 95 | 200 | ___ |
| **6015** | Sunoco 1-D Tank Car, *54–55* | | | |
| | (A) Painted tank | 105 | 373 | ___ |
| | (B) Unpainted tank | 4 | 13 | ___ |
| **6017** | Lionel Lines SP-type Caboose, *51–62* | | | |
| | (A) Glossy tuscan-painted orange mold | 35 | 140 | ___ |
| | (B) Semigloss tuscan-painted, orange mold | 10 | 40 | ___ |
| | (C) Common red, tuscan, and brown bodies | 3 | 11 | ___ |
| **6017** | SP-type Caboose, maroon, "Lionel" only, *56* | 14 | 34 | ___ |
| **6017-50** | U.S. Marine Corps SP-type Caboose, *58* | 29 | 75 | ___ |
| **6017-85** | LL SP-type Caboose, gray, *58* | 24 | 89 | ___ |
| **6017-100** | B&M SP-type Caboose, *59, 62, 65–66* | | | |
| | (A) Purple-blue | 209 | 513 | ___ |
| | (B) Medium or light blue | 11 | 39 | ___ |
| **6017-185** | ATSF SP-type Caboose, *59–60* | 13 | 33 | ___ |
| **6017-200** | U.S. Navy SP-type Caboose, *60* | 49 | 173 | ___ |
| **6017-225** | ATSF SP-type Caboose, *61–62* | 15 | 55 | ___ |
| **6017-235** | ATSF SP-type Caboose, *62* | 17 | 63 | ___ |
| **6019** | Remote Control Track (O27), *48–66* | 2 | 14 | ___ |
| **6024** | Nabisco Shredded Wheat Boxcar, *57* | 13 | 30 | ___ |
| **6024** | RCA Whirlpool Boxcar, *57 u* | 28 | 60 | ___ |

| | | Good | Exc | Cond/S |
|---|---|---|---|---|
| **6025** | Gulf 1-D Tank Car, *56–58* | | | |
| | (A) Gray body, blue lettering | 5 | 16 | ____ |
| | (B) Orange body, blue lettering | 5 | 12 | ____ |
| | (C) Black body, red-orange Gulf emblem | 5 | 14 | ____ |
| **6027** | Alaska SP-type Caboose, *59* | 28 | 80 | ____ |
| **6029** | Remote Control Uncoupling Track, *55–63* | 1 | 16 | ____ |
| **6032** | Short Gondola, black (027), *52–54* | 2 | 9 | ____ |
| **X6034** | Baby Ruth PRR Boxcar, *53–54* | | | |
| | (A) Orange, blue lettering | 5 | 11 | ____ |
| | (B) Red, white lettering | 5 | 11 | ____ |
| | (C) Orange, black lettering | 5 | 11 | ____ |
| **6035** | Sunoco 1-D Tank Car, *52–53* | 3 | 11 | ____ |
| **6037** | Lionel Lines SP-type Caboose, *52–54* | | | |
| | (A) Tuscan | 3 | 8 | ____ |
| | (B) Red | 5 | 15 | ____ |
| **6042** | Short Gondola, *59–61, 62–64 u* | 2 | 10 | ____ |
| **6044** | Airex Boxcar, orange lettering, *59–60 u* | | | |
| | (A) Medium blue | 8 | 23 | ____ |
| | (B) Teal blue | 35 | 80 | ____ |
| | (C) Purple-blue | 90 | 333 | ____ |
| **6044-1X** | Nestles/McCall's Boxcar, *62–63 u* | 304 | 755 | ____ |
| **6045** | Lionel Lines 2-D Tank Car, *59–64* | | | |
| | (A) Gray | 15 | 21 | ____ |
| | (B) Orange | 15 | 37 | ____ |
| **6045** | Cities Service 2-D Tank, *60 u* | 13 | 40 | ____ |
| **6047** | Lionel Lines SP-type Caboose, *62* | | | |
| | (A) Unpainted, medium red | 2 | 5 | ____ |
| | (B) Painted, brown | 100 | 300 | ____ |
| | (C) Unpainted, coral pink | 10 | 50 | ____ |
| **6050** | Lionel Savings Bank Boxcar, *61* | | | |
| | (A) Blt by Lionel, *61* | 32 | 59 | ____ |
| | (B) Built by Lionel | 100 | 225 | ____ |
| **6050** | Swift Reefer, *62–63* | | | |
| | (A) Red body | 11 | 24 | ____ |
| | (B) Dark red body, 2 open holes in roof walk | 35 | 150 | ____ |
| **6050** | Libby's Tomato Juice Boxcar, *63 u* | | | |
| | (A) Green stems on tomatoes | 18 | 38 | ____ |
| | (B) Green stems missing | 21 | 49 | ____ |
| **6057** | LL SP-type Caboose, *59–62* | | | |
| | (A) Unpainted | 3 | 9 | ____ |
| | (B) Painted | 32 | 150 | ____ |
| **6057-50** | LL SP-type Caboose, orange, *62* | 12 | 51 | ____ |

| | | Good | Exc | Cond/$ |
|---|---|---|---|---|
| **6058** | C&O SP-type Caboose, *61* | | | |
| | (A) Blue lettering | 19 | 57 | ___ |
| | (B) Black lettering | 34 | 103 | ___ |
| **6059** | M&StL SP-type Caboose, *61–69* | | | |
| | (A) Painted, red | 13 | 25 | ___ |
| | (B) Unpainted, red | 4 | 8 | ___ |
| | (C) Unpainted, maroon | 7 | 12 | ___ |
| **6062** | NYC Gondola with 3 cable reels, *59–62* | | | |
| | (A) No metal undercarriage | 14 | 34 | ___ |
| | (B) Metal undercarriage | 52 | 100 | ___ |
| **6062-50** | NYC Gondola with 2 canisters, *69* | 6 | 28 | ___ |
| **6067** | SP-type Caboose, unmarked, *61–62* | | | |
| | (A) Red | 3 | 8 | ___ |
| | (B) Yellow | 10 | 17 | ___ |
| | (C) Brown | 18 | 35 | ___ |
| **6076** | ATSF Hopper, *63 u* | 11 | 31 | ___ |
| **6076** | Lehigh Valley Hopper, short, *63* | | | |
| | (A) Gray body | 9 | 14 | ___ |
| | (B) Black body | 9 | 16 | ___ |
| | (C) Red body | 9 | 14 | ___ |
| | (D) Yellow body, unpainted | 9 | 13 | ___ |
| | (E) Yellow body, painted | 400 | 800 | ___ |
| **6076-100** | Hopper, gray, unmarked, *63* | 16 | 28 | ___ |
| **6110** | 2-4-2 Locomotive, 6001T Tender, *50–51* | 14 | 32 | ___ |
| **6111** | Flatcar with logs, *55–57* | 8 | 21 | ___ |
| **6112** | Short Gondola, *56–58* | | | |
| | (A) Black body | 3 | 19 | ___ |
| | (B) Blue body | 4 | 10 | ___ |
| | (C) White body | 11 | 43 | ___ |
| **6119** | DL&W Work Caboose, red, *55–56* | 13 | 33 | ___ |
| **6119-25** | DL&W Work Caboose, orange, *56–59* | 15 | 37 | ___ |
| **6119-50** | DL&W Work Caboose, brown, *56* | 20 | 59 | ___ |
| **6119-75** | DL&W Work Caboose, *57* | | | |
| | (A) Heat-stamped letters on frame | 14 | 36 | ___ |
| | (B) Closely spaced rubber-stamped letters on frame | 63 | 225 | ___ |
| | (C) Widely spaced rubber-stamped letters on frame | 50 | 175 | ___ |
| **6119-100** | DL&W Work Caboose, red cab, gray tool tray, *57–66, 69* | | | |
| | (A) Black frame, white letters | 11 | 36 | ___ |
| | (B) "Built By Lionel" builders plate, *66* | 64 | 136 | ___ |
| | (C) Black frame, white letters, red-painted cab | 65 | 225 | ___ |
| | (D) Santa Fe cab, gray tool box | 10 | 40 | ___ |
| **6119-125** | Work Caboose, olive, black frame, *64* | 55 | 180 | ___ |

| | | Good | Exc | Cond/$ |
|---|---|---|---|---|
| **6120** | Work Caboose, yellow, unmarked, *61–62* | 7 | 23 | ____ |
| **6121** | Flatcar with pipes, *56–57* | | | |
| | (A) Yellow, peach, red, or gray | 9 | 23 | ____ |
| | (B) Maroon | 28 | 99 | ____ |
| **6130** | ATSF Work Caboose, *61, 65–69* | | | |
| | (A) Red painted, no builders plate | 10 | 40 | ____ |
| | (B) Red unpainted, builders plate | 10 | 40 | ____ |
| | (C) Red painted, builders plate | 50 | 200 | ____ |
| **6139** | Remote Control Uncoupling Track (O27), *63* | 1 | 4 | ____ |
| **6142** | Short Gondola, *63–66, 69* | | | |
| | (A) Green, blue, or black | 3 | 8 | ____ |
| | (B) Olive drab | 32 | 125 | ____ |
| **6149** | Remote Control Uncoupling Track (O27), *64–69* | 1 | 5 | ____ |
| **6151** | Flatcar with patrol truck, *58* | | | |
| | (A) Yellow frame | 24 | 78 | ____ |
| | (B) Orange frame | 24 | 78 | ____ |
| | (C) Cream frame | 24 | 78 | ____ |
| **6162** | NYC Gondola, *59–68* | | | |
| | (A) Blue body | 5 | 11 | ____ |
| | (B) Red body | 73 | 324 | ____ |
| **6162-60** | Alaska Gondola, *59* | 38 | 80 | ____ |
| **6167** | LL SP-type Caboose, red, *63–64* | | | |
| | (A) Unpainted | 3 | 9 | ____ |
| | (B) Painted | 100 | 240 | ____ |
| **6167** | SP-type Caboose, unmarked, no end rails, *63–64* | | | |
| | (A) Red body | 3 | 9 | ____ |
| | (B) Brown body | 15 | 36 | ____ |
| **6167-50** | SP-type Caboose, unmarked, yellow | 11 | 26 | ____ |
| **6167-85** | Union Pacific SP-type Caboose, *69* | 10 | 43 | ____ |
| **6167-175** | SP-type Caboose, unmarked, olive | 113 | 488 | ____ |
| **6175** | Flatcar with rocket, *58–61* | | | |
| | (A) Black frame | 25 | 65 | ____ |
| | (B) Red frame | 25 | 70 | ____ |
| **6176** | Hopper, unmarked, *63–69* | | | |
| | (A) Dark yellow | 9 | 18 | ____ |
| | (B) Gray | 8 | 13 | ____ |
| | (C) Olive | 35 | 98 | ____ |
| | (D) Red | 20 | 40 | ____ |
| | (E) Bright yellow | 50 | 90 | ____ |

| | | Good | Exc | Cond/S |
|---|---|---|---|---|
| **6176** | Lehigh Valley Hopper, *64–66, 69* | | | |
| | (A) Dark yellow | 6 | 9 | ____ |
| | (B) Gray | 7 | 12 | ____ |
| | (C) Black | 3 | 8 | ____ |
| | (D) Red | 30 | 45 | ____ |
| | (E) Bright yellow | 20 | 75 | ____ |
| **6219** | C&O Work Caboose, *60* | 27 | 55 | ____ |
| **6220** | Santa Fe NW2 Switcher, *49–50* | | | |
| | (A) Large GM decal on cab | 125 | 280 | ____ |
| | (B) Small GM decal on side | 125 | 265 | ____ |
| **6250** | Seaboard NW2 Switcher, *54–55* | | | |
| | (A) Seaboard decal | 133 | 303 | ____ |
| | (B) Widely spaced rubber-stamped letters | 118 | 253 | ____ |
| | (C) Closely spaced rubber-stamped letters | 300 | 900 | ____ |
| **6257** | SP-type Caboose, *48–52* | 3 | 14 | ____ |
| **6257-25** | SP-type Caboose, circled-L logo, *53–55* | | | |
| | (A) Red painted | 5 | 25 | ____ |
| | (B) Unpainted red plastic | 4 | 9 | ____ |
| **6257-50** | SP-type Caboose, *56* | 4 | 13 | ____ |
| **6257-100** | Lionel Lines SP-type Caboose, smokestack, *63–64* | 9 | 24 | ____ |
| **6257X** | SP-type Caboose, red, 2 couplers, with box, *48* | 13 | 48 | ____ |
| **6262** | Flatcar with wheel load, *56–57* | | | |
| | (A) Black frame, *56–57* | 30 | 65 | ____ |
| | (B) Red frame, *56* | 165 | 510 | ____ |
| **6264** | Flatcar with lumber for 264 Fork Lift Platform, *57–60* | | | |
| | (A) No box | 18 | 57 | ____ |
| | (B) Separate-sale box and envelope | 75 | 262 | ____ |
| **6311** | Flatcar with 3 pipes, *55* | 20 | 45 | ____ |
| **6315** | Gulf 1-D Chemical Tank Car, *56–59, 68–69* | | | |
| | (A) Early, painted | 38 | 78 | ____ |
| | (B) Late, unpainted | 30 | 65 | ____ |
| | (C) Late, unpainted, built date | 43 | 218 | ____ |
| **6315** | Lionel Lines 1-D Tank Car, *63–66* | | | |
| | (A) Unpainted orange body | 15 | 23 | ____ |
| | (B) Painted orange body | 144 | 400 | ____ |
| **6342** | NYC Gondola, *56–58, 64–66* | 17 | 42 | ____ |
| **6343** | Barrel Ramp Car, *61–62* | 15 | 34 | ____ |
| **6346** | Alcoa Quad Hopper, *56* | 31 | 65 | ____ |
| **6352-1** | PFE Reefer from 352 Ice Depot, *55–57* | | | |
| | (A) 3 lines of data | 63 | 168 | ____ |
| | (B) 4 lines of data | 50 | 90 | ____ |
| | (C) Separate-sale box | 650 | 1700 | ____ |

| | | Good | Exc | Cond/$ |
|---|---|---|---|---|
| **6356** | NYC Stock Car, 2-level, *54–55* | | | |
| | (A) Heat-stamped lettering | 15 | 40 | ___ |
| | (B) Rubber-stamped lettering | 40 | 100 | ___ |
| **6357** | SP-type Caboose, *48–53* | 12 | 29 | |
| **6357** | SP-type Caboose, *57–61* | | | |
| | (A) Number to left | 10 | 38 | ___ |
| | (B) Number to right | 10 | 45 | ___ |
| **6357-25** | SP-type Caboose, *53–56* | | | |
| | (A) Maroon or tuscan body, black metal smokestack | 5 | 30 | ___ |
| | (B) Maroon body, maroon metal smokestack | 125 | 463 | ___ |
| **6357-50** | ATSF SP-type Caboose, lighted, *60* | 325 | 1000 | ___ |
| **6361** | Timber Transport Car, *60–61, 64–69* | | | |
| | (A) White lettering | 36 | 73 | ___ |
| | (B) No lettering | 75 | 150 | ___ |
| **6362** | Truck Car with 3 trucks, *55–56* | | | |
| | (A) Shiny orange | 24 | 55 | ___ |
| | (B) Dull orange | 80 | 130 | ___ |
| **6376** | LL Circus Stock Car, *56–57* | 43 | 68 | ___ |
| **6401** | Flatcar, no load, gray, *60* | 2 | 7 | ___ |
| **6401-25** | Flatcar with tank or jeep and cannon, *64–65* | 95 | 295 | ___ |
| **6402** | Flatcar with orange or gray reels, *62, 64–66* | 8 | 24 | ___ |
| **6402** | Flatcar with blue boat, *69* | 35 | 63 | ___ |
| **6404** | Black Flatcar with auto, *60* | | | |
| | (A) Red auto | 20 | 83 | ___ |
| | (B) Yellow auto | 20 | 200 | ___ |
| | (C) Brown auto | 50 | 398 | ___ |
| | (D) Green auto | 50 | 398 | ___ |
| **6405** | Flatcar with piggyback van, *61* | 15 | 53 | ___ |
| **6406** | Flatcar with auto, *61* | | | |
| | (A) Maroon frame, red auto | 22 | 58 | ___ |
| | (B) Maroon frame, yellow auto | 43 | 145 | ___ |
| | (C) Gray frame, dark brown auto | 98 | 328 | ___ |
| | (D) Gray frame, green auto | 98 | 325 | ___ |
| | (E) Gray frame, yellow auto | 35 | 75 | ___ |
| **6407** | Flatcar with rocket, *63* | 128 | 348 | ___ |
| **6408** | Flatcar with pipes, *63* | 14 | 43 | ___ |
| **6409-25** | Flatcar with pipes, *63* | 14 | 43 | ___ |
| **6410-25** | Flatcar with 2 automobiles, *63* | | | |
| | (A) Yellow autos | 180 | 600 | ___ |
| | (B) Brown autos | 240 | 800 | ___ |
| **6411** | Flatcar with logs, *48–50* | 15 | 33 | ___ |

| | | Good | Exc | Cond/$ |
|---|---|---|---|---|
| **6413** | Mercury Capsule Carrying Car, *62–63* | | | |
| | (A) Medium blue frame | 75 | 140 | ____ |
| | (B) Aquamarine frame | 95 | 163 | ____ |
| **6414** | Evans Auto Loader with 4 cars, *55–66* | | | |
| | (A) Premium cars (chrome bumpers, windows, rubber wheels): red, yellow, blue, and white | 55 | 115 | ____ |
| | (B) Cheapie cars (no wheels): 2 red and 2 yellow | 238 | 460 | ____ |
| | (C) Red cars with gray bumpers | 63 | 165 | ____ |
| | (D) Yellow cars with gray bumpers | 150 | 338 | ____ |
| | (E) Brown cars with gray bumpers | 350 | 775 | ____ |
| | (F) Green cars with gray bumpers | 380 | 875 | ____ |
| **6415** | Sunoco 3-D Tank Car, *53–55, 64–66, 69* | 12 | 43 | ____ |
| **6416** | Boat Transport Car, 4 boats, *61–63* | 110 | 253 | ____ |
| **6417** | PRR N5c Porthole Caboose, *53–57* | | | |
| | (A) New York Zone | 11 | 35 | ____ |
| | (B) without New York Zone | 105 | 285 | ____ |
| **6417-25** | Lionel Lines N5c Porthole Caboose, *54* | 15 | 37 | ____ |
| **6417-50** | LV N5c Porthole Caboose, *54* | | | |
| | (A) Tuscan | 368 | 1232 | ____ |
| | (B) Gray | 55 | 133 | ____ |
| **6418** | Machinery Car with 2 steel girders, *55–57* | | | |
| | (A) Black girders, "Lionel" in raised letters | 70 | 110 | ____ |
| | (B) Orange girders, "Lionel" in raised letters | 80 | 125 | ____ |
| | (C) Pinkish orange girders, U.S. Steel | 70 | 115 | ____ |
| | (D) Black girders, U.S. Steel | 70 | 110 | ____ |
| **6419** | DL&W Work Caboose, *48–50, 52–55* | 17 | 43 | ____ |
| **6419-25** | DL&W Work Caboose, one coupler, *54–55* | 16 | 41 | ____ |
| **6419-50** | DL&W Work Caboose, short smokestack, *56–57* | 17 | 50 | ____ |
| **6419-75** | DL&W Work Caboose, one coupler, *56–57* | 17 | 50 | ____ |
| **6419-100** | N&W Work Caboose, *57–58* | 39 | 120 | ____ |
| **6420** | DL&W Work Caboose with searchlight, *48–50* | | | |
| | (A) Heat-stamped serif lettering | 34 | 97 | ____ |
| | (B) Rubber-stamped sans serif lettering | 50 | 200 | ____ |
| | (A) Black frame, premium cars | 30 | 55 | ____ |
| **6424** | Twin Auto Flatcar, *56–59* | | | |
| | (B) 6805 slots and rail stops, *58–59* | 85 | 235 | ____ |
| | (C) 6805 slots, no rail stops | 50 | 200 | ____ |
| **6425** | Gulf 3-D Tank Car, *56–58* | 17 | 45 | ____ |
| **6427** | Lionel Lines N5c Porthole Caboose, *54–60* | 12 | 33 | ____ |
| **6427-60** | Virginian N5c Porthole Caboose, *58* | 155 | 464 | ____ |
| **6427-500** | PRR N5c Porthole Caboose, sky blue, from Girls Set, *57–58\** | 145 | 310 | ____ |
| **6428** | U.S. Mail Boxcar, *60–61, 65–66* | 20 | 44 | ____ |

| | | Good | Exc | Cond/$ |
|---|---|---|---|---|
| **6429** | DL&W Work Caboose, AAR trucks, *63* | 140 | 285 | ____ |
| **6430** | Flatcar with 2 trailers, *56–58* | | | |
| | (A) Gray Cooper-Jarrett trailers | 24 | 69 | ____ |
| | (B) White Cooper-Jarrett trailers | 22 | 75 | ____ |
| | (C) Green Fruehauf trailers | 25 | 100 | ____ |
| **6431** | Flatcar with 2 vans and Midge tractor, *66* | 90 | 225 | ____ |
| **6434** | Poultry Dispatch Stock Car, *58–59* | 42 | 70 | ____ |
| **6436-1** | LV Open Quad Hopper, black, *55* | | | |
| | (A) Spreader brace | 15 | 33 | ____ |
| | (B) No spreader brace | 20 | 93 | ____ |
| **6436-25** | LV Open Quad Hopper, maroon, *55–57* | 16 | 36 | ____ |
| **6436-110** | LV Quad Hopper, red, *63–68* | | | |
| | (A) No built date | 20 | 43 | ____ |
| | (B) Built date "New 3-55" | 40 | 145 | ____ |
| **6436-500** | LV Open Quad Hopper, lilac, from Girls Set, *57–58** | 93 | 420 | ____ |
| **6437** | PRR N5c Porthole Caboose, *61–68* | 16 | 53 | ____ |
| **6440** | Flatcar with vans, *61–63* | 31 | 85 | ____ |
| **6440** | Green Pullman Car, *48–49* | 28 | 70 | ____ |
| **6441** | Green Observation Car, *48–49* | 29 | 70 | ____ |
| **6442** | Brown Pullman Car, *49* | 31 | 75 | ____ |
| **6443** | Brown Observation Car, *49* | 35 | 60 | ____ |
| **6445** | Fort Knox Gold Reserve Boxcar with coin slot, *61–63* | 60 | 163 | ____ |
| **6446** | N&W Covered Quad Hopper, black or gray, *54–55* | 19 | 49 | ____ |
| **6446-25** | N&W Covered Quad Hopper, *55–57* | | | |
| | (A) Black, white lettering | 19 | 65 | ____ |
| | (B) Gray, black lettering | 20 | 75 | ____ |
| **6446-60** | LV Covered Quad Hopper, *63* | 100 | 275 | ____ |
| **6447** | PRR N5c Porthole Caboose, *63* | 155 | 450 | ____ |
| **6448** | Exploding Target Range Boxcar, *61–64* | | | |
| | (A) Red sides, white roof and ends | 17 | 38 | ____ |
| | (B) White sides, red roof and ends | 17 | 38 | ____ |
| **6452** | Pennsylvania Gondola, black, *48–49* | | | |
| | (A) Numbered "6462," *48* | 25 | 64 | ____ |
| | (B) Numbered "6452," *49* | 7 | 22 | ____ |
| **X6454** | Baby Ruth PRR Boxcar, *48* | 95 | 276 | ____ |
| **X6454** | Santa Fe Boxcar, *48* | 26 | 58 | ____ |
| **X6454** | NYC Boxcar, *48* | | | |
| | (A) Brown body | 24 | 52 | ____ |
| | (B) Orange body | 44 | 131 | ____ |
| | (C) Tan body | 21 | 43 | ____ |
| **X6454** | Erie Boxcar, *49–52* | 27 | 59 | ____ |
| **X6464** | Erie Replacement Boxcar Shell, *51* | | 125 | ____ |

| | | Good | Exc | Cond/$ |
|---|---|---|---|---|
| **X6454** | PRR Boxcar, *49–52* | 24 | 55 | \_\_\_\_ |
| **X6454** | SP Boxcar, *49–52* | | | |
| | (A) Break in herald circle between R and N, *49* | 25 | 86 | \_\_\_\_ |
| | (B) Complete herald circle | 15 | 47 | \_\_\_\_ |
| **6456** | Lehigh Valley Short Hopper, *48–55* | | | |
| | (A) Black | 10 | 20 | \_\_\_\_ |
| | (B) Maroon | 6 | 18 | \_\_\_\_ |
| | (C) Gray | 21 | 39 | \_\_\_\_ |
| | (D) Enamel red, yellow lettering | 60 | 170 | \_\_\_\_ |
| | (E) Enamel red, white lettering | 240 | 738 | \_\_\_\_ |
| **6457** | SP-type Caboose, *49–52* | 17 | 32 | \_\_\_\_ |
| **6460** | Bucyrus Erie Crane Car, 8-wheel, *52–54* | | | |
| | (A) Black cab | 18 | 50 | \_\_\_\_ |
| | (B) Red cab | 29 | 80 | \_\_\_\_ |
| **6460-25** | Bucyrus Erie Crane Car, red cab, 8-wheel, *54* | 48 | 140 | \_\_\_\_ |
| **6461** | Transformer Car, *49–50* | 25 | 70 | \_\_\_\_ |
| **6462** | NYC Gondola, black, *49–54* | 8 | 14 | \_\_\_\_ |
| **6462-25** | NYC Gondola, green, *54–57* | 12 | 35 | \_\_\_\_ |
| **6462-75** | NYC Gondola, red-painted, *52–55* | 12 | 28 | \_\_\_\_ |
| **6462-125** | NYC Gondola, red plastic, *55–57* | 15 | 33 | \_\_\_\_ |
| **6462-500** | NYC Gondola, pink, from Girls Set, *57–58** | 65 | 165 | \_\_\_\_ |
| **6463** | Rocket Fuel 2-D Tank Car, *62–63* | 17 | 96 | \_\_\_\_ |
| **6464-1** | WP Boxcar, *53–54* | | | |
| | (A) Blue lettering | 28 | 64 | \_\_\_\_ |
| | (B) Red lettering | 425 | 1175 | \_\_\_\_ |
| **6464-25** | GN Boxcar, *53–54* | 36 | 73 | \_\_\_\_ |
| **6464-50** | M&StL Boxcar, *53–56* | 42 | 70 | \_\_\_\_ |
| **6464-75** | RI Boxcar, green, *53–54, 69* | | | |
| | (A) Built date, *53–54* | 27 | 71 | \_\_\_\_ |
| | (B) No built date, *69* | 38 | 88 | \_\_\_\_ |
| **6464-100** | Western Pacific Boxcar, *54–55* | | | |
| | (A) Silver body, yellow feather | 48 | 140 | \_\_\_\_ |
| | (B) Orange body, blue feather | 279 | 714 | \_\_\_\_ |
| **6464-125** | NYC Pacemaker Boxcar, *54–56* | 52 | 125 | \_\_\_\_ |
| **6464-150** | MP Boxcar, *54–55, 57* | 56 | 126 | \_\_\_\_ |
| **6464-175** | Rock Island Boxcar, *54–55* | | | |
| | (A) Blue lettering | 47 | 125 | \_\_\_\_ |
| | (B) Black lettering | 413 | 908 | \_\_\_\_ |
| **6464-200** | Pennsylvania Boxcar, *54–55, 69* | 75 | 123 | \_\_\_\_ |
| **6464-225** | SP Boxcar, *54–56* | 60 | 107 | \_\_\_\_ |
| **6464-250** | WP Boxcar, *66* | 79 | 204 | \_\_\_\_ |
| **6464-275** | State of Maine Boxcar, *55, 57–59* | | | |
| | (A) Striped doors | 52 | 87 | \_\_\_\_ |
| | (B) Solid doors | 53 | 125 | \_\_\_\_ |

| | | Good | Exc | Cond/$ |
|---|---|---:|---:|---|
| **6464-300** | Rutland Boxcar, *55–56* | | | |
| | (A) Rubber-stamped lettering | 44 | 79 | ___ |
| | (B) Split door with bottom painted green | 305 | 625 | ___ |
| | (C) Rubber-stamped lettering with solid shield | 800 | 2400 | ___ |
| | (D) Heat-stamped lettering | 75 | 152 | ___ |
| **6464-325** | B&O Sentinel Boxcar, *56* | 266 | 525 | ___ |
| **6464-350** | MKT Boxcar, *56* | 150 | 288 | ___ |
| **6464-375** | Central of Georgia Boxcar, *56–57, 66* | | | |
| | (A) Unpainted maroon body | 55 | 105 | ___ |
| | (B) Painted red body | 775 | 1400 | ___ |
| **6464-400** | B&O Time-Saver Boxcar, *56–57, 69* | | | |
| | (A) BLT 5-54 | 41 | 118 | ___ |
| | (B) BLT 2-56 | 95 | 265 | ___ |
| **6464-425** | New Haven Boxcar, *56–58* | 23 | 44 | ___ |
| **6464-450** | Great Northern Boxcar, *56–57, 66* | 65 | 130 | ___ |
| **6464-475** | B&M Boxcar, *57–60, 65–66, 68* | | | |
| | (A) Medium blue-painted or unpainted plastic | 29 | 74 | ___ |
| | (B) Dark purple-painted, gray or blue mold | 60 | 250 | ___ |
| **6464-500** | Timken Boxcar, yellow body, white side band and charcoal lettering, *57–59, 69* | 75 | 150 | ___ |
| **6464-510** | NYC Pacemaker Boxcar, *57–58* | 345 | 740 | ___ |
| **6464-515** | MKT Boxcar, *57–58* | 315 | 545 | ___ |
| **6464-525** | M&StL Boxcar, *57–58, 64–66* | | | |
| | (A) Red, white lettering | 30 | 60 | ___ |
| | (B) Maroon, white lettering | | 530 | ___ |
| **6464-650** | D&RGW Boxcar, *57–58, 66* | | | |
| | (A) Yellow body, silver roof, black stripe | 50 | 120 | ___ |
| | (B) Yellow body, silver roof, no black stripe | 150 | 195 | ___ |
| | (C) Painted yellow body and yellow roof | 500 | 900 | ___ |
| **6464-700** | Santa Fe Boxcar, *61, 66* | 55 | 132 | ___ |
| **6464-725** | New Haven Boxcar, *62–66, 68* | | | |
| | (A) Orange body | 30 | 65 | ___ |
| | (B) Black body | 70 | 238 | ___ |
| **6464-825** | Alaska Boxcar, *59–60* | 160 | 390 | ___ |
| **6464-900** | NYC Boxcar, *60–66* | 73 | 134 | ___ |
| **6465** | Sunoco 2-D Tank Car, *48–56* | | | |
| | (A) Rubber-stamped "6465" | 6 | 20 | ___ |
| | (B) Rubber-stamped "6455" | 22 | 77 | ___ |
| | (C) No number | 7 | 21 | ___ |
| **6465-60** | Gulf 2-D Tank Car, *58* | | | |
| | (A) Black tank | 25 | 48 | ___ |
| | (B) Gray tank | 10 | 25 | ___ |
| **6465-85** | LL 2-D Tank Car, black, *59* | 38 | 93 | ___ |
| **6465-110** | Cities Service 2-D Tank, *60–62* | 17 | 45 | ___ |

| | | Good | Exc | Cond/$ |
|---|---|---|---|---|
| **6465-160** | LL 2-D Tank Car, orange with black ends, *63–64* | 8 | 21 | ___ |
| **6467** | Bulkhead Flatcar, *56* | 20 | 62 | ___ |
| **6468** | B&O Auto Boxcar, *53–55* | | | |
| | (A) Tuscan | 145 | 350 | ___ |
| | (B) Blue | 23 | 55 | ___ |
| **6468-25** | NH Auto Boxcar, *56–58* | | | |
| | (A) Black N over white H | 46 | 102 | ___ |
| | (B) White N over black H | 185 | 387 | ___ |
| **6469** | Liquefied Gas Tank Car, *63* | 50 | 135 | ___ |
| **6470** | Explosives Boxcar, *59–60* | 13 | 40 | ___ |
| **6472** | Refrigerator Car, *50–53* | 17 | 33 | ___ |
| **6473** | Horse Transport Car, *62–69* | 12 | 27 | ___ |
| **6475** | Libby's Crushed Pineapple Vat Car, *63 u* | 25 | 75 | ___ |
| **6475** | Pickles Vat Car, *60–62* | 26 | 78 | ___ |
| **6476** | LV Short Hopper, *57–63* | | | |
| | (A) Red body | 7 | 18 | ___ |
| | (B) Gray body | 7 | 14 | ___ |
| | (C) Black body | 7 | 19 | ___ |
| **6476-75** | LV Short Hopper, black, Type VI body, *63* | 5 | 25 | ___ |
| **6476-135** | LV Short Hopper, yellow, *64–66, 68* | 6 | 11 | ___ |
| **6476-160** | LV Short Hopper, black, *69* | 7 | 16 | ___ |
| **6476-185** | LV Short Hopper, yellow, *69* | 6 | 14 | ___ |
| **6477** | Bulkhead Car with pipes, *57–58* | 22 | 60 | ___ |
| **6480** | Explosives Boxcar, red, *61* | 28 | 49 | ___ |
| **6482** | Refrigerator Car, *57* | 17 | 49 | ___ |
| **6500** | Flatcar with Bonanza airplane, *62, 65* | | | |
| | (A) Plane, red top and wings | 333 | 637 | ___ |
| | (B) Plane, white top and wings | 358 | 700 | ___ |
| **6501** | Flatcar with jet boat, *62–63* | 70 | 198 | ___ |
| **6502** | Flatcar, black, with bridge girder, *62* | 21 | 56 | ___ |
| **6502-50** | Flatcar, blue or teal, no lettering, with bridge girder, *62* | 5 | 30 | ___ |
| **6511** | Flatcar with pipes, *53–56* | | | |
| | (A) Die-cast truck plates, *53* | 19 | 70 | ___ |
| | (B) Stamped metal truck plates | 19 | 40 | ___ |
| **6511-24** | Set of 6 pipes with box, *55–58* | 5 | 150 | ___ |
| **6512** | Cherry Picker Car, *62–63* | 33 | 95 | ___ |
| **6517** | LL Bay Window Caboose, *55–59* | | | |
| | (A) Built date underscored | 30 | 70 | ___ |
| | (B) Built date not underscored | 22 | 68 | ___ |
| **6517-75** | Erie Bay Window Caboose, *66* | 155 | 473 | ___ |
| **6518** | Transformer Car, *56–58* | 43 | 103 | ___ |

| | | Good | Exc | Cond/$ |
|---|---|---|---|---|
| **6519** | Allis-Chalmers Flatcar, *58–61* | | | |
| | (A) Dark or medium orange base | 35 | 70 | ____ |
| | (B) Dull light orange base | 40 | 100 | ____ |
| **6520** | Searchlight Car, *49–51* | | | |
| | (A) Tan generator | 350 | 625 | ____ |
| | (B) Green generator | 188 | 354 | ____ |
| | (C) Maroon generator | 20 | 61 | ____ |
| | (D) Orange generator | 24 | 65 | ____ |
| **6530** | Firefighting Instruction Car, *60–61* | | | |
| | (A) Red body, white lettering | 34 | 70 | ____ |
| | (B) Black body, white lettering | | 415 | ____ |
| **6536** | M&StL Open Quad Hopper, *58–59, 63* | 23 | 105 | ____ |
| **6544** | Missile Firing Car, 4 missiles, *60–64* | | | |
| | (A) White-lettered console | 45 | 170 | ____ |
| | (B) Black-lettered console | 160 | 320 | ____ |
| **6555** | Sunoco 1-D Tank Car, *49–50* | 16 | 44 | ____ |
| **6556** | MKT Stock Car, *58* | 95 | 365 | ____ |
| **6557** | SP-type Caboose, smoke, *58–59* | | | |
| | (A) Tuscan, with number on left | 95 | 224 | ____ |
| | (B) Brown, with number on right | 250 | 750 | ____ |
| **6560** | Bucyrus Erie Crane Car, smokestack, *55–58, 68–69* | | | |
| | (A) Black frame, red-orange or black cab | 65 | 170 | ____ |
| | (B) Black frame, gray cab | 40 | 78 | ____ |
| | (C) Black frame, red cab | 24 | 41 | ____ |
| | (D) Dark blue frame, red cab | 40 | 85 | ____ |
| | (E) Black frame, red cab, rubber-stamped "6560" | 75 | 300 | ____ |
| **6560-25** | Bucyrus Erie Crane Car, 8-wheel, *56* | 35 | 68 | ____ |
| **6561** | Cable Car, 2 reels, *53–56* | | | |
| | (A) Orange reels | 21 | 68 | ____ |
| | (B) Gray reels | 24 | 57 | ____ |
| **6562** | NYC Gondola with canisters, *56–58* | | | |
| | (A) Gray body, *56* | 16 | 41 | ____ |
| | (B) Red body, *56, 58* | 15 | 40 | ____ |
| | (C) Black body, *57* | 16 | 41 | ____ |
| **6572** | REA Reefer, *58–59, 63* | | | |
| | (A) Passenger trucks | 84 | 249 | ____ |
| | (B) Bar-end trucks | 43 | 108 | ____ |
| | (C) AAR trucks, *63* | 40 | 100 | ____ |
| **6630** | Missile Launching Car, *61* | 27 | 114 | ____ |
| **6636** | Alaska Open Quad Hopper, *59–60* | 30 | 148 | ____ |
| **6640** | USMC Missile Launching Car, *60* | 98 | 220 | ____ |
| **6646** | Lionel Lines Stock Car, *57* | 18 | 51 | ____ |

| | | Good | Exc | Cond/$ |
|---|---|---|---|---|
| **6650** | IRBM Rocket Launcher, *59–63* | 23 | 47 | ____ |
| **6650-80** | Missile, *60* | 3 | 9 | ____ |
| **6651** | USMC Cannon Car, *64 u* | 88 | 188 | ____ |
| **6656** | Lionel Lines Stock Car, *49–55* | | | |
| | (A) Brown Armour decal | 47 | 90 | ____ |
| | (B) No decal | 10 | 25 | ____ |
| **6657** | Rio Grande SP-type Caboose, *57–58* | | | |
| | (A) With ladder slots | 75 | 210 | ____ |
| | (B) Without ladder slots | 180 | 350 | ____ |
| **6660** | Boom Car, *58* | 33 | 80 | ____ |
| **6670** | Derrick Car, *59–60* | 22 | 63 | ____ |
| **6672** | Santa Fe Reefer, *54–56* | | | |
| | (A) Blue lettering, 2 lines of data | 29 | 65 | ____ |
| | (B) Black lettering, 2 lines of data | 25 | 65 | ____ |
| | (C) Blue lettering, 3 lines of data | 85 | 265 | ____ |
| **6736** | Detroit & Mackinac Open Quad Hopper, *60–62* | 13 | 34 | ____ |
| **6800** | Flatcar with airplane, *57–60* | | | |
| | (A) Plane, black top and wings | 78 | 154 | ____ |
| | (B) Plane, yellow top and wings | 75 | 155 | ____ |
| **6801** | Flatcar with boat, *57–60* | | | |
| | (A) Boat, blue hull with white deck | 45 | 88 | ____ |
| | (B) Boat, yellow hull with white deck | 45 | 95 | ____ |
| | (C) Boat, white hull with brown deck | 38 | 78 | ____ |
| **6802** | Flatcar with 2 U.S. Steel girders, *58–59* | 17 | 31 | ____ |
| **6803** | Flatcar with USMC tank and sound truck, *58–59* | 68 | 168 | ____ |
| **6804** | Flatcar with 2 USMC trucks, *58–59* | 73 | 179 | ____ |
| **6805** | Atomic Energy Disposal Flatcar, *58–59* | 57 | 192 | ____ |
| **6806** | Flatcar with 2 USMC trucks, *58–59* | 73 | 180 | ____ |
| **6807** | Flatcar with boat, *58–59* | 55 | 127 | ____ |
| **6808** | Flatcar with USMC tank and truck, *58–59* | 88 | 208 | ____ |
| **6809** | Flatcar with 2 USMC trucks, *58–59* | 73 | 183 | ____ |
| **6810** | Flatcar with trailer, *58* | 25 | 50 | ____ |
| **6812** | Track Maintenance Car, *59* | | | |
| | (A) Dark yellow superstructure | 18 | 80 | ____ |
| | (B) Black base, gray platform and crank handle | 18 | 80 | ____ |
| | (C) Gray base, black platform and crank handle | 18 | 80 | ____ |
| | (D) Cream superstructure | 19 | 153 | ____ |
| | (E) Light yellow superstructure | 18 | 80 | ____ |
| **6814** | Rescue Caboose, *59–61* | 33 | 128 | ____ |
| **6816** | Flatcar with Allis-Chalmers bulldozer, *59–60* | | | |
| | (A) Red car | 195 | 425 | ____ |
| | (B) Black car | 400 | 930 | ____ |

| | | Good | Exc | Cond/S |
|---|---|---|---|---|
| **6816-100** | Allis-Chalmers bulldozer, *59–60* | | | |
| | (A) No box | 100 | 250 | ____ |
| | (B) Separate-sale box | 300 | 1000 | ____ |
| **6817** | Flatcar with Allis-Chalmers motor scraper, *59–60* | | | |
| | (A) Red car | 203 | 490 | ____ |
| | (B) Black car | 425 | 1020 | ____ |
| **6817-100** | Allis-Chalmers motor scraper, *59–60* | | | |
| | (A) No box | 128 | 250 | ____ |
| | (B) Separate-sale box | 150 | 500 | ____ |
| **6818** | Transformer Car, *58* | 19 | 36 | ____ |
| **6819** | Flatcar with helicopter, *59–60* | 19 | 65 | ____ |
| **6820** | Aerial Missile Transport Car with helicopter, *60–61* | | | |
| | (A) Light blue frame | 80 | 228 | ____ |
| | (B) Medium blue frame | 63 | 189 | ____ |
| **6821** | Flatcar with crates, *59–60* | 22 | 38 | ____ |
| **6822** | Searchlight Car, *61–69* | | | |
| | (A) Black base, gray light | 20 | 40 | ____ |
| | (B) Gray base, black light | 21 | 52 | ____ |
| **6823** | Flatcar with 2 IRBM missiles, *59–60* | 33 | 80 | ____ |
| **6824** | USMC Work Caboose, *60* | 65 | 225 | ____ |
| **6824-50** | Rescue Caboose, white, *64* | 30 | 100 | ____ |
| **6825** | Flatcar with arch trestle bridge, *59–62* | 19 | 35 | ____ |
| **6826** | Flatcar with Christmas trees, *59–60* | 37 | 77 | ____ |
| **6827** | Flatcar with Harnischfeger power shovel, *60–63* | 60 | 180 | ____ |
| **6827-100** | Harnischfeger tractor shovel, *60* | | | |
| | (A) No box | 55 | 110 | ____ |
| | (B) Separate-sale box | 105 | 185 | ____ |
| **6828** | Flatcar with Harnischfeger crane, *60–63, 66* | | | |
| | (A) Black flatcar, light yellow crane cab | 58 | 195 | ____ |
| | (B) Black flatcar, dark yellow crane cab | 65 | 210 | ____ |
| | (C) Red flatcar, dark yellow crane cab | 250 | 1050 | ____ |
| **6828-100** | Harnischfeger construction crane, *60* | | | |
| | (A) No box | 33 | 105 | ____ |
| | (B) Separate-sale box | 68 | 175 | ____ |
| **6830** | Flatcar with submarine, *60–61* | 50 | 110 | ____ |
| **6844** | Missile Carrying Car, 6 missiles, *59–60* | | | |
| | (A) Black frame | 23 | 94 | ____ |
| | (B) Red frame | 317 | 813 | ____ |

## Other Track, Transformers, and Assorted Items

| | | Good | Exc | Cond/$ |
|---|---|---|---|---|
| **A** | Transformer, 90 watts, *47–48* | 25 | 70 | ____ |
| **CO-1** | Track Clips, dozen, with envelope (0), *49* | 4 | 12 | ____ |
| **CO-1** | Track Clips, box of 100 (0), *49* | 40 | 150 | ____ |
| **CTC** | Lockon (0 and 027), *47–69* | | 1 | ____ |
| **ECU-1** | Electronic Control Unit, *46* | 22 | 73 | ____ |
| **KW** | Transformer, 190 watts, *50–65* | 70 | 110 | ____ |
| **LTC** | Lockon (0 and 027), *50–69* | 2 | 3 | ____ |
| **LW** | Transformer, 125 watts, *55–56* | 70 | 78 | ____ |
| **027C-1** | Track Clips, dozen, with envelope (027), *49* | 4 | 12 | ____ |
| **027C-1** | Track Clips, box of 50 (027), *49* | 40 | 150 | ____ |
| **OC** | Curved Track (0), *45–61* | | 1 | ____ |
| **OC½** | Half Section Curved Track (0), *45–66* | | 1 | ____ |
| **OCS** | Curved Insulated Track (0), *46–50* | 40 | 75 | ____ |
| **OS** | Straight Track (0), *45–61* | | 1 | ____ |
| **OSS** | Straight Insulated Track, *46–50* | | 75 | ____ |
| **OTC** | Lockon Track (0 and 027) | | 3 | ____ |
| **Q** | Transformer, 75 watts, *46* | 20 | 50 | ____ |
| **R** | Transformer, 110 watts, *46–47* | 48 | 65 | ____ |
| **RCS** | Remote Control Track (0), *45–48* | 5 | 9 | ____ |
| **RW** | Transformer, 110 watts, *48–54* | 23 | 45 | ____ |
| **RX** | Transformer, 100 watts, *47–48* | 15 | 50 | ____ |
| **S** | Transformer, 80 watts, *47* | 29 | 46 | ____ |
| **SP** | Smoke Pellets, bottle, *48–69* | 7 | 23 | ____ |
| **SP-12** | Dealer Display Box with 12 full smoke bottles | | 400 | ____ |
| **SW** | Transformer, 130 watts, *61–66* | 49 | 70 | ____ |
| **TW** | Transformer, 175 watts, *53–60* | 55 | 81 | ____ |
| **TOC** | Curved Track (0), *62–66, 68–69* | | 1 | ____ |
| **TOC½** | Half Section Straight Track (0), *62–66* | | 1 | ____ |
| **TOS** | Straight Track (0), *62–69* | | 1 | ____ |
| **UCS** | Remote Control Track (0), *45–69* | 8 | 16 | ____ |
| **UTC** | Lockon (0, 027, Standard), *45* | | 1 | ____ |
| **V** | Transformer, 150 watts, *46–47* | 85 | 125 | ____ |
| **VW** | Transformer, 150 watts, *48–49* | 45 | 95 | ____ |
| **Z** | Transformer, 250 watts, *45–47* | 77 | 125 | ____ |
| **ZW** | Transformer, 250 watts, *48–49* | 80 | 153 | ____ |
| **ZW** | Transformer, 275 watts, *50–66* | 114 | 196 | ____ |

## Unnumbered Items

Flatcar (see 3413, 3510, 6111, 6121, 6151, 6401-1,
6401-25, 6401-50, 6402, 6402-50, 6406, 6407, 6408,
6409, 6469, 6500, 6501, 6502, 6512)

Gondola (see 6142)

Hopper (see 6076-100, 6176)

SP-type Caboose, (see 6067, 6167-25)

Turbo Missile Car (see 3309, 3349)

Work Caboose, (see 6119-125, 6120)

| | | Exc | Mint | Cond/$ |
|---|---|---|---|---|
| **366** | Menards C&NW 4-4-2 Locomotive with tender, *09* | 45 | 75 | ___ |
| **400** | Menards C&NW Chicago Combine Car, *09* | 25 | 40 | ___ |
| **403** | Menards C&NW Lake Superior Observation Car, *09* | 25 | 40 | ___ |
| **410** | Menards C&NW Lake Michigan Coach, *09* | 40 | 65 | ___ |
| **0512** | Toy Fair Reefer, *81 u* | 60 | 70 | ___ |
| **550C** | 31" Diameter Curved Track (O), *70* | 1 | 2 | ___ |
| **550S** | Straight Track (O), *70* | 1 | 2 | ___ |
| **634** | Santa Fe NW2 Switcher, *70 u* | 55 | 110 | ___ |
| **665E** | Johnny Cash *Blue Train* 4-6-4 Locomotive, *71 u* | | NRS | ___ |
| **1050** | New Englander Set, *80–81* | 155 | 205 | ___ |
| **1052** | Chesapeake Flyer Set, *80* | 140 | 150 | ___ |
| **1053** | James Gang Set, *80–82* | 155 | 195 | ___ |
| **1070** | Royal Limited Set, *80* | 285 | 350 | ___ |
| **1071** | Mid Atlantic Limited Set, *80* | 225 | 230 | ___ |
| **1072** | Cross Country Express Set, *80–81* | 240 | 385 | ___ |
| **1081** | *Wabash Cannonball* Set, *70–72* | 105 | 120 | ___ |
| **1082** | Yard Boss Set, *70* | 120 | 165 | ___ |
| **1083** | Pacemaker Set, *70* | 105 | 120 | ___ |
| **1084** | Grand Trunk Western Freight Set, *70* | 120 | 140 | ___ |
| **1085** | Santa Fe Express Diesel Freight Set, *70* | 175 | 190 | ___ |
| **1091** | Sears Special Steam Freight Set, *70 u* | 150 | 165 | ___ |
| **1092** | Sears GTW Steam Freight Set, *70 u* | 150 | 165 | ___ |
| **1100** | Happy Huff n' Puff, *74–75 u* | 55 | 70 | ___ |
| **1150** | L.A.S.E.R. Train Set, *81–82* | 155 | 195 | ___ |
| **1151** | Union Pacific Thunder Freight Set, *81–82* | 150 | 175 | ___ |
| **1153** | JCPenney Thunderball Freight Set, *81 u* | 165 | 180 | ___ |
| **1154** | Reading Yard King Set, *81–82* | 170 | 190 | ___ |
| **1155** | Cannonball Freight Set, *82* | 75 | 85 | ___ |
| **1157** | Lionel Leisure *Wabash Cannonball* Set, *81 u* | | 250 | ___ |
| **1158** | Maple Leaf Limited Set, *81* | 405 | 435 | ___ |
| **1159** | Toys "R" Us Midnight Flyer Set, *81 u* | 130 | 140 | ___ |
| **1160** | Great Lakes Limited Set, *81* | 280 | 330 | ___ |
| **T-1171** | CN Locomotive Set, *71 u* | 240 | 275 | ___ |
| **T-1172** | Yardmaster Set, *71 u* | | 200 | ___ |
| **T-1173** | Grand Trunk Western Freight Set, *71–73 u* | 175 | 195 | ___ |
| **T-1174** | Canadian National Set, *71–73 u* | 265 | 300 | ___ |
| **1182** | Yardmaster Set, *71–72* | 85 | 105 | ___ |
| **1183** | Silver Star Set, *71–72* | 65 | 80 | ___ |
| **1184** | Allegheny Set, *71* | 120 | 150 | ___ |
| **1186** | Cross Country Express Set, *71–72* | 210 | 260 | ___ |
| **1187** | Illinois Central Set (SSS), *71* | 400 | 485 | ___ |
| **1190** | Sears Special #1 Set, *71 u* | 85 | 100 | ___ |
| **1195** | JCPenney Special Set, *71 u* | 150 | 165 | ___ |

| | | Exc | Mint | Cond/$ |
|---|---|---|---|---|
| **1198** | Unnamed Set, *71 u* | | 175 | ____ |
| **1199** | Ford-Autolite Allegheny Set, *71 u* | 178 | 198 | ____ |
| **1200** | Gravel Gus, *75 u* | 75 | 100 | ____ |
| **1250** | New York Central Set (SSS), *72* | 315 | 380 | ____ |
| **1252** | Heavy Iron Set, *82–83* | 90 | 130 | ____ |
| **1253** | *Quicksilver* Express Set, *82–83* | 265 | 340 | ____ |
| **1254** | Black Cave Flyer Set, *82* | 75 | 105 | ____ |
| **1260** | Continental Limited Set, *82* | 290 | 385 | ____ |
| **1261** | Sears Black Cave Flyer Set, *82 u* | 165 | 195 | ____ |
| **1262** | Toys "R" Us Heavy Iron Set, *82 u* | 150 | 165 | ____ |
| **1263** | JCPenney Overland Freight Set, *82 u* | 150 | 165 | ____ |
| **1264** | Nibco Express Set, *82 u* | 190 | 195 | ____ |
| **1265** | Tappan Special Set, *82 u* | 130 | 155 | ____ |
| **T-1272** | Yardmaster Set, *72–73 u* | 150 | 165 | ____ |
| **T-1273** | Silver Star Set, *72–73 u* | 90 | 115 | ____ |
| **1280** | Kickapoo Valley & Northern Set, *72* | 60 | 75 | ____ |
| **1284** | Allegheny Set, *72* | 140 | 165 | ____ |
| **1285** | Santa Fe Twin Diesel Set, *72* | 95 | 140 | ____ |
| **1287** | Pioneer Dockside Switcher Set, *72* | 95 | 100 | ____ |
| **1290** | Sears Steam Freight Set, *72 u* | 150 | 165 | ____ |
| **1291** | Sears Steam Freight Set, *72 u* | 150 | 165 | ____ |
| **1300** | Gravel Gus Junior, *75 u* | 70 | 90 | ____ |
| **1350** | Canadian Pacific Set (SSS), *73* | 460 | 620 | ____ |
| **1351** | Baltimore & Ohio Set, *83–84* | 205 | 280 | ____ |
| **1352** | Rocky Mountain Freight Set, *83–84* | 75 | 95 | ____ |
| **1353** | Southern Streak Set, *83–85* | 75 | 95 | ____ |
| **1354** | Northern Freight Flyer Set, *83–85* | 230 | 280 | ____ |
| **1355** | Commando Assault Train, *83–84* | 175 | 248 | ____ |
| **1359** | Display Case for Set 1355, *83 u* | 75 | 95 | ____ |
| **1361** | Gold Coast Limited Set, *83* | 390 | 400 | ____ |
| **1362** | Lionel Leisure BN Express Set, *83 u* | 200 | 300 | ____ |
| **1380** | U.S. Steel Industrial Switcher Set, *73–75* | 60 | 75 | ____ |
| **1381** | Cannonball Set, *73–75* | 70 | 75 | ____ |
| **1382** | Yardmaster Set, *73–74* | 110 | 135 | ____ |
| **1383** | Santa Fe Freight Set, *73–75* | 100 | 125 | ____ |
| **1384** | Southern Express Set, *73–76* | 75 | 120 | ____ |
| **1385** | Blue Streak Freight Set, *73–74* | 100 | 120 | ____ |
| **1386** | Rock Island Express Set, *73–74* | 120 | 140 | ____ |
| **1387** | Milwaukee Road Special Set, *73* | 185 | 285 | ____ |
| **1388** | Golden State Arrow Set, *73–75* | 215 | 240 | ____ |
| **1390** | Sears 7-unit Steam Freight Set, *73 u* | 170 | 190 | ____ |
| **1392** | Sears 8-unit Steam Freight Set, *73 u* | 150 | 165 | ____ |
| **1393** | Sears 6-unit Diesel Freight Set, *73 u* | 150 | 165 | ____ |
| **1395** | JCPenney Set, *73 u* | 150 | 165 | ____ |
| **1400** | Happy Huff n' Puff Junior, *75 u* | 130 | 140 | ____ |
| **1402** | Chessie System Set, *84–85* | 125 | 150 | ____ |
| **1403** | Redwood Valley Express Set, *84–85* | 170 | 205 | ____ |
| **1450** | D&RGW Set (SSS), *74* | 335 | 415 | ____ |

| | | Exc | Mint | Cond/S |
|---|---|---|---|---|
| 1451 | Erie-Lackawanna Limited Set, *84* | 415 | 465 | ___ |
| 1460 | Grand National Set, *74* | 300 | 330 | ___ |
| 1461 | Black Diamond Set, *74 u, 75* | 100 | 120 | ___ |
| 1463 | Coca-Cola Special Set, *74 u, 75* | 194 | 242 | ___ |
| 1487 | Broadway Limited Set, *74–75* | 160 | 255 | ___ |
| 1489 | Santa Fe Double Diesel Set, *74–76* | 140 | 165 | ___ |
| 1492 | Sears 7-unit Steam Freight Set, *74 u* | 150 | 165 | ___ |
| 1493 | Sears 7-unit Steam Freight Set, *74 u* | 150 | 165 | ___ |
| 1499 | JCPenney Great Express Set, *74 u* | 150 | 165 | ___ |
| 1501 | Midland Freight Set, *85–86* | 75 | 95 | ___ |
| 1502 | Yard Chief Set, *85–86* | 205 | 230 | ___ |
| 1506 | Sears Centennial Chessie System Set, *85 u* | 165 | 195 | ___ |
| 1512 | JCPenney Midland Freight Set, *85 u* | 90 | 115 | ___ |
| 1549 | Toys "R" Us Heavy Iron Set, *85–89 u* | 180 | 215 | ___ |
| 1552 | Burlington Northern Limited Set, *85* | 500 | 570 | ___ |
| 1560 | North American Express Set, *75* | 275 | 365 | ___ |
| 1562 | Fast Freight Flyer Set, *85 u* | 120 | 140 | ___ |
| 1577 | Liberty Special Set, *75 u* | 209 | 211 | ___ |
| 1579 | Milwaukee Road Set (SSS), *75* | 325 | 410 | ___ |
| 1581 | Thunderball Freight Set, *75–76* | 90 | 100 | ___ |
| 1582 | Yard Chief Set, *75–76* | 115 | 155 | ___ |
| 1584 | N&W "Spirit of America" Set, *75* | 160 | 180 | ___ |
| 1585 | 75th Anniversary Special Set, *75–77* | 190 | 205 | ___ |
| 1586 | Chesapeake Flyer Set, *75–77* | 160 | 190 | ___ |
| 1587 | Capitol Limited Set, *75* | 270 | 300 | ___ |
| 1593 | Sears Set, *75 u* | | 100 | ___ |
| 1595 | Sears 6-unit Diesel Freight Set, *75 u* | 150 | 165 | ___ |
| 1602 | Nickel Plate Special Set, *86–91* | 120 | 125 | ___ |
| 1606 | Sears Centennial Nickel Plate Set, *86 u* | 165 | 195 | ___ |
| 1608 | American Express General Set, *86 u* | 205 | 320 | ___ |
| 1615 | Cannonball Express Set, *86–90* | 65 | 75 | ___ |
| 1632 | Santa Fe Work Train (SSS), *86* | 220 | 255 | ___ |
| 1652 | B&O Freight Set, *86* | 140 | 185 | ___ |
| 1658 | Town House TV and Appliances Set, *86 u* | 80 | 95 | ___ |
| 1660 | Yard Boss Set, *76* | 100 | 115 | ___ |
| 1661 | Rock Island Line Set, *76–77* | 80 | 100 | ___ |
| 1662 | Black River Freight Set, *76–78* | 75 | 95 | ___ |
| 1663 | Amtrak Lake Shore Limited Set, *76–77* | 215 | 265 | ___ |
| 1664 | Illinois Central Freight Set, *76–77* | 265 | 355 | ___ |
| 1665 | NYC Empire State Express Set, *76* | 310 | 435 | ___ |
| 1672 | Northern Pacific Set (SSS), *76* | 215 | 280 | ___ |
| 1685 | True Value Freight Flyer Set, *86–87 u* | 60 | 75 | ___ |
| 1686 | Kay Bee Toys Freight Flyer Set, *86 u* | 150 | 165 | ___ |
| 1687 | Freight Flyer Set, *87–90* | 39 | 47 | ___ |
| 1693 | Toys "R" Us Rock Island Line Set, *76 u* | 110 | 130 | ___ |
| 1694 | Toys "R" Us Black River Freight Set, *76 u* | 110 | 130 | ___ |
| 1696 | Sears Steam Freight Set, *76 u* | 110 | 130 | ___ |
| 1698 | True Value Rock Island Line Set, *76 u* | 125 | 145 | ___ |

| | | Exc | Mint | Cond/S |
|---|---|---|---|---|
| **1760** | Trains n' Truckin' Steel Hauler Set, *77–78* | 105 | 110 | ____ |
| **1761** | Trains n' Truckin' Cargo King Set, *77–78* | 95 | 165 | ____ |
| **1762** | *Wabash Cannonball* Set, *77* | 135 | 190 | ____ |
| **1764** | Heartland Express Set, *77* | 185 | 240 | ____ |
| **1765** | Rocky Mountain Special Set, *77* | 210 | 315 | ____ |
| **1766** | B&O Budd Car Set (SSS), *77* | 335 | 390 | ____ |
| **1776** | Seaboard U36B Diesel, *74–76* | 175 | 260 | ____ |
| **1790** | Lionel Leisure Steel Hauler Set, *77 u* | 150 | 200 | ____ |
| **1791** | Toys "R" Us Steel Hauler Set, *77 u* | 130 | 175 | ____ |
| **1792** | True Value Rock Island Line Set, *77 u* | 100 | 135 | ____ |
| **1793** | Toys "R" Us Black River Freight Set, *77 u* | 120 | 155 | ____ |
| **1796** | JCPenney Cargo Master Set, *77 u* | | 200 | ____ |
| **1860** | "Workin' on the Railroad" Timberline Set, *78* | 65 | 85 | ____ |
| **1862** | "Workin' on the Railroad" Logging Empire Set, *78* | 85 | 110 | ____ |
| **1864** | Santa Fe Double Diesel Set, *78–79* | 155 | 190 | ____ |
| **1865** | Chesapeake Flyer Set, *78–79* | 155 | 180 | ____ |
| **1866** | Great Plains Express Set, *78–79* | 195 | 285 | ____ |
| **1867** | Milwaukee Road Limited Set, *78* | 230 | 275 | ____ |
| **1868** | M&StL Set (SSS), *78* | 215 | 255 | ____ |
| **1892** | JCPenney Logging Empire Set, *78 u* | 95 | 125 | ____ |
| **1893** | Toys "R" Us Logging Empire Set, *78 u* | 175 | 225 | ____ |
| **1960** | Midnight Flyer Set, *79–81* | 55 | 75 | ____ |
| **1962** | *Wabash Cannonball* Set, *79* | 90 | 105 | ____ |
| **1963** | Black River Freight Set, *79–81* | 75 | 85 | ____ |
| **1965** | Smokey Mountain Line Set, *79* | 65 | 85 | ____ |
| **1970** | Southern Pacific Limited Set, *79 u* | 340 | 365 | ____ |
| **1971** | Quaker City Limited Set, *79* | 315 | 335 | ____ |
| **1990** | Mystery Glow Midnight Flyer Set, *79 u* | 75 | 90 | ____ |
| **1991** | JCPenney *Wabash Cannonball* Deluxe Express Set, *79 u* | 150 | 165 | ____ |
| **1993** | Toys "R" Us Midnight Flyer Set, *79 u* | 110 | 130 | ____ |
| **2110** | Graduated Trestle Set, 22 pieces, *70–88* | 9 | 13 | ____ |
| **2111** | Elevated Trestle Set, 10 pieces, *70–88* | 8 | 11 | ____ |
| **2113** | Tunnel Portals, pair, *84–87* | 11 | 17 | ____ |
| **2115** | Dwarf Signal, *84–87* | 12 | 13 | ____ |
| **2117** | Block Target Signal, *84–87* | 23 | 29 | ____ |
| **2122** | Extension Bridge, rock piers, *76–87* | 24 | 34 | ____ |
| **2125** | Whistling Freight Shed, *71* | 36 | 43 | ____ |
| **2126** | Whistling Freight Shed, *76–87* | 25 | 26 | ____ |
| **2127** | Diesel Horn Shed, *76–87* | 25 | 30 | ____ |
| **2128** | Operating Switchman, *83–86* | 26 | 29 | ____ |
| **2129** | Illuminated Freight Station, *83–86* | 30 | 33 | ____ |
| **2133** | Lighted Freight Station, *72–78, 80–84* | 34 | 38 | ____ |
| **2140** | Automatic Banjo Signal, *70–84* | 17 | 21 | ____ |
| **2145** | Automatic Gateman, *72–84* | 31 | 47 | ____ |
| **2151** | Operating Semaphore, *78–82* | 15 | 19 | ____ |
| **2152** | Automatic Crossing Gate, *70–84* | 21 | 25 | ____ |
| **2154** | Automatic Highway Flasher, *70–87* | 19 | 24 | ____ |

| | | Exc | Mint | Cond/$ |
|---|---|---|---|---|
| 2156 | Illuminated Station Platform, *70–71* | 26 | 34 | ____ |
| 2162 | Automatic Crossing Gate and Signal "262," *70–87, 94, 96–98, 05* | 16 | 27 | ____ |
| 2163 | Block Target Signal, *70–78* | 14 | 19 | ____ |
| 2170 | Street Lamps, set of 3, *70–87* | 13 | 19 | ____ |
| 2171 | Gooseneck Street Lamps, set of 2, *80–81, 83–84* | 15 | 18 | ____ |
| 2175 | "Sandy Andy" Gravel Loader Kit, *76–79* | 34 | 55 | ____ |
| 2180 | Road Signs, 16 pieces, *77–98* | | 6 | ____ |
| 2181 | Telephone Pole Set "150," *77–98* | | 5 | ____ |
| 2195 | Floodlight Tower, *70–71* | 38 | 50 | ____ |
| 2199 | Microwave Tower, *72–75* | 30 | 39 | ____ |
| 2214 | Girder Bridge, *70–71, 72 u, 73–87* | 5 | 9 | ____ |
| 2256 | Station Platform, *73–81* | 17 | 18 | ____ |
| 2260 | Illuminated Bumper, *70–71, 72 u, 73* | 23 | 35 | ____ |
| 2280 | Non-Illuminated Bumpers, set of 3, *73–84* | 2 | 4 | ____ |
| 2282 | Die-cast Bumpers, pair, *83 u* | 17 | 18 | ____ |
| 2283 | Die-cast Illuminated Bumpers "260," *84–99* | 15 | 16 | ____ |
| 2290 | Illuminated Bumpers, pair, *75 u, 76–86* | 10 | 11 | ____ |
| 2292 | Station Platform, *85–87* | 5 | 9 | ____ |
| 2300 | Operating Oil Drum Loader, *83–87* | 80 | 90 | ____ |
| 2301 | Operating Sawmill, *80–84* | 60 | 65 | ____ |
| 2302 | Union Pacific Manual Gantry Crane, *80–82* | 24 | 31 | ____ |
| 2303 | Santa Fe Manual Gantry Crane, *80–81, 83 u* | 17 | 21 | ____ |
| 2305 | Getty Operating Oil Derrick, *81–84* | 105 | 115 | ____ |
| 2306 | Operating Ice Station with 6700 Ice Car, *82–83* | 90 | 105 | ____ |
| 2307 | Lighted Billboard, *82–86* | 12 | 13 | ____ |
| 2308 | Animated Newsstand, *82–83* | 105 | 120 | ____ |
| 2309 | Mechanical Crossing Gate, *82–92* | 4 | 7 | ____ |
| 2310 | Mechanical Crossing Gate, *73–77* | 2 | 4 | ____ |
| 2311 | Mechanical Semaphore, *82–92* | 4 | 7 | ____ |
| 2312 | Mechanical Semaphore, *73–77* | 2 | 4 | ____ |
| 2313 | Floodlight Tower, *75–86* | 22 | 27 | ____ |
| 2314 | Searchlight Tower, *75–84* | 22 | 27 | ____ |
| 2315 | Operating Coaling Station, *83–84* | 80 | 83 | ____ |
| 2316 | N&W Operating Gantry Crane, *83–84* | 90 | 125 | ____ |
| 2317 | Operating Drawbridge, *75 u, 76–81* | 100 | 130 | ____ |
| 2318 | Operating Control Tower, *83–86* | 40 | 50 | ____ |
| 2319 | Illuminated Watchtower, *75–78, 80* | 29 | 46 | ____ |
| 2320 | Flagpole Kit, *83–87* | 10 | 14 | ____ |
| 2321 | Operating Sawmill, *84, 86–87* | 115 | 133 | ____ |
| 2323 | Operating Freight Station, *84–87* | 43 | 47 | ____ |
| 2324 | Operating Switch Tower, *84–87* | 60 | 65 | ____ |
| 2390 | Lionel Mirror, *82 u* | 65 | 105 | ____ |
| 2494 | Rotary Beacon, *72–74* | 37 | 44 | ____ |
| 2709 | Rico Station Kit, *81–98* | | 42 | ____ |
| 2710 | Billboards, set of 5, *70–84* | 4 | 10 | ____ |
| 2714 | Tunnel, *75 u, 76–77* | 36 | 43 | ____ |
| 2716 | Short Extension Bridge, *88–98* | 3 | 8 | ____ |

| | | Exc | Mint | Cond/$ |
|---|---|---|---|---|
| 2717 | Short Extension Bridge, *77–87* | 2 | 4 | ___ |
| 2718 | Barrel Platform Kit, *77–84* | 3 | 5 | ___ |
| 2719 | Watchman's Shanty Kit, *77–87* | 3 | 5 | ___ |
| 2720 | Lumber Shed Kit, *77–84, 87* | 3 | 5 | ___ |
| 2721 | Operating Log Mill Kit, *78* | 2 | 4 | ___ |
| 2722 | Barrel Loader Kit, *78* | 2 | 4 | ___ |
| 2783 | Freight Station Kit, *84* | 6 | 10 | ___ |
| 2784 | Freight Platform Kit, *81–90* | 5 | 8 | ___ |
| 2785 | Engine House Kit, *73–77* | 31 | 39 | ___ |
| 2786 | Freight Platform Kit, *73–77* | 4 | 6 | ___ |
| 2787 | Freight Station Kit, *73–77, 83* | 7 | 10 | ___ |
| 2788 | Coal Station Kit, *75 u, 76–77* | 18 | 30 | ___ |
| 2789 | Water Tower Kit, *75–77, 80* | 19 | 24 | ___ |
| 2791 | Cross Country Set, *70–71* | 22 | 30 | ___ |
| 2792 | Whistle Stop Set, *70–71* | 24 | 34 | ___ |
| 2792 | Layout Starter Pack, *80–84* | 9 | 21 | ___ |
| 2793 | Alamo Junction Set, *70–71* | 22 | 30 | ___ |
| 2796 | Grain Elevator Kit, *76 u, 77* | 43 | 47 | ___ |
| 2797 | Rico Station Kit, *76–77* | 23 | 37 | ___ |
| 2900 | Lockon, *70–98* | | 1 | ___ |
| 2901 | Track Clips, dozen (O27), *71–98* | | 6 | ___ |
| 2905 | Lockon and Wire, *74–00* | | 3 | ___ |
| 2909 | Smoke Fluid, *70–98* | | 4 | ___ |
| 2910 | OTC Contactor, *84–86, 88* | 4 | 7 | ___ |
| 2911 | Smoke Pellets, *70–73* | 10 | 30 | ___ |
| 2925 | Lubricant, *70–71, 72 u, 73–75* | | 2 | ___ |
| 2927 | Maintenance Kit, *70, 78–98* | | 11 | ___ |
| 2928 | Oil, *71* | | 2 | ___ |
| 2951 | Track Layout Book, *70–86* | 1 | 2 | ___ |
| 2952 | Train and Accessory Manual, *70–74* | 1 | 2 | ___ |
| 2953 | Train and Accessory Manual, *75–86* | 1 | 2 | ___ |
| 2960 | Lionel 75th Anniversary Book, *75 u, 76* | 13 | 24 | ___ |
| 2980 | Magnetic Conversion Coupler, *70–71* | 1 | 2 | ___ |
| 2985 | The Lionel Train Book, *86–98* | | 11 | ___ |
| 3100 | Great Northern 4-8-4 (FARR 3), *81* | 335 | 388 | ___ |
| 4044 | Transformer, 45-watt, *70–71* | 2 | 4 | ___ |
| 4045 | Safety Transformer, *70–71* | 2 | 3 | ___ |
| 4050 | Safety Transformer, *72–79* | 2 | 3 | ___ |
| 4060 | Power Master Transformer, *80–93* | | 13 | ___ |
| 4065 | DC Hobby Transformer, *81–83* | 2 | 3 | ___ |
| 4090 | Power Master Transformer, *70–84* | 47 | 65 | ___ |
| 4125 | Transformer, 25-watt, *72* | 2 | 3 | ___ |
| 4150 | Trainmaster Transformer, *72–73, 75–77* | 6 | 15 | ___ |
| 4250 | Trainmaster Transformer, *74* | 5 | 10 | ___ |
| 4651 | Trainmaster Transformer, *78–79* | 1 | 2 | ___ |
| 4690 | MW Transformer, *86–89* | 60 | 80 | ___ |
| 4851 | DC Transformer, *85–91, 94–96* | 5 | 10 | ___ |

| | | Exc | Mint | Cond/$ |
|---|---|---|---|---|
| **4870** | DC Hobby Transformer and Throttle Controller, *77–78* | 2 | 3 | ___ |
| **5012** | 27" Diameter Curved Track, card of 4 (027), *70–96* | | 17 | ___ |
| **5013** | 27" Diameter Curved Track (027), *70–78* | | 1 | ___ |
| **5014** | Half Curved Track (027), *70–98* | | 1 | ___ |
| **5016** | 36" Straight Track (027), *87–88* | 1 | 2 | ___ |
| **5017** | Straight Track, card of 4 (027), *70–96* | | 4 | ___ |
| **5018** | Straight Track (027), *70–78* | | 1 | ___ |
| **5019** | Half-Straight Track (027), *70–98* | | 1 | ___ |
| **5020** | 90-degree Crossover (027), *70–98* | | 7 | ___ |
| **5021** | 27" Manual Switch, left hand (027), *70–98* | | 15 | ___ |
| **5022** | 27" Manual Switch, right hand (027), *70–98* | | 15 | ___ |
| **5023** | 45-degree Crossover (027), *70–98* | | 6 | ___ |
| **5024** | 35" Straight Track (027), *88–98, 05* | | 3 | ___ |
| **5025** | Manumatic Uncoupler, *71–72* | 1 | 2 | ___ |
| **5027** | 27" Manual Switches, pair (027), *74–84* | 13 | 21 | ___ |
| **5030** | Track Expander Set (027), *71–84* | 18 | 26 | ___ |
| **5031** | Ford-Autolite Layout Expander Set, *71 u* | 50 | 65 | ___ |
| **5033** | 27" Diameter Curved Track (027), *79–98* | | 1 | ___ |
| **5038** | Straight Track (027), *79–98* | | 1 | ___ |
| **5041** | Insulator Pins, dozen (027), *70–98* | | 1 | ___ |
| **5042** | Steel Pins, dozen (027), *70–98* | | 1 | ___ |
| **5045** | 54" Diameter Curved Track Ballast (027), *87–88* | 1 | 2 | ___ |
| **5046** | 27" Diameter Curved Track Ballast (027), *87–88* | 1 | 2 | ___ |
| **5047** | Straight Track Ballast (027), *87–88* | 1 | 2 | ___ |
| **5049** | 42" Diameter Curved Track (027), *88–98* | 1 | 2 | ___ |
| **5090** | 27" Manual Switches, 3 pair (027), *78–84* | 55 | 70 | ___ |
| **5113** | 54" Diameter Curved Track (027), *79–98* | 1 | 2 | ___ |
| **5121** | 27" Remote Switch, left hand (027), *70–98* | 18 | 22 | ___ |
| **5122** | 27" Remote Switch, right hand (027), *70–98* | 20 | 22 | ___ |
| **5125** | 27" Remote Switches, pair (027), *71–83* | 20 | 30 | ___ |
| **5132** | 31" Remote Switch, right hand (0), *80–94* | 29 | 30 | ___ |
| **5133** | 31" Remote Switch, left hand (0), *80–94* | 22 | 30 | ___ |
| **5149** | Remote Uncoupling Section (027), *70–98* | | 7 | ___ |
| **5165** | 72" Remote Switch, right hand (0), *87–98* | 23 | 65 | ___ |
| **5166** | 72" Remote Switch, left hand (0), *87–98* | 23 | 75 | ___ |
| **5167** | 42" Remote Switch, right hand (027), *88–98* | 25 | 37 | ___ |
| **5168** | 42" Remote Switch, left hand (027), *88–98* | 25 | 37 | ___ |
| **5193** | 27" Remote Switches, 3 pair (027), *78–83* | 80 | 95 | ___ |
| **5500** | 10" Straight Track (0), *71–98* | | 1 | ___ |
| **5501** | 31" Diameter Curved Track (0), *71–98* | | 1 | ___ |
| **5502** | Remote Uncoupling Section (0), *71–72* | 7 | 9 | ___ |
| **5504** | Half Curved Track (0), *83–98* | | 1 | ___ |
| **5505** | Half Straight Track (0), *83–98* | | 1 | ___ |
| **5520** | 90-degree Crossover (0), *71–72* | 6 | 9 | ___ |
| **5522** | 36" Straight, *87–88* | | 3 | ___ |

| | | Exc | Mint | Cond/$ |
|---|---|---|---|---|
| **5523** | 40" Straight Track (O), *88–98* | | 4 | ___ |
| **5530** | Remote Uncoupling Section (O), *81–98* | 10 | 19 | ___ |
| **5540** | 90-degree Crossover (O), *81–98* | | 10 | ___ |
| **5543** | Insulator Pins, dozen (O), *70–98* | | 1 | ___ |
| **5545** | 45-degree Crossover (O), *83–98* | | 11 | ___ |
| **5551** | Steel Pins, dozen (O), *70–98* | | 1 | ___ |
| **5554** | 54" Diameter Curved Track (O), *90–98* | | 2 | ___ |
| **5560** | 72" Diameter Curved Track Ballast (O), *87–88* | 1 | 2 | ___ |
| **5561** | 31" Diameter Curved Track Ballast (O), *87–88* | 1 | 2 | ___ |
| **5562** | Straight Track Ballast (O), *87–88* | 1 | 2 | ___ |
| **5572** | 72" Diameter Curved Track (O), *79–98* | 2 | 3 | ___ |
| **5600** | Curved Track (Trutrack), *73–74* | 1 | 2 | ___ |
| **5601** | Curved Track, card of 4 (Trutrack), *73–74* | 6 | 10 | ___ |
| **5602** | Curved Track Ballast, card of 4 (Trutrack), *73–74* | 5 | 9 | ___ |
| **5605** | Straight Track (Trutrack), *73–74* | 1 | 2 | ___ |
| **5606** | Straight Track, card of 4 (Trutrack), *73–74* | 5 | 9 | ___ |
| **5607** | Straight Track Ballast, card of 4 (Trutrack), *73–74* | 5 | 9 | ___ |
| **5620** | Manual Switch, left hand (Trutrack), *73–74* | 4 | 13 | ___ |
| **5625** | Remote Switch, left hand (Trutrack), *73–74* | 9 | 17 | ___ |
| **5630** | Manual Switch, right hand (Trutrack), *73–74* | 4 | 13 | ___ |
| **5635** | Remote Switch, right hand (Trutrack), *73–74* | 9 | 17 | ___ |
| **5640** | Left Switch Ballast, card of 2 (Trutrack), *73–74* | 5 | 9 | ___ |
| **5650** | Right Switch Ballast, card of 2 (Trutrack), *73–74* | 5 | 9 | ___ |
| **5655** | Lockon (Trutrack), *73–74* | 1 | 2 | ___ |
| **5660** | Terminal Track with lockon (Trutrack), *74* | 1 | 3 | ___ |
| **5700** | Oppenheimer Reefer, *81* | 30 | 38 | ___ |
| **5701** | Dairymen's League Reefer, *81* | 21 | 23 | ___ |
| **5702** | National Dairy Despatch Reefer, *81* | 16 | 21 | ___ |
| **5703** | North American Despatch Reefer, *81* | 22 | 26 | ___ |
| **5704** | Budweiser Reefer, *81–82* | 63 | 68 | ___ |
| **5705** | Ball Glass Jars Reefer, *81–82* | 30 | 35 | ___ |
| **5706** | Lindsay Brothers Reefer, *81–82* | 26 | 27 | ___ |
| **5707** | American Refrigerator Reefer, *81–82* | 17 | 20 | ___ |
| **5708** | Armour Reefer, *82–83* | 16 | 21 | ___ |
| **5709** | REA Reefer, *82–83* | 22 | 26 | ___ |
| **5710** | Canadian Pacific Reefer, *82–83* | 22 | 25 | ___ |
| **5711** | Commercial Express Reefer, *82–83* | 13 | 15 | ___ |
| **5712** | Lionel Lines Reefer, *82 u* | 128 | 164 | ___ |
| **5713** | Cotton Belt Reefer, *83–84* | 19 | 22 | ___ |
| **5714** | Michigan Central Reefer, *83–84* | 17 | 24 | ___ |
| **5715** | Santa Fe Reefer, *83–84* | 19 | 26 | ___ |
| **5716** | Vermont Central Reefer, *83–84* | 20 | 23 | ___ |
| **5717** | Santa Fe Bunk Car, *83* | 22 | 30 | ___ |
| **5719** | Canadian National Reefer, *84* | 15 | 16 | ___ |
| **5720** | Great Northern Reefer, *84* | 75 | 90 | ___ |
| **5721** | Soo Line Reefer, *84* | 21 | 23 | ___ |

| | | Exc | Mint | Cond/$ |
|---|---|---|---|---|
| 5722 | NKP Reefer, *84* | 16 | 18 | ____ |
| 5724 | PRR Bunk Car, *84* | 15 | 23 | ____ |
| 5726 | Southern Bunk Car, *84 u* | 22 | 27 | ____ |
| 5727 | USMC Bunk Car, *84–85* | 25 | 30 | ____ |
| 5728 | Canadian Pacific Bunk Car, *86* | 18 | 23 | ____ |
| 5730 | Strasburg Reefer, *85–86* | 20 | 27 | ____ |
| 5731 | L&N Reefer, *85–86* | 19 | 24 | ____ |
| 5732 | Jersey Central Reefer, *85–86* | | 24 | ____ |
| 5733 | Lionel Lines Bunk Car, *86 u* | 18 | 24 | ____ |
| 5735 | NYC Bunk Car, *85–86* | 33 | 35 | ____ |
| 5739 | B&O Tool Car, *86* | 32 | 37 | ____ |
| 5745 | Santa Fe Bunk Car (SSS), *86* | 39 | 45 | ____ |
| 5760 | Santa Fe Tool Car (SSS), *86* | 30 | 35 | ____ |
| 5900 | AC/DC Converter, *79–83* | 3 | 5 | ____ |
| 6076 | LV Hopper (027), *70 u* | 17 | 21 | ____ |
| 6100 | Ontario Northland Covered Quad Hopper, *81–82* | 30 | 34 | ____ |
| 6101 | BN Covered Quad Hopper, *81–82* | 17 | 31 | ____ |
| 6102 | GN Covered Quad Hopper (FARR 3), *81* | 26 | 28 | ____ |
| 6103 | Canadian National Covered Quad Hopper, *81* | 35 | 38 | ____ |
| 6104 | Southern Quad Hopper with coal (FARR 4), *83* | 50 | 60 | ____ |
| 6105 | Reading Operating Hopper, *82* | 34 | 39 | ____ |
| 6106 | N&W Covered Quad Hopper, *82* | 30 | 40 | ____ |
| 6107 | Shell Covered Quad Hopper, *82* | 22 | 26 | ____ |
| 6109 | C&O Operating Hopper, *83* | 29 | 41 | ____ |
| 6110 | MP Covered Quad Hopper, *83–84* | 17 | 27 | ____ |
| 6111 | L&N Covered Quad Hopper, *83–84* | 13 | 20 | ____ |
| 6113 | Illinois Central Hopper (027), *83–85* | 15 | 25 | ____ |
| 6114 | C&NW Covered Quad Hopper, *83* | 63 | 80 | ____ |
| 6115 | Southern Hopper (027), *83–86* | 15 | 19 | ____ |
| 6116 | Soo Line Ore Car, *84* | 21 | 27 | ____ |
| 6117 | Erie Operating Hopper, *84* | 29 | 39 | ____ |
| 6118 | Erie Covered Quad Hopper, *84* | 31 | 45 | ____ |
| 6122 | Penn Central Ore Car, *84* | 20 | 25 | ____ |
| 6123 | PRR Covered Quad Hopper (FARR 5), *84–85* | 55 | 105 | ____ |
| 6124 | D&H Covered Quad Hopper, *84* | 19 | 32 | ____ |
| 6126 | Canadian National Ore Car, *86* | 18 | 24 | ____ |
| 6127 | Northern Pacific Ore Car, *86* | 20 | 24 | ____ |
| 6131 | Illinois Terminal Covered Quad Hopper, *85–86* | 15 | 21 | ____ |
| 6134 | BN 2-bay ACF Hopper (std O), *86 u* | 95 | 115 | ____ |
| 6135 | C&NW 2-bay ACF Hopper (std O), *86 u* | 65 | 80 | ____ |
| 6137 | NKP Hopper (027), *86–91* | 13 | 17 | ____ |
| 6138 | B&O Quad Hopper with coal, *86* | 21 | 28 | ____ |
| 6142 | Gondola, black, *70* | 20 | 33 | ____ |
| 6150 | Santa Fe Hopper (027), *85–86, 92 u* | 10 | 15 | ____ |
| 6177 | Reading Hopper (027), *86–90* | 14 | 19 | ____ |
| 6200 | FEC Gondola with canisters, *81–82* | 13 | 24 | ____ |
| 6201 | Union Pacific Animated Gondola, *82–83* | 19 | 25 | ____ |
| 6202 | WM Gondola with coal, *82* | 34 | 36 | ____ |

| | | Exc | Mint | Cond/$ |
|---|---|---|---|---|
| **6203** | Black Cave Gondola (027), *82* | 2 | 4 | ____ |
| **6205** | CP Gondola with canisters, *83* | 18 | 26 | ____ |
| **6206** | C&IM Gondola with canisters, *83–85* | 18 | 26 | ____ |
| **6207** | Southern Gondola with canisters (027), *83–85* | 6 | 8 | ____ |
| **6208** | Chessie System Gondola with canisters, *83 u* | 21 | 24 | ____ |
| **6209** | NYC Gondola with coal (std O), *84–85* | 42 | 46 | ____ |
| **6210** | Erie-Lackawanna Gondola with canisters, *84* | 21 | 30 | ____ |
| **6211** | C&O Gondola with canisters, *84–85* | | 10 | ____ |
| **6214** | Lionel Lines Gondola with canisters, *84 u* | 38 | 45 | ____ |
| **6230** | Erie-Lackawanna Reefer (std O), *86 u* | 95 | 120 | ____ |
| **6231** | Railgon Gondola with coal (std O), *86 u* | 66 | 76 | ____ |
| **6232** | Illinois Central Boxcar (std O), *86 u* | 65 | 80 | ____ |
| **6233** | CP Flatcar with stakes (std O), *86 u* | 47 | 50 | ____ |
| **6234** | Burlington Northern Boxcar (std O), *85* | 55 | 75 | ____ |
| **6235** | Burlington Northern Boxcar (std O), *85* | 33 | 43 | ____ |
| **6236** | Burlington Northern Boxcar (std O), *85* | 33 | 43 | ____ |
| **6237** | Burlington Northern Boxcar (std O), *85* | 32 | 47 | ____ |
| **6238** | Burlington Northern Boxcar (std O), *85* | 33 | 43 | ____ |
| **6239** | Burlington Northern Boxcar (std O), *86 u* | 37 | 55 | ____ |
| **6251** | NYC Coal Dump Car, *85* | 25 | 42 | ____ |
| **6254** | NKP Gondola with canisters, *86–91* | 10 | 11 | ____ |
| **6258** | Santa Fe Gondola with canisters (027), *85–86, 92 u* | | 3 | ____ |
| **X6260** | NYC Gondola with canisters, *85–86* | 13 | 15 | ____ |
| **6272** | Santa Fe Gondola with cable reels (SSS), *86* | 20 | 25 | ____ |
| **6300** | Corn Products 3-D Tank Car, *81–82* | 19 | 25 | ____ |
| **6301** | Gulf 1-D Tank Car, *81* | 20 | 26 | ____ |
| **6302** | Quaker State 3-D Tank Car, *81* | 38 | 42 | ____ |
| **6304** | GN 1-D Tank Car (FARR 3), *81* | 44 | 55 | ____ |
| **6305** | British Columbia 1-D Tank Car, *81* | 55 | 76 | ____ |
| **6306** | Southern 1-D Tank Car (FARR 4), *83* | 45 | 50 | ____ |
| **6307** | PRR 1-D Tank Car (FARR 5), *84–85* | 70 | 75 | ____ |
| **6308** | Alaska 1-D Tank Car (027), *82–83* | 27 | 35 | ____ |
| **6310** | Shell 2-D Tank Car (027), *83–84* | 19 | 24 | ____ |
| **6312** | C&O 2-D Tank Car (027), *84–85* | 18 | 26 | ____ |
| **6313** | Lionel Lines 1-D Tank Car, *84 u* | 43 | 50 | ____ |
| **6314** | B&O 3-D Tank Car, *86* | 31 | 38 | ____ |
| **6317** | Gulf 2-D Tank Car (027), *84–85* | 18 | 22 | ____ |
| **6357** | Frisco 1-D Tank Car, *83* | 42 | 50 | ____ |
| **6401** | Virginian Bay Window Caboose, *81* | 37 | 47 | ____ |
| **6403** | Amtrak Vista Dome Car (027), *76–77* | 30 | 31 | ____ |
| **6404** | Amtrak Passenger Coach (027), *76–77* | 24 | 31 | ____ |
| **6405** | Amtrak Passenger Coach (027), *76–77* | 24 | 31 | ____ |
| **6406** | Amtrak Observation Car (027), *76–77* | 22 | 29 | ____ |
| **6410** | Amtrak Passenger Coach (027), *77* | 28 | 48 | ____ |
| **6411** | Amtrak Passenger Coach (027), *77* | 24 | 35 | ____ |
| **6412** | Amtrak Vista Dome Car (027), *77* | 22 | 33 | ____ |
| **6420** | Reading Transfer Caboose, *81–82* | 20 | 28 | ____ |

| | | Exc | Mint | Cond/$ |
|---|---|---|---|---|
| 6421 | Joshua L. Cowen Bay Window Caboose, *82* | 34 | 40 | _____ |
| 6422 | DM&IR Bay Window Caboose, *81* | 32 | 38 | _____ |
| 6425 | Erie-Lackawanna Bay Window Caboose, *83–84* | 35 | 43 | _____ |
| 6426 | Reading Transfer Caboose, *82–83* | 14 | 24 | _____ |
| 6427 | BN Transfer Caboose, *83–84* | 12 | 21 | _____ |
| 6428 | C&NW Transfer Caboose, *83–85* | 22 | 25 | _____ |
| 6430 | Santa Fe SP-type Caboose, *83–89* | 4 | 14 | _____ |
| 6431 | Southern Bay Window Caboose (FARR 4), *83* | 42 | 55 | _____ |
| 6432 | Union Pacific SP-type Caboose, *81–82* | 9 | 10 | _____ |
| 6433 | Canadian Pacific Bay Window Caboose, *81* | 60 | 70 | _____ |
| 6435 | U.S. Marines Transfer Caboose, *83–84* | 9 | 17 | _____ |
| 6438 | GN Bay Window Caboose (FARR 3), *81* | 48 | 65 | _____ |
| 6439 | Reading Bay Window Caboose, *84–85* | 22 | 30 | _____ |
| 6441 | Alaska Bay Window Caboose, *82–83* | 45 | 50 | _____ |
| 6446-25 | N&W Covered Quad Hopper, *70 u* | 203 | 340 | _____ |
| 6449 | Wendy's N5c Caboose, *81–82* | 54 | 64 | _____ |
| 6464-500 | Timken Boxcar, orange, *70 u* | 225 | 290 | _____ |
| 6464-500 | Timken Boxcar, yellow, *70 u* | 210 | 350 | _____ |
| 6476-135 | LV Hopper "25000" (027), *70–71 u* | 6 | 11 | _____ |
| 6478 | Black Cave SP-type Caboose, *82* | 5 | 9 | _____ |
| 6482 | Nibco Express SP-type Caboose, *82 u* | 26 | 34 | _____ |
| 6485 | Chessie System SP-type Caboose, *84–85* | 6 | 10 | _____ |
| 6486 | Southern SP-type Caboose, *83–85* | 5 | 7 | _____ |
| 6490 | NKP N5c Caboose, *84 u* | | NRS | _____ |
| 6491 | Erie-Lackawanna Transfer Caboose, *85–86* | 9 | 17 | _____ |
| 6493 | L&C Bay Window Caboose, *86–87* | 21 | 36 | _____ |
| 6494 | Santa Fe Bobber Caboose, *85–86* | 7 | 9 | _____ |
| 6496 | Santa Fe Work Caboose (SSS), *86* | 21 | 29 | _____ |
| 6504 | L.A.S.E.R. Flatcar with helicopter (027), *81–82* | 18 | 26 | _____ |
| 6505 | L.A.S.E.R. Radar Car, *81–82* | 17 | 25 | _____ |
| 6506 | L.A.S.E.R. Security Car, *81–82* | 18 | 26 | _____ |
| 6507 | L.A.S.E.R. Flatcar with cruise missile, *81–82* | 21 | 30 | _____ |
| 6508 | Canadian Pacific Crane Car, *81* | 50 | 70 | _____ |
| 6509 | Depressed Center Flatcar with girders, *81* | 60 | 85 | _____ |
| 6510 | Union Pacific Crane Car, *82* | 55 | 60 | _____ |
| 6515 | Union Pacific Flatcar (027), *83–84, 86* | 5 | 9 | _____ |
| 6521 | NYC Flatcar with stakes (std O), *84–85* | 29 | 35 | _____ |
| 6522 | C&NW Searchlight Car, *83–85* | 27 | 30 | _____ |
| 6524 | Erie Crane Car, *84* | 55 | 60 | _____ |
| 6526 | Searchlight Car, *84–85* | 23 | 25 | _____ |
| 6529 | NYC Searchlight Car, *85–86* | 21 | 27 | _____ |
| 6531 | Express Mail Flatcar with trailers, *85–86* | 23 | 32 | _____ |
| 6560 | Bucyrus Erie Crane Car, *71* | 100 | 130 | _____ |
| 6561 | Flatcar with cruise missile (027), *83–84* | 13 | 26 | _____ |
| 6562 | Flatcar with fences (027), *83–84* | 13 | 21 | _____ |
| 6564 | U.S. Marines Flatcar with 2 tanks (027), *83–84* | 13 | 21 | _____ |
| 6573 | Redwood Valley Express Log Dump Car (027), *84–85* | 8 | 13 | _____ |

| | | Exc | Mint | Cond/$ |
|---|---|---|---|---|
| **6574** | Redwood Valley Express Crane Car (027), *84–85* | 7 | 13 | \_\_\_\_ |
| **6575** | Redwood Valley Express Flatcar with fences (027), *84–85* | 7 | 13 | \_\_\_\_ |
| **6576** | Santa Fe Crane Car (027), *85–86, 92 u* | 7 | 10 | \_\_\_\_ |
| **6579** | NYC Crane Car, *85–86* | 36 | 44 | \_\_\_\_ |
| **6585** | PRR Flatcar with fences (027), *86–90* | 5 | 9 | \_\_\_\_ |
| **6587** | W&ARR Flatcar with horses, *86 u* | 18 | 26 | \_\_\_\_ |
| **6593** | Santa Fe Crane Car (SSS), *86* | 41 | 48 | \_\_\_\_ |
| **6700** | PFE Ice Car, *82–83* | | 70 | \_\_\_\_ |
| **6900** | N&W Extended Vision Caboose, *82* | 60 | 65 | \_\_\_\_ |
| **6901** | Ontario Northland Extended Vision Caboose, *82 u* | 44 | 55 | \_\_\_\_ |
| **6903** | Santa Fe Extended Vision Caboose, *83* | 80 | 95 | \_\_\_\_ |
| **6904** | Union Pacific Extended Vision Caboose, *83* | 115 | 135 | \_\_\_\_ |
| **6905** | NKP Extended Vision Caboose, *83 u* | 50 | 65 | \_\_\_\_ |
| **6906** | Erie-Lack. Extended Vision Caboose, *84* | 75 | 90 | \_\_\_\_ |
| **6907** | NYC Wood-sided Caboose (std O), *86 u* | 90 | 92 | \_\_\_\_ |
| **6908** | PRR N5c Caboose (FARR 5), *84–85* | 43 | 47 | \_\_\_\_ |
| **6910** | NYC Extended Vision Caboose, *84 u* | 55 | 60 | \_\_\_\_ |
| **6912** | Redwood Valley Express SP-type Caboose, *84–85* | 9 | 16 | \_\_\_\_ |
| **6913** | Burlington Northern Extended Vision Caboose, *85* | 70 | 90 | \_\_\_\_ |
| **6916** | NYC Work Caboose, *85–86* | 16 | 22 | \_\_\_\_ |
| **6917** | Jersey Central Extended Vision Caboose, *86* | 36 | 50 | \_\_\_\_ |
| **6918** | B&O SP-type Caboose, *86* | 10 | 15 | \_\_\_\_ |
| **6919** | Nickel Plate Road SP-type Caboose, *86–91* | 5 | 9 | \_\_\_\_ |
| **6920** | B&A Wood-sided Caboose (std O), *86 u* | 65 | 80 | \_\_\_\_ |
| **26604** | Halloween Spooky Grave Gondola, *09* | | 58 | \_\_\_\_ |
| **6921** | PRR SP-type Caboose, *86–90* | 5 | 9 | \_\_\_\_ |
| **7200** | *Quicksilver* Passenger Coach (027), *82–83* | 26 | 34 | \_\_\_\_ |
| **7201** | *Quicksilver* Passenger Coach (027), *82–83* | 26 | 34 | \_\_\_\_ |
| **7202** | *Quicksilver* Observation Car (027), *82–83* | 26 | 34 | \_\_\_\_ |
| **7203** | N&W Diner "491," *82 u* | 130 | 180 | \_\_\_\_ |
| **7204** | Southern Pacific Diner, *82 u* | 190 | 235 | \_\_\_\_ |
| **7207** | NYC Diner, *83 u* | 70 | 140 | \_\_\_\_ |
| **7208** | PRR Diner, *83 u* | 80 | 90 | \_\_\_\_ |
| **7210** | Union Pacific Diner, *84* | 85 | 110 | \_\_\_\_ |
| **7211** | Southern Pacific Vista Dome Car, *83 u* | 145 | 185 | \_\_\_\_ |
| **7215** | B&O Passenger Coach, *83–84* | 43 | 50 | \_\_\_\_ |
| **7216** | B&O Passenger Coach, *83–84* | 43 | 50 | \_\_\_\_ |
| **7217** | B&O Baggage Car, *83–84* | 43 | 50 | \_\_\_\_ |
| **7220** | Illinois Central Baggage Car, *85, 87* | 105 | 135 | \_\_\_\_ |
| **7221** | Illinois Central Combination Car, *85, 87* | 85 | 105 | \_\_\_\_ |
| **7222** | Illinois Central Passenger Coach, *85, 87* | 85 | 105 | \_\_\_\_ |
| **7223** | Illinois Central Passenger Coach, *85, 87* | 85 | 105 | \_\_\_\_ |
| **7224** | Illinois Central Diner, *85, 87* | 75 | 90 | \_\_\_\_ |
| **7225** | Illinois Central Observation Car, *85, 87* | 95 | 115 | \_\_\_\_ |

| | | Exc | Mint | Cond/$ |
|---|---|---|---|---|
| 7227 | Wabash Diner (FF 1), *86–87* | 115 | 130 | _____ |
| 7228 | Wabash Baggage Car (FF 1), *86–87* | 90 | 100 | _____ |
| 7229 | Wabash Combination Car (FF 1), *86–87* | 90 | 100 | _____ |
| 7230 | Wabash Passenger Coach (FF 1), *86–87* | 90 | 100 | _____ |
| 7231 | Wabash Passenger Coach (FF 1), *86–87* | 90 | 100 | _____ |
| 7232 | Wabash Observation Car (FF 1), *86–87* | 85 | 95 | _____ |
| 7241 | W&ARR Passenger Coach, *86 u* | 43 | 50 | _____ |
| 7242 | W&ARR Baggage Car, *86 u* | 43 | 50 | _____ |
| 7301 | Norfolk & Western Stock Car, *82* | 44 | 45 | _____ |
| 7302 | Texas & Pacific Stock Car (O27), *83–84* | 11 | 14 | _____ |
| 7303 | Erie Stock Car, *84* | 41 | 50 | _____ |
| 7304 | Southern Stock Car (FARR 4), *83 u* | 41 | 45 | _____ |
| 7309 | Southern Stock Car (O27), *85–86* | 12 | 16 | _____ |
| 7312 | W&ARR Stock Car (O27), *86 u* | 25 | 30 | _____ |
| 7401 | Chessie System Stock Car (O27), *84–85* | 13 | 17 | _____ |
| 7404 | Jersey Central Boxcar, *86* | 26 | 40 | _____ |
| 7500 | Lionel 75th Anniversary U36B Diesel, *75–77* | 118 | 138 | _____ |
| 7501 | Lionel 75th Anniversary Boxcar, *75–77* | 23 | 32 | _____ |
| 7502 | Lionel 75th Anniversary Reefer, *75–77* | 26 | 35 | _____ |
| 7503 | Lionel 75th Anniversary Reefer, *75–77* | 28 | 39 | _____ |
| 7504 | Lionel 75th Anniversary Covered Quad Hopper, *75–77* | 26 | 39 | _____ |
| 7505 | Lionel 75th Anniversary Boxcar, *75–77* | 26 | 37 | _____ |
| 7506 | Lionel 75th Anniversary Boxcar, *75–77* | 15 | 20 | _____ |
| 7507 | Lionel 75th Anniversary Reefer, *75–77* | 26 | 37 | _____ |
| 7508 | Lionel 75th Anniversary N5c Caboose, *75–77* | 22 | 27 | _____ |
| 7509 | Kentucky Fried Chicken Reefer, *81–82* | 49 | 59 | _____ |
| 7510 | Red Lobster Reefer, *81–82* | 49 | 57 | _____ |
| 7511 | Pizza Hut Reefer, *81–82* | 49 | 57 | _____ |
| 7512 | Arthur Treacher's Reefer, *82* | 48 | 54 | _____ |
| 7513 | Bonanza Reefer, *82* | 47 | 54 | _____ |
| 7514 | Taco Bell Reefer, *82* | 58 | 87 | _____ |
| 7515 | Denver Mint Car, *81* | 65 | 70 | _____ |
| 7517 | Philadelphia Mint Car, *82* | 38 | 39 | _____ |
| 7518 | Carson City Mint Car, *83* | 34 | 43 | _____ |
| 7519 | Toy Fair Reefer, *82 u* | 35 | 42 | _____ |
| 7520 | Nibco Express Boxcar, *82 u* | 265 | 440 | _____ |
| 7521 | Toy Fair Reefer, *83 u* | 50 | 65 | _____ |
| 7522 | New Orleans Mint Car, *84 u* | 33 | 38 | _____ |
| 7523 | Toy Fair Reefer, *84 u* | 44 | 49 | _____ |
| 7524 | Toy Fair Reefer, *85 u* | 55 | 60 | _____ |
| 7525 | Toy Fair Boxcar, *86 u* | 65 | 80 | _____ |
| 7530 | Dahlonega Mint Car, *86 u* | 37 | 48 | _____ |
| 7600 | Frisco "Spirit of '76" N5c Caboose, *74–76* | 33 | 39 | _____ |
| 7601 | Delaware Boxcar, *74–76* | 16 | 19 | _____ |
| 7602 | Pennsylvania Boxcar, *74–76* | 23 | 27 | _____ |
| 7603 | New Jersey Boxcar, *74–76* | 23 | 24 | _____ |
| 7604 | Georgia Boxcar, *74 u, 75–76* | 22 | 26 | _____ |

| | | Exc | Mint | Cond/$ |
|---|---|---|---|---|
| **7605** | Connecticut Boxcar, *74 u, 75–76* | 22 | 32 | ____ |
| **7606** | Massachusetts Boxcar, *74 u, 75–76* | 25 | 29 | ____ |
| **7607** | Maryland Boxcar, *74 u, 75–76* | 22 | 34 | ____ |
| **7608** | South Carolina Boxcar, *75 u, 76* | 38 | 50 | ____ |
| **7609** | New Hampshire Boxcar, *75 u, 76* | 38 | 46 | ____ |
| **7610** | Virginia Boxcar, *75 u, 76* | 155 | 200 | ____ |
| **7611** | New York Boxcar, *75 u, 76* | 50 | 65 | ____ |
| **7612** | North Carolina Boxcar, *75 u, 76* | 35 | 60 | ____ |
| **7613** | Rhode Island Boxcar, *75 u, 76* | 36 | 50 | ____ |
| **7700** | Uncle Sam Boxcar, *75 u* | 44 | 51 | ____ |
| **7701** | Camel Boxcar, *76–77* | 49 | 59 | ____ |
| **7702** | Prince Albert Boxcar, *76–77* | 53 | 70 | ____ |
| **7703** | Beechnut Boxcar, *76–77* | 29 | 47 | ____ |
| **7704** | Toy Fair Boxcar, *76 u* | 110 | 120 | ____ |
| **7705** | Canadian Toy Fair Boxcar, *76 u* | 130 | 145 | ____ |
| **7706** | Sir Walter Raleigh Boxcar, *77–78* | 49 | 59 | ____ |
| **7707** | White Owl Boxcar, *77–78* | 49 | 65 | ____ |
| **7708** | Winston Boxcar, *77–78* | 51 | 67 | ____ |
| **7709** | Salem Boxcar, *78* | 51 | 59 | ____ |
| **7710** | Mail Pouch Boxcar, *78* | 53 | 64 | ____ |
| **7711** | El Producto Boxcar, *78* | 50 | 66 | ____ |
| **7712** | Santa Fe Boxcar (FARR 1), *79* | 25 | 44 | ____ |
| **7800** | Pepsi Boxcar, *76 u, 77* | 65 | 68 | ____ |
| **7801** | A&W Boxcar, *76 u, 77* | 41 | 55 | ____ |
| **7802** | Canada Dry Boxcar, *76 u, 77* | 43 | 55 | ____ |
| **7803** | Trains n' Truckin' Boxcar, *77 u* | 20 | 26 | ____ |
| **7806** | Season's Greetings Boxcar, *76 u* | 70 | 95 | ____ |
| **7807** | Toy Fair Boxcar, *77 u* | 70 | 95 | ____ |
| **7808** | Northern Pacific Stock Car, *77* | 37 | 44 | ____ |
| **7809** | Vernors Boxcar, *77 u, 78* | 50 | 65 | ____ |
| **7810** | Orange Crush Boxcar, *77 u, 78* | 40 | 55 | ____ |
| **7811** | Dr Pepper Boxcar, *77 u, 78* | 44 | 60 | ____ |
| **7813** | "Season's Greetings" Boxcar, *77 u* | 65 | 90 | ____ |
| **7814** | "Season's Greetings" Boxcar, *78 u* | 70 | 95 | ____ |
| **7815** | Toy Fair Boxcar, *78 u* | 65 | 85 | ____ |
| **7816** | Toy Fair Boxcar, *79 u* | 65 | 85 | ____ |
| **7817** | Toy Fair Boxcar, *80 u* | 95 | 105 | ____ |
| **7900** | D&RGW Operating Cowboy Car (O27), *82–83* | 22 | 26 | ____ |
| **7901** | LL Cop and Hobo Car (O27), *82–83* | 24 | 27 | ____ |
| **7902** | Santa Fe Boxcar (O27), *82–85* | 5 | 9 | ____ |
| **7903** | Rock Island Boxcar (O27), *83* | 8 | 13 | ____ |
| **7904** | San Diego Zoo Giraffe Car (O27), *83–84* | 44 | 55 | ____ |
| **7905** | Black Cave Boxcar (O27), *82* | 6 | 9 | ____ |
| **7908** | Tappan Boxcar (O27), *82 u* | 39 | 55 | ____ |
| **7909** | L&N Boxcar (O27), *83–84* | 40 | 49 | ____ |
| **7910** | Chessie System Boxcar (O27), *84–85* | 18 | 23 | ____ |
| **7912** | Toys "R" Us Giraffe Car (O27), *82–84 u* | 70 | 80 | ____ |
| **7913** | Turtleback Zoo Giraffe Car (O27), *85–86* | 50 | 60 | ____ |

Exc Mint Cond/$

| | | Exc | Mint | Cond/$ |
|---|---|---|---|---|
| 7914 | Toys "R" Us Giraffe Car (027), *85–89 u* | 70 | 90 | ____ |
| 7920 | Sears Centennial Boxcar (027), *85–86 u* | 39 | 44 | ____ |
| 7925 | Erie-Lackawanna Boxcar (027), *86–90* | 10 | 18 | ____ |
| 7926 | NKP Boxcar (027), *86–91* | 8 | 10 | ____ |
| 7930 | True Value Boxcar (027), *86–87 u* | 34 | 50 | ____ |
| 7931 | Town House TV and Appliances Boxcar (027), *86 u* | 31 | 39 | ____ |
| 7932 | Kay Bee Toys Boxcar (027), *86–87 u* | 40 | 49 | ____ |
| 8001 | NKP 2-6-4 Locomotive, *80 u* | 55 | 65 | ____ |
| 8002 | Union Pacific 2-8-4 Locomotive (FARR 2), *80* | 310 | 345 | ____ |
| 8003 | Chessie System 2-8-4 Locomotive, *80* | 360 | 540 | ____ |
| 8004 | Rock Island 4-4-0 Locomotive, *80–82* | 190 | 220 | ____ |
| 8005 | Santa Fe 4-4-0 Locomotive, *80–82* | 65 | 75 | ____ |
| 8006 | ACL 4-6-4 Locomotive, *80 u* | 245 | 340 | ____ |
| 8007 | NYNH&H 2-6-4 Locomotive, *80–81* | 65 | 75 | ____ |
| 8008 | Chessie System 4-4-2 Locomotive, *80* | 65 | 75 | ____ |
| 8010 | Santa Fe NW2 Switcher, *70, 71 u* | 25 | 65 | ____ |
| 8020 | Santa Fe Alco Diesel A Unit, *70–72, 74–76* | 65 | 85 | ____ |
| 8020 | Santa Fe Alco Diesel A Unit, dummy, *70* | 45 | 60 | ____ |
| 8021 | Santa Fe Alco Diesel B Unit, *71–72, 74–76* | 47 | 70 | ____ |
| 8022 | Santa Fe Alco Diesel A Unit, *71 u* | 80 | 105 | ____ |
| 8025 | CN Alco Diesel A Unit, *71–73 u* | 85 | 105 | ____ |
| 8025 | CN Alco Diesel A Unit, dummy, *71–73 u* | 45 | 65 | ____ |
| 8030 | Illinois Central GP9 Diesel, *70–72* | 125 | 145 | ____ |
| 8031 | Canadian National GP7 Diesel, *71–73 u* | 80 | 150 | ____ |
| 8031 | Illinois Central GP9 Diesel Dummy Unit, *70* | | NRS | ____ |
| 8040 | Canadian National 2-4-2 Locomotive, *71 u* | 43 | 85 | ____ |
| 8040 | NKP 2-4-2 Locomotive, *70–72* | 26 | 34 | ____ |
| 8041 | NYC 2-4-2 Locomotive, *70* | 55 | 65 | ____ |
| 8041 | PRR 2-4-2 Locomotive, *71 u* | 55 | 65 | ____ |
| 8042 | GTW 2-4-2 Locomotive, *70, 71–73 u* | 26 | 34 | ____ |
| 8043 | NKP 2-4-2 Locomotive, *70 u* | 45 | 65 | ____ |
| 8050 | D&H U36C Diesel, *80* | 105 | 220 | ____ |
| 8051 | D&H U36C Diesel Dummy Unit, *80* | 95 | 115 | ____ |
| 8054/55 | Burlington F3 Diesel AA Set, *80* | 360 | 385 | ____ |
| 8056 | C&NW FM Train Master Diesel, *80* | 175 | 225 | ____ |
| 8057 | Burlington NW2 Switcher, *80* | 100 | 115 | ____ |
| 8059 | Pennsylvania F3 Diesel B Unit, *80 u* | 190 | 290 | ____ |
| 8060 | Pennsylvania F3 Diesel B Unit, *80 u* | 335 | 420 | ____ |
| 8061 | Chessie System U36C Diesel, *80* | 110 | 140 | ____ |
| 8062 | Burlington F3 Diesel B Unit, *80 u* | 205 | 255 | ____ |
| 8063 | Seaboard SD9 Diesel, *80* | 80 | 100 | ____ |
| 8064 | Florida East Coast GP9 Diesel, *80* | 150 | 200 | ____ |
| 8065 | Florida East Coast GP9 Diesel Dummy Unit, *80* | 95 | 120 | ____ |
| 8066 | TP&W GP20 Diesel, *80–81, 83 u* | 65 | 80 | ____ |
| 8071 | Virginian SD18 Diesel, *80 u* | 135 | 155 | ____ |
| 8072 | Virginian SD18 Diesel Dummy Unit, *80 u* | 75 | 110 | ____ |
| 8100 | Norfolk & Western 4-8-4 "611," *81* | 360 | 402 | ____ |

| | | Exc | Mint | Cond/$ |
|---|---|---|---|---|
| 8101 | Chicago & Alton 4-6-4 Locomotive "659," *81* | 275 | 445 | ____ |
| 8102 | Union Pacific 4-4-2 Locomotive, *81–82* | 49 | 65 | ____ |
| 8104 | Union Pacific 4-4-0 Locomotive "3," *81 u* | 180 | 235 | ____ |
| 8111 | DT&I NW2 Switcher, *71–74* | 55 | 65 | ____ |
| 8140 | Southern 2-4-0 Locomotive, *71 u* | 22 | 30 | ____ |
| 8141 | PRR 2-4-2 Locomotive, *71–72* | 41 | 43 | ____ |
| 8142 | C&O 4-4-2 Locomotive, *71–72* | | 55 | ____ |
| 8150 | PRR GG1 Electric Locomotive "4935," *81* | 330 | 395 | ____ |
| 8151 | Burlington SD28 Diesel, *81* | 120 | 145 | ____ |
| 8152 | Canadian Pacific SD24 Diesel, *81* | 170 | 180 | ____ |
| 8153 | Reading NW2 Switcher, *81–82* | 100 | 155 | ____ |
| 8154 | Alaska NW2 Switcher, *81–82* | 120 | 160 | ____ |
| 8155 | Monon U36B Diesel, *81–82* | 110 | 135 | ____ |
| 8156 | Monon U36B Diesel Dummy Unit, *81–82* | | 65 | ____ |
| 8157 | Santa Fe FM Train Master, *81* | 280 | 325 | ____ |
| 8158 | DM&IR GP35 Diesel, *81–82* | 90 | 150 | ____ |
| 8159 | DM&IR GP35 Diesel Dummy Unit, *81–82* | 55 | 75 | ____ |
| 8160 | Burger King GP20 Diesel, *81–82* | 94 | 114 | ____ |
| 8161 | L.A.S.E.R. Switcher, *81–82* | 23 | 55 | ____ |
| 8162 | Ontario Northland SD18 Diesel, *81 u* | 150 | 210 | ____ |
| 8163 | Ontario Northland SD18 Diesel Dummy Unit, *81 u* | 95 | 140 | ____ |
| 8164 | Pennsylvania F3 Diesel B Unit, *81 u* | 340 | 370 | ____ |
| 8182 | Nibco Express NW2 Switcher, *82 u* | 90 | 130 | ____ |
| 8190 | Diesel Horn Kit, *81 u* | | 30 | ____ |
| 8200 | Kickapoo Dockside 0-4-0T, *72* | 30 | 39 | ____ |
| 8203 | PRR 2-4-2 Locomotive, *72, 74 u, 75* | 26 | 34 | ____ |
| 8204 | C&O 4-4-2 Locomotive, *72* | 55 | 60 | ____ |
| 8206 | NYC 4-6-4 Locomotive, *72–75* | 140 | 155 | ____ |
| 8209 | *Pioneer* Dockside 0-4-0T with tender, *72* | 45 | 65 | ____ |
| 8209 | *Pioneer* Dockside 0-4-0T, no tender, *73–76* | 42 | 55 | ____ |
| 8210 | Joshua L. Cowen 4-6-4 Locomotive, *82* | 245 | 350 | ____ |
| 8212 | Black Cave 0-4-0 Locomotive, *82* | 30 | 49 | ____ |
| 8213 | D&RGW 2-4-2 Locomotive, *82–83, 84–91 u* | 65 | 70 | ____ |
| 8214 | Pennsylvania 2-4-2 Locomotive, *82–83* | 55 | 65 | ____ |
| 8215 | Nickel Plate Road 2-8-4 Locomotive "779," *82 u* | 245 | 285 | ____ |
| 8250 | Santa Fe GP9 Diesel, *72, 74–75* | 120 | 145 | ____ |
| 8251-50 | Horn/Whistle Controller, *72–74* | 1 | 2 | ____ |
| 8252 | D&H Alco Diesel A Unit, *72* | 85 | 125 | ____ |
| 8253 | D&H Alco Diesel B Unit, *72* | 50 | 70 | ____ |
| 8254 | Illinois Central GP9 Diesel Dummy Unit, *72* | 60 | 65 | ____ |
| 8255 | Santa Fe GP9 Diesel Dummy Unit, *72* | 60 | 65 | ____ |
| 8258 | Canadian National GP7 Diesel Dummy Unit, *72–73 u* | 65 | 85 | ____ |
| 8260/62 | Southern Pacific F3 Diesel AA Set, *82* | 490 | 520 | ____ |
| 8261 | Southern Pacific F3 Diesel B Unit, *82 u* | 435 | 445 | ____ |
| 8263 | Santa Fe GP7 Diesel, *82* | 65 | 80 | ____ |
| 8264 | CP Vulcan Switcher Snowplow, *82* | 80 | 100 | ____ |

| | | Exc | Mint | Cond/$ |
|---|---|---|---|---|
| 8265 | Santa Fe SD40 Diesel, *82* | 205 | 225 | ____ |
| 8266 | Norfolk & Western SD24 Diesel, *82* | 150 | 225 | ____ |
| 8268 | *Quicksilver* Alco Diesel A Unit, *82–83* | 85 | 105 | ____ |
| 8269 | *Quicksilver* Alco Diesel A Unit, dummy, *82–83* | 55 | 65 | ____ |
| 8272 | Pennsylvania EP-5 Electric Locomotive, *82 u* | 205 | 265 | ____ |
| 8300 | Santa Fe 2-4-0 Locomotive, *73–74* | 22 | 25 | ____ |
| 8302 | Southern 2-4-0 Locomotive, *73–76* | 29 | 30 | ____ |
| 8303 | Jersey Central 2-4-2 Locomotive, *73–74* | 55 | 59 | ____ |
| 8304 | B&O 4-4-2 Locomotive, *75* | 75 | 105 | ____ |
| 8304 | C&O 4-4-2 Locomotive, *75–77* | 75 | 105 | ____ |
| 8304 | Pennsylvania 4-4-2 Locomotive, *74–75* | 75 | 105 | ____ |
| 8304 | Rock Island 4-4-2 Locomotive, *73–75* | 85 | 105 | ____ |
| 8305 | Milwaukee Road 4-4-2 Locomotive, *73* | 95 | 120 | ____ |
| 8307 | Southern Pacific 4-8-4 Locomotive "4449," *83* | 490 | 560 | ____ |
| 8308 | Jersey Central 2-4-2 Locomotive, *73–74 u* | 36 | 43 | ____ |
| 8309 | Southern 2-8-2 Locomotive "4501" (FARR 4), *83* | 385 | 495 | ____ |
| 8310 | Jersey Central 2-4-0 Locomotive, *74–75 u* | 26 | 50 | ____ |
| 8310 | Nickel Plate Road 2-4-0 Locomotive, *73 u* | 26 | 50 | ____ |
| 8310 | Santa Fe 2-4-0 Locomotive, *74–75 u* | 26 | 34 | ____ |
| 8311 | Southern 0-4-0 Locomotive, *73 u* | 26 | 34 | ____ |
| 8313 | Santa Fe 0-4-0 Locomotive, *83–84* | 13 | 17 | ____ |
| 8314 | Southern 2-4-0 Locomotive, *83–85* | 17 | 21 | ____ |
| 8315 | B&O 4-4-0 Locomotive, *83–84* | 85 | 120 | ____ |
| 8341 | ACL SP-type Caboose, *86 u, 87–90* | 6 | 8 | ____ |
| 8350 | U.S. Steel Switcher, *73–75* | 18 | 26 | ____ |
| 8351 | Santa Fe Alco Diesel A Unit, *73–75* | 60 | 65 | ____ |
| 8352 | Santa Fe GP20 Diesel, *73–75* | 65 | 105 | ____ |
| 8353 | Grand Trunk Western GP7 Diesel, *73–75* | 90 | 120 | ____ |
| 8354 | Erie NW2 Switcher, *73, 75* | 80 | 105 | ____ |
| 8355 | Santa Fe GP20 Diesel Dummy Unit, *73–74* | 65 | 90 | ____ |
| 8356 | Grand Trunk Western GP7 Diesel Dummy Unit, *73–75* | 65 | 75 | ____ |
| 8357 | PRR GP9 Diesel, *73–75* | 100 | 120 | ____ |
| 8358 | PRR GP9 Diesel Dummy Unit, *73–75* | 55 | 100 | ____ |
| 8359 | Chessie System GP7 Diesel "GM50," *73* | 95 | 120 | ____ |
| 8360 | Long Island GP20 Diesel, *73–74* | 70 | 105 | ____ |
| 8361 | Western Pacific Alco Diesel A Unit, *73–75* | 50 | 70 | ____ |
| 8362 | Western Pacific Alco Diesel B Unit, *73–75* | 45 | 65 | ____ |
| 8363 | B&O F3 Diesel A Unit, *73–75* | 280 | 310 | ____ |
| 8364 | B&O F3 Diesel A Unit, dummy, *73–75* | 120 | 160 | ____ |
| 8365/66 | CP F3 Diesel AA Set (SSS), *73* | 355 | 405 | ____ |
| 8367 | Long Island GP20 Diesel Dummy Unit, *73–75* | 80 | 100 | ____ |
| 8368 | Alaska Vulcan Switcher, *83* | 120 | 129 | ____ |
| 8369 | Erie-Lackawanna GP20 Diesel, *83–85* | 125 | 140 | ____ |
| 8370/72 | NYC F3 Diesel AA Set, *83* | 330 | 435 | ____ |
| 8371 | NYC F3 Diesel B Unit, *83* | 105 | 150 | ____ |
| 8374 | Burlington Northern NW2 Switcher, *83–85* | 105 | 110 | ____ |
| 8375 | C&NW GP7 Diesel, *83–85* | 135 | 165 | ____ |

| | | Exc | Mint | Cond/$ |
|---|---|---|---|---|
| 8376 | Union Pacific SD40 Diesel, *83* | 175 | 200 | ____ |
| 8377 | U.S. Marines Switcher, *83–84* | 55 | 65 | ____ |
| 8378 | Wabash FM Train Master Diesel "550," *83 u* | 500 | 690 | ____ |
| 8379 | PRR Fire Car, *83 u* | 80 | 100 | ____ |
| 8380 | Lionel Lines SD28 Diesel, *83 u* | 235 | 315 | ____ |
| 8402 | Reading 4-4-2 Locomotive, *84–85* | 47 | 55 | ____ |
| 8403 | Chessie System 4-4-2 Locomotive, *84–85* | 55 | 65 | ____ |
| 8404 | PRR 6-8-6 "6200" (FARR 5), *84–85* | 360 | 460 | ____ |
| 8406 | NYC 4-6-4 Locomotive "783," *84* | 445 | 571 | ____ |
| 8410 | Redwood Valley Express 4-4-0 Locomotive, *84–85* | 34 | 50 | ____ |
| 8452 | Erie Alco Diesel A Unit, *74–75* | 75 | 95 | ____ |
| 8453 | Erie Alco Diesel B Unit, *74–75* | 55 | 75 | ____ |
| 8454 | D&RGW GP7 Diesel, *74–75* | 80 | 110 | ____ |
| 8455 | D&RGW GP7 Diesel Dummy Unit, *74–75* | 50 | 85 | ____ |
| 8458 | Erie-Lackawanna SD40 Diesel, *84* | 160 | 190 | ____ |
| 8459 | D&RGW Vulcan Rotary Snowplow, *84* | 125 | 146 | ____ |
| 8460 | MKT NW2 Switcher, *74–75* | 45 | 65 | ____ |
| 8463 | Chessie System GP20 Diesel, *74 u* | 130 | 190 | ____ |
| 8464/65 | D&RGW F3 Diesel AA Set (SSS), *74* | 220 | 325 | ____ |
| 8466 | Amtrak F3 Diesel A Unit, *74–76* | 225 | 250 | ____ |
| 8467 | Amtrak F3 Diesel A Unit, dummy, *74–76* | 80 | 90 | ____ |
| 8468 | B&O F3 Diesel B Unit, *74–75* | 95 | 100 | ____ |
| 8469 | CP F3 Diesel B Unit (SSS), *74* | 85 | 110 | ____ |
| 8470 | Chessie System U36B Diesel, *74* | 80 | 110 | ____ |
| 8471 | Pennsylvania NW2 Switcher, *74–76* | 170 | 195 | ____ |
| 8473 | Coca-Cola NW2 Switcher, *74 u, 75* | 98 | 123 | ____ |
| 8474 | D&RGW F3 Diesel B Unit (SSS), *74* | 95 | 110 | ____ |
| 8475 | Amtrak F3 Diesel B Unit, *74* | 85 | 105 | ____ |
| 8477 | NYC GP9 Diesel, *84 u* | 150 | 205 | ____ |
| 8480/82 | Union Pacific F3 Diesel AA Set, *84* | 280 | 365 | ____ |
| 8481 | Union Pacific F3 Diesel B Unit, *84* | 150 | 155 | ____ |
| 8485 | USMC NW2 Switcher, *84–85* | 105 | 135 | ____ |
| 8500 | Pennsylvania 2-4-0 Locomotive, *75–76* | 17 | 21 | ____ |
| 8502 | Santa Fe 2-4-0 Locomotive, *75* | 17 | 21 | ____ |
| 8506 | PRR 0-4-0 Locomotive, *75–77* | 75 | 90 | ____ |
| 8507 | Santa Fe 2-4-0 Locomotive, *75 u* | 25 | 30 | ____ |
| 8512 | Santa Fe 0-4-0T Locomotive, *85–86* | 22 | 30 | ____ |
| 8516 | NYC 0-4-0 Locomotive, *85–86* | 115 | 140 | ____ |
| 8550 | Jersey Central GP9 Diesel, *75–76* | 120 | 155 | ____ |
| 8551 | Pennsylvania EP-5 Electric Locomotive, *75–76* | 115 | 120 | ____ |
| 8552/53/54 | SP Alco Diesel ABA Set, *75–76* | 200 | 245 | ____ |
| 8555/57 | Milwaukee Road F3 Diesel AA Set (SSS), *75* | 240 | 315 | ____ |
| 8556 | Chessie System NW2 Switcher, *75–76* | 160 | 200 | ____ |
| 8558 | Milwaukee Road EP-5 Electric Locomotive, *76–77* | 160 | 195 | ____ |
| 8559 | N&W GP9 Diesel "1776," *75* | 115 | 145 | ____ |
| 8560 | Chessie System U36B Diesel Dummy Unit, *75* | 85 | 130 | ____ |
| 8561 | Jersey Central GP9 Diesel Dummy Unit, *75–76* | 70 | 95 | ____ |

Exc Mint Cond/S

| | | Exc | Mint | Cond/S |
|---|---|---|---|---|
| 8562 | Missouri Pacific GP20 Diesel, *75–76* | 130 | 145 | ____ |
| 8563 | Rock Island Alco Diesel A Unit, *75–76 u* | 65 | 90 | ____ |
| 8564 | Union Pacific U36B Diesel, *75* | 110 | 155 | ____ |
| 8565 | Missouri Pacific GP20 Diesel Dummy Unit, *75–76* | 55 | 70 | ____ |
| 8566 | Southern F3 Diesel A Unit, *75–77* | 220 | 370 | ____ |
| 8567 | Southern F3 Diesel A Unit, dummy, *75–77* | 105 | 135 | ____ |
| 8568 | Preamble Express F3 Diesel A Unit, *75 u* | 90 | 115 | ____ |
| 8569 | Soo Line NW2 Switcher, *75–77* | 60 | 65 | ____ |
| 8570 | Liberty Special Alco Diesel A Unit, *75 u* | 75 | 90 | ____ |
| 8571 | Frisco U36B Diesel, *75–76* | 75 | 95 | ____ |
| 8572 | Frisco U36B Diesel Dummy Unit, *75–76* | | 55 | ____ |
| 8573 | Union Pacific U36B Diesel Dummy Unit, *75 u* | 145 | 190 | ____ |
| 8575 | Milwaukee Road F3 Diesel B Unit (SSS), *75* | 105 | 160 | ____ |
| 8576 | Penn Central GP7 Diesel, *75 u, 76–77* | 90 | 120 | ____ |
| 8578 | NYC Ballast Tamper, *85, 87* | 85 | 90 | ____ |
| 8580/82 | Illinois Central F3 Diesel AA Set, *85, 87* | 420 | 485 | ____ |
| 8581 | Illinois Central F3 Diesel B Unit, *85, 87* | 130 | 155 | ____ |
| 8585 | Burlington Northern SD40 Diesel, *85* | 355 | 385 | ____ |
| 8587 | Wabash GP9 Diesel "484," *85 u* | 250 | 280 | ____ |
| 8600 | NYC 4-6-4 Locomotive, *76* | 175 | 195 | ____ |
| 8601 | Rock Island 0-4-0 Locomotive, *76–77* | 17 | 21 | ____ |
| 8602 | D&RGW 2-4-0 Locomotive, *76–78* | 22 | 26 | ____ |
| 8603 | C&O 4-6-4 Locomotive, *76–77* | 135 | 190 | ____ |
| 8604 | Jersey Central 2-4-2 Locomotive, *76 u* | 39 | 44 | ____ |
| 8606 | B&A 4-6-4 Locomotive "784," *86 u* | 720 | 760 | ____ |
| 8610 | Wabash 4-6-2 "672" (FF 1), *86–87* | 435 | 610 | ____ |
| 8615 | L&N 2-8-4 Locomotive "1970," *86 u* | 540 | 630 | ____ |
| 8616 | Santa Fe 4-4-2 Locomotive, *86* | 60 | 65 | ____ |
| 8617 | Nickel Plate Road 4-4-2 Locomotive, *86–91* | 60 | 65 | ____ |
| 8625 | Pennsylvania 2-4-0 Locomotive, *86–90* | 21 | 34 | ____ |
| 8630 | W&ARR 4-4-0 Locomotive "3," *86 u* | 125 | 150 | ____ |
| 8635 | Santa Fe 0-4-0 (SSS), *86* | 80 | 100 | ____ |
| 8650 | Burlington Northern U36B Diesel, *76–77* | 120 | 170 | ____ |
| 8651 | Burlington Northern U36B Diesel Dummy Unit, *76–77* | 70 | 90 | ____ |
| 8652 | Santa Fe F3 Diesel A Unit, *76–77* | 260 | 510 | ____ |
| 8653 | Santa Fe F3 Diesel A Unit, dummy, *76–77* | 135 | 160 | ____ |
| 8654 | Boston & Maine GP9 Diesel, *76–77* | 155 | 195 | ____ |
| 8655 | Boston & Maine GP9 Diesel Dummy Unit, *76–77* | 90 | 110 | ____ |
| 8656 | Canadian National Alco Diesel A Unit, *76* | 150 | 195 | ____ |
| 8657 | Canadian National Alco Diesel B Unit, *76* | 60 | 75 | ____ |
| 8658 | CN Alco Diesel A Unit, dummy, *76* | 85 | 170 | ____ |
| 8659 | Virginian Electric Locomotive, *76–77* | 125 | 137 | ____ |
| 8660 | CP Rail NW2 Switcher, *76–77* | 100 | 135 | ____ |
| 8661 | Southern F3 Diesel B Unit, *76* | 165 | 170 | ____ |
| 8662 | B&O GP7 Diesel, *86* | 120 | 130 | ____ |
| 8664 | Amtrak Alco Diesel A Unit, *76–77* | 85 | 120 | ____ |

| | | Exc | Mint | Cond/$ |
|---|---|---|---|---|
| 8665 | BAR *Jeremiah O'Brien* GP9 Diesel "1776," *76 u* | 100 | 170 | ____ |
| 8666 | Northern Pacific GP9 Diesel (SSS), *76* | 125 | 175 | ____ |
| 8667 | Amtrak Alco Diesel B Unit, *76–77* | 60 | 80 | ____ |
| 8668 | Northern Pacific GP9 Diesel Dummy Unit (SSS), *76* | 100 | 130 | ____ |
| 8669 | Illinois Central Gulf U36B Diesel, *76–77* | 125 | 165 | ____ |
| 8670 | Chessie System Switcher, *76* | 30 | 55 | ____ |
| 8679 | Northern Pacific GP20 Diesel, *86* | 90 | 105 | ____ |
| 8687 | Jersey Central FM Train Master Diesel, *86* | 198 | 276 | ____ |
| 8690 | Lionel Lines Trolley, *86* | 105 | 115 | ____ |
| 8701 | W&ARR 4-4-0 Locomotive "3," *77–79* | 285 | 300 | ____ |
| 8702 | Southern 4-6-4 Locomotive, *77–78* | 280 | 398 | ____ |
| 8703 | Wabash 2-4-2 Locomotive, *77* | 22 | 30 | ____ |
| 8750 | Rock Island GP7 Diesel, *77–78* | 110 | 125 | ____ |
| 8751 | Rock Island GP7 Diesel Dummy Unit, *77–78* | 50 | 70 | ____ |
| 8753 | Pennsylvania GG1 Electric Locomotive, *77 u* | 290 | 315 | ____ |
| 8754 | New Haven Electric Locomotive, *77–78* | 100 | 115 | ____ |
| 8755 | Santa Fe U36B Diesel, *77–78* | 130 | 150 | ____ |
| 8756 | Santa Fe U36B Diesel Dummy Unit, *77–78* | 75 | 95 | ____ |
| 8757 | Conrail GP9 Diesel, *76 u, 77–78* | 110 | 140 | ____ |
| 8758 | Southern GP7 Diesel Dummy Unit, *77 u, 78* | 75 | 95 | ____ |
| 8759 | Erie-Lackawanna GP9 Diesel, *77–79* | 115 | 175 | ____ |
| 8760 | Erie-Lackawanna GP9 Diesel Dummy Unit, *77–79* | 95 | 115 | ____ |
| 8761 | GTW NW2 Switcher, *77–78* | 95 | 130 | ____ |
| 8762 | Great Northern EP-5 Electric Locomotive, *77–78* | 130 | 140 | ____ |
| 8763 | Norfolk & Western GP9 Diesel, *76 u, 77–78* | 110 | 120 | ____ |
| 8764 | B&O Budd RDC Passenger (SSS), *77* | 110 | 135 | ____ |
| 8765 | B&O Budd RDC Baggage Dummy Unit (SSS), *77* | 80 | 100 | ____ |
| 8766 | B&O Budd RDC Baggage (SSS), *77* | | 310 | ____ |
| 8767 | B&O Budd RDC Passenger Dummy Unit (SSS), *77* | 85 | 105 | ____ |
| 8768 | B&O Budd RDC Passenger Dummy Unit (SSS), *77* | 85 | 105 | ____ |
| 8769 | Republic Steel Switcher, *77–78* | 22 | 39 | ____ |
| 8770 | NW2 Switcher, *77–78* | | 65 | ____ |
| 8771 | Great Northern U36B Diesel, *77* | 110 | 140 | ____ |
| 8772 | GM&O GP20 Diesel, *77* | 85 | 95 | ____ |
| 8773 | Mickey Mouse U36B Diesel, *77–78* | 470 | 630 | ____ |
| 8774 | Southern GP7 Diesel, *77 u, 78* | 110 | 135 | ____ |
| 8775 | Lehigh Valley GP9 Diesel, *77 u, 78* | 85 | 105 | ____ |
| 8776 | C&NW GP20 Diesel, *77 u, 78* | 87 | 129 | ____ |
| 8777 | Santa Fe F3 Diesel B Unit (SSS), *77* | 160 | 175 | ____ |
| 8778 | Lehigh Valley GP9 Diesel Dummy Unit, *77 u, 78* | 90 | 110 | ____ |
| 8779 | C&NW GP20 Diesel Dummy Unit, *77 u, 78* | 73 | 109 | ____ |
| 8800 | Lionel Lines 4-4-2 Locomotive, *78–81* | 75 | 105 | ____ |
| 8801 | *Blue Comet* 4-6-4 Locomotive, *78–80* | 380 | 500 | ____ |
| 8803 | Santa Fe 0-4-0 Locomotive, *78* | 14 | 24 | ____ |

| | | Exc | Mint | Cond/S |
|---|---|---|---|---|
| **8850** | Penn Central GG1 Electric Locomotive, *78 u, 79* | 250 | 305 | ___ |
| **8851/52** | New Haven F3 Diesel AA Set, *78 u, 79* | 320 | 430 | ___ |
| **8854** | CP Rail GP9 Diesel, *78–79* | 100 | 120 | ___ |
| **8855** | Milwaukee Road SD18 Diesel, *78* | | 115 | ___ |
| **8857** | Northern Pacific U36B Diesel, *78–80* | 140 | 180 | ___ |
| **8858** | Northern Pacific U36B Diesel Dummy Unit, *78–80* | 55 | 85 | ___ |
| **8859** | Conrail Electric Locomotive, *78–82* | 105 | 150 | ___ |
| **8860** | Rock Island NW2 Switcher, *78–79* | 85 | 100 | ___ |
| **8861** | Santa Fe Alco Diesel A Unit, *78–79* | 65 | 85 | ___ |
| **8862** | Santa Fe Alco Diesel B Unit, *78–79* | 36 | 43 | ___ |
| **8864** | New Haven F3 Diesel B Unit, *78* | 85 | 105 | ___ |
| **8866** | M&StL GP9 Diesel (SSS), *78* | 85 | 120 | ___ |
| **8867** | M&StL GP9 Diesel Dummy Unit (SSS), *78* | 65 | 95 | ___ |
| **8868** | Amtrak Budd RDC Baggage, *78, 80* | 195 | 235 | ___ |
| **8869** | Amtrak Budd RDC Passenger Dummy Unit, *78, 80* | 75 | 95 | ___ |
| **8870** | Amtrak Budd RDC Passenger Dummy Unit, *78, 80* | 85 | 115 | ___ |
| **8871** | Amtrak Budd RDC Baggage Dummy Unit, *78, 80* | 85 | 105 | ___ |
| **8872** | Santa Fe SD18 Diesel, *78 u* | 125 | 155 | ___ |
| **8873** | Santa Fe SD18 Diesel Dummy Unit, *78 u* | 60 | 85 | ___ |
| **8900** | Santa Fe 4-6-4 Locomotive (FARR 1), *79* | 270 | 310 | ___ |
| **8902** | ACL 2-4-0 Locomotive, *79–82, 86 u, 87–90* | 13 | 17 | ___ |
| **8903** | D&RGW 2-4-2 Locomotive, *79–81* | 17 | 21 | ___ |
| **8904** | Wabash 2-4-2 Locomotive, *79, 81 u* | 30 | 34 | ___ |
| **8905** | Smokey Mountain Dockside 0-4-0T Locomotive, *79* | 9 | 17 | ___ |
| **8950** | Virginian FM Train Master Diesel, *79* | 230 | 285 | ___ |
| **8951** | Southern Pacific FM Train Master Diesel, *79* | 245 | 338 | ___ |
| **8952/53** | PRR F3 Diesel AA Set, *79* | 350 | 500 | ___ |
| **8955** | Southern U36B Diesel, *79* | 120 | 195 | ___ |
| **8956** | Southern U36B Diesel Dummy Unit, *79* | 80 | 125 | ___ |
| **8957** | Burlington Northern GP20 Diesel, *79* | 120 | 150 | ___ |
| **8958** | Burlington Northern GP20 Diesel Dummy Unit, *79* | 85 | 90 | ___ |
| **8960** | Southern Pacific U36C Diesel, *79 u* | 130 | 180 | ___ |
| **8961** | Southern Pacific U36C Diesel Dummy Unit, *79 u* | 70 | 80 | ___ |
| **8962** | Reading U36B Diesel, *79* | 115 | 130 | ___ |
| **8970/71** | PRR F3 Diesel AA Set, *79 u, 80* | 330 | 425 | ___ |
| **9001** | Conrail Boxcar (027), *86–87 u, 88–90* | 5 | 10 | ___ |
| **9010** | GN Hopper (027), *70–71* | 6 | 8 | ___ |
| **9011** | GN Hopper (027), *70 u, 75–76, 78–83* | 8 | 10 | ___ |
| **9012** | TA&G Hopper (027), *71–72* | 7 | 8 | ___ |
| **9013** | Canadian National Hopper (027), *72–76* | 5 | 8 | ___ |
| **9015** | Reading Hopper (027), *73–75* | 17 | 21 | ___ |
| **9016** | Chessie System Hopper (027), *75–79, 87–88, 89 u* | 4 | 6 | ___ |

Exc  Mint  Cond/S

| | | Exc | Mint | Cond/S |
|---|---|---|---|---|
| **9017** | Wabash Gondola with canisters (027), *78–82* | 3 | 5 | ____ |
| **9018** | DT&I Hopper (027), *78–79, 81–82* | 6 | 7 | ____ |
| **9019** | Flatcar (027), *78* | 2 | 3 | ____ |
| **9020** | Union Pacific Flatcar (027), *70–78* | 3 | 5 | ____ |
| **9021** | Santa Fe Work Caboose, *70–71, 73–75* | 9 | 13 | ____ |
| **9022** | Santa Fe Bulkhead Flatcar (027), *70–72, 75–79* | 7 | 13 | ____ |
| **9023** | MKT Bulkhead Flatcar (027), *73–74* | 7 | 10 | ____ |
| **9024** | C&O Flatcar (027), *73–75* | 3 | 6 | ____ |
| **9025** | DT&I Work Caboose, *71–74, 77–78* | 8 | 10 | ____ |
| **9026** | Republic Steel Flatcar (027), *75–82* | 5 | 7 | ____ |
| **9027** | Soo Line Work Caboose, *75–76* | 7 | 9 | ____ |
| **9030** | Kickapoo Gondola (027), *72, 79* | 5 | 9 | ____ |
| **9031** | NKP Gondola with canisters (027), *73–75, 82–83, 84–91 u* | 4 | 7 | ____ |
| **9032** | SP Gondola with canisters (027), *75–78* | | 3 | ____ |
| **9033** | PC Gondola with canisters (027), *76–78, 82, 86 u, 87–90, 92 u* | | 3 | ____ |
| **9034** | Lionel Leisure Hopper (027), *77 u* | 30 | 34 | ____ |
| **9035** | Conrail Boxcar (027), *78–82* | 5 | 9 | ____ |
| **9036** | Mobilgas 1-D Tank Car (027), *78–82* | 7 | 19 | ____ |
| **9037** | Conrail Boxcar (027), *78 u, 80* | 7 | 10 | ____ |
| **9038** | Chessie System Hopper (027), *78 u, 80* | 15 | 19 | ____ |
| **9039** | Mobilgas 1-D Tank Car (027), *78 u, 80* | 10 | 15 | ____ |
| **9040** | General Mills Wheaties Boxcar (027), *70–72* | 9 | 13 | ____ |
| **9041** | Hershey's Boxcar (027), *70–71, 73–76* | 16 | 25 | ____ |
| **9042** | Ford-Autolite Boxcar (027), *71 u, 72 74–76* | 13 | 21 | ____ |
| **9043** | Erie-Lackawanna Boxcar (027), *73–75* | 13 | 20 | ____ |
| **9044** | D&RGW Boxcar (027), *75–76* | 5 | 8 | ____ |
| **9045** | Toys "R" Us Boxcar (027), *75 u* | 35 | 42 | ____ |
| **9046** | True Value Boxcar (027), *76 u* | 26 | 34 | ____ |
| **9047** | Toys "R" Us Boxcar (027), *76 u* | 40 | 43 | ____ |
| **9048** | Toys "R" Us Boxcar (027), *76 u* | 33 | 41 | ____ |
| **9049** | Toys "R" Us Boxcar (027), *78 u* | | NRS | ____ |
| **9050** | Sunoco 1-D Tank Car (027), *70–71* | 17 | 23 | ____ |
| **9051** | Firestone 1-D Tank Car (027), *74–75, 78* | 15 | 19 | ____ |
| **9052** | Toys "R" Us Boxcar (027), *77 u* | 26 | 34 | ____ |
| **9053** | True Value Boxcar (027), *77 u* | 28 | 40 | ____ |
| **9054** | JCPenney Boxcar (027), *77 u* | 14 | 19 | ____ |
| **9055** | Republic Steel Gondola with canisters, *78 u* | 9 | 10 | ____ |
| **9057** | CP Rail SP-type Caboose, *78–79* | 10 | 15 | ____ |
| **9058** | Lionel Lines SP-type Caboose, *78–79, 83* | 5 | 7 | ____ |
| **9059** | Lionel Lines SP-type Caboose, *79 u, 81 u* | 7 | 9 | ____ |
| **9060** | Nickel Plate Road SP-type Caboose, *70–72* | 5 | 7 | ____ |
| **9061** | Santa Fe SP-type Caboose, *70–76* | 5 | 8 | ____ |
| **9062** | Penn Central SP-type Caboose, *70–72, 74–76* | 5 | 9 | ____ |
| **9063** | GTW SP-type Caboose, *70, 71–73 u* | 15 | 19 | ____ |
| **9064** | C&O SP-type Caboose, *71–72, 75–77* | 7 | 10 | ____ |
| **9065** | Canadian National SP-type Caboose, *71–73 u* | 19 | 24 | ____ |

| | | Exc | Mint | Cond/$ |
|---|---|---|---|---|
| 9066 | Southern SP-type Caboose, 73–76 | 7 | 9 | ____ |
| 9067 | Kickapoo Valley Bobber Caboose, 72 | 6 | 9 | ____ |
| 9068 | Reading Bobber Caboose, 73–76 | 5 | 7 | ____ |
| 9069 | Jersey Central SP-type Caboose, 73–74, 75–76 u | 5 | 8 | ____ |
| 9070 | Rock Island SP-type Caboose, 73–74 | 13 | 17 | ____ |
| 9071 | Santa Fe Bobber Caboose, 74 u, 77–78 | 7 | 9 | ____ |
| 9073 | Coca-Cola SP-type Caboose, 74 u, 75 | 17 | 22 | ____ |
| 9075 | Rock Island SP-type Caboose, 75–76 u | 13 | 17 | ____ |
| 9076 | "We The People" SP-type Caboose, 75 u | 19 | 28 | ____ |
| 9077 | D&RGW SP-type Caboose, 76–83, 84–91 u | 7 | 8 | ____ |
| 9078 | Rock Island Bobber Caboose, 76–77 | 5 | 7 | ____ |
| 9079 | GTW Hopper (O27), 77 | 28 | 32 | ____ |
| 9080 | Wabash SP-type Caboose, 77 | 9 | 10 | ____ |
| 9085 | Santa Fe Work Caboose, 79–82 | 4 | 5 | ____ |
| 9090 | General Mills Mini-Max Car, 71 | 24 | 28 | ____ |
| 9106 | Miller Vat Car, 84–85 | 34 | 48 | ____ |
| 9107 | Dr Pepper Vat Car, 86–87 | 27 | 34 | ____ |
| 9110 | B&O Quad Hopper, 71 | 25 | 30 | ____ |
| 9111 | N&W Quad Hopper, 72–75 | 15 | 20 | ____ |
| 9112 | D&RGW Covered Quad Hopper, 73–75 | 20 | 23 | ____ |
| 9113 | Norfolk & Western Quad Hopper (SSS), 73 | 27 | 32 | ____ |
| 9114 | Morton Salt Covered Quad Hopper, 74–76 | 20 | 27 | ____ |
| 9115 | Planter's Covered Quad Hopper, 74–76 | 21 | 33 | ____ |
| 9116 | Domino Sugar Covered Quad Hopper, 74–76 | 22 | 29 | ____ |
| 9117 | Alaska Covered Quad Hopper (SSS), 74–76 | 29 | 33 | ____ |
| 9119 | Detroit & Mackinac Covered Hopper, 75 u | | 20 | ____ |
| 9120 | Northern Pacific Flatcar with trailers, 70–71 | 33 | 38 | ____ |
| 9121 | L&N Flatcar with bulldozer and scraper, 71–79 | 47 | 50 | ____ |
| 9122 | Northern Pacific Flatcar with trailers, 72–75 | 19 | 32 | ____ |
| 9123 | C&O Auto Carrier, 3-tier, 72 u, 73–74 | 18 | 27 | ____ |
| 9124 | P&LE Flatcar with logs, 73–74 | 18 | 25 | ____ |
| 9125 | Norfolk & Western Auto Carrier, 2-tier, 73–77 | 23 | 28 | ____ |
| 9126 | C&O Auto Carrier, 3-tier, 73–75 | 23 | 34 | ____ |
| 9128 | Heinz Vat Car, 74–76 | 23 | 30 | ____ |
| 9129 | N&W Auto Carrier, 3-tier, 75–76 | 17 | 19 | ____ |
| 9130 | B&O Quad Hopper, 70 | 23 | 24 | ____ |
| 9131 | D&RGW Gondola with canisters, 73–77 | 5 | 8 | ____ |
| 9132 | Libby's Vat Car (SSS), 75–77 | 16 | 23 | ____ |
| 9133 | BN Flatcar with trailers, 76–77, 80 | 20 | 28 | ____ |
| 9134 | Virginian Covered Quad Hopper, 76–77 | | 32 | ____ |
| 9135 | N&W Covered Quad Hopper, 70 u, 71, 75 | 19 | 23 | ____ |
| 9136 | Republic Steel Gondola with canisters, 72–76, 79 | 8 | 11 | ____ |
| 9138 | Sunoco 3-D Tank Car (SSS), 78 | 33 | 37 | ____ |
| 9139 | PC Auto Carrier, 3-tier, 76–77 | 21 | 29 | ____ |
| 9140 | Burlington Gondola with canisters, 70, 73–82, 87–89 | 7 | 9 | ____ |
| 9141 | BN Gondola with canisters, 70–72 | 8 | 10 | ____ |

| | | Exc | Mint | Cond/$ |
|---|---|---|---|---|
| **9143** | CN Gondola with canisters, *71–73 u* | 30 | 34 | ____ |
| **9144** | D&RGW Gondola with canisters (SSS), *74–76* | 9 | 13 | ____ |
| **9145** | ICG Auto Carrier, 3-tier, *77–80* | 21 | 29 | ____ |
| **9146** | Mogen David Vat Car, *77–81* | 21 | 26 | ____ |
| **9147** | Texaco 1-D Tank Car, *77–78* | 39 | 55 | ____ |
| **9148** | Du Pont 3-D Tank Car, *77–81* | 25 | 28 | ____ |
| **9149** | CP Rail Flatcar with trailers, *77–78* | 22 | 35 | ____ |
| **9150** | Gulf 1-D Tank Car, *70 u, 71* | 22 | 28 | ____ |
| **9151** | Shell 1-D Tank Car, *72* | 27 | 31 | ____ |
| **9152** | Shell 1-D Tank Car, *73–76* | 25 | 34 | ____ |
| **9153** | Chevron 1-D Tank Car, *74–76* | 25 | 30 | ____ |
| **9154** | Borden 1-D Tank Car, *75–76* | 33 | 47 | ____ |
| **9156** | Mobilgas 1-D Tank Car, *76–77* | 30 | 40 | ____ |
| **9157** | C&O Crane Car, *76–78, 81–82* | 35 | 44 | ____ |
| **9158** | PC Flatcar with shovel, *76–77, 80* | 40 | 55 | ____ |
| **9159** | Sunoco 1-D Tank Car, *76* | 35 | 50 | ____ |
| **9160** | Illinois Central N5c Caboose, *70–72* | 17 | 23 | ____ |
| **9161** | CN N5c Caboose, *72–74* | 14 | 25 | ____ |
| **9162** | PRR N5c Caboose, *72–76* | 25 | 30 | ____ |
| **9163** | Santa Fe N5c Caboose, *73–76* | 17 | 24 | ____ |
| **9165** | Canadian Pacific N5c Caboose (SSS), *73* | 21 | 30 | ____ |
| **9166** | D&RGW SP-type Caboose (SSS), *74–75* | 20 | 25 | ____ |
| **9167** | Chessie System N5c Caboose, *74–76* | 24 | 31 | ____ |
| **9168** | Union Pacific N5c Caboose, *75–77* | 17 | 19 | ____ |
| **9169** | Milwaukee Road SP-type Caboose (SSS), *75* | 16 | 19 | ____ |
| **9170** | N&W N5c Caboose "1776," *75* | 27 | 30 | ____ |
| **9171** | MP SP-type Caboose, *75 u, 76–77* | 19 | 20 | ____ |
| **9172** | Penn Central SP-type Caboose, *75 u, 76–77* | 23 | 31 | ____ |
| **9173** | Jersey Central SP-type Caboose, *75 u, 76–77* | 22 | 33 | ____ |
| **9174** | NYC (P&E) Bay Window Caboose, *76* | 65 | 70 | ____ |
| **9175** | Virginian N5c Caboose, *76–77* | 24 | 26 | ____ |
| **9176** | BAR N5c Caboose, *76 u* | 18 | 30 | ____ |
| **9177** | Northern Pacific Bay Window Caboose (SSS), *76* | 25 | 35 | ____ |
| **9178** | ICG SP-type Caboose, *76–77* | 19 | 24 | ____ |
| **9179** | Chessie System Bobber Caboose, *76* | 7 | 11 | ____ |
| **9180** | Rock Island N5c Caboose, *77–78* | 12 | 23 | ____ |
| **9181** | B&M N5c Caboose, *76 u, 77* | 39 | 49 | ____ |
| **9182** | N&W N5c Caboose, *76 u, 77–80* | 20 | 26 | ____ |
| **9183** | Mickey Mouse N5c Caboose, *77–78* | 32 | 50 | ____ |
| **9184** | Erie Bay Window Caboose, *77–78* | 24 | 30 | ____ |
| **9185** | GTW N5c Caboose, *77* | 21 | 28 | ____ |
| **9186** | Conrail N5c Caboose, *76 u, 77–78* | 27 | 29 | ____ |
| **9187** | Gulf, Mobile & Ohio SP-type Caboose, *77* | 10 | 16 | ____ |
| **9188** | GN Bay Window Caboose, *77* | 22 | 27 | ____ |
| **9189** | Gulf 1-D Tank Car, *77* | 40 | 60 | ____ |
| **9193** | Budweiser Vat Car, *83–84* | 83 | 108 | ____ |
| **9200** | Illinois Central Boxcar, *70–71* | 19 | 25 | ____ |

| | | Exc | Mint | Cond/S |
|---|---|---|---|---|
| 9201 | Penn Central Boxcar, 70 | 17 | 25 | ____ |
| 9202 | Santa Fe Boxcar, 70 | 20 | 24 | ____ |
| 9203 | Union Pacific Boxcar, 70 | | 21 | ____ |
| 9204 | Northern Pacific Boxcar, 70 | | 21 | ____ |
| 9205 | Norfolk & Western Boxcar, 70 | 22 | 25 | ____ |
| 9206 | Great Northern Boxcar, 70–71 | | 20 | ____ |
| 9207 | Soo Line Boxcar, 71 | 11 | 18 | ____ |
| 9208 | CP Rail Boxcar, 71 | 21 | 23 | ____ |
| 9209 | Burlington Northern Boxcar, 71–72 | 16 | 21 | ____ |
| 9210 | B&O DD Boxcar, 71 | 16 | 20 | ____ |
| 9211 | Penn Central Boxcar, 71 | 17 | 28 | ____ |
| 9213 | M&StL Covered Quad Hopper (SSS), 78 | 20 | 29 | ____ |
| 9214 | Northern Pacific Boxcar, 71–72 | 16 | 21 | ____ |
| 9215 | Norfolk & Western Boxcar, 71 | 19 | 24 | ____ |
| 9216 | Great Northern Auto Carrier, 3-tier, 78 | 25 | 39 | ____ |
| 9217 | Soo Line Operating Boxcar, 82–84 | 29 | 36 | ____ |
| 9218 | Monon Operating Boxcar, 81 | 25 | 30 | ____ |
| 9219 | Missouri Pacific Operating Boxcar, 83 | 27 | 33 | ____ |
| 9220 | Borden Operating Milk Car, 83–86 | 95 | 113 | ____ |
| 9221 | Poultry Dispatch Operating Chicken Car, 83–85 | 45 | 50 | ____ |
| 9222 | L&N Flatcar with trailers, 83–84 | 38 | 60 | ____ |
| 9223 | Reading Operating Boxcar, 84 | 33 | 40 | ____ |
| 9224 | Churchill Downs Operating Horse Car, 84–86 | 85 | 110 | ____ |
| 9225 | Conrail Operating Barrel Car, 84 | 42 | 55 | ____ |
| 9226 | Delaware & Hudson Flatcar with trailers, 84–85 | 31 | 34 | ____ |
| 9228 | Canadian Pacific Operating Boxcar, 86 | 24 | 37 | ____ |
| 9229 | Express Mail Operating Boxcar, 85–86 | 21 | 27 | ____ |
| 9230 | Monon Boxcar (SSS), 71, 72 u | 17 | 24 | ____ |
| 9231 | Reading Bay Window Caboose, 79 | 24 | 32 | ____ |
| 9232 | Allis-Chalmers Condenser Car, 80–81, 83 u | 42 | 50 | ____ |
| 9233 | Depressed Center Flatcar with transformer, 80 | 55 | 65 | ____ |
| 9234 | Radioactive Waste Car, 80 | 50 | 75 | ____ |
| 9235 | Union Pacific Derrick Car, 83–84 | 16 | 22 | ____ |
| 9236 | C&NW Derrick Car, 83–85 | 22 | 30 | ____ |
| 9238 | Northern Pacific Log Dump Car, 84 | 16 | 24 | ____ |
| 9239 | Lionel Lines N5c Caboose, 83 u | 50 | 60 | ____ |
| 9240 | NYC Hopper (O27), 87 u | 20 | 29 | ____ |
| 9240 | NYC Operating Hopper, 86 | 32 | 39 | ____ |
| 9241 | PRR Log Dump Car, 85–86 | 21 | 27 | ____ |
| 9250 | WaterPoxy 3-D Tank Car, 70–71 | 23 | 26 | ____ |
| 9260 | Reynolds Aluminum Covered Quad Hopper, 75–77 | 19 | 22 | ____ |
| 9261 | Sun-Maid Raisins Covered Quad Hopper, 75 u, 76 | 20 | 26 | ____ |
| 9262 | Ralston Purina Covered Quad Hopper, 75 u, 76 | 34 | 55 | ____ |
| 9263 | PRR Covered Quad Hopper, 75 u, 76–77 | 23 | 30 | ____ |
| 9264 | Illinois Central Covered Quad Hopper, 75 u, 76–77 | 28 | 39 | ____ |

| | | Exc | Mint | Cond/$ |
|---|---|---|---|---|
| 9265 | Chessie System Covered Quad Hopper, *75 u, 76–77* | 21 | 27 | \_\_\_\_ |
| 9266 | Southern "Big John" Covered Quad Hopper, *76* | 46 | 65 | \_\_\_\_ |
| 9267 | Alcoa Covered Quad Hopper (SSS), *76* | 20 | 25 | \_\_\_\_ |
| 9268 | Northern Pacific Bay Window Caboose, *77 u* | 33 | 40 | \_\_\_\_ |
| 9269 | Milwaukee Road Bay Window Caboose, *78* | 34 | 47 | \_\_\_\_ |
| 9270 | Northern Pacific N5c Caboose, *78* | 14 | 27 | \_\_\_\_ |
| 9271 | M&StL Bay Window Caboose (SSS), *78–79* | 18 | 30 | \_\_\_\_ |
| 9272 | New Haven Bay Window Caboose, *78–80* | 20 | 34 | \_\_\_\_ |
| 9273 | Southern Bay Window Caboose, *78 u* | 36 | 45 | \_\_\_\_ |
| 9274 | Santa Fe Bay Window Caboose, *78 u* | 40 | 47 | \_\_\_\_ |
| 9276 | Peabody Quad Hopper, *78* | 19 | 28 | \_\_\_\_ |
| 9277 | Cities Service 1-D Tank Car, *78* | 41 | 45 | \_\_\_\_ |
| 9278 | Life Savers 1-D Tank Car, *78–79* | 105 | 145 | \_\_\_\_ |
| 9279 | Magnolia 3-D Tank Car, *78, 79 u* | 13 | 19 | \_\_\_\_ |
| 9280 | Santa Fe Operating Stock Car (027), *77–81* | 20 | 24 | \_\_\_\_ |
| 9281 | Santa Fe Auto Carrier, 3-tier, *78–80* | 21 | 27 | \_\_\_\_ |
| 9282 | GN Flatcar with trailers, *78–79, 81–82* | 22 | 28 | \_\_\_\_ |
| 9283 | Union Pacific Gondola with canisters, *77* | 15 | 21 | \_\_\_\_ |
| 9284 | Santa Fe Gondola with canisters, *77* | 16 | 27 | \_\_\_\_ |
| 9285 | ICG Flatcar with trailers, *77* | 47 | 48 | \_\_\_\_ |
| 9286 | B&LE Covered Quad Hopper, *77* | 14 | 26 | \_\_\_\_ |
| 9287 | Southern N5c Caboose, *77 u, 78* | 18 | 30 | \_\_\_\_ |
| 9288 | Lehigh Valley N5c Caboose, *77 u, 78, 80* | 25 | 31 | \_\_\_\_ |
| 9289 | C&NW N5c Caboose, *77 u, 78, 80* | 25 | 36 | \_\_\_\_ |
| 9290 | Union Pacific Operating Barrel Car, *83* | 65 | 75 | \_\_\_\_ |
| 9300 | PC Log Dump Car, *70–75, 77* | 18 | 24 | \_\_\_\_ |
| 9301 | U.S. Mail Operating Boxcar, *73–84* | 32 | 42 | \_\_\_\_ |
| 9302 | L&N Searchlight Car, *72 u, 73–78* | 21 | 24 | \_\_\_\_ |
| 9303 | Union Pacific Log Dump Car, *74–78, 80* | 17 | 22 | \_\_\_\_ |
| 9304 | C&O Coal Dump Car, *74–78* | 12 | 23 | \_\_\_\_ |
| 9305 | Santa Fe Operating Cowboy Car (027), *80–82* | 16 | 23 | \_\_\_\_ |
| 9306 | Santa Fe Flatcar with horses, *80–82* | 18 | 26 | \_\_\_\_ |
| 9307 | Erie Gondola, animated, *80–84* | 55 | 70 | \_\_\_\_ |
| 9308 | Aquarium Car, *81–84* | 125 | 129 | \_\_\_\_ |
| 9309 | TP&W Bay Window Caboose, *80–81, 83 u* | 19 | 25 | \_\_\_\_ |
| 9310 | Santa Fe Log Dump Car, *78 u, 79–83* | 13 | 24 | \_\_\_\_ |
| 9311 | Union Pacific Coal Dump Car, *78 u, 79–82* | 13 | 24 | \_\_\_\_ |
| 9312 | Conrail Searchlight Car, *78 u, 79–83* | 18 | 27 | \_\_\_\_ |
| 9313 | Gulf 3-D Tank Car, *79 u* | 43 | 50 | \_\_\_\_ |
| 9315 | Southern Pacific Gondola with canisters, *79 u* | 16 | 23 | \_\_\_\_ |
| 9316 | Southern Pacific Bay Window Caboose, *79 u* | 47 | 50 | \_\_\_\_ |
| 9317 | Santa Fe Bay Window Caboose, *79* | 21 | 36 | \_\_\_\_ |
| 9320 | Fort Knox Mint Car, *79 u* | 110 | 135 | \_\_\_\_ |
| 9321 | Santa Fe 1-D Tank Car (FARR 1), *79* | 25 | 31 | \_\_\_\_ |
| 9322 | Santa Fe Covered Quad Hopper (FARR 1), *79* | 30 | 38 | \_\_\_\_ |
| 9323 | Santa Fe Bay Window Caboose (FARR 1), *79* | 39 | 49 | \_\_\_\_ |
| 9324 | Tootsie Roll 1-D Tank Car, *79–81* | 63 | 88 | \_\_\_\_ |

| | | Exc | Mint | Cond/$ |
|---|---|---|---|---|
| 9325 | Norfolk & Western Flatcar with fences, *79–81 u* | 6 | 10 | ____ |
| 9326 | Burlington Northern Bay Window Caboose, *79–80* | 34 | 44 | ____ |
| 9327 | Bakelite 3-D Tank Car, *80* | 19 | 29 | ____ |
| 9328 | Chessie System Bay Window Caboose, *80* | 33 | 42 | ____ |
| 9329 | Chessie System Crane Car, *80* | 40 | 47 | ____ |
| 9330 | Kickapoo Dump Car, *72, 79* | 3 | 7 | ____ |
| 9331 | Union 76 1-D Tank Car, *79* | 39 | 44 | ____ |
| 9332 | Reading Crane Car, *79* | 37 | 50 | ____ |
| 9333 | Southern Pacific Flatcar with trailers, *79–80* | 33 | 47 | ____ |
| 9334 | Humble 1-D Tank Car, *79* | 21 | 26 | ____ |
| 9335 | B&O Log Dump Car, *86* | 16 | 22 | ____ |
| 9336 | CP Rail Gondola with canisters, *79* | 20 | 29 | ____ |
| 9338 | Pennsylvania Power & Light Quad Hopper, *79* | 60 | 75 | ____ |
| 9339 | GN Boxcar (027), *79–83, 85 u, 86* | 7 | 10 | ____ |
| 9340 | Illinois Central Gondola with canisters (027), *79–81, 82 u, 83* | 5 | 9 | ____ |
| 9341 | ACL SP-type Caboose, *79–82, 86 u 87–90* | 6 | 8 | ____ |
| 9344 | Citgo 3-D Tank Car, *80* | 23 | 38 | ____ |
| 9345 | Reading Searchlight Car, *84–85* | 20 | 25 | ____ |
| 9346 | Wabash SP-type Caboose, *79* | 6 | 10 | ____ |
| 9348 | Santa Fe Crane Car (FARR 1), *79 u* | 60 | 70 | ____ |
| 9349 | San Francisco Mint Car, *80* | 55 | 70 | ____ |
| 9351 | PRR Auto Carrier, 3-tier, *80* | 23 | 40 | ____ |
| 9352 | Trailer Train Flatcar with C&NW trailers, *80* | 29 | 55 | ____ |
| 9353 | Crystal Line 3-D Tank Car, *80* | 18 | 26 | ____ |
| 9354 | Pennzoil 1-D Tank Car, *80, 81 u* | 60 | 85 | ____ |
| 9355 | Delaware & Hudson Bay Window Caboose, *80* | 37 | 45 | ____ |
| 9357 | Smokey Mountain Bobber Caboose, *79* | 8 | 10 | ____ |
| 9359 | National Basketball Association Boxcar (027), *79–80 u* | 19 | 24 | ____ |
| 9360 | National Hockey League Boxcar (027), *79–80 u* | 21 | 26 | ____ |
| 9361 | C&NW Bay Window Caboose, *80* | 47 | 50 | ____ |
| 9362 | Major League Baseball Boxcar (027), *79–80 u* | 17 | 21 | ____ |
| 9363 | N&W Log Dump Car "9325" (027), *79* | 4 | 7 | ____ |
| 9364 | N&W Crane Car "9325" (027), *79* | 7 | 9 | ____ |
| 9365 | Toys "R" Us Boxcar (027), *79 u* | 30 | 37 | ____ |
| 9366 | UP Covered Quad Hopper (FARR 2), *80* | 19 | 23 | ____ |
| 9367 | Union Pacific 1-D Tank Car (FARR 2), *80* | 21 | 30 | ____ |
| 9368 | Union Pacific Bay Window Caboose (FARR 2), *80* | 30 | 36 | ____ |
| 9369 | Sinclair 1-D Tank Car, *80* | 60 | 85 | ____ |
| 9370 | Seaboard Gondola with canisters, *80* | 19 | 21 | ____ |
| 9371 | Atlantic Sugar Covered Quad Hopper, *80* | 19 | 22 | ____ |
| 9372 | Seaboard Bay Window Caboose, *80* | 30 | 41 | ____ |
| 9373 | Getty 1-D Tank Car, *80–81, 83 u* | 31 | 42 | ____ |
| 9374 | Reading Covered Quad Hopper, *80–81, 83 u* | 39 | 40 | ____ |
| 9376 | Soo Line Boxcar (027), *81 u* | 40 | 50 | ____ |
| 9378 | Derrick Car, *80–82* | 18 | 22 | ____ |

| | | Exc | Mint | Cond/$ |
|---|---|---|---|---|
| 9379 | Santa Fe Gondola with canisters, *80–81, 83 u* | 22 | 30 | ____ |
| 9380 | NYNH&H SP-type Caboose, *80–81* | 9 | 10 | ____ |
| 9381 | Chessie System SP-type Caboose, *80* | 7 | 9 | ____ |
| 9382 | Florida East Coast Bay Window Caboose, *80* | 34 | 48 | ____ |
| 9383 | UP Flatcar with trailers (FARR 2), *80 u* | 27 | 34 | ____ |
| 9384 | Great Northern Operating Hopper, *81* | 50 | 55 | ____ |
| 9385 | Alaska Gondola with canisters, *81* | 27 | 34 | ____ |
| 9386 | Pure Oil 1-D Tank Car, *81* | 38 | 50 | ____ |
| 9387 | Burlington Bay Window Caboose, *81* | 46 | 52 | ____ |
| 9388 | Toys "R" Us Boxcar (027), *81 u* | 38 | 45 | ____ |
| 9389 | Radioactive Waste Car, *81–82* | 60 | 75 | ____ |
| 9398 | PRR Coal Dump Car, *83–84* | 28 | 38 | ____ |
| 9399 | C&NW Coal Dump Car, *83–85* | 17 | 22 | ____ |
| 9400 | Conrail Boxcar, *78* | 14 | 20 | ____ |
| 9401 | Great Northern Boxcar, *78* | 18 | 23 | ____ |
| 9402 | Susquehanna Boxcar, *78* | 30 | 33 | ____ |
| 9403 | Seaboard Coast Line Boxcar, *78* | 12 | 17 | ____ |
| 9404 | NKP Boxcar, *78* | 19 | 21 | ____ |
| 9405 | Chattahoochee Boxcar, *78* | 14 | 19 | ____ |
| 9406 | D&RGW Boxcar, *78–79* | 17 | 21 | ____ |
| 9407 | Union Pacific Stock Car, *78* | 24 | 25 | ____ |
| 9408 | Lionel Lines Circus Stock Car (SSS), *78* | 31 | 40 | ____ |
| 9411 | Lackawanna Phoebe Snow Boxcar, *78* | 35 | 43 | ____ |
| 9412 | RF&P Boxcar, *79* | 21 | 27 | ____ |
| 9413 | Napierville Junction Boxcar, *79* | 18 | 24 | ____ |
| 9414 | Cotton Belt Boxcar, *79* | 19 | 23 | ____ |
| 9415 | Providence & Worcester Boxcar, *79* | 17 | 25 | ____ |
| 9416 | MD&W Boxcar, *79, 81* | 13 | 19 | ____ |
| 9417 | CP Rail Boxcar, *79* | 45 | 50 | ____ |
| 9418 | FARR Boxcar, *79 u* | 50 | 60 | ____ |
| 9419 | Union Pacific Boxcar (FARR 2), *80* | 15 | 17 | ____ |
| 9420 | B&O Sentinel Boxcar, *80* | 25 | 28 | ____ |
| 9421 | Maine Central Boxcar, *80* | 10 | 17 | ____ |
| 9422 | EJ&E Boxcar, *80* | 12 | 20 | ____ |
| 9423 | NYNH&H Boxcar, *80* | 14 | 22 | ____ |
| 9424 | TP&W Boxcar, *80* | 17 | 21 | ____ |
| 9425 | British Columbia DD Boxcar, *80* | 27 | 35 | ____ |
| 9426 | Chesapeake & Ohio Boxcar, *80* | 19 | 30 | ____ |
| 9427 | Bay Line Boxcar, *80–81* | 12 | 17 | ____ |
| 9428 | TP&W Boxcar, *80–81, 83 u* | | 23 | ____ |
| 9429 | "The Early Years" Boxcar, *80* | 20 | 27 | ____ |
| 9430 | "The Standard Gauge Years" Boxcar, *80* | 22 | 25 | ____ |
| 9431 | "The Prewar Years" Boxcar, *80* | 20 | 25 | ____ |
| 9432 | "The Postwar Years" Boxcar, *80* | 50 | 55 | ____ |
| 9433 | "The Golden Years" Boxcar, *80* | 33 | 43 | ____ |
| 9434 | Joshua Lionel Cowen "The Man" Boxcar, *80 u* | 29 | 37 | ____ |
| 9436 | Burlington Boxcar, *81* | 25 | 30 | ____ |
| 9437 | Northern Pacific Stock Car, *81* | 22 | 36 | ____ |

| | | Exc | Mint | Cond/$ |
|---|---|---|---|---|
| **9438** | Ontario Northland Boxcar, *81* | 25 | 31 | ___ |
| **9439** | Ashley Drew & Northern Boxcar, *81* | 11 | 19 | ___ |
| **9440** | Reading Boxcar, *81* | 50 | 65 | ___ |
| **9441** | Pennsylvania Boxcar, *81* | 32 | 42 | ___ |
| **9442** | Canadian Pacific Boxcar, *81* | 13 | 21 | ___ |
| **9443** | Florida East Coast Boxcar, *81* | 19 | 24 | ___ |
| **9444** | Louisiana Midland Boxcar, *81* | 14 | 18 | ___ |
| **9445** | Vermont Northern Boxcar, *81* | 14 | 17 | ___ |
| **9446** | Sabine River & Northern Boxcar, *81* | 15 | 21 | ___ |
| **9447** | Pullman Standard Boxcar, *81* | 16 | 21 | ___ |
| **9448** | Santa Fe Stock Car, *81–82* | 34 | 40 | ___ |
| **9449** | Great Northern Boxcar (FARR 3), *81* | 27 | 31 | ___ |
| **9450** | Great Northern Stock Car (FARR 3), *81 u* | 50 | 60 | ___ |
| **9451** | Southern Boxcar (FARR 4), *83* | 26 | 32 | ___ |
| **9452** | Western Pacific Boxcar, *82–83* | 12 | 16 | ___ |
| **9453** | MPA Boxcar, *82–83* | 14 | 19 | ___ |
| **9454** | New Hope & Ivyland Boxcar, *82–83* | 21 | 27 | ___ |
| **9455** | Milwaukee Road Boxcar, *82–83* | 15 | 19 | ___ |
| **9456** | PRR DD Boxcar (FARR 5), *84–85* | 24 | 30 | ___ |
| **9461** | Norfolk & Southern Boxcar, *82* | 25 | 43 | ___ |
| **9462** | Southern Pacific Boxcar, *83–84* | 18 | 23 | ___ |
| **9463** | Texas & Pacific Boxcar, *83–84* | 15 | 19 | ___ |
| **9464** | NC&StL Boxcar, *83–84* | 16 | 22 | ___ |
| **9465** | Santa Fe Boxcar, *83–84* | 12 | 19 | ___ |
| **9466** | Wanamaker Boxcar, *82 u* | 60 | 70 | ___ |
| **9467** | Tennessee World's Fair Boxcar, *82 u* | 26 | 31 | ___ |
| **9468** | Union Pacific DD Boxcar, *83* | 31 | 34 | ___ |
| **9469** | NYC Pacemaker Boxcar (std O), *84–85* | 37 | 53 | ___ |
| **9470** | Chicago Beltline Boxcar, *84* | 15 | 20 | ___ |
| **9471** | Atlantic Coast Line Boxcar, *84* | 13 | 19 | ___ |
| **9472** | Detroit & Mackinac Boxcar, *84* | 22 | 26 | ___ |
| **9473** | Lehigh Valley Boxcar, *84* | 24 | 28 | ___ |
| **9474** | Erie-Lackawanna Boxcar, *84* | 31 | 35 | ___ |
| **9475** | D&H "I Love NY" Boxcar, *84 u* | 28 | 37 | ___ |
| **9476** | PRR Boxcar (FARR 5), *84–85* | 27 | 36 | ___ |
| **9480** | MN&S Boxcar, *85–86* | 15 | 18 | ___ |
| **9481** | Seaboard System Boxcar, *85–86* | 15 | 18 | ___ |
| **9482** | Norfolk & Southern Boxcar, *85–86* | 13 | 17 | ___ |
| **9483** | Manufacturers Railway Boxcar, *85–86* | 14 | 19 | ___ |
| **9484** | Lionel 85th Anniversary Boxcar, *85* | 22 | 26 | ___ |
| **9486** | GTW "I Love Michigan" Boxcar, *86* | 23 | 34 | ___ |
| **9490** | Christmas Boxcar for Lionel Employees, *85 u* | | 1750 | ___ |
| **9491** | Christmas Boxcar, *86 u* | 26 | 37 | ___ |
| **9492** | Lionel Lines Boxcar, *86* | 23 | 29 | ___ |
| **9500** | Milwaukee Road Passenger Coach, *73* | 28 | 75 | ___ |
| **9501** | Milwaukee Road Passenger Coach, *73 u, 74–76* | 33 | 37 | ___ |
| **9502** | Milwaukee Road Observation Car, *73* | 30 | 48 | ___ |

| | | Exc | Mint | Cond/$ |
|---|---|---|---|---|
| 9503 | Milwaukee Road Passenger Coach, *73* | 33 | 48 | ____ |
| 9504 | Milwaukee Road Passenger Coach, *73 u, 74–76* | 33 | 37 | ____ |
| 9505 | Milwaukee Road Passenger Coach, *73 u, 74–76* | 35 | 38 | ____ |
| 9506 | Milwaukee Road Combination Car, *74 u, 75–76* | 32 | 37 | ____ |
| 9507 | PRR Passenger Coach, *74–75* | 34 | 55 | ____ |
| 9508 | PRR Passenger Coach, *74–75* | 32 | 50 | ____ |
| 9509 | PRR Observation Car, *74–75* | 41 | 60 | ____ |
| 9510 | PRR Combination Car, *74 u, 75–76* | 30 | 47 | ____ |
| 9511 | Milwaukee Road Passenger Coach, *74 u* | 33 | 48 | ____ |
| 9513 | PRR Passenger Coach, *75–76* | 25 | 44 | ____ |
| 9514 | PRR Passenger Coach, *75–76* | 23 | 36 | ____ |
| 9515 | PRR Passenger Coach, *75–76* | 22 | 34 | ____ |
| 9516 | B&O Passenger Coach, *76* | 27 | 42 | ____ |
| 9517 | B&O Passenger Coach, *75* | 45 | 65 | ____ |
| 9518 | B&O Observation Car, *75* | 45 | 65 | ____ |
| 9519 | B&O Combination Car, *75* | 55 | 85 | ____ |
| 9521 | PRR Baggage Car, *75 u, 76* | 65 | 95 | ____ |
| 9522 | Milwaukee Road Baggage Car, *75 u, 76* | 65 | 80 | ____ |
| 9523 | B&O Baggage Car, *75 u, 76* | 60 | 70 | ____ |
| 9524 | B&O Passenger Coach, *76* | 27 | 37 | ____ |
| 9525 | B&O Passenger Coach, *76* | 30 | 43 | ____ |
| 9527 | Milwaukee Road Campaign Observation Car, *76 u* | 50 | 75 | ____ |
| 9528 | PRR Campaign Observation Car, *76 u* | 65 | 95 | ____ |
| 9529 | B&O Campaign Observation Car, *76 u* | 44 | 70 | ____ |
| 9530 | Southern Baggage Car, *77–78* | 45 | 65 | ____ |
| 9531 | Southern Combination Car, *77–78* | 29 | 37 | ____ |
| 9532 | Southern Passenger Coach, *77–78* | 33 | 47 | ____ |
| 9533 | Southern Passenger Coach, *77–78* | 27 | 38 | ____ |
| 9534 | Southern Observation Car, *77–78* | 31 | 47 | ____ |
| 9536 | *Blue Comet* Baggage Car, *78–80* | 39 | 55 | ____ |
| 9537 | *Blue Comet* Combination Car, *78–80* | 35 | 50 | ____ |
| 9538 | *Blue Comet* Passenger Coach, *78–80* | 35 | 47 | ____ |
| 9539 | *Blue Comet* Passenger Coach, *78–80* | 35 | 48 | ____ |
| 9540 | *Blue Comet* Observation Car, *78–80* | 27 | 40 | ____ |
| 9541 | Santa Fe Baggage Car, *80–82* | 21 | 30 | ____ |
| 9545 | Union Pacific Baggage Car, *84* | 135 | 200 | ____ |
| 9546 | Union Pacific Combination Car, *84* | 85 | 105 | ____ |
| 9547 | Union Pacific Observation Car, *84* | 85 | 105 | ____ |
| 9548 | UP *Placid Bay* Passenger Coach, *84* | 90 | 110 | ____ |
| 9549 | UP *Ocean Sunset* Passenger Coach, *84* | 85 | 105 | ____ |
| 9551 | W&ARR Baggage Car, *77 u, 78–80* | 36 | 48 | ____ |
| 9552 | W&ARR Passenger Coach, *77 u, 78–80* | 46 | 60 | ____ |
| 9553 | W&ARR Flatcar with horses, *77 u, 78–80* | 32 | 50 | ____ |
| 9554 | Chicago & Alton Baggage Car, *81* | 55 | 85 | ____ |
| 9555 | Chicago & Alton Combination Car, *81* | 50 | 75 | ____ |
| 9556 | Chicago & Alton *Wilson* Passenger Coach, *81* | 50 | 75 | ____ |

| | | Exc | Mint | Cond/$ |
|---|---|---|---|---|
| 9557 | Chicago & Alton *Webster Groves* Passenger Coach, *81* | 45 | 65 | ____ |
| 9558 | Chicago & Alton Observation Car, *81* | 50 | 75 | ____ |
| 9559 | Rock Island Baggage Car, *81–82* | 42 | 65 | ____ |
| 9560 | Rock Island Passenger Coach, *81–82* | 43 | 65 | ____ |
| 9561 | Rock Island Passenger Coach, *81–82* | 42 | 65 | ____ |
| 9562 | N&W Baggage Car "577," *81* | 80 | 110 | ____ |
| 9563 | N&W Combination Car "578," *81* | 80 | 105 | ____ |
| 9564 | N&W Passenger Coach "579," *81* | 90 | 100 | ____ |
| 9565 | N&W Passenger Coach "580," *81* | 85 | 100 | ____ |
| 9566 | N&W Observation Car "581," *81* | 90 | 95 | ____ |
| 9567 | N&W Vista Dome Car "582," *81 u* | 160 | 255 | ____ |
| 9569 | PRR Combination Car, *81 u* | 115 | 160 | ____ |
| 9570 | PRR Baggage Car, *79* | 85 | 115 | ____ |
| 9571 | PRR Passenger Coach, *79* | 125 | 145 | ____ |
| 9572 | PRR Passenger Coach, *79* | 110 | 125 | ____ |
| 9573 | PRR Vista Dome Car, *79* | 95 | 120 | ____ |
| 9574 | PRR Observation Car, *79* | 75 | 100 | ____ |
| 9575 | PRR Passenger Coach, *79–80 u* | 100 | 135 | ____ |
| 9576 | Burlington Baggage Car, *80* | 145 | 175 | ____ |
| 9577 | Burlington Passenger Coach, *80* | 95 | 105 | ____ |
| 9578 | Burlington Passenger Coach, *80* | 105 | 110 | ____ |
| 9579 | Burlington Vista Dome Car, *80* | 95 | 110 | ____ |
| 9580 | Burlington Observation Car, *80* | 95 | 110 | ____ |
| 9581 | Chessie System Baggage Car, *80* | 55 | 62 | ____ |
| 9582 | Chessie System Combination Car, *80* | 47 | 55 | ____ |
| 9583 | Chessie System Passenger Coach, *80* | 40 | 47 | ____ |
| 9584 | Chessie System Passenger Coach, *80* | 31 | 37 | ____ |
| 9585 | Chessie System Observation Car, *80* | 55 | 65 | ____ |
| 9586 | Chessie System Diner, *86 u* | 85 | 90 | ____ |
| 9588 | Burlington Vista Dome Car, *80 u* | 110 | 120 | ____ |
| 9589 | Southern Pacific Baggage Car, *82–83* | 110 | 135 | ____ |
| 9590 | Southern Pacific Combination Car, *82–83* | 90 | 105 | ____ |
| 9591 | Southern Pacific Pullman Passenger Coach, *82–83* | 85 | 105 | ____ |
| 9592 | Southern Pacific Pullman Passenger Coach, *82–83* | 85 | 105 | ____ |
| 9593 | Southern Pacific Observation Car, *82–83* | 100 | 130 | ____ |
| 9594 | NYC Baggage Car, *83–84* | 105 | 130 | ____ |
| 9595 | NYC Combination Car, *83–84* | 75 | 85 | ____ |
| 9596 | NYC *Wayne County* Passenger Coach, *83–84* | 80 | 95 | ____ |
| 9597 | NYC *Hudson River* Passenger Coach, *83–84* | 70 | 85 | ____ |
| 9598 | NYC Observation Car, *83–84* | 75 | 85 | ____ |
| 9599 | Chicago & Alton Diner, *86 u* | 80 | 90 | ____ |
| 9600 | Chessie System Hi-Cube Boxcar, *75 u, 76–77* | 19 | 25 | ____ |
| 9601 | ICG Hi-Cube Boxcar, *75 u, 76–77* | 20 | 21 | ____ |
| 9602 | Santa Fe Hi-Cube Boxcar, *75 u, 76–77* | 17 | 20 | ____ |
| 9603 | Penn Central Hi-Cube Boxcar, *76–77* | 17 | 18 | ____ |
| 9604 | Norfolk & Western Hi-Cube Boxcar, *76–77* | 23 | 26 | ____ |

| | | Exc | Mint | Cond/$ |
|---|---|---|---|---|
| **9605** | NH Hi-Cube Boxcar, *76–77* | 17 | 21 | ____ |
| **9606** | Union Pacific Hi-Cube Boxcar, *76 u, 77* | 16 | 17 | ____ |
| **9607** | Southern Pacific Hi-Cube Boxcar, *76 u, 77* | 12 | 15 | ____ |
| **9608** | Burlington Northern Hi-Cube Boxcar, *76 u, 77* | 21 | 23 | ____ |
| **9610** | Frisco Hi-Cube Boxcar, *77* | 25 | 34 | ____ |
| **9620** | NHL Wales Boxcar, *80* | 27 | 35 | ____ |
| **9621** | NHL Campbell Boxcar, *80* | 27 | 34 | ____ |
| **9622** | NBA Western Boxcar, *80* | 24 | 30 | ____ |
| **9623** | NBA Eastern Boxcar, *80* | 26 | 34 | ____ |
| **9624** | National League Baseball Boxcar, *80* | 27 | 34 | ____ |
| **9625** | American League Baseball Boxcar, *80* | 27 | 35 | ____ |
| **9626** | Santa Fe Hi-Cube Boxcar, *82–84* | 10 | 14 | ____ |
| **9627** | Union Pacific Hi-Cube Boxcar, *82–83* | 15 | 21 | ____ |
| **9628** | Burlington Northern Hi-Cube Boxcar, *82–84* | 14 | 19 | ____ |
| **9629** | Chessie System Hi-Cube Boxcar, *83–84* | 23 | 34 | ____ |
| **9660** | Mickey Mouse Hi-Cube Boxcar, *77–78* | 25 | 37 | ____ |
| **9661** | Goofy Hi-Cube Boxcar, *77–78* | 49 | 56 | ____ |
| **9662** | Donald Duck Hi-Cube Boxcar, *77–78* | 34 | 46 | ____ |
| **9663** | Dumbo Hi-Cube Boxcar, *77 u, 78* | 40 | 55 | ____ |
| **9664** | Cinderella Hi-Cube Boxcar, *77 u, 78* | 55 | 85 | ____ |
| **9665** | Peter Pan Hi-Cube Boxcar, *77 u, 78* | 48 | 75 | ____ |
| **9666** | Pinocchio Hi-Cube Boxcar, *78* | 105 | 155 | ____ |
| **9667** | Snow White Hi-Cube Boxcar, *78* | 338 | 445 | ____ |
| **9668** | Pluto Hi-Cube Boxcar, *78* | 145 | 185 | ____ |
| **9669** | Bambi Hi-Cube Boxcar, *78 u* | 65 | 100 | ____ |
| **9670** | *Alice In Wonderland* Hi-Cube Boxcar, *78 u* | 60 | 90 | ____ |
| **9671** | *Fantasia* Hi-Cube Boxcar, *78 u* | 55 | 90 | ____ |
| **9672** | Mickey Mouse 50th Anniversary Hi-Cube Boxcar, *78 u* | 350 | 415 | ____ |
| **9700** | Southern Boxcar, *72–73* | 22 | 30 | ____ |
| **9701** | B&O DD Boxcar, *72* | 14 | 19 | ____ |
| **9702** | Soo Line Boxcar, *72–73* | 15 | 21 | ____ |
| **9703** | CP Rail Boxcar, *72* | 34 | 44 | ____ |
| **9704** | Norfolk & Western Boxcar, *72* | 10 | 17 | ____ |
| **9705** | D&RGW Boxcar, *72* | 13 | 20 | ____ |
| **9706** | C&O Boxcar, *72* | 17 | 19 | ____ |
| **9707** | MKT Stock Car, *72–75* | 14 | 22 | ____ |
| **9708** | U.S. Mail Boxcar, *72–75* | 18 | 23 | ____ |
| **9708** | U.S. Mail Toy Fair Boxcar, *73 u* | 85 | 95 | ____ |
| **9709** | BAR State of Maine Boxcar (SSS), *72–74* | 29 | 32 | ____ |
| **9710** | Rutland Boxcar (SSS), *72–74* | 24 | 28 | ____ |
| **9711** | Southern Boxcar, *74–75* | 19 | 25 | ____ |
| **9712** | B&O DD Boxcar, *73–74* | 31 | 34 | ____ |
| **9713** | CP Rail Boxcar, *73–74* | 24 | 30 | ____ |
| **9713** | CP Rail "Season's Greetings" Boxcar, *74 u* | 95 | 120 | ____ |
| **9714** | D&RGW Boxcar, *73–74* | 16 | 20 | ____ |
| **9715** | C&O Boxcar, *73–74* | 17 | 22 | ____ |
| **9716** | Penn Central Boxcar, *73–74* | 15 | 20 | ____ |

| | | Exc | Mint | Cond/$ |
|---|---|---|---|---|
| 9717 | Union Pacific Boxcar, *73–74* | 21 | 25 | ____ |
| 9718 | Canadian National Boxcar, *73–74* | 23 | 31 | ____ |
| 9719 | New Haven DD Boxcar, *73 u* | 23 | 32 | ____ |
| 9723 | Western Pacific Boxcar (SSS), *73–74* | 27 | 29 | ____ |
| 9723 | Western Pacific Toy Fair Boxcar, *74 u* | 20 | 60 | ____ |
| 9724 | Missouri Pacific Boxcar (SSS), *73–74* | 21 | 24 | ____ |
| 9725 | MKT Stock Car (SSS), *73–75* | 15 | 18 | ____ |
| 9726 | Erie-Lackawanna Boxcar (SSS), *78* | 25 | 30 | ____ |
| 9729 | CP Rail Boxcar, *78* | | 34 | ____ |
| 9730 | CP Rail Boxcar, *74–75* | 23 | 27 | ____ |
| 9731 | Milwaukee Road Boxcar, *74–75* | 16 | 21 | ____ |
| 9732 | Southern Pacific Boxcar, *79 u* | 24 | 31 | ____ |
| 9734 | Bangor & Aroostook Boxcar, *79* | 30 | 38 | ____ |
| 9735 | Grand Trunk Western Boxcar, *74–75* | 15 | 21 | ____ |
| 9737 | Vermont Central Boxcar, *74–76* | 27 | 34 | ____ |
| 9738 | Illinois Terminal Boxcar, *82* | 43 | 45 | ____ |
| 9739 | D&RGW Boxcar (SSS), *74–76* | 17 | 25 | ____ |
| 9740 | Chessie System Boxcar, *74–75* | 15 | 19 | ____ |
| 9742 | M&StL Boxcar, *73 u* | 17 | 19 | ____ |
| 9742 | M&StL "Season's Greetings" Boxcar, *73 u* | 85 | 105 | ____ |
| 9743 | Sprite Boxcar, *74 u, 75* | 19 | 27 | ____ |
| 9744 | Tab Boxcar, *74 u, 75* | 17 | 24 | ____ |
| 9745 | Fanta Boxcar, *74 u, 75* | 19 | 29 | ____ |
| 9747 | Chessie System DD Boxcar, *75–76* | 24 | 28 | ____ |
| 9748 | CP Rail Boxcar, *75–76* | 16 | 20 | ____ |
| 9749 | Penn Central Boxcar, *75–76* | 16 | 21 | ____ |
| 9750 | DT&I Boxcar, *75–76* | 13 | 15 | ____ |
| 9751 | Frisco Boxcar, *75–76* | 21 | 23 | ____ |
| 9752 | L&N Boxcar, *75–76* | 20 | 23 | ____ |
| 9753 | Maine Central Boxcar, *75–76* | 16 | 22 | ____ |
| 9754 | NYC Pacemaker Boxcar (SSS), *75–77* | 20 | 30 | ____ |
| 9755 | Union Pacific Boxcar, *75–76* | 20 | 24 | ____ |
| 9757 | Central of Georgia Boxcar, *74 u* | 16 | 19 | ____ |
| 9758 | Alaska Boxcar (SSS), *75–77* | 24 | 31 | ____ |
| 9759 | Paul Revere Boxcar, *75 u* | 36 | 43 | ____ |
| 9760 | Liberty Bell Boxcar, *75 u* | 30 | 40 | ____ |
| 9761 | George Washington Boxcar, *75 u* | 36 | 43 | ____ |
| 9762 | Toy Fair Boxcar, *75 u* | 125 | 170 | ____ |
| 9763 | D&RGW Stock Car, *76–77* | 15 | 20 | ____ |
| 9764 | GTW DD Boxcar, *76–77* | 40 | 55 | ____ |
| 9767 | Railbox Boxcar, *76–77* | 15 | 20 | ____ |
| 9768 | B&M Boxcar, *76–77* | 18 | 27 | ____ |
| 9769 | B&LE Boxcar, *76–77* | 17 | 21 | ____ |
| 9770 | Northern Pacific Boxcar, *76–77* | 14 | 18 | ____ |
| 9771 | Norfolk & Western Boxcar, *76–77* | 16 | 24 | ____ |
| 9772 | Great Northern Boxcar, *76* | 60 | 85 | ____ |
| 9773 | NYC Stock Car, *76* | 32 | 39 | ____ |
| 9775 | M&StL Boxcar (SSS), *76* | 19 | 23 | ____ |

| | | Exc | Mint | Cond/$ |
|---|---|---|---|---|
| 9776 | SP Overnight Boxcar (SSS), *76* | 32 | 34 | ____ |
| 9777 | Virginian Boxcar, *76–77* | 22 | 25 | ____ |
| 9778 | "Season's Greetings" Boxcar, *75 u* | 165 | 185 | ____ |
| 9780 | Johnny Cash Boxcar, *76 u* | 50 | 54 | ____ |
| 9781 | Delaware & Hudson Boxcar, *77–78* | 19 | 23 | ____ |
| 9782 | Rock Island Boxcar, *77–78* | 14 | 17 | ____ |
| 9783 | B&O Time-Saver Boxcar, *77–78* | 25 | 27 | ____ |
| 9784 | Santa Fe Boxcar, *77–78* | 13 | 17 | ____ |
| 9785 | Conrail Boxcar, *77–78* | 20 | 23 | ____ |
| 9786 | C&NW Boxcar, *77–79* | 18 | 27 | ____ |
| 9787 | Jersey Central Boxcar, *77–79* | 18 | 19 | ____ |
| 9788 | Lehigh Valley Boxcar, *77–79* | 17 | 21 | ____ |
| 9789 | Pickens Boxcar, *77* | 25 | 33 | ____ |
| 9801 | B&O Sentinel Boxcar (std 0), *73–75* | 18 | 26 | ____ |
| 9802 | Miller High Life Reefer (std 0), *73–75* | 28 | 33 | ____ |
| 9803 | Johnson Wax Boxcar (std 0), *73–75* | 27 | 33 | ____ |
| 9805 | Grand Trunk Western Reefer (std 0), *73–75* | 30 | 31 | ____ |
| 9806 | Rock Island Boxcar (std 0), *74–75* | 38 | 46 | ____ |
| 9807 | Stroh's Beer Reefer (std 0), *74–76* | 60 | 70 | ____ |
| 9808 | Union Pacific Boxcar (std 0), *75–76* | 36 | 50 | ____ |
| 9809 | Clark Reefer (std 0), *75–76* | 33 | 41 | ____ |
| 9811 | Pacific Fruit Express Reefer (FARR 2), *80* | 26 | 33 | ____ |
| 9812 | Arm & Hammer Reefer, *80* | 24 | 30 | ____ |
| 9813 | Ruffles Reefer, *80* | 18 | 26 | ____ |
| 9814 | Perrier Reefer, *80* | 21 | 30 | ____ |
| 9815 | NYC "Early Bird" Reefer (std 0), *84–85* | 34 | 40 | ____ |
| 9816 | Brach's Candy Reefer, *80* | 21 | 26 | ____ |
| 9817 | Bazooka Bubble Gum Reefer, *80* | 24 | 31 | ____ |
| 9818 | Western Maryland Reefer, *80* | 18 | 23 | ____ |
| 9819 | Western Fruit Express Reefer (FARR 3), *81* | 22 | 29 | ____ |
| 9820 | Wabash Gondola with coal (std 0), *73–74* | 24 | 38 | ____ |
| 9821 | SP Gondola with coal (std 0), *73–75* | 28 | 32 | ____ |
| 9822 | GTW Gondola with coal (std 0), *74–75* | 24 | 29 | ____ |
| 9823 | Santa Fe Flatcar with crates (std 0), *75–76* | 34 | 44 | ____ |
| 9824 | NYC Gondola with coal (std 0), *75–76* | 41 | 56 | ____ |
| 9825 | Schaefer Reefer (std 0), *76–77* | 45 | 60 | ____ |
| 9826 | P&LE Boxcar (std 0), *76–77* | 34 | 39 | ____ |
| 9827 | Cutty Sark Reefer, *84* | 29 | 37 | ____ |
| 9828 | J&B Reefer, *84* | 29 | 38 | ____ |
| 9829 | Dewar's White Label Reefer, *84* | 29 | 37 | ____ |
| 9830 | Johnnie Walker Red Label Reefer, *84* | 29 | 38 | ____ |
| 9831 | Pepsi Cola Reefer, *82* | 68 | 78 | ____ |
| 9832 | Cheerios Reefer, *82* | 147 | 171 | ____ |
| 9833 | Vlasic Pickles Reefer, *82* | 23 | 29 | ____ |
| 9834 | Southern Comfort Reefer, *83–84* | 25 | 42 | ____ |
| 9835 | Jim Beam Reefer, *83–84* | 32 | 47 | ____ |
| 9836 | Old Grand-Dad Reefer, *83–84* | 29 | 41 | ____ |
| 9837 | Wild Turkey Reefer, *83–84* | 51 | 80 | ____ |

| | | Exc | Mint | Cond/$ |
|---|---|---|---|---|
| **9840** | Fleischmann's Gin Reefer, *85* | 33 | 37 | ____ |
| **9841** | Calvert Gin Reefer, *85* | 33 | 38 | ____ |
| **9842** | Seagram's Gin Reefer, *85* | 33 | 37 | ____ |
| **9843** | Tanqueray Gin Reefer, *85* | 34 | 38 | ____ |
| **9844** | Sambuca Reefer, *86* | 33 | 43 | ____ |
| **9845** | Baileys Irish Cream Reefer, *86* | 48 | 74 | ____ |
| **9846** | Seagram's Vodka Reefer, *86* | 31 | 39 | ____ |
| **9847** | Wolfschmidt Vodka Reefer, *86* | 33 | 38 | ____ |
| **9849** | Lionel Lines Reefer, *83 u* | 30 | 32 | ____ |
| **9850** | Budweiser Reefer, *72 u, 73–75* | 48 | 58 | ____ |
| **9851** | Schlitz Reefer, *72 u, 73–75* | 28 | 34 | ____ |
| **9852** | Miller Reefer, *72 u, 73–77* | 32 | 38 | ____ |
| **9853** | Cracker Jack Reefer, *72 u, 73–75* | | | |
| | (A) Caramel-colored body | 29 | 34 | ____ |
| | (B) White body, black logo border | 23 | 28 | ____ |
| **9854** | Baby Ruth Reefer, *72 u, 73–76* | 22 | 26 | ____ |
| **9855** | Swift Reefer, *72 u, 73–77* | 23 | 28 | ____ |
| **9856** | Old Milwaukee Reefer, *75–76* | 30 | 37 | ____ |
| **9858** | Butterfinger Reefer, *73 u, 74–76* | 21 | 26 | ____ |
| **9859** | Pabst Reefer, *73 u, 74–75* | 34 | 41 | ____ |
| **9860** | Gold Medal Reefer, *73 u, 74–76* | 12 | 21 | ____ |
| **9861** | Tropicana Reefer, *75–77* | 23 | 35 | ____ |
| **9862** | Hamm's Reefer, *75–76* | 28 | 39 | ____ |
| **9863** | REA Reefer (SSS), *74–76* | 24 | 28 | ____ |
| **9866** | Coors Reefer, *76–77* | 40 | 55 | ____ |
| **9867** | Hershey's Reefer, *76–77* | 63 | 73 | ____ |
| **9869** | Santa Fe Reefer (SSS), *76* | 32 | 37 | ____ |
| **9870** | Old Dutch Cleanser Reefer, *77–78, 80* | 15 | 21 | ____ |
| **9871** | Carling Black Label Reefer, *77–78, 80* | 33 | 45 | ____ |
| **9872** | Pacific Fruit Express Reefer, *77–79* | 24 | 28 | ____ |
| **9873** | Ralston Purina Reefer, *78* | 30 | 38 | ____ |
| **9874** | Miller Lite Beer Reefer, *78–79* | 43 | 54 | ____ |
| **9875** | A&P Reefer, *78–79* | 23 | 31 | ____ |
| **9876** | Vermont Central Reefer, *78* | 26 | 31 | ____ |
| **9877** | Gerber Reefer, *79–80* | 65 | 75 | ____ |
| **9878** | Good and Plenty Reefer, *79* | 24 | 31 | ____ |
| **9879** | Hills Bros. Reefer, *79–80* | 23 | 29 | ____ |
| **9880** | Santa Fe Reefer (FARR 1), *79* | 27 | 31 | ____ |
| **9881** | Rath Packing Reefer, *79 u* | 23 | 31 | ____ |
| **9882** | NYC "Early Bird" Reefer, *79* | 25 | 29 | ____ |
| **9883** | Nabisco Oreo Reefer, *79* | 80 | 85 | ____ |
| **9884** | Fritos Reefer, *81–82* | 24 | 33 | ____ |
| **9885** | Lipton Tea Reefer, *81–82* | 30 | 38 | ____ |
| **9886** | Mounds Reefer, *81–82* | 24 | 30 | ____ |
| **9887** | Fruit Growers Express Reefer (FARR 4), *83* | 29 | 38 | ____ |
| **9888** | Green Bay & Western Reefer, *83* | 42 | 49 | ____ |
| **11000** | Holiday Express Freight Set, *08* | | 280 | ____ |
| **11004** | NASCAR Diesel Freight Set, *06–07* | | 300 | ____ |

| | | | |
|---|---|---|---|
| **11005** | Dale Earnhardt Jr. Diesel Freight Set, *06–07* | 240 | ____ |
| **11006** | Kasey Kahne Expansion Pack, *06–07* | 130 | ____ |
| **11006** | Lionel Lion Set, *03 u* | 230 | ____ |
| **11007** | Dale Earnhardt Sr. Expansion Pack, *06–07* | 130 | ____ |
| **11008** | Dale Earnhardt Jr. Expansion Pack, *06–07* | 130 | ____ |
| **11009** | Tony Stewart Expansion Pack, *06–07* | 130 | ____ |
| **11010** | Jimmie Johnson Expansion Pack, *06–07* | 130 | ____ |
| **11011** | Jeff Gordon Expansion Pack, *06–07* | 130 | ____ |
| **11020** | Harry Potter *Hogwarts Express* Steam Passenger Set, *08–10* | 330 | ____ |
| **11025** | Jimmie Johnson 2006 Champion Boxcar, *07* | 45 | ____ |
| **11038** | Snow-covered Straight Track 4-pack, *08* | 14 | ____ |
| **11041** | Holiday Calliope Car, *08* | 45 | ____ |
| **11067** | Lionel Bear, *08* | 25 | ____ |
| **11077** | Harry Potter Figures, *08* | 27 | ____ |
| **11096** | Engineer Hat, *08* | 15 | ____ |
| **11098** | Holiday Toy Soldier Car, *08* | 50 | ____ |
| **11100** | PRR 2-8-2 Mikado Locomotive "9631," CC, *07* | 370 | ____ |
| **11101** | LL 2-8-4 Berkshire Locomotive "737," CC, *06* | 350 | ____ |
| **11103** | Southern PS-4 4-6-2 Pacific Locomotive "1403," CC, *06* | 1000 | ____ |
| **11104** | UP Big Boy Locomotive "4014," CC, *06* | 1700 | ____ |
| **11105** | NYC L-2A 4-8-2 Mohawk Locomotive "2770," CC, *06* | 1100 | ____ |
| **11107** | LionMaster SP Cab Forward Locomotive "4276," RailSounds, *06–07* | 850 | ____ |
| **11108** | C&O F-19 4-6-2 Pacific Locomotive "494," CC, *06–07* | 1160 | ____ |
| **11109** | C&O 0-8-0 Locomotive "79," TrainSounds, *06* | 420 | ____ |
| **11110** | NYC 0-8-0 Locomotive "7805," TrainSounds, *06* | 420 | ____ |
| **11116** | UP 4-8-4 FEF-3 Locomotive "844," gray, CC, *08–09* | 1160 | ____ |
| **11117** | Santa Fe E6 4-4-2 Atlantic Locomotive "1484," CC, *07–09* | 600 | ____ |
| **11119** | Southern 0-8-0 Locomotive "6535," TrainSounds, *07* | 420 | ____ |
| **11122** | UP Big Boy Locomotive "4024," CC, *06* | 1700 | ____ |
| **11123** | UP Big Boy Locomotive "4023," CC, *06* | 1700 | ____ |
| **11127** | SP GS-4 4-8-4 Northern Locomotive "4436," CC, *07–09* | 1200 | ____ |
| **11128** | C&O F-19 4-6-2 Pacific Locomotive "490," CC, *07* | 1160 | ____ |
| **11131** | UP 4-8-4 FEF-3 Locomotive "844," black, CC, *08–09* | 1160 | ____ |
| **11132** | Reading 2-8-0 Consolidation Locomotive "1914," RailSounds, *08* | 450 | ____ |
| **11133** | NYC 2-8-0 Consolidation Locomotive "1149," RailSounds, *08* | 450 | ____ |
| **11134** | WM 2-8-0 Consolidation Locomotive "729," RailSounds, *08* | 450 | ____ |
| **11135** | B&O 2-8-0 Consolidation Locomotive "2784," RailSounds, *08* | 450 | ____ |

Exc  Mint  Cond/$

| | | Exc | Mint | Cond/$ |
|---|---|---|---|---|
| 11136 | WP 2-8-2 Mikado Locomotive "322," CC, *08* | | 800 | ___ |
| 11137 | UP 2-8-2 Mikado Locomotive "1925," CC, *08* | | 800 | ___ |
| 11138 | ATSF 2-8-2 Mikado Locomotive "3156," CC, *08* | | 800 | ___ |
| 11139 | MILW 2-8-2 Mikado Locomotive "462," CC, *08* | | 800 | ___ |
| 11140 | Cass Scenic Shay Locomotive "7," CC, *07* | | 800 | ___ |
| 11141 | Birch Valley Lumber Shay Locomotive "5," CC, *07* | | 800 | ___ |
| 11142 | *Hogwarts Express* Add-on 2-pack, *09–10* | | 120 | ___ |
| 11143 | SP AC-4 Cab Forward Locomotive "4100," CC, *08* | | 1670 | ___ |
| 11146 | Pere Marquette 2-8-4 Berkshire Locomotive "1225," CC, *08* | | 1290 | ___ |
| 11147 | PRR 4-8-2 Mib Locomotive "6750," CC, *08* | | 1290 | ___ |
| 11148 | NYC Dreyfuss J-3a 4-6-4 Hudson Locomotive "5448," CC, *08* | | 1130 | ___ |
| 11149 | LionMaster UP Big Boy 4-8-8-4 Locomotive "4006," CC, *08* | | 860 | ___ |
| 11150 | NYC F-12e 4-6-0 10-wheel Locomotive "827," CC, *08* | | 700 | ___ |
| 11151 | *Polar Express* Tender, RailSounds, *08–10* | | 440 | ___ |
| 11152 | D&RGW LionMaster 4-6-6-4 Challenger Locomotive "3805," CC, *09* | | 900 | ___ |
| 11153 | Stourbridge Lion Steam Locomotive, *09–10* | | 430 | ___ |
| 11154 | PRR CC2s 0-8-8-0 Mallet Locomotive "8183," CC, *09–10* | | 2000 | ___ |
| 11155 | ATSF 2-10-10-2 Mallet Locomotive "3000," CC, *09–10* | | 2500 | ___ |
| 11156 | C&O 4-6-0 Ten-Wheeler Locomotive, CC, *10* | | 740 | ___ |
| 11157 | WM Shay Locomotive "6," CC, *10* | | 800 | ___ |
| 11162 | Lone Ranger Add-on 3-pack, *10* | | 165 | ___ |
| 11164 | Dewitt Clinton Passenger Set, *10* | | 630 | ___ |
| 11165 | Dewitt Clinton Add-on Coach, *10* | | 700 | ___ |
| 11166 | CSX Merger Freight 2-pack #1, *10* | | 130 | ___ |
| 11167 | CSX Merger Freight 2-pack #2, *10* | | 105 | ___ |
| 11168 | CSX Merger Freight 2-pack #3, *10* | | 130 | ___ |
| 11169 | Strasburg Freight Add-on 2-pack, *10* | | 100 | ___ |
| 11170 | Three Rivers Fast Freight Set, *10* | | 400 | ___ |
| 11173 | Texan Freight Add-on 2-pack, *10* | | 130 | ___ |
| 11174 | Maple Leaf Freight Add-on 2-pack, *10* | | 110 | ___ |
| 11175 | Operation Eagle Justice Add-on 2-pack, *10* | | 125 | ___ |
| 11200 | UP LionMaster Challenger Locomotive "3985," CC, *10* | | 900 | ___ |
| 11201 | WM LionMaster Challenger Locomotive "1204," CC, *10* | | 900 | ___ |
| 11202 | CP 4-6-0 Ten-Wheeler Locomotive "914," CC, *10* | | 740 | ___ |
| 11203 | Pere Marquette Berkshire Locomotive "1225," CC, *09* | | 980 | ___ |
| 11204 | Pere Marquette Tender, RailSounds, *09* | | 440 | ___ |
| 11207 | PRR LionMaster T1 Duplex Locomotive "5511," CC, *10* | | 800 | ___ |

## MODERN ERA 1970-2011

| | | Exc | Mint | Cond/$ |
|---|---|---|---|---|
| 11208 | UP LionMaster Big Boy Locomotive "4011," CC, *10* | | 900 | ____ |
| 11209 | Vision NYC Hudson Locomotive "5344," CC, *10* | | 1600 | ____ |
| 11210 | UP Challenger Locomotive "3967," CC, *10* | | 1825 | ____ |
| 11211 | UP 4-6-6-4 Challenger Locomotive "3976," CC, *10* | | 1825 | ____ |
| 11212 | NKP Berkshire Locomotive "765," CC, *10* | | 1400 | ____ |
| 11215 | LV 4-6-0 Camelback Locomotive "1598," CC, *10* | | 550 | ____ |
| 11216 | Jersey Central 4-6-0 Camelback Locomotive, CC, *10* | | 550 | ____ |
| 11217 | PRR 4-6-0 Camelback Locomotive "822," CC, *10* | | 550 | ____ |
| 11218 | Vision NYC Hudson Locomotive "5331," CC, *10* | | 1600 | ____ |
| 11219 | Clinchfield Challenger Locomotive "672," CC, *10* | | 1825 | ____ |
| 11220 | UP Challenger Locomotive "3989," CC, *10* | | 1825 | ____ |
| 11221 | UP Challenger Locomotive "3983," CC, *10* | | 1825 | ____ |
| 11650 | Alderney Dairy General American Milk Car 2-pack (std O), *07* | | 130 | ____ |
| 11651 | Freeport General American Milk Car 2-pack (std O), *07* | | 130 | ____ |
| 11652 | BNSF Mechanical Refrigerator Car 2-pack (std O), *07–09* | | 140 | ____ |
| 11653 | SPFE Mechanical Refrigerator Car 2-pack (std O), *07* | | 140 | ____ |
| 11654 | UPFE Mechanical Refrigerator Car 2-pack (std O), *07* | | 140 | ____ |
| 11655 | GN WFE Mechanical Refrigerator Car 2-pack (std O), *07* | | 140 | ____ |
| 11657 | PFE Wood-sided Reefer 3-pack (std O), *06* | | 190 | ____ |
| 11658 | *John Bull* Add-on Coach, *08* | | 80 | ____ |
| 11700 | Conrail Limited Set, *87* | 320 | 370 | ____ |
| 11701 | Rail Blazer Set, *87–88* | | 60 | ____ |
| 11702 | Black Diamond Set, *87* | 195 | 265 | ____ |
| 11703 | Iron Horse Freight Set, *88–91* | 100 | 105 | ____ |
| 11704 | Southern Freight Runner Set (SSS), *87* | 210 | 285 | ____ |
| 11705 | Chessie System Unit Train, *88* | 360 | 450 | ____ |
| 11706 | Dry Gulch Line Set (SSS), *88* | 190 | 260 | ____ |
| 11707 | Silver Spike Set, *88–89* | 175 | 245 | ____ |
| 11708 | Midnight Shift Set, *88 u, 89* | 60 | 75 | ____ |
| 11710 | CP Rail Freight Set, *89* | 375 | 447 | ____ |
| 11711 | Santa Fe F3 Diesel ABA Set, *91* | 480 | 590 | ____ |
| 11712 | Great Lakes Express Set (SSS), *90* | 260 | 280 | ____ |
| 11713 | Santa Fe Dash 8-40B Set, *90* | 395 | 480 | ____ |
| 11714 | Badlands Express Set, *90–91* | 49 | 60 | ____ |
| 11715 | Lionel 90th Anniversary Set, *90* | 296 | 324 | ____ |
| 11716 | Lionelville Circus Special Set, *90–91* | 155 | 190 | ____ |
| 11717 | CSX Freight Set, *90* | 230 | 240 | ____ |
| 11718 | Norfolk Southern Dash 8-40C Unit Train, *92* | 445 | 481 | ____ |
| 11719 | Coastal Freight Set (SSS), *91* | 165 | 215 | ____ |

| | | Exc | Mint | Cond/$ |
|---|---|---|---|---|
| 11720 | Santa Fe Special Set, *91* | 49 | 60 | ____ |
| 11721 | Mickey's World Tour Train Set, *91, 92 u* | 115 | 155 | ____ |
| 11722 | Girl's Train Set, *91* | 545 | 815 | ____ |
| 11723 | Amtrak Maintenance Train, *91, 92 u* | 210 | 245 | ____ |
| 11724 | GN F3 Diesel ABA Set, *92* | 730 | 840 | ____ |
| 11726 | Erie-Lackawanna Freight Set, *91 u* | 225 | 275 | ____ |
| 11727 | Coastal Limited Set, *92* | 90 | 110 | ____ |
| 11728 | High Plains Runner Set, *92* | 120 | 130 | ____ |
| 11733 | Feather River Set (SSS), *92* | 285 | 330 | ____ |
| 11734 | Erie Alco Diesel ABA Set (FF 7), *93* | 250 | 305 | ____ |
| 11735 | NYC Flyer Freight Set "1735WS," *93–99* | 125 | 160 | ____ |
| 11736 | Union Pacific Express Set, *93–95* | 110 | 130 | ____ |
| 11738 | Soo Line Set (SSS), *93* | 250 | 280 | ____ |
| 11739 | *Super Chief* Set, *93–94* | 135 | 155 | ____ |
| 11740 | Conrail Consolidated Set, *93* | 200 | 240 | ____ |
| 11741 | Northwest Express Set, *93* | 130 | 155 | ____ |
| 11742 | Coastal Limited Set, *93 u* | 90 | 115 | ____ |
| 11743 | Chesapeake & Ohio Freight Set, *94* | 240 | 280 | ____ |
| 11744 | NYC Passenger/Freight Set (SSS), *94* | 295 | 335 | ____ |
| 11745 | U.S. Navy Set, *94–95* | 240 | 283 | ____ |
| 11746 | Seaboard Freight Set, *94, 95 u* | 90 | 115 | ____ |
| 11747 | Lionel Lines Steam Set, *95* | 310 | 340 | ____ |
| 11748 | Amtrak Alco Diesel Passenger Set, *95–96* | 130 | 185 | ____ |
| 11749 | Western Maryland Set (SSS), *95* | 275 | 300 | ____ |
| 11750 | McDonald's Nickel Plate Special Set, *87 u* | 143 | 153 | ____ |
| 11751 | Sears PRR Passenger Set, *87 u* | 120 | 155 | ____ |
| 11752 | JCPenney Timber Master Set, *87 u* | 75 | 115 | ____ |
| 11753 | Kay Bee Toys Rail Blazer Set, *87 u* | 80 | 100 | ____ |
| 11754 | Key America Set, *87 u* | 150 | 165 | ____ |
| 11755 | Timber Master Set, *87 u* | 150 | 165 | ____ |
| 11756 | Hawthorne Freight Flyer Set, *87–88 u* | 65 | 85 | ____ |
| 11757 | Chrysler Mopar Express Set, *88 u* | 288 | 335 | ____ |
| 11758 | Desert King Set (SSS), *89* | 195 | 250 | ____ |
| 11759 | JCPenney Silver Spike Set, *88 u* | 175 | 250 | ____ |
| 11761 | JCPenney Iron Horse Freight Set, *88 u* | 120 | 125 | ____ |
| 11762 | True Value Cannonball Express Set, *89 u* | 95 | 145 | ____ |
| 11763 | United Model Freight Hauler Set, *88 u* | 135 | 145 | ____ |
| 11764 | Sears Iron Horse Freight Set, *88 u* | 155 | 190 | ____ |
| 11765 | Spiegel Silver Spike Set, *88 u* | 175 | 250 | ____ |
| 11767 | Shoprite Freight Flyer Set, *88 u* | 80 | 125 | ____ |
| 11769 | JCPenney Midnight Shift Set, *89 u* | 100 | 175 | ____ |
| 11770 | Sears Circus Set, *89 u* | 185 | 220 | ____ |
| 11771 | K-Mart Microracers Set, *89 u* | 80 | 110 | ____ |
| 11772 | Macy's Freight Flyer Set, *89 u* | 170 | 220 | ____ |
| 11773 | Sears NYC Passenger Set, *89 u* | 175 | 200 | ____ |
| 11774 | Ace Hardware Cannonball Express Set, *89 u* | 145 | 175 | ____ |
| 11775 | Anheuser-Busch Set, *89–92 u* | 228 | 323 | ____ |
| 11776 | Pace Iron Horse Freight Set, *89 u* | 115 | 135 | ____ |

| | | Exc | Mint | Cond/$ |
|---|---|---|---|---|
| 11777 | Sears Lionelville Circus Set, *90 u* | 175 | 190 | ____ |
| 11778 | Sears Badlands Express Set, *90 u* | 49 | 60 | ____ |
| 11779 | Sears CSX Freight Set, *90 u* | 190 | 230 | ____ |
| 11780 | Sears NP Passenger Set, *90 u* | 155 | 190 | ____ |
| 11781 | True Value Cannonball Express Set, *90 u* | 75 | 115 | ____ |
| 11783 | Toys "R" Us Heavy Iron Set, *90–91 u* | 135 | 160 | ____ |
| 11784 | Pace Iron Horse Freight Set, *90 u* | 115 | 135 | ____ |
| 11785 | Costco Union Pacific Express Set, *90 u* | 200 | 230 | ____ |
| 11789 | Sears Illinois Central Passenger Set, *91 u* | 170 | 200 | ____ |
| 11793 | Santa Fe Set, *91 u* | 49 | 60 | ____ |
| 11794 | Mickey's World Tour Set, *91 u* | 80 | 100 | ____ |
| 11796 | Union Pacific Express Set, *91 u* | 150 | 160 | ____ |
| 11797 | Sears Coastal Limited Set, *92 u* | 80 | 100 | ____ |
| 11800 | Toys "R" Us Heavy Iron Thunder Limited Set, *92–93 u* | 235 | 295 | ____ |
| 11803 | Nickel Plate Special Set, *92 u* | 135 | 145 | ____ |
| 11804 | K-Mart Coastal Limited Set, *92 u* | 80 | 100 | ____ |
| 11809 | Village Trolley Set, *95–97* | 55 | 85 | ____ |
| 11810 | Budweiser Modern Era Set, *93–94 u* | 194 | 201 | ____ |
| 11811 | United Auto Workers Set, *93 u* | 185 | 443 | ____ |
| 11812 | Coastal Limited Special Set, *93 u* | 95 | 115 | ____ |
| 11813 | Crayola Activity Train Set, *94 u, 95* | 95 | 115 | ____ |
| 11814 | Ford Limited Edition Set, *94 u* | 196 | 243 | ____ |
| 11818 | Chrysler Mopar Set, *94 u* | 212 | 246 | ____ |
| 11819 | Georgia Power Set, *95 u* | 502 | 527 | ____ |
| 11820 | Red Wing Shoes NYC Flyer Set, *95 u* | 248 | 300 | ____ |
| 11821 | Sears Zenith Set, *95 u* | | 755 | ____ |
| 11822 | Chevrolet Set, *96 u* | 268 | 307 | ____ |
| 11825 | Bloomingdale's Set, *96 u* | | 313 | ____ |
| 11826 | Sears Freight Set, *95–96 u* | | 755 | ____ |
| 11827 | Zenith Employees Set, *96 u* | | 755 | ____ |
| 11828 | NJ Transit Passenger Set, *96 u* | | 180 | ____ |
| 11833 | NJ Transit GP38 Diesel Passenger Set, *97* | 275 | 300 | ____ |
| 11837 | Union Pacific GP9 Diesel Set, *97* | | 520 | ____ |
| 11838 | ATSF Warhorse Hudson Freight Set, *97* | | 810 | ____ |
| 11839 | SP&S 4-6-2 Steam Freight Set, *97* | | 280 | ____ |
| 11841 | Bloomingdale's Set, *97 u* | | 287 | ____ |
| 11843 | Boston & Maine GP9 Diesel ABA Set, *98* | | 510 | ____ |
| 11844 | Union Pacific Die-cast Ore Cars 4-pack, *98* | | 225 | ____ |
| 11846 | Kal Kan Pet Care Train Set, *97 u* | | 763 | ____ |
| 11849 | Lionel Centennial Series Reefer 4-pack, *98* | | 105 | ____ |
| 11850 | Rice A Roni Trolley Set, *02 u* | | 260 | ____ |
| 11851 | PFE Reefer 6-pack (std O), *02* | 225 | 255 | ____ |
| 11852 | Clinchfield PS-2 2-bay Hopper, *04* | | 70 | ____ |
| 11853 | B&M PS-2 2-bay Hopper 2-pack, *05* | | 110 | ____ |
| 11854 | N&W PS-2 Covered Hopper 2-pack, *04* | | 70 | ____ |
| 11855 | GN Offset Hopper with coal, 2-pack, *05* | | 120 | ____ |
| 11856 | Green Bay & Western Offset Hopper 2-pack, *05* | | 120 | ____ |

| | | Exc | Mint | Cond/$ |
|---|---|---|---|---|
| **11857** | Baltimore & Ohio Offset Hopper 2-pack, *05* | | 120 | ___ |
| **11858** | PRR PS-4 Flatcar with trailers, 2-pack (std O), *05* | | 160 | ___ |
| **11859** | GN PS-4 Flatcar with trailers (std O), *05* | | 160 | ___ |
| **11860** | SP PS-4 Flatcar with trailers (std O), *05* | | 160 | ___ |
| **11861** | C&O PS-4 Flatcar with trailers (std O), *05* | | 160 | ___ |
| **11863** | Southern Pacific GP9 Diesel "2383," *98* | | 225 | ___ |
| **11864** | New York Central GP9 Diesel "2383," *98* | | 275 | ___ |
| **11865** | Alaska GP7 Diesel "1802," *98–99* | | 90 | ___ |
| **11866** | Govt. of Canada Cylindrical Hopper 2-pack (std O), *05* | | 120 | ___ |
| **11867** | CN Cylindrical Hopper 2-pack (std O), *05* | | 120 | ___ |
| **11868** | BN Husky Stack Car 2-pack (std O), *05* | | 160 | ___ |
| **11869** | SP Husky Stack Car 2-pack (std O), *05* | | 160 | ___ |
| **11870** | CSX Husky Stack Car 2-pack (std O), *05* | | 220 | ___ |
| **11871** | TTX Trailer Train Stack Car 2-pack (std O), *05* | | 160 | ___ |
| **11872** | PFE Orange Steel-sided Reefer 3-pack (std O), *05* | | 130 | ___ |
| **11873** | C&O Offset Hopper 3-pack (std O), *05* | | 130 | ___ |
| **11874** | PFE Orange Steel-sided Reefer 3-pack (std O), *05* | | 130 | ___ |
| **11875** | NP Steel-sided Reefer 3-pack (std O), *05* | | 130 | ___ |
| **11876** | PFE Silver Steel-sided Reefer 3-pack (std O), *05* | | 130 | ___ |
| **11877** | C&NW Steel-sided Reefer 3-pack (std O), *05* | | 130 | ___ |
| **11878** | Santa Fe PS-2 2-bay Covered Hopper 3-pack (std O), *06* | | 125 | ___ |
| **11879** | MKT PS-2 2-bay Covered Hopper 3-pack (std O), *06* | | 125 | ___ |
| **11880** | Boraxo PS-2 2-bay Covered Hopper 3-pack (std O), *06* | | 125 | ___ |
| **11881** | PRR PS-2 2-bay Covered Hopper 3-pack (std O), *06* | | 125 | ___ |
| **11882** | RI Offset Hopper with gravel, 3-pack (std O), *06* | | 125 | ___ |
| **11883** | CNJ Offset Hopper 3-pack (std O), *06* | | 145 | ___ |
| **11884** | Maine Central Offset Hopper 3-pack (std O), *06* | | 145 | ___ |
| **11891** | Pennsylvania 3-bay Hopper 3-pack (std O), *06* | | 155 | ___ |
| **11892** | Conrail ACF 3-bay Hopper 3-pack (std O), *06* | | 155 | ___ |
| **11893** | N&W 3-bay Hopper 3-pack (std O), *06* | | 155 | ___ |
| **11894** | UP 3-bay Hopper 3-pack (std O), *06* | | 155 | ___ |
| **11895** | GN Steel-sided Reefer 3-pack (std O), *06* | | 145 | ___ |
| **11896** | Santa Fe Steel-sided Reefer 3-pack (std O), *06* | | 145 | ___ |
| **11897** | Pepper Packing Steel-sided Reefer 3-pack (std O), *06* | | 145 | ___ |
| **11900** | SF Steam Freight Set (O), *96–01* | | 130 | ___ |
| **11903** | ACL F3 Diesel ABA Set, *96* | | 716 | ___ |
| **11905** | U.S. Coast Guard Set, *96* | 160 | 180 | ___ |
| **11906** | Factory Selection Special Set, *95 u* | | 85 | ___ |
| **11909** | N&W J 4-8-4 Warhorse Set, *96* | 560 | 720 | ___ |
| **11910** | Lionel Lines Set (027), *96* | 140 | 160 | ___ |

Exc  Mint  Cond/S

| | | Exc | Mint | Cond/S |
|---|---|---|---|---|
| 11912 | "57" Switcher Service Exclusive, *96* | | 310 | ___ |
| 11913 | SP GP9 Diesel Freight Set, *97* | | 440 | ___ |
| 11914 | NYC GP9 Diesel Freight Set, *97* | | 370 | ___ |
| 11918 | Conrail SD20 Service Exclusive "X1144" (SSS), *97* | | 255 | ___ |
| 11919 | Docksider Set (O), *97* | | 70 | ___ |
| 11920 | Port of Lionel City Dive Team Set, *97* | | 185 | ___ |
| 11921 | Lionel Lines Freight Set, *97* | | 130 | ___ |
| 11929 | ATSF Warbonnet Passenger Set, *97–99* | | 132 | ___ |
| 11930 | ATSF Warbonnet Passenger Car 2-pack, *97–99* | | 80 | ___ |
| 11931 | Chessie Flyer Freight Set "1931S" (O), *97–99* | | 165 | ___ |
| 11933 | Dodge Motorsports Freight Set, *96 u* | | 265 | ___ |
| 11934 | Virginian Electric Locomotive Freight Set, *97–99* | | 260 | ___ |
| 11935 | NYC Flyer Freight Set, *97* | | 155 | ___ |
| 11936 | Little League Baseball Steam Set, *97* | 212 | 274 | ___ |
| 11939 | SP&S 4-6-2 Steam Freight Set, *97* | | 220 | ___ |
| 11940 | Southern Pacific SD40 Warhorse Coal Set, *98* | | 600 | ___ |
| 11944 | Lionel Lines 4-4-2 Steam Freight Set, *98* | | 175 | ___ |
| 11956 | UP GP9 Diesel Set, *97* | 325 | 375 | ___ |
| 11957 | Mobil Oil Steam Special Set, *97* | | 372 | ___ |
| 11971 | D&H 4-4-2 Steam Freight Set, *98* | 125 | 155 | ___ |
| 11972 | Alaska GP7 Diesel Set, *98–99* | 180 | 215 | ___ |
| 11974 | Station Accessory Set, *98* | | 22 | ___ |
| 11975 | Freight Accessory Pack, *98* | | 23 | ___ |
| 11977 | NP Freight Cars 4-pack, *98* | | 170 | ___ |
| 11979 | N&W 4-4-2 Steam Freight Set, *98* | | 75 | ___ |
| 11981 | 1998 Holiday Trolley Set, *98* | | 75 | ___ |
| 11982 | New Jersey Transit Ore Car Set, *98* | | 250 | ___ |
| 11983 | Farmrail Agricultural Set, *99* | | 442 | ___ |
| 11984 | Corvette GP7 Diesel Set, *99* | | 438 | ___ |
| 11988 | NYC Firecar "18444" and Instruction Car "19853," *99* | | 210 | ___ |
| 12014 | 10" Straight Track (FasTrack), *03–10* | | 5 | ___ |
| 12015 | O36 Curved Track (FasTrack), *03–10* | | 4 | ___ |
| 12016 | 10" Terminal Track (FasTrack), *03–10* | | 8 | ___ |
| 12017 | O36 Manual Switch, left hand (FasTrack), *03–10* | | 45 | ___ |
| 12018 | O36 Manual Switch, right hand (FasTrack), *03–10* | | 45 | ___ |
| 12019 | 90-degree Crossover (FasTrack), *03–10* | | 23 | ___ |
| 12020 | 5" Uncoupling Track (FasTrack), *03–10* | | 42 | ___ |
| 12022 | O36 Half Curved Track (FasTrack), *03–10* | | 5 | ___ |
| 12023 | O36 Quarter Curved Track (FasTrack), *03–10* | | 5 | ___ |
| 12024 | Half Straight Track (FasTrack), *03–10* | | 5 | ___ |
| 12025 | 4½" Straight Track (FasTrack), *03–10* | | 5 | ___ |
| 12026 | 1¾" Straight Track (FasTrack), *03–10* | | 5 | ___ |
| 12027 | 5" Insulated Track (FasTrack), *03–10* | | 5 | ___ |
| 12028 | Inner Passing Loop Track Pack (FasTrack), *03–10* | | 100 | ___ |

Exc  Mint  Cond/S

| No. | Description | Exc | Mint | Cond/S |
|---|---|---|---|---|
| 12029 | Accessory Activator Pack (FasTrack), *03–10* | | 14 | ___ |
| 12030 | Figure 8 Track Pack (FasTrack), *03–10* | | 67 | ___ |
| 12031 | Outer Passing Loop Track Pack (FasTrack), *03–10* | | 115 | ___ |
| 12032 | 10" Straight Track 4-pack (FasTrack), *03–10* | | 21 | ___ |
| 12033 | O36 Curved Track, card of 4 (FasTrack), *03–10* | | 21 | ___ |
| 12035 | FasTrack Lighted Bumper 2-pack, *05–10* | | 30 | ___ |
| 12036 | Grade Crossing (FasTrack), *05–10* | | 14 | ___ |
| 12037 | Graduated Trestle Set (FasTrack), *05–10* | | 75 | ___ |
| 12038 | Elevated Trestle Set (FasTrack), *05–10* | | 40 | ___ |
| 12039 | Railer (FasTrack), *04–10* | | 9 | ___ |
| 12040 | O Gauge Transition Piece (FasTrack), *04–10* | | 9 | ___ |
| 12041 | O72 Curved Track (FasTrack), *04–10* | | 7 | ___ |
| 12042 | 30" Straight Track (FasTrack), *04–10* | | 15 | ___ |
| 12043 | O48 Curved Track (FasTrack), *04–10* | | 5 | ___ |
| 12044 | Siding Track Add-on Track Pack (FasTrack), *04–10* | | 106 | ___ |
| 12045 | O36 Remote Switch, left hand (FasTrack), *04–10* | | 92 | ___ |
| 12046 | O36 Remote Switch, right hand (FasTrack), *04–10* | | 92 | ___ |
| 12047 | O72 Wye Remote Switch (FasTrack), *04–10* | | 97 | ___ |
| 12048 | O72 Remote Switch, left hand (FasTrack), *04–10* | | 104 | ___ |
| 12049 | O72 Remote Switch, right hand (FasTrack), *04–10* | | 104 | ___ |
| 12050 | 22½-degree Crossover (FasTrack), *04–10* | | 46 | ___ |
| 12051 | 45-degree Crossover (FasTrack), *04–10* | | 24 | ___ |
| 12052 | Grade Crossing with flashers (FasTrack), *05–10* | | 92 | ___ |
| 12053 | Accessory Power Wire (FasTrack), *04–10* | | 6 | ___ |
| 12054 | Operating Track with half straight (FasTrack), *05–10* | | 43 | ___ |
| 12055 | O72 Half Curved Track (FasTrack), *04–10* | | 6 | ___ |
| 12056 | O60 Curved Track (FasTrack), *05–10* | | 7 | ___ |
| 12057 | O60 Remote Switch, left hand, *05–10* | | 104 | ___ |
| 12058 | O60 Remote Switch, right hand (FasTrack), *05–10* | | 104 | ___ |
| 12059 | Earthen Bumper (FasTrack), *04–10* | | 9 | ___ |
| 12060 | Block Section (FasTrack), *05–10* | | 9 | ___ |
| 12061 | O84 Curved Track (FasTrack), *05–10* | | 7 | ___ |
| 12062 | Grade Crossing with gates and flashers (FasTrack), *06–10* | | 160 | ___ |
| 12065 | O48 Remote Switch, left hand (FasTrack), *07–10* | | 104 | ___ |
| 12066 | O48 Remote Switch, right hand (FasTrack), *07–10* | | 104 | ___ |
| 12073 | 1⅜" Track Section (FasTrack), *07–10* | | 5 | ___ |
| 12074 | 1⅜" Track Section, no roadbed (FasTrack), *07–10* | | 5 | ___ |
| 12080 | 42" Path Remote Switch, right hand, *07–10* | | 80 | ___ |
| 12081 | 42" Path Remote Switch, left hand, *07–10* | | 80 | ___ |

| | | Exc | Mint | Cond/S |
|---|---|---|---|---|
| **12700** | Erie Magnetic Gantry Crane, *87* | 125 | 150 | ____ |
| **12701** | Operating Fueling Station, *87* | 60 | 74 | ____ |
| **12702** | Control Tower, *87* | 60 | 75 | ____ |
| **12703** | Icing Station, *88–89* | 60 | 65 | ____ |
| **12704** | Dwarf Signal, *88–93* | 9 | 11 | ____ |
| **12705** | Lumber Shed Kit, *88–99* | | 9 | ____ |
| **12706** | Barrel Loader Building Kit, *87–99* | | 10 | ____ |
| **12707** | Billboards, set of 3, *87–99* | | 5 | ____ |
| **12708** | Street Lamps, set of 3, *88–93* | 6 | 9 | ____ |
| **12709** | Banjo Signal, *87–91, 95–00* | | 29 | ____ |
| **12710** | Engine House Kit, *87–91* | 21 | 25 | ____ |
| **12711** | Water Tower Kit, *87–99* | | 13 | ____ |
| **12712** | Automatic Ore Loader, *87–88* | 17 | 21 | ____ |
| **12713** | Automatic Gateman, *87–88, 94–00* | 30 | 40 | ____ |
| **12714** | Crossing Gate, *87–91, 93–10* | | 20 | ____ |
| **12715** | Illuminated Bumpers, set of 2, *87–10* | | 11 | ____ |
| **12716** | Searchlight Tower, *87–89, 91–92* | 19 | 22 | ____ |
| **12717** | Non-Illuminated Bumpers, set of 3, *87–10* | | 5 | ____ |
| **12718** | Barrel Shed Kit, *87–99* | | 10 | ____ |
| **12719** | Animated Refreshment Stand, *88–89* | 65 | 70 | ____ |
| **12720** | Rotary Beacon, *88–89* | 40 | 45 | ____ |
| **12721** | Illuminated Extension Bridge, rock piers, *89* | 26 | 38 | ____ |
| **12722** | Roadside Diner, smoke, *88–89* | 27 | 38 | ____ |
| **12723** | Microwave Tower, *88–91, 94–95* | 14 | 19 | ____ |
| **12724** | Double Signal Bridge, *88–90* | 39 | 50 | ____ |
| **12725** | Lionel Tractor and Trailer, *88–89* | 16 | 18 | ____ |
| **12726** | Grain Elevator Kit, *88–91, 94–99* | | 36 | ____ |
| **12727** | Operating Semaphore, *89–99* | | 26 | ____ |
| **12728** | Illuminated Freight Station, *89* | 29 | 38 | ____ |
| **12729** | Mail Pickup Set, *88–91, 95* | 12 | 16 | ____ |
| **12730** | Girder Bridge, *88–03, 08–10* | | 10 | ____ |
| **12731** | Station Platform, *88–00* | | 8 | ____ |
| **12732** | Coal Bag, *88–10* | | 5 | ____ |
| **12733** | Watchman Shanty Kit, *88–99* | | 5 | ____ |
| **12734** | Passenger/Freight Station, *89–99* | | 18 | ____ |
| **12735** | Diesel Horn Shed, *88–91* | 19 | 24 | ____ |
| **12736** | Coaling Station Kit, *88–91* | 21 | 31 | ____ |
| **12737** | Whistling Freight Shed, *88–99* | | 28 | ____ |
| **12739** | Lionel Gas Company Tractor and Tanker, *89* | 20 | 25 | ____ |
| **12740** | Genuine Wood Logs, set of 3, *88–92, 94–95, 97–99* | | 5 | ____ |
| **12741** | Union Pacific Intermodal Crane, *89* | 165 | 185 | ____ |
| **12742** | Gooseneck Lamps, set of 2, *89–00* | | 21 | ____ |
| **12743** | Track Clips, dozen (O), *89–10* | | 12 | ____ |
| **12744** | Rock Piers, set of 2, *89–92, 94–05, 08* | | 13 | ____ |
| **12745** | Barrel Pack, set of 6, *89–10* | | 6 | ____ |
| **12746** | Operating/Uncoupling Track (O27), *89–10* | | 10 | ____ |
| **12748** | Illuminated Passenger Platform, *89–99* | | 18 | ____ |

| | | Exc | Mint | Cond/$ |
|---|---|---|---|---|
| 12749 | Rotary Radar Antenna, *89–92, 95* | 28 | 38 | _____ |
| 12750 | Crane Kit, *89–91* | 8 | 10 | _____ |
| 12751 | Shovel Kit, *89–91* | 8 | 10 | _____ |
| 12752 | History of Lionel Trains Video, *89–92, 94* | 19 | 21 | _____ |
| 12753 | Ore Load, set of 2, *89–91, 95* | 1 | 2 | _____ |
| 12754 | Graduated Trestle Set, 22 pieces, *89–10* | | 15 | _____ |
| 12755 | Elevated Trestle Set, 10 pieces, *89–10* | | 15 | _____ |
| 12756 | The Making of the Scale Hudson Video, *91–94* | 20 | 22 | _____ |
| 12759 | Floodlight Tower, *90–00* | | 25 | _____ |
| 12760 | Automatic Highway Flasher, *90–91* | 23 | 27 | _____ |
| 12761 | Animated Billboard, *90–91, 93, 95* | 22 | 23 | _____ |
| 12763 | Single Signal Bridge, *90–91, 93* | 31 | 35 | _____ |
| 12767 | Steam Clean and Wheel Grind Shop, *92–93, 95* | 240 | 290 | _____ |
| 12768 | Burning Switch Tower, *90, 93* | 85 | 90 | _____ |
| 12770 | Arch-Under Bridge, *90–03, 08–10* | | 21 | _____ |
| 12771 | Mom's Roadside Diner, smoke, *90–91* | 34 | 50 | _____ |
| 12772 | Truss Bridge, flasher and piers, *90–10* | | 35 | _____ |
| 12773 | Freight Platform Kit, *90–98* | | 32 | _____ |
| 12774 | Lumber Loader Kit, *90–99* | | 19 | _____ |
| 12777 | Chevron Tractor and Tanker, *90–91* | 9 | 15 | _____ |
| 12778 | Conrail Tractor and Trailer, *90* | 9 | 16 | _____ |
| 12779 | Lionelville Grain Company Tractor and Trailer, *90* | 11 | 19 | _____ |
| 12780 | RS-1 50-watt Transformer, *90–93* | 95 | 130 | _____ |
| 12781 | N&W Intermodal Crane, *90–91* | 145 | 160 | _____ |
| 12782 | Lift Bridge, *91–92* | 425 | 510 | _____ |
| 12783 | Monon Tractor and Trailer, *91* | 11 | 19 | _____ |
| 12784 | Intermodal Containers, set of 3, *91* | 12 | 17 | _____ |
| 12785 | Lionel Gravel Company Tractor and Trailer, *91* | 9 | 15 | _____ |
| 12786 | Lionel Steel Company Tractor and Trailer, *91* | 10 | 16 | _____ |
| 12791 | Animated Passenger Station, *91* | 45 | 60 | _____ |
| 12794 | Lionel Tractor, *91* | 7 | 13 | _____ |
| 12795 | Cable Reels, pair, *91–98* | 3 | 5 | _____ |
| 12798 | Forklift Loader Station, *92–95* | 33 | 44 | _____ |
| 12800 | Scale Hudson Replacement Pilot Truck, *91 u* | 13 | 17 | _____ |
| 12802 | Chat & Chew Roadside Diner, smoke and lights, *92–95* | 41 | 50 | _____ |
| 12804 | Highway Lights, set of 4, *92–99, 02–04* | 9 | 13 | _____ |
| 12805 | Intermodal Containers, set of 3, *92* | 10 | 14 | _____ |
| 12806 | Lionel Lumber Company Tractor and Trailer, *92* | 10 | 15 | _____ |
| 12807 | Little Caesars Tractor and Trailer, *92* | 9 | 14 | _____ |
| 12808 | Mobil Tractor and Tanker, *92* | 8 | 13 | _____ |
| 12809 | Animated Billboard, *92–93* | 20 | 22 | _____ |
| 12810 | American Flyer Tractor and Trailer, *94* | 12 | 18 | _____ |
| 12811 | Alka Seltzer Tractor and Trailer, *92* | 11 | 19 | _____ |
| 12812 | Illuminated Freight Station, *93–00* | | 27 | _____ |
| 12818 | Animated Freight Station, *92, 94–95* | 50 | 60 | _____ |
| 12819 | Inland Steel Tractor and Trailer, *92* | 9 | 16 | _____ |
| 12821 | Lionel Catalog Video, *92* | 13 | 17 | _____ |

| | | Exc | Mint | Cond/S |
|---|---|---|---|---|
| **12826** | Intermodal Containers, set of 3, *93* | 10 | 16 | ____ |
| **12831** | Rotary Beacon, *93–95* | 22 | 32 | ____ |
| **12832** | Block Target Signal, *93–98* | | 25 | ____ |
| **12833** | RoadRailer Tractor and Trailer, *93* | 9 | 15 | ____ |
| **12834** | Pennsylvania Magnetic Gantry Crane, *93* | 130 | 170 | ____ |
| **12835** | Operating Fueling Station, *93* | 55 | 60 | ____ |
| **12836** | Santa Fe Quantum Tractor and Trailer, *93* | 8 | 14 | ____ |
| **12837** | Humble Oil Tractor and Tanker, *93* | 9 | 16 | ____ |
| **12838** | Crate Load, set of 2, *93–97* | | 3 | ____ |
| **12839** | Grade Crossings, set of 2, *93–10* | | 6 | ____ |
| **12840** | Insulated Straight Track (O), *93–10* | | 8 | ____ |
| **12841** | Insulated Straight Track (O27), *93–10* | | 5 | ____ |
| **12842** | Dunkin' Donuts Tractor and Trailer, *92 u* | 23 | 25 | ____ |
| **12843** | Die-cast Sprung Trucks, pair, *93–99* | | 10 | ____ |
| **12844** | Coil Covers, pair (O), *93–98* | | 3 | ____ |
| **12847** | Animated Ice Depot, *94–99* | | 65 | ____ |
| **12848** | Lionel Oil Company Derrick, *94* | 55 | 75 | ____ |
| **12849** | Lionel Controller with wall pack, *94, 95 u* | | NRS | ____ |
| **12852** | Die-cast Intermodal Trailer Frame, *94–01* | | 6 | ____ |
| **12853** | Coil Covers, pair (std O), *94–98* | | 7 | ____ |
| **12854** | U.S. Navy Tractor and Tanker, *94–95* | | 33 | ____ |
| **12855** | Intermodal Containers, set of 3, *94–95* | 9 | 13 | ____ |
| **12860** | Lionel Visitor's Center Tractor and Trailer, *94 u* | 10 | 14 | ____ |
| **12861** | Lionel Leasing Company Tractor, *94* | 8 | 13 | ____ |
| **12862** | Oil Drum Loader, *94–95* | 75 | 85 | ____ |
| **12864** | Little Caesars Tractor and Trailer, *94* | 8 | 14 | ____ |
| **12865** | Wisk Tractor and Trailer, *94* | 12 | 55 | ____ |
| **12866** | TMCC 135-watt PowerHouse Power Supply, *94 u, 95–03* | | 46 | ____ |
| **12867** | TMCC 135 PowerMaster Power Distribution Center, *94 u, 95–04* | | 49 | ____ |
| **12868** | TMCC CAB-1 Remote Controller, *94 u, 95–09* | | 115 | ____ |
| **12869** | Marathon Oil Tractor and Tanker, *94* | 13 | 19 | ____ |
| **12873** | Operating Sawmill, *95–97* | | 70 | ____ |
| **12874** | Classic Street Lamps, set of 3, *94–00* | | 13 | ____ |
| **12877** | Operating Fueling Station, *95* | 75 | 85 | ____ |
| **12878** | Control Tower, *95* | 49 | 60 | ____ |
| **12881** | Chrysler Mopar Tractor and Trailer, *94 u* | 37 | 46 | ____ |
| **12882** | Lighted Billboard, *95* | 9 | 14 | ____ |
| **12883** | Dwarf Signal, *95–10* | | 23 | ____ |
| **12884** | Truck Loading Dock Kit, *95–98* | | 16 | ____ |
| **12885** | 40-watt Control System, *94 u, 95–05* | | 35 | ____ |
| **12886** | Floodlight Tower, *95–98* | | 31 | ____ |
| **12888** | Railroad Crossing Flasher, *95–10* | | 45 | ____ |
| **12889** | Operating Windmill, *95–98* | | 34 | ____ |
| **12890** | Big Red Control Button, *94 u, 95–00* | | 43 | ____ |
| **12891** | LL Refrigerator Tractor and Trailer, *95* | 12 | 16 | ____ |
| **12892** | Automatic Flagman, *92–98* | | 25 | ____ |

| | | Exc | Mint | Cond/$ |
|---|---|---|---|---|
| **12893** | TMCC PowerMaster Power Adapter Cable, *94 u, 95–09* | | 9 | ___ |
| **12894** | Signal Bridge, *95–01* | | 22 | ___ |
| **12895** | Double-track Signal Bridge, *95–00* | | 44 | ___ |
| **12896** | Tunnel Portals, pair, *95–10* | | 11 | ___ |
| **12897** | Engine House Kit, *96–98* | | 29 | ___ |
| **12898** | Flagpole, *95–97* | | 8 | ___ |
| **12899** | Searchlight Tower, *95–98* | | 25 | ___ |
| **12900** | Crane Kit, *95–98* | | 8 | ___ |
| **12901** | Shovel Kit, *95–98* | | 7 | ___ |
| **12902** | Marathon Oil Derrick, *94 u, 95* | 105 | 151 | ___ |
| **12903** | Diesel Horn Shed, *95–98* | | 29 | ___ |
| **12904** | Coaling Station Kit, *95–98* | | 19 | ___ |
| **12905** | Factory Kit, *95–98* | | 20 | ___ |
| **12906** | Maintenance Shed Kit, *95–98* | | 20 | ___ |
| **12907** | Intermodal Containers, set of 3, *95* | 9 | 14 | ___ |
| **12911** | TMCC Command Base, *95–09* | | 80 | ___ |
| **12912** | Oil Pumping Station, *95–98* | 38 | 65 | ___ |
| **12914** | SC-1 Switch and Accessory Controller, *95–98* | | 35 | ___ |
| **12915** | Log Loader, *96* | | 115 | ___ |
| **12916** | Water Tower, *96–97* | | 56 | ___ |
| **12917** | Animated Switch Tower, *96–98* | | 29 | ___ |
| **12922** | NYC Operating Gantry Crane, coil covers, *96* | 75 | 90 | ___ |
| **12923** | Red Wing Shoes Tractor and Trailer, *95 u* | 32 | 35 | ___ |
| **12925** | 42" Diameter Curved Track Section (O), *96–10* | | 4 | ___ |
| **12926** | Globe Street Lamps, set of 3, *96–03, 08–09* | | 10 | ___ |
| **12927** | Yard Light, *96–10* | | 10 | ___ |
| **12929** | Rail-truck Loading Dock, *96* | | 44 | ___ |
| **12930** | Lionelville Oil Company Derrick, *95 u, 96* | 55 | 75 | ___ |
| **12931** | Electrical Substation, *96* | | 22 | ___ |
| **12932** | Laimbeer Packaging Tractor and Trailer Set, *96* | | 14 | ___ |
| **12933** | GM Parts Tractor and Trailer, *95* | | NRS | ___ |
| **12935** | Zenith Tractor and Trailer, *96* | | 22 | ___ |
| **12936** | SP Intermodal Crane, *97* | | 195 | ___ |
| **12937** | NS Intermodal Crane, *97* | | 200 | ___ |
| **12938** | PowerStation Controller and PowerHouse 135-watt Power Supply, *97–00* | | 150 | ___ |
| **12943** | Illuminated Station Platform, *97–00* | | 24 | ___ |
| **12944** | Sunoco Oil Derrick, *97* | | 85 | ___ |
| **12945** | Sunoco Pumping Oil Station, *97* | | 80 | ___ |
| **12948** | Bascule Bridge, *97* | | 315 | ___ |
| **12949** | Billboards, set of 3, *97–00* | | 7 | ___ |
| **12951** | Airplane Hangar Kit, *97–98* | | 29 | ___ |
| **12952** | Big L Diner Kit, *97* | | 24 | ___ |
| **12953** | Linex Gas Tall Oil Tank, *97* | | 9 | ___ |
| **12954** | Linex Gas Wide Oil Tank, *97* | | 10 | ___ |
| **12955** | Road Runner and Wile E. Coyote Ambush Shack, *97* | | 93 | ___ |
| **12958** | Industrial Water Tower, *97–98* | | 50 | ___ |

| | | Exc | Mint | Cond/$ |
|---|---|---|---|---|
| **12960** | Rotary Radar Antenna, *97* | | 26 | ____ |
| **12961** | Newsstand with diesel horn, *97* | | 30 | ____ |
| **12962** | LL Passenger Service Train Whistle, *97–99* | | 30 | ____ |
| **12964** | Donald Duck Radar Antenna, *97* | | 59 | ____ |
| **12965** | Goofy Rotary Beacon, *97* | | 52 | ____ |
| **12966** | Rotary Aircraft Beacon, *97–00* | | 35 | ____ |
| **12968** | Girder Bridge Building Kit, *97* | | 22 | ____ |
| **12969** | TMCC Command Set, *97–09* | | 148 | ____ |
| **12974** | Blinking Light Billboard, *97–00* | | 15 | ____ |
| **12975** | Steiner Victorian Building Kit, *97–98* | | 33 | ____ |
| **12976** | Dobson Victorian Building Kit, *97–98* | | 24 | ____ |
| **12977** | Kindler Victorian Building Kit, *97–98* | | 35 | ____ |
| **12982** | Culvert Loader, conventional, *98–00* | | 190 | ____ |
| **12983** | Culvert Unloader, conventional, *99* | | 185 | ____ |
| **12987** | Intermodal Contianers, set of 3, *98* | | 15 | ____ |
| **12989** | Lionel Tractor and Trailer, *98* | | 16 | ____ |
| **12991** | Linex Gas Tractor-Tanker, *98* | | 16 | ____ |
| **13113** | Electric Trolley and Trail Car (std), *07* | | 450 | ____ |
| **14000** | Operating Forklift Platform, *00* | | 160 | ____ |
| **14001** | Operating Belt Lumber Loader, *00* | | 95 | ____ |
| **14002** | ZW Amp/Volt Meter, *00–04* | | 80 | ____ |
| **14003** | 80-watt Transformer/Controller, *00–03* | | 70 | ____ |
| **14004** | Operating Coal Loader, *00* | | 135 | ____ |
| **14005** | Operating Coal Ramp, *00* | | 130 | ____ |
| **14018** | ElectroCoupler Kit for Command Upgradeable GP9s, *00* | | 20 | ____ |
| **14062** | O31 Remote Switch, left hand, *01–10* | | 55 | ____ |
| **14063** | 31" Path Remote Switch, right hand, *01–10* | | 75 | ____ |
| **14065** | Nuclear Reactor, *00* | | 230 | ____ |
| **14071** | Yard Light, *00–10* | | 18 | ____ |
| **14072** | Haunted House, *01* | | 178 | ____ |
| **14073** | History of Lionel, The First 90 Years Video, *00* | | 15 | ____ |
| **14075** | A Century of Lionel, 1900-1969 Video, *00* | | 15 | ____ |
| **14076** | A Century of Lionel, 1970-2000 Video, *00* | | 15 | ____ |
| **14077** | ZW Amp/Volt Meter, *00–03* | | 70 | ____ |
| **14078** | Die-cast Sprung Trucks, *00–05, 07–10* | | 17 | ____ |
| **14079** | Operating North Pole Pylon, *01* | | 70 | ____ |
| **14080** | Hobo Hotel, *01* | 30 | 65 | ____ |
| **14081** | Shell Oil Derrick, *01* | | 100 | ____ |
| **14082** | Pedestrian Walkover, speed sensor, *01–03* | | 50 | ____ |
| **14083** | Pedestrian Walkover, *01–03, 08* | | 30 | ____ |
| **14084** | Lionel Heliport, *01* | | 85 | ____ |
| **14085** | Newsstand, *01* | | 75 | ____ |
| **14086** | Water Tower, *00* | | 105 | ____ |
| **14087** | Lighthouse, *01* | | 95 | ____ |
| **14090** | Banjo Signal, *01–10* | | 50 | ____ |
| **14091** | Automatic Gateman, *01–03, 07–09* | | 45 | ____ |
| **14092** | Floodlight Tower, *01–05, 08–10* | | 35 | ____ |

| | | Exc | Mint | Cond/$ |
|---|---|---|---|---|
| **14093** | Single Signal Bridge, *01–04, 08* | 22 | | |
| **14094** | Double Signal Bridge, *01–04, 08* | 30 | | |
| **14095** | Illuminated Station Platform, *01–04* | 20 | | |
| **14096** | Station Platform, *01–04* | 10 | | |
| **14097** | Rotary Aircraft Beacon, *01–04, 07–10* | 40 | | |
| **14098** | Auto Crossing Gate, *01–10* | 90 | | |
| **14099** | Block Target Signal, *01–04, 07–08* | 22 | | |
| **14100** | Blinking Light Billboard, *01–03* | 23 | | |
| **14101** | Red Baron Pylon, *01* | 85 | | |
| **14102** | Rocket Launcher, *01* | 250 | | |
| **14104** | Burning Switch Tower, *00* | 70 | | |
| **14105** | Aquarium, *01* | 175 | | |
| **14106** | Operating Freight Station, *00* | 70 | | |
| **14107** | Coaling Station, *01–03* | 95 | | |
| **14109** | Carousel, *01* | 230 | | |
| **14110** | Operating Ferris Wheel, *01–02, 04* | 170 | | |
| **14111** | 1531R Controller, *00–10* | 40 | | |
| **14112** | Lighted Lockon, *01–10* | 6 | | |
| **14113** | Engine Transfer Table, *01* | 210 | | |
| **14114** | Engine Transfer Table Extension, *01* | 75 | | |
| **14116** | PRR Die-cast Girder Bridge, *01* | 20 | | |
| **14117** | NYC Die-cast Girder Bridge, *01* | 20 | | |
| **14119** | Gooseneck Lamps, set of 2, *01–04, 07* | 22 | | |
| **14121** | Classic Billboards, set of 3, *01–03* | 10 | | |
| **14124** | ZW Controller with 2 transformers, *01* | 300 | | |
| **14125** | Christmas Tree with 400E Train, *00* | 65 | | |
| **14133** | Madison Hobby Shop, *01* | 290 | | |
| **14134** | Triple Action Magnetic Crane, *01* | 230 | | |
| **14135** | NS Black Die-cast Girder Bridge, *02* | 15 | | |
| **14137** | Die-cast Girder Bridge, *01–07* | 25 | | |
| **14138** | Snap-On Tool Animated Billboard, *01 u* | NRS | | |
| **14142** | Industrial Smokestack, *02–04* | 50 | | |
| **14143** | Industrial Tank, *02–04* | 40 | | |
| **14145** | Operating Lumberjacks, *02–03* | 65 | | |
| **14147** | Die-cast Old Style Clock Tower, *02–04, 08–09* | 42 | | |
| **14148** | Operating Billboard Signmen, *02–03* | 60 | | |
| **14149** | Scale-sized Banjo Signal, *02–05* | 40 | | |
| **14151** | Mainline Dwarf Signal, *02–08* | 43 | | |
| **14152** | Passenger Station, *02–04* | 37 | | |
| **14153** | Lion Oil Derrick, *02–03* | 50 | | |
| **14154** | Water Tower, *01–02* | 65 | | |
| **14155** | Floodlight Tower, *02–03* | 55 | | |
| **14156** | Lion Oil Diesel Fueling Station, *02–03* | 70 | | |
| **14157** | Coal Loader, *01–03* | 120 | | |
| **14158** | Icing Station, *01–02* | 75 | | |
| **14159** | Animated Billboard, *02–04* | 20 | | |
| **14160** | Frank's Hotdog Stand, *03–04* | 55 | | |
| **14161** | Smoking Hobo Shack, *02* | 60 | | |

| | | Exc | Mint | Cond/$ |
|---|---|---|---|---|
| 14162 | Missile Launching Platform, *02–03* | | 48 | ___ |
| 14163 | Industrial Power Station, *02–03* | | 550 | ___ |
| 14164 | Lionelville Bandstand, *02* | | 140 | ___ |
| 14166 | Train Orders Building, *04–05* | | 49 | ___ |
| 14167 | Operating Lift Bridge, *02* | | 380 | ___ |
| 14168 | Operating Harry's Barber Shop, *02–04* | | 100 | ___ |
| 14170 | Amusement Park Swing Ride, *03–04* | | 150 | ___ |
| 14171 | Pirate Ship Ride, *02–04* | | 130 | ___ |
| 14172 | NYC Railroad Tugboat, *02* | | 180 | ___ |
| 14173 | Drawbridge, *02–04* | | 70 | ___ |
| 14175 | Santa Fe Die-cast Girder Bridge, *01–03* | | 17 | ___ |
| 14176 | Norfolk Southern Die-cast Girder Bridge, *02–03* | | 18 | ___ |
| 14178 | TMCC Direct Lockon, *02–03* | | 25 | ___ |
| 14179 | TMCC Track Power Controller, *02–10* | | 130 | ___ |
| 14180 | B&O Railroad Tugboat, *02–03* | | 155 | ___ |
| 14181 | TMCC Action Recorder Controller, *02–10* | | 100 | ___ |
| 14182 | TMCC Accessory Switch Controller, *02–10* | | 90 | ___ |
| 14183 | TMCC Accessory Motor Controller, *02–10* | | 100 | ___ |
| 14184 | TMCC Block Power Controller, *02–10* | | 90 | ___ |
| 14185 | TMCC Operating Track Controller, *02–10* | | 79 | ___ |
| 14186 | TMCC Accessory Voltage Controller, *02–10* | | 140 | ___ |
| 14187 | TMCC How-to Video, *02–04* | | 11 | ___ |
| 14189 | TMCC Track Power Controller, *02–10* | | 148 | ___ |
| 14190 | The Lionel Train Book, *04–10* | | 30 | ___ |
| 14191 | TMCC Command Base Cable, 6 feet, *02–10* | | 11 | ___ |
| 14192 | TMCC 3-wire Command Base Cable, *02–10* | | 12 | ___ |
| 14193 | TMCC Controller to Controller Cable, 1 foot, *02–10* | | 4 | ___ |
| 14194 | TMCC TPC Cable Set, *02–10* | | 14 | ___ |
| 14195 | TMCC Command Base Cable, 20 feet, *02–07* | | 12 | ___ |
| 14196 | TMCC Controller to Controller Cable, 6 feet, *02–10* | | 7 | ___ |
| 14197 | TMCC Controller to Controller Cable, 20 feet, *02–07* | | 9 | ___ |
| 14198 | CW-80 80-watt Transformer, *03–10* | | 55 | ___ |
| 14199 | Playground Swings, *03–04, 08–09* | | 50 | ___ |
| 14201 | Burning Switch Tower, *05* | | 70 | ___ |
| 14202 | Water Tower, *05* | | 140 | ___ |
| 14203 | Amusement Park Swing Ride, *06–07* | | 230 | ___ |
| 14209 | U.S. Steel Gantry Crane, *05* | | 180 | ___ |
| 14210 | Pony Ride, *06–07* | | 70 | ___ |
| 14211 | Road Crew, *07–08* | | 90 | ___ |
| 14214 | Lionelville Mini Golf, *06* | | 80 | ___ |
| 14215 | Tug-of-War, *06–08* | | 60 | ___ |
| 14217 | Helicopter Pylon, *06–09* | | 140 | ___ |
| 14218 | Downtown People Pack, *06–10* | | 23 | ___ |
| 14219 | Ice Rink, *06–08* | | 80 | ___ |
| 14220 | Lionelville Water Tower, *06–08* | | 21 | ___ |
| 14221 | Witches Cauldron, *06–08* | | 70 | ___ |

| | | Exc | Mint | Cond/$ |
|---|---|---|---|---|
| 14222 | Die-cast Girder Bridge, *06–09* | | 30 | ___ |
| 14225 | Sunoco Industrial Tank, *06–09* | | 70 | ___ |
| 14227 | Yard Tower, *06–08* | | 45 | ___ |
| 14229 | Crossing Shanty, *06–09* | | 20 | ___ |
| 14230 | Milk Bottle Toss Midway Game, *06* | | 20 | ___ |
| 14231 | Cotton Candy Midway Booth, *06* | | 20 | ___ |
| 14236 | Operating Freight Station, *06–07* | | 105 | ___ |
| 14237 | Rocket Launcher, *06–07* | | 320 | ___ |
| 14240 | Ice Block Pack, *06–10* | | 5 | ___ |
| 14241 | Work Crew People Pack, *06–10* | | 23 | ___ |
| 14242 | Hard Rock Cafe, *06* | | 50 | ___ |
| 14243 | U.S. Army Water Tower, *06–08* | | 95 | ___ |
| 14244 | Ammo Loader, *06–07* | | 105 | ___ |
| 14251 | Die-cast Sprung Trucks, rotating bearing caps, *07–10* | | 17 | ___ |
| 14255 | Sand Tower, *06–10* | | 29 | ___ |
| 14257 | Passenger Station, *06–10* | | 55 | ___ |
| 14258 | North Pole Passenger Station, *06–10* | | 53 | ___ |
| 14259 | Christmas People Pack, *06–10* | | 23 | ___ |
| 14260 | Christmas Tractor and Trailer, *06–08* | | 25 | ___ |
| 14261 | Christmas Tree Lot, *06* | | 70 | ___ |
| 14262 | Elevated Tank, *07* | | 70 | ___ |
| 14265 | Sawmill with sound, *08* | | 130 | ___ |
| 14267 | Sir Topham Hatt Gateman, *07–09* | | 80 | ___ |
| 14273 | *Polar Express* Add-on Figures, *06–07* | | 27 | ___ |
| 14289 | Operating Santa Gateman, *08* | | 80 | ___ |
| 14290 | UPS Store, *06* | | 30 | ___ |
| 14291 | Operating Milk Loading Depot, *08* | | 100 | ___ |
| 14291 | Operating Milk Loading Depot, K-Line, *06* | | 100 | ___ |
| 14294 | 993 Legacy Expansion Set, *07–10* | | 250 | ___ |
| 14295 | 990 Legacy Command Set, *07–10* | | 300 | ___ |
| 14297 | Halloween Witch Pylon, *07–08* | | 140 | ___ |
| 14500 | KCS F3 Diesel AA Set, Railsounds, CC, *01* | 380 | 660 | ___ |
| 14512 | F3 Diesel ABA Demonstrator "291," CC, *01* | 360 | 425 | ___ |
| 14517 | Santa Fe F3 Diesel B Unit "2343C," powered, *01* | | 280 | ___ |
| 14518 | CP F3 Diesel B Unit "2373C," RailSounds, CC, *01* | | 345 | ___ |
| 14520 | *Texas Special* F3 Diesel B Unit, RailSounds, *01* | | 360 | ___ |
| 14521 | Rock Island E6 Diesel AA Set, *01* | | 530 | ___ |
| 14524 | Atlantic Coast Line E6 Diesel AA Set, *01* | | 630 | ___ |
| 14536 | Santa Fe F3 Diesel AA Set, RailSounds, CC, *03–04* | | 800 | ___ |
| 14539 | Santa Fe F3 Diesel B Unit, *03* | | 300 | ___ |
| 14540 | D&RGW F3 Diesel B Unit, RailSounds, CC, *01* | | 315 | ___ |
| 14541 | C&O F3 Diesel B Unit, RailSounds, CC, *01* | | 300 | ___ |
| 14542 | KCS F3 Diesel B Unit "2388C," RailSounds, CC, *01* | | 375 | ___ |
| 14543 | SP F3 Diesel B Unit, RailSounds, CC, *01* | | 282 | ___ |
| 14544 | Southern E6 AA Diesel Set, CC, *02* | | 560 | ___ |

| | | Exc | Mint | Cond/S |
|---|---|---|---|---|
| **14547** | Burlington E5 AA Diesel Set, CC, *02* | | 570 | ___ |
| **14552** | NYC F3 Diesel AA Set, RailSounds, CC, *03–04* | | 740 | ___ |
| **14555** | NYC F3 Diesel B Unit, *03* | | 200 | ___ |
| **14557** | WP F3 Diesel B Unit, nonpowered, *03–04* | | 190 | ___ |
| **14558** | B&O F3 Diesel B Unit, nonpowered, *03–04* | | 155 | ___ |
| **14559** | D&RGW F3 Diesel AA Set, *01* | | 620 | ___ |
| **14560** | NP F3 Diesel A Unit "2390B," freight, *02* | | 175 | ___ |
| **14561** | NP F3 Diesel A Unit "2390B," passenger, *02* | | 190 | ___ |
| **14562** | Milwaukee Road F3 Diesel A Unit "75C," *02* | | 190 | ___ |
| **14563** | Erie-Lackawanna F3 Diesel A Unit "7094," *02* | | 175 | ___ |
| **14564** | CP F3 Diesel B Unit "237C," CC, *02* | | 350 | ___ |
| **14565** | B&O F3 Diesel AA Set, *03–04* | | 650 | ___ |
| **14568** | WP F3 Diesel AA Set, *03–04* | | 780 | ___ |
| **14571** | Santa Fe PA Diesel AA Set, CC, *03* | | 660 | ___ |
| **14574** | D&H PA Diesel AA Set, CC, *03* | | 580 | ___ |
| **14584** | Wabash F3 Diesel A Unit, nonpowered, *03* | | 180 | ___ |
| **14586** | D&H PB Unit, *03* | | 125 | ___ |
| **14587** | Santa Fe PB Unit, *03* | | 125 | ___ |
| **14588** | Santa Fe F3 Diesel ABA Set, CC, *04–05* | | 980 | ___ |
| **14592** | PRR F3 Diesel ABA Set, CC, *04–05* | | 750 | ___ |
| **14596** | NH Alco PA Diesel AA Set, *04–05* | | 700 | ___ |
| **14599** | NH Alco PB Diesel B Unit "0767-B," *04–05* | | 150 | ___ |
| **15000** | D&RGW Waffle-sided Boxcar, *95* | 16 | 18 | ___ |
| **15001** | Seaboard Waffle-sided Boxcar, *95* | 14 | 19 | ___ |
| **15002** | Chesapeake & Ohio Waffle-sided Boxcar, *96* | 16 | 20 | ___ |
| **15003** | Green Bay & Western Waffle-sided Boxcar, *96* | 16 | 20 | ___ |
| **15004** | Bloomingdale's Boxcar, *97 u* | | 40 | ___ |
| **15005** | "I Love NY" Boxcar, *97 u* | | 65 | ___ |
| **15008** | CP Rail Boxcar | | 30 | ___ |
| **15013** | L&N Waffle-sided Boxcar "102402," *00* | | 29 | ___ |
| **15014** | Seaboard Waffle-sided Boxcar "125925," *00* | | 25 | ___ |
| **15015** | C&NW Waffle-sided Boxcar "161013," *03* | | 18 | ___ |
| **15016** | IC Waffle-sided Boxcar "12981," *04* | | 20 | ___ |
| **15017** | CSX Waffle-sided Boxcar, *05* | | 27 | ___ |
| **15018** | D&H Waffle-sided Boxcar "24052," *06* | | 30 | ___ |
| **15020** | NH Waffle-sided Boxcar, *07* | | 30 | ___ |
| **15021** | MKT Waffle-sided Boxcar, *08* | | 35 | ___ |
| **15024** | UP Waffle Boxcar "960860," *09* | | 40 | ___ |
| **15028** | Southern Waffle-sided Boxcar "539889," *10* | | 40 | ___ |
| **15029** | Western & Atlantic Wood-sided Reefer, *10* | | 53 | ___ |
| **15060** | K-Line Boxcar, *06* | | 40 | ___ |
| **15100** | Amtrak Passenger Coach, *95–97* | | 35 | ___ |
| **15101** | Reading Baggage Car (O27), *96* | | 34 | ___ |
| **15102** | Reading Combination Car (O27), *96* | | 23 | ___ |
| **15103** | Reading Passenger Coach (O27), *96* | | 23 | ___ |
| **15104** | Reading Vista Dome Car (O27), *96* | | 26 | ___ |
| **15105** | Reading Full Vista Dome Car (O27), *96* | | 26 | ___ |
| **15106** | Reading Observation Car (O27), *96* | | 23 | ___ |

Exc Mint Cond/$

| | | Exc | Mint | Cond/$ |
|---|---|---|---|---|
| 15107 | Amtrak Vista Dome Car, *96* | | 38 | ___ |
| 15108 | Northern Pacific Vista Dome Car, *96* | | 34 | ___ |
| 15109 | ATSF Combine Car "2407," *97* | | 35 | ___ |
| 15110 | ATSF Vista Dome Car 2404," *97* | | 35 | ___ |
| 15111 | ATSF Observation Car "2406," *97* | | 35 | ___ |
| 15112 | ATSF *Albuquerque* Coach "2405," *97* | | 34 | ___ |
| 15113 | ATSF *Culebra* Vista Dome Car "2404," *97* | | 34 | ___ |
| 15114 | NJ Transit Coach "5610," *96 u* | | 45 | ___ |
| 15115 | NJ Transit Coach "5611," *96 u* | | 45 | ___ |
| 15116 | NJ Transit Coach "5612," *96 u* | | 45 | ___ |
| 15117 | Annie Passenger Coach, *97* | | 26 | ___ |
| 15118 | Clarabel Passenger Coach, *97* | | 26 | ___ |
| 15122 | NJ Transit Passenger Coach "5613," *97 u* | | 45 | ___ |
| 15123 | NJ Transit Passenger Coach "5614," *97 u* | | 45 | ___ |
| 15124 | NJ Transit Passenger Coach "5615," *97 u* | | 45 | ___ |
| 15125 | Amtrak Observation Car, *97 u* | | 50 | ___ |
| 15126 | Stars & Stripes *Abraham Lincoln* General Coach, *99* | | 60 | ___ |
| 15127 | Stars & Stripes *Ulysses S. Grant* General Coach, *99* | | 60 | ___ |
| 15128 | Pride of Richmond *Robert E. Lee* General Coach, *99* | | 60 | ___ |
| 15129 | Pride of Richmond *Jefferson Davis* General Coach, *99* | | 60 | ___ |
| 15136 | Custom Series Short Observation Car, blue, *99* | | 40 | ___ |
| 15137 | Custom Series Short Observation Car, red, *99* | | 34 | ___ |
| 15138 | Pratt's Hollow Baggage Car, *98* | | 100 | ___ |
| 15139 | Pratt's Hollow Vista Dome Car, *98* | | 100 | ___ |
| 15140 | Pratt's Hollow Coach, *98* | | 100 | ___ |
| 15141 | Pratt's Hollow Observation, *98* | | 100 | ___ |
| 15142 | U.S. Army Baby Heavyweight Coach, *00* | | 50 | ___ |
| 15143 | U.S. Army Baby Heavyweight Coach, *00* | | 50 | ___ |
| 15153 | Pullman Baby Madison Set 4-pack, *01* | | 190 | ___ |
| 15163 | T&P Baby Heavyweight Coach, *01* | | 30 | ___ |
| 15166 | Union Pacific Whistling Baggage Car, *04* | | 41 | ___ |
| 15169 | C&O Streamliner Car 4-pack, *03* | | 140 | ___ |
| 15170 | L&N Streamliner Car 4-pack, *03* | | 140 | ___ |
| 15180 | NYC Streamliner Car 4-pack, *04* | | 340 | ___ |
| 15185 | UP Streamliner Car 4-pack, *04* | | 340 | ___ |
| 15300 | NYC Superliner Aluminum Passenger Car 4-pack, *02* | | 360 | ___ |
| 15301 | NYC *Manhattan* Superliner Passenger Coach, *02* | | 90 | ___ |
| 15302 | NYC *Queens* Superliner Passenger Coach, *02* | | 90 | ___ |
| 15304 | NYC *Staten Island* Superliner Passenger Coach, *02* | | 90 | ___ |
| 15305 | NYC *Brooklyn* Superliner Passenger Coach, *02* | | 90 | ___ |
| 15311 | CB&Q *California Zephyr* Aluminum Passenger Car 4-pack, *03* | | 350 | ___ |
| 15312 | Santa Fe *Super Chief* Aluminum Passenger Car 4-pack, *03* | | 275 | ___ |

Exc Mint Cond/$

| | | Exc | Mint | Cond/$ |
|---|---|---|---|---|
| 15313 | D&H Aluminum Passenger Car 4-pack, *03* | | 350 | ____ |
| 15313 | D&H Aluminum Passenger Car 4-pack, *05* | | 480 | ____ |
| 15314 | Amtrak Superliner 2-pack, *03* | | 220 | ____ |
| 15315 | Santa Fe Superliner 2-pack, *03* | | 200 | ____ |
| 15316 | NYC Superliner 2-pack, *03* | | 195 | ____ |
| 15317 | Southern Aluminum Passenger Car 4-pack, *03* | | 350 | ____ |
| 15318 | Lionel Lines Aluminum Passenger Car 2-pack, *03* | | 125 | ____ |
| 15319 | Santa Fe Superliner Aluminum Passenger Car 2-pack, *03* | | 145 | ____ |
| 15326 | NYC *20th Century Limited* Aluminum Passenger Car 6-pack, *02* | | 485 | ____ |
| 15333 | N&W *Powhatan Arrow* Aluminum Passenger Car 6-pack, *02* | | 435 | ____ |
| 15340 | PRR *South Wind* Aluminum Passenger Car 6-pack, *02* | | 435 | ____ |
| 15379 | Lionel Lines *Silver Valley* Aluminum Combination Car, *03* | | 100 | ____ |
| 15380 | Lionel Lines *Silver Spoon* Aluminum Diner, *03* | | 100 | ____ |
| 15381 | Santa Fe Aluminum Baggage Car "2571," *03* | | 100 | ____ |
| 15382 | Santa Fe *Regal Dome* Aluminum Vista Dome Car, *03* | | 100 | ____ |
| 15383 | NYC *20th Century Limited* Diner, StationSounds, *03* | | 195 | ____ |
| 15384 | N&W *Powhatan Arrow* Diner, StationSounds, *03* | | 190 | ____ |
| 15385 | Pennsylvania *South Wind* Diner, StationSounds, *03* | | 190 | ____ |
| 15394 | Amtrak Streamliner Car 4-pack, *03–04* | | 450 | ____ |
| 15395 | Alaska Streamliner Car 4-pack, *03–04* | | 355 | ____ |
| 15396 | Amtrak Superliner Diner, StationSounds, *03* | | 220 | ____ |
| 15397 | Santa Fe Superliner Diner, StationSounds, *03* | | 200 | ____ |
| 15398 | NYC Superliner Diner, StationSounds, *03* | | 200 | ____ |
| 15405 | 50th Anniversary *Hillside* Heavyweight Diner, StationSounds, *02* | | 195 | ____ |
| 15406 | Blue Comet *Giacobini* Heavyweight Diner, StationSounds, *02* | | 300 | ____ |
| 15504 | *Alton Limited* Diner, StationSounds, *03* | | 230 | ____ |
| 15507 | Phantom III Passenger Car 4-pack (15508 Baggage, 15509 Vista Dome, 15510 Coach, 15511 Observation), *02* | | 245 | ____ |
| 15512 | Phantom II Passenger Car 4-pack, *02* | | 250 | ____ |
| 15517 | Southern *Crescent Limited* Heavyweight Passenger Car 2-pack, *03–04* | | 205 | ____ |
| 15520 | Southern *Crescent Limited* Heavyweight Diner, StationSounds, *03–04* | | 220 | ____ |
| 15521 | NYC *20th Century Limited* Heavyweight Passenger Car 4-pack, *04* | | 345 | ____ |
| 15526 | Santa Fe *Chief* Heavyweight Passenger Car 4-pack, *04* | | 370 | ____ |
| 15538 | NYC *20th Century Limited* Heavyweight Passenger Car 2-pack, *04* | | 200 | ____ |

| | | Exc | Mint | Cond/S |
|---|---|---|---|---|
| **15541** | NYC *20th Century Limited* Heavyweight Diner, StationSounds, *04* | | 200 | ___ |
| **15542** | Santa Fe *Chief* Heavyweight Passenger Car 2-pack, *04* | | 195 | ___ |
| **15545** | Santa Fe *Chief* Heavyweight Diner, StationSounds, *04* | | 200 | ___ |
| **15546** | Napa Valley Wine Train Heavyweight 2-pack, *05* | | 250 | ___ |
| **15549** | Napa Valley Wine Train Diner, StationSounds, *05* | | 280 | ___ |
| **15554** | Pennsylvania Heavyweight Car 3-pack (std O), *05* | | 375 | ___ |
| **15558** | Pennsylvania Heavyweight Add-on Coach (std O), *05* | | 140 | ___ |
| **15559** | PRR Reading Seashore Heavyweight Car 3-pack (std O), *05* | | 370 | ___ |
| **15563** | PRR Reading Seashore Heavyweight Add-on Coach, *05* | | 130 | ___ |
| **15564** | LIRR Heavyweight Car 3-pack (std O), *05* | | 370 | ___ |
| **15568** | LIRR Heavyweight Add-on Coach (std O), *05* | | 130 | ___ |
| **15570** | LIRR Heavyweight Car 3-pack (std O), *06* | | 230 | ___ |
| **15574** | LIRR Heavyweight Car Add-on (std O), *06* | | 140 | ___ |
| **15575** | C&O Heavyweight Diner, StationSounds (std O), *06–07* | | 295 | ___ |
| **15576** | C&O Heavyweight Passenger Car 2-pack (std O), *06–07* | | 265 | ___ |
| **15577** | NYC Heavyweight 3-pack (std O), *05–06* | | 370 | ___ |
| **15581** | NYC Heavyweight Add-on Coach (std O), *05–06* | | 130 | ___ |
| **15584** | Amtrak Acela Passenger Car 3-pack (std O), *06* | | 580 | ___ |
| **15588** | Southern Heavyweight Passenger Car 4-pack, *06* | | 495 | ___ |
| **15593** | Southern Heavyweight Passenger Car 2-pack, *06* | | 265 | ___ |
| **15596** | Southern Heavyweight Diner, StationSounds, *06* | | 295 | ___ |
| **15597** | C&O Heavyweight Passenger Car 4-pack (std O), *06–07* | | 495 | ___ |
| **15906** | RailSounds Trigger Button, *90–95* | | 12 | ___ |
| **16000** | PRR Vista Dome Car (027), *87–88* | 37 | 55 | ___ |
| **16001** | PRR Passenger Coach (027), *87–88* | 33 | 41 | ___ |
| **16002** | PRR Passenger Coach (027), *87–88* | 24 | 29 | ___ |
| **16003** | PRR Observation Car (027), *87–88* | 24 | 29 | ___ |
| **16009** | PRR Combination Car (027), *88* | 36 | 38 | ___ |
| **16010** | Virginia & Truckee Passenger Coach (SSS), *88* | 36 | 47 | ___ |
| **16011** | Virginia & Truckee Passenger Coach (SSS), *88* | 36 | 47 | ___ |
| **16012** | Virginia & Truckee Baggage Car (SSS), *88* | 36 | 47 | ___ |
| **16013** | Amtrak Combination Car (027), *88–89* | 21 | 34 | ___ |
| **16014** | Amtrak Vista Dome Car (027), *88–89* | 21 | 34 | ___ |
| **16015** | Amtrak Observation Car (027), *88–89* | 21 | 34 | ___ |
| **16016** | NYC Baggage Car (027), *89* | 36 | 55 | ___ |
| **16017** | NYC Combination Car (027), *89* | 21 | 29 | ___ |
| **16018** | NYC Passenger Coach (027), *89* | 21 | 29 | ___ |
| **16019** | NYC Vista Dome Car (027), *89* | 21 | 29 | ___ |
| **16020** | NYC Passenger Coach (027), *89* | 23 | 33 | ___ |

| | | Exc | Mint | Cond/$ |
|---|---|---|---|---|
| **16021** | NYC Observation Car (027), *89* | 20 | 28 | ____ |
| **16022** | Pennsylvania Baggage Car (027), *89* | 27 | 38 | ____ |
| **16023** | Amtrak Passenger Coach (027), *89* | 21 | 30 | ____ |
| **16024** | Northern Pacific Diner (027), *92* | 39 | 44 | ____ |
| **16027** | LL Combination Car (027, SSS), *90* | 39 | 48 | ____ |
| **16028** | LL Passenger Coach (SSS, 027), *90* | 35 | 42 | ____ |
| **16029** | LL Passenger Coach (SSS, 027), *90* | 35 | 42 | ____ |
| **16030** | LL Observation Car (SSS, 027), *90* | 35 | 42 | ____ |
| **16031** | Pennsylvania Diner (027), *90* | 35 | 39 | ____ |
| **16033** | Amtrak Baggage Car (027), *90* | 28 | 38 | ____ |
| **16034** | NP Baggage Car (027), *90–91* | 30 | 45 | ____ |
| **16035** | NP Combination Car (027), *90–91* | 18 | 26 | ____ |
| **16036** | NP Passenger Coach (027), *90–91* | 21 | 30 | ____ |
| **16037** | NP Vista Dome Car (027), *90–91* | 18 | 26 | ____ |
| **16038** | NP Passenger Coach (027), *90–91* | 17 | 25 | ____ |
| **16039** | NP Observation Car (027), *90–91* | 21 | 30 | ____ |
| **16040** | Southern Pacific Baggage Car, *90–91* | 22 | 30 | ____ |
| **16041** | NYC Diner (027), *91* | 37 | 37 | ____ |
| **16042** | Illinois Central Baggage Car (027), *91* | 24 | 34 | ____ |
| **16043** | Illinois Central Combination Car (027), *91* | 22 | 30 | ____ |
| **16044** | Illinois Central Passenger Coach (027), *91* | 24 | 34 | ____ |
| **16045** | Illinois Central Vista Dome Car (027), *91* | 22 | 30 | ____ |
| **16046** | Illinois Central Passenger Coach (027), *91* | 24 | 34 | ____ |
| **16047** | Illinois Central Observation Car (027), *91* | 24 | 34 | ____ |
| **16048** | Amtrak Diner (027), *91–92* | 33 | 40 | ____ |
| **16049** | Illinois Central Diner (027), *92* | 27 | 38 | ____ |
| **16050** | C&NW Baggage Car "6620," *93* | 44 | 55 | ____ |
| **16051** | C&NW Combination Car "6630," *93* | 40 | 50 | ____ |
| **16052** | C&NW Passenger Coach "6616," *93* | 34 | 42 | ____ |
| **16053** | C&NW Passenger Coach "6602," *93* | 37 | 46 | ____ |
| **16054** | C&NW Observation Car "6603," *93* | 38 | 47 | ____ |
| **16055** | Santa Fe Passenger Coach (027), *93–94* | 29 | 38 | ____ |
| **16056** | Santa Fe Vista Dome Car (027), *93–94* | 25 | 32 | ____ |
| **16057** | Santa Fe Passenger Coach (027), *93–94* | 30 | 40 | ____ |
| **16058** | Santa Fe Combination Car (027), *93–94* | 27 | 35 | ____ |
| **16059** | Santa Fe Vista Dome Car (027), *93–94* | 26 | 34 | ____ |
| **16060** | Santa Fe Observation Car (027), *93–94* | 25 | 31 | ____ |
| **16061** | N&W Baggage Car "6061," *94* | 60 | 85 | ____ |
| **16062** | N&W Combination Car "6062," *94* | 38 | 50 | ____ |
| **16063** | N&W Passenger Coach "6063," *94* | 43 | 55 | ____ |
| **16064** | N&W Passenger Coach "6064," *94* | 43 | 55 | ____ |
| **16065** | N&W Observation Car "6065," *94* | 36 | 48 | ____ |
| **16066** | NYC Combination Car "6066" (SSS), *94* | 55 | 70 | ____ |
| **16067** | NYC Passenger Coach "6067" (SSS), *94* | 38 | 47 | ____ |
| **16068** | UP Baggage Car "6068" (027), *94* | 50 | 65 | ____ |
| **16069** | UP Combination Car "6069" (027), *94* | 36 | 43 | ____ |
| **16070** | UP Passenger Coach "6070" (027), *94* | 36 | 43 | ____ |
| **16071** | UP Diner "6071" (027), *94* | 36 | 46 | ____ |

| | | Exc | Mint | Cond/$ |
|---|---|---|---|---|
| 16072 | UP Vista Dome Car "6072" (027), *94* | 36 | 43 | ____ |
| 16073 | UP Passenger Coach "6073" (027), *94* | 36 | 42 | ____ |
| 16074 | UP Observation Car "6074" (027), *94* | 36 | 43 | ____ |
| 16075 | Missouri Pacific Baggage Car "6620," *95* | 44 | 55 | ____ |
| 16076 | Missouri Pacific Combination Car "6630," *95* | 34 | 41 | ____ |
| 16077 | Missouri Pacific Passenger Coach "6616," *95* | 34 | 41 | ____ |
| 16078 | Missouri Pacific Passenger Coach "7805," *95* | 34 | 39 | ____ |
| 16079 | Missouri Pacific Observation Car "6609," *95* | 34 | 41 | ____ |
| 16080 | New Haven Baggage Car "6080" (027), *95* | 35 | 44 | ____ |
| 16081 | New Haven Combination Car "6081" (027), *95* | 28 | 37 | ____ |
| 16082 | New Haven Passenger Coach "6082" (027), *95* | 28 | 37 | ____ |
| 16083 | New Haven Vista Dome Car "6083" (027), *95* | 30 | 39 | ____ |
| 16084 | New Haven Full Vista Dome Car "6084" (027), *95* | 33 | 39 | ____ |
| 16086 | New Haven Observation Car "6086" (027), *95* | 31 | 40 | ____ |
| 16087 | NYC Baggage Car "6087" (SSS), *95* | 48 | 65 | ____ |
| 16088 | NYC Passenger Coach "6088" (SSS), *95* | 36 | 43 | ____ |
| 16089 | NYC Diner "6089" (SSS), *95* | 36 | 43 | ____ |
| 16090 | NYC Observation Car "6090" (SSS), *95* | 38 | 46 | ____ |
| 16091 | NYC Passenger Cars, set of 4 (SSS), *95* | 140 | 165 | ____ |
| 16092 | Santa Fe Full Vista Dome Car (027), *95* | 30 | 38 | ____ |
| 16093 | Illinois Central Full Vista Dome Car (027), *95* | 29 | 38 | ____ |
| 16094 | Pennsylvania Full Vista Dome Car (027), *95* | 30 | 39 | ____ |
| 16095 | Amtrak Combination Car (027), *95* | 19 | 23 | ____ |
| 16096 | Amtrak Vista Dome Car (027), *95* | 19 | 23 | ____ |
| 16097 | Amtrak Observation Car (027), *95* | 19 | 23 | ____ |
| 16098 | Amtrak Passenger Coach, *95–97* | 20 | 33 | ____ |
| 16099 | Amtrak Vista Dome Car, *95–97* | 20 | 33 | ____ |
| 16102 | Southern 3-D Tank Car (SSS), *87* | 23 | 30 | ____ |
| 16103 | Lehigh Valley 2-D Tank Car (027), *88* | 19 | 25 | ____ |
| 16104 | Santa Fe 2-D Tank Car (027), *89* | 19 | 23 | ____ |
| 16105 | D&RGW 3-D Tank Car (SSS), *89* | 48 | 65 | ____ |
| 16106 | Mopar Express 3-D Tank Car, *88 u* | 93 | 163 | ____ |
| 16107 | Sunoco 2-D Tank Car (027), *90* | 16 | 20 | ____ |
| 16108 | Racing Fuel 1-D Tank Car "6108" (027), *89 u, 92 u* | 9 | 13 | ____ |
| 16109 | B&O 1-D Tank Car (SSS), *91* | 29 | 34 | ____ |
| 16110 | Circus Animals Operating Stock Car "1989" (027), *89 u* | 24 | 34 | ____ |
| 16111 | Alaska 1-D Tank Car (027), *90–91* | 22 | 27 | ____ |
| 16112 | Dow Chemical 3-D Tank Car, *90* | 20 | 26 | ____ |
| 16113 | Diamond Shamrock 2-D Tank Car (027), *91* | 20 | 25 | ____ |
| 16114 | Hooker Chemicals 1-D Tank Car (027), *91* | 13 | 17 | ____ |
| 16115 | MKT 3-D Tank Car, *92* | 13 | 16 | ____ |
| 16116 | U.S. Army 1-D Tank Car, *91 u* | 36 | 42 | ____ |
| 16119 | MKT 2-D Tank Car (027), *92, 93 u* | 14 | 19 | ____ |
| 16121 | C&NW Stock Car (SSS), *92* | 33 | 43 | ____ |
| 16123 | Union Pacific 3-D Tank Car, *93–95* | 16 | 22 | ____ |
| 16124 | Penn Salt 3-D Tank Car, *93* | 21 | 26 | ____ |

| | | Exc | Mint | Cond/$ |
|---|---|---|---|---|
| **16125** | Virginian Stock Car, *93* | 19 | 24 | ___ |
| **16126** | Jefferson Lake 3-D Tank Car, *93* | 22 | 26 | ___ |
| **16127** | Mobil 1-D Tank Car, *93* | 25 | 30 | ___ |
| **16128** | Alaska 1-D Tank Car, *94* | 24 | 29 | ___ |
| **16129** | Alaska 1-D Tank Car (027), *93 u, 94* | 21 | 28 | ___ |
| **16130** | SP Stock Car (027), *93 u, 94* | 10 | 13 | ___ |
| **16131** | T&P Reefer, *94* | 19 | 24 | ___ |
| **16132** | Deep Rock 3-D Tank Car, *94* | 25 | 30 | ___ |
| **16133** | Santa Fe Reefer, *94* | 22 | 28 | ___ |
| **16134** | Reading Reefer, *94* | 17 | 21 | ___ |
| **16135** | C&O Stock Car, *94* | 23 | 27 | ___ |
| **16136** | B&O 1-D Tank Car, *94* | 28 | 32 | ___ |
| **16137** | Ford 1-D Tank Car "12," *94 u* | 34 | 39 | ___ |
| **16138** | Goodyear 1-D Tank Car, *95* | 28 | 34 | ___ |
| **16140** | Domino Sugar 1-D Tank Car, *95* | 24 | 29 | ___ |
| **16141** | Erie Stock Car, *95* | 22 | 30 | ___ |
| **16142** | Santa Fe 1-D Tank Car, *95* | 26 | 30 | ___ |
| **16143** | Reading Reefer, *95* | 18 | 23 | ___ |
| **16144** | San Angelo 3-D Tank Car, *95* | 22 | 25 | ___ |
| **16146** | Dairy Despatch Reefer, *95* | 15 | 20 | ___ |
| **16147** | Clearly Canadian 1-D Tank Car (027), *94 u* | 25 | 40 | ___ |
| **16149** | Zep Chemical 1-D Tank Car (027), *95 u* | 47 | 59 | ___ |
| **16150** | Sunoco 1-D Tank Car "6315," *97* | 35 | 38 | ___ |
| **16152** | Sunoco 3-D Tank Car "6415," *97* | | 26 | ___ |
| **16153** | AEC Reactor Fluid 1-D Tank Car "6515-1," *97* | | 76 | ___ |
| **16154** | AEC Reactor Fluid 1-D Tank Car "6515-2," *97* | | 89 | ___ |
| **16155** | AEC Reactor Fluid 1-D Tank Car "6515-3," *97* | | 89 | ___ |
| **16157** | Gatorade Little League Baseball 1-D Tank Car "6315," *97 u* | | 53 | ___ |
| **16160** | AEC Tank Car "6515" with reactor fluid, *98* | | 69 | ___ |
| **16162** | Hooker 1-D Tank Car "6315-1," *97* | | 50 | ___ |
| **16163** | Hooker 1-D Tank Car "6315-2," *97* | | 50 | ___ |
| **16164** | Hooker 1-D Tank Car "6315-3," *97* | | 50 | ___ |
| **16165** | Mobilfuel 3-D Tank Car "6415," *97 u* | | 50 | ___ |
| **16171** | Alaska 1-D Tank Car "6171," *98–99* | | 33 | ___ |
| **16173** | Harold the Helicopter Flatcar, *98* | 45 | 60 | ___ |
| **16175** | NJ Transit Port Morris Ore Car "9125," *98* | | 45 | ___ |
| **16176** | NJ Transit Raritan Yard Ore Car "9126," *98 u* | | 45 | ___ |
| **16177** | NJ Transit Gladstone Yard Ore Car "9127," *98 u* | | 45 | ___ |
| **16178** | NJ Transit Bay Head Yard Ore Car "9128," *98 u* | | 45 | ___ |
| **16179** | NJ Transit Dover Yard Ore Car "9129," *98 u* | | 45 | ___ |
| **16180** | Tabasco 1-D Tank Car, *98* | 55 | 71 | ___ |
| **16181** | Biohazard Tank Car with Lights, *98* | | 69 | ___ |
| **16182** | Gatorade 1-D Tank Car "6315," *98 u* | | 59 | ___ |
| **16187** | Linex 3-D Tank Car "6425," *99* | | 30 | ___ |
| **16188** | Kodak 1-D Tank Car "6515," *99* | 70 | 83 | ___ |
| **16199** | UP 1-D Tank Car "6035," *99–00* | | 25 | ___ |
| **16200** | Rock Island Boxcar (027), *87–88* | 7 | 10 | ___ |

| | | Exc | Mint | Cond/S |
|---|---|---|---|---|
| 16201 | Wabash Boxcar (027), *88–91* | 7 | 10 | ___ |
| 16203 | Key America Boxcar (027), *87 u* | 45 | 65 | ___ |
| 16204 | Hawthorne Boxcar (027), *87 u* | 50 | 85 | ___ |
| 16205 | Mopar Express Boxcar "1987" (027), *87–88 u* | 50 | 60 | ___ |
| 16206 | D&RGW Boxcar (SSS), *89* | 37 | 42 | ___ |
| 16207 | True Value Boxcar (027), *88 u* | 32 | 47 | ___ |
| 16208 | PRR Auto Carrier, 3-tier, *89* | 24 | 37 | ___ |
| 16209 | Disney Magic Boxcar (027), *88 u* | 90 | 110 | ___ |
| 16211 | Hawthorne Boxcar (027), *88 u* | 45 | 65 | ___ |
| 16213 | Shoprite Boxcar (027), *88 u* | 55 | 80 | ___ |
| 16214 | D&RGW Auto Carrier, *90* | 24 | 32 | ___ |
| 16215 | Conrail Auto Carrier, *90* | 27 | 38 | ___ |
| 16217 | Burlington Northern Auto Carrier, *92* | 24 | 36 | ___ |
| 16219 | True Value Boxcar (027), *89 u* | 55 | 75 | ___ |
| 16220 | Ace Hardware Boxcar (027), *89 u* | 55 | 80 | ___ |
| 16221 | Macy's Boxcar (027), *89 u* | 55 | 80 | ___ |
| 16222 | Great Northern Boxcar (027), *90–91* | 8 | 15 | ___ |
| 16223 | Budweiser Reefer, *89–92 u* | 51 | 71 | ___ |
| 16224 | True Value "Lawn Chief" Boxcar (027), *90 u* | 45 | 60 | ___ |
| 16225 | Budweiser Vat Car, *90–91 u* | 114 | 149 | ___ |
| 16226 | Union Pacific Boxcar "6226" (027), *90–91 u* | 15 | 19 | ___ |
| 16227 | Santa Fe Boxcar (027), *91* | 13 | 17 | ___ |
| 16228 | Union Pacific Auto Carrier, *92* | 26 | 33 | ___ |
| 16229 | Erie-Lackawanna Auto Carrier, *91 u* | 45 | 55 | ___ |
| 16232 | Chessie System Boxcar, *92, 93 u, 94, 95 u* | 25 | 30 | ___ |
| 16233 | MKT DD Boxcar, *92* | 20 | 29 | ___ |
| 16234 | ACY Boxcar (SSS), *92* | 34 | 41 | ___ |
| 16235 | Railway Express Agency Reefer, *92* | 19 | 23 | ___ |
| 16236 | NYC Pacemaker Boxcar, *92 u* | 18 | 24 | ___ |
| 16237 | Railway Express Agency Boxcar, *92 u* | 21 | 23 | ___ |
| 16238 | NYNH&H Boxcar, *93–95* | | 3 | ___ |
| 16239 | Union Pacific Boxcar, *93–95* | 15 | 20 | ___ |
| 16241 | Toys "R" Us Boxcar, *92–93 u* | 35 | 45 | ___ |
| 16242 | Grand Trunk Western Auto Carrier, *93* | 35 | 40 | ___ |
| 16243 | Conrail Boxcar, *93* | 26 | 34 | ___ |
| 16244 | Duluth, South Shore & Atlantic Boxcar, *93* | 20 | 24 | ___ |
| 16245 | Contadina Boxcar, *93* | 16 | 20 | ___ |
| 16247 | ACL Boxcar, *94* | 15 | 19 | ___ |
| 16248 | Budweiser Boxcar, *93–94 u* | 34 | 49 | ___ |
| 16249 | United Auto Workers Boxcar, *93 u* | | 55 | ___ |
| 16250 | Santa Fe Boxcar (027), *93 u, 94* | 8 | 10 | ___ |
| 16251 | Columbus & Greenville Boxcar, *94* | 14 | 15 | ___ |
| 16252 | U.S. Navy Boxcar "6106888," *94–95* | | 30 | ___ |
| 16253 | Santa Fe Auto Carrier, *94* | 32 | 38 | ___ |
| 16255 | Wabash DD Boxcar, *95* | 20 | 26 | ___ |
| 16256 | Ford DD Boxcar, *94 u* | 30 | 34 | ___ |
| 16257 | Crayola Boxcar, *94 u, 95* | 17 | 23 | ___ |
| 16258 | Lehigh Valley Boxcar, *95* | 17 | 22 | ___ |

| | | Exc | Mint | Cond/$ |
|---|---|---|---|---|
| **16259** | Chrysler Mopar Boxcar, *97 u* | 31 | 35 | _____ |
| **16260** | Chrysler Mopar Auto Carrier, *96 u* | 57 | 67 | _____ |
| **16261** | Union Pacific DD Boxcar, *95* | 26 | 29 | _____ |
| **16263** | ATSF Boxcar, *96–99* | | 25 | _____ |
| **16264** | Red Wing Shoes Boxcar, *95* | 22 | 27 | _____ |
| **16265** | Georgia Power "Atlanta '96" Boxcar, *95 u* | 169 | 219 | _____ |
| **16266** | Crayola Boxcar, *95* | 17 | 23 | _____ |
| **16267** | Sears Zenith Boxcar, *95–96 u* | | 51 | _____ |
| **16268** | GM/AC Delco Boxcar, *95 u* | | 51 | _____ |
| **16269** | Lionel Lines Boxcar, *96* | | 10 | _____ |
| **16272** | Christmas Boxcar, *97* | | 36 | _____ |
| **16273** | Lionel Employee Christmas Boxcar, *97* | | 55 | _____ |
| **16274** | Marvin the Martian Boxcar, *97* | | 39 | _____ |
| **16279** | Dodge Motorsports Boxcar, *96 u* | 118 | 158 | _____ |
| **16284** | Galveston Wharves Boxcar, *98* | | 28 | _____ |
| **16285** | Savannah State Docks Boxcar, *98* | | 26 | _____ |
| **16291** | Christmas Boxcar, *98* | | 34 | _____ |
| **16292** | Lionel Employee Christmas Boxcar, *98* | 305 | 365 | _____ |
| **16293** | JCPenney Boxcar, *97* | | 100 | _____ |
| **16294** | Pedigree Boxcar, *97* | 131 | 149 | _____ |
| **16295** | Kal Kan Boxcar, *97* | 127 | 150 | _____ |
| **16296** | Whiskas Boxcar, *97* | 125 | 148 | _____ |
| **16297** | Sheba Boxcar, *97* | 120 | 143 | _____ |
| **16298** | Mobil Boxcar, *97* | | 48 | _____ |
| **16300** | Rock Island Flatcar with fences (O27), *87–88* | 8 | 10 | _____ |
| **16301** | Lionel Barrel Ramp Car, *87* | 14 | 19 | _____ |
| **16303** | PRR Flatcar with trailers, *87* | 26 | 33 | _____ |
| **16304** | RI Gondola with cable reels (O27), *87–88* | 5 | 9 | _____ |
| **16305** | Lehigh Valley Ore Car, *87* | 80 | 130 | _____ |
| **16306** | Santa Fe Barrel Ramp Car, *88* | 12 | 16 | _____ |
| **16307** | NKP Flatcar with trailers, *88* | 30 | 40 | _____ |
| **16308** | Burlington Northern Flatcar with trailer, *88–89* | 20 | 25 | _____ |
| **16309** | Wabash Gondola with canisters, *88–91* | 9 | 13 | _____ |
| **16310** | Mopar Express Gondola with canisters, *87–88 u* | 32 | 37 | _____ |
| **16311** | Mopar Express Flatcar with trailers, *87–88 u* | 108 | 154 | _____ |
| **16313** | PRR Gondola with cable reels (O27), *88 u, 89* | 9 | 10 | _____ |
| **16314** | Wabash Flatcar with trailers, *89* | 26 | 30 | _____ |
| **16315** | PRR Flatcar with fences (O27), *88 u, 89* | 7 | 9 | _____ |
| **16317** | PRR Barrel Ramp Car, *89* | 18 | 22 | _____ |
| **16318** | LL Depressed Center Flatcar with cable reels, *89* | 22 | 26 | _____ |
| **16320** | Great Northern Barrel Ramp Car, *90* | 13 | 19 | _____ |
| **16321/22** | Sealand TTUX Flatcar Set with trailers, *90* | 65 | 73 | _____ |
| **16323** | Lionel Lines Flatcar with trailers, *90* | 21 | 25 | _____ |
| **16324** | PRR Depressed Center Flatcar with cable reels, *90* | 16 | 20 | _____ |
| **16325** | Microracers Exhibition Ramp Car, *89 u* | 20 | 27 | _____ |

| | | Exc | Mint | Cond/$ |
|---|---|---|---|---|
| 16326 | Santa Fe Depressed Center Flatcar with cable reels, *91* | 16 | 21 | _____ |
| 16327 | "The Big Top" Circus Gondola with canisters, *89 u* | 19 | 24 | _____ |
| 16328 | NKP Gondola with cable reels, *90–91* | 17 | 23 | _____ |
| 16329 | SP Flatcar with horses (O27), *90–91* | 19 | 24 | _____ |
| 16330 | MKT Flatcar with trailers, *91* | 25 | 30 | _____ |
| 16332 | LL Depressed Center Flatcar with transformer, *91* | 28 | 33 | _____ |
| 16333 | Frisco Bulkhead Flatcar with lumber, *91* | 17 | 22 | _____ |
| 16334 | C&NW Flatcar Set ("16337, 16338") with trailers, *91* | 55 | 60 | _____ |
| 16335 | NYC Pacemaker Flatcar with trailer (SSS), *91* | 46 | 65 | _____ |
| 16336 | UP Gondola "6336" with canisters, *90–91 u* | 17 | 21 | _____ |
| 16339 | Mickey's World Tour Gondola with canisters (O27), *91, 92 u* | 17 | 21 | _____ |
| 16341 | NYC Depressed Center Flatcar with transformer, *92* | 29 | 32 | _____ |
| 16342 | CSX Gondola with coil covers, *92* | 18 | 23 | _____ |
| 16343 | Burlington Gondola with coil covers, *92* | 20 | 23 | _____ |
| 16345/46 | SP TTUX Flatcar Set with trailers, *92* | 55 | 65 | _____ |
| 16347 | Ontario Northland Bulkhead Flatcar with pulp load, *92* | 22 | 26 | _____ |
| 16348 | Erie Liquefied Petroleum Car, *92* | 23 | 25 | _____ |
| 16349 | Allis Chalmers Condenser Car, *92* | 28 | 35 | _____ |
| 16350 | CP Rail Bulkhead Flatcar with lumber, *91 u* | 20 | 29 | _____ |
| 16351 | Flatcar with U.S. Navy submarine, *92* | 27 | 33 | _____ |
| 16352 | U.S. Military Flatcar with cruise missile, *92* | 33 | 43 | _____ |
| 16353 | B&M Gondola with coil covers, *91 u* | 33 | 39 | _____ |
| 16355 | Burlington Gondola, *92, 93 u, 94–95* | 11 | 17 | _____ |
| 16356 | MKT Depressed Center Flatcar with cable reels, *92* | 17 | 21 | _____ |
| 16357 | L&N Flatcar with trailer, *92* | 24 | 31 | _____ |
| 16358 | L&N Gondola with coil covers, *92* | 17 | 21 | _____ |
| 16359 | Pacific Coast Gondola with coil covers (SSS), *92* | 33 | 38 | _____ |
| 16360 | N&W Maxi-Stack Flatcar Set ("16361" and "16362") with containers, *93* | 44 | 55 | _____ |
| 16363 | Southern TTUX Flatcar Set ("16364" and "16365") with trailers, *93* | 38 | 49 | _____ |
| 16367 | Clinchfield Gondola with coil covers, *93* | 18 | 21 | _____ |
| 16368 | MKT Liquid Oxygen Car, *93* | 21 | 22 | _____ |
| 16369 | Amtrak Flatcar with wheel load, *92 u* | 19 | 28 | _____ |
| 16370 | Amtrak Flatcar with rail load, *92 u* | 19 | 28 | _____ |
| 16371 | BN I-Beam Flatcar with load, *92 u* | 24 | 29 | _____ |
| 16372 | Southern I-Beam Flatcar with load, *92 u* | 24 | 34 | _____ |
| 16373 | Erie-Lackawanna Flatcar with stakes, *93* | 19 | 23 | _____ |
| 16374 | D&RGW Flatcar with trailer, *93* | 25 | 28 | _____ |
| 16375 | NYC Bulkhead Flatcar, *93–95* | 21 | 25 | _____ |
| 16376 | UP Flatcar with trailer, *93–95* | 31 | 37 | _____ |
| 16378 | Toys "R" Us Flatcar with trailer, *92–93 u* | 60 | 95 | _____ |

| | | Exc | Mint | Cond/S |
|---|---|---|---|---|
| 16379 | NP Bulkhead Flatcar with pulp load, *93* | 16 | 23 | ___ |
| 16380 | UP I-Beam Flatcar with load, *93* | 20 | 26 | ___ |
| 16381 | CSX I-Beam Flatcar with load, *93* | 20 | 25 | ___ |
| 16382 | Kansas City Southern Bulkhead Flatcar, *93* | 14 | 18 | ___ |
| 16383 | Conrail Flatcar with trailer, *93* | 50 | 58 | ___ |
| 16384 | Soo Line Gondola with cable reels, *93* | 14 | 19 | ___ |
| 16385 | Soo Line Ore Car, *93* | 65 | 75 | ___ |
| 16386 | SP Flatcar with lumber, *94* | 15 | 19 | ___ |
| 16387 | KCS Gondola with coil covers, *94* | 13 | 16 | ___ |
| 16388 | LV Gondola with canisters, *94* | 16 | 20 | ___ |
| 16389 | PRR Flatcar with wheel load, *94* | 27 | 32 | ___ |
| 16390 | Flatcar with water tank, *94* | 24 | 27 | ___ |
| 16391 | Lionel Lines Gondola, *93 u* | | 15 | ___ |
| 16392 | Wabash Gondola with canisters (O27), *93 u, 94* | 7 | 9 | ___ |
| 16393 | Wisconsin Central Bulkhead Flatcar, *94* | 13 | 19 | ___ |
| 16394 | Vermont Central Bulkhead Flatcar, *94* | 20 | 30 | ___ |
| 16395 | CP Flatcar with rail load, *94* | 18 | 23 | ___ |
| 16396 | Alaska Bulkhead Flatcar, *94* | 17 | 22 | ___ |
| 16397 | Milwaukee Road I-Beam Flatcar with load, *94* | 30 | 34 | ___ |
| 16398 | C&O Flatcar with trailer, *94* | 80 | 85 | ___ |
| 16399 | Western Pacific I-Beam Flatcar with load, *94* | 31 | 35 | ___ |
| 16400 | PRR Hopper (O27), *88 u, 89* | 15 | 18 | ___ |
| 16402 | Southern Quad Hopper with coal (SSS), *87* | 30 | 42 | ___ |
| 16406 | CSX Quad Hopper with coal, *90* | 29 | 34 | ___ |
| 16407 | B&M Covered Quad Hopper (SSS), *91* | 28 | 37 | ___ |
| 16408 | UP Hopper "6408" (O27), *90–91 u* | 17 | 21 | ___ |
| 16410 | MKT Hopper (O27), *92, 93 u* | 19 | 24 | ___ |
| 16411 | L&N Quad Hopper with coal, *92* | 28 | 32 | ___ |
| 16412 | C&NW Covered Quad Hopper, *94* | 16 | 21 | ___ |
| 16413 | Clinchfield Quad Hopper with coal, *94* | 16 | 22 | ___ |
| 16414 | CCC&StL Hopper (O27), *94* | 18 | 25 | ___ |
| 16416 | D&RGW Covered Quad Hopper, *95* | 16 | 20 | ___ |
| 16417 | Wabash Quad Hopper with coal, *95* | 19 | 21 | ___ |
| 16418 | C&NW Hopper with coal (O27), *95* | 15 | 21 | ___ |
| 16419 | Tennessee Central Hopper, *96* | | 17 | ___ |
| 16420 | WM Quad Hopper with coal (SSS), *95* | 30 | 34 | ___ |
| 16421 | WM Quad Hopper with coal (SSS), *95* | 30 | 33 | ___ |
| 16422 | WM Quad Hopper with coal (SSS), *95* | | 33 | ___ |
| 16423 | WM Quad Hopper with coal (SSS), *95* | | 30 | ___ |
| 16424 | WM Covered Quad Hopper (SSS), *95* | 34 | 39 | ___ |
| 16425 | WM Covered Quad Hopper (SSS), *95* | 25 | 29 | ___ |
| 16426 | WM Covered Quad Hopper (SSS), *95* | 24 | 27 | ___ |
| 16427 | WM Covered Quad Hopper (SSS), *95* | 27 | 30 | ___ |
| 16429 | WM Quad Hopper with coal, set of 2 | | 70 | ___ |
| 16430 | Georgia Power Quad Hopper "82947" with coal, *95 u* | | 105 | ___ |
| 16431 | Lionel Corporation 2-bay Hopper "6456-1," *96* | | 30 | ___ |
| 16432 | Lionel Corporation 2-bay Hopper "6456-2," *96* | | 17 | ___ |

Exc Mint Cond/$

| | | Exc | Mint | Cond/$ |
|---|---|---|---|---|
| 16433 | Lionel Corporation 2-bay Hopper "6456-3," *96* | | 18 | ___ |
| 16434 | LV 2-bay Hopper "6456," "TLDX," *97* | | 25 | ___ |
| 16435 | Virginian 2-bay Hopper "6456-1," *97* | | 30 | ___ |
| 16436 | N&W 2-bay Hopper "6456-2," *97* | | 33 | ___ |
| 16437 | C&O 2-bay Hopper "6456-3," *97* | | 33 | ___ |
| 16438 | Frisco 4-bay Covered Hopper "87538," *98* | | 34 | ___ |
| 16439 | Southern 4-bay Covered Hopper "77836," *98* | | 34 | ___ |
| 16440 | Alaska 2-bay Hopper "7100," *98–99* | | 35 | ___ |
| 16441 | New York Central 4-bay Hopper, *99* | | 26 | ___ |
| 16442 | Bethlehem Gondola "6462" (SSS), *99* | | 40 | ___ |
| 16443 | GN 2-bay Hopper "172364," *99–00* | | 20 | ___ |
| 16444 | CNJ 2-bay Hopper "643," *00* | | 20 | ___ |
| 16445 | Frisco 2-bay Hopper "93108," *00* | | 20 | ___ |
| 16446 | Burlington 2-bay Hopper, *00* | | 20 | ___ |
| 16447 | PRR Tuscan 2-bay Hopper, *00 u* | | 30 | ___ |
| 16448 | PRR Gray 2-bay Hopper, *00 u* | | 30 | ___ |
| 16449 | PRR Black 2-bay Hopper, *00 u* | | 30 | ___ |
| 16450 | PRR Green 2-bay Hopper, *00 u* | | 30 | ___ |
| 16451 | Lionel Mines 2-bay Hopper, *00 u* | | 50 | ___ |
| 16453 | SP 2-bay Hopper "460604," *01* | | 15 | ___ |
| 16454 | Bethlehem Steel Hopper "41025," *01* | | 37 | ___ |
| 16455 | Pioneer Seed 2-bay Hopper, *00 u* | | 50 | ___ |
| 16456 | B&O 2-bay Hopper, *01* | | 20 | ___ |
| 16459 | LV 2-bay Hopper "51102," *01* | | 23 | ___ |
| 16460 | Reading 2-bay Hopper "79636," *02* | | 25 | ___ |
| 16463 | Rio Grande Icebreaker Tunnel Car "18936," *02* | | 32 | ___ |
| 16464 | NYC Icebreaker Tunnel Car "X3200," *02* | | 32 | ___ |
| 16465 | WP 2-bay Hopper "100340," *03* | | 19 | ___ |
| 16466 | Pennsylvania Icebreaker Tunnel Car "16466," *03* | | 33 | ___ |
| 16467 | "Naughty and Nice" Hopper 2-pack, *02* | | 60 | ___ |
| 16469 | B&O Hopper "435351," *02* | | 22 | ___ |
| 16470 | "Naughty and Nice" Ore Car 2-pack, *03* | | 43 | ___ |
| 16473 | Rock Island Ore Car "99122," *03* | | 18 | ___ |
| 16474 | Alaska Ore Car "16474," *04* | | 21 | ___ |
| 16475 | Santa Fe Hopper "16475," *04* | | 18 | ___ |
| 16480 | Lionelville Snow Transport Quad Hopper, *04* | | 45 | ___ |
| 16482 | Norfolk Southern Hopper, traditional, *05* | | 27 | ___ |
| 16489 | BNSF Ore Car, traditional, *05* | | 15 | ___ |
| 16490 | Sodor Mining Hopper, *05* | | 35 | ___ |
| 16491 | CNJ Hopper "60714," *06* | | 30 | ___ |
| 16492 | C&NW Ore Car "114023," *06* | | 30 | ___ |
| 16493 | Christmas Ice Breaker Car, *06* | | 55 | ___ |
| 16500 | Rock Island Bobber Caboose, *87–88* | 9 | 13 | ___ |
| 16501 | Lehigh Valley SP-type Caboose, *87* | 19 | 24 | ___ |
| 16503 | NYC Transfer Caboose, *87* | 16 | 22 | ___ |
| 16504 | Southern N5c Caboose (SSS), *87* | 17 | 30 | ___ |
| 16505 | Wabash SP-type Caboose, *88–91* | 10 | 15 | ___ |
| 16506 | Santa Fe Bay Window Caboose, *88* | 18 | 28 | ___ |

| | | Exc | Mint | Cond/$ |
|---|---|---|---|---|
| **16507** | Mopar Express SP-type Caboose, *87–88 u* | 41 | 50 | ___ |
| **16508** | Lionel Lines SP-type Caboose "6508," *89 u* | 13 | 17 | ___ |
| **16509** | D&RGW SP-type Caboose (SSS), *89* | 19 | 24 | ___ |
| **16510** | New Haven Bay Window Caboose, *89* | 25 | 30 | ___ |
| **16511** | PRR Bobber Caboose, *88 u, 89* | 9 | 13 | ___ |
| **16513** | Union Pacific SP-type Caboose, *89* | 14 | 21 | ___ |
| **16515** | Lionel Lines SP-type Caboose, RailScope, *89* | 20 | 23 | ___ |
| **16516** | Lehigh Valley SP-type Caboose, *90* | 15 | 26 | ___ |
| **16517** | Atlantic Coast Line Bay Window Caboose, *90* | 22 | 26 | ___ |
| **16518** | Chessie System Bay Window Caboose, *90* | 41 | 50 | ___ |
| **16519** | Rock Island Transfer Caboose, *90* | 13 | 17 | ___ |
| **16520** | "Welcome to the Show" Circus SP-type Caboose, *89 u* | 13 | 21 | ___ |
| **16521** | PRR SP-type Caboose, *90–91* | 8 | 11 | ___ |
| **16522** | "Chills & Thrills" Circus N5c Caboose, *90–91* | 10 | 15 | ___ |
| **16523** | Alaska SP-type Caboose, *91* | 24 | 31 | ___ |
| **16524** | Anheuser-Busch SP-type Caboose, *89–92 u* | 31 | 41 | ___ |
| **16525** | D&H Bay Window Caboose (SSS), *91* | 30 | 39 | ___ |
| **16526** | Kansas City Southern SP-type Caboose, *91* | 17 | 21 | ___ |
| **16528** | UP SP-type Caboose "6528," *90–91 u* | 17 | 21 | ___ |
| **16529** | Santa Fe SP-type Caboose "16829," *91* | 9 | 13 | ___ |
| **16530** | Mickey's World Tour SP-type Caboose "16830," *91, 92 u* | 13 | 17 | ___ |
| **16531** | Texas &Pacific SP-type Caboose, *92* | 18 | 23 | ___ |
| **16533** | C&NW Bay Window Caboose, *92* | 29 | 40 | ___ |
| **16534** | Delaware & Hudson SP-type Caboose, *92* | 14 | 19 | ___ |
| **16535** | Erie-Lackawanna Bay Window Caboose, *91 u* | 42 | 50 | ___ |
| **16536** | Chessie System SP-type Caboose, *92, 93 u, 94, 95 u* | | 23 | ___ |
| **16537** | MKT SP-type Caboose, *92, 93 u* | 17 | 21 | ___ |
| **16538** | L&N Bay Window Caboose "1041," *92 u* | 29 | 33 | ___ |
| **16539** | WP Steelside Caboose "539," smoke, SSS (std O), *92* | 50 | 55 | ___ |
| **16541** | Montana Rail Link Extended Vision Caboose "10131" with smoke, *93* | 55 | 65 | ___ |
| **16543** | NYC SP-type Caboose, *93–95* | | 20 | ___ |
| **16544** | Union Pacific SP-type Caboose, *93–95* | 22 | 26 | ___ |
| **16546** | Clinchfield SP-type Caboose, *93* | 22 | 26 | ___ |
| **16547** | "Happy Holidays" SP-type Caboose, *93–95* | 46 | 55 | ___ |
| **16548** | Conrail SP-type Caboose, *93* | 15 | 20 | ___ |
| **16549** | Soo Line Work Caboose, *93* | 18 | 26 | ___ |
| **16550** | U.S. Navy Searchlight Caboose, *94–95* | 17 | 21 | ___ |
| **16551** | Budweiser SP-type Caboose, *93–94 u* | 24 | 29 | ___ |
| **16552** | Frisco Searchlight Caboose, *94* | 23 | 26 | ___ |
| **16553** | United Auto Workers SP-type Caboose, *93 u* | | 40 | ___ |
| **16554** | GT Extended Vision Caboose "79052," smoke, *94* | 40 | 47 | ___ |
| **16555** | C&O SP-type Caboose, *94* | 22 | 26 | ___ |
| **16557** | Ford SP-type Caboose, *94 u* | 19 | 24 | ___ |
| **16558** | Crayola SP-type Caboose, *94 u, 95* | 17 | 21 | ___ |

| | | Exc | Mint | Cond/$ |
|---|---|---|---|---|
| 16559 | Seaboard Center Cupola Caboose "5658," *95* | 23 | 24 | ___ |
| 16560 | Chrysler Mopar Caboose, *94 u* | 23 | 25 | ___ |
| 16561 | UP Center Cupola Caboose "25766," *95* | 27 | 31 | ___ |
| 16562 | Reading Center Cupola Caboose, *95* | 25 | 29 | ___ |
| 16563 | Lionel Lines SP-type Caboose, *95* | 22 | 26 | ___ |
| 16564 | Western Maryland Center Cupola Caboose (SSS), *95* | 30 | 34 | ___ |
| 16565 | Milwaukee Road Bay Window Caboose, *95* | 50 | 60 | ___ |
| 16566 | U.S. Army SP-type Caboose "907," *95* | | 28 | ___ |
| 16568 | ATSF SP-type Caboose, *96–99* | | 23 | ___ |
| 16571 | Georgia Power SP-type Caboose "52789," *95 u* | | 65 | ___ |
| 16575 | Sears Zenith SP-type Caboose, *95* | | 38 | ___ |
| 16577 | U.S. Coast Guard Work Caboose, *96* | | 26 | ___ |
| 16578 | Lionel Lines SP-type Caboose, *95 u* | | 20 | ___ |
| 16579 | GM/AC Delco, SP-type Caboose, *95* | | 35 | ___ |
| 16580 | SP-type Caboose, *96–99* | | 11 | ___ |
| 16581 | UP Illuminated Caboose, *96* | | 30 | ___ |
| 16586 | SP Illuminated Caboose "6357," *97* | | 30 | ___ |
| 16590 | Dodge Motorsports SP-type Caboose "6950," *96* | | 48 | ___ |
| 16591 | Little League Baseball SP-type Caboose "6397," *97* | | 38 | ___ |
| 16593 | Lionel Belt Line Caboose "6257," *98* | | 32 | ___ |
| 16594 | Caboose "6357," *98* | | 29 | ___ |
| 16600 | Illinois Central Coal Dump Car, *88* | 14 | 23 | ___ |
| 16601 | Canadian National Searchlight Car, *88* | 19 | 24 | ___ |
| 16602 | Erie-Lackawanna Coal Dump Car, *87* | 16 | 26 | ___ |
| 16603 | Detroit Zoo Giraffe Car (O27), *87* | 40 | 49 | ___ |
| 16604 | NYC Log Dump Car, *87* | 15 | 27 | ___ |
| 16605 | Bronx Zoo Giraffe Car (O27), *88* | 39 | 44 | ___ |
| 16606 | Southern Searchlight Car, *87* | 13 | 21 | ___ |
| 16607 | Southern Coal Dump Car "16707" (SSS), *87* | 18 | 26 | ___ |
| 16608 | Lehigh Valley Searchlight Car, *87* | 22 | 30 | ___ |
| 16609 | Lehigh Valley Derrick Car, *87* | 22 | 30 | ___ |
| 16610 | Track Maintenance Car, *87–88* | 15 | 25 | ___ |
| 16611 | Santa Fe Log Dump Car, *88* | 15 | 23 | ___ |
| 16612 | Soo Line Log Dump Car, *89* | 14 | 24 | ___ |
| 16613 | MKT Coal Dump Car, *89* | 17 | 26 | ___ |
| 16614 | Reading Cop and Hobo Car (O27), *89* | 24 | 25 | ___ |
| 16615 | Lionel Lines Extension Searchlight Car, *89* | 20 | 28 | ___ |
| 16616 | D&RGW Searchlight Car (SSS), *89* | 22 | 30 | ___ |
| 16617 | C&NW Boxcar with ETD, *89* | 23 | 34 | ___ |
| 16618 | Santa Fe Track Maintenance Car, *89* | 11 | 19 | ___ |
| 16619 | Wabash Coal Dump Car, *90* | 14 | 25 | ___ |
| 16620 | C&O Track Maintenance Car, *90–91* | 16 | 19 | ___ |
| 16621 | Alaska Log Dump Car, *90* | 24 | 31 | ___ |
| 16622 | CSX Boxcar with ETD, *90–91* | 20 | 28 | ___ |
| 16623 | MKT DD Boxcar with ETD, *91* | 16 | 23 | ___ |
| 16624 | NH Cop and Hobo Car (O27), *90–91* | 23 | 31 | ___ |
| 16625 | NYC Extension Searchlight Car, *90* | 22 | 30 | ___ |

| | | Exc | Mint | Cond/$ |
|---|---|---|---|---|
| **16626** | CSX Searchlight Car, *90* | 18 | 26 | ___ |
| **16627** | CSX Log Dump Car, *90* | 19 | 23 | ___ |
| **16628** | Cop and Hobo Circus Gondola, *90–91* | 36 | 43 | ___ |
| **16629** | Operating Circus Elephant Car (O27), *90–91* | 38 | 50 | ___ |
| **16630** | SP Operating Cowboy Car (O27), *90–91* | 22 | 26 | ___ |
| **16631** | RI Boxcar, steam RailSounds, *90* | 110 | 130 | ___ |
| **16632** | BN Boxcar, diesel RailSounds, *90* | 90 | 100 | ___ |
| **16634** | WM Coal Dump Car, *91* | 26 | 32 | ___ |
| **16636** | D&RGW Log Dump Car, *91* | 19 | 25 | ___ |
| **16637** | WP Extension Searchlight Car, *91* | 27 | 30 | ___ |
| **16638** | Operating Circus Animal Car (O27), *91* | 50 | 55 | ___ |
| **16639** | B&O Boxcar, steam RailSounds, *91* | 100 | 120 | ___ |
| **16640** | Rutland Boxcar, diesel RailSounds, *91* | 100 | 120 | ___ |
| **16641** | Toys "R" Us Giraffe Car (O27), *90–91 u* | 45 | 65 | ___ |
| **16642** | Mickey's World Tour Goofy Car (O27), *91, 92 u* | 33 | 41 | ___ |
| **16644** | Amtrak Crane Car, *91, 92 u* | 36 | 42 | ___ |
| **16645** | Amtrak Searchlight Caboose, *91* | 27 | 30 | ___ |
| **16649** | Railway Express Agency Boxcar, steam RailSounds, *92* | 110 | 140 | ___ |
| **16650** | NYC Pacemaker Boxcar, diesel RailSounds, *92* | 100 | 135 | ___ |
| **16651** | Operating Circus Clown Car (O27), *92* | 24 | 30 | ___ |
| **16652** | Radar Car, *92* | 25 | 29 | ___ |
| **16653** | Western Pacific Crane Car (SSS), *92* | 44 | 60 | ___ |
| **16655** | Steam Tender "1993," RailSounds, *93* | 115 | 140 | ___ |
| **16656** | Burlington Log Dump Car, *92 u* | 18 | 25 | ___ |
| **16657** | Lehigh Valley Coal Dump Car, *92 u* | 22 | 29 | ___ |
| **16658** | Erie-Lackawanna Crane Car, *93* | 47 | 65 | ___ |
| **16659** | Union Pacific Searchlight Car, *93–95* | 15 | 18 | ___ |
| **16660** | Fire Car with ladders, *93–94* | 28 | 33 | ___ |
| **16661** | Flatcar with boat, *93* | 20 | 22 | ___ |
| **16662** | Bugs Bunny and Yosemite Sam Outlaw Car (O27), *93–94* | 27 | 28 | ___ |
| **16663** | Missouri Pacific Searchlight Car, *93* | 16 | 19 | ___ |
| **16664** | L&N Coal Dump Car, *93* | 22 | 25 | ___ |
| **16665** | Maine Central Log Dump Car, *93* | 23 | 27 | ___ |
| **16666** | Toxic Waste Car, *93–94* | 25 | 32 | ___ |
| **16667** | Conrail Searchlight Car, *93* | 27 | 30 | ___ |
| **16668** | Ontario Northland Log Dump Car, *93* | 20 | 24 | ___ |
| **16669** | Soo Line Searchlight Car, *93* | 17 | 21 | ___ |
| **16670** | TV Car, *93–94* | 20 | 22 | ___ |
| **16673** | Lionel Lines Tender, whistle, *94–97* | 33 | 42 | ___ |
| **16674** | Pinkerton Animated Gondola, *94* | 28 | 32 | ___ |
| **16675** | Great Northern Log Dump Car, *94* | 21 | 25 | ___ |
| **16676** | Burlington Coal Dump Car, *94* | 23 | 28 | ___ |
| **16677** | NATO Flatcar with Royal Navy submarine, *94* | 34 | 44 | ___ |
| **16678** | Rock Island Searchlight Car, *94* | 21 | 23 | ___ |
| **16679** | U.S. Mail Operating Boxcar, *94* | 45 | 50 | ___ |
| **16680** | Cherry Picker Car, *94* | 25 | 28 | ___ |
| **16681** | Aquarium Car, *95* | 35 | 44 | ___ |

| | | Exc | Mint | Cond/S |
|---|---|---|---|---|
| 16682 | Lionelville Farms Operating Stock Car (O27), *94* | 23 | 27 | ____ |
| 16683 | Los Angeles Zoo Elephant Car (O27), *94* | 22 | 26 | ____ |
| 16684 | U.S. Navy Crane Car, *94–95* | 35 | 40 | ____ |
| 16685 | Erie Extension Searchlight Car, *95* | 30 | 34 | ____ |
| 16686 | Mickey Mouse Animated Boxcar, *95* | 28 | 35 | ____ |
| 16687 | U.S. Mail Operating Boxcar, *94* | 29 | 37 | ____ |
| 16688 | Fire Car with ladders, *94* | 34 | 45 | ____ |
| 16689 | Toxic Waste Car, *94* | 29 | 32 | ____ |
| 16690 | Bugs Bunny and Yosemite Sam Outlaw Car (O27), *94* | 30 | 34 | ____ |
| 16701 | Southern Tool Car (SSS), *87* | 43 | 55 | ____ |
| 16702 | Amtrak Bunk Car, *91, 92 u* | 25 | 27 | ____ |
| 16703 | NYC Tool Car, *92* | 24 | 31 | ____ |
| 16704 | TV Car, *94* | 27 | 29 | ____ |
| 16705 | Chesapeake & Ohio Cop and Hobo Car, *95* | 28 | 34 | ____ |
| 16706 | Animal Transport Service Giraffe Car, *95* | 27 | 30 | ____ |
| 16708 | C&NW Track Maintenance Car, *95* | 24 | 31 | ____ |
| 16709 | New York Central Derrick Car, *95* | 22 | 28 | ____ |
| 16710 | U.S. Army Operating Missile Car, *95* | 40 | 42 | ____ |
| 16711 | Pennsylvania Searchlight Car, *95* | 27 | 31 | ____ |
| 16712 | Pinkerton Animated Gondola, *95* | 34 | 39 | ____ |
| 16715 | ATSF Log Dump Car, *96–99* | | 24 | ____ |
| 16717 | Jersey Central Crane Car, *96* | | 41 | ____ |
| 16718 | USMC Missile Launching Flatcar, *96* | 26 | 31 | ____ |
| 16719 | Exploding Boxcar, *96* | | 38 | ____ |
| 16720 | Lionel Lines Searchlight Car "3650," *96–97* | | 50 | ____ |
| 16724 | Mickey and Friends Submarine Car, *96* | | 39 | ____ |
| 16725 | Rhino Transport Car, *97* | | 31 | ____ |
| 16726 | U.S. Army Fire Ladder Car, *96* | | 43 | ____ |
| 16734 | U.S. Coast Guard Searchlight Car, *96* | | 30 | ____ |
| 16735 | U.S. Coast Guard Flatcar with radar, *96* | 28 | 35 | ____ |
| 16736 | U.S. Coast Guard Derrick Car, *96* | | 34 | ____ |
| 16737 | Road Runner and Wile E. Coyote Gondola "3444," *96* | | 58 | ____ |
| 16738 | Pepe LePew Boxcar "3370," *96* | | 38 | ____ |
| 16739 | Foghorn Leghorn Poultry Car "6434," *96* | | 41 | ____ |
| 16740 | Lionel Corporation Mail Car "3428," *96* | | 37 | ____ |
| 16741 | Union Pacific Illuminated Bunk Car, *97* | | 25 | ____ |
| 16742 | Trout Ranch Aquarium Car "3435," *96* | | 32 | ____ |
| 16744 | Port of Lionel City Searchlight Car, *97* | | 30 | ____ |
| 16745 | Port of Lionel City Flatcar with radar, *97* | | 30 | ____ |
| 16746 | Port of Lionel City Derrick Car, *97* | | 30 | ____ |
| 16747 | Breyer Animated Horse Car "6473," *97* | | 34 | ____ |
| 16748 | U.S. Forest Service Log-Dump Car "3361," *97* | | 30 | ____ |
| 16749 | Midget Mines Ore-Dump Car "3479," *97* | | 36 | ____ |
| 16750 | Lionel City Aquarium Car "3436," *97* | | 32 | ____ |
| 16751 | AIREX Sports Channel TV Car "3545," *97* | | 25 | ____ |
| 16752 | Marvin the Martian Missile Launching Flatcar "6655," *97* | 108 | 123 | ____ |

| | | Exc | Mint | Cond/$ |
|---|---|---|---|---|
| **16754** | Porky Pig and Instant Martians Flatcar "6805," *97* | 115 | 159 | ____ |
| **16755** | Daffy Duck Animated Balloon Car "3470," *97* | 111 | 150 | ____ |
| **16760** | Pluto and Cats Animated Gondola "3444," *97* | | 55 | ____ |
| **16765** | Bureau of Land Management Log Car "3351," *98* | | 30 | ____ |
| **16766** | Bureau of Land Management Ore Car "3479," *98* | | 31 | ____ |
| **16767** | New York Central Ice Docks Ice Car "6352," *98* | | 47 | ____ |
| **16776** | Holiday Boxcar, RailSounds, *98* | | 68 | ____ |
| **16777** | Animated Cola Car and Platform, *98* | | 100 | ____ |
| **16782** | Bethlehem Ore Dump Car "3479," *99* | | 95 | ____ |
| **16783** | Westside Lumber Log Dump Car "3351," *99* | | 32 | ____ |
| **16784** | Pratt's Hollow Seed Dump Car "3479," *99* | | 36 | ____ |
| **16785** | "Happy Holidays" Music Reefer "5700," *99* | | 100 | ____ |
| **16789** | Easter Operating Boxcar, *99* | | 39 | ____ |
| **16790** | UP Stock Car "3356," Crowsounds, *99* | | 90 | ____ |
| **16791** | New York City Lights Boxcar, *99* | | 44 | ____ |
| **16792** | Constellation Boxcar "9600," *99* | | 37 | ____ |
| **16793** | Animated Glow-in-the-Dark Alien Boxcar, *99* | | 44 | ____ |
| **16794** | Wicked Witch Halloween Boxcar, *99* | | 46 | ____ |
| **16795** | Elf Chasing Rudolph Gondola "6462," *99* | | 55 | ____ |
| **16796** | Snowman Loading Ice Car "6352," *99* | | 55 | ____ |
| **16805** | Budweiser Malt Nutrine Reefer "3285," *91–92 u* | 68 | 95 | ____ |
| **16806** | Toys "R" Us Boxcar, *92 u* | 21 | 26 | ____ |
| **16807** | H.J. Heinz Reefer "301," *93* | 23 | 27 | ____ |
| **16808** | Toys "R" Us Boxcar, *93 u* | 28 | 30 | ____ |
| **16817** | Ambassador 1-D Tank Car, *00 u* | | 154 | ____ |
| **16818** | Engineer Award Tank Car, *00 u* | | 690 | ____ |
| **16819** | JLC Award Tank Car, *00 u* | | 750 | ____ |
| **16820** | Ambassador Boxcar, *00 u* | 305 | 498 | ____ |
| **16822** | CSX Water Tower, *08* | | 23 | ____ |
| **16824** | O36 Command Control Switch, left hand (FasTrack), *09–10* | | 110 | ____ |
| **16825** | O36 Command Control Switch, right hand (FasTrack), *09–10* | | 110 | ____ |
| **16826** | O72 Command Control Switch, left hand (FasTrack), *09–10* | | 120 | ____ |
| **16827** | O72 Command Control Switch, right hand (FasTrack), *09–10* | | 120 | ____ |
| **16828** | O60 Command Control Switch, left hand (FasTrack), *09–10* | | 120 | ____ |
| **16829** | O60 Command Control Switch, right hand (FasTrack), *09–10* | | 120 | ____ |
| **16830** | O48 Command Control Switch, left hand (FasTrack), *09–10* | | 120 | ____ |
| **16831** | O48 Command Control Switch, right hand (FasTrack), *09–10* | | 120 | ____ |
| **16832** | O72 Command Control Wye Switch (FasTrack), *09–10* | | 115 | ____ |

| | | Exc | Mint | Cond/S |
|---|---|---|---|---|
| **16834** | O48 Half-Curved Track (FasTrack), *09–10* | | 5 | ___ |
| **16835** | O48 Quarter-Curved Track (FasTrack), *09–10* | | 5 | ___ |
| **16836** | Christmas Girder Bridge, *09* | | 21 | ___ |
| **16837** | Christmas Operating Billboard, *09* | | 45 | ___ |
| **16841** | Halloween Gateman, *09* | | 80 | ___ |
| **16842** | Big Moe Crane, *10* | | 70 | ___ |
| **16843** | City and Western Diorama, *10* | | 15 | ___ |
| **16845** | Bookstore, *09–10* | | 60 | ___ |
| **16846** | Burning Hobo Depot, *09* | | 90 | ___ |
| **16847** | Legacy Hotel, *10* | | 70 | ___ |
| **16848** | Creature Comforts Pet Store, sound, *09–10* | | 80 | ___ |
| **16849** | Rotary Dumper with coal conveyor, CC, *10* | | 600 | ___ |
| **16850** | Operating Wind Turbine, 3-pack, *09–10* | | 225 | ___ |
| **16851** | Sunoco Cylindrical Oil Tank, gray, *10* | | 100 | ___ |
| **16852** | Sunoco Cylindrical Oil Tank, yellow, *10* | | 90 | ___ |
| **16853** | *Polar Express* Diorama, *09–10* | | 18 | ___ |
| **16854** | MTA LIRR Blinking Billboard, *09* | | 30 | ___ |
| **16855** | MTA LIRR Illuminated Station Platform, *09* | | 37 | ___ |
| **16856** | MTA LIRR Passenger Station, *09* | | 60 | ___ |
| **16857** | Thomas & Friends Diorama, *10* | | 18 | ___ |
| **16859** | Grand Central Terminal, *09* | | 1500 | ___ |
| **16861** | 50,000-gallon Water Tank, *09–10* | | 150 | ___ |
| **16863** | Santa's Christmas Wish Station, *09* | | 125 | ___ |
| **16868** | Straight O Gauge Tunnel, *09–10* | | 40 | ___ |
| **16871** | Winter Wonderland Diorama, *09* | | 15 | ___ |
| **16872** | Illuminated Christmas Station Platform, *09* | | 35 | ___ |
| **16873** | Bathtub Gondola Coal Load 3-pack, *10* | | 20 | ___ |
| **16874** | Coaling Station, *10* | | 80 | ___ |
| **16880** | Freight Platform, *10* | | 30 | ___ |
| **16881** | Barrel Shed, *10* | | 30 | ___ |
| **16882** | 12" Covered Bridge, *10* | | 38 | ___ |
| **16883** | Neil's Guitar Shop, *10* | | 60 | ___ |
| **16891** | Tank Car Accident, *10* | | 130 | ___ |
| **16896** | Flagpole with lights, *10* | | 25 | ___ |
| **16897** | 75th Anniversary Gateman, *10* | | 75 | ___ |
| **16903** | CP Bulkhead Flatcar with pulp load (SSS), *94* | 22 | 25 | ___ |
| **16904** | NYC Pacemaker Flatcar Set with trailers, *94* | 55 | 60 | ___ |
| **16907** | Flatcar with farm tractors, *94* | 27 | 33 | ___ |
| **16908** | U.S. Navy Flatcar "04039" with submarine, *94–95* | 39 | 46 | ___ |
| **16909** | U.S. Navy Gondola "16556" with canisters, *94–95* | 16 | 22 | ___ |
| **16910** | Missouri Pacific Flatcar with trailer, *94* | 22 | 27 | ___ |
| **16911** | B&M Flatcar with trailer, *94* | 28 | 34 | ___ |
| **16912** | CN Maxi-Stack Flatcar Set with containers, *94* | 70 | 75 | ___ |
| **16915** | Lionel Lines Gondola (O27), *93–94 u* | 7 | 10 | ___ |
| **16916** | Ford Flatcar with trailer, *94 u* | 38 | 45 | ___ |
| **16917** | Crayola Gondola with crayons, *94 u, 95* | 8 | 9 | ___ |

| | | Exc | Mint | Cond/$ |
|---|---|---|---|---|
| **16919** | Chrysler Mopar Gondola with coil covers, *94–96* | 33 | 36 | ____ |
| **16922** | Chesapeake & Ohio Flatcar with trailer, *95* | 25 | 31 | ____ |
| **16923** | Intermodal Service Flatcar with wheel chocks, *95* | 15 | 22 | ____ |
| **16924** | Lionel Corporation Flatcar "6424" with trailer, *96* | | 24 | ____ |
| **16925** | New York Central Flatcar with trailer, *95* | 65 | 85 | ____ |
| **16926** | Frisco Flatcar with trailers, *95* | 24 | 31 | ____ |
| **16927** | New York Central Flatcar with gondola, *95* | 17 | 22 | ____ |
| **16928** | Soo Line Flatcar with dump bin (O27), *95* | 12 | 15 | ____ |
| **16929** | BC Rail Gondola with cable reels, *95* | 21 | 25 | ____ |
| **16930** | Santa Fe Flatcar with wheel load, *95* | 20 | 25 | ____ |
| **16932** | Erie Flatcar with rail load, *95* | 17 | 22 | ____ |
| **16933** | Lionel Lines Flatcar with autos, *95* | 23 | 25 | ____ |
| **16934** | Pennsylvania Flatcar with Ertl road grader, *95* | 28 | 39 | ____ |
| **16935** | UP Depressed Center Flatcar with Ertl bulldozer, *95* | 22 | 35 | ____ |
| **16936** | Sealand Maxi-Stack Flatcar Set with containers, *95* | 70 | 85 | ____ |
| **16939** | U.S. Navy Flatcar "04040" with boat, *95* | 25 | 30 | ____ |
| **16940** | ATSF Flatcar with trailer, *96–99* | | 40 | ____ |
| **16941** | ATSF Flatcar with autos, *96–99* | | 25 | ____ |
| **16943** | Jersey Central Gondola, *96* | | 18 | ____ |
| **16944** | Georgia Power Depressed Center Flatcar "31438" with transformer, *95 u* | | 50 | ____ |
| **16945** | Georgia Power Depressed Center Flatcar "31950" with cable reels, *95 u* | | 53 | ____ |
| **16946** | C&O F9 Well Car "3840," *96* | | 31 | ____ |
| **16951** | Southern I-Beam Flatcar "9823" with load, *97* | | 25 | ____ |
| **16952** | U.S. Navy Flatcar with Ertl helicopter, *96* | | 25 | ____ |
| **16953** | NYC Flatcar with Red Wing Shoes trailer, *95 u* | 39 | 45 | ____ |
| **16954** | NYC Flatcar "6424" with Ertl scraper, *96* | | 30 | ____ |
| **16955** | ATSF Flatcar with Ertl Challenger, *96* | | 30 | ____ |
| **16956** | Zenith Flatcar with trailer, *95 u* | | 130 | ____ |
| **16957** | Depressed Center Flatcar "6461" with Ertl Case tractor, *96* | | 29 | ____ |
| **16958** | Flatcar with Ertl New Holland loader, *96* | | 26 | ____ |
| **16960** | U.S. Coast Guard Flatcar with boat, *96* | | 40 | ____ |
| **16961** | GM/AC Delco Flatcar with trailer, *95* | | 73 | ____ |
| **16963** | Lionel Corporation Flatcar "6411," *96–97* | | 34 | ____ |
| **16964** | Lionel Corporation Gondola "6462," *97* | | 22 | ____ |
| **16965** | Scout Flatcar "6424" with stakes, *96–97* | | 20 | ____ |
| **16967** | Depressed Center Flatcar "6461" with transformer, *96* | | 21 | ____ |
| **16968** | Depressed Center Flatcar "6461" with Ertl Helicopter, *96* | | 35 | ____ |
| **16969** | Flatcar "6411" with Beechcraft Bonanza, *96* | | 33 | ____ |
| **16970** | LA County Flatcar "6424" with motorized powerboat, *96* | | 20 | ____ |
| **16971** | Port of Lionel City Flatcar with boat, *97* | | 35 | ____ |

| | | Exc | Mint | Cond/S |
|---|---|---|---|---|
| **16972** | P&LE Gondola "6462," *97* | | 22 | ___ |
| **16975** | Well Car Doublestack Set, *97* | | 75 | ___ |
| **16978** | MILW Flatcar "6424" with P&H shovel, *97* | | 43 | ___ |
| **16980** | Speedy Gonzales Missile Flatcar "6823," *97* | | 41 | ___ |
| **16982** | BC Rail Bulkhead Flatcar "9823" with lumber, *97* | | 28 | ___ |
| **16983** | PRR F9 Well Car "6983" with cable reels, *97* | | 39 | ___ |
| **16986** | Sears Zenith Bulkhead Flatcar, *96 u* | | 45 | ___ |
| **16987** | Musco Lighting Bulkhead Flatcar, *97 u* | | 35 | ___ |
| **16997** | Lionel Lines Recovery Crane Car, *99* | | 50 | ___ |
| **17002** | Conrail 2-bay ACF Hopper (std O), *87* | 42 | 47 | ___ |
| **17003** | Du Pont 2-bay ACF Hopper (std O), *90* | 39 | 45 | ___ |
| **17004** | MKT 2-bay ACF Hopper (std O), *91* | 23 | 27 | ___ |
| **17005** | Cargill 2-bay ACF Hopper (std O), *92* | 29 | 37 | ___ |
| **17006** | Soo Line 2-bay ACF Hopper (std O, SSS), *93* | 31 | 36 | ___ |
| **17007** | GN 2-bay ACF Hopper "173872" (std O), *94* | 26 | 31 | ___ |
| **17008** | D&RGW 2-bay ACF Hopper "10009" (std O), *95* | | 31 | ___ |
| **17009** | New York Central 2-bay ACF Hopper, *96* | | 35 | ___ |
| **17010** | Govt. of Canada ACF 2-bay Covered Hopper "7000," *98* | | 32 | ___ |
| **17011** | NP ACF 2-bay Covered Hopper "75052," *98* | | 44 | ___ |
| **17012** | Govt. of Canada ACF 2-bay Covered Hopper "7001," *98* | | 30 | ___ |
| **17013** | NYC Graffiti 2-bay Covered Hopper "7000," *99* | | 55 | ___ |
| **17014** | Graffiti 2-bay Covered Hopper "7000" (std O), *99* | | 45 | ___ |
| **17015** | Corning 2-bay Hopper "90409" (std O), *01* | | 40 | ___ |
| **17016** | C&NW 2-bay Hopper "96644" (std O), *01* | | 46 | ___ |
| **17017** | Chessie System 2-bay Hopper "605527" (std O), *02* | | 32 | ___ |
| **17018** | Nickel Plate Road Offset Hopper "33074," *02* | | 43 | ___ |
| **17019** | Santa Fe Offset Hopper "78299," *02* | | 43 | ___ |
| **17020** | Frisco Offset Hopper "92092," *02* | | 43 | ___ |
| **17021** | NYC Offset Hopper "867999," *02* | | 43 | ___ |
| **17022** | Burlington 2-bay ACF Hopper "183925" (std O), *03* | | 30 | ___ |
| **17023** | BNSF 2-bay Hopper "409038" (std O), *04* | | 30 | ___ |
| **17024** | Reading Offset Hopper "81089" (std O), *03–04* | | 43 | ___ |
| **17025** | C&O Offset Hopper "300027" (std O), *03–04* | | 43 | ___ |
| **17026** | D&H Offset Hopper "7215" (std O), *03–04* | | 41 | ___ |
| **17027** | IC Offset Hopper "92142" (std O), *03–04* | | 49 | ___ |
| **17028** | GE PS-2 2-bay Covered Hopper "326" (std O), *03–04* | | 35 | ___ |
| **17029** | CNJ PS-2 2-bay Covered Hopper "803" (std O), *03–04* | | 35 | ___ |
| **17030** | MILW PS-2 2-bay Covered Hopper "99708" (std O), *03–04* | | 35 | ___ |
| **17031** | SP PS-2 2-bay Covered Hopper "401306" (std O), *03–04* | | 38 | ___ |
| **17038** | Clinchfield PS-2 Covered Hopper, *05* | | 70 | ___ |

| | | Exc | Mint | Cond/$ |
|---|---|---|---|---|
| **17039** | Boston & Maine PS-2 2-bay Covered Hopper, *05* | | 55 | ___ |
| **17040** | Norfolk & Western PS-2 2-bay Covered Hopper, *05* | | 55 | ___ |
| **17041** | Great Northern Offset Hopper, *05* | | 60 | ___ |
| **17042** | Green Bay & Western Offset Hopper, *05* | | 60 | ___ |
| **17043** | Baltimore & Ohio Offset Hopper, *05* | | 60 | ___ |
| **17063** | Santa Fe PS-2 2-bay Covered Hopper "82297" (std O), *06* | | 55 | ___ |
| **17064** | MKT PS-2 2-bay Covered Hopper "1311" (std O), *06* | | 55 | ___ |
| **17065** | Boraxo PS-2 2-bay Covered Hopper "31062" (std O), *06* | | 55 | ___ |
| **17066** | PRR PS-2 2-bay Covered Hopper "256177" (std O), *06* | | 55 | ___ |
| **17067** | Rock Island Offset Hopper "89500" with gravel (std O), *06* | | 65 | ___ |
| **17068** | CNJ Offset Hopper "61261" (std O), *06* | | 65 | ___ |
| **17069** | Maine Central Offset Hopper "3785" (std O), *06* | | 65 | ___ |
| **17070** | P&LE Offset Hopper "4990" (std O), *06* | | 65 | ___ |
| **17083** | C&O Offset Hopper "47386" (std O), *05* | | 40 | ___ |
| **17100** | Chessie System 3-bay ACF Hopper | 49 | 85 | ___ |
| **17101** | Chessie System 3-bay ACF Hopper (std O), *88* | 37 | 45 | ___ |
| **17102** | Chessie System 3-bay ACF Hopper (std O), *88* | 35 | 41 | ___ |
| **17103** | Chessie System 3-bay ACF Hopper (std O), *88* | 31 | 34 | ___ |
| **17104** | Chessie System 3-bay ACF Hopper (std O), *88* | 38 | 46 | ___ |
| **17105** | Chessie System 3-bay ACF Hopper (std O), *88* | 39 | 46 | ___ |
| **17107** | Sinclair 3-bay ACF Hopper (std O), *89* | 40 | 48 | ___ |
| **17108** | Santa Fe 3-bay ACF Hopper (std O), *90* | 42 | 48 | ___ |
| **17109** | N&W 3-bay ACF Hopper (std O), *91* | 24 | 31 | ___ |
| **17110** | UP Hopper with coal (std O), *91* | 24 | 30 | ___ |
| **17111** | Reading Hopper with coal (std O), *91* | 23 | 28 | ___ |
| **17112** | Erie-Lack. 3-bay ACF Hopper (std O), *92* | 24 | 34 | ___ |
| **17113** | LV Hopper with coal (std O), *92–93* | 25 | 32 | ___ |
| **17114** | Peabody Hopper with coal (std O), *92–93* | 26 | 30 | ___ |
| **17118** | Archer Daniels Midland 3-bay ACF Hopper "60029" (std O), *93* | 28 | 35 | ___ |
| **17120** | CSX Hopper "295110" with coal (std O), *94* | 28 | 30 | ___ |
| **17121** | ICG Hopper "72867" with coal (std O), *94* | 26 | 33 | ___ |
| **17122** | RI 3-bay ACF Hopper "800200" (std O), *94* | 32 | 39 | ___ |
| **17123** | Cargill Covered Grain Hopper "844304" (std O), *95* | 25 | 34 | ___ |
| **17124** | Archer Daniels Midland 3-bay ACF Hopper "50224" (std O), *95* | 24 | 30 | ___ |
| **17127** | Delaware & Hudson 3-bay Hopper, *96* | | 34 | ___ |
| **17128** | Chesapeake & Ohio 3-bay Hopper, *96* | | 30 | ___ |
| **17129** | WM 3-bay Hopper "9300" with coal (std O), *97* | | 34 | ___ |
| **17132** | PRR 3-bay ACF Hopper "260815," *98* | | 40 | ___ |
| **17133** | BNSF ACF 3-bay Covered Hopper "403698," *98* | | 38 | ___ |
| **17134** | BNSF 3-bay Covered Hopper "403698" (std O), *01* | | 38 | ___ |

Exc Mint Cond/$

| | | Exc | Mint | Cond/$ |
|---|---|---|---|---|
| 17135 | BNSF ACF 3-bay Covered Hopper with ETD, *98* | | 39 | ___ |
| 17137 | Cargill 3-bay Covered Hopper "1219" (std O), *99* | | 45 | ___ |
| 17138 | Farmers Elevator 3-bay Covered Hopper (std O), *99* | | 45 | ___ |
| 17139 | "Grain Train" 3-bay Hopper "BLMR 1025," *99–00* | | 39 | ___ |
| 17140 | Virginian 3-bay Hopper 6-pack, "5260-5265," *99* | | 230 | ___ |
| 17147 | C&O 3-bay Hopper 6-pack, "156330-156335," *99* | | 230 | ___ |
| 17154 | Alberta Cylindrical Hopper "628373" (std O), *01* | | 40 | ___ |
| 17155 | Shell Cylindrical Hopper "3527" (std O), *01* | | 40 | ___ |
| 17156 | ACF Pressureaide 3-bay Hopper "59267" (std O), *01* | | 27 | ___ |
| 17157 | Wonder Bread "56670" 3-bay Hopper (std O), *01* | | 40 | ___ |
| 17158 | Conrail Coal Hopper "487739" (std O), *01* | | 42 | ___ |
| 17159 | N&W Coal Hopper "1776" (std O), *01* | | 45 | ___ |
| 17163 | C&O 3-bay Hopper (std O), *01* | | 30 | ___ |
| 17170 | General Mills 3-bay Covered Hopper (std O), *00 u* | | 60 | ___ |
| 17171 | Lionel Lion Cylindrical Hopper (std O), *01* | | 45 | ___ |
| 17172 | CP Rail Cylindrical Hopper "385206" (std O), *02* | | 37 | ___ |
| 17173 | Govt. of Canada Cylindrical Hopper "111031" (std O), *02* | | 33 | ___ |
| 17174 | GN 3-bay Hopper "171250" (std O), *02* | | 29 | ___ |
| 17175 | IC PS-2CD 4427 Covered Hopper "57031" (std O), *02* | | 40 | ___ |
| 17176 | Cargill PS-2CD 4427 Covered Hopper "2514" (std O), *02* | | 46 | ___ |
| 17177 | PS-2CD 4427 Covered Hopper "2500" (std O), *02* | | 40 | ___ |
| 17178 | Santa Fe PS-2CD 4427 Covered Hopper "304774" (std O), *02* | | 40 | ___ |
| 17179 | Indianapolis Power & Light Coal Hopper "10074" (std O), *02* | | 40 | ___ |
| 17180 | Rock Island Coal Hopper "700665" (std O), *02* | | 40 | ___ |
| 17181 | NYC 4-bay ACF Centerflow Hopper "892138" (std O), *03* | | 45 | ___ |
| 17182 | Sigco Hybrids 4-bay ACF Centerflow Hopper "1100" (std O), *03* | | 46 | ___ |
| 17183 | C&O Hopper "156341" (std O), *01* | | 30 | ___ |
| 17184 | Virginian Hopper "5271" (std O), *01* | | 30 | ___ |
| 17185 | LLCX Bathtub Gondola "877900" (std O), *01* | | 36 | ___ |
| 17186 | Cannonaide 4-bay ACF Centerflow Hopper "96169" (std O), *03* | | 40 | ___ |
| 17187 | Rio Grande 4-bay ACF Centerflow Hopper "15521" (std O), *03* | | 40 | ___ |
| 17188 | Govt. of Canada 3-bay Cylindrical Hopper (std O), *03* | | 48 | ___ |
| 17189 | Saskatchewan Grain 3-bay Cylindrical Hopper (std O), *03* | | 48 | ___ |

| | | Exc | Mint | Cond/$ |
|---|---|---|---|---|
| 17190 | Soo/CP 3-bay ACF Hopper "119303" (std O), *03* | | 37 | ____ |
| 17191 | BN PS-2CD 4427 Hopper "450669" (std O), *03–04* | | 45 | ____ |
| 17192 | Lehigh Valley PS-2CD 4427 Hopper "51118" (std O), *03–04* | | 40 | ____ |
| 17193 | Chessie System/WM PS-2CD 4427 Hopper "4673" (std O), *03–04* | | 30 | ____ |
| 17194 | MKT PS-2CD 4427 Hopper "1122" (std O), *03–04* | | 40 | ____ |
| 17195 | L&N 3-bay Hopper "240850" (std O), *04* | | 40 | ____ |
| 17196 | Firestone 4-bay Hopper "53240" (std O), *04* | | 40 | ____ |
| 17197 | Diamond Chemicals 4-bay Hopper "53286" (std O), *04* | | 40 | ____ |
| 17198 | Hercules 4-bay Hopper "50503" (std O), *04* | | 40 | ____ |
| 17199 | Conrail 4-bay Hopper "888367" (std O), *04* | | 46 | ____ |
| 17200 | Canadian Pacific Boxcar (std O), *89* | 26 | 32 | ____ |
| 17201 | Conrail Boxcar (std O), *87* | 33 | 38 | ____ |
| 17202 | Santa Fe Boxcar (std O), diesel RailSounds, *90* | 80 | 85 | ____ |
| 17203 | Cotton Belt DD Boxcar (std O), *91* | 33 | 38 | ____ |
| 17204 | Missouri Pacific DD Boxcar (std O), *91* | 27 | 30 | ____ |
| 17207 | C&IM DD Boxcar (std O), *92* | 36 | 42 | ____ |
| 17208 | Union Pacific DD Boxcar (std O), *92* | 35 | 40 | ____ |
| 17209 | B&O DD Boxcar "296000" (std O), *93* | 37 | 43 | ____ |
| 17210 | Chicago & Illinois Midland Boxcar "16021" (std O), *92 u* | 30 | 39 | ____ |
| 17211 | Chicago & Illinois Midland Boxcar "16022" (std O), *92 u* | 30 | 39 | ____ |
| 17212 | Chicago & Illinois Midland Boxcar "16023" (std O), *92 u* | 24 | 31 | ____ |
| 17213 | Susquehanna Boxcar "501" (std O), *93* | 28 | 31 | ____ |
| 17214 | Railbox Boxcar (std O), diesel RailSounds, *93* | 75 | 85 | ____ |
| 17216 | PRR DD Boxcar "60155" (std O), *94* | 34 | 38 | ____ |
| 17217 | New Haven State of Maine Boxcar "45003" (std O), *95* | 28 | 35 | ____ |
| 17218 | BAR State of Maine Boxcar "2184" (std O), *95* | 23 | 36 | ____ |
| 17219 | Tazmanian Devil 40th Birthday Boxcar (std O), *95* | 37 | 48 | ____ |
| 17220 | Pennsylvania Boxcar (std O), *96* | | 23 | ____ |
| 17221 | NYC Boxcar (std O), *96* | | 34 | ____ |
| 17222 | Western Pacific Boxcar (std O), *96* | 28 | 34 | ____ |
| 17223 | Milwaukee Road DD Boxcar (std O), *96* | | 34 | ____ |
| 17224 | Central of Georgia Boxcar "9464-197" (std O), *97* | 15 | 29 | ____ |
| 17225 | Penn Central Boxcar "9464-297" (std O), *97* | 13 | 26 | ____ |
| 17226 | Milwaukee Road Boxcar "9464-397" (std O), *97* | | 23 | ____ |
| 17227 | UP DD Boxcar "9200" (std O), *97* | | 35 | ____ |
| 17231 | Wisconsin Central DD Boxcar "9200" with auto frames, *98* | | 40 | ____ |
| 17232 | SP/UP Merger DD Boxcar "9200," *98* | | 33 | ____ |
| 17233 | Western Pacific Boxcar "9464-198," *98* | | 27 | ____ |

| | | Exc | Mint | Cond/S |
|---|---|---|---|---|
| 17234 | Port Huron & Detroit Boxcar "9464-298," *98* | 33 | | |
| 17235 | Boston & Maine Boxcar "9464-398," *98* | 41 | | |
| 17239 | ATSF "Texas Chief" Boxcar "9464-1," *97* | 50 | | |
| 17240 | ATSF "Super Chief" Boxcar "9464-2," *97* | 50 | | |
| 17241 | ATSF" El Capitan" Boxcar "9464-3," *97* | 50 | | |
| 17242 | ATSF "Grand Canyon" Boxcar "9464-4," *97* | 60 | | |
| 17243 | NP Boxcar "8722," *98* | 48 | | |
| 17244 | Santa Fe "Chief" Boxcar, *98* | 37 | | |
| 17245 | C&O Boxcar with Chessie kitten, *98* | 44 | | |
| 17246 | NYC Pacemaker Rolling Stock 4-pack, *98* | 200 | | |
| 17247 | NYC 9464 Boxcar "174940," *98* | 135 | | |
| 17248 | NYC 9464 Boxcar "174945," *98* | 115 | | |
| 17249 | NYC 9464 Boxcar "174949," *98* | 60 | | |
| 17250 | UP Boxcar "507406" (std O), *99* | 45 | | |
| 17251 | BNSF Boxcar "103277," *99* | 41 | | |
| 17252 | NS Boxcar "564824" (std O), *99* | 41 | | |
| 17253 | CSX Boxcar "141756" (std O), *99* | 35 | | |
| 17254 | UP Boxcar "551967" (std O), *99* | 42 | | |
| 17257 | Atlantic Coast Line Boxcar "28809" (std O), *99* | 36 | | |
| 17258 | D&H 9464 Boxcar "29055" std O, *99* | 41 | | |
| 17259 | MKT 9464 Boxcar "1422" (std O), *99* | 34 | | |
| 17260 | CP Rail 9464 Boxcar "286138" (std O), silver, *00* | 45 | | |
| 17261 | CP Rail 9464 Boxcar "85154," green, *00* | 44 | | |
| 17262 | CP Rail 9464 Boxcar "56776," red (std O), *00* | 48 | | |
| 17263 | NYC Boxcar "45725" (std O), *00* | 46 | | |
| 17264 | C&O Boxcar "6054" (std O), *00* | 44 | | |
| 17265 | U.S. Army Boxcar (std O), *00* | 35 | | |
| 17266 | Monon Boxcar "911" (std O), *00* | 45 | | |
| 17268 | C&O 9464 Boxcar "12700" (std O), *01* | 44 | | |
| 17269 | Western Maryland 9464 Boxcar "29140" (std O), *01* | 44 | | |
| 17270 | B&O Time-Saver 9464 Boxcar "467439" (std O), *01* | 42 | | |
| 17271 | "The Rock" Boxcar "300324" (std O), *01* | 37 | | |
| 17272 | Railbox Boxcar "15150" (std O), *01* | 27 | | |
| 17273 | DT&I DD Boxcar "26852" (std O), *01* | 44 | | |
| 17274 | Soo Line DD Boxcar "177587" (std O), *01* | 42 | | |
| 17275 | NYC PS-1 Boxcar "175008" (std O), *02* | 43 | | |
| 17276 | Cotton Belt PS-1 Boxcar "75000" (std O), *02* | 44 | | |
| 17277 | Rio Grande PS-1 Boxcar "69676" (std O), *02* | 40 | | |
| 17278 | WP PS-1 Boxcar "1953" (std O), *02* | 44 | | |
| 17279 | Ontario Northland Boxcar "7428" (std O), *02* | 40 | | |
| 17280 | Santa Fe Boxcar "600194" with auto frames (std O), *02* | 45 | | |
| 17281 | PRR DD Boxcar "83158" (std O), *04* | 42 | | |
| 17282 | UP DD Boxcar "160300" (std O), *04* | 42 | | |
| 17283 | GM&O DD Boxcar "9077" (std O), *04* | 41 | | |
| 17284 | Erie DD Boxcar "66000" (std O), *04* | 41 | | |
| 17285 | CSX Big Blue Boxcar "151296" (std O), *03* | 36 | | |

| | | Exc | Mint | Cond/$ |
|---|---|---|---|---|
| **17287** | BAR Boxcar "5976" (std O), *03* | | 35 | ____ |
| **17288** | NYC PS-1 Boxcar "175012" (std O), *03–04* | | 38 | ____ |
| **17289** | GN PS-1 Boxcar "18485" (std O), *03* | | 40 | ____ |
| **17290** | Seaboard PS-1 Boxcar "24452" (std O), *03–04* | | 42 | ____ |
| **17291** | RI PS-1 Boxcar "21110" (std O), *03–04* | | 42 | ____ |
| **17292** | B&M PS-1 Boxcar "76182" (std O), *04* | | 34 | ____ |
| **17293** | IC PS-1 Boxcar "400666" (std O), *04* | | 40 | ____ |
| **17294** | TP&W PS-1 Boxcar "5036" (std O), *04* | | 36 | ____ |
| **17295** | Santa Fe PS-1 Boxcar "276749" (std O), *04* | | 40 | ____ |
| **17297** | UP PS-1 Boxcar, *03* | | 100 | ____ |
| **17300** | Canadian Pacific Reefer (std O), *89* | 28 | 33 | ____ |
| **17301** | Conrail Reefer (std O), *87* | 35 | 42 | ____ |
| **17302** | Santa Fe Reefer with ETD (std O), *90* | 35 | 41 | ____ |
| **17303** | C&O Reefer "7890" (std O), *93* | 23 | 30 | ____ |
| **17304** | Wabash Reefer "26269" (std O), *94* | 29 | 37 | ____ |
| **17305** | Pacific Fruit Express Reefer "459400" (std O), *94* | 27 | 40 | ____ |
| **17306** | Pacific Fruit Express Reefer "459401" (std O), *94* | 19 | 27 | ____ |
| **17307** | Tropicana Reefer "300" (std O), *95* | 44 | 65 | ____ |
| **17308** | Tropicana Reefer "301" (std O), *95* | 22 | 35 | ____ |
| **17309** | Tropicana Reefer "302" (std O), *95* | 21 | 29 | ____ |
| **17310** | Tropicana Reefer "303" (std O), *95* | 20 | 27 | ____ |
| **17311** | REA Reefer (std O), *96* | 28 | 30 | ____ |
| **17314** | PFE Reefer "9800-198," *98* | | 42 | ____ |
| **17315** | PFE Reefer "9800-298," *98* | | 39 | ____ |
| **17316** | NP Reefer "98583," *98* | | 50 | ____ |
| **17317** | PRR Reefer FGE "91904," *98* | | 36 | ____ |
| **17318** | UP Reefer "170650" (std O), *99* | | 47 | ____ |
| **17319** | PFE Reefer 6-pack (std O), *01* | | 300 | ____ |
| **17331** | Hood's General American Milk Car "802" (std O), *02* | | 100 | ____ |
| **17332** | Pfaudler General American Milk Car "501" (std O), *02* | | 70 | ____ |
| **17334** | REA General American Milk Car "1741" (std O), *02* | | 100 | ____ |
| **17335** | New Haven General American Milk Car "102" (std O), *02* | | 75 | ____ |
| **17336** | PFE Steel-sided Reefer "17760" (std O), *03* | | 45 | ____ |
| **17337** | CN Steel-sided Reefer "209712" (std O), *03* | | 38 | ____ |
| **17338** | Merchants Dispatch Transit Steel-sided Reefer "12322" (std O), *03* | | 39 | ____ |
| **17339** | Burlington Steel-sided Reefer "74825" (std O), *03* | | 45 | ____ |
| **17340** | White Bros. General American Milk Car "891" (std O), *03* | | 44 | ____ |
| **17341** | Dairymen's League General American Milk Car "779" (std O), *03* | | 43 | ____ |
| **17342** | Miller Beer Steel-sided Reefer (std O), *03 u* | | 53 | ____ |
| **17343** | Miller Beer Steel-sided Reefer (std O), *03 u* | | 59 | ____ |

Exc Mint Cond/$

| | | Exc | Mint | Cond/$ |
|---|---|---|---|---|
| 17349 | NYC General American Milk Car "6581" (std O), *03 u* | | 42 | ___ |
| 17350 | Hood's General American Milk Car "503" (std O), *03 u* | | 45 | ___ |
| 17351 | Santa Fe Steel-sided Reefer "3526" (std O), *04* | | 43 | ___ |
| 17352 | PFE Steel-sided Reefer "20043" (std O), *04* | | 41 | ___ |
| 17353 | Needham Packing Steel-sided Reefer "60507" (std O), *04* | | 44 | ___ |
| 17354 | Swift Steel-sided Reefer "15392" (std O), *04* | | 42 | ___ |
| 17355 | Hood's Steel-sided Reefer "550" (std O), *04* | | 40 | ___ |
| 17356 | Nestle Nesquik Steel-sided Reefer (std O), *04* | | 44 | ___ |
| 17357 | Borden's Steel-sided Reefer "522" (std O), *04* | | 47 | ___ |
| 17358 | Fairfield Farms Steel-sided Reefer (std O), *04* | | 44 | ___ |
| 17360 | Hood's General American Milk Car "810" (std O), *03* | | 46 | ___ |
| 17361 | Hood's General American Milk Car "811" (std O), *03* | | 43 | ___ |
| 17362 | Pfaudler General American Milk Car "502" (std O), *03* | | 47 | ___ |
| 17363 | Pfaudler General American Milk Car "503" (std O), *03* | | 40 | ___ |
| 17364 | REA General American Milk Car "1742" (std O), *03* | | 38 | ___ |
| 17365 | REA General American Milk Car "1743" (std O), *03* | | 44 | ___ |
| 17366 | NH General American Milk Car "103" (std O), *03* | | 43 | ___ |
| 17367 | NH General American Milk Car "104" (std O), *03* | | 47 | ___ |
| 17368 | White Brothers General American Milk Car "892" (std O), *03* | | 43 | ___ |
| 17369 | White Brothers General American Milk Car "893" (std O), *03* | | 47 | ___ |
| 17370 | Dairymen's League General American Milk Car "780" (std O), *03* | | 47 | ___ |
| 17371 | Dairymen's League Milk Car "781" (std O), *03* | | 47 | ___ |
| 17372 | NYC General American Milk Car "6582" (std O), *03* | | 47 | ___ |
| 17373 | NYC General American Milk Car "6583" (std O), *03* | | 40 | ___ |
| 17374 | Hood's General American Milk Car "504" (std O), *03* | | 43 | ___ |
| 17375 | Hood's General American Milk Car "505" (std O), *03* | | 47 | ___ |
| 17377 | Railway Express Operating Milk Car "302" (std O), *05* | | 172 | ___ |
| 17378 | Supplee General American Milk Car (std O), *05* | | 63 | ___ |
| 17379 | NP Steel-sided Reefer "91353" (std O), *05* | | 60 | ___ |
| 17380 | PFE Silver Steel-sided Reefer "45698" (std O), *05* | | 60 | ___ |
| 17381 | North Western Steel-sided Reefer "751" (std O), *05* | | 40 | ___ |
| 17397 | PFE Steel-sided Reefer "47767" (std O), *05* | | 45 | ___ |

| | | Exc | Mint | Cond/$ |
|---|---|---|---|---|
| 17398 | A&P General American Milk Car "737" (std O), *06* | | 65 | ___ |
| 17399 | Bowman Dairy General American Milk Car "117" (std O), *06* | | 65 | ___ |
| 17400 | CP Rail Gondola with coal (std O), *89* | 30 | 34 | ___ |
| 17401 | Conrail Gondola with coal (std O), *87* | 24 | 26 | ___ |
| 17402 | Santa Fe Gondola with coal (std O), *90* | 19 | 25 | ___ |
| 17403 | Chessie System Gondola "371629" with coil covers (std O), *93* | 24 | 25 | ___ |
| 17404 | ICG Gondola "245998" with coil covers (std O), *93* | 26 | 32 | ___ |
| 17405 | Reading Gondola "24876" with coil covers (std O), *94* | 27 | 31 | ___ |
| 17406 | PRR Gondola "385405" with coil covers (std O), *95* | 37 | 42 | ___ |
| 17407 | NKP Gondola with scrap load, *96* | | 24 | ___ |
| 17408 | Cotton Belt Gondola "9820" with scrap load (std O), *97* | | 32 | ___ |
| 17410 | UP Gondola "903004" with scrap load (std O), *99* | | 30 | ___ |
| 17412 | Gondola, blue, online store, *98* | | 20 | ___ |
| 17413 | Service Center Gondola with parts load (SSS), *00* | | 24 | ___ |
| 17414 | Nickel Plate PS-5 Gondola "44801" (std O), *01–02* | | 40 | ___ |
| 17415 | Frisco PS-5 Gondola "61878" (std O), *01–02* | | 35 | ___ |
| 17416 | D&H Gondola "14011" with scrap load (std O), *01* | | 33 | ___ |
| 17417 | BN Rotary Bathtub Gondola 3-pack, *01* | | 140 | ___ |
| 17421 | CSX Rotary Bathtub Gondola 3-pack, *01* | | 135 | ___ |
| 17425 | Western Maryland PS-5 Gondola "354903" (std O), *01–02* | | 36 | ___ |
| 17426 | Maine Central PS-5 Gondola "1116" (std O), *01–02* | | 40 | ___ |
| 17427 | CSX Rotary Bathtub Gondola Add-on Unit (std O), *02* | | 47 | ___ |
| 17428 | BN Rotary Bathtub Gondola Add-on Unit (std O), *02* | | 42 | ___ |
| 17429 | Conrail Rotary Bathtub Gondola 3-pack (std O), *02–03* | | 115 | ___ |
| 17433 | BNSF Rotary Bathtub Gondola 3-pack (std O), *02–03* | | 145 | ___ |
| 17439 | UP PS-5 Gondola "229606" (std O), *03* | | 35 | ___ |
| 17440 | Algoma Central PS-5 Gondola "801" (std O), *03* | | 32 | ___ |
| 17441 | Conrail Rotary Bathtub Gondola "507673" (std O), *03* | | 39 | ___ |
| 17442 | BNSF Rotary Bathtub Gondola "668330" (std O), *03* | | 46 | ___ |
| 17443 | NS Rotary Bathtub Gondola 3-pack (std O), *03* | | 90 | ___ |
| 17447 | UP Rotary Bathtub Gondola 3-pack (std O), *03* | | 100 | ___ |
| 17457 | GN PS-5 Gondola "72839" (std O), *03* | | 35 | ___ |
| 17458 | Reading PS-5 Gondola "33267" (std O), *03* | | 35 | ___ |
| 17459 | CP Rail PS-5 Gondola "338966" (std O), *04* | | 35 | ___ |

| | | Exc | Mint | Cond/$ |
|---|---|---|---|---|
| 17460 | NYC PS-5 Gondola "749592" (std O), *04* | | 40 | ___ |
| 17461 | Pennsylvania PS-5 Gondola "374256" (std O), *04* | | 36 | ___ |
| 17462 | Santa Fe PS-5 Gondola "167340" (std O), *04* | | 35 | ___ |
| 17463 | NS Bathtub Gondola "10303" (std O), *04* | | 40 | ___ |
| 17464 | UP Bathtub Gondola "28100" (std O), *04* | | 35 | ___ |
| 17465 | CP Rail Bathtub Gondola 3-pack (std O), *04* | | 105 | ___ |
| 17470 | CP Rail Bathtub Gondola, *05* | | 50 | ___ |
| 17471 | Burlington PS-5 Gondola with covers (std O), *05* | | 44 | ___ |
| 17472 | New Haven PS-5 Gondola with covers (std O), *05* | | 53 | ___ |
| 17473 | NYC PS-5 Gondola "502351" (std O), *06–07* | | 65 | ___ |
| 17474 | D&H PS-5 Gondola "13816" (std O), *06–07* | | 65 | ___ |
| 17475 | Koppers PS-5 Gondola "213" (std O), *06–07* | | 65 | ___ |
| 17477 | L&N PS-5 Gondola "170012" (std O), *06–07* | | 46 | ___ |
| 17478 | N&W PS-5 Gondola "275005" with containers (std O), *08* | | 70 | ___ |
| 17479 | LV PS-5 Gondola "33455" with containers (std O), *08* | | 70 | ___ |
| 17480 | RI PS-5 Gondola with coke containers (std O), *08–09* | | 70 | ___ |
| 17488 | UP Bathtub Gondola 3-pack (std O), *09* | | 190 | ___ |
| 17500 | CP Flatcar with logs (std O), *89* | 27 | 29 | ___ |
| 17501 | Conrail Flatcar with stakes (std O), *87* | 37 | 45 | ___ |
| 17502 | Santa Fe Flatcar with trailer (std O), *90* | 70 | 75 | ___ |
| 17503 | NS Flatcar with trailer (std O), *92* | 55 | 65 | ___ |
| 17504 | NS Flatcar with trailer (std O), *92* | 55 | 65 | ___ |
| 17505 | NS Flatcar with trailer (std O), *92* | 50 | 55 | ___ |
| 17506 | NS Flatcar with trailer (std O), *92* | 46 | 55 | ___ |
| 17507 | NS Flatcar with trailer (std O), *92* | 50 | 55 | ___ |
| 17510 | NP Flatcar "61200" with logs (std O), *94* | 31 | 36 | ___ |
| 17511 | WM Flatcar with logs, set of 3 (std O), *95* | | 145 | ___ |
| 17512 | WM Flatcar with logs (std O), *95* | 35 | 41 | ___ |
| 17513 | WM Flatcar with logs (std O), *95* | 43 | 50 | ___ |
| 17514 | WM Flatcar with logs (std O), *95* | 39 | 45 | ___ |
| 17515 | Norfolk Southern Flatcar with tractors (std O), *95* | 24 | 42 | ___ |
| 17516 | T&P Flatcar "9823" with 2 Beechcraft Bonanzas (std O), *97* | | 50 | ___ |
| 17517 | WP Flatcar "9823" with Ertl Caterpillar frontloader (std O), *97* | | 39 | ___ |
| 17518 | PRR Flatcar "9823" with 2 Corgi Mack trucks (std O), *97* | 49 | 50 | ___ |
| 17522 | Flatcar with Plymouth Prowler, *98* | | 41 | ___ |
| 17527 | Flatcar with 2 Dodge Vipers, *98* | | 38 | ___ |
| 17529 | ATSF Flatcar "90010" with Ford milk truck, *99* | | 55 | ___ |
| 17533 | MTTX Ford Flatcar with auto frames, *99* | | 38 | ___ |
| 17534 | Diamond T Flatcar with Mack trucks, *99* | | 55 | ___ |
| 17536 | Route 66 Flatcar "9823-3" with 2 luxury coupes, *99* | | 37 | ___ |

| | | Exc | Mint | Cond/$ |
|---|---|---|---|---|
| **17537** | Route 66 Flatcar "9823-4" with 2 touring coupes, *99* | | 32 | ___ |
| **17538** | NYC Flatcar with Ford tow truck, *99* | | 43 | ___ |
| **17539** | Flatcar "9823" with 2 Corvettes (std O), *99* | | 70 | ___ |
| **17540** | Flatcar "9823" with 2 Corvettes (std O), *99* | | 70 | ___ |
| **17546** | LL Recovery Flatcar "6424" with rail load, *99* | | 50 | ___ |
| **17547** | Lionel Lines Recovery Flatcar "6429" with machinery, *99* | | 50 | ___ |
| **17548** | Route 66 Flatcar "9823-6" with 2 luxury coupes, *99* | | 42 | ___ |
| **17549** | Route 66 Flatcar "9823-5" with station wagon and trailer, *99* | | 42 | ___ |
| **17550** | BN Center Beam Flatcar "6216" with lumber (std O), *99* | | 39 | ___ |
| **17551** | NYC Flatcar with NYC pickups "499," *99* | | 49 | ___ |
| **17553** | Trailer Train Flatcar "98102" with combine (std O), *99* | | 125 | ___ |
| **17554** | GN Flatcar "61042" with logs, *00* | | 32 | ___ |
| **17555** | Ford Mustang Flatcar with 2 cars (std O), *01* | | NRS | ___ |
| **17556** | Ford Mustang Flatcar with 2 cars (std O), *01* | | NRS | ___ |
| **17557** | Route 66 Flatcar "9823-7" with black sedans, *99–00* | | 39 | ___ |
| **17558** | Route 66 Flatcar "9823-8" with brown sedans, *99* | | 39 | ___ |
| **17559** | Route 66 Flatcar "9823-9" with 2 wagons (std O), *01* | | 40 | ___ |
| **17560** | Route 66 Flatcar "9823-10" with 2 sedans (std O), *01* | | 40 | ___ |
| **17563** | Santa Fe Flatcar "90011" with pickup trucks (std O), *01* | | 49 | ___ |
| **17564** | West Side Lumber Shay Log Car 3-pack #2 (std O), *01* | | 95 | ___ |
| **17568** | PRR Flatcar "470333" with pickup trucks (std O), *02* | | 50 | ___ |
| **17571** | UP Flatcar "909231" with pickup trucks (std O), *03* | | 50 | ___ |
| **17572** | Pioneer Seed Flatcar with pedal cars, *02 u* | | 190 | ___ |
| **17573** | WM PS-4 Flatcar "2631" (std O), *03* | | 35 | ___ |
| **17574** | Santa Fe PS-4 Flatcar "90081" (std O), *03* | | 35 | ___ |
| **17575** | NYC PS-4 Flatcar "506098" (std O), *03* | | 40 | ___ |
| **17576** | Ontario Northland PS-4 Flatcar "2020" (std O), *03* | | 35 | ___ |
| **17577** | B&O PS-4 Flatcar "8651" (std O), *04* | | 35 | ___ |
| **17578** | B&M PS-4 Flatcar "34007" (std O), *04* | | 35 | ___ |
| **17579** | Milwaukee Road PS-4 Flatcar "64073" (std O), *04* | | 35 | ___ |
| **17580** | UP PS-4 Flatcar "54603" (std O), *04* | | 35 | ___ |
| **17581** | GN Flatcar "X4168" with pickup trucks (std O), *04* | | 42 | ___ |
| **17582** | PRR PS-4 Flatcar "469617" with trailers (std O), *05* | | 110 | ___ |
| **17583** | GN PS-4 Flatcar with trailers, *05* | | 80 | ___ |

Exc Mint Cond/$

| | | Exc | Mint | Cond/$ |
|---|---|---|---|---|
| 17584 | SP PS-4 Flatcar with trailers, *05* | | 80 | ___ |
| 17585 | C&O PS-4 Flatcar "81000" with trailers (std O), *05* | | 80 | ___ |
| 17586 | BN Husky Stack Car "63322" (std O), *05* | | 80 | ___ |
| 17587 | SP Husky Stack Car "513915" (std O), *05* | | 80 | ___ |
| 17588 | CSX Husky Stack Car "620350" (std O), *05* | | 80 | ___ |
| 17589 | TTX Trailer Train Husky Stack Car "456249" (std O), *05* | | 65 | ___ |
| 17600 | NYC Wood-sided Caboose (std O), *87 u* | 35 | 45 | ___ |
| 17601 | Southern Wood-sided Caboose (std O), *88* | 35 | 44 | ___ |
| 17602 | Conrail Wood-sided Caboose (std O), *87* | 65 | 75 | ___ |
| 17603 | RI Wood-sided Caboose (std O), *88* | 19 | 34 | ___ |
| 17604 | Lackawanna Wood-sided Caboose (std O), *88* | 42 | 53 | ___ |
| 17605 | Reading Wood-sided Caboose (std O), *89* | 34 | 37 | ___ |
| 17606 | NYC Steel-sided Caboose, smoke (std O), *90* | 49 | 65 | ___ |
| 17607 | Reading Steel-sided Caboose, smoke (std O), *90* | 55 | 65 | ___ |
| 17608 | C&O Steel-sided Caboose, smoke (std O), *91* | 46 | 55 | ___ |
| 17610 | Wabash Steel-sided Caboose, smoke (std O), *91* | 39 | 55 | ___ |
| 17611 | NYC Wood-sided Caboose "6003" (std O), *90 u* | 40 | 55 | ___ |
| 17612 | NKP Steel-sided Caboose, smoke (FF 6), *92* | 60 | 65 | ___ |
| 17613 | Southern Steel-sided Caboose "7613," smoke (std O), *92* | 60 | 65 | ___ |
| 17615 | NP Wood-sided Caboose, smoke (std O), *92* | 65 | 70 | ___ |
| 17617 | D&RGW Steel-sided Caboose (std O), *95* | 50 | 55 | ___ |
| 17618 | Frisco Wood-sided Caboose (std O), *95* | 65 | 75 | ___ |
| 17620 | NP Wood-sided Caboose "1746," *98* | | 70 | ___ |
| 17623 | Farmrail Extended Vision Caboose, *99* | | 65 | ___ |
| 17624 | Conrail Extended Vision Caboose "6900," *99* | | 43 | ___ |
| 17625 | Burlington Northern Steel-sided Caboose "7606," *99* | | 65 | ___ |
| 17626 | Service Center Extended Vision Caboose (SSS), *00* | | 29 | ___ |
| 17627 | C&O Extended Vision Caboose, *01* | | 65 | ___ |
| 17628 | BNSF Extended Vision Caboose, *01* | | 65 | ___ |
| 17629 | Santa Fe Extended Vision Caboose, *01* | | 80 | ___ |
| 17630 | UP Extended Vision Caboose, *01* | | 85 | ___ |
| 17631 | Virginian Bay Window Caboose, *01* | | 85 | ___ |
| 17632 | CSX Bay Window Caboose, *01* | | 75 | ___ |
| 17633 | NYC Bay Window Caboose, *01* | | 90 | ___ |
| 17634 | Delaware & Hudson Bay Window Caboose, *01* | | 75 | ___ |
| 17635 | 100th Anniversary Die-cast Gold Caboose, *00* | | 345 | ___ |
| 17636 | NYC Die-cast Caboose "18096," *00–01* | | 100 | ___ |
| 17637 | NYC "Quicker via Peoria" Die-cast Caboose, *00* | | 135 | ___ |
| 17638 | RI Extended Vision Caboose "17011" (std O), *02* | | 55 | ___ |
| 17639 | Chessie Extended Vision Caboose "3322" (std O), *02* | | 55 | ___ |

| | | Exc | Mint | Cond/S |
|---|---|---|---|---|
| **17640** | CP Extended Vision Caboose "434604" (std O), *02* | | 57 | ___ |
| **17641** | Soo Line Extended Vision Caboose "2" (std O), *02* | | 55 | ___ |
| **17642** | Conrail Bay Window Caboose "21023" (std O), *02* | | 65 | ___ |
| **17643** | NKP Bay Window Caboose "480" (std O), *02* | | 60 | ___ |
| **17644** | Erie Bay Window Caboose "C307," (std O), *02* | | 55 | ___ |
| **17645** | N&W Bay Window Caboose "C-6," (std O), *02* | | 55 | ___ |
| **17646** | UP Bay Window Caboose "24555," (std O), *02* | | 65 | ___ |
| **17647** | B&O Caboose "C-2820" (std O), *03–04* | | 65 | ___ |
| **17648** | Chessie System Caboose "C-2800" (std O), *03–04* | | 75 | ___ |
| **17649** | Lionel Lines Caboose "7649" (std O), *03–04* | | 65 | ___ |
| **17650** | Rio Grande Extended Vision Caboose "01500" (std O), *03* | | 65 | ___ |
| **17651** | BN Extended Vision Caboose "10531" (std O), *03–05* | | 80 | ___ |
| **17652** | NYC Bay Window Caboose "20200" (std O), *03* | | 75 | ___ |
| **17653** | SP Bay Window Caboose "1337" (std O), *03* | | 65 | ___ |
| **17654** | Alaska Extended Vision Caboose "989" (std O), *03* | | 75 | ___ |
| **17655** | WP Bay Window Caboose "448" (std O), *03–04* | | 75 | ___ |
| **17658** | Burlington Extended Vision Caboose "13611" (std O), *04* | | 70 | ___ |
| **17659** | CN Extended Vision Caboose "79646" (std O), *04* | | 70 | ___ |
| **17660** | Seaboard Extended Vision Caboose "5700" (std O), *04* | | 65 | ___ |
| **17661** | C&NW Bay Window Caboose "10871" (std O), *04* | | 65 | ___ |
| **17662** | PC Bay Window Caboose "21001" (std O), *04* | | 65 | ___ |
| **17663** | Southern Bay Window Caboose "X546" (std O), *04* | | 65 | ___ |
| **17664** | B&O Caboose "C-2824" (std O), *03–04* | | 65 | ___ |
| **17665** | Chessie System Caboose "C-2802" (std O), *03–04* | | 75 | ___ |
| **17669** | NYC Bay Window Caboose, smoke, *05* | | 85 | ___ |
| **17670** | CP Rail Bay Window Caboose, smoke, *05* | | 85 | ___ |
| **17671** | Burlington Northern Extended Vision Caboose, *05* | | 85 | ___ |
| **17672** | GN Extended Vision Caboose "X-106" (std O), *05* | | 85 | ___ |
| **17673** | Santa Fe Extended Vision Caboose, *05* | | 85 | ___ |
| **17674** | Reading Extended Vision Caboose "94119" (std O), *05* | | 75 | ___ |
| **17675** | Rio Grande Extended Vision Caboose "01507" (std O), *06* | | 90 | ___ |
| **17676** | NYC Bay Window Caboose "20300," *07* | | 60 | ___ |
| **17677** | Erie-Lack. Bay Window Caboose "C359" (std O), *06* | | 90 | ___ |
| **17678** | B&O I-12 Caboose "C2421" (std O), *06* | | 90 | ___ |

| | | Exc | Mint | Cond/$ |
|---|---|---|---|---|
| 17679 | Long Island Bay Window Caboose "C-62" (std O), *06* | | 90 | ___ |
| 17682 | Reading Northeastern Caboose "92841" (std O), *06–07* | | 85 | ___ |
| 17683 | Chessie System Northeastern Caboose "1893" (std O), *07* | | 85 | ___ |
| 17684 | Conrail Northeastern Caboose "18873" (std O), *07* | | 85 | ___ |
| 17685 | Jersey Central Northeastern Caboose "91533" (std O), *07* | | 85 | ___ |
| 17690 | UP CA-4 Caboose "3826" (std O), *06* | | 90 | ___ |
| 17691 | UP CA-4 Caboose "25103" (std O), *06* | | 90 | ___ |
| 17692 | LL CA-4 B22 Caboose "7629" (std O), *06* | | 90 | ___ |
| 17693 | Chessie Extended Vision Caboose "3285" (std O), *06* | | 90 | ___ |
| 17694 | NS Extended Vision Caboose "555582" (std O), *06* | | 90 | ___ |
| 17695 | Alaska I-12 Caboose "1001" (std O), *06* | | 90 | ___ |
| 17696 | CP Bay Window Caboose "437266" (std O), *06* | | 90 | ___ |
| 17697 | CN Extended Vision Caboose "78128" (std O), *06* | | 90 | ___ |
| 17699 | UP Ca-4 Caboose "25193" (std O), *07* | | 90 | ___ |
| 17700 | UP ACF 40-ton Stock Car "47456" (std O), *01–02* | | 85 | ___ |
| 17701 | Rio Grande ACF 40-ton Stock Car "39269" (std O), *01–02* | | 60 | ___ |
| 17702 | CP ACF 40-ton Stock Car "277083" (std O), *01–02* | | 75 | ___ |
| 17703 | NYC ACF 40-ton Stock Car "23334" (std O), *01–02* | | 85 | ___ |
| 17704 | B&O ACF 40-ton Stock Car "110234" std O, *02* | | 40 | ___ |
| 17705 | CB&Q ACF 40-ton Stock Car "52886" std O, *02* | | 40 | ___ |
| 17707 | PRR ARF 40-ton Stock Car "128994" (std O), *03* | | 35 | ___ |
| 17708 | CP Rail ACF 40-ton Stock Car "277313" (std O), *03* | | 38 | ___ |
| 17709 | UP Stock Car "48154" (std O), *04* | | 45 | ___ |
| 17710 | Great Northern Stock Car "56385" (std O), *04* | | 40 | ___ |
| 17711 | C&O ACF 40-ton Stock Car "95237" (std O), *06* | | 60 | ___ |
| 17712 | N&W ACF 40-ton Stock Car "33000" (std O), *06* | | 60 | ___ |
| 17713 | MKT ACF 40-ton Stock Car "47150" (std O), *06* | | 60 | ___ |
| 17714 | CN 40-ton Stock Car "172755" (std O), *06* | | 60 | ___ |
| 17715 | MP 40-ton Stock Car "52428" (std O), *06* | | 60 | ___ |
| 17716 | CGW 40-ton Stock Car "838," *08* | | 60 | ___ |
| 17717 | UP 40-ton Stock Car "48217," *08* | | 60 | ___ |
| 17719 | C&BQ ACF Stock Car "52925" (std O), *09* | | 70 | ___ |
| 17720 | UP ACF Stock Car (std O), *10* | | 70 | ___ |
| 17721 | Postwar Scale Stock Car 2-pack, *10* | | 140 | ___ |
| 17800 | Ontario Northland Ore Car "6126," *00* | | 30 | ___ |
| 17801 | CN Ore Car "345165," *00* | | 37 | ___ |
| 17802 | CP Ore Car "377249," *00* | | 28 | ___ |

Exc Mint Cond/S

| | | Exc | Mint | Cond/S |
|---|---|---|---|---|
| **17803** | DMIR Ore Car "51456," *00* | | 30 | |
| **17804** | UP Ore Car "8023," *01* | | 29 | |
| **17805** | CP Rail Ore Car "377238," *01* | | 29 | |
| **17806** | UP Ore Car "27250," *03* | | 30 | |
| **17807** | BN Ore Car "95887," *02* | | 28 | |
| **17900** | Santa Fe Unibody Tank Car (std O), *90* | 37 | 46 | |
| **17901** | Chevron Unibody Tank Car (std O), *90* | 24 | 28 | |
| **17902** | NJ Zinc Unibody Tank Car (std O), *91* | 26 | 34 | |
| **17903** | Conoco Unibody Tank Car (std O), *91* | 24 | 29 | |
| **17904** | Texaco Unibody Tank Car (std O), *92* | 31 | 41 | |
| **17905** | Archer Daniels Midland Unibody Tank Car (std O), *92* | 26 | 26 | |
| **17906** | SCM Unibody Tank Car "78286" (std O), *93* | 47 | 55 | |
| **17908** | Marathon Oil Unibody Tank Car (std O), *95* | 45 | 51 | |
| **17909** | Hooker Chemicals Unibody Tank Car (std O), *96* | | 55 | |
| **17910** | Sunoco Unibody Tank Car "7900," *97* | | 37 | |
| **17913** | J.M. Huber Tank Car, *98* | | 29 | |
| **17914** | Englehard Tank Car, *98* | | 36 | |
| **17915** | Gulf Unibody Tank Car "8438," *00* | | 43 | |
| **17916** | Burlington Unibody Tank Car "130000," *00* | 24 | 38 | |
| **17918** | Southern Unibody Tank Car, *01* | | 32 | |
| **17919** | Koppers Unibody Tank Car, *01* | | 39 | |
| **17924** | Safety Kleen Unibody Tank Car "77603" (std O), *02* | | 40 | |
| **17925** | Beefmaster Unibody Tank Car "120021" (std O), *02* | | 38 | |
| **17926** | Cargill Unibody 1-D Tank Car "5836" (std O), *03* | | 40 | |
| **17927** | Union Starch Unibody 1-D Tank Car "59137" (std O), *03* | | 35 | |
| **17928** | Merck 1-D Tank Car "25421" (std O), *03* | | 35 | |
| **17929** | Wyandotte Chemicals 1-D Tank Car "1325" (std O), *03* | | 34 | |
| **17930** | CSX Unibody Tank Car "993369" (std O), *04* | | 35 | |
| **17931** | UP Unibody Tank Car "6" (std O), *04* | | 35 | |
| **17932** | CIBRO TankTrain Intermediate Car "26263" (std O), *04* | | 35 | |
| **17933** | GATX TankTrain Intermediate Car 3-pack (std O), *04* | | 100 | |
| **17946** | Candy Cane Unibody Tank Car, *04* | | 60 | |
| **17948** | Philadelphia Quartz 1-D Tank Car "806" (std O), *06* | | 55 | |
| **17949** | Skelly Oil 1-D Tank Car "2293" (std O), *06* | | 55 | |
| **17950** | ADM Unibody Tank Car "19020" (std O), *06* | | 60 | |
| **17951** | Cerestar Unibody Tank Car "190177" (std O), *06* | | 60 | |
| **17959** | Dow 1-D Tank Car "310101" (std O), *07* | | 55 | |
| **17960** | Amaizo 1-D Tank Car "15440" (std O), *07* | | 55 | |
| **17962** | Domino Sugar 1-D Tank Car "3008" (std O), *07* | | 60 | |
| **17966** | Procor 1-D Tank Car "82607" (std O), *07* | | 60 | |

| | | Exc | Mint | Cond/$ |
|---|---|---|---|---|
| 17972 | Union Starch 1-D Tank Car "724" (std O), *08* | | 60 | ____ |
| 17973 | UP 1-D Tank Car "907838" (std O), *08* | | 60 | ____ |
| 17975 | Cargill Foods Unibody Tank Car 3-pack (std O), *08–09* | | 195 | ____ |
| 17976 | Huber Unibody Tank Car 3-pack (std O), *08–09* | | 195 | ____ |
| 17983 | GATX TankTrain Intermediate Car 3-pack, *08* | | 195 | ____ |
| 18000 | PRR 0-6-0 Locomotive "8977," *89, 91* | 315 | 434 | ____ |
| 18001 | Rock Island 4-8-4 Locomotive "5100," *87* | 305 | 315 | ____ |
| 18002 | NYC 4-6-4 Locomotive "785," *87 u* | 510 | 576 | ____ |
| 18003 | DL&W 4-8-4 Locomotive "1501," *88* | 235 | 294 | ____ |
| 18004 | Reading 4-6-2 Locomotive "8004," *89* | 185 | 205 | ____ |
| 18005 | NYC 4-6-4 Locomotive "5340," display case, *90* | 860 | 898 | ____ |
| 18006 | Reading 4-8-4 Locomotive "2100," *89 u* | 490 | 528 | ____ |
| 18007 | Southern Pacific 4-8-4 Locomotive "4410," *91* | 374 | 392 | ____ |
| 18008 | Disneyland 35th Anniversary 4-4-0 Locomotive, display case, *90* | 228 | 288 | ____ |
| 18009 | NYC 4-8-2 Locomotive "3000," *90 u, 91* | 370 | 561 | ____ |
| 18010 | PRR 6-8-6 Steam Turbine Locomotive "6200," *91–92* | 900 | 1041 | ____ |
| 18011 | Chessie System 4-8-4 Locomotive "2101," *91* | 440 | 536 | ____ |
| 18012 | NYC 4-6-4 Locomotive "5340," *90* | 710 | 900 | ____ |
| 18013 | Disneyland 35th Anniversary 4-4-0 Locomotive, *90* | 230 | 270 | ____ |
| 18014 | Lionel Lines 2-6-4 Locomotive "8014," *91* | 145 | 190 | ____ |
| 18016 | Northern Pacific 4-8-4 Locomotive "2626," *92* | 385 | 440 | ____ |
| 18018 | Southern 2-8-2 Locomotive "4501," *92* | 640 | 650 | ____ |
| 18022 | Pere Marquette 2-8-4 Locomotive "1201," *93* | 550 | 650 | ____ |
| 18023 | Western Maryland Shay Locomotive "6," *92* | 1050 | 1350 | ____ |
| 18024 | Sears T&P 4-8-2 Locomotive "907," display case, *92 u* | 750 | 790 | ____ |
| 18025 | T&P 4-8-2 Locomotive "907," *92 u* | | 640 | ____ |
| 18026 | NYC 4-6-4 Dreyfuss Hudson Locomotive, 2-rail, *92 u* | | 2350 | ____ |
| 18027 | NYC 4-6-4 Dreyfuss Hudson Locomotive, 3-rail, *93 u* | | 1450 | ____ |
| 18028 | Smithsonian PRR 4-6-2 Locomotive "3768," 2-rail, *93 u* | | 2150 | ____ |
| 18029 | NYC 4-6-4 Dreyfuss Hudson Locomotive, 3-rail, *93 u* | 1900 | 2150 | ____ |
| 18030 | Frisco 2-8-2 Locomotive "4100," *93 u* | 530 | 625 | ____ |
| 18031 | 2-10-0 Bundesbahn BR-50 Locomotive, 2-rail, *93 u* | | NRS | ____ |
| 18034 | Santa Fe 2-8-2 Locomotive "3158," *94* | 540 | 620 | ____ |
| 18035 | 2-10-0 Reichsbahn BR-50 Locomotive, 2-rail, *93 u* | | NRS | ____ |
| 18036 | 2-10-0 French BR-50 Locomotive, 2-rail, *93 u* | | NRS | ____ |
| 18040 | N&W 4-8-4 Locomotive "612," *95* | 640 | 710 | ____ |
| 18042 | Boston & Albany 4-6-4 Locomotive "618," *95* | | 250 | ____ |
| 18043 | Chesapeake & Ohio 4-6-4 Locomotive "490," *95* | 680 | 750 | ____ |

Exc Mint Cond/S

| | | Exc | Mint | Cond/S |
|---|---|---|---|---|
| **18044** | Southern 4-6-2 Locomotive "1390," *96* | | 255 | ___ |
| **18045** | Commodore Vanderbilt Locomotive "777," *96* | | 678 | ___ |
| **18046** | Wabash 4-6-4 Locomotive "700," *96* | 190 | 375 | ___ |
| **18049** | N&W Warhorse 4-8-4 Locomotive "600," *96* | | 490 | ___ |
| **18050** | JCPenney 4-6-2 Locomotive "2055," *96* | 235 | 245 | ___ |
| **18052** | Pennsylvania Torpedo Locomotive "238E," *97* | | 455 | ___ |
| **18054** | NYC 0-4-0 Switcher "1665," black, *97* | | 145 | ___ |
| **18056** | NYC J1-e Hudson Locomotive "763E," Vanderbilt tender, *97* | | 603 | ___ |
| **18062** | ATSF 4-6-4 Hudson Locomotive "3447," *97* | | 680 | ___ |
| **18063** | NYC 4-6-4 Commodore Vanderbilt Locomotive, *99* | | 952 | ___ |
| **18064** | NYC 4-8-2 Mohawk L-3A Locomotive "3000," tender, *98* | 540 | 740 | ___ |
| **18067** | NYC Weathered Commodore Vanderbilt Scale Hudson Locomotive, *97* | | 840 | ___ |
| **18071** | Southern Pacific Daylight Locomotive "4449," *98* | | 680 | ___ |
| **18072** | Lionel Lines Torpedo Locomotive, tender, *98* | | 360 | ___ |
| **18079** | NYC 2-8-2 Mikado Locomotive "1967," *99* | | 710 | ___ |
| **18080** | D&RGW 2-8-2 Mikado Locomotive "1210," *99* | | 720 | ___ |
| **18082** | NYC 4-6-4 Hudson Locomotive "5404," *99* | | 230 | ___ |
| **18083** | C&O 4-6-4 Hudson Locomotive "305," *99* | | 205 | ___ |
| **18084** | Santa Fe 4-6-4 Hudson Locomotive "305," *99* | | 225 | ___ |
| **18085** | NH 4-6-2 Pacific Locomotive "1334," *99* | | 275 | ___ |
| **18086** | NYC 4-6-2 Pacific Locomotive "4929," *99* | | 235 | ___ |
| **18087** | Santa Fe 4-6-2 Pacific Locomotive "3448," *99* | | 265 | ___ |
| **18088** | SP 4-6-2 Pacific Locomotive "1407," *99* | | 350 | ___ |
| **18089** | CNJ 4-6-0 Camelback Locomotive "771," *99* | | 405 | ___ |
| **18091** | PRR 4-6-0 Camelback Locomotive "821," *99* | | 405 | ___ |
| **18092** | SP 4-6-0 Camelback Locomotive "2283," *99* | | 395 | ___ |
| **18093** | C&NW 4-6-0 Camelback Locomotive "3006," *99* | | 285 | ___ |
| **18094** | B&O 4-4-2 E6 Atlantic Locomotive, CC, *99–00* | | 345 | ___ |
| **18095** | PRR 4-4-2 E6 Atlantic Locomotive, CC, *99–00* | 275 | 455 | ___ |
| **18096** | ATSF 4-4-2 E6 Atlantic Locomotive, CC, *99–00* | | 370 | ___ |
| **18097** | CNJ 4-6-0 Camelback Locomotive "770," *99* | | 330 | ___ |
| **18098** | PRR 4-6-0 Camelback Locomotive "820," *99* | | 355 | ___ |
| **18099** | SP 4-6-0 Camelback Locomotive "2282," *99* | | 360 | ___ |
| **18100** | Santa Fe F3 Diesel A Unit "8100" (see 11711) | | NRS | ___ |
| **18101** | Santa Fe F3 Diesel B Unit "8101" (see 11711) | | NRS | ___ |
| **18102** | Santa Fe F3 Diesel A Unit "8102," dummy (see 11711) | | NRS | ___ |
| **18103** | Santa Fe F3 Diesel B Unit "8103," dummy, *91 u* | 180 | 190 | ___ |
| **18104** | GN F3 Diesel A Unit "366A," dummy (see 11724) | | 500 | ___ |
| **18105** | GN F3 Diesel B Unit "370B," dummy (see 11724) | | NRS | ___ |
| **18106** | GN F3 Diesel A Unit "351C," dummy (see 11724) | | NRS | ___ |

| | | Exc | Mint | Cond/$ |
|---|---|---|---|---|
| 18107 | D&RGW Alco PA1 Diesel ABA Set, *92* | 640 | 740 | ___ |
| 18108 | Great Northern F3 Diesel B Unit "371B," *93* | 85 | 105 | ___ |
| 18109 | Erie Alco Diesel A Unit "725A" (see 11734) | | NRS | ___ |
| 18110 | Erie Alco Diesel B Unit "725B" (see 11734) | | 160 | ___ |
| 18111 | Erie Alco Diesel A Unit "736A," dummy (see 11734) | | NRS | ___ |
| 18115 | Santa Fe F3 Diesel B Unit, *93* | 90 | 115 | ___ |
| 18116 | Erie-Lackawanna Alco PA1 Diesel AA Set, *93* | 450 | 490 | ___ |
| 18117/18 | Santa Fe F3 Diesel AA Set "200," *93* | 330 | 410 | ___ |
| 18119/20 | UP Alco Diesel AA Set, *94* | 200 | 235 | ___ |
| 18121 | Santa Fe F3 Diesel B Unit "200A," *94* | 75 | 95 | ___ |
| 18122 | Santa Fe F3 Diesel B Unit "200B," *95* | 140 | 150 | ___ |
| 18123 | ACL F3 Diesel A Unit "342" (see 11903) | | NRS | ___ |
| 18124 | ACL F3 Diesel B Unit "342B" (see 11903) | | NRS | ___ |
| 18125 | ACL F3 Diesel A Unit "343," dummy (see 11903) | | NRS | ___ |
| 18128 | Santa Fe F3 Diesel A Unit "2343," *96* | | 435 | ___ |
| 18129 | Santa Fe F3 Diesel B Unit "2343C," *96* | | 245 | ___ |
| 18130 | Santa Fe F3 Diesel AB Set, *96* | | 580 | ___ |
| 18131 | NP F3 Diesel AB Set, "2390A, 2390C," *97* | 295 | 360 | ___ |
| 18132 | Santa Fe F3 Diesel A Unit, powered (see 18130) | | NRS | ___ |
| 18133 | Santa Fe F3 Diesel A Unit, dummy (see 18130) | | NRS | ___ |
| 18134 | Santa Fe F3 Diesel A Unit "2343," dummy, *97* | | 195 | ___ |
| 18136 | ATSF F3 Diesel B Unit "2343C," RailSounds, *97* | 135 | 240 | ___ |
| 18138 | Milwaukee Road F3 Diesel A Unit "75A," *98* | | 400 | ___ |
| 18139 | Milwaukee Road F3 Diesel B Unit "2378B," *98* | | 250 | ___ |
| 18140 | Milwaukee Road F3 Diesel AB Set, *98* | 390 | 600 | ___ |
| 18145 | NP F3 Diesel A Unit "2390A," *97* | 300 | 360 | ___ |
| 18146 | NP F3 Diesel B Unit "2390C," *97* | | 170 | ___ |
| 18147 | NP F3 Diesel AB Set, *97* | 450 | 580 | ___ |
| 18149 | UP Veranda Gas Turbine Locomotive "61," *98* | 860 | 900 | ___ |
| 18154 | Deluxe Santa Fe FT Diesel AA Set, *98–00* | | 375 | ___ |
| 18155 | Deluxe Santa Fe FT Diesel A Unit, powered (see 18154) | | NRS | ___ |
| 18156 | Deluxe Santa Fe FT Diesel A Unit, dummy (see 18154) | | NRS | ___ |
| 18157 | Santa Fe FT Diesel AA Set, *98–00* | | 240 | ___ |
| 18158 | Santa Fe FT Diesel A Unit, powered (see 18157) | | NRS | ___ |
| 18159 | Santa Fe FT Diesel A Unit, dummy (see 18157) | | NRS | ___ |
| 18160 | NYC Deluxe FT Diesel AA Set, "1602, 1603," *98–00* | | 500 | ___ |
| 18163 | NYC FT Diesel AA Set, "1600, 2400," *98–00* | | 300 | ___ |
| 18166 | B&O FT Diesel AA Set, CC, *99–00* | | 340 | ___ |
| 18169 | B&O FT Diesel AA Set, traditional, *99–00* | | 240 | ___ |
| 18189 | Army of Potomac Operating Stock Car, *99* | | 45 | ___ |
| 18190 | McNeil's Rangers Operating Stock Car "2," *99* | | 45 | ___ |
| 18191 | WP F3 Diesel AA Set, *98* | 153 | 570 | ___ |
| 18192 | WP F3 Diesel A Unit, powered, *98* | | 485 | ___ |

| | | Exc | Mint | Cond/$ |
|---|---|---|---|---|
| **18193** | WP F3 Diesel A Unit, dummy, *98* | | 495 | ____ |
| **18197** | WP F3 Diesel B Unit "2355C," *99* | 88 | 255 | ____ |
| **18198** | WP F3 Diesel B Unit "2345C" CC, *99* | | 360 | ____ |
| **18200** | Conrail SD40 Diesel "8200," *87* | 180 | 200 | ____ |
| **18201** | Chessie System SD40 Diesel "8201," *88* | 245 | 340 | ____ |
| **18202** | Erie-Lack. SD40 Diesel Unit "8459," dummy, *89 u* | 90 | 140 | ____ |
| **18203** | CP Rail SD40 Diesel "8203," *89* | 195 | 250 | ____ |
| **18204** | Chessie SD40 Diesel Unit "8204," dummy, *90 u* | 135 | 190 | ____ |
| **18205** | Union Pacific Dash 8-40C Diesel "9100," *89* | 275 | 335 | ____ |
| **18206** | Santa Fe Dash 8-40B Diesel "8206," *90* | 195 | 235 | ____ |
| **18207** | Norfolk Southern Dash 8-40C Diesel "8689," *92* | 230 | 270 | ____ |
| **18208** | BN SD40 Diesel Dummy Unit "8586," *91 u* | 115 | 165 | ____ |
| **18209** | CP Rail SD40 Diesel Dummy Unit "8209," *92 u* | 135 | 165 | ____ |
| **18210** | Illinois Central SD40 "6006," *93* | 220 | 250 | ____ |
| **18211** | Susquehanna Dash 8-40B Diesel "4002," *93* | 145 | 165 | ____ |
| **18212** | Santa Fe Dash 8-40B Diesel Dummy Unit "8212," *93* | 155 | 180 | ____ |
| **18213** | Norfolk Southern Dash 8-40C Diesel "8688," *94* | 225 | 240 | ____ |
| **18214** | CSX Dash 8-40C Diesel "7500," *94* | 235 | 255 | ____ |
| **18215** | CSX Dash 8-40C Diesel "7643," *94* | 240 | 260 | ____ |
| **18216** | Conrail SD-60M Diesel "5500," *94* | 355 | 380 | ____ |
| **18217** | Illinois Central SD40 Diesel "6007," *94* | 170 | 175 | ____ |
| **18218** | Susquehanna Dash 8-40B Diesel "4004," *94* | 205 | 225 | ____ |
| **18219** | C&NW Dash 8-40C Diesel "8501," *95* | 325 | 330 | ____ |
| **18220** | C&NW Dash 8-40C Diesel "8502," *95* | 215 | 315 | ____ |
| **18221** | D&RGW SD50 Diesel "5512," *95* | 455 | 520 | ____ |
| **18222** | D&RGW SD50 Diesel "5517," *95* | 280 | 325 | ____ |
| **18223** | Milwaukee Road SD40 Diesel "154," *95* | 375 | 380 | ____ |
| **18224** | Milwaukee Road SD40 Diesel "155," *95* | 240 | 265 | ____ |
| **18226** | GE Dash 9 Diesel, *97* | | 295 | ____ |
| **18228** | SP Dash 9 Diesel "8228," gray with red nose, *97* | | 340 | ____ |
| **18229** | SP SD40 Diesel "7333," *98* | 300 | 425 | ____ |
| **18231** | BNSF Dash 9 Diesel "739," *98* | | 435 | ____ |
| **18232** | Soo Line SD60 Diesel "5500," *97* | | 350 | ____ |
| **18233** | BNSF Dash 9 Diesel "745," *98* | | 330 | ____ |
| **18234** | BNSF Dash 9 Diesel "740," CC, *98–99* | | 405 | ____ |
| **18235** | BNSF Dash 9 Diesel 2-pack, "739, 740," *98* | | 710 | ____ |
| **18238** | Conrail SD70 Diesel "4145," *99–00* | | 300 | ____ |
| **18240** | Conrail Dash 8-40B Diesel "5065" CC, *98* | | 260 | ____ |
| **18241** | BN SD70 Diesel "9413," *99–00* | | 345 | ____ |
| **18245** | PRR Alco PA1 Diesel AA Set, *99* | | 495 | ____ |
| **18248** | PRR Alco PB-1 Diesel "5750B," *99* | | 215 | ____ |
| **18249** | Erie Alco PB-1 Diesel "850B," *00* | | 250 | ____ |
| **18250** | BNSF SD70 Diesel "9870," *99–00* | | 365 | ____ |
| **18251** | CSX SD60 Diesel "8701," *99–00* | | 300 | ____ |

| | | Exc | Mint | Cond/$ |
|---|---|---|---|---|
| 18252 | Amtrak Dash 9 Diesel, CC, *99* | | 285 | ____ |
| 18253 | BNSF Dash 9 Diesel, CC, *99* | | 305 | ____ |
| 18254 | ATSF Dash 9 Diesel, CC, *99* | | 340 | ____ |
| 18255 | NS Dash 9 Diesel, CC, *99* | | 315 | ____ |
| 18256 | Amtrak Dash 9 Diesel, traditional, *99* | | 200 | ____ |
| 18257 | BNSF Dash 9 Diesel, traditional, *99* | | 190 | ____ |
| 18258 | ATSF Dash 9 Diesel, traditional, *99* | | 205 | ____ |
| 18259 | NS Dash 9 Diesel, traditional, *99* | | 215 | ____ |
| 18260 | Conrail SD70 Diesel "4144," *99–00* | | 280 | ____ |
| 18261 | BN SD60 Diesel "9412," *99–00* | | 255 | ____ |
| 18262 | BNSF SD70 Diesel "9869," *99–00* | | 250 | ____ |
| 18263 | CSX SD60 Diesel "8700," *99–00* | | 255 | ____ |
| 18264 | Southern Pacific SD70M Diesel "8238," *99–00* | | 245 | ____ |
| 18265 | Southern Pacific SD70M Diesel "9803," *99–00* | | 340 | ____ |
| 18266 | Norfolk Southern SD60 Diesel "6552," CC, *01–02* | | 400 | ____ |
| 18268 | Lionel Centennial SD90MAC Diesel, CC, *00* | | 378 | ____ |
| 18269 | UP SD90MAC Diesel "8006," CC, *00* | | 405 | ____ |
| 18271 | CP SD90MAC Diesel "9129," CC, *00* | | 440 | ____ |
| 18273 | UP SD40 Diesel "8071," *99–00* | | 330 | ____ |
| 18274 | Burlington U30C Diesel "891," CC, *01* | | 370 | ____ |
| 18276 | Seaboard U30C Diesel "7274," CC, *01* | | 325 | ____ |
| 18278 | UP U30C Diesel "2938," CC, *01* | | 330 | ____ |
| 18280 | Maersk SD70 Diesel, CC, *00* | | 345 | ____ |
| 18281 | BNSF Dash 9-44CW Diesel "788," CC, *00* | | 340 | ____ |
| 18282 | BNSF Dash 9-44CW Diesel "789," traditional, *00* | | 225 | ____ |
| 18283 | CSX Dash 9-44CW Diesel "9019," CC, *00* | | 340 | ____ |
| 18284 | CSX Dash 9-44CW Diesel "9020," traditional, *00* | | 300 | ____ |
| 18285 | UP Dash 9-44C Diesel "9659," CC, *01* | | 325 | ____ |
| 18286 | UP Dash 9-44CW Diesel "9717," CC, *01* | | 355 | ____ |
| 18287 | CN Dash 9-44C Diesel "2529," CC, *01* | | 460 | ____ |
| 18288 | Odyssey System SD70 Diesel, CC, *00 u* | | 400 | ____ |
| 18290 | Amtrak Dash 8-32BWH Diesel "509," CC, *01* | | 325 | ____ |
| 18291 | BNSF Dash 8-32BWH Diesel "580," CC, *02* | | 340 | ____ |
| 18292 | Chessie GE U30C Diesel "3312," CC, *02* | | 340 | ____ |
| 18293 | Santa Fe U30C Diesel, CC, *03* | | 395 | ____ |
| 18294 | Alaska SD70MAC Diesel "4005," CC, *01–02* | | 435 | ____ |
| 18295 | Conrail SD80MAC Diesel "7200," CC, *02–03* | | 365 | ____ |
| 18296 | CSX SD80MAC Diesel "801," CC, *02–03* | | 405 | ____ |
| 18297 | NYC SD80MAC Diesel "9914," CC, *02–03* | | 405 | ____ |
| 18298 | UP "Desert Victory" SD40-2 Diesel "3593," CC, *02–03* | | 380 | ____ |
| 18299 | CP Rail SD40-2 Diesel "5420," CC, *02–03* | | 375 | ____ |
| 18300 | PRR GG1 Electric Locomotive "8300," *87* | 285 | 335 | ____ |
| 18301 | Southern FM Train Master Diesel "8301," *88* | 175 | 230 | ____ |
| 18302 | GN EP-5 Electric Locomotive "8302" (FF 3), *88* | 190 | 250 | ____ |
| 18303 | Amtrak GG1 Electric Locomotive "8303," *89* | 275 | 338 | ____ |
| 18304 | Lackawanna MU Commuter Car Set, *91* | 380 | 435 | ____ |
| 18305 | Lackawanna MU Commuter Car Dummy Set, *92* | 230 | 255 | ____ |

| | | Exc | Mint | Cond/$ |
|---|---|---|---|---|
| 18306 | PRR MU Commuter Car Set, *92* | 260 | 330 | ___ |
| 18307 | PRR FM Train Master Diesel "8699," *94* | 190 | 234 | ___ |
| 18308 | PRR GG1 Electric Locomotive "4866," *92* | 235 | 305 | ___ |
| 18309 | Reading FM Train Master Diesel "863," *93* | 195 | 253 | ___ |
| 18310 | PRR MU Commuter Car Dummy Set, *93* | 265 | 345 | ___ |
| 18311 | Disney EP-5 Electric Locomotive "8311," *94* | 293 | 394 | ___ |
| 18313 | Pennsylvania GG1 Electric Locomotive "4907," *96* | | 343 | ___ |
| 18314 | PRR GG1 Electric Locomotive "2332," 5 gold stripes, *97* | 500 | 507 | ___ |
| 18315 | Virginian E33 Electric Locomotive "2329," *97* | | 240 | ___ |
| 18319 | New Haven EP-5 Electric Locomotive, *99* | 300 | 365 | ___ |
| 18321 | CNJ Train Master Diesel "2341," *99* | | 405 | ___ |
| 18322 | Lackawanna Train Master Diesel "2321," *99* | | 465 | ___ |
| 18326 | PRR Congressional GG1 Electric Locomotive, *00* | | 600 | ___ |
| 18327 | Virginian FM Train Master Diesel "2331," *99–00* | | 410 | ___ |
| 18328 | NH MU Commuter Car Set, CC, *00* | | 385 | ___ |
| 18331 | Reading MU Commuter Car Set, CC, *00* | | 460 | ___ |
| 18334 | NH MU Commuter Car Dummy Set, CC, *01* | | 180 | ___ |
| 18337 | Reading MU Commuter Car Dummy Set, CC, *01* | | 200 | ___ |
| 18343 | PRR GG1 Electric Locomotive "2332," CC, *01* | | 610 | ___ |
| 18344 | LIRR MU Commuter Car Set, powered, CC, *01* | | 470 | ___ |
| 18347 | IC MU Commuter Car Set, powered, CC, *01* | | 470 | ___ |
| 18351 | NYC S1 Electric Locomotive, *03* | | 400 | ___ |
| 18352 | JCPenney SP MU Commuter Car, display case, *02* | | 140 | ___ |
| 18353 | Pennsylvania E33 Electric Locomotive "4403," CC, *02* | | 280 | ___ |
| 18354 | PRR GG1 Electric Locomotive "4918," tuscan, CC, *04* | | 790 | ___ |
| 18355 | PRR GG1 Electric Locomotive "4876," green, CC, *04* | | 900 | ___ |
| 18356 | Penn Central GG1 Electric Locomotive "4901," CC, *04* | | 1050 | ___ |
| 18364 | PRR BB1 Electric Locomotive "3900," CC, *05–07* | | 530 | ___ |
| 18367 | LIRR BB3 Electric Locomotive "328 A," CC, *05* | | 530 | ___ |
| 18371 | PRR GG1 Electric Locomotive "4912," tuscan, 5 stripes, CC, *05–07* | | 780 | ___ |
| 18372 | PRR GG1 Electric Locomotive "4925," green, 1 stripe, CC, *05–07* | | 780 | ___ |
| 18373 | NYC S2 Electric Locomotive "125," CC, *05–07* | | 410 | ___ |
| 18374 | PRR GG1 Electric Locomotive "4866," silver, CC, *06–08* | | 900 | ___ |
| 18375 | Lackawanna FM Train Master Diesel "850," CC, *06* | | 400 | ___ |
| 18376 | Lackawanna FM Train Master Diesel "851," nonpowered (std O), *06* | | 130 | ___ |
| 18378 | New York City R27 Subway Car 2-pack, *07* | | 360 | ___ |
| 18384 | MILW EP-2 Electric Locomotive, CC, *07–08* | | 950 | ___ |

| | | Exc | Mint | Cond/S |
|---|---|---|---|---|
| **18385** | NYC H-16-44 Diesel "7001," *07–09* | | 233 | ___ |
| **18386** | NYC H-16-44 Diesel "7002," nonpowered (std O), *07–09* | | 140 | ___ |
| **18389** | MILW EP-2 Electric Locomotive "E-1," CC, *07–08* | | 950 | ___ |
| **18399** | NH EF-4 Rectifier Locomotive "306," CC, *09* | | 360 | ___ |
| **18400** | Santa Fe Vulcan Rotary Snowplow "8400," *87* | 135 | 170 | ___ |
| **18401** | Workmen Handcar, *87–88* | 30 | 37 | ___ |
| **18402** | Lionel Lines Burro Crane, *88* | 65 | 80 | ___ |
| **18403** | Santa Claus Handcar, *88* | 26 | 29 | ___ |
| **18404** | San Francisco Trolley "8404," *88* | 55 | 85 | ___ |
| **18405** | Santa Fe Burro Crane, *89* | 70 | 83 | ___ |
| **18406** | Track Maintenance Car, *89, 91* | 34 | 49 | ___ |
| **18407** | Snoopy and Woodstock Handcar, *90–91* | 80 | 96 | ___ |
| **18408** | Santa Claus Handcar, *89* | 26 | 35 | ___ |
| **18410** | PRR Burro Crane, *90* | 100 | 115 | ___ |
| **18411** | Canadian Pacific Fire Car, *90* | 70 | 98 | ___ |
| **18413** | Charlie Brown and Lucy Handcar, *91* | 34 | 61 | ___ |
| **18416** | Bugs Bunny and Daffy Duck Handcar, *92–93* | 104 | 147 | ___ |
| **18417** | Section Gang Car, *93* | 65 | 80 | ___ |
| **18419** | Lionelville Electric Trolley "8419," *94* | 75 | 90 | ___ |
| **18421** | Sylvester and Tweety Handcar, *94* | 44 | 50 | ___ |
| **18422** | Santa and Snowman Handcar, *94* | 32 | 37 | ___ |
| **18423** | On-track Step Van, *95* | 23 | 28 | ___ |
| **18424** | On-track Pickup Truck, *95* | 20 | 25 | ___ |
| **18425** | Goofy and Pluto Handcar, *95* | 30 | 46 | ___ |
| **18426** | Santa and Snowman Handcar, *95* | 25 | 30 | ___ |
| **18427** | Tie-Jector Car "55," *97* | | 60 | ___ |
| **18429** | Workmen Handcar, *96* | 28 | 34 | ___ |
| **18430** | Crew Car, *96* | | 28 | ___ |
| **18431** | Trolley Car, *96–97* | | 46 | ___ |
| **18433** | Mickey and Minnie Handcar, *96–97* | 37 | 78 | ___ |
| **18434** | Porky and Petunia Handcar, *96* | | 34 | ___ |
| **18436** | Dodge Ram Track Inspection Vehicle, *97* | | 39 | ___ |
| **18438** | PRR High-rail Inspection Vehicle, *98* | | 50 | ___ |
| **18439** | Union Pacific High-rail Inspection Vehicle, *98* | | 42 | ___ |
| **18440** | NJ Transit High-rail Inspection Vehicle, *98* | | 50 | ___ |
| **18444** | Lionelville Fire Car (SSS), *98* | | 150 | ___ |
| **18445** | NYC Fire Car, *98* | | 90 | ___ |
| **18446** | Postwar "58" GN Rotary Snowplow, *99* | | 181 | ___ |
| **18447** | Executive Inspection Vehicle, *99* | | 125 | ___ |
| **18452** | Boston Trolley "3321," *99–00* | | 65 | ___ |
| **18454** | Executive Inspection Vehicle, blue, *00* | | 105 | ___ |
| **18455** | NYC Tie-Jector Car "X-2," *00–01* | | 74 | ___ |
| **18456** | Postwar "59" Minuteman Motorized Unit, *01–02* | | 290 | ___ |
| **18457** | Postwar "65" Handcar, *00–01* | | 45 | ___ |
| **18458** | Postwar "53" D&RGW Snowplow, *00* | | 160 | ___ |
| **18459** | Christmas Handcar, *01* | | 35 | ___ |

| | | Exc | Mint | Cond/S |
|---|---|---|---|---|
| 18461 | Track Cleaning Car, *02–03* | | 90 | ___ |
| 18463 | Hot Rod Inspection Vehicle, *01–02* | | 100 | ___ |
| 18464 | Postwar "54" Track Ballast Tamper, *02–03* | | 170 | ___ |
| 18465 | Postwar "50" Gang Car, *03* | | 78 | ___ |
| 18466 | UP Rotary Snow Plow, *01–02* | | 150 | ___ |
| 18467 | Train Robbery Handcar, *02* | | 45 | ___ |
| 18468 | CN Railroad Speeder, *03–04* | | 49 | ___ |
| 18469 | Chessie System Railroad Speeder, *03–04* | | 49 | ___ |
| 18470 | Postwar "52" Fire Car, *02* | | 105 | ___ |
| 18471 | UP GP20 Diesel "1977," *03* | | 105 | ___ |
| 18473 | Lehigh Valley GP38 Diesel "310," *03* | | 160 | ___ |
| 18474 | Postwar "41" U.S. Army Switcher, *03–04* | | 145 | ___ |
| 18475 | *Toy Story* Handcar, *03* | | 55 | ___ |
| 18476 | Mickey and Minnie Mouse Handcar, *03–04* | | 55 | ___ |
| 18480 | Hobo Motorized Handcar, *03–04* | | 35 | ___ |
| 18481 | Christmas Yuletide Trolley, *03* | | 50 | ___ |
| 18482 | New Haven Rail Bonder "16," *04* | | 35 | ___ |
| 18483 | C&O Ballast Tamper "48," *04* | | 55 | ___ |
| 18484 | NS Dodge Inspection Vehicle, *04–05* | | 50 | ___ |
| 18485 | NYC Gang Car, *04–05* | | 100 | ___ |
| 18486 | Donald and Daisy Duck Handcar, *04–05* | | 50 | ___ |
| 18487 | Postwar "56" M&StL Mine Transport Car, *04–05* | | 230 | ___ |
| 18489 | Great Northern Rail Bonder "HR-73," *04* | | 35 | ___ |
| 18490 | UP Ballast Tamper, *04–05* | | 150 | ___ |
| 18491 | M.O.W. Ballast Tamper "325," *04* | | 44 | ___ |
| 18492 | M.O.W. Rail Bonder "58," *04* | | 35 | ___ |
| 18493 | Santa's Speeder, *05* | | 60 | ___ |
| 18497 | N&W Speeder "541005," traditional, *05* | | 65 | ___ |
| 18498 | New York Central Rotary Snowplow, *05* | | 210 | ___ |
| 18500 | Milwaukee Road GP9 Diesel "8500" (FF 2), *87* | 175 | 230 | ___ |
| 18501 | WM NW2 Switcher "8501" (FF 4), *89* | 185 | 215 | ___ |
| 18502 | LL 90th Anniversary GP9 Diesel "1900," *90* | 145 | 170 | ___ |
| 18503 | Southern Pacific NW2 Switcher "8503," *90* | 250 | 280 | ___ |
| 18504 | Frisco GP7 Diesel "504" (FF 5), *91* | 155 | 240 | ___ |
| 18505 | NKP GP7 Diesel Set "400, 401" (FF 6) | 295 | 365 | ___ |
| 18506 | CN Budd RDC Set, "D202, D203" | 210 | 261 | ___ |
| 18507 | CN Budd RDC Baggage Car "D202," powered, *92* | 50 | 75 | ___ |
| 18508 | CN Budd RDC Passenger Dummy Unit "D203," *92* | 125 | 150 | ___ |
| 18510 | CN Budd RDC Passenger Dummy Unit "D200" | 50 | 75 | ___ |
| 18511 | CN Budd RDC Passenger Dummy Unit "D250" | 50 | 75 | ___ |
| 18512 | CN Budd RDC Dummy Set, "D200, D250," *93* | 125 | 195 | ___ |
| 18513 | NYC GP7 Diesel "7420," *94* | 90 | 125 | ___ |
| 18514 | Missouri Pacific GP7 Diesel "4124," *95* | 245 | 310 | ___ |
| 18515 | Lionel Steel Vulcan Diesel "57" (SSS), *96* | | 190 | ___ |
| 18516 | Phantom III Locomotive, CC, *02* | | 345 | ___ |

| | | Exc | Mint | Cond/$ |
|---|---|---|---|---|
| **18550** | JCPenney MILW GP9 Diesel "8500," display case, *87 u* | 180 | 245 | ____ |
| **18551** | JCPenney Susquehanna RS3 Diesel "8809," display case, *89 u* | 180 | 195 | ____ |
| **18552** | JCPenney DM&IR SD18 Diesel "8813," display case, *90 u* | 170 | 195 | ____ |
| **18553** | Sears UP GP9 Diesel "150," display case, *91 u* | 150 | 151 | ____ |
| **18554** | JCPenney GM&O RS3 "721," display case, *92–93 u* | 160 | 180 | ____ |
| **18555** | Sears C&IM SD9 Diesel "52," *92 u* | 165 | 190 | ____ |
| **18556** | Sears Chicago & Illinois Midland Freight Car Set, *92 u* | 110 | 120 | ____ |
| **18557** | Chessie System 4-8-4 Locomotive "2101," display case, export, *92 u* | | NRS | ____ |
| **18558** | JCPenney MKT GP9 Diesel "91," display case, *94 u* | 160 | 180 | ____ |
| **18562** | SP GP9 Diesel "2380," *96* | | 195 | ____ |
| **18563** | NYC GP9 Diesel "2380," *96* | | 230 | ____ |
| **18564** | CP GP9 Diesel "2380," *97* | | 265 | ____ |
| **18565** | Milwaukee Road GP9 Diesel "2338," *97* | | 220 | ____ |
| **18566** | CR SD20 Diesel "8495" (SSS), *97* | | 150 | ____ |
| **18567** | PRR GP9 Diesel "2028," *97* | | 225 | ____ |
| **18569** | CB&Q GP9 Diesel "2380," *98* | | 190 | ____ |
| **18573** | Santa Fe GP9 Diesel "2380," *98* | | 155 | ____ |
| **18574** | Milwaukee Road GP20 Diesel "975," *98* | | 250 | ____ |
| **18575** | Custom Series I GP9 Diesel "2398," *98* | | 350 | ____ |
| **18576** | SP GP9 Diesel B Unit "2385," nonpowered, *98* | | 135 | ____ |
| **18577** | NYC GP9 Diesel B Unit "2385," nonpowered, *98* | | 145 | ____ |
| **18579** | MILW GP9 Diesel "2384," nonpowered, *99* | | 135 | ____ |
| **18580** | Pennsylvania GP9 Diesel B Unit "2027," *98* | | 165 | ____ |
| **18582** | Seaboard NW2 Switcher, *98* | 450 | 455 | ____ |
| **18583** | AEC Switcher "57," *98* | | 200 | ____ |
| **18585** | Centennial SD40 Diesel, *99* | | 443 | ____ |
| **18587** | NKP Alco C420 Switcher "577," CC, *99–01* | 215 | 255 | ____ |
| **18588** | D&H Alco C420 Switcher "412," CC, *99–01* | 250 | 275 | ____ |
| **18589** | LV Alco C420 Switcher "409," CC, *99–01* | 255 | 300 | ____ |
| **18590** | NKP Alco C420 Switcher "578," traditional, *99–01* | | 170 | ____ |
| **18591** | D&H Alco C420 Switcher "411," traditional, *99–01* | | 215 | ____ |
| **18592** | LV Alco C420 Switcher "410," traditional, *99–01* | | 175 | ____ |
| **18596** | D&H Alco RS11 Switcher "5001," CC, *99–01* | | 370 | ____ |
| **18598** | NYC Alco RS11 Switcher "8010," CC, *99–01* | | 380 | ____ |
| **18599** | C&O GP38 Diesel "3855," *99–00* | | 145 | ____ |
| **18600** | ACL 4-4-2 Locomotive "8600," *87 u* | 65 | 75 | ____ |
| **18601** | Great Northern 4-4-2 Locomotive "8601," *88* | 80 | 95 | ____ |
| **18602** | PRR 4-4-2 Locomotive "8602," *87* | 75 | 85 | ____ |
| **18604** | Wabash 4-4-2 Locomotive "8604," *88–91* | 65 | 75 | ____ |
| **18605** | Mopar Express 4-4-2 Locomotive "1987," *87–88 u* | 75 | 120 | ____ |

| | | Exc | Mint | Cond/S |
|---|---|---|---|---|
| **18606** | NYC 2-6-4 Locomotive "8606," *89* | 170 | 190 | ____ |
| **18607** | Union Pacific 2-6-4 Locomotive "8607," *89* | 130 | 155 | ____ |
| **18608** | D&RGW 2-6-4 Locomotive "8608" (SSS), *89* | 90 | 105 | ____ |
| **18609** | Northern Pacific 2-6-4 Locomotive "8609," *90* | 170 | 195 | ____ |
| **18610** | Rock Island 0-4-0 Locomotive "8610," *90* | 105 | 115 | ____ |
| **18611** | Lionel Lines 2-6-4 Locomotive (SSS), *90* | 125 | 140 | ____ |
| **18612** | C&NW 4-4-2 Locomotive "8612," *89* | 75 | 100 | ____ |
| **18613** | NYC 4-4-2 Locomotive "8613," *89 u* | 75 | 95 | ____ |
| **18614** | Circus Train 4-4-2 Locomotive "1989," *89 u* | 95 | 125 | ____ |
| **18615** | GTW 4-4-2 Locomotive "8615," *90* | 70 | 85 | ____ |
| **18616** | Northern Pacific 4-4-2 Locomotive "8616," *90 u* | 85 | 110 | ____ |
| **18617** | Adolphus III 4-4-2 Locomotive, *89–92 u* | 100 | 125 | ____ |
| **18620** | Illinois Central 2-6-2 Locomotive "8620," *91* | 165 | 190 | ____ |
| **18622** | Union Pacific 4-4-2 Locomotive "8622," *90–91 u* | 65 | 80 | ____ |
| **18623** | Texas & Pacific 4-4-2 Locomotive "8623," *92* | 80 | 110 | ____ |
| **18625** | Illinois Central 4-4-2 Locomotive "8625," *91 u* | 70 | 95 | ____ |
| **18626** | Delaware & Hudson 2-6-2 Locomotive "8626," *92* | 105 | 115 | ____ |
| **18627** | C&O 4-4-2 Locomotive "8627" or "8633," *92, 93 u, 94, 95 u* | 75 | 95 | ____ |
| **18628** | MKT 4-4-2 Locomotive "8628," *92, 93 u* | 70 | 85 | ____ |
| **18630** | C&NW 4-6-2 Locomotive "2903," *93* | 325 | 370 | ____ |
| **18632** | C&O Columbia 4-4-2 Locomotive "8632," *97–99* | 75 | 95 | ____ |
| **18632** | NYC 4-4-2 Locomotive "8632," *93–95* | 75 | 95 | ____ |
| **18633** | C&O 4-4-2 Locomotive "8633," *94–95* | 65 | 85 | ____ |
| **18633** | UP 4-4-2 Locomotive "8633," *93–95* | 65 | 85 | ____ |
| **18635** | Santa Fe 2-6-4 Locomotive "8625," *93* | 135 | 155 | ____ |
| **18636** | B&O 4-6-2 Locomotive "5300," *94* | 295 | 315 | ____ |
| **18637** | United Auto Workers 4-4-2 Locomotive "8633," *93 u* | | 90 | ____ |
| **18638** | Norfolk & Western 2-6-4 Locomotive "638," *94* | 170 | 220 | ____ |
| **18639** | Reading 4-6-2 Locomotive "639," *95* | 145 | 170 | ____ |
| **18640** | Union Pacific 4-6-2 Locomotive "8640," *95* | 110 | 130 | ____ |
| **18641** | Ford 4-4-2 Locomotive "8641," *94 u* | 65 | 85 | ____ |
| **18642** | Lionel Lines 4-6-2 Locomotive, *95* | 110 | 130 | ____ |
| **18644** | ATSF 4-4-2 Columbia Locomotive "8644," *96–99* | 75 | 90 | ____ |
| **18648** | Sears Zenith 4-4-2 Locomotive "8632," *96 u* | | 100 | ____ |
| **18649** | Chevrolet 4-4-2 Locomotive "USA-1," *96 u* | | 100 | ____ |
| **18650** | LL 4-4-2 Columbia Locomotive "X-1110," *96–99* | 95 | 120 | ____ |
| **18653** | B&A 4-6-2 Pacific Locomotive "2044," *97* | | 140 | ____ |
| **18654** | SP 4-6-2 Pacific Locomotive "2044," *97* | | 140 | ____ |
| **18656** | Bloomingdale's 4-4-2 Columbia Locomotive "8632," *96* | | 108 | ____ |
| **18657** | Sears Zenith 4-4-2 Columbia Locomotive "8632," *96* | | 108 | ____ |

| | | Exc | Mint | Cond/S |
|---|---|---|---|---|
| 18658 | LL Little League 4-4-2 Columbia Locomotive "X-1110," *97* | | 90 | ___ |
| 18660 | CN 4-6-2 Locomotive "2044," tender, *98* | | 175 | ___ |
| 18661 | N&W 4-6-2 Locomotive "2044," tender, *98* | | 160 | ___ |
| 18662 | Pennsylvania 0-4-0 Switcher, *98* | 165 | 230 | ___ |
| 18666 | SP&S 4-6-2 Pacific Locomotive "2044," *97* | | 200 | ___ |
| 18668 | Bloomingdale's 4-4-2 Columbia Locomotive "8632," *97* | | 130 | ___ |
| 18669 | JCPenney IC 4-6-2 Pacific Locomotive "2099," *98* | | 205 | ___ |
| 18670 | D&H Columbia 4-4-2 Locomotive "1400," *98* | | 80 | ___ |
| 18671 | N&W Columbia 4-4-2 Locomotive "1201," *98* | | 70 | ___ |
| 18678 | Quaker Oats Columbia 4-4-2 Locomotive "8632," *98* | | 155 | ___ |
| 18679 | JCPenney T&P 4-6-2 Locomotive "2000," traditional, *99, 00 u* | | 250 | ___ |
| 18681 | PRR 4-4-2 Locomotive "460," *99* | | 75 | ___ |
| 18682 | Santa Fe 4-4-2 Columbia Locomotive "524," traditional, *00–01* | | 70 | ___ |
| 18696 | ACL 4-6-4 Locomotive "1800," *01* | | 120 | ___ |
| 18697 | Santa Fe 4-6-4 Locomotive "3465," *01* | | 100 | ___ |
| 18699 | Alaska 4-4-2 Locomotive "64," *01* | | 105 | ___ |
| 18700 | Rock Island 0-4-0T Locomotive "8700," *87–88* | 36 | 43 | ___ |
| 18702 | V&TRR 4-4-0 Locomotive "8702" (SSS), *88* | 160 | 195 | ___ |
| 18704 | Lionel Lines 2-4-0 Locomotive, *89 u* | 36 | 43 | ___ |
| 18705 | Neptune 0-4-0T Locomotive "8705," *90–91* | 35 | 42 | ___ |
| 18706 | Santa Fe 2-4-0 Locomotive "8706," *91* | 36 | 43 | ___ |
| 18707 | Mickey's World Tour 2-4-0 Locomotive "8707," *91, 92 u* | 55 | 65 | ___ |
| 18709 | Lionel Employee Learning Center 0-4-0T Locomotive, *92 u* | | 135 | ___ |
| 18710 | SP 2-4-0 Locomotive "2000," *93* | 30 | 38 | ___ |
| 18711 | Southern 2-4-0 Locomotive "2000," *93* | 30 | 38 | ___ |
| 18712 | Jersey Central 2-4-0 Locomotive "2000," *93* | 30 | 38 | ___ |
| 18713 | Chessie System 2-4-0 Locomotive "1993," *94–95* | 30 | 38 | ___ |
| 18716 | Lionelville Circus 4-4-0 Locomotive, *90–91* | 90 | 110 | ___ |
| 18718 | LL 0-4-0 Dockside Switcher "8200," *97–98* | | 40 | ___ |
| 18719 | Thomas the Tank Engine "1," *97* | | 158 | ___ |
| 18720 | Union 4-4-0 General Locomotive "1865," *99* | | 175 | ___ |
| 18721 | Confederate 4-4-0 General Locomotive "1861," *99* | | 175 | ___ |
| 18722 | Percy the Tank Engine "6," *99* | | 170 | ___ |
| 18723 | Union Pacific 4-4-0 General Locomotive, *05* | | 100 | ___ |
| 18730 | Transylvania RR 4-4-0 Locomotive "13," traditional, *05* | | 105 | ___ |
| 18732 | North Pole Central 4-4-0 Locomotive "25," *06* | | 110 | ___ |
| 18733 | Percy the Tank Engine "6," *05–10* | | 120 | ___ |
| 18734 | James the Tank Engine "5," *06–10* | | 120 | ___ |
| 18741 | Thomas the Tank Engine, *08–09* | | 120 | ___ |
| 18799 | Bethlehem Steel Switcher "44," *99* | | 100 | ___ |

Exc Mint Cond/$

| | | Exc | Mint | Cond/$ |
|---|---|---|---|---|
| **18800** | Lehigh Valley GP9 Diesel "8800," *87* | 80 | 95 | ___ |
| **18801** | Santa Fe U36B Diesel "8801," *87* | 100 | 120 | ___ |
| **18802** | Southern GP9 Diesel "8802" (SSS), *87* | 100 | 115 | ___ |
| **18803** | Santa Fe RS3 Diesel "8803," *88* | 90 | 105 | ___ |
| **18804** | Soo Line RS3 Diesel "8804," *88* | 95 | 115 | ___ |
| **18805** | Union Pacific RS3 Diesel "8805," *89* | 100 | 125 | ___ |
| **18806** | New Haven SD18 Diesel "8806," *89* | 100 | 115 | ___ |
| **18807** | Lehigh Valley RS3 Diesel "8807," *90* | 90 | 120 | ___ |
| **18808** | ACL SD18 Diesel "8808," *90* | 85 | 105 | ___ |
| **18809** | Susquehanna RS3 Diesel "8809," *89 u* | | 130 | ___ |
| **18810** | CSX SD18 Diesel "8810," *90* | 95 | 130 | ___ |
| **18811** | Alaska SD9 Diesel "8811," *91* | 95 | 135 | ___ |
| **18812** | Kansas City Southern GP38 Diesel "4000," *91* | 120 | 140 | ___ |
| **18813** | DM&IR SD18 Diesel "8813," *90 u* | 90 | 145 | ___ |
| **18814** | D&H RS3 Diesel "8814" (SSS), *91* | 90 | 120 | ___ |
| **18815** | Amtrak RS3 Diesel "1815," *91, 92 u* | 100 | 130 | ___ |
| **18816** | C&NW GP38-2 Diesel "4600," *92* | 105 | 130 | ___ |
| **18817** | UP GP9 Diesel "150" (see 18553), *91 u* | | 135 | ___ |
| **18819** | L&N GP38-2 Diesel "4136," *92* | 115 | 145 | ___ |
| **18820** | WP GP9 Diesel "8820" (SSS), *92* | 120 | 140 | ___ |
| **18821** | Clinchfield GP38-2 Diesel "6005," *93* | 125 | 150 | ___ |
| **18822** | Gulf, Mobile & Ohio RS3 Diesel "721," *92–93 u* | | NRS | ___ |
| **18823** | Chicago & Illinois Midland SD9 Diesel "52," *92 u* | | 235 | ___ |
| **18824** | Montana Rail Link SD9 Diesel "600," *93* | 185 | 230 | ___ |
| **18825** | Soo Line GP38-2 Diesel "4000" (SSS), *93* | 120 | 145 | ___ |
| **18826** | Conrail GP7 Diesel "5808," *93* | 100 | 120 | ___ |
| **18827** | "Happy Holidays" RS3 Diesel "8827," *93* | 165 | 220 | ___ |
| **18830** | Budweiser GP9 Diesel "1947," *93–94 u* | 115 | 155 | ___ |
| **18831** | SP GP20 Diesel "4060," *94* | 105 | 120 | ___ |
| **18832** | PRR RSD-4 Diesel "8446," *95* | 110 | 135 | ___ |
| **18833** | Milwaukee Road RS3 Diesel "2487," *94* | 100 | 110 | ___ |
| **18834** | C&O SD28 Diesel "8834," *94* | 110 | 140 | ___ |
| **18835** | NYC RS3 Diesel "8223" (SSS), *94* | 135 | 195 | ___ |
| **18836** | CN (Grand Trunk) GP38-2 Diesel "5800," *94* | 135 | 160 | ___ |
| **18837** | "Happy Holidays" RS3 Diesel "8837," *94–95* | 150 | 190 | ___ |
| **18838** | Seaboard RSC-3 Diesel "1538," *95* | 110 | 140 | ___ |
| **18840** | U.S. Army GP7 Diesel "1821," *95* | 85 | 124 | ___ |
| **18841** | Western Maryland GP20 Diesel "27" (SSS), *95* | 120 | 150 | ___ |
| **18842** | JCPenney B&LE SD38 Diesel "868," *95 u* | | 265 | ___ |
| **18843** | Great Northern RS3 Diesel "197," *96* | | 145 | ___ |
| **18845** | D&RGW RS3 Diesel "5204," *97* | | 100 | ___ |
| **18846** | Lionel Centennial Series GP9 Diesel, *98* | | 385 | ___ |
| **18847** | Santa Fe H-12-44 Switcher "602," *99* | | 385 | ___ |
| **18848** | PRR H-12-44 Switcher "9087," *99* | | 420 | ___ |
| **18853** | JCPenney Santa Fe GP9 Diesel "2370," *97 u* | | 150 | ___ |
| **18854** | UP GP9 Diesel Dummy Set, "2380, 2387," *97* | | 450 | ___ |
| **18856** | NJ Transit GP38-2 Diesel "4303," *99* | | 315 | ___ |

Exc Mint Cond/$

| | | Exc | Mint | Cond/$ |
|---|---|---|---|---|
| 18857 | Union Pacific GP9 Diesel "2397," 97 | | 240 | ____ |
| 18858 | Lionel Centennial GP20 Diesel, 98 | | 405 | ____ |
| 18859 | Phantom II, 99 | | 360 | ____ |
| 18860 | Pratt's Hollow Collection I: Phantom, 98 | | 400 | ____ |
| 18864 | Southern Pacific GP9 Diesel B Unit, 98 | | 140 | ____ |
| 18865 | New York Central GP9 Diesel B Unit, 98 | | 170 | ____ |
| 18866 | Milwaukee Road GP7 Diesel "2383," 98 | | 205 | ____ |
| 18868 | NJ Transit GP38-2 Diesel "4300," 98 u | | 140 | ____ |
| 18870 | Pennsylvania GP9 Diesel "2029," 98 | | 180 | ____ |
| 18872 | Wabash GP7 Diesel Set, "453, 454, 455," 99 | | 560 | ____ |
| 18876 | C&NW H-12-44 Switcher "1053," 99 | 125 | 363 | ____ |
| 18877 | Union Pacific GP9 Diesel "2399," nonpowered, 99 | | 175 | ____ |
| 18878 | Alaska GP7 Diesel "1803," 99 | | 115 | ____ |
| 18879 | B&O GP9 Diesel "5616," 99 | | 260 | ____ |
| 18881 | Custom GP9 Diesel "5616," 99 | | 350 | ____ |
| 18892 | Burlington GP9 Diesel "2328," 99 | | 205 | ____ |
| 18897 | Christmas GP7 Diesel "1999," 99 | | 200 | ____ |
| 18900 | PRR Switcher "8900," 88 u, 89 | 26 | 34 | ____ |
| 18901/02 | PRR Alco Diesel AA Set, 88 | 110 | 130 | ____ |
| 18903/04 | Amtrak Alco Diesel AA Set, 88–89 | 90 | 130 | ____ |
| 18903 | Amtrak "Mopar Express," 99 | | 500 | ____ |
| 18905 | PRR 44-ton Switcher "9312," 92 | 80 | 116 | ____ |
| 18906 | Erie-Lackawanna RS3 Diesel "8906," 91 u | 70 | 90 | ____ |
| 18907 | Rock Island 44-ton Switcher "371," 93 | 95 | 110 | ____ |
| 18908/09 | NYC Alco Diesel AA Set, 93 | 105 | 115 | ____ |
| 18910 | CSX Switcher "8910," 93 | 40 | 46 | ____ |
| 18911 | UP Switcher "8911," 93 | 33 | 37 | ____ |
| 18912 | Amtrak Switcher "8912," 93 | 37 | 43 | ____ |
| 18913 | Santa Fe Alco Diesel A Unit "8913," 93–94 | 55 | 65 | ____ |
| 18915 | WM Alco Diesel A Unit "8915," 93 | 65 | 80 | ____ |
| 18916 | WM Alco Diesel A Unit "8916," dummy, 93 | 38 | 42 | ____ |
| 18917 | Soo Line NW2 Switcher, 93 | 65 | 75 | ____ |
| 18918 | B&M NW2 Switcher "8918," 93 | 75 | 90 | ____ |
| 18919 | Santa Fe Alco Diesel A Unit "8919," dummy, 93–94 | 36 | 55 | ____ |
| 18920 | Frisco NW2 Switcher "254," 94 | 70 | 75 | ____ |
| 18921 | C&NW NW2 Switcher "1017," 94 | 60 | 80 | ____ |
| 18922 | New Haven Alco Diesel A Unit "8922," 94 | 75 | 105 | ____ |
| 18923 | New Haven Alco Diesel A Unit "8923," dummy, 94 | 50 | 55 | ____ |
| 18924 | IC Switcher "8924," 94–95 | 37 | 44 | ____ |
| 18925 | D&RGW Switcher "8925," 94–95 | 32 | 37 | ____ |
| 18926 | Reading Switcher "8926," 94–95 | 31 | 39 | ____ |
| 18927 | U.S. Navy NW2 Switcher "65-00637," 94–95 | 65 | 85 | ____ |
| 18928 | C&NW NW2 Switcher Calf Unit, 95 | 50 | 55 | ____ |
| 18929 | B&M NW2 Switcher Calf Unit, 95 | 44 | 49 | ____ |
| 18930 | Crayola Switcher, 94 u, 95 | 27 | 30 | ____ |
| 18931 | Chrysler Mopar NW2 Switcher "1818," 94 u | 70 | 85 | ____ |

| | | Exc | Mint | Cond/$ |
|---|---|---|---|---|
| 18932 | Jersey Central NW2 Switcher "8932," *96* | | 65 | ____ |
| 18933 | Jersey Central NW2 Switcher Calf Unit "8933," *96* | | 55 | ____ |
| 18934/35 | Reading Alco Diesel AA Set, *95* | 75 | 95 | ____ |
| 18936 | Amtrak Alco Diesel A Unit "8936," *95* | | 65 | ____ |
| 18937 | Amtrak FA2 Alco Diesel, nonpowered, *95–97* | | 50 | ____ |
| 18938 | U.S. Navy NW2 Switcher Calf Unit, *95* | 55 | 65 | ____ |
| 18939 | Union Pacific NW2 Switcher Set, *96* | | 145 | ____ |
| 18943 | Georgia Power NW2 Switcher "1960," *95 u* | | 170 | ____ |
| 18946 | U.S. Coast Guard NW2 Switcher "8946," *96* | | 80 | ____ |
| 18947 | Port of Lionel City Alco FA2 Diesel "2030," *97* | | 70 | ____ |
| 18948 | Port of Lionel City Alco FB2 Diesel "2030B," *97* | | 45 | ____ |
| 18952 | ATSF Alco PA1 Diesel "2000," *97* | | 345 | ____ |
| 18953 | NYC Alco PA1 Diesel "2000," *97* | | 260 | ____ |
| 18954 | ATSF Alco FA2 Diesel "212," powered, *97–99* | | 80 | ____ |
| 18955 | NJ Transit NW2 Switcher "500," *96 u* | | 110 | ____ |
| 18956 | Dodge Motorsports NW2 Switcher "8956," *96 u* | | 163 | ____ |
| 18959 | New York Central NW2 Switcher "622," *97* | | 475 | ____ |
| 18961 | Erie Alco PA1 Diesel "850," *98* | | 315 | ____ |
| 18965 | Santa Fe Alco PB1 Diesel, *98* | | 255 | ____ |
| 18966 | New York Central Alco BP1 Diesel "2008," *98* | | 250 | ____ |
| 18971 | Alco Diesel A Unit, nonpowered, *98* | | 60 | ____ |
| 18973 | RI Alco FA2 Diesel "2031," powered, *98–99* | | NRS | ____ |
| 18974 | RI Alco FA2 Diesel Dummy Unit, *98–99* | | NRS | ____ |
| 18975 | Southern 44-ton Switcher "1955," *99* | | 190 | ____ |
| 18978 | C&O NW2 Switcher "624," *99–00* | | 410 | ____ |
| 18981 | Pennsylvania Railroad Speeder "16," *04* | | 45 | ____ |
| 18982 | Santa Fe Railroad Speeder "122," *04–05* | | 65 | ____ |
| 18988 | MP15 Diesel, K-Line, *06* | | 140 | ____ |
| 18989 | Bethlehem Steel Plymouth Switcher, traditional, K-Line, *06* | | 100 | ____ |
| 18992 | SP S2 Diesel Switcher "1440," CC, *08* | | 410 | ____ |
| 18993 | C&NW S2 Diesel Switcher "1031," CC, *08* | | 410 | ____ |
| 18994 | Lionel Lines FA Diesel, traditional, *08–09* | | 90 | ____ |
| 19000 | *Blue Comet* Diner, *87 u* | 60 | 75 | ____ |
| 19001 | Southern Diner, *87 u* | 55 | 65 | ____ |
| 19002 | Pennsylvania Diner, *88 u* | 29 | 41 | ____ |
| 19003 | Milwaukee Road Diner, *88 u* | 29 | 44 | ____ |
| 19010 | B&O Diner, *89 u* | 36 | 55 | ____ |
| 19011 | Lionel Lines Baggage Car, *93* | 268 | 398 | ____ |
| 19015 | Lionel Lines Passenger Coach, *91* | 125 | 180 | ____ |
| 19016 | Lionel Lines Passenger Coach, *91* | 100 | 135 | ____ |
| 19017 | Lionel Lines Passenger Coach, *91* | 85 | 110 | ____ |
| 19018 | Lionel Lines Observation Car, *91* | 95 | 120 | ____ |
| 19019 | SP Baggage Car "9019," *93* | 120 | 153 | ____ |
| 19023 | SP Passenger Coach "9023," *92* | 125 | 160 | ____ |
| 19024 | SP Passenger Coach "9024," *92* | 85 | 100 | ____ |
| 19025 | SP Passenger Coach "9025," *92* | 100 | 115 | ____ |
| 19026 | SP Observation Car "9026," *92* | 85 | 100 | ____ |

| | | Exc | Mint | Cond/S |
|---|---|---|---|---|

| | | Exc Mint Cond/S |
|---|---|---|
| **19038** | *Adolphus Busch* Observation Car, *92–93 u* | 85 ____ |
| **19039** | Pere Marquette Baggage Car, *93* | 75 ____ |
| **19040** | Pere Marquette Passenger Coach "1115," *93* | 75 ____ |
| **19041** | Pere Marquette Passenger Coach "1116," *93* | 75 ____ |
| **19042** | Pere Marquette Observation Car "36," *93* | 75 ____ |
| **19047** | Baltimore & Ohio Combination Car "9047," *96* | 55 ____ |
| **19048** | Baltimore & Ohio Passenger Coach "9048," *96* | 50 ____ |
| **19049** | Baltimore & Ohio Diner "9049," *96* | 42 ____ |
| **19050** | Baltimore & Ohio Observation Car "9050," *96* | 42 ____ |
| **19056** | NYC Heavyweight Baggage Car, *96* | 105 ____ |
| **19057** | NYC *Willow Run* Heavyweight Coach, *96* | 95 ____ |
| **19058** | NYC *Willow Trail* Heavyweight Coach, *96* | 90 ____ |
| **19059** | NYC *Seneca Valley* Heavyweight Observation Car, *96* | 100 ____ |
| **19060** | Pullman Heavyweight Set, *96* | 473 ____ |
| **19061** | Wabash Passenger Set, *97* | 235 ____ |
| **19062** | Wabash *City of Columbia* Coach "2361," *97* | 90 ____ |
| **19063** | Wabash *City of Danville* Coach "2362," *97* | 75 ____ |
| **19064** | Wabash REA Baggage Car "2360," *97* | 47 ____ |
| **19065** | Wabash *Windy City* Observation Car "2363," *97* | 90 ____ |
| **19066** | Commodore Vanderbilt Pullman Heavyweight 2-pack, *97* | 190 ____ |
| **19067** | Commodore Vanderbilt *Willow River* Pullman "2543," *97* | 115 ____ |
| **19068** | Commodore Vanderbilt *Willow Valley* Pullman "2544," *97* | 100 ____ |
| **19069** | Pullman Baby Madison Set "9500-02," *97* | 155 ____ |
| **19070** | Baby Madison Combination Car "9501," *97* | 40 ____ |
| **19071** | *Laurel Gap* Baby Madison Coach "9500," *97* | 34 ____ |
| **19072** | *Laurel Summit* Baby Madison Coach "9500," *97* | 40 ____ |
| **19073** | *Catskill Valley* Baby Madison Observation Car "9502," *97* | 34 ____ |
| **19074** | Legends of Lionel Madison Set, *97* | 385 ____ |
| **19075** | *Mazzone* Lionel Legends Coach "2621," *97* | 105 ____ |
| **19076** | *Caruso* Lionel Legends Coach "2624," *97* | 90 ____ |
| **19077** | *Raphael* Lionel Legends Coach "2652," *97* | 90 ____ |
| **19078** | *Cowen* Lionel Legends Observation Car "2600," *97* | 95 ____ |
| **19079** | NYC Heavyweight Passenger Car Set, *97* | 275 ____ |
| **19080** | NYC Heavyweight REA Baggage Car "2564," *97* | 100 ____ |
| **19081** | NYC *Park Place* Heavyweight Coach "2565," *97* | 100 ____ |
| **19082** | NYC *Star Beam* Heavyweight Coach "2566," *97* | 100 ____ |
| **19083** | NYC *Hudson Valley* Heavyweight Observation Car "2566," *97* | 100 ____ |
| **19087** | C&O Heavyweight Passenger Car 4-pack, "2571-74," *97* | 290 ____ |
| **19088** | C&O Heavyweight Baggage Car "2571," *97* | 100 ____ |
| **19089** | C&O Heavyweight Sleeper Car "2572," *97* | 100 ____ |
| **19090** | C&O Heavyweight Diner "2573," *97* | 110 ____ |
| **19091** | C&O Heavyweight Observation Car "2574," *97* | 100 ____ |

| | | Exc | Mint | Cond/$ |
|---|---|---|---|---|
| **19093** | Commodore Vanderbilt Heavyweight Sleeper Car 2-pack, *98* | | 170 | ____ |
| **19094** | Commodore Vanderbilt *Niagara Falls* Sleeper, *98* | | 75 | ____ |
| **19095** | Commodore Vanderbilt *Highland Falls* Sleeper, *98* | | 75 | ____ |
| **19096** | Legends of Lionel Madison Car 2-pack, *98* | | 130 | ____ |
| **19097** | *Bonnano* Lionel Legends Coach "2653," *98* | | 80 | ____ |
| **19098** | *Pagano* Lionel Legends Coach "2654," *98* | | 105 | ____ |
| **19099** | PRR *Liberty Gap* Baggage Car "2623," *99* | | 80 | ____ |
| **19100** | Amtrak Baggage Car "9100," *89* | 125 | 165 | ____ |
| **19101** | Amtrak Combination Car "9101," *89* | 75 | 85 | ____ |
| **19102** | Amtrak Passenger Coach "9102," *89* | 75 | 85 | ____ |
| **19103** | Amtrak Vista Dome Car "9103," *89* | 70 | 90 | ____ |
| **19104** | Amtrak Diner "9104," *89* | 65 | 80 | ____ |
| **19105** | Amtrak Full Vista Dome Car "9105," *89 u* | 70 | 80 | ____ |
| **19106** | Amtrak Observation Car "9106," *89* | 75 | 90 | ____ |
| **19107** | SP Full Vista Dome Car, *90 u* | 70 | 88 | ____ |
| **19108** | N&W Full Vista Dome Car "576," *91 u* | 75 | 85 | ____ |
| **19109** | Santa Fe Baggage Car "3400," *91* | 225 | 300 | ____ |
| **19110** | Santa Fe Combination Car "3500," *91* | 80 | 110 | ____ |
| **19111** | Santa Fe Diner "601," *91* | 100 | 135 | ____ |
| **19112** | Santa Fe Passenger Coach, *91* | 125 | 175 | ____ |
| **19113** | Santa Fe Vista Dome Car, *91* | 100 | 135 | ____ |
| **19116** | Great Northern Baggage Car "1200," *92* | 135 | 165 | ____ |
| **19117** | Great Northern Combination Car "1240," *92* | 65 | 80 | ____ |
| **19118** | Great Northern Passenger Coach "1212," *92* | 75 | 95 | ____ |
| **19119** | Great Northern Vista Dome Car "1322," *92* | 75 | 95 | ____ |
| **19120** | Great Northern Observation Car "1192," *92* | 75 | 95 | ____ |
| **19121** | Union Pacific Vista Dome Car "9121," *92 u* | 90 | 100 | ____ |
| **19122** | D&RGW *California Zephyr* Baggage Car, *93* | 170 | 210 | ____ |
| **19123** | D&RGW California Zephyr *Silver Bronco* Vista Dome Car, *93* | 95 | 115 | ____ |
| **19124** | D&RGW California Zephyr *Silver Colt* Vista Dome Car, *93* | 95 | 115 | ____ |
| **19125** | D&RGW California Zephyr *Silver Mustang* Vista Dome Car, *93* | 100 | 125 | ____ |
| **19126** | D&RGW California Zephyr *Silver Pony* Vista Dome Car, *93* | 95 | 115 | ____ |
| **19127** | D&RGW *California Zephyr* Vista Dome Car, *93* | 85 | 100 | ____ |
| **19128** | Santa Fe Full Vista Dome Car "507," *92 u* | 175 | 185 | ____ |
| **19129** | IC Full Vista Dome Car "9129," *93* | 75 | 85 | ____ |
| **19130** | Lackawanna Passenger Cars, set of 4, *94* | 280 | 350 | ____ |
| **19131** | Lackawanna Baggage Car "2000" (see 19130) | | 150 | ____ |
| **19132** | Lackawanna Diner "469" (see 19130) | | 100 | ____ |
| **19133** | Lackawanna Passenger Coach "260" (see 19130) | | 100 | ____ |
| **19134** | Lackawanna Observation Car "789" (see 19130) | | 85 | ____ |
| **19135** | Lackawanna Combination Car "425," *94* | 85 | 100 | ____ |
| **19136** | Lackawanna Passenger Coach "211," *94* | 65 | 75 | ____ |
| **19137** | New York Central Roomette Car, *95* | 90 | 105 | ____ |
| **19138** | Santa Fe Roomette Car, *95* | 75 | 95 | ____ |

| | | Exc | Mint | Cond/S |
|---|---|---|---|---|
| 19139 | N&W Baggage Car "577," *95* | 150 | 200 | ____ |
| 19140 | N&W Combination Car "494," *95* | 60 | 80 | ____ |
| 19141 | N&W Diner "495," *95* | 105 | 135 | ____ |
| 19142 | N&W Passenger Coach "538," *95* | 75 | 95 | ____ |
| 19143 | N&W Passenger Coach "537," *95* | 75 | 95 | ____ |
| 19144 | N&W Observation Car "582," *95* | 80 | 95 | ____ |
| 19145 | C&O Combination Car "1403," *96* | | 65 | ____ |
| 19146 | C&O Passenger Coach "1623," *96* | | 60 | ____ |
| 19147 | C&O Passenger Coach "1803," *96* | | 55 | ____ |
| 19148 | C&O Chessie Club Coach "1903," *96* | | 55 | ____ |
| 19149 | C&O Coach/Diner "1950," *96* | | 50 | ____ |
| 19150 | C&O Observation Car "2504," *96* | | 55 | ____ |
| 19151 | Norfolk & Western Duplex Roomette car, *96* | | 108 | ____ |
| 19152 | Union Pacific Duplex Roomette Car, *96* | | 75 | ____ |
| 19153 | C&O Passenger Cars, set of 4, *96* | | 340 | ____ |
| 19154 | Atlantic Coast Line Passenger Car Set, *96* | | 340 | ____ |
| 19155 | ACL Combination Car "101," *96* | | 90 | ____ |
| 19156 | ACL *Talladega* Diner, *96* | | 90 | ____ |
| 19157 | ACL *Moultrie* Coach, *96* | | 95 | ____ |
| 19158 | ACL Observation Car "256," *96* | | 90 | ____ |
| 19159 | N&W Passenger Cars, set of 4, *95 u* | 300 | 385 | ____ |
| 19160 | LL REA Baggage Car, *96* | | 90 | ____ |
| 19161 | LL *Silver Mesa* Coach, *96* | | 80 | ____ |
| 19162 | LL *Silver Sky* Vista Dome Car, *96* | | 75 | ____ |
| 19163 | LL *Silver Rail* Observation Car, *96* | | 75 | ____ |
| 19164 | Chesapeake & Ohio Passenger Cars, *96* | | 160 | ____ |
| 19165 | ATSF *Super Chief* Set, *96* | | 305 | ____ |
| 19166 | NP Vista Dome Car Set, *97* | | 305 | ____ |
| 19167 | NP Pullman Coach "2571," *97* | | 105 | ____ |
| 19168 | NP Pullman Coach "2571," *97* | | 105 | ____ |
| 19169 | NP Pullman Coach "2570," *97* | | 95 | ____ |
| 19170 | NP Pullman Coach "2571," *97* | | 100 | ____ |
| 19171 | NYC Streamliner Car 4-pack, *97* | | 285 | ____ |
| 19172 | NYC Aluminum Passenger/Baggage Car "2570," *97* | | 95 | ____ |
| 19173 | NYC *Manhattan Island* Aluminum Passenger Diner, *97* | | 100 | ____ |
| 19174 | NYC *Queensboro Bridge* Aluminum Passenger Coach, *97* | | 100 | ____ |
| 19175 | NYC *Windgate Brook* Aluminum Observation Car, *97* | | 90 | ____ |
| 19176 | ATSF *Indian Arrow* Diner "2572," *97* | | 90 | ____ |
| 19177 | ATSF *Grass Valley* Coach "2573," *97* | | 90 | ____ |
| 19178 | ATSF *Citrus Valley* Coach "2574," *97* | | 90 | ____ |
| 19179 | ATSF *Vista Heights* Coach "2575," *97* | | 90 | ____ |
| 19180 | ATSF Surfliner Passenger Car 4-pack, *97* | | 250 | ____ |
| 19181 | GN Empire Builder *Prairie View* Full Vista Dome Car, *98* | | 75 | ____ |
| 19182 | GN Empire Builder *River View* Full Vista Dome Car, *98* | | 75 | ____ |

| | | Exc | Mint | Cond/$ |
|---|---|---|---|---|
| 19183 | GN *Empire Builder* Vista Dome Car 2-pack, *98* | | 125 | ____ |
| 19184 | Milwaukee Road Passenger Car 4-pack, *99* | | 390 | ____ |
| 19185 | MILW *Red River Valley* Aluminum Passenger Coach "194," *99* | | 125 | ____ |
| 19186 | MILW Aluminum Coach/Diner "170," *99* | | 110 | ____ |
| 19187 | MILW *Cedar Rapids* Aluminum Observation Car "186 ," *99* | | 120 | ____ |
| 19188 | MILW Aluminum REA Passenger/Baggage Car "1336," *99* | | 95 | ____ |
| 19194 | KCS Aluminum Passenger Car 4-pack, *00* | | 380 | ____ |
| 19200 | Tidewater Southern Boxcar, *87* | 13 | 21 | ____ |
| 19201 | Lancaster & Chester Boxcar, *87* | 23 | 37 | ____ |
| 19202 | PRR Boxcar, *87* | 22 | 30 | ____ |
| 19203 | D&TS Boxcar, *87* | 11 | 18 | ____ |
| 19204 | Milwaukee Road Boxcar (FF 2), *87* | 29 | 41 | ____ |
| 19205 | Great Northern DD Boxcar (FF 3), *88* | 20 | 24 | ____ |
| 19206 | Seaboard System Boxcar, *88* | 18 | 23 | ____ |
| 19207 | CP Rail DD Boxcar, *88* | 17 | 22 | ____ |
| 19208 | Southern DD Boxcar, *88* | 11 | 13 | ____ |
| 19209 | Florida East Coast Boxcar, *88* | 15 | 19 | ____ |
| 19210 | Soo Line Boxcar, *89* | 19 | 23 | ____ |
| 19211 | Vermont Railway Boxcar, *89* | 18 | 21 | ____ |
| 19212 | PRR Boxcar, *89* | 21 | 25 | ____ |
| 19213 | SP&S DD Boxcar, *89* | 16 | 19 | ____ |
| 19214 | Western Maryland Boxcar (FF 4), *89* | 23 | 27 | ____ |
| 19215 | Union Pacific DD Boxcar, *90* | 17 | 21 | ____ |
| 19216 | Santa Fe Boxcar, *90* | 17 | 22 | ____ |
| 19217 | Burlington Boxcar, *90* | 16 | 21 | ____ |
| 19218 | New Haven Boxcar, *90* | 16 | 20 | ____ |
| 19219 | Lionel Lines 1900-1906 Boxcar, diesel RailSounds, *90* | 120 | 145 | ____ |
| 19220 | Lionel Lines 1926-1934 Boxcar, *90* | 27 | 30 | ____ |
| 19221 | Lionel Lines 1935-1937 Boxcar, *90* | 27 | 30 | ____ |
| 19222 | Lionel Lines 1948-1950 Boxcar, *90* | 27 | 30 | ____ |
| 19223 | Lionel Lines 1979-1989 Boxcar, *90* | 23 | 25 | ____ |
| 19228 | Cotton Belt Boxcar, *91* | 21 | 22 | ____ |
| 19229 | Frisco Boxcar, diesel RailSounds (FF 5), *91* | 75 | 90 | ____ |
| 19230 | Frisco DD Boxcar (FF 5), *91* | 21 | 26 | ____ |
| 19231 | TA&G DD Boxcar, *91* | 13 | 16 | ____ |
| 19232 | Rock Island DD Boxcar, *91* | 17 | 20 | ____ |
| 19233 | Southern Pacific Boxcar, *91* | 15 | 19 | ____ |
| 19234 | NYC Boxcar, *91* | 60 | 65 | ____ |
| 19235 | MKT Boxcar, *91* | 55 | 65 | ____ |
| 19236 | NKP DD Boxcar (FF 6), *92* | 22 | 30 | ____ |
| 19237 | C&IM Boxcar, *92* | 17 | 24 | ____ |
| 19238 | Kansas City Southern Boxcar, *92* | 18 | 23 | ____ |
| 19239 | Toronto, Hamilton & Buffalo DD Boxcar, *92* | 15 | 20 | ____ |
| 19240 | Great Northern DD Boxcar, *92* | 15 | 20 | ____ |

| | | Exc | Mint | Cond/$ |
|---|---|---|---|---|
| **19241** | Mickey Mouse 60th Anniversary Hi-Cube Boxcar, *91 u* | 128 | 168 | ___ |
| **19242** | Donald Duck 50th Anniversary Hi-Cube Boxcar, *91 u* | 125 | 132 | ___ |
| **19243** | Clinchfield Boxcar "9790," *91 u* | 35 | 41 | ___ |
| **19244** | L&N Boxcar "9791," *92* | 35 | 38 | ___ |
| **19245** | Mickey's World Tour Hi-Cube Boxcar, *92 u* | 35 | 40 | ___ |
| **19246** | Disney World 20th Anniversary Hi-Cube Boxcar, *92 u* | 33 | 40 | ___ |
| **19247** | Postwar "6464" Series Boxcar Set I, 3 cars, *93* | 445 | 610 | ___ |
| **19248** | Western Pacific Boxcar "6464," *93* | 75 | 95 | ___ |
| **19249** | Great Northern Boxcar "6464," *93* | 75 | 95 | ___ |
| **19250** | M&StL Boxcar "6464," *93* | 80 | 105 | ___ |
| **19251** | Montana Rail Link DD Boxcar "10001," *93* | 21 | 27 | ___ |
| **19254** | Erie Boxcar (FF 7), *93* | 21 | 25 | ___ |
| **19255** | Erie DD Boxcar (FF 7), *93* | 22 | 26 | ___ |
| **19256** | Goofy Hi-Cube Boxcar, *93* | 23 | 26 | ___ |
| **19257** | Postwar "6464" Series Boxcar Set II, 3 cars, *94* | 80 | 97 | ___ |
| **19258** | Rock Island Boxcar "6464," *94* | 25 | 34 | ___ |
| **19259** | Western Pacific Boxcar "6464100," *94* | 33 | 46 | ___ |
| **19260** | Western Pacific Boxcar "6464100," *94* | 35 | 49 | ___ |
| **19261** | Perils of Mickey Hi-Cube Boxcar #1, *93* | 28 | 30 | ___ |
| **19262** | Perils of Mickey Hi-Cube Boxcar #2, *93* | 20 | 28 | ___ |
| **19263** | NYC DD Boxcar (SSS), *94* | 36 | 42 | ___ |
| **19264** | Perils of Mickey Hi-Cube Boxcar #3, *94* | 28 | 31 | ___ |
| **19265** | Mickey Mouse 65th Anniversary Hi-Cube Boxcar, *94* | 42 | 44 | ___ |
| **19266** | Postwar "6464" Series Boxcar Set III, 3 cars, *95* | 75 | 90 | ___ |
| **19267** | NYC Pacemaker Boxcar "6464125," *95* | 37 | 42 | ___ |
| **19268** | Missouri Pacific Boxcar "6464150," *95* | 25 | 29 | ___ |
| **19269** | Rock Island Boxcar "6464," *95* | 25 | 26 | ___ |
| **19270** | Donald Duck 60th Anniversary Hi-Cube Boxcar, *95* | 30 | 34 | ___ |
| **19271** | Minnie Mouse Hi-Cube Boxcar, *95* | 41 | 43 | ___ |
| **19272** | Postwar "6464" Series Boxcar Set IV, 3 cars, *96* | 70 | 85 | ___ |
| **19273** | BAR State of Maine Boxcar "6464275," *96* | | 35 | ___ |
| **19274** | SP Overnight Boxcar "6464225," *96* | | 28 | ___ |
| **19275** | Pennsylvania Boxcar "6464," *96* | | 44 | ___ |
| **19276** | Postwar "6464" Series Boxcar Set V, 3 cars, *96* | 65 | 85 | ___ |
| **19277** | Rutland Boxcar "6464-300," *96* | | 26 | ___ |
| **19278** | B&O Boxcar "6464-325," *96* | | 30 | ___ |
| **19279** | Central of Georgia Boxcar "6464-375," *96* | | 29 | ___ |
| **19280** | Mickey's Wheat Hi-Cube Boxcar, *96* | | 32 | ___ |
| **19281** | Mickey's Carrots Hi-Cube Boxcar, *96* | | 40 | ___ |
| **19282** | Santa Fe "Super Chief" Boxcar "6464-196," *96* | | 24 | ___ |

| | | Exc | Mint | Cond/$ |
|---|---|---|---|---|
| 19283 | Erie Boxcar "6464-296," *96* | | 22 | ____ |
| 19284 | Northern Pacific Boxcar "6464-396," *96* | | 29 | ____ |
| 19285 | B&A State of Maine Boxcar "6464-275," *96* | | 27 | ____ |
| 19286 | Tweety and Sylvester Boxcar, *96* | | 46 | ____ |
| 19287 | NYC/PC Merger Boxcar "6464-125X" (SSS), *97* | 50 | 75 | ____ |
| 19288 | PRR/CR Merger Boxcar "6464-200X" (SSS), *97* | 43 | 56 | ____ |
| 19289 | Monon "Hoosier Line" Boxcar "6464," *97* | | 27 | ____ |
| 19290 | Seaboard "Silver Meteor" Boxcar "6464," *97* | | 24 | ____ |
| 19291 | GN Boxcar "6464-397," *97* | | 26 | ____ |
| 19292 | Postwar "6464" Series Boxcar Set VI, 3 cars, *97* | | 90 | ____ |
| 19293 | MKT Boxcar "6464-350," *97* | 28 | 32 | ____ |
| 19294 | B&O Boxcar "6464-400," *97* | 27 | 34 | ____ |
| 19295 | NH Boxcar "6464-425," *97* | 25 | 34 | ____ |
| 19300 | PRR Ore Car, *87* | 15 | 23 | ____ |
| 19301 | Milwaukee Road Ore Car, *87* | 20 | 25 | ____ |
| 19302 | Milwaukee Road Quad Hopper with coal (FF 2), *87* | 24 | 35 | ____ |
| 19303 | Lionel Lines Quad Hopper with coal, *87 u* | 20 | 31 | ____ |
| 19304 | GN Covered Quad Hopper (FF 3), *88* | 24 | 25 | ____ |
| 19305 | Chessie System Ore Car, *88* | 18 | 23 | ____ |
| 19307 | B&LE Ore Car with load, *89* | 19 | 25 | ____ |
| 19308 | GN Ore Car with load, *89* | 18 | 23 | ____ |
| 19309 | Seaboard Covered Quad Hopper, *89* | 16 | 19 | ____ |
| 19310 | L&C Quad Hopper with coal, *89* | 16 | 30 | ____ |
| 19311 | SP Covered Quad Hopper, *90* | 14 | 19 | ____ |
| 19312 | Reading Quad Hopper with coal, *90* | 21 | 36 | ____ |
| 19313 | B&O Ore Car with load, *90–91* | 20 | 25 | ____ |
| 19315 | Amtrak Ore Car with load, *91* | 22 | 30 | ____ |
| 19316 | Wabash Covered Quad Hopper, *91* | 18 | 23 | ____ |
| 19317 | Lehigh Valley Quad Hopper with coal, *91* | 47 | 55 | ____ |
| 19318 | NKP Quad Hopper with coal (FF 6), *92* | 30 | 34 | ____ |
| 19319 | Union Pacific Covered Quad Hopper, *92* | 19 | 23 | ____ |
| 19320 | PRR Ore Car with load, *92* | 21 | 30 | ____ |
| 19321 | B&LE Ore Car with load, *92* | 21 | 30 | ____ |
| 19322 | C&NW Ore Car with load, *93* | 27 | 34 | ____ |
| 19323 | Detroit & Mackinac Ore Car with load, *93* | 20 | 29 | ____ |
| 19324 | Erie Quad Hopper with coal (FF 7), *93* | 25 | 33 | ____ |
| 19325 | N&W 4-bay Hopper "6446-1" with coal, *97* | | 65 | ____ |
| 19326 | N&W 4-bay Hopper with coal, *96* | | 60 | ____ |
| 19327 | N&W 4-bay Hopper "6446-3" with coal, *96* | | 60 | ____ |
| 19328 | N&W 4-bay Hopper "6446-4" with coal, *96* | | 60 | ____ |
| 19329 | N&W 4-bay Hopper "6436" with coal, *97* | | 55 | ____ |
| 19330 | Cotton Belt 4-bay Hopper "64661" with coal, *98* | | 45 | ____ |
| 19331 | Cotton Belt 4-bay Hopper "64662" with coal, *98* | | 45 | ____ |
| 19332 | Cotton Belt 4-bay Hopper "64663" with coal, *98* | | 45 | ____ |
| 19333 | Cotton Belt 4-bay Hopper "64664" with coal, *98* | | 45 | ____ |
| 19338 | Cotton Belt 4-bay Hopper 2-pack, *99* | | 120 | ____ |
| 19339 | Cotton Belt 4-bay Hopper "64469," *99* | | NRS | ____ |

| | | Exc | Mint | Cond/$ |
|---|---|---|---|---|
| 19340 | Cotton Belt 4-bay Hopper "64470," 99 | | NRS | ___ |
| 19341 | LV 2-bay Hopper "6456," 99 | | 30 | ___ |
| 19344 | D&RGW 3-bay Cylindrical Hopper "15990," 99–00 | | 42 | ___ |
| 19345 | CN 3-bay Cylindrical Hopper "370708," 99–00 | | 95 | ___ |
| 19346 | PRR 4-bay Hopper with coal "744433," 01 | | 40 | ___ |
| 19347 | LV 2-bay Hopper "643657," 01 | | 40 | ___ |
| 19348 | Duluth, Missabe & Iron Range Ore Car "28000," 03 | | 25 | ___ |
| 19349 | U.S. Steel Ore Car "19349," 03 | | 29 | ___ |
| 19350 | Postwar "6636" Alaska Quad Hopper, 03 | | 34 | ___ |
| 19357 | N&W Hopper "6446-25," Archive Collection, 07 | | 50 | ___ |
| 19361 | Twizzlers Quad Hopper, 10 | | 55 | ___ |
| 19362 | Coursers Christmas Hopper with gifts, 10 | | 60 | ___ |
| 19365 | Coca-Cola Quad Hopper, 10 | | 60 | ___ |
| 19366 | Santa's Little Hopper, 10 | | 55 | ___ |
| 19371 | Burlington Northern I-Beam Car, 04 | | 60 | ___ |
| 19400 | Milwaukee Road Gondola with cable reels (FF 2), 87 | 23 | 31 | ___ |
| 19401 | GN Gondola with coal (FF 3), 88 | 14 | 16 | ___ |
| 19402 | GN Crane Car (FF 3), 88 | 47 | 65 | ___ |
| 19403 | WM Gondola with coal (FF 4), 89 | 20 | 25 | ___ |
| 19404 | Trailer Train Flatcar with WM trailers (FF 4), 89 | 29 | 33 | ___ |
| 19405 | Southern Crane Car, 91 | 42 | 65 | ___ |
| 19406 | West Point Mint Car, 91 u | 38 | 50 | ___ |
| 19408 | Frisco Gondola with coil covers (FF 5), 91 | 26 | 31 | ___ |
| 19409 | Southern Flatcar with stakes, 91 | 18 | 22 | ___ |
| 19410 | NYC Gondola with canisters, 91 | 47 | 55 | ___ |
| 19411 | NKP Flatcar with Sears trailer (FF 6), 92 | 50 | 59 | ___ |
| 19412 | Frisco Crane Car, 92 | 49 | 65 | ___ |
| 19413 | Frisco Flatcar with stakes, 92 | 16 | 21 | ___ |
| 19414 | Union Pacific Flatcar with stakes (SSS), 92 | 19 | 26 | ___ |
| 19415 | Erie Flatcar with trailer "7200" (FF 7), 93 | 28 | 39 | ___ |
| 19416 | ICG TTUX Flatcar Set with trailers (SSS), 93 | 70 | 75 | ___ |
| 19419 | Charlotte Mint Car, 93 | 25 | 32 | ___ |
| 19420 | Lionel Lines Vat Car, 94 | 18 | 22 | ___ |
| 19421 | Hirsch Brothers Vat Car, 95 | 20 | 21 | ___ |
| 19423 | Circle L Racing Flatcar "6424" with stock cars, 96 | | 27 | ___ |
| 19424 | Edison Electric Depressed Center Flatcar "6461" with transformer, 97 | | 31 | ___ |
| 19427 | Evans Auto Loader "6414," 99 | | 55 | ___ |
| 19428 | Evans Boat Loader "6414," 99 | | 70 | ___ |
| 19429 | Culvert Gondola "6342," 98–99 | | 48 | ___ |
| 19430 | ATSF Flatcar "6411" with Beechcraft Bonanza, 98 | | 47 | ___ |
| 19438 | Christmas Gondola (std 0), 98 | | 42 | ___ |
| 19439 | Flatcar with safes, 98 | | 35 | ___ |
| 19440 | Flatcar with FedEx trailer, 98 | | 34 | ___ |

| | | Exc | Mint | Cond/$ |
|---|---|---|---|---|
| **19441** | Lobster Vat Car, *98* | | 32 | ___ |
| **19442** | Water Supply Flatcar with tank (SSS), *98* | | 31 | ___ |
| **19444** | Flatcar with VW Bug, *98* | | 38 | ___ |
| **19445** | Borden Milk Tank Car "520," *99* | | 38 | ___ |
| **19446** | Pittsburgh Paint Vat Car, *99* | | 43 | ___ |
| **19447** | Mama's Baked Beans Vat Car, *99* | | 35 | ___ |
| **19448** | Easter Gondola "6462" with candy, *99* | | 27 | ___ |
| **19449** | Liquified Gas Tank Car "6469," *99* | | 31 | ___ |
| **19450** | Barrel Ramp Car "6343," *99* | | 31 | ___ |
| **19451** | Wheel Car "6262," *99* | | 32 | ___ |
| **19454** | PRR Flatcar "6424" with gondola, *99* | | 25 | ___ |
| **19455** | Lionel Lines Flatcar "6430" with Cooper-Jarrett trailers, *99* | | 60 | ___ |
| **19457** | Lionel Lines Extension Searchlight Car, *99* | | 40 | ___ |
| **19459** | Valentine Gondola "6462" with candy, *99* | | 50 | ___ |
| **19471** | Mobil Flatcar with 2 trailers, *00 u* | | 93 | ___ |
| **19472** | Mobil Bulkhead Flatcar with tank, *00 u* | | 68 | ___ |
| **19474** | L&N Flatcar "6424" with trailer frames, *99* | | 26 | ___ |
| **19476** | Zoo Gondola "6462" with animals, *99–00* | | 43 | ___ |
| **19477** | Monday Night Football Flatcar with trailer, *01* | | 30 | ___ |
| **19478** | Culvert Gondola "6342," *99* | | 45 | ___ |
| **19479** | Borden Milk Car "521," *00* | | 38 | ___ |
| **19480** | Valentine's Vat Car "6475," *99–00* | | 30 | ___ |
| **19481** | Easter Vat Car, *99–00* | | 38 | ___ |
| **19482** | NYC Flat with trailer "6424," *00* | | 50 | ___ |
| **19483** | VW Beetle Flatcar, *00* | | 48 | ___ |
| **19484** | Flatcar "6264" with timber, *00* | | 34 | ___ |
| **19485** | PRR Culvert Gondola "347004," *01* | | 41 | ___ |
| **19486** | NYC Lumber Flatcar, *01* | | 34 | ___ |
| **19487** | Flatcar "6800" with airplane, *00* | | 41 | ___ |
| **19489** | Evans Auto Loader "500085," *00* | | 50 | ___ |
| **19490** | Postwar "6475" Libby's Vat Car, *01–02* | | 36 | ___ |
| **19491** | Christmas Vat Car, *01* | | 30 | ___ |
| **19492** | WM Skeleton Log Car 3-pack, *01* | | 95 | ___ |
| **19496** | Westside Lumber Skeleton Log Car 3-pack, *01* | | 112 | ___ |
| **19500** | Milwaukee Road Reefer (FF 2), *87* | 30 | 39 | ___ |
| **19502** | C&NW Reefer, *87* | 30 | 33 | ___ |
| **19503** | Bangor & Aroostook Reefer, *87* | 22 | 25 | ___ |
| **19504** | Northern Pacific Reefer, *87* | 20 | 22 | ___ |
| **19505** | Great Northern Reefer (FF 3), *88* | 29 | 35 | ___ |
| **19506** | Thomas Newcomen Reefer, *88* | 18 | 23 | ___ |
| **19507** | Thomas Edison Reefer, *88* | 21 | 27 | ___ |
| **19508** | Leonardo da Vinci Reefer, *89* | 19 | 27 | ___ |
| **19509** | Alexander Graham Bell Reefer, *89* | 17 | 20 | ___ |
| **19510** | PRR Stock Car (FARR 5), *89 u* | 25 | 26 | ___ |
| **19511** | WM Reefer (FF 4), *89* | 22 | 28 | ___ |
| **19512** | Wright Brothers Reefer, *90* | 17 | 21 | ___ |
| **19513** | Ben Franklin Reefer, *90* | 17 | 20 | ___ |

| | | Exc | Mint | Cond/S |
|---|---|---|---|---|
| 19515 | Milwaukee Road Stock Car (FF 2), *90 u* | 33 | 41 | ___ |
| 19516 | George Washington Reefer, *89 u, 91* | 14 | 19 | ___ |
| 19517 | Civil War Reefer, *89 u, 91* | 14 | 19 | ___ |
| 19518 | Man on the Moon Reefer, *89 u, 91* | 13 | 17 | ___ |
| 19519 | Frisco Stock Car (FF 5), *91* | 26 | 31 | ___ |
| 19520 | CSX Reefer, *91* | 18 | 23 | ___ |
| 19522 | Guglielmo Marconi Reefer, *91* | 19 | 23 | ___ |
| 19523 | Dr. Robert Goddard Reefer, *91* | 19 | 23 | ___ |
| 19524 | Delaware & Hudson Reefer (SSS), *91* | 29 | 32 | ___ |
| 19525 | Speedy Alka Seltzer Reefer, *91 u* | 31 | 32 | ___ |
| 19526 | Jolly Green Giant Reefer, *91 u* | 21 | 33 | ___ |
| 19527 | Nickel Plate Road Reefer (FF 6), *92* | 20 | 29 | ___ |
| 19528 | Joshua L. Cowen Reefer, *92* | 23 | 28 | ___ |
| 19529 | A.C. Gilbert Reefer, *92* | 18 | 23 | ___ |
| 19530 | Rock Island Stock Car, *92 u* | 34 | 38 | ___ |
| 19531 | Rice Krispies Reefer, *92 u* | 23 | 33 | ___ |
| 19532 | Hormel Reefer "901," *92 u* | 18 | 24 | ___ |
| 19535 | Erie Reefer (FF 7), *93* | 23 | 26 | ___ |
| 19536 | Soo Line REA Reefer (SSS), *93* | 25 | 30 | ___ |
| 19538 | Hormel Reefer "102," *94* | 22 | 25 | ___ |
| 19539 | Heinz Reefer, *94* | 37 | 46 | ___ |
| 19540 | Broken Arrow Ranch Stock Car "3356," *97* | | 28 | ___ |
| 19552 | Rutland Reefer "395" (std O), *00* | | 32 | ___ |
| 19553 | ATSF Stock Car "23003," *00* | | 37 | ___ |
| 19554 | Postwar Celebration Milk Car "36621," *00* | | 125 | ___ |
| 19555 | Swift Reefer "5839," red, *01* | | 33 | ___ |
| 19556 | Swift Reefer "1020," silver, *01* | | 31 | ___ |
| 19557 | Circus Stock Car "6376," *00* | | 32 | ___ |
| 19558 | Postwar "6556" MKT Stock Car, *02* | | 27 | ___ |
| 19559 | MKT Stock Car, girls set add-on, *02* | | 95 | ___ |
| 19560 | NP 2-door Stock Car "6356," Archive Collection, *02* | | 33 | ___ |
| 19564 | Postwar "6672" Santa Fe Reefer, *03* | | 35 | ___ |
| 19565 | Burlington Reefer "6672," Archive Collection, *03* | | 35 | ___ |
| 19567 | Postwar "6572" Railway Express Agency Reefer, *05* | | 45 | ___ |
| 19568 | GN Reefer, Archive Collection, *05* | | 45 | ___ |
| 19569 | Pillsbury Reefer, traditional, *05* | | 53 | ___ |
| 19570 | Nestle Nesquik Reefer, traditional, *05* | | 53 | ___ |
| 19572 | NYC Reefer "6672," Archive Collection, *06* | | 45 | ___ |
| 19573 | Postwar "6356" NYC Stock Car, *06–07* | | 50 | ___ |
| 19574 | GN Stock Car, *08* | | 50 | ___ |
| 19575 | REA Reefer "6721," *08–09* | | 50 | ___ |
| 19576 | Alaska Reefer, *08* | | 50 | ___ |
| 19577 | Krey's Reefer, *10* | | 60 | ___ |
| 19578 | Granny Smith Apples Wood-sided Reefer, *10* | | 53 | ___ |
| 19585 | NS Transparent Instruction Car, *10* | | 75 | ___ |
| 19586 | Alaska Husky Transport Car, *10* | | 75 | ___ |

Exc Mint Cond/$

| | | Exc | Mint | Cond/$ |
|---|---|---|---|---|
| 19587 | Hershey's Chocolate Wood-sided Reefer, *10* | | 55 | ___ |
| 19588 | Santa's Wish Transparent Gift Car, *10* | | 75 | ___ |
| 19589 | Blood Transfusion Bunk Car, *10* | | 60 | ___ |
| 19590 | Wood-sided Reefer 2-pack, *10* | | 110 | ___ |
| 19599 | Old Glory Reefers, set of 3, *89 u, 91* | 37 | 43 | ___ |
| 19600 | Milwaukee Road 1-D Tank Car (FF 2), *87* | 33 | 40 | ___ |
| 19601 | North American 1-D Tank Car (FF 4), *89* | 27 | 29 | ___ |
| 19602 | Johnson 1-D Tank Car (FF 5), *91* | 24 | 30 | ___ |
| 19603 | GATX 1-D Tank Car (FF 6), *92* | 32 | 41 | ___ |
| 19604 | Goodyear 1-D Tank Car (SSS), *93* | 33 | 36 | ___ |
| 19605 | Hudson's Bay 1-D Tank Car (SSS), *94* | 25 | 29 | ___ |
| 19607 | Sunoco 1-D Tank Car "6315," *96* | | 23 | ___ |
| 19608 | Sunoco Aviation Services 1-D Tank Car "6315" (SSS), *97* | | 38 | ___ |
| 19611 | Gulf Oil 1-D Tank Car "6315," *98* | | 33 | ___ |
| 19612 | Gulf Oil 3-D Tank Car "6425," *98* | | 30 | ___ |
| 19614 | BASF 1-D Tank Car "UTLX 78252," *99–00* | | 25 | ___ |
| 19615 | Vulcan Chemicals 1-D Tank Car, *99–00* | | 25 | ___ |
| 19621 | Centennial 1-D Tank Car "6015-1," *99* | | 45 | ___ |
| 19622 | Centennial 1-D Tank Car "6015-2," *99* | | 49 | ___ |
| 19623 | Centennial 1-D Tank Car "6015-3," *99* | | 48 | ___ |
| 19624 | Centennial 1-D Tank Car "6015-4," *99* | | 45 | ___ |
| 19625 | Ethyl Tank Car " 6236," *01* | | 31 | ___ |
| 19626 | Diamond Chemical Tank Car "19419," *01* | | 29 | ___ |
| 19627 | Shell 1-D Tank Car "1227," *01* | | 37 | ___ |
| 19628 | Lion Oil 1-D Tank Car "2256," *01* | | 35 | ___ |
| 19634 | General American 1-D Tank Car, *01* | | 30 | ___ |
| 19635 | U.S. Army 1-D Tank Car "10936," *01* | | 31 | ___ |
| 19636 | Hooker Chemicals 1-D Tank Car "6180," *01* | | 36 | ___ |
| 19637 | GATX TankTrain Intermediate Car "44589" (std O), *02* | | 55 | ___ |
| 19638 | CN TankTrain Intermediate Car "75571" (std O), *02* | | 65 | ___ |
| 19639 | GATX TankTrain Intermediate Car 3-pack (std O), *02* | | 140 | ___ |
| 19644 | Union Texas 1-D Tank Car "9922," *02* | | 33 | ___ |
| 19645 | Penn Salt 1-D Tank Car "4730," *02* | | 33 | ___ |
| 19646 | CN TankTrain Intermediate Car "75571" (std O), *03* | | 45 | ___ |
| 19647 | GATX TankTrain Intermediate Car "44589" (std O), *03* | | 45 | ___ |
| 19649 | Scrooge McDuck Mint Car, *05* | | 188 | ___ |
| 19651 | Santa Fe Tool Car, *87* | 30 | 35 | ___ |
| 19652 | Jersey Central Bunk Car, *88* | 25 | 33 | ___ |
| 19653 | Jersey Central Tool Car, *88* | 26 | 28 | ___ |
| 19654 | Amtrak Bunk Car, *89* | 22 | 25 | ___ |
| 19655 | Amtrak Tool Car, *90–91* | 23 | 30 | ___ |
| 19656 | Milwaukee Road Bunk Car, smoke, *90* | 40 | 50 | ___ |
| 19657 | Wabash Bunk Car, smoke, *91–92* | 36 | 42 | ___ |
| 19658 | Norfolk & Western Tool Car, *91* | 24 | 29 | ___ |

| | | Exc | Mint | Cond/$ |
|---|---|---|---|---|
| **19660** | Mint Car, *98* | | 40 | ____ |
| **19663** | Pratt's Hollow Bunk Car "5717," *99* | | 40 | ____ |
| **19664** | Ambassador Award Bunk Car, bronze, *99 u* | | 369 | ____ |
| **19665** | Ambassador Engineer Bunk Car, silver, *99 u* | | 564 | ____ |
| **19666** | Ambassador Cowen Bunk Car, gold, *99 u* | | 394 | ____ |
| **19667** | Wellspring Gold Bullion Car, *99* | | 50 | ____ |
| **19669** | King Tut Museum Car "9660," *99* | | 68 | ____ |
| **19670** | NY Federal Reserve Bullion Car "6445," *00* | | 44 | ____ |
| **19671** | Lionel Model Shop Display Car "6445-01," *99–00* | | 50 | ____ |
| **19672** | Lionel Mines Mint Car, *00 u* | | 250 | ____ |
| **19673** | Wellspring Capital Management Mint Car, *99 u* | | 208 | ____ |
| **19674** | Lionel Lines Platinum Car, *00* | | 43 | ____ |
| **19675** | Lionel Model Shop Display "6445-2," *01* | | 42 | ____ |
| **19676** | Philadelphia Mint Car, *01* | | 40 | ____ |
| **19677** | Fort Knox Mint Car "6445," *00* | | 50 | ____ |
| **19678** | U.S. Army Bunk Car, *02* | | 45 | ____ |
| **19679** | St. Louis Federal Reserve Mint Car, *02* | | 38 | ____ |
| **19681** | Area 51 Alien Suspension Car, *02* | | 47 | ____ |
| **19682** | Alaska Klondike Mining Mint Car, *02* | | 40 | ____ |
| **19683** | Pony Express Mint Car, *02* | | 50 | ____ |
| **19686** | Chicago Federal Reserve Mint Car "6445," *03–04* | | 45 | ____ |
| **19687** | UP Bunk Car "3887," smoke, *03* | | 40 | ____ |
| **19688** | Postwar "6445" Fort Knox Mint Car, *02–03* | | 39 | ____ |
| **19689** | CIBRO TankTrain Intermediate Car 3-pack (std O), *03* | | 100 | ____ |
| **19694** | Pony Express Mint Car, *03* | | 50 | ____ |
| **19696** | U.S. Savings Bond Mint Car, *00* | | 150 | ____ |
| **19697** | U.S. Bureau of Engraving and Printing Mint Car "19697," *04* | | 40 | ____ |
| **19698** | San Francisco Federal Reserve Mint Car, *04* | | 40 | ____ |
| **19700** | Chessie System Extended Vision Caboose, *88* | 43 | 50 | ____ |
| **19701** | Milwaukee Road N5c Caboose (FF 2), *88* | 50 | 65 | ____ |
| **19702** | PRR N5c Caboose, *87* | 44 | 55 | ____ |
| **19703** | GN Extended Vision Caboose (FF 3), *88* | 42 | 49 | ____ |
| **19704** | WM Extended Vision Caboose, smoke (FF 4), *89* | 42 | 49 | ____ |
| **19705** | CP Rail Extended Vision Caboose, smoke, *89* | 43 | 47 | ____ |
| **19706** | UP Extended Vision Caboose "9706," smoke, *89* | 40 | 56 | ____ |
| **19707** | SP Work Caboose with searchlight, smoke, *90* | 55 | 60 | ____ |
| **19708** | Lionel Lines Bay Window Caboose, *90* | 43 | 46 | ____ |
| **19709** | PRR Work Caboose, smoke, *89, 91* | 55 | 70 | ____ |
| **19710** | Frisco Extended Vision Caboose, smoke (FF 5), *91* | 43 | 47 | ____ |
| **19711** | NS Extended Vision Caboose, smoke, *92* | 47 | 65 | ____ |
| **19712** | PRR N5c Caboose, *91* | 44 | 47 | ____ |
| **19714** | NYC Work Caboose with searchlight, smoke, *92* | 100 | 130 | ____ |
| **19715** | DM&IR Extended Vision Caboose "C-217," *92 u* | 50 | 60 | ____ |
| **19716** | IC Extended Vision Caboose "9405," smoke, *93* | 105 | 135 | ____ |

| | | Exc | Mint | Cond/$ |
|---|---|---|---|---|
| **19717** | Susquehanna Bay Window Caboose "0121," *93* | 44 | 55 | ____ |
| **19718** | C&IM Extended Vision Caboose "74," *92 u* | 38 | 45 | ____ |
| **19719** | Erie Bay Window Caboose "C-300" (FF 7), *93* | 47 | 55 | ____ |
| **19720** | Soo Line Extended Vision Caboose (SSS), *93* | 32 | 41 | ____ |
| **19721** | GM&O Extended Vision Caboose "2956," *93 u* | 47 | 50 | ____ |
| **19723** | Disney Extended Vision Caboose, *94* | 36 | 45 | ____ |
| **19724** | JCPenney MKT Extended Vision Caboose "125," *94 u* | 38 | 43 | ____ |
| **19726** | NYC Bay Window Caboose (SSS), *95* | 50 | 60 | ____ |
| **19727** | Pennsylvania N5c Caboose "477938," *96* | | 30 | ____ |
| **19728** | N&W Bay Window Caboose, *96* | | 70 | ____ |
| **19732** | ATSF Bay Window Caboose "6517," *96* | | 43 | ____ |
| **19733** | New York Central Caboose "6357," *96* | | 30 | ____ |
| **19734** | Southern Pacific Caboose "6357," *96* | | 26 | ____ |
| **19736** | PRR N5c Caboose "6417," *97* | | 27 | ____ |
| **19737** | Lackawanna Searchlight Caboose "2420," *97* | | 75 | ____ |
| **19738** | Conrail N5c Caboose "6417" (SSS), *97* | | 55 | ____ |
| **19739** | NYC Wood-sided Caboose "6907," *97* | | 60 | ____ |
| **19740** | Virginian N5c Caboose "6427," *97 u* | | 65 | ____ |
| **19741** | Pennsylvania N5c Caboose "6417," *98* | | 50 | ____ |
| **19742** | Erie Bay Window Caboose "C301," Caboose Talk, *98* | | 95 | ____ |
| **19748** | SP&S Bay Window Caboose "6517," *97 u* | | 50 | ____ |
| **19749** | SP Bay Window Caboose "6517," *98* | | 100 | ____ |
| **19750** | Holiday Music Bay Window Caboose, *98* | | 160 | ____ |
| **19751** | PRR N5c Caboose "492418," *98* | | 30 | ____ |
| **19752** | NP Bay Window Caboose "407," *98* | | 50 | ____ |
| **19753** | UP Extended Vision Caboose "25641," *98* | | 55 | ____ |
| **19754** | NYC Caboose "20112," *98* | | 55 | ____ |
| **19755** | Centennial Porthole Caboose, *99* | | 53 | ____ |
| **19756** | Lionel Lines Bay Window Caboose, *99* | | 50 | ____ |
| **19758** | DL&W Work Caboose "6419," *99* | | 55 | ____ |
| **19759** | Corvette N5c Caboose, *99* | | 60 | ____ |
| **19772** | Lionel Visitor's Center Vat Car, *99 u* | | 40 | ____ |
| **19773** | Lionel Kids Club Barrel Ramp Car "6343," *96 u* | | 45 | ____ |
| **19778** | Case Cutlery Wood-sided Caboose "1889" (std O), *99 u* | | NRS | ____ |
| **19779** | SP Bay Window Caboose "1908," *99* | | 65 | ____ |
| **19780** | LV Porthole Caboose "641751," *99–00* | | 43 | ____ |
| **19781** | Vapor Records Holiday Porthole Caboose "6417," *99–00* | | 40 | ____ |
| **19782** | NYC Bay Window Caboose "21719," *00* | | 65 | ____ |
| **19783** | Ford Mustang Extended Vision Caboose, *01* | | 50 | ____ |
| **19785** | SP Bay Window Caboose "6517," *00* | | 55 | ____ |
| **19786** | PRR Extended Vision Caboose, *00 u* | | 40 | ____ |
| **19787** | PRR Extended Vision Caboose "477927," *01* | | 40 | ____ |
| **19790** | Postwar "6417" Lehigh Valley Caboose, *02* | | 41 | ____ |
| **19792** | Postwar "C301" Erie Bay Window Caboose, *03* | | 45 | ____ |
| **19796** | C&O Bay Window Caboose, *03* | | 50 | ____ |

| | | Exc | Mint | Cond/S |
|---|---|---|---|---|
| 19800 | Circle L Ranch Operating Cattle Car, *88* | 75 | 95 | ___ |
| 19801 | Poultry Dispatch Chicken Car, *87* | 20 | 27 | ___ |
| 19802 | Carnation Milk Car, *87* | 85 | 100 | ___ |
| 19803 | Reading Ice Car, *87* | 38 | 44 | ___ |
| 19804 | Wabash Operating Hopper, *87* | 25 | 34 | ___ |
| 19805 | Santa Fe Operating Boxcar, *87* | 28 | 36 | ___ |
| 19806 | PRR Operating Hopper, *88* | 28 | 32 | ___ |
| 19807 | PRR Extended Vision Caboose, smoke, *88* | 39 | 47 | ___ |
| 19808 | NYC Ice Car, *88* | 38 | 49 | ___ |
| 19809 | Erie-Lackawanna Operating Boxcar, *88* | 27 | 35 | ___ |
| 19810 | Bosco Milk Car, *88* | 80 | 89 | ___ |
| 19811 | Monon Brakeman Car, *90* | 50 | 55 | ___ |
| 19813 | Northern Pacific Ice Car, *89 u* | 41 | 46 | ___ |
| 19815 | Delaware & Hudson Brakeman Car, *92* | 49 | 60 | ___ |
| 19816 | Madison Hardware Operating Boxcar "190991," *91 u* | 80 | 102 | ___ |
| 19817 | Virginian Ice Car, *94* | 31 | 35 | ___ |
| 19818 | Dairymen's League Milk Car "788," *94* | 65 | 80 | ___ |
| 19819 | Poultry Dispatch Car (SSS), *94* | 36 | 43 | ___ |
| 19820 | Die-cast Tender, RailSounds II, *95–96* | | 175 | ___ |
| 19821 | UP Operating Boxcar, *95* | 31 | 36 | ___ |
| 19822 | Pork Dispatch Car, *95* | 29 | 39 | ___ |
| 19823 | Burlington Ice Car, *94 u, 95* | 39 | 49 | ___ |
| 19824 | U.S. Army Target Launcher, *96* | | 30 | ___ |
| 19825 | Generator Car, *96* | | 48 | ___ |
| 19827 | NYC Operating Boxcar, *97* | | 37 | ___ |
| 19828 | C&NW Animated Stock Car "3356" and Stockyard, *96–97* | | 100 | ___ |
| 19830 | U.S. Mail Operating Boxcar "3428," *97* | | 39 | ___ |
| 19831 | GM Generator Car "3530," power pole and wire, *97* | | 46 | ___ |
| 19832 | Cola Ice Car "6352," *97* | | 47 | ___ |
| 19833 | Tender "2426RS," RailSounds II, *97* | | 240 | ___ |
| 19834 | LL 6-wheel Crane Car "2460," *97* | | 60 | ___ |
| 19835 | FedEx Animated Boxcar "3464X," *97* | | 38 | ___ |
| 19837 | Bucyrus 6-wheel Crane Car "2460," *99* | | 49 | ___ |
| 19845 | Aquarium Car "3435," CC, *98* | | 151 | ___ |
| 19846 | Animated Giraffe Car "3376C," *98* | | 105 | ___ |
| 19850 | Stock Car "33760," RailSounds, *00* | | 130 | ___ |
| 19853 | Firefighting Instruction Generator Car (SSS), *98* | | 60 | ___ |
| 19854 | Lionelville Fire Car (SSS), *98* | | 55 | ___ |
| 19855 | Christmas Aquarium Car, *98* | | 60 | ___ |
| 19856 | Mermaid Transport, *98* | | 65 | ___ |
| 19857 | NYC Firefighting Instruction Car "19853," *98–99* | | 175 | ___ |
| 19858 | Lionelville Operating Searchlight Car "19854," *99* | | 65 | ___ |
| 19859 | REA Boxcar "6267," steam RailSounds, *99* | | 170 | ___ |
| 19860 | Conrail Boxcar "169671," diesel RailSounds, *99* | | 140 | ___ |

| | | Exc | Mint | Cond/$ |
|---|---|---|---|---|
| **19864** | Animated Ostrich Boxcar, *99* | | 37 | ____ |
| **19867** | Operating Poultry Dispatch Car "3434," *99* | | 48 | ____ |
| **19868** | Shark Aquarium Car "3435," *99* | | 190 | ____ |
| **19869** | Alien Aquarium Car "3435," *99* | | 49 | ____ |
| **19877** | ATSF Operating Barrel Car, *99* | | 55 | ____ |
| **19878** | Operating Helium Tank Flatcar "3362," *99* | | 40 | ____ |
| **19880** | Lionel Lines Extension Searchlight Car, *00* | | 50 | ____ |
| **19882** | Sanderson Farms Poultry Car "3434," *99* | | 41 | ____ |
| **19883** | LL Bucyrus Erie Crane Car "64608," *99* | | 45 | ____ |
| **19884** | Atlantis Travel Aquarium Car, *00 u* | | 95 | ____ |
| **19885** | N&W Operating Hopper Car, *00* | | 31 | ____ |
| **19886** | Seaboard Boxcar "16126," steam RailSounds, *00* | | 140 | ____ |
| **19887** | SP Boxcar "651663," diesel RailSounds, *00* | | 140 | ____ |
| **19888** | Christmas Music Boxcar, *01* | | 65 | ____ |
| **19889** | PRR Bay Window Caboose "477719," Crewtalk, *00* | | 140 | ____ |
| **19890** | Santa Fe Bay Window Caboose "999211," Crewtalk, *00* | | 100 | ____ |
| **19894** | Hood's Operating Milk Car with platform, *03–04* | | 95 | ____ |
| **19894** | Pony Express Mint Car, *03* | | 50 | ____ |
| **19895** | 3356 Santa Fe Horse Car with corral, *04* | | 120 | ____ |
| **19896** | USMC Missile Launch Sound Car "45," *03–04* | | 165 | ____ |
| **19897** | NYC Crane Car, TMCC, *04* | | 255 | ____ |
| **19898** | Nestle Nesquik Operating Milk Car with platform, *04* | | 95 | ____ |
| **19899** | Pennsylvania Crane Car "19899" CC, *03–05* | | 260 | ____ |
| **19900** | Toy Fair Boxcar, *87 u* | 65 | 80 | ____ |
| **19901** | "I Love Virginia" Boxcar, *87* | 25 | 35 | ____ |
| **19902** | Toy Fair Boxcar, *88 u* | 55 | 80 | ____ |
| **19903** | Christmas Boxcar, *87 u* | 32 | 34 | ____ |
| **19904** | Christmas Boxcar, *88 u* | 32 | 43 | ____ |
| **19905** | "I Love California" Boxcar, *88* | 20 | 24 | ____ |
| **19906** | "I Love Pennsylvania" Boxcar, *89* | 26 | 32 | ____ |
| **19907** | Toy Fair Boxcar, *89 u* | 38 | 55 | ____ |
| **19908** | Christmas Boxcar, *89 u* | 30 | 39 | ____ |
| **19909** | "I Love New Jersey" Boxcar, *90* | 19 | 25 | ____ |
| **19910** | Christmas Boxcar, *90 u* | 35 | 38 | ____ |
| **19911** | Toy Fair Boxcar, *90 u* | 75 | 95 | ____ |
| **19912** | "I Love Ohio" Boxcar, *91* | 21 | 28 | ____ |
| **19913** | Christmas Boxcar, *91* | 34 | 52 | ____ |
| **19913** | Lionel Employee Christmas Boxcar, *91 u* | 150 | 200 | ____ |
| **19914** | Toy Fair Boxcar, *91 u* | 38 | 50 | ____ |
| **19915** | "I Love Texas" Boxcar, *92* | 35 | 60 | ____ |
| **19916** | Lionel Employee Christmas Boxcar, *92 u* | 190 | 220 | ____ |
| **19917** | Toy Fair Boxcar, *92 u* | 45 | 53 | ____ |
| **19918** | Christmas Boxcar, *92 u* | 49 | 70 | ____ |
| **19919** | "I Love Minnesota" Boxcar, *93* | 40 | 60 | ____ |

| No. | Description | Exc | Mint | Cond/$ |
|---|---|---|---|---|
| 19920 | Lionel Visitor's Center Boxcar, *92 u* | 26 | 28 | ___ |
| 19921 | Lionel Employee Christmas Boxcar, *93 u* | 140 | 185 | ___ |
| 19922 | Christmas Boxcar, *93* | 33 | 41 | ___ |
| 19923 | Toy Fair Boxcar, *93 u* | 65 | 95 | ___ |
| 19925 | Lionel Employee Learning Center Boxcar, *93 u* | 55 | 63 | ___ |
| 19926 | "I Love Nevada" Boxcar, *94* | 21 | 26 | ___ |
| 19927 | Lionel Visitor's Center Boxcar, *93 u* | 26 | 33 | ___ |
| 19928 | Lionel Employee Christmas Boxcar, *94 u* | 205 | 230 | ___ |
| 19929 | Christmas Boxcar, *94* | 30 | 40 | ___ |
| 19931 | Toy Fair Boxcar, *94 u* | 49 | 65 | ___ |
| 19932 | Lionel Visitor's Center Boxcar, *94 u* | 26 | 33 | ___ |
| 19933 | "I Love Illinois" Boxcar, *95* | 21 | 27 | ___ |
| 19934 | Lionel Visitor's Center Boxcar, *95 u* | 18 | 22 | ___ |
| 19937 | Toy Fair Boxcar, *95 u* | 55 | 75 | ___ |
| 19938 | Christmas Boxcar, *95* | 26 | 34 | ___ |
| 19939 | Lionel Employee Christmas Boxcar, *95 u* | 100 | 128 | ___ |
| 19941 | "I Love Colorado" Boxcar, *95* | 23 | 30 | ___ |
| 19942 | "I Love Florida" Boxcar, *96* | 19 | 27 | ___ |
| 19943 | "I Love Arizona" Boxcar, *96* | 20 | 25 | ___ |
| 19944 | Lionel Visitor's Center Tank Car, *96 u* | | 35 | ___ |
| 19945 | Holiday Boxcar, *96* | | 29 | ___ |
| 19946 | Lionel Employee Christmas Boxcar, *96 u* | | 195 | ___ |
| 19947 | Lionel Toy Fair Boxcar, *96 u* | | 200 | ___ |
| 19948 | Visitor's Center Flatcar with trailer, *96 u* | | 34 | ___ |
| 19949 | "I Love NY" Boxcar, *97* | | 50 | ___ |
| 19950 | "I Love Montana" Boxcar, *97* | | 30 | ___ |
| 19951 | "I Love Massachusetts" Boxcar, *98* | | 26 | ___ |
| 19952 | "I Love Indiana" Boxcar, *98* | | 31 | ___ |
| 19955 | Lionel Visitor's Center Gondola with coil covers, *98 u* | | 20 | ___ |
| 19956 | Toy Fair Boxcar "777," *98 u* | | 65 | ___ |
| 19957 | Ambassador Caboose, *97 u* | | 454 | ___ |
| 19958 | Ambassador Caboose, silver (std O), *98 u* | | 543 | ___ |
| 19959 | Ambassador Caboose, gold (std O), *98 u* | | 731 | ___ |
| 19964 | U.S. JCI Senate Boxcar, *92 u* | 55 | 63 | ___ |
| 19968 | "I Love Maine" Boxcar, *99* | | 40 | ___ |
| 19969 | "I Love Vermont" Boxcar, *99* | | 40 | ___ |
| 19970 | "I Love New Hampshire" Boxcar, *99* | | 34 | ___ |
| 19971 | "I Love Rhode Island" Boxcar, *99* | | 34 | ___ |
| 19976 | Lionel Employee Holiday Boxcar, *99 u* | | 150 | ___ |
| 19977 | Toy Fair Boxcar, *99 u* | | 50 | ___ |
| 19981 | Lionel Centennial Boxcar, *99* | | 30 | ___ |
| 19982 | Lionel Centennial Boxcar, *99* | | 30 | ___ |
| 19983 | Lionel Centennial Boxcar, *99* | | 30 | ___ |
| 19984 | Lionel Centennial Boxcar, *99* | | 30 | ___ |
| 19985 | "I Love Georgia" Boxcar, *99–00* | | 45 | ___ |
| 19986 | "I Love North Carolina" Boxcar, *99–00* | | 40 | ___ |
| 19987 | "I Love South Carolina" Boxcar, *99–00* | | 40 | ___ |

Exc Mint Cond/$

| | | Exc | Mint | Cond/$ |
|---|---|---|---|---|
| 19988 | "I Love Tennessee" Boxcar, *99–00* | | 55 | ___ |
| 19989 | Toy Fair Boxcar, *00 u* | | 55 | ___ |
| 19996 | Toy Fair Boxcar, *01 u* | | 50 | ___ |
| 19997 | Lionel Employee Boxcar, *01 u* | | 120 | ___ |
| 19998 | Christmas Boxcar, *01* | | 33 | ___ |
| 19999 | Lionel Visitor's Center 4-bay Hopper, *02 u* | | 150 | ___ |
| 21029 | World of Little Choo Choo Set, *94u, 95* | 36 | 43 | ___ |
| 21141 | North Dakota State Quarter Gondola Bank, *07* | | 60 | ___ |
| 21142 | South Dakota State Quarter Hopper Bank, *07* | | 60 | ___ |
| 21163 | SuperStreets FasTrack Grade Crossing, *08–10* | | 20 | ___ |
| 21164 | SuperStreets 10" Transition to FasTrack, *08–10* | | 9 | ___ |
| 21165 | SuperStreets Transition to FasTrack, 2 pieces, *08–10* | | 17 | ___ |
| 21168 | City Traction Trolley Add-on, *08* | | 75 | ___ |
| 21169 | City Traction Speeder Add-on, *08* | | 75 | ___ |
| 21170 | NYC 15" Heavyweight Passenger Car 4-pack, *07* | | 250 | ___ |
| 21175 | NYC 15" Heavyweight Passenger Car 2-pack, *07* | | 125 | ___ |
| 21198 | ATSF Alco Diesel AA Set, horn, *08* | | 200 | ___ |
| 21199 | ATSF *Midnight Chief* Streamliner Car 4-pack, *08* | | 200 | ___ |
| 21204 | ATSF *Midnight Chief* Streamliner Car 2-pack, *08* | | 100 | ___ |
| 21207 | SP Diesel Work Train, *07* | | 175 | ___ |
| 21212 | NH Diesel Freight Set, *07* | | 250 | ___ |
| 21217 | Southern Diesel Executive Inspection Train, *07* | | 175 | ___ |
| 21229 | Ringling Bros. S2 Diesel Switcher, horn, *07* | | 80 | ___ |
| 21230 | Ringling Bros. Porter Locomotive, *07* | | 105 | ___ |
| 21231 | Ringling Bros. Streamliner Car 4-pack, *07* | | 210 | ___ |
| 21234 | Ringling Bros. Streamliner Car 2-pack, *07* | | 105 | ___ |
| 21237 | Ringling Bros. Flatcar with 3 wagons, *07* | | 50 | ___ |
| 21238 | Ringling Bros. Flatcar with 3 wagons, *07* | | 50 | ___ |
| 21239 | Ringling Bros. Flatcar with crates, *07* | | 45 | ___ |
| 21240 | Ringling Bros. Flatcar with front end loader and poles, *07* | | 45 | ___ |
| 21252 | Boy Flying Kite, *08* | | 60 | ___ |
| 21253 | Operating Bunk Car Yard Office, *07* | | 80 | ___ |
| 21261 | SuperStreets 2.5" Straight-to-Curve Connector, 4 pieces, *08–10* | | 9 | ___ |
| 21265 | Operating Voltmeter Car, *07* | | 75 | ___ |
| 21266 | SuperStreets Intersection, 4 pieces, *08–10* | | 40 | ___ |
| 21267 | PRR Boxcab Electric Locomotive, horn, *07* | | 77 | ___ |
| 21271 | WP Operating Coal Dump Car with vehicle, *07* | | 33 | ___ |
| 21276 | Congressional Diner, smoke, *07* | | 110 | ___ |
| 21277 | Operating Flagman's Shanty, *08* | | 70 | ___ |
| 21279 | Roach Wranglers Pest Control Van, *08* | | 30 | ___ |
| 21281 | SuperStreets D21 Curve, *08–10* | | 3 | ___ |
| 21282 | SuperStreets 2.5" Curve-to-Curve Connector, 4 pieces, *08–10* | | 9 | ___ |

Exc Mint Cond/$

| | | Exc | Mint | Cond/$ |
|---|---|---|---|---|
| 21283 | SuperStreets Tubular Track Grade Crossing, *08–10* | 18 | | |
| 21284 | SuperStreets 10" Tubular Transition, *08–10* | 8 | | |
| 21285 | SuperStreets 10" Tubular Transition, 2 pieces, *08–10* | 14 | | |
| 21286 | SuperStreets Intersection, *08–10* | 10 | | |
| 21287 | SuperStreets Y Roadway, *08–10* | 12 | | |
| 21288 | SuperStreets O Gauge Conversion Pins, *08–10* | 2 | | |
| 21289 | SuperStreets Connector Pins, *08–10* | 2 | | |
| 21290 | SuperStreets Hookup Wires, 2 pieces, *08–10* | 3 | | |
| 21291 | Dogbone Expander pack, *08–10* | 25 | | |
| 21296 | City Traction Classic Truck, *07* | 30 | | |
| 21298 | NYC 4-6-4 Hudson Locomotive "5279," CC, *07* | 500 | | |
| 21316 | PE RS3 Diesel "2815," CC, *07* | 350 | | |
| 21324 | Acrobats and Clowns Figures, 10 pieces, *08–10* | 12 | | |
| 21325 | Ringmaster Circus Figures, 5, with accessories, *08–10* | 12 | | |
| 21326 | PRR 15" Interurban Car 2-pack, *07* | 200 | | |
| 21354 | Fresh Never Frozen Fish Transport Car, *07* | 80 | | |
| 21355 | Dump Bin, *08–10* | 20 | | |
| 21358 | Special Addition Boxcar, Girl, *08–10* | 25 | | |
| 21359 | Special Addition Boxcar, Boy, *08–10* | 25 | | |
| 21368 | Passenger Coach Figures, 9 pieces, *08–10* | 11 | | |
| 21369 | Walking Figures, 8 pieces, *08–10* | 11 | | |
| 21370 | Sitting Figures, 6, with benches, *08–10* | 11 | | |
| 21371 | Standing Figures, 8 pieces, *08–10* | 11 | | |
| 21372 | Railroad Station Figures, 6, with accessories, *08–10* | 11 | | |
| 21373 | School Figures, 7, with accessories, *08–10* | 11 | | |
| 21374 | Service Station Figures, 5, with accessories, *08–10* | 11 | | |
| 21375 | Police Figures, 10, with dog, *08* | 20 | | |
| 21376 | Seated Passenger Figures, 40 pieces, *08* | 27 | | |
| 21377 | Mounted Police, 3, with horses, *08–10* | 11 | | |
| 21378 | Factory, *08–10* | 18 | | |
| 21379 | Police Station, *08–10* | 16 | | |
| 21380 | Colonial House, *08–10* | 16 | | |
| 21381 | Suburban Station, *08–10* | 16 | | |
| 21382 | School, *08–10* | 17 | | |
| 21383 | Suburban Ranch House, *08–10* | 15 | | |
| 21384 | Service Station with gas pumps, *08–10* | 17 | | |
| 21385 | Barn and Chicken Coop, *08–10* | 20 | | |
| 21386 | Firehouse, *08–10* | 17 | | |
| 21387 | Church, *08–10* | 15 | | |
| 21388 | Country L-shaped Ranch House, *08–10* | 16 | | |
| 21389 | Supermarket, *08–10* | 12 | | |
| 21390 | Diner, *08–10* | 15 | | |
| 21394 | Rotating Beacon, *08–09* | 31 | | |
| 21396 | Single Tunnel Portals, pair, *08–10* | 15 | | |

| | | Exc | Mint | Cond/S |
|---|---|---|---|---|
| **21397** | SuperSnap 31" Remote Switch, left hand, *08–09* | | 55 | ___ |
| **21398** | SuperSnap 31" Remote Switch, right hand, *08–09* | | 55 | ___ |
| **21399** | SuperSnap 72" Remote Switch, left hand, *08–09* | | 70 | ___ |
| **21400** | SuperSnap 72" Remote Switch, right hand, *08–09* | | 70 | ___ |
| **21412** | NYC Plymouth Switcher Freight Set, *07* | | 155 | ___ |
| **21430** | SuperStreets D16 Curve, *08–10* | | 2 | ___ |
| **21431** | SuperStreets 10" Straight Track, *08–10* | | 2 | ___ |
| **21432** | SuperStreets D16 Curved Track, 8 pieces, *08–10* | | 18 | ___ |
| **21433** | SuperStreets 5" Straight Track, 4 pieces, *08–10* | | 14 | ___ |
| **21434** | SuperStreets 10" Straight Track, 8 pieces, *08–10* | | 19 | ___ |
| **21435** | World War II Seated Soldiers, 9, with benches, *08–10* | | 20 | ___ |
| **21436** | Rings and Things Circus Accessories, *08–09* | | 10 | ___ |
| **21438** | Remote Controller, *07–10* | | 35 | ___ |
| **21442** | City Figures, 7, with scooter, *08–10* | | 11 | ___ |
| **21443** | Factory Figures, 6, with accessories, *08–10* | | 11 | ___ |
| **21444** | Church Figures, 5, with accessories, *08–10* | | 11 | ___ |
| **21445** | Firefighting Figures, 11, with accessories, *08–10* | | 20 | ___ |
| **21449** | Operating Loading Platform with flatcar, *07–08* | | 80 | ___ |
| **21450** | Unloading Station with dumb bins, *07* | | 100 | ___ |
| **21451** | Girder Bridge with stone piers, *07* | | 40 | ___ |
| **21452** | Graduated Trestle Set, 26 pieces, *07* | | 50 | ___ |
| **21453** | Elevated Trestle Set, 10 pieces, *07* | | 40 | ___ |
| **21454** | Double Tunnel Portals, 2 pieces, *08–10* | | 20 | ___ |
| **21456** | UPS Step Van, *07* | | 30 | ___ |
| **21466** | Ringling Bros. 15" Aluminum Advertising Car, *07* | | 110 | ___ |
| **21469** | Ringling Bros. Flatcar, white, with container, *07* | | 45 | ___ |
| **21470** | Ringling Bros. Flatcar, blue, with container, *07* | | 45 | ___ |
| **21471** | Ringling Bros. Flatcar with 2 trailers, *08–10* | | 60 | ___ |
| **21472** | Ringling Bros. Flatcar with 2 trailers, *08–10* | | 60 | ___ |
| **21476** | Strasburg Plymouth Diesel Switcher, *07* | | 100 | ___ |
| **21494** | WM RS3 Diesel "189," CC, *07* | | 350 | ___ |
| **21529** | Montana State Quarter Boxcar Bank, *08* | | 45 | ___ |
| **21542** | Washington State Quarter Tank Car Bank, *08* | | 45 | ___ |
| **21543** | Boyd Bros. Ford Classic Truck, *08* | | 33 | ___ |
| **21549** | Ringling Bros. Crew Bus, *08* | | 33 | ___ |
| **21552** | S.W.A.T. Team Step Van, *08* | | 30 | ___ |
| **21560** | Reading Flatcar with rail load, *07* | | 25 | ___ |
| **21567** | School Bus SuperStreets Set, *08* | | 110 | ___ |
| **21568** | Dirty Dogz Van SuperStreets Set, *08* | | 100 | ___ |
| **21569** | Angelo's Pizza Delivery Van, *08* | | 30 | ___ |
| **21570** | Flying Colors Painting Van, *08* | | 30 | ___ |

Exc Mint Cond/$

| | | Exc | Mint | Cond/$ |
|---|---|---|---|---|
| 21571 | SuperStreets 10" Insulated Roadway, 2 pieces, *08–10* | 8 | | ___ |
| 21572 | SuperStreets 5" Straight School, 2 pieces, *08–10* | 8 | | ___ |
| 21573 | SuperStreets 5" Straight Stop Ahead, 2 pieces, *08–10* | 8 | | ___ |
| 21574 | SuperStreets 5" Straight Crosswalk, 2 pieces, *08–10* | 8 | | ___ |
| 21575 | SuperStreets 10" Crossing, 2 pieces, *08–10* | 10 | | ___ |
| 21576 | SuperStreets Skid Mark Roadway Pack, *08–10* | 13 | | ___ |
| 21577 | Snack-On Step Van, *08* | 30 | | ___ |
| 21582 | Keystone Coal Porter Locomotive, *08* | 100 | | ___ |
| 21583 | Keystone Coal Freight Car 4-pack, *08* | 100 | | ___ |
| 21590 | ATSF "Midnight Chief" 2-bay Hopper "162277," *08* | 25 | | ___ |
| 21591 | ATSF "Midnight Chief" Flatcar "94468" with trailer, *08* | 43 | | ___ |
| 21592 | ATSF "Midnight Chief" Caboose, *08* | 25 | | ___ |
| 21593 | ATSF "Midnight Chief" Boxcar "621593," *08* | 35 | | ___ |
| 21594 | NYC Empire State Express 15" Aluminum Car 4-pack, *08–09* | 420 | | ___ |
| 21599 | SP flatcar with wheel load, *07* | 35 | | ___ |
| 21600 | B&M RS3 Diesel "1538," CC, *08–09* | 350 | | ___ |
| 21607 | Jack Frost Hopper "327" with sugar load, *08* | 25 | | ___ |
| 21609 | Elephants and Giraffes, 2 pair, *08–10* | 13 | | ___ |
| 21610 | Lions and Tigers, 2 pair, *08–10* | 13 | | ___ |
| 21611 | Horses, 4 pieces, *08* | 13 | | ___ |
| 21621 | ATSF Operating Boxcar "22658," *08–09* | 90 | | ___ |
| 21623 | Rutland Operating Milk Car with platform, *08–10* | 150 | | ___ |
| 21626 | Rath Wood-sided Reefer "622," *09* | 45 | | ___ |
| 21627 | Greenlee Packing Wood-sided Reefer "3862," *10* | 45 | | ___ |
| 21628 | CNJ Reefer "1438," *08–09* | 35 | | ___ |
| 21629 | C&O Reefer "7783," *08–09* | 35 | | ___ |
| 21630 | UP Stock Car "42005," *09* | 45 | | ___ |
| 21631 | Reading Boxcar "107984," *08–09* | 35 | | ___ |
| 21632 | GN Boxcar "34285," *08–09* | 35 | | ___ |
| 21633 | RI "Route of the Rockets" Boxcar "21110," *09–10* | 40 | | ___ |
| 21634 | Tidewater Flying A 1-D Tank Car "1367," *09* | 40 | | ___ |
| 21635 | Southern Depressed Center Flatcar, 2 transformers, *09* | 43 | | ___ |
| 21636 | NS Flatcar with bulkheads and stakes, *08–09* | 35 | | ___ |
| 21637 | Ontario Northland Ribbed Hopper with coal, *09* | 40 | | ___ |
| 21639 | Pan Am Boxcar "32126," *08–09* | 55 | | ___ |
| 21640 | UP Modern Steel-sided Reefer "499030," *08–09* | 55 | | ___ |
| 21641 | Ringling Bros. Merchandise Flatcar, *08* | 50 | | ___ |
| 21643 | PRR Die-cast Gondola with covers, *09* | 73 | | ___ |
| 21644 | PRR 16-wheel Flatcar with transformer, *08–09* | 80 | | ___ |

| | | Exc | Mint | Cond/S |
|---|---|---|---|---|
| 21646 | DT&I Work Crane and Boom Car, *09* | | 85 | ___ |
| 21649 | City Traction Trolley with Ringling Bros. banner, *08–09* | | 80 | ___ |
| 21651 | Moo-Town Creamery Step Van, *08–09* | | 38 | ___ |
| 21656 | Quikrete Step Van, *08–09* | | 42 | ___ |
| 21658 | Ringling Bros. Vintage Truck, *08–09* | | 42 | ___ |
| 21659 | DT&I Flatcar "90059" with Ford trailer, *08–09* | | 60 | ___ |
| 21662 | Moo-Town Creamery Vending Machine, *08–09* | | 13 | ___ |
| 21663 | Moo-Town Creamery Bunk Car Ice Cream Shop, *08–09* | | 115 | ___ |
| 21664 | RI Operating Coal Dump Car with vehicle, *08–09* | | 40 | ___ |
| 21665 | Alaska Operating Log Dump Car with vehicle, *09* | | 40 | ___ |
| 21667 | Red River Lumber Boxcab Diesel with horn, *08–09* | | 100 | ___ |
| 21668 | CP Operating Hopper "9628," *08–09* | | 45 | ___ |
| 21675 | Mountain View Creamery Loading Depot, *08–10* | | 130 | ___ |
| 21676 | Beaver Creek Logging Die-cast Porter Locomotive, *08–09* | | 120 | ___ |
| 21677 | Ford Factory, *09* | | 22 | ___ |
| 21679 | Assured Comfort HVAC Van, *08–09* | | 38 | ___ |
| 21680 | Division of Prisons Bus SuperStreets Set, *08–09* | | 150 | ___ |
| 21688 | Ringling Bros. Heavyweight Coach 2-pack, *08–10* | | 240 | ___ |
| 21691 | Ringling Bros. Flatcar with 2 trailers, *08–10* | | 60 | ___ |
| 21692 | C&NW MP15 Diesel with Ringling Bros. banner, *08–09* | | 140 | ___ |
| 21693 | Southern MP15 Diesel Pair, powered and dummy, *10* | | 200 | ___ |
| 21696 | Ford Flatcar with 2 trucks, *08–09* | | 53 | ___ |
| 21698 | Lionel Van SuperStreets Set, *08–10* | | 130 | ___ |
| 21701 | Star Spangled GG1 Electric Locomotive "4837," *08–10* | | 260 | ___ |
| 21702 | Milwaukee Road Girder Bridge, *08–09* | | 15 | ___ |
| 21703 | ATSF *Black Mesa* Aluminum Business Car, *09–10* | | 160 | ___ |
| 21704 | C&O Double Searchlight Car with vehicle, *08–09* | | 50 | ___ |
| 21706 | Chatham Police Van, *08–09* | | 38 | ___ |
| 21707 | NYC Aluminum Business Car, *09* | | 160 | ___ |
| 21708 | CN Operating Log Dump Car, *10* | | 120 | ___ |
| 21709 | PRR Girder Bridge, *08–09* | | 15 | ___ |
| 21715 | Ringling Bros. Stock Car, *08–09* | | 60 | ___ |
| 21717 | Pullman-Standard 1-D Tank Car, *08–09* | | 35 | ___ |
| 21719 | NYC Bay Window Caboose, *99* | | 70 | ___ |
| 21720 | Ringling Bros. Billboard Set #2, *08–09* | | 10 | ___ |
| 21721 | Warning Sign Pack, 12 pieces, *08–10* | | 25 | ___ |
| 21730 | Regulatory Sign Pack, 12 pieces, *08–10* | | 25 | ___ |

Exc Mint Cond/S

| Number | Description | Exc | Mint | Cond/S |
|---|---|---|---|---|
| 21738 | Railroad Crossing Sign Pack, 6 pieces, *08–10* | | 21 | ___ |
| 21750 | NKP Rolling Stock 4-pack, *98* | | 160 | ___ |
| 21751 | PRR Rolling Stock 4-pack, *98* | | 145 | ___ |
| 21752 | Conrail Unit Trailer Train, *98* | | 285 | ___ |
| 21753 | Service Station Fire Rescue Train, *98* | 495 | 580 | ___ |
| 21754 | BNSF 3-bay Covered Hopper 2-pack (std O), *98* | | 65 | ___ |
| 21755 | 4-bay Covered Hoppers 2-pack, *98* | | 65 | ___ |
| 21756 | 6464-style Overstamped Boxcars 2-pack, *98* | | 65 | ___ |
| 21757 | UP Freight Car Set, *98* | | 185 | ___ |
| 21758 | Bethlehem Steel "44" (SSS), *99* | | 375 | ___ |
| 21759 | Canadian Pacific F3 Diesel Passenger Set, *99* | | 930 | ___ |
| 21761 | B&M Boxcar Set, 4-pack, *99* | | 180 | ___ |
| 21763 | New Haven Freight Set, *99* | | 265 | ___ |
| 21766 | ACL Passenger Car 2-pack, *99* | | 385 | ___ |
| 21769 | Centennial 1-D Tank Car Set, 4-pack, *99* | | 195 | ___ |
| 21770 | NYC Reefer Set, 4-pack, *99* | | 225 | ___ |
| 21771 | D&RGW Stock Car Set, 4-pack, *99* | | 230 | ___ |
| 21774 | Custom Series Consist I, 3-pack, *99* | | 150 | ___ |
| 21775 | Train Wreck Recovery Set, *99* | | 190 | ___ |
| 21778 | ATSF Train Master Diesel Freight Set, *99* | | NRS | ___ |
| 21779 | Seaboard Freight Car Set, *99* | | 280 | ___ |
| 21780 | NYC Aluminum Passenger Car 2-pack, *99* | | 160 | ___ |
| 21781 | Case Cutlery Freight Set, *99 u* | | 950 | ___ |
| 21782 | PRR Congressional Set, *00* | | 930 | ___ |
| 21783 | Monday Night Football 2-pack, *01–02* | | 50 | ___ |
| 21784 | QVC PRR Coal Freight Steam Set, *00 u* | | 348 | ___ |
| 21785 | QVC Gold Mine Freight Steam Set, *00 u* | | 380 | ___ |
| 21786 | Santa Fe F3 Diesel ABBA Passenger Set, *00* | | 1500 | ___ |
| 21787 | *Blue Comet* Steam Passenger Set, *01–02* | | 1050 | ___ |
| 21788 | Postwar Missile Launch Freight Set, *02–03* | | 350 | ___ |
| 21789 | Norfolk Southern Piggyback Set, CC (SSS), *01* | | 370 | ___ |
| 21790 | CN TankTrain Dash 9 Diesel Freight Set, *02* | | 630 | ___ |
| 21791 | Freedom Train Diesel Passenger Set, RailSounds, *03* | | 540 | ___ |
| 21792 | C&O Coal Hopper 6-pack #2 (std O), *01* | | 145 | ___ |
| 21793 | Virginian Coal Hopper 6-pack #2 (std O), *01* | | 160 | ___ |
| 21794 | Pioneer Seed GP7 Diesel Freight Set, *01 u* | | 820 | ___ |
| 21795 | Case Farmall Freight Set, *01 u* | | 940 | ___ |
| 21796 | NJ Medical Steam Freight Set, *01 u* | | 448 | ___ |
| 21797 | SP Daylight Passenger Set, *01* | | 670 | ___ |
| 21852 | MILW PS-2CD Hopper 3-pack (std O), *06* | | 155 | ___ |
| 21853 | BNSF PS-2CD Hopper 3-pack (std O), *06* | | 155 | ___ |
| 21854 | N&W PS-2CD Hopper 3-pack (std O), *06* | | 155 | ___ |
| 21855 | A&P Milk Car 3-pack, *06* | | 150 | ___ |
| 21856 | Bowman Dairy Milk Car 3-pack (std O), *06* | | 150 | ___ |
| 21857 | Western Dairy Milk Car 3-pack (std O), *06* | | 150 | ___ |
| 21858 | NP PS-4 Flatcar with trailers, 2-pack (std O), *06* | | 170 | ___ |

| | | Exc | Mint | Cond/$ |
|---|---|---|---|---|
| 21859 | C&NW PS-4 Flatcar with trailers, 2-pack (std O), 06 | | 170 | |
| 21860 | UP PS-4 Flatcar with trailers, 2-pack (std O), 06 | | 170 | |
| 21861 | PRR PS-4 Flatcar with trailers (std O), 06 | | 170 | |
| 21863 | ADM Unibody Tank Car 3-pack (std O), 06 | | 135 | |
| 21864 | Cerestar Unibody Tank Car 3-pack (std O), 06 | | 135 | |
| 21865 | Coe Rail Husky Stack Car 2-pack (std O), 06 | | 170 | |
| 21866 | Santa Fe Husky Stack Car 2-pack (std O), 06 | | 170 | |
| 21872 | C&O Offset Hopper 3-pack (std O), 05 | | 130 | |
| 21873 | P&LE Offset Hopper 3-pack (std O), 06 | | 145 | |
| 21874 | TTX Trailer Train 2-pack (std O), 06 | | 170 | |
| 21875 | CSX Husky Stack Car 2-pack (std O), 06 | | 170 | |
| 21876 | Disney Villain Hi-Cube Boxcar 3-pack, 05–06 | | 130 | |
| 21877 | Domino Sugar 1-D Tank Car 3-pack (std O), 07 | | 135 | |
| 21878 | Procor 1-D Tank Car 3-pack (std O), 07 | | 135 | |
| 21879 | C&EI Offset Hopper 3-pack (std O), 07 | | 145 | |
| 21880 | Erie Offset Hopper 3-pack (std O), 07 | | 145 | |
| 21881 | Frisco Offset Hopper 3-pack (std O), 07–08 | | 200 | |
| 21882 | Chessie System Offset Hopper 3-pack (std O), 07 | | 145 | |
| 21883 | C&O 3-bay Hopper 2-pack (std O), 07–08 | | 140 | |
| 21884 | Pennsylvania Power & Light 3-bay Hopper 2-pack (std O), 07 | | 140 | |
| 21885 | Santa Fe 3-bay Hopper 2-pack (std O), 07 | | 140 | |
| 21886 | C&NW 3-bay Hopper 2-pack (std O), 07–08 | | 140 | |
| 21888 | IMC Canada Cylindrical Hopper 2-pack, 06 | | 130 | |
| 21893 | Greenbrier Husky Stack Car 2-pack (std O), 07 | | 170 | |
| 21894 | CSX Husky Stack Car 2-pack (std O), 07 | | 170 | |
| 21895 | BN Husky Stack Car 2-pack (std O), 07 | | 170 | |
| 21896 | Arizona & California Husky Stack Car 2-pack (std O), 07 | | 170 | |
| 21897 | REA PS-4 Flatcar with trailers, 2-pack (std O), 07–08 | | 170 | |
| 21898 | NYC PS-4 Flatcar with trailers, 2-pack (std O), 07–08 | | 170 | |
| 21899 | Lackawanna PS-4 Flatcar with trailers, 2-pack (std O), 07 | | 170 | |
| 21900 | Civil War Union Train Set, 99 | | 375 | |
| 21901 | Civil War Confederate Train Set, 99 | | 375 | |
| 21902 | Construction Zone Set, 99 u | | 87 | |
| 21902 | MILW PS-4 Flatcar with trailers, 2-pack (std O), 07–08 | | 170 | |
| 21904 | Safari Adventure Set, 99 u | | 90 | |
| 21904 | UP PS-2 Covered Hopper 2-pack (std O), 07 | | 120 | |
| 21905 | NYC Flyer Set, 99 u | | 100 | |
| 21909 | AGFA Film Steam Freight Set, 98 u | | 1155 | |
| 21914 | Lionel Lines Freight Set, 99 | | 120 | |
| 21916 | Lionel Village Trolley, 99 | | 75 | |
| 21917 | N&W Freight Set, 99 | | 70 | |

| | | Exc | Mint | Cond/$ |
|---|---|---|---|---|
| 21918 | PC PS-2 Covered Hopper 2-pack (std O), *07* | | 120 | ____ |
| 21918 | Thomas Circus Play Set, *00* | | 100 | ____ |
| 21921 | Imco PS-2 Covered Hopper 2-pack (std O), *07–08* | | 120 | ____ |
| 21924 | Holiday Trolley Set, *99* | | 65 | ____ |
| 21925 | Thomas the Tank Engine Island of Sodor Train Set, *99–00* | | 150 | ____ |
| 21930 | NYC PS-2 Covered Hopper 2-pack (std O), *07* | | 120 | ____ |
| 21932 | JCPenney NYC Freight Flyer Steam Set, *00 u* | | 170 | ____ |
| 21934 | Custom Series Consist II, 3-pack, *99* | | 140 | ____ |
| 21936 | Looney Tunes Train Set, *00 u* | | 363 | ____ |
| 21937 | NYC Steel-sided Reefer 2-pack (std O), *07* | | 130 | ____ |
| 21939 | Dubuque Steel-sided Reefer 2-pack (std O), *07–08* | | 130 | ____ |
| 21940 | ADM Steel-sided Reefer 2-pack (std O), *07* | | 130 | ____ |
| 21941 | National Car Steel-sided Reefer 2-pack (std O), *07* | | 130 | ____ |
| 21944 | "Celebrate a Lionel Christmas" Steam Set, *00–01* | | 165 | ____ |
| 21945 | Christmas Trolley Set, *00* | | 100 | ____ |
| 21948 | NYC Freight Flyer Set, air whistle, *00* | | 240 | ____ |
| 21950 | Maersk SD70 Diesel Maxi-Stack Set, *00* | 560 | 700 | ____ |
| 21951 | World War II Troop Train, *00* | | 410 | ____ |
| 21952 | Lionel Lines Service Station Special Set, *00* | | 288 | ____ |
| 21953 | Ford Mustang GP7 Diesel Set, CC, *01* | | 345 | ____ |
| 21955 | D&RGW F3 Diesel AA Passenger Set, CC, *01* | | 740 | ____ |
| 21956 | New York Central Freight Set, *99–00* | | 355 | ____ |
| 21969 | Lionel Village Trolley Set, *00* | | 85 | ____ |
| 21970 | SP RS3 Diesel Freight Set, horn, *00–01* | | 110 | ____ |
| 21971 | Pennsylvania Flyer Steam Set, *00* | | 150 | ____ |
| 21972 | Frisco GP7 Diesel Freight Set, horn, *00* | | 150 | ____ |
| 21973 | ATSF Passenger Set, RailSounds, *00–01* | | 375 | ____ |
| 21974 | ATSF Passenger Set, SignalSounds, *00–01* | | 240 | ____ |
| 21975 | Burlington Steam Freight Set, SignalSounds, *00* | | 275 | ____ |
| 21976 | Centennial Steam Freight Starter Set, *00* | | 585 | ____ |
| 21977 | NYC Train Master Steam Freight Set, *99–00* | | 620 | ____ |
| 21978 | ATSF Train Master Diesel Freight Set, *99–00* | | 500 | ____ |
| 21981 | JCPenney NYC Flyer Set, *00 u* | | 150 | ____ |
| 21988 | NYC Freight Set, RailSounds, *00* | | 325 | ____ |
| 21989 | Burlington Steam Freight Set, RailSounds, *00* | | 300 | ____ |
| 21990 | NYC Flyer Freight Set, RailSounds, *00* | | 175 | ____ |
| 21999 | Whirlpool Steam Freight Set, *00 u* | | 698 | ____ |
| 22103 | PRR A5 Scale Switcher "411," CC, *08–09* | | 330 | ____ |
| 22104 | PRR Freight Car 3-pack, *08* | | 135 | ____ |
| 22105 | NYC *Empire State Express* 4-6-4 Hudson Locomotive "5429," CC, *08–09* | | 420 | ____ |
| 22113 | NYC *Empire State Express* 15" Aluminum Car 2-pack, *08–10* | | 210 | ____ |
| 22116 | Ringling Bros. Diesel Freight Set, *08–10* | | 245 | ____ |
| 22121 | Ringling Bros. Freight Set, *08–10* | | 390 | ____ |

Exc Mint Cond/$

| | | Exc | Mint | Cond/$ |
|---|---|---|---|---|
| **22126** | Ringling Bros. Expansion Pack, *08–10* | 135 | | ___ |
| **22131** | NH Streamliner Car 3-pack, *07* | 150 | | ___ |
| **22135** | CB&Q S2 Diesel Switcher "9305," horn, *07* | 80 | | ___ |
| **22136** | Erie S2 Diesel Switcher "522," horn, *07* | 80 | | ___ |
| **22137** | Alaska MP15 Diesel "1552," horn, *07* | 100 | | ___ |
| **22138** | Astoria Heat & Power Porter Locomotive "4," *07* | 100 | | ___ |
| **22139** | LIRR Speeder, *08* | 50 | | ___ |
| **22140** | CNJ Boxcab Diesel "1000," horn, *08* | 90 | | ___ |
| **22141** | Lackawanna 15" Interurban Car 2-pack, *07* | 200 | | ___ |
| **22142** | FEC Operating Dump Car, *07* | 70 | | ___ |
| **22143** | B&A Operating Log Dump Car, *08–09* | 70 | | ___ |
| **22144** | Alaska Operating Coal Dump Car with vehicle, *08* | 33 | | ___ |
| **22145** | WM Operating Log Dump Car with vehicle, *08* | 33 | | ___ |
| **22146** | PFE Operating Boxcar, *08* | 80 | | ___ |
| **22147** | B&O Operating Hopper with coal, *08* | 35 | | ___ |
| **22148** | GN Operating Hopper with coal, *08* | 35 | | ___ |
| **22149** | Dairymen's League Operating Milk Car, green, with platform, *08* | 140 | | ___ |
| **22150** | D&RGW Bunk Car, smoke, *08* | 65 | | ___ |
| **22151** | Alaska Searchlight Car with vehicle, *08* | 45 | | ___ |
| **22152** | NKP 2-bay Outside-braced Hopper "31299," *08* | 50 | | ___ |
| **22153** | L&N 2-bay Offset Hopper "78660," *08* | 50 | | ___ |
| **22154** | D&H 2-bay Rib Side Hopper "5737," *07* | 50 | | ___ |
| **22155** | Erie-Lack. 2-bay Aluminum Hopper "21353," *08* | 60 | | ___ |
| **22156** | ACF Demonstrator 2-bay Aluminum Hopper "44586," *07* | 60 | | ___ |
| **22157** | GN Aluminum Tank Car "74787," *08* | 60 | | ___ |
| **22158** | MILW Bulkhead Flatcar "967116" with wood, *08–09* | 43 | | ___ |
| **22159** | BNSF Flatcar "585011" with trailer, *08* | 43 | | ___ |
| **22160** | UP Flatcar "58059" with container, *08* | 43 | | ___ |
| **22161** | Conrail Flatcar "705910" with NS container, *08* | 43 | | ___ |
| **22161** | NS Flatcar with container, *07* | 43 | | ___ |
| **22162** | Foppiano Wine 3-D Tank Car "1112," *08* | 45 | | ___ |
| **22163** | PRR Weed Control Car "6321226," *07* | 45 | | ___ |
| **22166** | PRR Reefer "19492," *08* | 25 | | ___ |
| **22167** | Seaboard Reefer "16622," *08* | 25 | | ___ |
| **22168** | N&W Boxcar "645772," *08* | 25 | | ___ |
| **22169** | ATSF Reefer "11744," *07* | 25 | | ___ |
| **22170** | P&LE Reefer "22300," *07* | 25 | | ___ |
| **22171** | B&O DD Boxcar "495289," *08* | 25 | | ___ |
| **22172** | CB&Q Stock Car "52731," *08* | 25 | | ___ |
| **22174** | Erie-Lack. Transfer Caboose, *07* | 25 | | ___ |
| **22176** | PRR Caboose "478884," *07* | 25 | | ___ |
| **22177** | L&N Caboose "100," *07* | 25 | | ___ |
| **22179** | NYC Depressed Center Flatcar "66256" with 2 girders, *08* | 25 | | ___ |

Exc Mint Cond/S

| | | Exc | Mint | Cond/S |
|---|---|---|---|---|
| 22180 | IC Depressed Center Flatcar with 2 transformers, *07* | | 25 | ___ |
| 22182 | RI Gondola "180043" with coils, *08* | | 25 | ___ |
| 22184 | B&O Covered Hopper "604321," *08* | | 25 | ___ |
| 22185 | UP Covered Hopper "53186," *08* | | 25 | ___ |
| 22186 | P&LE (NYC) Gondola "17243," *08–09* | | 35 | ___ |
| 22187 | PRR 2-D Tank Car "6351815," *07* | | 25 | ___ |
| 22188 | Deep Rock 3-D Tank Car "2152," *08* | | 25 | ___ |
| 22189 | NP Java Diner, smoke, *08* | | 110 | ___ |
| 22190 | C&O Operating Billboard, *08* | | 65 | ___ |
| 22191 | Operating Passenger Station, *08–09* | | 105 | ___ |
| 22192 | Hot Box Operating BBQ Shack, *07* | | 80 | ___ |
| 22193 | Cold Drinks Vending Machine, *08* | | 12 | ___ |
| 22194 | Water Tower with light, *08–09* | | 20 | ___ |
| 22199 | City Traction Trolley Barn, *08–09* | | 65 | ___ |
| 22202 | Loading Ramp, *08–10* | | 20 | ___ |
| 22203 | Dairymen's League Operating Milk Car, white, with platform, *07* | | 140 | ___ |
| 22204 | Snacks Vending Machine, *08* | | 12 | ___ |
| 22205 | Soup and Sandwich Vending Machine, *08* | | 12 | ___ |
| 22206 | PRR Crew Bus, *08* | | 30 | ___ |
| 22222 | Ringling Bros. Speeder Chase Set, *08–10* | | 92 | ___ |
| 22225 | Ringling Bros. *Jomar* Heavyweight Private Car, *08–10* | | 120 | ___ |
| 22226 | Ringling Bros. 18" *Caledonia* Heavyweight Private Car, *08* | | 100 | ___ |
| 22227 | Ringling Bros. 18" Advertising Car, *08* | | 100 | ___ |
| 22228 | Ringling Bros. Flatcar with 3 wagons, *08* | | 50 | ___ |
| 22231 | Ringling Bros. Flatcar with 3 wagons, *08* | | 50 | ___ |
| 22235 | Ringling Bros. Flatcar with pole wagon and truck, *08* | | 75 | ___ |
| 22238 | Ringling Bros. Work Caboose with calliope wagon, *08* | | 40 | ___ |
| 22240 | Ringling Bros. Flatcar/Stock Car with wagon, *08* | | 50 | ___ |
| 22243 | Ringling Bros. Human Cannonball Car, *08* | | 45 | ___ |
| 22244 | Ringling Bros. Operating Searchlight Car with 3 spotlights, *08* | | 60 | ___ |
| 22247 | Ringling Bros. Stock Car "54," *08* | | 50 | ___ |
| 22248 | Ringling Bros. Stock Car "47," *08* | | 50 | ___ |
| 22249 | Ringling Bros. Dining Dept. Billboard Reefer, *08* | | 80 | ___ |
| 22250 | Ringling Bros. Dining Dept. Wood-sided Reefer, *08–09* | | 90 | ___ |
| 22251 | Ringling Bros. Dormitory Bunk Car "22," *08* | | 75 | ___ |
| 22252 | Ringling Bros. Operating Billboard, *08–09* | | 75 | ___ |
| 22253 | Ringling Bros. Vintage Billboard Set #1, *08* | | 9 | ___ |
| 22255 | Ringling Bros. Aluminum Coach "40010," *08–10* | | 165 | ___ |
| 22257 | Ringling Bros. Aluminum Shop Car "63002," *08–10* | | 165 | ___ |

Exc Mint Cond/$

| | | Exc | Mint | Cond/$ |
|---|---|---|---|---|
| 22258 | Ringling Bros. 18" Aluminum Large Animal Car, *08–10* | 165 | | |
| 22259 | Ringling Bros. Flatcar with trailer, *08* | 53 | | |
| 22260 | Ringling Bros. Tractor Trailer, *08* | 30 | | |
| 22261 | Idaho State Quarter Hopper Bank, *08* | 65 | | |
| 22262 | Wyoming State Quarter Tank Car Bank, *08* | 50 | | |
| 22263 | Utah State Quarter Boxcar Bank, *08* | 45 | | |
| 22264 | SuperStreets Figure-8 Expander Pack, *08–10* | 35 | | |
| 22267 | Mulligan Spring Water Step Van, *08* | 30 | | |
| 22270 | Quikrete Classic Truck with 2 pallets, *08* | 33 | | |
| 22271 | MILW EP-5 Electric Locomotive "E20," CC, *08–09* | 460 | | |
| 22272 | MILW Olympian *Hiawatha* 18" Aluminum Car 4-pack, *08* | 480 | | |
| 22277 | MILW Olympian *Hiawatha* 18" Aluminum Car 2-pack, *08* | 250 | | |
| 22280 | Erie-Lack. RS3 Diesel "933," CC, *08–09* | 350 | | |
| 22281 | Southern Train Master Diesel "6300," CC, *08–09* | 420 | | |
| 22282 | Southern Bay Window Caboose "X270," *08–09* | 70 | | |
| 22283 | UP S2 Diesel Switcher "1103" and Caboose "25384," *08* | 130 | | |
| 22286 | GN Boxcab Electric Locomotive "5008-A," horn, *08* | 90 | | |
| 22287 | North Shore Line 15" Interurban Car 2-pack, *08* | 230 | | |
| 22288 | Commuter Train Station, 6 road name stickers, *09* | 25 | | |
| 22289 | Ringling Bros. 18" Aluminum Passenger Car 2-pack, *08* | 270 | | |
| 22290 | Erie Boxcar "86448" with graffiti, *08* | 46 | | |
| 22291 | C&NW Stock Car "14303," *08* | 46 | | |
| 22292 | Land o' Lakes Butter Billboard Reefer, *08* | 75 | | |
| 22293 | PRR 4-bay Hopper "253776," *08* | 65 | | |
| 22294 | Montana Rail Link 3-bay Aluminum Hopper "50049," *08* | 70 | | |
| 22295 | Canada Wheat 4-bay Aluminum Hopper "606418," *08* | 73 | | |
| 22296 | Eaglebrook Aluminum Tank Car "19039," *08* | 70 | | |
| 22297 | Petri Wine 3-D Tank Car "904," *08–09* | 45 | | |
| 22298 | Cotton Belt Offset Cupola Wood-sided Caboose "2230," *08* | 80 | | |
| 22299 | MILW Bay Window Caboose "980502," *08–09* | 70 | | |
| 22300 | Detroit, Toledo & Ironton Coil Car "1352," *08* | 60 | | |
| 22301 | NYC Flatcar "506090" with freight kit, *08* | 35 | | |
| 22302 | C&O Flatcar "80951" with freight kit, *08* | 35 | | |
| 22303 | Extruded Aluminum I-Beam, 3 pieces, *08–09* | 6 | | |
| 22304 | Rails, 12 pieces, *08–09* | 6 | | |
| 22305 | Small Transformer Load, pair, *08–09* | 15 | | |
| 22306 | Large Transformer Load, *08* | 19 | | |
| 22307 | Forklifts, 3, with pallets, *08–09* | 27 | | |

| | | Exc | Mint | Cond/$ |
|---|---|---|---|---|
| **22308** | Loaders with crates, pair, *08–09* | | 13 | _____ |
| **22309** | Loaders with logs, pair, *08–09* | | 13 | _____ |
| **22310** | KBL Logistics Container 2-pack, *08* | | 40 | _____ |
| **22312** | Commemorative Quarter Extended Vision Caboose, *09* | | 80 | _____ |
| **22313** | ATSF Boxcar "137460," *08* | | 25 | _____ |
| **22314** | Coastal King Seafood Wood-sided Reefer, *08* | | 25 | _____ |
| **22315** | Wisconsin & Southern "God Bless America" Boxcar, *09* | | 43 | _____ |
| **22316** | NP Depressed Center Flatcar "66130" with water tank, *08* | | 25 | _____ |
| **22317** | U.S. Air Force Hopper "55175" with ballast load, *08* | | 25 | _____ |
| **22318** | DM&IR Ore Car "29991," *08* | | 25 | _____ |
| **22319** | Celanese Chemicals 1-D Tank Car "12730," *08* | | 25 | _____ |
| **22320** | Baldwin Locomotives Works 1-D Tank Car "6809," *08* | | 25 | _____ |
| **22321** | B&O Operating Boxcar, *08* | | 45 | _____ |
| **22322** | PRR Operating Ballast Dump Car, *08* | | 75 | _____ |
| **22323** | FEMA Voltmeter Car, *08* | | 75 | _____ |
| **22324** | C&NW Cop and Robber Chase Gondola, *08–09* | | 55 | _____ |
| **22325** | White Milk Cans, 10 pieces, *08–10* | | 8 | _____ |
| **22326** | Twin Searchlight Tower, *08–10* | | 33 | _____ |
| **22327** | Tommy's Bunk Car Grill, *08–09* | | 100 | _____ |
| **22328** | Santa Fe Operating Freight Transfer Platform, *08–09* | | 130 | _____ |
| **22329** | Dual Track Signal Bridge, *08–10* | | 45 | _____ |
| **22330** | Stella's Heavyweight Diner, smoke, *08–09* | | 140 | _____ |
| **22331** | Coffee Vending Machine, *08* | | 12 | _____ |
| **22332** | Spring Water Vending Machine, *08* | | 12 | _____ |
| **22333** | Candy Vending Machine, *08* | | 12 | _____ |
| **22334** | Ford Plymouth Diesel Switcher and Ore Car 6-pack, *08* | | 200 | _____ |
| **22335** | NS Operating Paint Shop with boxcar, *08–09* | | 140 | _____ |
| **22344** | KBL Logistics ISO Tank, *08* | | 19 | _____ |
| **22346** | Tableau Circus Wagons, *08* | | 13 | _____ |
| **22349** | Forklift with 6 pallets, *08–09* | | 23 | _____ |
| **22350** | Twin Lamp Posts, 3 pieces, *08–09* | | 22 | _____ |
| **22352** | Lamp Posts, 4 pieces, *08–09* | | 20 | _____ |
| **22354** | Portable Spotlights, 3 pieces, *08–09* | | 15 | _____ |
| **22356** | High Tension Poles, 4 pieces, *08–09* | | 8 | _____ |
| **22358** | Rail Yard Signs, 12 pieces, *08–09* | | 10 | _____ |
| **22360** | Telephone Poles, 6 pieces, *08–09* | | 7 | _____ |
| **22362** | Girder Bridge, *08–09* | | 8 | _____ |
| **22363** | Stone Bridge Piers, pair, *08–10* | | 27 | _____ |
| **22365** | Heavyweight Passenger Coach 6-wheel Scale Trucks, pair, *08–09* | | 25 | _____ |
| **22366** | Aluminum Passenger Coach 4-wheel Scale Trucks, pair, *08–09* | | 25 | _____ |
| **22367** | Timkin Scale Sprung Trucks, pair, *08–09* | | 19 | _____ |

Exc Mint Cond/$

| | | Exc Mint | Cond/$ |
|---|---|---|---|
| 22368 | Bettendorf Scale Sprung Trucks, pair, *08–09* | 19 | ___ |
| 22369 | Scale Couplers, pair, *08–09* | 6 | ___ |
| 22379 | SuperStreets Barricade, 2 pieces, *08–10* | 11 | ___ |
| 22387 | Kiosk with 3 vending machines, *08–09* | 40 | ___ |
| 22391 | Ford MP15 Diesel "10021," horn, *08* | 115 | ___ |
| 22392 | Ford Farming Boxcar "1681," *08* | 30 | ___ |
| 22393 | Ford Stampings DD Boxcar "101," *08* | 35 | ___ |
| 22394 | Ford 2-bay Covered Hopper "1667," *08* | 30 | ___ |
| 22395 | Ford Speeder "14," *08* | 65 | ___ |
| 22396 | Ford Water Tower, *08* | 25 | ___ |
| 22397 | Ford Rotating Sign Tower, *08* | 55 | ___ |
| 22398 | Boyd Bros. and Ford Barn and Chicken Coop, *08* | 25 | ___ |
| 22399 | Ford ISO Tank, *08–09* | 21 | ___ |
| 22402 | PRR Streamlined K4 4-6-2 Pacific Locomotive, tender, *09–10* | 500 | ___ |
| 22408 | Ringling Bros. Tractor Trailer #1, *08–09* | 35 | ___ |
| 22411 | Tableau Wagon Set #2, *08–10* | 18 | ___ |
| 22412 | PRR Operating Flagman's Shanty, *08–09* | 90 | ___ |
| 22414 | Linde Union Carbide Boxcar with aluminum tank, *08–09* | 70 | ___ |
| 22415 | Ringling Bros. Flatcar with circus wagon, *08* | 50 | ___ |
| 22417 | Ringling Bros. Flatcar with container, *09* | 55 | ___ |
| 22420 | PRR *Broadway Limited* Aluminum Passenger Car 2-pack, *09–10* | 300 | ___ |
| 22423 | GN Aluminum Passenger Car 2-pack, *09–10* | 360 | ___ |
| 22426 | Ford Gondola "13447" with coils, *08–09* | 43 | ___ |
| 22427 | Ford Operating Billboard, *08–09* | 75 | ___ |
| 22428 | Ford Tin Sign Replica 4-pack, *08–09* | 17 | ___ |
| 22433 | PRR *Broadway Limited* Aluminum Passenger Car 4-pack, *09–10* | 600 | ___ |
| 22438 | Mail Crane, *08–10* | 30 | ___ |
| 22439 | Milwaukee Road Aluminum Passenger Car 2-pack, *09–10* | 360 | ___ |
| 22447 | Wabash Die-cast 2-bay Ribbed Hopper "37751," *08–09* | 60 | ___ |
| 22449 | UP Crew Bus, *08–09* | 38 | ___ |
| 22450 | Seaboard Die-cast Hopper with gravel, *10* | 80 | ___ |
| 22454 | Oklahoma State Quarter Die-cast Hopper Bank, *08–09* | 75 | ___ |
| 22455 | New Mexico State Quarter Die-cast Gondola Bank, *08–09* | 74 | ___ |
| 22456 | Arizona State Quarter Tank Car Bank, *08–09* | 55 | ___ |
| 22457 | Alaska State Quarter Boxcar Bank, *09* | 55 | ___ |
| 22458 | Hawaii State Quarter Die-cast Hopper Bank, *09* | 75 | ___ |
| 22459 | Southern Aluminum Passenger Car 2-pack #1, *09* | 300 | ___ |
| 22460 | Southern Aluminum Passenger Car 2-pack #2, *09* | 300 | ___ |
| 22461 | Scale Skeleton Log Car 4-pack, *08–09* | 160 | ___ |
| 22467 | Railroad Water Tower, *08–09* | 23 | ___ |

Exc Mint Cond/S

| | | Exc | Mint | Cond/S |
|---|---|---|---|---|
| 22468 | Fast Eddie's Used Car Lot with 2 die-cast vehicles, *08–09* | | 50 | ___ |
| 22469 | Cola Illuminated Vending Machine, *08–09* | | 13 | ___ |
| 22470 | SuperStreets Guard Rails, *08–10* | | 20 | ___ |
| 22472 | Ringling Bros. Tin Sign Replica 4-pack, *08–09* | | 17 | ___ |
| 22477 | Lionel Tin Sign Replica 4-pack, *08–09* | | 15 | ___ |
| 22482 | Vintage Tin Sign Replica 4-pack, *08–09* | | 15 | ___ |
| 22487 | Scooter Gang with scooters, *09–10* | | 13 | ___ |
| 22492 | Airport Revolving Searchlight, *10* | | 40 | ___ |
| 22493 | Ringling Bros. Lighted Clown Wood-sided Reefer, *09* | | 75 | ___ |
| 22494 | Ford Flatcar with 2 Thunderbird convertibles, *09* | | 53 | ___ |
| 22496 | Vita O Flavored Water Vending Machine, *09* | | 13 | ___ |
| 22497 | Top Pop Soda Illuminated Vending Machine, *09* | | 13 | ___ |
| 22498 | Ringling Bros. Flatcar with 3 circus wagons, *09–10* | | 55 | ___ |
| 22500 | Defense Dept. Flatcar with 2 jeeps and soldier, *09* | | 50 | ___ |
| 22501 | C&NW Railroad Van, CC, *09–10* | | 100 | ___ |
| 22502 | Ringling Bros. Flatcar with 3 circus wagons, *09–10* | | 55 | ___ |
| 22504 | Ford Water Tower with vintage Ford logo, *09–10* | | 25 | ___ |
| 22505 | Sparkling Springs Beverage Truck, *09* | | 45 | ___ |
| 22506 | SuperStreets Fishtail Roadway, *09* | | 25 | ___ |
| 22507 | Ringling Bros. Flatcar with boxcar and ticket wagon, *09* | | 60 | ___ |
| 22509 | Pallet Pack with banded loads, *09* | | 20 | ___ |
| 22510 | Lionel Step Van, CC, *09–10* | | 100 | ___ |
| 22511 | BNSF Flatcar with helicopter, *09* | | 50 | ___ |
| 22513 | Ringling Bros. Heavyweight Advertising Car, *09* | | 120 | ___ |
| 22514 | NYC Girder Bridge, *09–10* | | 15 | ___ |
| 22515 | Milwaukee Road/REA Scale Boxcar "6436," *09* | | 55 | ___ |
| 22516 | BNSF MP15 Diesel "3704" with horn, *09* | | 120 | ___ |
| 22517 | Quick Lane Ford Motorcraft Auto Parts Van, *09–10* | | 42 | ___ |
| 22518 | Lionel Tank Container Leasing ISO Tank, *09–10* | | 23 | ___ |
| 22519 | Roma Wine Wood-sided Billboard Reefer, *09–10* | | 70 | ___ |
| 22520 | WWII Soldiers in Action, 10 pieces, *09–10* | | 20 | ___ |
| 22521 | 1959 Ford Billboard Set, *09* | | 10 | ___ |
| 22523 | American Flyer Vintage Truck, *09* | | 38 | ___ |
| 22524 | Ford Coil Car "749772," *09* | | 73 | ___ |
| 22525 | Vermont Railway Operating Boxcar "177," *09* | | 50 | ___ |
| 22526 | Crabby Matt's Smoking Heavyweight Diner, *09* | | 150 | ___ |
| 22527 | Toledo, Peoria & Western Boxcar "5067," *09–10* | | 55 | ___ |
| 22528 | GN Stock Car "55973," *09–10* | | 55 | ___ |
| 22529 | U.S. Army 1-D Tank Car "11278," *09* | | 35 | ___ |

| | | Exc | Mint | Cond/$ |
|---|---|---|---|---|
| **22530** | Milwaukee Road Aluminum Coach "627," *09–10* | | 180 | ___ |
| **22531** | Southern Girder Bridge, *09* | | 15 | ___ |
| **22532** | Montana Rail Link 1-D Tank Car "100017," *09* | | 35 | ___ |
| **22533** | GN Aluminum Coach "1377," *09–10* | | 180 | ___ |
| **22534** | SuperStreets D16 Curve Guard Rails, *09–10* | | 20 | ___ |
| **22536** | SuperStreets D21 Curve Guard Rails, *09–10* | | 22 | ___ |
| **22538** | Ford Modern Aluminum Tank Car "30166," *09* | | 90 | ___ |
| **22539** | BNSF Flatcar "922267" with Ford trailer, *09–10* | | 60 | ___ |
| **22542** | PRR Flatcar "480227" with freight kit, *09* | | 40 | ___ |
| **22543** | Biodiesel 2-D Tank Car "1544," *09* | | 40 | ___ |
| **22544** | Ringling Bros. Wood-sided Gondola with equipment, *09* | | 63 | ___ |
| **22548** | Kiosk #2 with 3 illuminated vending machines, *09* | | 40 | ___ |
| **22553** | Convenience Mart, *09–10* | | 25 | ___ |
| **22554** | Auto Parts Store, *09–10* | | 20 | ___ |
| **22555** | Ringling Bros. Tractor with Gold Tour container, *09–10* | | 55 | ___ |
| **22558** | PRR Flatcar "469301" with milk containers, *09* | | 50 | ___ |
| **22559** | UP Gondola "229794" with freight kit, *09–10* | | 80 | ___ |
| **22560** | CB&Q Wood-sided Gondola "85150" with spools, *09–10* | | 60 | ___ |
| **22561** | Gondola Scrap Load, *09* | | 9 | ___ |
| **22562** | Operation Lifesaver Boxcar with flashing LEDs, *09* | | 65 | ___ |
| **22563** | Ringling Bros. Handcar and Trailer Set, *10* | | 70 | ___ |
| **22566** | SuperStreets 2.5" Straight Roadway, 4 pieces, *10* | | 12 | ___ |
| **22568** | Generators, 2 pieces, *09* | | 9 | ___ |
| **22570** | Large transformer, *09* | | 22 | ___ |
| **22571** | Cage Wagon Set, *09–10* | | 18 | ___ |
| **22573** | Display Base, *09* | | 20 | ___ |
| **22574** | Ringling Bros. Flatcar "39" with trailer, *09* | | 60 | ___ |
| **22577** | Biodiesel Storage Tank with 2 figures, *09–10* | | 40 | ___ |
| **22578** | Ringling Bros. Heavyweight Coach "70," *09* | | 120 | ___ |
| **22579** | Circus Horses, 4 pieces, *09–10* | | 15 | ___ |
| **22580** | Bollards and Chains, *09–10* | | 20 | ___ |
| **22582** | Pipe Stack Load, *09* | | 30 | ___ |
| **22583** | KBL Operating Wind Turbine, *09–10* | | 75 | ___ |
| **22584** | KBL Die-cast 16-wheel Flatcar "34807," *09* | | 85 | ___ |
| **22587** | Old Reading Flatcar Foot Bridge with stone piers, *09–10* | | 50 | ___ |
| **22590** | Roadside Fender Bender, *09–10* | | 75 | ___ |
| **22592** | SuperStreets D16 Turn Roadways, left and right, *10* | | 35 | ___ |
| **22595** | SuperStreets D21 Turn Roadways, left and right, *10* | | 39 | ___ |
| **22598** | SuperStreets Adjustable Straight Kit, *09–10* | | 20 | ___ |
| **22600** | Wire Spool Load, 6 pieces, *09* | | 20 | ___ |

| No. | Description | Exc/Mint | Cond/$ |
|---|---|---|---|
| 22610 | Napa Valley Wine Train Alco FA Diesel AA Set, *10* | 230 | ____ |
| 22613 | Napa Valley Wine Train 15" Passenger Car 4-pack, *10* | 450 | ____ |
| 22618 | Signal Oil Co. 1-D Tank Car, *10* | 40 | ____ |
| 22619 | PRR Paoli MU Commuter Train 2-pack, *10* | 290 | ____ |
| 22622 | RR Paoli Motorized Combine, *10* | 200 | ____ |
| 22623 | PRR Commuter Train Station, *10* | 35 | ____ |
| 22624 | NH Die-cast Plymouth Switcher with snowplow, *10* | 160 | ____ |
| 22625 | Ringling Bros. 18" Aluminum Generator Car, *10* | 180 | ____ |
| 22627 | Ringling Bros. Lighted Clown Wood-sided Reefer, *10* | 90 | ____ |
| 22628 | Ringling Bros. 18" Aluminum Advertising Car, *10* | 180 | ____ |
| 22629 | Ringling Bros. Stock Car, *10* | 60 | ____ |
| 22630 | Ringling Bros. Tractor and Trailer, *10* | 35 | ____ |
| 22633 | Ringling Bros. 18" Aluminum Coach, *10* | 180 | ____ |
| 22634 | Ringling Bros. 18" Heavyweight Advertising Car, *10* | 146 | ____ |
| 22635 | Ringling Bros. Operating Dual Searchlight Car, *10* | 60 | ____ |
| 22637 | Quikrete Step Van, *10* | 48 | ____ |
| 22638 | PRR Crew Bus, *10* | 45 | ____ |
| 22639 | B&O Boxcab Diesel "195," *10* | 100 | ____ |
| 22640 | Central of Georgia Boxcar "5823," *10* | 45 | ____ |
| 22641 | New Haven Boxcar "36438," *10* | 45 | ____ |
| 22642 | Ringling Bros. Operating Large Animal Feed Car, *10* | 150 | ____ |
| 22643 | Ford MP15 Diesel "10022," *10* | 135 | ____ |
| 22644 | Ford Motorcraft 48' Aluminum Tank Car, *10* | 95 | ____ |
| 22645 | Ringling Bros. Operating Tent Pole Dump Car, *10* | 130 | ____ |
| 22646 | Ford Speeder, *10* | 75 | ____ |
| 22647 | Rock Island Gondola "180044," *10* | 35 | ____ |
| 22648 | PRR Gondola "353381," *10* | 35 | ____ |
| 22651 | Central Vermont Operating Milk Car with platform, *10* | 175 | ____ |
| 22653 | Starlite Diner with parking lot, *10* | 200 | ____ |
| 22654 | Ringling Bros. Flatcar with 3 circus wagons, *10* | 60 | ____ |
| 22656 | Ringling Bros. Flatcar with 3 circus wagons, *10* | 60 | ____ |
| 22658 | Operating Flagman's Shanty, *10* | 100 | ____ |
| 22659 | Union 76 1-D Tank Car "6322," *10* | 40 | ____ |
| 22660 | Moose Pond Creamery Operating Loading Depot, *10* | 140 | ____ |
| 22661 | WM 2-Bay Covered Hopper "5051," *10* | 35 | ____ |
| 22662 | PRR Reefer "19494," *10* | 45 | ____ |
| 22663 | New Haven Illuminated Caboose, *10* | 40 | ____ |
| 22667 | Acme Scrap Platform Crane, *10* | 60 | ____ |
| 22670 | ATSF Operating Boxcar, *10* | 140 | ____ |
| 22671 | Smoking Southern Bay-Window Caboose, *10* | 90 | ____ |

Exc  Mint  Cond/$

| | | Exc | Mint | Cond/$ |
|---|---|---|---|---|
| **22672** | Ringling Bros. 18" Sarasota Observation Car, *10* | | 146 | ___ |
| **22673** | Ford Water Tower with light, *10* | | 27 | ___ |
| **22674** | MILW 21" Aluminum Passenger Car 2-pack, *10* | | 400 | ___ |
| **22679** | Ringling Bros. Operating Billboard, *10* | | 100 | ___ |
| **22902** | Quonset Hut, *98–99* | | 22 | ___ |
| **22907** | Die-cast Girder Bridge, *98–01* | | 10 | ___ |
| **22910** | Gilbert Tractor Trailer, *98* | | 20 | ___ |
| **22914** | PowerHouse Lockon, *98–01* | | 24 | ___ |
| **22915** | Municipal Building, *98–99* | | 28 | ___ |
| **22916** | 190-watt Power Accessory System, *98* | | 425 | ___ |
| **22918** | Locomotive Backshop, *98* | 300 | 460 | ___ |
| **22919** | ElectroCouplers Kit for GP9 Diesel, *98–00* | | 20 | ___ |
| **22922** | Intermodal Crane, *98* | | 195 | ___ |
| **22931** | Die-cast Cantilever Signal Bridge, *98–06* | | 35 | ___ |
| **22934** | Walkout Cantilever Signal, *98–03* | | 42 | ___ |
| **22936** | Coaling Tower, 3 pieces, *98* | | 85 | ___ |
| **22940** | Mast Signal, *98–00* | | 37 | ___ |
| **22942** | Accessories Box, *98–01* | | 20 | ___ |
| **22944** | Automatic Operating Semaphore, *98–03, 08* | | 35 | ___ |
| **22945** | Block Target Signal, *98–00* | | 39 | ___ |
| **22946** | Automatic Crossing Gate and Signal, *98–99* | | 45 | ___ |
| **22947** | Auto Crossing Gate, *98–00* | | 36 | ___ |
| **22948** | Gooseneck Street Lamps, set of 2, *98–00* | | 165 | ___ |
| **22949** | Highway Lights, set of 4, *98–99* | | 20 | ___ |
| **22950** | Classic Street Lamps, set of 3, *98–02* | | 20 | ___ |
| **22951** | Dwarf Signal, *98–00* | | 24 | ___ |
| **22952** | Classic Billboards, set of 3, *98–00* | | 15 | ___ |
| **22953** | Linex Gasoline Tall Oil Tank, *98–99* | | 6 | ___ |
| **22954** | Linex Gasoline Wide Oil Tank, *98–99* | | 6 | ___ |
| **22955** | ElectroCouplers Kit for J Class and B&A tenders, *98–00* | | 20 | ___ |
| **22956** | ElectroCouplers Kit for NW2 Switcher, *98* | | 20 | ___ |
| **22957** | ElectroCouplers Kit for F3 Diesel, *98–01* | | 20 | ___ |
| **22958** | ElectroCouplers Kit for Dash 9 Diesel, *98–01* | | 20 | ___ |
| **22959** | ElectroCoupler Conversion Kit for Atlantic Locomotive, *98–01* | | 13 | ___ |
| **22960** | Trainmaster Command Basic Upgrade Kit, *98–01* | | 34 | ___ |
| **22961** | Standard GP9 Diesel B Unit Upgrade Kit, *98–01* | | 30 | ___ |
| **22962** | Deluxe GP9 Diesel B Unit Upgrade Kit, black trucks, *98–01* | | 44 | ___ |
| **22963** | RailSounds Upgrade Kit, steam RailSounds, *98–01* | | 55 | ___ |
| **22964** | RailSounds Upgrade Kit, diesel RailSounds, *98–01* | | 55 | ___ |
| **22965** | Culvert Loader, CC, *98–01* | | 255 | ___ |
| **22966** | Figure-8 Add-on Track Pack (O27), *98–10* | | 17 | ___ |
| **22967** | Double Loop Add-on Track Pack (O27), *98–10* | | 62 | ___ |
| **22968** | Double Loop Track Pack (O27), *98–03* | | 65 | ___ |

Exc Mint Cond/S

| | | Exc | Mint | Cond/S |
|---|---|---|---|---|
| 22969 | Deluxe Complete Track Pack (O), *98–10* | | 120 | ___ |
| 22972 | Bascule Bridge, *98–99* | | 337 | ___ |
| 22973 | Lionel Corporation Tractor and Trailer, *98* | | 15 | ___ |
| 22975 | Culvert Unloader, CC, *99–00* | | 225 | ___ |
| 22979 | GP9 Diesel B-Unit Deluxe Upgrade Kit, silver trucks, *98–01* | | 34 | ___ |
| 22980 | TMCC SC-2 Switch Controller, *99–10* | | 105 | ___ |
| 22982 | Postwar ZW Controller and Transformer Set, *98* | | 265 | ___ |
| 22983 | 180-watt PowerHouse Power Supply, *99–10* | | 100 | ___ |
| 22990 | Flatcar with Route 66 autos, 4-pack, *99* | | 37 | ___ |
| 22991 | Christmas Tree and *Blue Comet* Train, *99–00* | | 60 | ___ |
| 22993 | Route 66 Sinclair Dino Cafe, *99–00* | | 210 | ___ |
| 22997 | Oil Drum Loader, *99–00* | | 100 | ___ |
| 22998 | Triple Action Magnetic Crane, *99* | | 220 | ___ |
| 22999 | Sound Dispatching Station, *99–00* | | 90 | ___ |
| 23000 | NYC Dreyfuss Hudson Operating Base, 2-rail, *92 u* | | 190 | ___ |
| 23001 | NYC Dreyfuss Hudson Operating Base, 3-rail, *93 u* | | 190 | ___ |
| 23002 | NYC Hudson Operating Base, *92 u, 93–94* | | 190 | ___ |
| 23003 | PRR B-6 Switcher Operating Base, *92 u, 93–94* | | 190 | ___ |
| 23004 | NP 4-8-4 Operating Base, *92 u, 93–94* | | 190 | ___ |
| 23005 | Reading T-1 Operating Base, *92 u, 93–94* | | 190 | ___ |
| 23006 | Chessie System T-1 Operating Base, *92 u, 93–94* | | 190 | ___ |
| 23007 | SP Daylight Operating Base, *92 u, 93–94* | | 190 | ___ |
| 23008 | NYC L-3 Mohawk Operating Base, *92 u, 93–94* | | 190 | ___ |
| 23009 | PRR S2 Turbine Locomotive Operating Base, *92 u, 93–94* | | 190 | ___ |
| 23010 | 31" Remote Switch, left hand (O), *95–99* | 30 | 37 | ___ |
| 23011 | 31" Remote Switch, right hand (O), *95–99* | 28 | 30 | ___ |
| 23012 | F3 Diesel ABA Operating Base, *92 u, 93–94* | | 190 | ___ |
| 24101 | Mainline Color Position Signal, *04–08* | | 25 | ___ |
| 24102 | Industrial Water Tower, *03* | | 55 | ___ |
| 24103 | Double Floodlight Tower, *03, 05–09* | | 42 | ___ |
| 24104 | Hobo Tower, *03–05* | | 70 | ___ |
| 24105 | Track Gang, *03–06* | | 70 | ___ |
| 24106 | Exploding Ammunition Dump, *02* | | 25 | ___ |
| 24107 | Missile Firing Range Set, *02* | | 60 | ___ |
| 24108 | World War II Pylon, *03* | | 80 | ___ |
| 24109 | Santa Fe Railroad Tugboat, *03* | | 125 | ___ |
| 24110 | Pennsylvania Railroad Tugboat, *03* | | 118 | ___ |
| 24111 | Swing Bridge, *03* | | 215 | ___ |
| 24112 | Oil Field with bubble tubes, *03* | | 44 | ___ |
| 24113 | Lionelville Ford Auto Dealership, *03* | | 225 | ___ |
| 24114 | AMC/ARC Gantry Crane, CC, *03* | | 195 | ___ |
| 24115 | AMC/ARC Log Loader, CC, *03, 06–07* | | 140 | ___ |
| 24117 | Covered Bridge, *02–10* | | 45 | ___ |
| 24119 | Big Bay Lighthouse, *04–05* | | 170 | ___ |

| | | Exc | Mint | Cond/$ |
|---|---|---|---|---|
| **24122** | Lionelville People Pack, *03, 08–09* | | 15 | ___ |
| **24123** | Passenger Station People Pack, *03, 08–09* | | 15 | ___ |
| **24124** | Carnival People Pack, *03, 08–10* | 5 | 15 | ___ |
| **24130** | TMCC 135/180 PowerMaster, *04–10* | | 79 | ___ |
| **24131** | Dumbo Pylon, *03* | | 70 | ___ |
| **24134** | Bethlehem Steel Gantry Crane, *02* | | 200 | ___ |
| **24135** | Lionel Lighthouse, *02–03* | | 100 | ___ |
| **24137** | Mr. Spiff and Puddles, *03, 08* | | 34 | ___ |
| **24138** | Playtime Playground, *03, 08* | | 50 | ___ |
| **24139** | Duck Shooting Gallery, *03* | | 110 | ___ |
| **24140** | Charles Bowdish Homestead, *03* | | 60 | ___ |
| **24147** | Lionel Sawmill, *03* | | 90 | ___ |
| **24148** | Coal Tipple Coal Pack, *02, 08–10* | | 20 | ___ |
| **24149** | NYC Hobo Hotel, *02* | | 42 | ___ |
| **24151** | Hobo Campfire, *03* | | 25 | ___ |
| **24152** | Conveyor Lumber Loader, *03* | | 65 | ___ |
| **24153** | Railroad Control Tower, *03, 08–10* | | 40 | ___ |
| **24154** | Maiden Rescue, *03* | | 35 | ___ |
| **24155** | Blinking Light Billboard, *04–10* | | 21 | ___ |
| **24156** | Lionelville Street Lamps, set of 4, *04–05, 07–10* | | 23 | ___ |
| **24159** | Illuminated Station Platform, *04–08* | | 32 | ___ |
| **24160** | Rub-a-Dub-Dub, *04* | | 42 | ___ |
| **24161** | Test O' Strength, *04–06* | | 70 | ___ |
| **24164** | Summer Vacation, *04–05* | | 80 | ___ |
| **24168** | Tire Swing, *04–05* | | 70 | ___ |
| **24170** | Rover's Revenge, *04–05* | | 70 | ___ |
| **24171** | Campbell's Soup Water Tower, *04* | | 45 | ___ |
| **24172** | Balancing Man, *04–05* | | 70 | ___ |
| **24173** | Derrick Platform, *03–05* | | 60 | ___ |
| **24174** | Icing Station, *04–06* | | 100 | ___ |
| **24176** | Irene's Diner, *06–07* | | 65 | ___ |
| **24177** | Hot Air Balloon Ride, *04, 06* | | 95 | ___ |
| **24179** | Scrambler Amusement Ride, *04–07* | | 165 | ___ |
| **24180** | Choo Choo Barn Lionelville Zoo, *04–05* | | 105 | ___ |
| **24182** | Lionelville Firehouse, *04* | | 100 | ___ |
| **24183** | Lionelville Gas Station, *04, 06–09* | | 115 | ___ |
| **24187** | Classic Billboard Set: 3 stands and 5 inserts, *04–08* | | 10 | ___ |
| **24190** | Station Platform, *05–09* | | 17 | ___ |
| **24191** | Park People Pack, *04–10* | | 23 | ___ |
| **24192** | Park Benches People Pack, *04–09* | | 23 | ___ |
| **24193** | Railroad Yard People Pack, *04–08* | | 23 | ___ |
| **24194** | Civil Servants People Pack, *04–10* | | 23 | ___ |
| **24196** | Farm People Pack, *04–09* | | 23 | ___ |
| **24197** | City Accessory Pack, *04–10* | | 23 | ___ |
| **24200** | Lionel FasTrack Book, *07–10* | | 35 | ___ |
| **24201** | UPS Centennial Operating Billboard Signmen, *07* | | 100 | ___ |
| **24203** | *Polar Express* Original Figures, 4 pieces, *08–10* | | 27 | ___ |

| | | Exc | Mint | Cond/S |
|---|---|---|---|---|
| 24204 | Christmas Tractor Trailer with trees, *08* | | 25 | ___ |
| 24205 | Classic Billboard Set, *08–10* | | 20 | ___ |
| 24206 | M.O.W. Gantry Crane, *08* | | 280 | ___ |
| 24212 | Lionel Art Blinking Billboard, *08–09* | | 23 | ___ |
| 24214 | Postwar "395" Floodlight Tower, *08* | | 75 | ___ |
| 24215 | MTA Metro-North Passenger Station, *07* | | 53 | ___ |
| 24218 | Sunoco Elevated Tank, *08–09* | | 75 | ___ |
| 24219 | PRR Plastic Girder Bridge, *08* | | 18 | ___ |
| 24220 | ATSF Girder Bridge, *08–09* | | 18 | ___ |
| 24221 | UP Die-cast Girder Bridge, *08* | | 30 | ___ |
| 24222 | UPS Die-cast Girder Bridge, *08* | | 30 | ___ |
| 24223 | Santa's Sleigh Pylon, *08* | | 150 | ___ |
| 24224 | Postwar "38" Water Tower, *08–09* | | 150 | ___ |
| 24226 | Christmas Toy Store, *08* | | 52 | ___ |
| 24227 | Halloween Animated Billboard, *08–09* | | 50 | ___ |
| 24228 | Christmas Operating Billboard, *08* | | 38 | ___ |
| 24229 | Pennsylvania Water Tower, *08–09* | | 23 | ___ |
| 24230 | Maiden Rescue, *08* | | 60 | ___ |
| 24232 | Burning Switch Tower, *08* | | 80 | ___ |
| 24233 | Exploding Ammunition Dump, *08* | | 36 | ___ |
| 24234 | Missile Firing Range, *08* | | 43 | ___ |
| 24235 | UPS Water Tower, *08* | | 80 | ___ |
| 24236 | Wimpy's All-Star Burger Stand, *08* | | 97 | ___ |
| 24238 | Sunoco Oil Derrick, *08* | | 90 | ___ |
| 24240 | MTA Metro-North Blinking Billboard, *07* | | 21 | ___ |
| 24242 | Postwar "352" Icing Station, *08* | | 100 | ___ |
| 24243 | Rosie's Roadside Diner, *08* | | 85 | ___ |
| 24244 | Commuter People, *08* | | 23 | ___ |
| 24245 | MTA Metro-North Illuminated Station Platform, *07* | | 32 | ___ |
| 24248 | Manual Crossing Gate, *08–10* | | 16 | ___ |
| 24250 | Mainline Gooseneck Lamps, pair, *08–09* | | 32 | ___ |
| 24251 | *Polar Express* Caribou, *08–10* | | 23 | ___ |
| 24252 | *Polar Express* Wolves and Rabbits, *08–10* | | 23 | ___ |
| 24264 | Halloween People, *08–10* | | 23 | ___ |
| 24265 | Trick or Treat People, *08–10* | | 23 | ___ |
| 24270 | Operating Forklift Platform, *08–09* | | 280 | ___ |
| 24272 | Train Orders Building, *08* | | 80 | ___ |
| 24273 | Christmas Water Tower, *08–10* | | 23 | ___ |
| 24274 | Christmas Girder Bridge, *08* | | 18 | ___ |
| 24279 | PowerMaster Bridge, *08–10* | | 55 | ___ |
| 24283 | NYC Girder Bridge, *09–10* | | 21 | ___ |
| 24284 | Halloween Girder Bridge, *09–10* | | 21 | ___ |
| 24285 | CP Rail Girder Bridge, *08–09* | | 30 | ___ |
| 24286 | *Polar Express* Girder Bridge, *09–10* | | 21 | ___ |
| 24287 | ATSF Blinking Light Water Tower, *09* | | 30 | ___ |
| 24288 | NYC Blinking Light Water Tower, *09* | | 30 | ___ |
| 24293 | Legacy Module Garage, *08–09* | | 50 | ___ |

| | | Exc | Mint | Cond/$ |
|---|---|---|---|---|
| 24294 | AEC Nuclear Reactor, *09–10* | | 300 | ___ |
| 24295 | Cowen's Corner Hobby Shop, *09* | | 420 | ___ |
| 24296 | Engine House, *09–10* | | 80 | ___ |
| 24299 | Main Street Ice Cream Parlor, *08* | | 37 | ___ |
| 24928 | Franklin Mutual Bank, *08* | | 60 | ___ |
| 24500 | D&RGW Alco PA Diesel AA Set, *04* | | 530 | ___ |
| 24503 | D&RGW Alco PB Diesel, *04* | | 150 | ___ |
| 24504 | Santa Fe E6 Diesel AA Set, CC, *03* | | 530 | ___ |
| 24507 | Milwaukee Road E6 Diesel AA Set, CC, *03* | | 530 | ___ |
| 24511 | Burlington FT Diesel AA Set, RailSounds, *03* | | 225 | ___ |
| 24516 | Santa Fe F3 Diesel B Unit, *03* | | 235 | ___ |
| 24517 | NYC F3 Diesel B Unit "2404," powered, CC, *03* | | 250 | ___ |
| 24518 | WP F3 Diesel B Unit, *03* | | 275 | ___ |
| 24519 | B&O F3 Diesel B Unit, *03* | | 270 | ___ |
| 24520 | Alaska F3 Diesel AA Set, *03* | | 650 | ___ |
| 24521 | Alaska F3 Diesel B Unit, nonpowered, *03* | | 200 | ___ |
| 24522 | Alaska F3 Diesel B Unit "1519," powered, CC, *03* | | 300 | ___ |
| 24528 | Postwar "2379T" Rio Grande F3 Diesel A Unit, nonpowered, *04* | | 175 | ___ |
| 24529 | Santa Fe F3 Diesel AA Set, CC, *04* | | 690 | ___ |
| 24532 | Santa Fe F3 Diesel B Unit "18A," nonpowered, *04* | | 150 | ___ |
| 24533 | Santa Fe F3 Diesel B Unit "18B," *04* | | 200 | ___ |
| 24534 | Erie-Lack. F3 Diesel ABA Set, CC, *05* | | 900 | ___ |
| 24538 | Erie-Lack. F3 Diesel B Unit "8042," powered, CC, *05* | | 225 | ___ |
| 24544 | NYC FA2 Diesel AA Set, CC, *05* | | 600 | ___ |
| 24547 | NYC FB2 Diesel B Unit "3330" (std O), *05* | | 150 | ___ |
| 24548 | CN FPA-4 Diesel AA Set, CC, *05* | | 600 | ___ |
| 24551 | CN FPB-4 Diesel B Unit "6865" (std O), *05* | | 150 | ___ |
| 24552 | UP F3 Diesel ABA Set, CC, *05* | | 680 | ___ |
| 24556 | UP F3 Diesel B Unit "900C," powered, CC, *05* | | 285 | ___ |
| 24562 | Santa Fe F3 Diesel B Unit, powered, *04–05* | | 300 | ___ |
| 24563 | PRR F3 Diesel B Unit, powered, *04–05* | | 195 | ___ |
| 24570 | Santa Fe FT Diesel B Unit, nonpowered, *05* | | 85 | ___ |
| 24573 | Postwar "2383C" Santa Fe F3 Diesel B Unit, nonpowered, *05* | | 180 | ___ |
| 24574 | UP E7 Diesel AA Set, CC, *06* | | 700 | ___ |
| 24577 | UP E7 Diesel B Unit "990," nonpowered (std O), *06* | | 150 | ___ |
| 24578 | UP E7 Diesel B Unit "988," powered, *06* | | 300 | ___ |
| 24579 | NYC E7 Diesel AA Set, CC, *06* | | 700 | ___ |
| 24582 | NYC E7 Diesel B Unit "4105," nonpowered (std O), *06* | | 150 | ___ |
| 24583 | NYC E7 Diesel B Unit "4104," powered, *06* | | 300 | ___ |
| 24584 | Pennsylvania F7 Diesel ABA Set, CC, *06* | | 900 | ___ |
| 24588 | Pennsylvania F7 Diesel B Unit "9643B," powered, *06–07* | | 300 | ___ |
| 24589 | Santa Fe F7 Diesel ABA Set, CC, *06–07* | | 900 | ___ |

| | | Exc | Mint | Cond/$ |
|---|---|---|---|---|
| 24593 | Santa Fe F7 Diesel B Unit "332B," powered, *06–07* | | 300 | ___ |
| 24594 | PRR F7 Diesel Breakdown B Unit, RailSounds, *06–07* | | 160 | ___ |
| 24595 | Santa Fe F7 Diesel Breakdown B Unit, RailSounds, *06–07* | | 270 | ___ |
| 24596 | UP E7 Diesel Breakdown B Unit, RailSounds, *06* | | 270 | ___ |
| 24597 | NYC E7 Diesel Breakdown B Unit, RailSounds, *06* | | 270 | ___ |
| 25008 | Holiday Boxcar, *06* | | 50 | ___ |
| 25009 | Santa Fe Hi-Cube Boxcar "14064," *06* | | 30 | ___ |
| 25010 | NP Boxcar "48189," *06* | | 30 | ___ |
| 25011 | Angela Trotta Thomas "Santa's Break" Boxcar, *06* | | 50 | ___ |
| 25025 | Reading Boxcar "106502," *07–08* | | 35 | ___ |
| 25026 | RI Hi-Cube Boxcar, *07–08* | | 35 | ___ |
| 25030 | Billboard Boxcar with catalog art, *06* | | 20 | ___ |
| 25033 | Holiday Boxcar, *07* | | 50 | ___ |
| 25034 | Angela Trotta Thomas "Santa's Workshop" Boxcar, *07* | | 50 | ___ |
| 25041 | UPS Centennial Boxcar #1, *06* | | 50 | ___ |
| 25042 | UPS Centennial Boxcar #2, *07* | | 50 | ___ |
| 25043 | Macy's Boxcar, *07* | | 66 | ___ |
| 25050 | British Columbia Hi-Cube Boxcar "8008," *08* | | 35 | ___ |
| 25051 | Seaboard Boxcar, *08* | | 35 | ___ |
| 25053 | NYC DD Boxcar "75500," *08* | | 55 | ___ |
| 25054 | Angela Trotta Thomas "Christmas Memories" Boxcar, *08* | | 55 | ___ |
| 25059 | Democrat 2008 Election Boxcar, *08* | | 50 | ___ |
| 25060 | Republican 2008 Election Boxcar, *08* | | 50 | ___ |
| 25061 | Holiday Boxcar, *08* | | 55 | ___ |
| 25063 | Conrail Boxcar "25063," *09* | | 40 | ___ |
| 25064 | CP Rail Hi-Cube Boxcar, *09–10* | | 40 | ___ |
| 25066 | Holiday Boxcar, *09* | | 65 | ___ |
| 25067 | Angela Trotta Thomas "General Delivery" Boxcar, *09* | | 65 | ___ |
| 25077 | Milwaukee Road Boxcar "8484," *09–10* | | 40 | ___ |
| 25087 | Wabash Boxcar "6439," *10* | | 40 | ___ |
| 25103 | Chessie "Steam Special" Madison Car 2-pack, *05* | | 100 | ___ |
| 25106 | Pennsylvania Madison Car 4-pack, *05* | | 210 | ___ |
| 25111 | Pennsylvania Madison Car 2-pack, *05* | | 120 | ___ |
| 25114 | Lionel Lines Passenger Car 3-pack, *05* | | 120 | ___ |
| 25118 | Lionel Lines Passenger Car 2-pack, *05* | | 80 | ___ |
| 25121 | Southern Streamliner Car 4-pack, *05* | | 210 | ___ |
| 25126 | Southern Streamliner Car 2-pack, *05–06* | | 120 | ___ |
| 25134 | *Polar Express* Add-on Diner, *05–10* | | 47 | ___ |
| 25135 | *Polar Express* Add-on Baggage Car, *05–10* | | 60 | ___ |
| 25148 | B&O Madison Car 4-pack, *06–07* | | 220 | ___ |
| 25153 | B&O Madison Car 2-pack, *06–07* | | 125 | ___ |

Exc Mint Cond/$

| No. | Description | Exc | Mint | Cond/$ |
|---|---|---|---|---|
| 25156 | *California Zephyr* Streamliner Car 4-pack (std O), *06–07* | | 220 | ___ |
| 25161 | *California Zephyr* Streamliner Car 2-pack, *06–07* | | 125 | ___ |
| 25164 | UP Madison Car 4-pack, *06–07* | | 220 | ___ |
| 25169 | UP Madison Car 2-pack, *06–07* | | 125 | ___ |
| 25176 | B&O Baggage Car, TrainSounds, *06–07* | | 160 | ___ |
| 25177 | UP Baggage Car, TrainSounds, *06–07* | | 160 | ___ |
| 25178 | *California Zephyr* Streamliner Baggage Car, TrainSounds, *06–07* | | 160 | ___ |
| 25186 | *Polar Express* Hot Chocolate Car Add-on, *06–10* | | 60 | ___ |
| 25187 | GN Streamliner Car 4-pack, *07* | | 220 | ___ |
| 25188 | GN Streamliner Car 2-pack, *07* | | 125 | ___ |
| 25189 | GN Streamliner Baggage Car, TrainSounds, *07* | | 160 | ___ |
| 25196 | North Pole Central Vista Dome Car, *07–08* | | 45 | ___ |
| 25197 | North Pole Central Baggage Car, *07–10* | | 45 | ___ |
| 25198 | PRR Vista Dome Car "4058," *07–08* | | 45 | ___ |
| 25199 | PRR Baggage Car "9359," *07–09* | | 45 | ___ |
| 25404 | FEC *Champion* Aluminum Passenger Car 2-pack, *04–05* | | 290 | ___ |
| 25407 | FEC *Champion* Aluminum Diner, StationSounds, *04–05* | | 290 | ___ |
| 25408 | Santa Fe *El Capitan* Aluminum Passenger Car 2-pack, *05* | | 290 | ___ |
| 25411 | Santa Fe *El Capitan* Aluminum Diner, StationSounds, *05* | | 290 | ___ |
| 25412 | B&O *Columbian* Aluminum Passenger Car 2-pack, *05* | | 275 | ___ |
| 25415 | B&O *Columbian* Aluminum Diner, StationSounds, *05* | | 290 | ___ |
| 25416 | SP Daylight Aluminum Passenger Car 2-pack, *04–05* | | 290 | ___ |
| 25419 | SP Daylight Aluminum Diner, StationSounds, *04–05* | | 290 | ___ |
| 25420 | PRR *Trail Blazer* Aluminum Passenger Car 2-pack, *04–05* | | 290 | ___ |
| 25423 | PRR *Trail Blazer* Aluminum Diner, StationSounds, *04–05* | | 290 | ___ |
| 25433 | UP *City of Denver* Aluminum Passenger Car 4-pack (std O), *05* | | 1000 | ___ |
| 25438 | Union Pacific Aluminum Passenger Car 2-pack, *05* | | 250 | ___ |
| 25441 | UP *City of Denver* 18" Aluminum Diner, StationSounds, *05* | | 290 | ___ |
| 25446 | Santa Fe *Super Chief* Streamliner Car 2-pack, *05* | | 150 | ___ |
| 25450 | PRR Congressional Aluminum Passenger Car 4-pack (std O), *06–07* | | 580 | ___ |
| 25455 | PRR Congressional Aluminum Passenger Car 2-pack (std O), *06–07* | | 300 | ___ |
| 25458 | PRR Congressional Diner, StationSounds (std O), *06–07* | | 300 | ___ |

| | | Exc | Mint | Cond/$ |
|---|---|---|---|---|
| 25473 | NYC Commodore Vanderbilt Aluminum Passenger Car 2-pack (std O), *06* | | 300 | ___ |
| 25476 | NYC Commodore Vanderbilt Diner, StationSounds (std O), *06* | | 300 | ___ |
| 25496 | *Texas Special* 21" Streamliner Diner, StationSounds (std O), *07* | | 300 | ___ |
| 25503 | Santa Fe Heavyweight Passenger Car 4-pack (std O), *07–09* | | 495 | ___ |
| 25504 | Santa Fe Heavyweight Passenger Car 2-pack (std O), *07–09* | | 265 | ___ |
| 25505 | Santa Fe Heavyweight Diner, StationSounds (std O), *07–09* | | 295 | ___ |
| 25506 | SP Heavyweight Passenger Car 4-pack (std O), *07* | | 495 | ___ |
| 25507 | SP Heavyweight Passenger Car 2-pack (std O), *07–08* | | 265 | ___ |
| 25508 | SP Heavyweight Diner, StationSounds (std O), *07–08* | | 295 | ___ |
| 25512 | *Texas Special* Streamliner Car 2-pack (std O), *07* | | 300 | ___ |
| 25515 | MILW Heavyweight Passenger Car 4-pack (std O), *07* | | 495 | ___ |
| 25516 | MILW Heavyweight Passenger Car 2-pack (std O), *07* | | 265 | ___ |
| 25517 | MILW Heavyweight Diner, StationSounds (std O), *07–08* | | 295 | ___ |
| 25518 | PRR Heavyweight Passenger Car 4-pack (std O), *07* | | 495 | ___ |
| 25519 | PRR Heavyweight Passenger Car 2-pack (std O), *07* | | 265 | ___ |
| 25520 | PRR Heavyweight Diner, StationSounds (std O), *07–08* | | 295 | ___ |
| 25521 | B&O Heavyweight Passenger Car 4-pack (std O), *07* | | 495 | ___ |
| 25522 | B&O Heavyweight Passenger Car 2-pack (std O), *07* | | 265 | ___ |
| 25523 | B&O Heavyweight Diner, StationSounds (std O), *07–08* | | 295 | ___ |
| 25559 | Phantom IV Passenger Car 4-pack, *08* | | 380 | ___ |
| 25574 | UP Streamlined Diner, StationSounds (std O), *08* | | 325 | ___ |
| 25575 | *Polar Express* Heavyweight Car 2-pack, *09* | | 400 | ___ |
| 25578 | *Polar Express* Heavyweight Add-on Coach, *09* | | 200 | ___ |
| 25582 | New York City Transit R30 Subway 2-pack, *10* | | 400 | ___ |
| 25586 | *Polar Express* Heavyweight Baggage Car, *10* | | 200 | ___ |
| 25587 | *Polar Express* Abandoned Toy Car, *10* | | 200 | ___ |
| 25595 | New York City Transit R16 Subway 2-pack, *10* | | 400 | ___ |
| 26000 | C&O Flatcar with pipes, *01* | | 20 | ___ |
| 26001 | BP Flatcar "6424" with trailers, *01 u* | | 150 | ___ |
| 26002 | Monopoly Flatcar with airplane, *00 u* | | NRS | ___ |
| 26003 | Lackawanna Flatcar with NH trailer, *01* | | 60 | ___ |
| 26004 | Conrail Flatcar "71693" with trailer, *01* | | 50 | ___ |
| 26005 | Nickel Plate Flatcar with trailer, *01* | | 55 | ___ |

Exc Mint Cond/$

| | | Exc | Mint | Cond/$ |
|---|---|---|---|---|
| 26006 | Southern Flatcar "50126" with trailer, 01 | | 50 | ___ |
| 26007 | NW Flatcar "203029" with trailer, 01 | | 50 | ___ |
| 26008 | Farmall Flatcar, 01 u | | NRS | ___ |
| 26011 | B&M Bulkhead Flatcar, 01 u | | NRS | ___ |
| 26013 | CN Flatcar with Zamboni ice resurfacing machine, 01 | | 48 | ___ |
| 26014 | JCPenney Flatcar, 01 u | | 145 | ___ |
| 26016 | Soo Line Flatcar with trucks, 01 u | | NRS | ___ |
| 26017 | Soo Line Flatcar with trailer, 01 u | | NRS | ___ |
| 26018 | Soo Line Flatcar with trailer, 01 u | | NRS | ___ |
| 26019 | Alaska Gondola "13801," 02 | | 30 | ___ |
| 26020 | Postwar "3830" Flatcar with submarine, 02 | | 46 | ___ |
| 26021 | CN Flatcar with trailer, 02 | | 44 | ___ |
| 26022 | PFE Flatcar with trailer, 02 | | 32 | ___ |
| 26023 | Postwar "6816" Flatcar with bulldozer, 02 | | 65 | ___ |
| 26024 | Postwar "6817" Flatcar with scraper, 02 | | 65 | ___ |
| 26025 | Postwar "6407" Flatcar with rocket, 02 | | 42 | ___ |
| 26026 | Postwar "6413" Flatcar with Mercury capsules, 02 | | 95 | ___ |
| 26027 | Flatcar "6425" with U.S. Army boat, 02 | | 30 | ___ |
| 26028 | Conrail Well Car "768121," 02 | | 40 | ___ |
| 26030 | NYC Flatcar "601172" with stakes and bulkheads, 02 | | 22 | ___ |
| 26033 | NYC Gondola "6462," 01 | | 30 | ___ |
| 26035 | LL Flatcar with traffic helicopter, 01 | | 50 | ___ |
| 26039 | Lions Flatcar with 2 Zamboni ice resurfacing machines, 02 | | 39 | ___ |
| 26042 | B&O Gondola "601272" with canisters, 03 | | 19 | ___ |
| 26043 | Seaboard Flatcar "48109" with trailer, 03 | | 30 | ___ |
| 26044 | NYC Flatcar "506089" with trailers, 03 | | 35 | ___ |
| 26045 | Postwar "2411" Flatcar with pipes, 03 | | 40 | ___ |
| 26046 | Postwar "6561" Flatcar with cable reels, 03 | | 30 | ___ |
| 26047 | Postwar "2461" Flatcar with transformer, 03 | | 25 | ___ |
| 26048 | Postwar "6801" Flatcar with boat, 02 | | 29 | ___ |
| 26049 | Speedboat Willie Flatcar with boat, 03 | | 29 | ___ |
| 26056 | Southern Bulkhead Flatcar "50125," 02 | | 19 | ___ |
| 26057 | SP Flatcar "599365" with tractors, 02 | | 37 | ___ |
| 26058 | SP Flatcar "599366" with trailer frames, 02 | | 35 | ___ |
| 26061 | Lionelville Tree Transport Gondola, 03 | | 40 | ___ |
| 26062 | NYC Gondola "26062" with cable reels, 03 | | 19 | ___ |
| 26063 | Pennsylvania Bulkhead Flatcar "26063," 03 | | 19 | ___ |
| 26064 | Rock Island Flatcar "90088" with trailer, 04 | | 34 | ___ |
| 26065 | REA Flatcar with trailers "TLCX2," 04 | | 35 | ___ |
| 26066 | Great Northern Bulkhead Flatcar "26066," 04 | | 20 | ___ |
| 26067 | Southern Gondola "60141" with cable reels, 04 | | 20 | ___ |
| 26070 | Nestle Nesquik Flatcar "26070" with trailer, 03 | | 41 | ___ |
| 26077 | LL Flatcar "6424" with autos, girls set add-on, 03 | | 44 | ___ |
| 26078 | LL Flatcar "6801" with boat, boys set add-on, 03 | | 40 | ___ |

| | | Exc | Mint | Cond/S |
|---|---|---|---|---|
| 26080 | NJ Medical School Flatcar with handcar, *03* | | 75 | ___ |
| 26082 | Frisco Auto Carrier, 2-tier, *04* | | 20 | ___ |
| 26085 | New York Auto Carrier, 2-tier, *05* | | 27 | ___ |
| 26086 | Alaska Bulkhead Flatcar, traditional, *05* | | 27 | ___ |
| 26087 | Rock Island Gondola with canisters, traditional, *05* | | 27 | ___ |
| 26091 | Elvis Flatcar with tractor and trailer, traditional, *05* | | 60 | ___ |
| 26099 | PRR Auto Carrier "500423," 3-tier, *07* | | 30 | ___ |
| 26100 | PRR 1-D Tank Car, *00* | | 27 | ___ |
| 26101 | Lenoil 1-D Tank Car "6015," *00* | | 34 | ___ |
| 26102 | AEC Glow-in-Dark 1-D Tank Car, *00* | | 41 | ___ |
| 26103 | GATX Tank Train 1-D Tank Car "44588," *00* | | 34 | ___ |
| 26107 | BP Petroleum 3-D Tank Car, *00 u* | | 98 | ___ |
| 26108 | Lionel Visitor's Center Reefer "206482," *00 u* | | 38 | ___ |
| 26109 | NYC (P&LE) 1-D Tank Car, *00* | | 42 | ___ |
| 26110 | SP 3-D Tank Car "6415," *00–01* | | 15 | ___ |
| 26111 | Frisco Tank Car, *00* | | 29 | ___ |
| 26112 | Gulf Oil Tank Car, *00* | | 40 | ___ |
| 26113 | U.S. Army 1-D Tank Car, *00* | | 35 | ___ |
| 26114 | Service Station 1-D Tank Car (SSS), *00* | | 32 | ___ |
| 26115 | Lionel Centennial Tank Car, *00 u* | | 83 | ___ |
| 26116 | Pepe LePew 1-D Tank Car, *00 u* | | 90 | ___ |
| 26118 | NYC Tank Car "101900," *01* | | 23 | ___ |
| 26119 | Protex 3-D Tank Car "1054," *00* | | 29 | ___ |
| 26120 | KCS Tank Car "1229," *00* | | 32 | ___ |
| 26122 | Pioneer Seed Tank Car, *00 u* | | NRS | ___ |
| 26123 | Santa Fe Stock Car "23002," *01* | | 35 | ___ |
| 26124 | C&O 1-D Tank Car "X1019," *01* | | 30 | ___ |
| 26125 | Winter Wonderland Clear Tank Car with confetti, *00* | | 50 | ___ |
| 26126 | Cheerios Boxcar, *98* | | 53 | ___ |
| 26127 | Wellspring Capital Management Tank Car with confetti, *00 u* | | 214 | ___ |
| 26131 | Santa Fe 1-D Tank Car "335268," *02* | | 22 | ___ |
| 26132 | UP 1-D Tank Car "69015, *02* | | 40 | ___ |
| 26133 | Tootsie Roll 1-D Tank Car "26133," *02* | | 37 | ___ |
| 26135 | Whirlpool Tank Car, *01* | | NRS | ___ |
| 26136 | Southern 1-D Tank Car "8790011," *03* | | 20 | ___ |
| 26137 | Jack Frost 1-D Tank Car "106," *03* | | 32 | ___ |
| 26138 | Nestle Nesquik 1-D Tank Car "26138," *03* | | 40 | ___ |
| 26139 | Lionel Lines Stock Car "26139" with horses, *03* | | 39 | ___ |
| 26141 | Whirlpool 1-D Tank Car, *03 u* | | 89 | ___ |
| 26144 | Chessie System 1-D Tank Car "2233," *02* | | 22 | ___ |
| 26145 | Do It Best 1-D Tank Car, *03 u* | | 80 | ___ |
| 26146 | Do It Best 1-D Tank Car, *03 u* | | 95 | ___ |
| 26147 | Diamond Chemicals 1-D Tank Car "6315," Archive Collection, *02* | | 33 | ___ |
| 26149 | Egg Nog 1-D Tank Car, *03* | | 43 | ___ |

| | | Exc | Mint | Cond/S |
|---|---|---|---|---|
| 26150 | Alaska 3-D Tank Car "26150," *03* | 23 | | |
| 26151 | NP Wood-sided Reefer "26151," *03* | 19 | | |
| 26152 | Morton Salt 1-D Tank Car "26152," *04* | 40 | | |
| 26153 | Pillsbury 1-D Tank Car "26153," *04* | 40 | | |
| 26154 | NYC 3-D Tank Car "26154," *04* | 25 | | |
| 26155 | Pennsylvania 1-D Tank Car "26155," *04* | 20 | | |
| 26156 | North Western Wood-sided Reefer "15356," *04* | 20 | | |
| 26157 | Ballyhoo Brothers Circus Stock Car "26157," *04* | 35 | | |
| 26158 | Campbell's Soup 1-D Tank Car, *04* | 35 | | |
| 26164 | LL 1-D Tank Car "6315," girls set add-on, *03* | 43 | | |
| 26167 | New Haven 1-D Tank Car, traditional, *05* | 27 | | |
| 26168 | Conrail 3-D Tank Car, traditional, *05* | 27 | | |
| 26169 | Santa Fe Wood-sided Reefer, traditional, *05* | 27 | | |
| 26176 | Tidmouth Milk 1-D Tank Car, *05* | 35 | | |
| 26179 | GN 3-D Tank Car, *06* | 30 | | |
| 26180 | DM&IR 1-D Tank Car "S15," *06* | 30 | | |
| 26181 | NYC Wood-sided Reefer, *06* | 30 | | |
| 26196 | Candy Cane 1-D Tank Car, *06* | 60 | | |
| 26197 | D&H 1-D Tank Car "55," *07–08* | 35 | | |
| 26198 | D&RGW 3-D Tank Car, *07* | 30 | | |
| 26199 | WP PFE Wood-sided Reefer "55327," *07* | 30 | | |
| 26200 | NKP Boxcar "18211," *98* | 35 | | |
| 26201 | Operation Lifesaver Boxcar, *98* | 29 | | |
| 26203 | D&H Boxcar "1829," *98* | 25 | | |
| 26204 | Alaska Boxcar "10806," *98–99* | 35 | | |
| 26205 | Rocky & Bullwinkle Boxcar, *99* | 36 | | |
| 26206 | Curious George Boxcar, *99* | 40 | | |
| 26208 | Vapor Records Boxcar #2, *98* | 40 | | |
| 26214 | Celebrate the Century Stamp Boxcar, *98 u* | 90 | | |
| 26215 | AEC Glow-in-the-Dark Boxcar, *98* | 79 | | |
| 26216 | Cheerios Boxcar, *98 u* | 65 | | |
| 26218 | Quaker Oats Boxcar, *98 u* | 398 | | |
| 26219 | Ace Hardware Boxcar, *98 u* | NRS | | |
| 26220 | Smuckers Boxcar, *98 u* | 78 | | |
| 26222 | Penn Central Boxcar "125962," *99* | 31 | | |
| 26223 | FEC Boxcar "5027," *99* | 31 | | |
| 26224 | D&H Boxcar, *99* | 24 | | |
| 26228 | Vapor Records Holiday Boxcar, *99 u* | 98 | | |
| 26230 | AEC Glow-in-the-Dark Boxcar #2, *99* | 39 | | |
| 26232 | Martin Guitar Lumber Boxcar "9823," *99* | 41 | | |
| 26234 | NYC Boxcar, *99* | 29 | | |
| 26235 | Valentine Boxcar, *99* | 40 | | |
| 26236 | Aircraft Boxcar, *99* | 28 | | |
| 26237 | Boy Scout Boxcar, *99* | 85 | | |
| 26238 | Detroit Historical Museum Boxcar, *99* | 29 | | |
| 26239 | M.A.D.D. Boxcar, *99* | 19 | | |
| 26240 | RailBox Boxcar, *99–00* | 24 | | |
| 26241 | Norfolk & Western Boxcar, *99–00* | 17 | | |

Exc Mint Cond/$

| | | Exc | Mint | Cond/$ |
|---|---|---|---|---|
| 26242 | D.A.R.E. Boxcar, 99 | | 30 | ___ |
| 26243 | Christmas Boxcar, 99 | | 35 | ___ |
| 26244 | Woody Woodpecker Boxcar, 99 | | 43 | ___ |
| 26247 | Lionel Lines Boxcar, 99 | | 38 | ___ |
| 26253 | Acme Explosives Boxcar, 99 u | | NRS | ___ |
| 26254 | Keebler Boxcar, 99 u | | NRS | ___ |
| 26255 | NYC Boxcar "200495," 99 u | | 30 | ___ |
| 26256 | Salvation Army Charity Boxcar, 99 | | 29 | ___ |
| 26257 | Wheaties Boxcar, 99 | | 73 | ___ |
| 26264 | Lionel Station Boxcar, 99 | | 44 | ___ |
| 26265 | NYC Pacemaker Boxcar, 00 | | 30 | ___ |
| 26271 | AEC Glow-in-the-Dark Boxcar, 99 | | 48 | ___ |
| 26272 | Christmas Boxcar, 00 | | 42 | ___ |
| 26275 | Boy Scout Boxcar, 00 | | 55 | ___ |
| 26276 | C&O Boxcar "23296," 99–00 | | 23 | ___ |
| 26277 | UP Boxcar "491050," 00 | | 20 | ___ |
| 26278 | Cap'n Crunch Christmas Boxcar, 99 | | 587 | ___ |
| 26280 | Tinsel Town Express Boxcar, music, 00 | | 50 | ___ |
| 26284 | Toy Fair Preview Boxcar, 99 u | | 725 | ___ |
| 26285 | NYC Pacemaker Boxcar, 00 | | 40 | ___ |
| 26288 | AEC Glow-in-Dark Boxcar, 99 | | 44 | ___ |
| 26290 | SP Boxcar, 00 | | 20 | ___ |
| 26291 | Pennsylvania Boxcar "47158," 00 | | 20 | ___ |
| 26292 | Frisco Boxcar "22015," 00 | | 20 | ___ |
| 26293 | Burlington Boxcar, 00 | | 30 | ___ |
| 26294 | Centennial Express Boxcar, 00 | | NRS | ___ |
| 26295 | Trainmaster Boxcar, 99 u | | 55 | ___ |
| 26296 | Service Station Boxcar Set (SSS), 00 | | 105 | ___ |
| 26298 | Taz Bobbing Boxcar, 00 | | 65 | ___ |
| 26300 | UPS Flatcar with trailers, 04 | | 50 | ___ |
| 26301 | UPS Flatcar with airplane, traditional, 05 | | 53 | ___ |
| 26302 | Troublesome Truck #1, 05 | | 35 | ___ |
| 26303 | Troublesome Truck #2, 05 | | 35 | ___ |
| 26305 | SP Auto Carrier, 2-tier, 06 | | 30 | ___ |
| 26306 | D&RGW Gondola "56135" with canisters, 06 | | 30 | ___ |
| 26307 | Chessie System Bulkhead Flatcar, 06 | | 30 | ___ |
| 26308 | Hard Rock Cafe Flatcar with billboards, 06 | | 55 | ___ |
| 26309 | Alaska Flatcar with cable reels, 06 | | 55 | ___ |
| 26310 | CGW Flatcar "3707" with trailer, 06 | | 55 | ___ |
| 26311 | Santa Fe Flatcar with pickups, 06 | | 60 | ___ |
| 26330 | Gondola with trees and presents, 06 | | 60 | ___ |
| 26331 | Lionel Lines Bulkhead Flatcar, 07 | | 30 | ___ |
| 26332 | CP Rail Gondola "337061" with canisters, 07 | | 30 | ___ |
| 26335 | Domino Sugar Flatcar with trailer, 07–08 | | 60 | ___ |
| 26357 | CSX Flatcar "600514" with pipes, 07–08 | | 50 | ___ |
| 26366 | REA Flatcar with trailers, 07 | | 60 | ___ |
| 26367 | Santa's Egg Nog Flatcar with container, 07 | | 60 | ___ |
| 26368 | Gondola with trees and presents, 07 | | 60 | ___ |

| | | Exc | Mint | Cond/$ |
|---|---|---|---|---|
| 26378 | Conrail Auto Carrier "786414," 2-tier, *08* | | 35 | ___ |
| 26379 | PRR Gondola with cable reels, *08–09* | | 35 | ___ |
| 26380 | NYC Bulkhead Flatcar, *08* | | 35 | ___ |
| 26389 | ATSF Flatcar "108477" with 2 pickups, *08* | | 60 | ___ |
| 26390 | ATSF Flatcar with bulkheads, *09–10* | | 40 | ___ |
| 26391 | NYC Gondola "263910" with containers, *09* | | 40 | ___ |
| 26392 | BNSF Auto Carrier, *09* | | 40 | ___ |
| 26400 | C&NW Hopper, *07–08* | | 35 | ___ |
| 26401 | NP Ore Car "78540," *08* | | 35 | ___ |
| 26410 | Chessie System Hopper "47806," *08* | | 35 | ___ |
| 26411 | Lionel Lines Ore Car "2026," *08–09* | | 35 | ___ |
| 26412 | Chessie System 4-bay Hopper "60573," *08* | | 35 | ___ |
| 26418 | B&M Hopper, *09* | | 40 | ___ |
| 26422 | White Pass Ice Breaker Car, *09* | | 50 | ___ |
| 26423 | Soo Line Ore Car, *10* | | 40 | ___ |
| 26502 | UP Bay Window Caboose "6517," *97* | | 47 | ___ |
| 26503 | ATSF High-Cupola Caboose "7606R," *97* | | 85 | ___ |
| 26504 | Mobil Oil Square Window Caboose "6257," *97 u* | | 35 | ___ |
| 26505 | Rescue Unit Caboose, *98* | | 50 | ___ |
| 26506 | N&W Square Window Caboose "562748," *98* | | 15 | ___ |
| 26507 | D&H Square Window Caboose "35707," *98* | | 20 | ___ |
| 26508 | Alaska Square Window Caboose "1081," *98* | | 28 | ___ |
| 26511 | Quaker Oats Square Window Caboose, *98 u* | | 44 | ___ |
| 26513 | NYC Emergency Caboose "26505," *99* | | 47 | ___ |
| 26515 | Lionel Lines Bobber Caboose, *99* | | 10 | ___ |
| 26516 | Safari Bobber Caboose, *99 u* | | 10 | ___ |
| 26519 | Christmas Work Caboose "6496," *99* | | 41 | ___ |
| 26520 | Bethlehem Steel Work Caboose "6130" (SSS), *99* | | 55 | ___ |
| 26523 | Keebler Cheezit Square Window Caboose, *99 u* | | NRS | ___ |
| 26524 | NYC Square Window Caboose "295," *99 u* | | 20 | ___ |
| 26526 | Santa Fe Square Window Caboose "999471," *01* | | 30 | ___ |
| 26527 | Christmas Work Caboose with presents, *02* | | 27 | ___ |
| 26528 | PRR Square Window Caboose "6257," *99* | | 21 | ___ |
| 26530 | LL Square Window Caboose "6257," *99* | | 22 | ___ |
| 26532 | NYC Square Window Caboose "296," *00* | | 20 | ___ |
| 26533 | SP Square Window Caboose, *00* | | 20 | ___ |
| 26534 | PRR Square Window Caboose "6257," *00* | | 20 | ___ |
| 26535 | Frisco Square Window Caboose "1700," *00* | | 20 | ___ |
| 26536 | Centennial Express Square Window Caboose, *00* | | NRS | ___ |
| 26537 | Lionel Mines Square Window Caboose, *00 u* | | 45 | ___ |
| 26539 | Whirlpool Square Window Caboose, *00 u* | | NRS | ___ |
| 26542 | ACL Square Window Caboose "069," *01* | | 31 | ___ |
| 26543 | GN Square Window Caboose "X66," *00–01* | | 28 | ___ |
| 26544 | Alaska Square Window Caboose "1084," *01* | | 25 | ___ |
| 26545 | Snap-On Square Window Caboose, *00 u* | | NRS | ___ |
| 26548 | Pioneer Seed Square Window Caboose, *00 u* | | NRS | ___ |
| 26549 | PRR Square Window Caboose "4977947," *01* | | 20 | ___ |

| | | Exc | Mint | Cond/$ |
|---|---|---|---|---|
| 26550 | NYC Square Window Caboose "19293," *01* | | 20 | ___ |
| 26551 | Chessie System Center Cupola Caboose, *01* | | 25 | ___ |
| 26552 | Santa Fe Square Window Caboose "999472," *01* | | 25 | ___ |
| 26553 | C&O Center Cupola Caboose "A918," *01* | | 30 | ___ |
| 26554 | Monopoly Short Line Square Window Caboose, *00 u* | | NRS | ___ |
| 26556 | NH Center Cupola Caboose, *01* | | 35 | ___ |
| 26557 | Farmall Square Window Caboose, *01 u* | | NRS | ___ |
| 26559 | N&W Center Cupola Caboose "518408," *01* | | 20 | ___ |
| 26560 | B&M Square Window Caboose, *01 u* | | 20 | ___ |
| 26564 | Soo Line Center Cupola Caboose, *01 u* | | 20 | ___ |
| 26565 | Lionel Employee Square Window Caboose, *01 u* | | 139 | ___ |
| 26566 | WP Square Window Caboose "731," *02* | | 25 | ___ |
| 26568 | NKP Square Window Caboose "1155," *02* | | 25 | ___ |
| 26569 | Southern Square Window Caboose "252," *02* | | 25 | ___ |
| 26570 | B&O Square Window Caboose "295," *02* | | 25 | ___ |
| 26572 | Lionel 20th Century Square Window Caboose, *00 u* | | 25 | ___ |
| 26580 | Wabash Square Window Caboose "2805," *03* | | 22 | ___ |
| 26581 | C&O Square Window Caboose "C-1831," *03* | | 20 | ___ |
| 26582 | L&N Square Window Caboose "318," *03* | | 20 | ___ |
| 26583 | PRR Square Window Caboose "477814," *03* | | 25 | ___ |
| 26594 | Ontario Northland Work Caboose "26594," *03* | | 25 | ___ |
| 26595 | UP Caboose "26595," *03* | | 18 | ___ |
| 26596 | NYC Caboose "17716," *04* | | 25 | ___ |
| 26597 | Great Northern Caboose "X295," *04* | | 25 | ___ |
| 26598 | UP Caboose "26598," *04* | | 25 | ___ |
| 26599 | DM&IR Work Caboose "26599," *04* | | 25 | ___ |
| 26600 | American Fire and Rescue Water Tank Car, *09–10* | | 55 | ___ |
| 26603 | LV Depressed Flatcar with reels, *09* | | 40 | ___ |
| 26612 | Christmas Gifts Gondola, *09* | | 60 | ___ |
| 26614 | Tupelo Dairy Farms Milk Car, *10* | | 60 | ___ |
| 26616 | UP Bulkhead Flatcar with pipes, *10* | | 40 | ___ |
| 26617 | B&O Depressed Center Flatcar with generator, *10* | | 40 | ___ |
| 26661 | Reindeer Feed Barrel Ramp Car, *09* | | 60 | ___ |
| 26706 | Lighted Christmas Boxcar, *00* | | 47 | ___ |
| 26707 | Lionel Steel Operating Welding Flatcar "1108," *00* | | 90 | ___ |
| 26709 | Flatcar "6511" with psychedelic submarine, *99* | | 32 | ___ |
| 26710 | Southern Stock Car, Carsounds, *99* | | 95 | ___ |
| 26712 | Churchill Downs Horse Car "6473," *99–00* | | 38 | ___ |
| 26713 | Shay Log Car 3-pack, *99* | | 105 | ___ |
| 26714 | Westside Lumber Flatcar with logs (std O), *99* | | 45 | ___ |
| 26715 | Westside Lumber Flatcar with logs (std O), *99* | | 45 | ___ |
| 26716 | Westside Lumber Flatcar with logs (std O), *99* | | 45 | ___ |
| 26717 | Orion Star Boxcar 9600, *00* | | 30 | ___ |
| 26718 | Christmas Boxcar, RailSounds, *00* | | 160 | ___ |

| | | Exc | Mint | Cond/S |
|---|---|---|---|---|
| 26719 | Bobbing Ghost Halloween Boxcar, *00* | | 46 | ___ |
| 26721 | Lionel Lines Coal Dump Car "3379," *00* | | 31 | ___ |
| 26722 | Lionel Lines Log Dump Car "3351," *00* | | 31 | ___ |
| 26723 | Lion Chasing Trainer Gondola "3444," *00* | | 49 | ___ |
| 26724 | Veterans Day Boxcar, *00* | | 70 | ___ |
| 26725 | NYC Jumping Hobo Boxcar "88160," *00* | | 38 | ___ |
| 26726 | T. Rex Bobbing Boxcar, *00* | | 41 | ___ |
| 26727 | San Francisco City Lights Boxcar, *00* | | 50 | ___ |
| 26736 | Lionel Birthday Boxcar, *02 u* | | 40 | ___ |
| 26737 | Operating Santa Gondola "6462," *00 u* | | 65 | ___ |
| 26738 | Lionel Mines Gondola, *00 u* | | NRS | ___ |
| 26739 | Santa and Snowman Boxcar, *00* | | 46 | ___ |
| 26740 | Reindeer Car, *00* | | 43 | ___ |
| 26741 | Operating Santa Boxcar, *00* | | 50 | ___ |
| 26743 | Christmas Reindeer Car, *01* | | 55 | ___ |
| 26745 | Traveling Aquarium Car "506," *01* | | 70 | ___ |
| 26746 | Bobbing Vampire Boxcar, *01* | | 46 | ___ |
| 26747 | Halloween Bats Aquarium Car, *01* | | 75 | ___ |
| 26748 | T&P Operating Hopper Car "9699," *01* | | 38 | ___ |
| 26749 | Alaska Log Dump Car, *01* | | 29 | ___ |
| 26751 | Chessie Coal Dump Car, *01* | | 27 | ___ |
| 26752 | Christmas Aquarium Car, *01* | | 55 | ___ |
| 26753 | Christmas Operating Dump Car, *01* | | 43 | ___ |
| 26757 | Operating Barrel Car "35621," *00* | | 55 | ___ |
| 26758 | AEC Nuclear Gondola "719766," *01* | | 85 | ___ |
| 26759 | Postwar "3459" Coal Dump Car, *02* | | 60 | ___ |
| 26760 | Postwar "3461" Log Dump Car, *02* | | 60 | ___ |
| 26761 | AEC Security Caboose 3535, *01* | | 60 | ___ |
| 26762 | Postwar "3665" Minuteman Car, *01* | | 55 | ___ |
| 26763 | Postwar "6448" Exploding Boxcar, *01* | | 40 | ___ |
| 26764 | Bethlehem Steel Operating Welding Car, *01* | | 75 | ___ |
| 26765 | Postwar "3370" Sheriff and Outlaw Car, *01–02* | 40 | 49 | ___ |
| 26766 | Priority Mail Operating Boxcar, *01–02* | | 32 | ___ |
| 26768 | Postwar "6520" Searchlight Car, *02* | | 49 | ___ |
| 26769 | Santa Fe Crane Car "199793," CC, *03* | | 255 | ___ |
| 26770 | Wabash Brakeman Car "3424," *01* | | 70 | ___ |
| 26773 | Chessie Searchlight Car, *01* | | 20 | ___ |
| 26774 | Santa Fe Log Dump Car, *01* | | 25 | ___ |
| 26775 | U.S. Army Searchlight Car, *00* | | 50 | ___ |
| 26776 | U.S. Army Operating Boxcar "26413," *00* | | 55 | ___ |
| 26777 | U.S. Flag Boxcar, *01 u* | | 250 | ___ |
| 26779 | Burlington Operating Hopper "189312," *02* | | 40 | ___ |
| 26780 | Postwar "3376" Bronx Zoo Giraffe Car, *02* | 35 | 36 | ___ |
| 26781 | Postwar "3540" Operating Radar Car, *02* | | 35 | ___ |
| 26782 | Lenny the Lion Bobbing Head Car, *02* | | 38 | ___ |
| 26784 | Stingray Express Aquarium Car, *02* | | 35 | ___ |
| 26785 | Flatcar with powerboat, *02* | | 31 | ___ |
| 26786 | Lionelville Operating Parade Car, *02* | | 40 | ___ |

Exc Mint Cond/$

| | | Exc | Mint | Cond/$ |
|---|---|---|---|---|
| 26787 | Erie Jumping Hobo Boxcar, *01–02* | | 43 | ___ |
| 26788 | Christmas Music Boxcar, *02* | | 46 | ___ |
| 26789 | Kiss Kringle Chase Gondola, *02* | | 35 | ___ |
| 26790 | Lighted Christmas Boxcar, *02* | | 34 | ___ |
| 26791 | UP Animated Gondola, *02* | 40 | 50 | ___ |
| 26792 | REA Operating Boxcar "6299," *03* | | 39 | ___ |
| 26793 | Alaska Extension Searchlight Car, *01* | | 44 | ___ |
| 26794 | Postwar "6352" PFE Ice Car, *01–02* | | 85 | ___ |
| 26795 | NYC Stock Car "3121," Cattle Sounds, *02* | | 50 | ___ |
| 26796 | Lionel Farms Poultry Dispatch Car, *01* | | 55 | ___ |
| 26797 | GN Log Dump Car "60011," *02* | | 48 | ___ |
| 26798 | Bethlehem Steel Coal Dump Car "26798," *02* | | 70 | ___ |
| 26801 | Jumping Bart Simpson Boxcar, *04* | | 44 | ___ |
| 26802 | *Simpsons* Animated Gondola, *04* | | 46 | ___ |
| 26803 | Santa Fe Derrick Car "26803," *04* | | 25 | ___ |
| 26804 | NYC Coal Dump Car "26804," *04* | | 22 | ___ |
| 26805 | Pennsylvania Log Dump Car "26805," *04* | | 24 | ___ |
| 26806 | Pillsbury Operating Boxcar "3428," Archive Collection, *04* | | 40 | ___ |
| 26807 | Blue Chip Line Motorized Animated Gondola, *04* | | 40 | ___ |
| 26808 | Egg Nog Barrel Car, *04* | | 55 | ___ |
| 26809 | Santa's Extension Searchlight Car, *04* | | 42 | ___ |
| 26810 | NYC Operating Searchlight Car, *05* | | 33 | ___ |
| 26811 | Pennsylvania Coal Dump Car, *05* | | 33 | ___ |
| 26812 | Santa Fe Log Dump Car, *05* | | 33 | ___ |
| 26813 | Lionel Lines Derrick Car, *05* | | 33 | ___ |
| 26814 | NYC Walking Brakeman Car "174226," *05* | | 40 | ___ |
| 26815 | PRR "Workin' on the Railroad" Boxcar "24255," *05* | | 42 | ___ |
| 26816 | REA Boxcar, steam TrainSounds, *05* | | 105 | ___ |
| 26817 | Alaska Boxcar, diesel TrainSounds, *05* | | 145 | ___ |
| 26818 | Christmas Music Boxcar, *05* | | 63 | ___ |
| 26819 | Holiday Animated Gondola, *05* | | 55 | ___ |
| 26820 | Penguin Transport Aquarium Car, *05* | | 60 | ___ |
| 26821 | NP Moe & Joe Lumber Flatcar, *05* | | 75 | ___ |
| 26827 | UPS Operating Boxcar "9237," Archive Collection, *05* | | 63 | ___ |
| 26828 | Tornado Chaser Radar Tracking Car, *05* | | 63 | ___ |
| 26829 | UPS Holiday Operating Boxcar, *05* | | 59 | ___ |
| 26832 | Lionel Lines Tender, TrainSounds, *07–08* | | 105 | ___ |
| 26834 | PFE Ice Car "20042" (std O), *05–06* | | 63 | ___ |
| 26835 | M.O.W. Track Cleaning Car, *05* | | 140 | ___ |
| 26836 | Halloween Boxcar, SpookySounds, *05* | | 105 | ___ |
| 26841 | PRR Log Dump Car, *05* | | 27 | ___ |
| 26842 | NYC Coal Dump Car, *05* | | 27 | ___ |
| 26845 | Southern Derrick Car, *06* | | 35 | ___ |
| 26846 | GN Coal Dump Car, *06* | | 38 | ___ |
| 26847 | C&O Coal Dump Car, *06–07* | | 80 | ___ |
| 26848 | Lionel Lines Moe & Joe Flatcar, *06* | | 80 | ___ |

| | | Exc | Mint | Cond/$ |
|---|---|---|---|---|
| 26849 | SP Log Dump Car, *06–07* | | 80 | ___ |
| 26850 | D&RGW Searchlight Car, *06* | | 75 | ___ |
| 26851 | WM Log Dump Car, *06* | | 35 | ___ |
| 26852 | Postwar "3562-25" Santa Fe Barrel Car, *06* | | 75 | ___ |
| 26853 | SeaWorld Aquarium Car, *06* | | 75 | ___ |
| 26854 | UP Walking Brakeman Car, *06–07* | | 75 | ___ |
| 26855 | Halloween Animated Gondola, *06* | | 65 | ___ |
| 26856 | Christmas Chase Gondola, *06* | | 65 | ___ |
| 26857 | Alien Radar Tracking Car, *06* | | 65 | ___ |
| 26858 | Christmas Music Boxcar, *06* | | 65 | ___ |
| 26859 | Christmas Parade Boxcar, *06* | | 75 | ___ |
| 26860 | B&O Boxcar "466035," steam TrainSounds (std O), *06–07* | | 75 | ___ |
| 26861 | Santa Fe Boxcar, diesel TrainSounds (std O), *06–07* | | 110 | ___ |
| 26863 | Railway Express Operating Milk Car with platform, *06* | | 140 | ___ |
| 26864 | Domino Sugar Operating Boxcar, *06–07* | | 40 | ___ |
| 26865 | CP Animated Caboose, *06–07* | | 80 | ___ |
| 26867 | Boxcar, AlienSounds, *06–07* | | 110 | ___ |
| 26868 | U.S. Steel Operating Welding Car, *06* | | 75 | ___ |
| 26869 | REA Jumping Hobo Boxcar, *06–07* | | 70 | ___ |
| 26870 | Christmas Dump Car with presents, *06* | | 80 | ___ |
| 26871 | PRR Tender, steam TrainSounds (std O), *06* | | 105 | ___ |
| 26872 | U.S. Army Security Car, *06* | | 75 | ___ |
| 26876 | Missile Firing Trail Car, *06* | | 75 | ___ |
| 26877 | U.S. Army Missile Launch Car, *06–07* | | 190 | ___ |
| 26891 | PRR Coal Dump Car, *05* | | 30 | ___ |
| 26898 | NYC Log Dump Car, *05* | | 25 | ___ |
| 26905 | Bethlehem Steel Gondola "6462" with canisters, *98* | | 29 | ___ |
| 26906 | SP Flatcar "9823" with Corgi '57 Chevy, *98* | | 40 | ___ |
| 26908 | TTUX Flatcar "6300" with Apple trailers, *98* | | 70 | ___ |
| 26913 | East St. Louis Gondola "9820," *98* | | 29 | ___ |
| 26920 | Union Pacific Die-cast Ore Car "64861," *97* | | 70 | ___ |
| 26921 | Union Pacific Die-cast Ore Car "64862," *97* | | 55 | ___ |
| 26922 | Union Pacific Die-cast Ore Car "64863," *97* | | 65 | ___ |
| 26923 | Union Pacific Die-cast Ore Car "64864," *97* | | 55 | ___ |
| 26924 | Union Pacific Die-cast Ore Car "64865," *97* | | 55 | ___ |
| 26925 | Union Pacific Die-cast Ore Car "64866," *97* | | 60 | ___ |
| 26926 | Union Pacific Die-cast Ore Car, *98* | | 55 | ___ |
| 26927 | Union Pacific Die-cast Ore Car, *98* | | 55 | ___ |
| 26928 | Union Pacific Die-cast Ore Car, *98* | | 55 | ___ |
| 26929 | Union Pacific Die-cast Ore Car, *98* | | 40 | ___ |
| 26936 | Die-cast Tank Car 4-pack, *98* | | 335 | ___ |
| 26937 | Die-cast Hopper 4-pack, *98* | | 325 | ___ |
| 26938 | NYC Reefer, *99* | | 80 | ___ |
| 26940 | Rio Grande Stock Car "37710," *99* | | 80 | ___ |
| 26946 | D&H Semi-Scale Hopper "9642" | | 85 | ___ |

| | | Exc | Mint | Cond/$ |
|---|---|---|---|---|
| 26947 | Gulf Die-cast Tank Car, *98* | | 120 | ___ |
| 26948 | P&LE Die-cast Hopper, *98* | | 65 | ___ |
| 26949 | NP Flatcar with trailer "6424-2017," *98* | | 47 | ___ |
| 26950 | NP Flatcar with trailer "6424-2016," *98* | | 47 | ___ |
| 26951 | TTX Flatcar "475185" with PRR trailer, *98* | | 55 | ___ |
| 26952 | J.B. Hunt Flatcar with trailer, *98* | | 40 | ___ |
| 26953 | J.B. Hunt Flatcar with trailer, *98* | | 40 | ___ |
| 26954 | J.B. Hunt Flatcar with trailer, *98* | | 40 | ___ |
| 26955 | J.B. Hunt Flatcar with trailer, *98* | | 40 | ___ |
| 26956 | C&O Gondola (027), *98–99* | | 15 | ___ |
| 26957 | Delaware & Hudson Flatcar with stakes, *98* | | 20 | ___ |
| 26971 | Lionel Steel 16-wheel Depressed Center Flatcar, *98* | | 135 | ___ |
| 26972 | Pony Express Animated Gondola, *98* | | 36 | ___ |
| 26973 | Getty Die-cast Tank Car 3-pack, *98* | | 270 | ___ |
| 26974 | Getty Die-cast 1-D Tank Car "4003," *98* | | 80 | ___ |
| 26975 | Getty Die-cast 1-D Tank Car "4004," *98* | | 90 | ___ |
| 26976 | Getty Die-cast 1-D Tank Car "4005," *98* | | 80 | ___ |
| 26977 | Sinclair Die-cast Tank Car 3-pack, *98* | | 275 | ___ |
| 26978 | Sinclair Tank Car UTLX "64026," *98* | | 105 | ___ |
| 26979 | Sinclair Tank Car UTLX "64027," *98* | | 85 | ___ |
| 26980 | Sinclair Tank UTLX "64028," *98* | | 90 | ___ |
| 26981 | Gulf Die-cast Tank Car 2-pack, *99* | | 165 | ___ |
| 26985 | B&O Die-cast Hopper 2-pack, *99* | | 160 | ___ |
| 26987 | Chessie System (B&O) Die-cast 4-bay Hopper "235154," *99* | | 90 | ___ |
| 26991 | Lionelville Ladder Fire Car, *99* | | 47 | ___ |
| 26992 | NYC Reefer, *99* | | 75 | ___ |
| 26993 | NYC Reefer, *99* | | 85 | ___ |
| 26994 | NYC Reefer, *99* | | 135 | ___ |
| 26995 | Rio Grande Stock Car "37714," *99* | | 80 | ___ |
| 26996 | Rio Grande Stock Car "37715," *99* | | 80 | ___ |
| 26997 | Rio Grande Stock Car "37716," *99* | | 80 | ___ |
| 27000 | C&EI Offset Hopper "97393" (std 0), *07* | | 65 | ___ |
| 27001 | Erie Offset Hopper "28001" (std 0), *07* | | 65 | ___ |
| 27002 | Frisco Offset Hopper "92399" (std 0), *07* | | 65 | ___ |
| 27003 | Chessie System Offset Hopper "234355" (std 0), *07* | | 65 | ___ |
| 27016 | UP PS-2 Covered Hopper "1312" (std 0), *07–08* | | 60 | ___ |
| 27019 | Imco PS-2 Covered Hopper "41001" (std 0), *07–08* | | 60 | ___ |
| 27022 | PC PS-2 Covered Hopper "74217" (std 0), *07* | | 60 | ___ |
| 27025 | NYC PS-2 Covered Hopper "883180" (std 0), *07* | | 60 | ___ |
| 27029 | ATSF Offset Hopper 3-pack (std 0), *08–09* | | 200 | ___ |
| 27030 | Monon Offset Hopper 3-pack (std 0), *08–09* | | 200 | ___ |
| 27031 | MoPac Offset Hopper 3-pack (std 0), *08–09* | | 200 | ___ |
| 27032 | NYC Offset Hopper 3-pack (std 0), *08–09* | | 200 | ___ |
| 27033 | Chessie System PS-2 Hopper 3-pack (std 0), *08–09* | | 180 | ___ |

| | | Exc | Mint | Cond/$ |
|---|---|---|---|---|
| **27034** | Nickel Plate Road PS-2 Hopper 3-pack (std O), *08–09* | 180 | | |
| **27053** | CB&Q ACF 2-bay Covered Hopper "183925" (std O), *08–09* | 55 | | |
| **27059** | Bakelite Plastics PS-2 Hopper "61445" (std O), *10* | 70 | | |
| **27061** | Clinchfield Freight Car 2-pack (std O), *10* | 150 | | |
| **27100** | C&NW PS-2CD 4427 Hopper "450669" (std O), *04* | 40 | | |
| **27101** | Morton Salt PS-2CD 4427 Hopper "504" (std O), *04* | 43 | | |
| **27102** | Pillsbury PS-2CD 4427 Hopper "3980" (std O), *04* | 42 | | |
| **27103** | Soo Line PS-2CD 4427 Hopper "70207" (std O), *04* | 49 | | |
| **27104** | Wabash Cylindrical Hopper "33007" (std O), *03* | 43 | | |
| **27105** | PC Cylindrical Hopper "884312" (std O), *03* | 42 | | |
| **27113** | Govt. of Canada Cylindrical Hopper, *04–05* | 60 | | |
| **27114** | Canadian National Cylindrical Hopper, *04–05* | 60 | | |
| **27115** | D&H 3-bay ACF Hopper "3454" (std O), *05–06* | 65 | | |
| **27116** | NYC 3-bay ACF Hopper "886270" (std O), *05–06* | 65 | | |
| **27117** | DM&IR 3-bay ACF Hopper "5017" (std O), *05* | 65 | | |
| **27118** | WP 3-bay ACF Hopper "11774" (std O), *05–06* | 65 | | |
| **27129** | N&W 3-bay ACF Hopper "10717" (std O), *06* | 70 | | |
| **27130** | PRR 3-bay ACF Hopper "180658" (std O), *06* | 70 | | |
| **27131** | Conrail 3-bay ACF Hopper "473877" (std O), *06* | 70 | | |
| **27132** | UP 3-bay ACF Hopper "18137" (std O), *06* | 70 | | |
| **27133** | MILW PS-2CD Hopper "98606" (std O), *06* | 70 | | |
| **27134** | BNSF PS-2CD Hopper "414367" (std O), *06* | 70 | | |
| **27135** | N&W PS-2CD Hopper "71573" (std O), *06* | 70 | | |
| **27142** | CP Rail 3-bay Hopper, *06* | 48 | | |
| **27146** | CP Soo 3-bay Hopper, *06* | 48 | | |
| **27165** | C&O 3-bay Hopper "86912" (std O), *07* | 70 | | |
| **27166** | Pennsylvania Power & Light 3-bay Hopper "347" (std O), *07* | 70 | | |
| **27167** | Santa Fe 3-bay Hopper "178558" (std O), *07–08* | 70 | | |
| **27168** | C&NW 3-bay Hopper "135000" (std O), *07* | 70 | | |
| **27169** | CN Cylindrical Hopper "370708" (std O), *06* | 65 | | |
| **27172** | IMC Canada Cylindrical Hopper "45726" (std O), *06* | 65 | | |
| **27177** | Union Starch Cylindrical Hopper 3-pack (std O), *08* | 210 | | |
| **27186** | PRR Cylindrical Hopper 3-pack (std O), *08* | 210 | | |
| **27187** | TH&B Cylindrical Hopper 3-pack (std O), *08* | 210 | | |
| **27188** | KCS 3-bay Covered Hopper 3-pack, *08* | 225 | | |
| **27189** | BNSF 3-bay Aluminum Covered Hopper 3-pack, *08* | 225 | | |
| **27190** | C&NW PS-2CD Covered Hopper 3-pack (std O), *08* | 225 | | |

| | | Exc Mint | Cond/$ |
|---|---|---|---|
| 27191 | RI PS-2CD Covered Hopper 3-pack, *08* | 225 | |
| 27192 | NP PS-2CD Covered Hopper 3-pack (std O), *08* | 225 | |
| 27203 | NYC DD Boxcar "75509" (std O), *05* | 63 | |
| 27204 | Grand Trunk Western DD Boxcar "596377" (std O), *05* | 63 | |
| 27205 | D&RGW DD Boxcar "63798" (std O), *05* | 40 | |
| 27206 | UP PS 60' Boxcar "960342" (std O), *08* | 75 | |
| 27207 | IC PS 60' Boxcar "44295" (std O), *08* | 75 | |
| 27208 | ATSF PS 60' Boxcar "37287" (std O), *08* | 75 | |
| 27209 | D&RGW PS 60' Boxcar "63835" (std O), *08* | 75 | |
| 27210 | PRR PS-1 Boxcar "47009" (std O), *05* | 60 | |
| 27211 | MKT PS-1 Boxcar "948" (std O), *05* | 60 | |
| 27212 | Rutland PS-1 Boxcar "358" (std O), *05* | 60 | |
| 27213 | N&W DD Boxcar, *05* | 35 | |
| 27214 | Chessie System PS-1 Boxcar "23770" (std O), *06* | 60 | |
| 27215 | Rock Island PS-1 Boxcar "57607" (std O), *06* | 60 | |
| 27216 | Erie-Lack. PS-1 Boxcar "84433" (std O), *06* | 60 | |
| 27217 | Frisco PS-1 Boxcar "17826" (std O), *06* | 19 | |
| 27218 | Santa Fe DD Boxcar "9870" (std O), *06–07* | 70 | |
| 27219 | GN DD Boxcar "35449" (std O), *06–07* | 70 | |
| 27220 | L&N DD Boxcar "41237" (std O), *06–07* | 70 | |
| 27221 | CB&Q DD Boxcar "48500" (std O), *06–07* | 70 | |
| 27224 | CGW PS-1 Boxcar "5180" (std O), *06* | 60 | |
| 27225 | WP PS-1 Boxcar "19528" (std O), *06* | 60 | |
| 27226 | NH PS-1 Boxcar "32196" (std O), *06* | 60 | |
| 27227 | UP PS-1 Boxcar "100306" (std O), *06* | 60 | |
| 27228 | UP DD Boxcar "454400" (std O), *07* | 70 | |
| 27229 | Nickel Plate Road DD Boxcar "87100" (std O), *08* | 70 | |
| 27230 | LV DD Boxcar "8505" (std O), *08* | 70 | |
| 27231 | GN USRA Double-sheathed Boxcar (std O), *07* | 65 | |
| 27232 | UP USRA Double-sheathed Boxcar (std O), *07* | 65 | |
| 27233 | Cotton Belt USRA Double-sheathed Boxcar (std O), *07* | 65 | |
| 27234 | C&NW USRA Double-sheathed Boxcar (std O), *07* | 65 | |
| 27235 | Railbox Boxcar "10011" (std O), *07* | 55 | |
| 27239 | SP DD Boxcar "232852" with auto rack (std O), *08* | 75 | |
| 27240 | Pere Marquette DD Boxcar with auto rack (std O), *08* | 75 | |
| 27241 | C&O PS-1 Boxcar "18719," *08* | 60 | |
| 27242 | LV PS-1 Boxcar "62080," *08* | 60 | |
| 27243 | SP PS-1 Boxcar "128131," *08* | 60 | |
| 27244 | GN PS-1 Boxcar "39404," *08* | 60 | |
| 27246 | SP Double-sheathed Boxcar "133" (std O), *08* | 70 | |
| 27247 | MP Double-sheathed Boxcar "45111" (std O), *08* | 70 | |
| 27249 | GN Express Boxcar "2500" (std O), *08* | 65 | |
| 27250 | CN Express Boxcar "11061" (std O), *08–09* | 65 | |

Exc Mint Cond/$

| | | Exc | Mint | Cond/$ |
|---|---|---|---|---|
| 27251 | WP Express Boxcar "220116," *08–09* | | 65 | ___ |
| 27254 | Western Pacific UP Heritage Boxcar (std O), *09–10* | | 85 | ___ |
| 27259 | PRR ACF Stock Car "128988" (std O), *10* | | 70 | ___ |
| 27260 | ATSF Tool Car "190021" (std O), *09–10* | | 80 | ___ |
| 27261 | D&RGW Double-sheathed Boxcar "3282," *09* | | 80 | ___ |
| 27263 | Polar Railroad PS-1 Boxcar, *09* | | 70 | ___ |
| 27264 | C&O Double-sheathed Boxcar "3502," *10* | | 80 | ___ |
| 27265 | Virginian PS-1 Boxcar "63300" (std O), *10* | | 70 | ___ |
| 27266 | PRR Express Boxcar "504141" (std O), *10* | | 70 | ___ |
| 27267 | SP UP Heritage 60' Boxcar "6991" (std O), *10* | | 85 | ___ |
| 27270 | B&O PS-1 Boxcar 2-pack (std O), *10* | | 140 | ___ |
| 27274 | Polar Railroad Double-sheathed Boxcar "1201" *10* | | 70 | ___ |
| 27275 | SP Overnight PS-1 Boxcar "97938" (std O), *10* | | 70 | ___ |
| 27276 | NKP Double-sheathed Boxcar "10580" (std O), *10* | | 70 | ___ |
| 27278 | Cryo-Trans Trans-Mechanical Reefer (std O), *10* | | 95 | ___ |
| 27282 | UP DD Boxcar "163100" (std O), *10* | | 70 | ___ |
| 27283 | Postwar Scale Boxcar 2-pack, *10* | | 140 | ___ |
| 27287 | LV Boxcar and Caboose Set (std O), *10* | | 160 | ___ |
| 27289 | Jersey Central Boxcar and Caboose Set (std O), *10* | | 160 | ___ |
| 27291 | PRR Double-sheathed Boxcar "539335" (std O), *10* | | 70 | ___ |
| 27300 | Western Dairy General American Milk Car (std O), *06* | | 65 | ___ |
| 27305 | GN Steel-sided Reefer "70290" (std O), *06* | | 65 | ___ |
| 27306 | Santa Fe Steel-sided Reefer "3494" (std O), *06* | | 42 | ___ |
| 27307 | Pepper Packing Steel-sided Reefer "2330" (std O), *06* | | 65 | ___ |
| 27327 | BNSF Mechanical Reefer "798870" (std O), *07* | | 70 | ___ |
| 27328 | SP Fruit Express Reefer "456465" (std O), *07–09* | | 70 | ___ |
| 27329 | UP Fruit Express Reefer "55962" (std O), *07* | | 70 | ___ |
| 27330 | Great Northern WFE Reefer "8873" (std O), *07–08* | | 70 | ___ |
| 27331 | Alderney Dairy General American Milk Car (std O), *07* | | 65 | ___ |
| 27332 | Freeport General American Milk Car (std O), *07* | | 65 | ___ |
| 27349 | ADM Steel-sided Reefer "7019" (std O), *07* | | 65 | ___ |
| 27350 | National Car Steel-sided Reefer "2430" (std O), *07* | | 48 | ___ |
| 27355 | NYC Steel-sided Reefer "2570" (std O), *07–08* | | 65 | ___ |
| 27358 | Dubuque Steel-sided Reefer "63648" (std O), *07* | | 65 | ___ |
| 27361 | PFE Wood-sided Reefer "97680" (std O), *06* | | 65 | ___ |
| 27365 | Sheffield Farms Milk Car 2-pack (std O), *08* | | 140 | ___ |
| 27369 | Borden's Milk Car 2-pack (std O), *08* | | 140 | ___ |
| 27372 | PFE Steel-sided Reefer 3-pack (std O), *08* | | 210 | ___ |
| 27373 | MILW Reefer 3-pack (std O), *08–09* | | 225 | ___ |

Exc Mint Cond/S

| | | Exc | Mint | Cond/S |
|---|---|---|---|---|
| 27374 | Alaska Reefer 3-pack (std O), *08–09* | | 225 | ___ |
| 27375 | NP Reefer 3-pack (std O), *08–09* | | 225 | ___ |
| 27394 | Detroit, Toledo & Ironton Steel-sided Reefer (std O), *09–10* | | 80 | ___ |
| 27395 | Amtrak ExpressTrak Baggage Car, *10* | | 75 | ___ |
| 27396 | C&NW UP Heritage Mechanical Reefer (std O), *10* | | 85 | ___ |
| 27409 | ATSF Water Tank Car "100844" (std O), *09–10* | | 70 | ___ |
| 27410 | Modern 30,000-gallon Ethanol Tank Car 3-pack, sound, *09* | | 270 | ___ |
| 27411 | Modern 30,000-gallon Ethanol Tank Car 3-pack, *09* | | 210 | ___ |
| 27412 | GATX TankTrain Car "53782" (std O), *10* | | 70 | ___ |
| 27418 | PRR NS Heritage Unibody Tank Car (std O), *10* | | 70 | ___ |
| 27419 | Pennsylvania Power & Light 3-bay Open Hopper, *08* | | 80 | ___ |
| 27421 | MoPac UP Heritage Cylindrical Hopper (std O), *09* | | 80 | ___ |
| 27422 | N&W 3-bay Open Hopper "1776" (std O), *09* | | 80 | ___ |
| 27424 | Penn Central PS-2 Hopper "440774" (std O), *10* | | 80 | ___ |
| 27425 | Saskatchewan Cylindrical Hopper "397015" (std O), *09* | | 80 | ___ |
| 27426 | Stourbridge Lion Anthracite Coal Car 2-pack, *09–10* | | 130 | ___ |
| 27429 | MKT UP Heritage PS2-CD Hopper (std O), *09* | | 80 | ___ |
| 27432 | UP 3-bay Open Hopper "78123" (std O), *10* | | 80 | ___ |
| 27433 | Conrail NS Heritage Cylindrical Hopper (std O), *10* | | 80 | ___ |
| 27434 | D&RGW UP Heritage PS2-CD Hopper (std O), *10* | | 80 | ___ |
| 27435 | Polar Railroad Tank Car, *09* | | 70 | ___ |
| 27436 | Alberta Cylindrical Hopper "396363" (std O), *10* | | 80 | ___ |
| 27438 | Virginian NS Heritage 3-bay Open Hopper (std O), *10* | | 80 | ___ |
| 27439 | NS Heritage Unibody Tank Car "14098" (std O), *10* | | 70 | ___ |
| 27440 | BN Cylindrical Hopper "458456" (std O), *10* | | 80 | ___ |
| 27445 | N&W NS Heritage PS-2CD Hopper (std O), *10* | | 80 | ___ |
| 27446 | Southern NS Heritage Cylindrical Hopper (std O), *10* | | 80 | ___ |
| 27510 | WP PS-4 Flatcar "2001" (std O), *05–06* | | 53 | ___ |
| 27511 | P&LE PS-4 Flatcar "1154" (std O), *05–06* | | 35 | ___ |
| 27512 | Reading PS-4 Flatcar "9314" (std O), *05* | | 53 | ___ |
| 27513 | UP 40' Flatcar "51219" (std O), *06* | | 55 | ___ |
| 27514 | CP 40' Flatcar "307401" (std O), *06* | | 55 | ___ |
| 27515 | Pennsylvania 40' Flatcar "473567" (std O), *06* | | 55 | ___ |
| 27516 | N&W 40' Flatcar "32900" (std O), *06* | | 55 | ___ |
| 27517 | NP PS-4 Flatcar "62829" with trailers (std O), *06* | | 85 | ___ |
| 27518 | C&NW PS-4 Flatcar "44503" with trailers (std O), *06* | | 85 | ___ |

| | | Exc | Mint | Cond/S |
|---|---|---|---|---|
| **27519** | UP PS-4 Flatcar "53007" with trailers (std O), *06* | | 85 | ___ |
| **27520** | Coe Rail Husky Stack Car "5540" (std O), *06* | | 85 | ___ |
| **27521** | Santa Fe Husky Stack Car "254220" (std O), *06* | | 85 | ___ |
| **27537** | UP Flatcar with wood load, *06* | | 39 | ___ |
| **27541** | NYC 40' Flatcar "496299" with load (std O), *07* | | 63 | ___ |
| **27542** | NH 40' Flatcar "17808" with load (std O), *07–08* | | 70 | ___ |
| **27543** | ATSF 40' Flatcar "191549" with load (std O), *07–08* | | 70 | ___ |
| **27544** | GT 40' Flatcar "64301" with load (std O), *07–08* | | 70 | ___ |
| **27545** | REA PS-4 Flatcar "81003" with trailers (std O), *07–08* | | 85 | ___ |
| **27546** | Greenbrier Husky Stack Car "1993" (std O), *07* | | 85 | ___ |
| **27552** | Arizona & California Husky Stack Car (std O), *07* | | 85 | ___ |
| **27562** | NYC PS-4 Flatcar "506075" with trailers (std O), *07–08* | | 85 | ___ |
| **27563** | Lackawanna PS-4 Flatcar "16540" with trailers (std O), *07* | | 85 | ___ |
| **27564** | Milwaukee Road PS-4 Flatcar with trailers "64074" (std O), *07–08* | | 85 | ___ |
| **27583** | UP 40' Flatcar "59292" with load (std O), *08* | | 70 | ___ |
| **27584** | Reading Flatcar with covered load (std O), *08–09* | | 70 | ___ |
| **27585** | B&M 40' Flatcar "33773" with stakes (std O), *08–09* | | 65 | ___ |
| **27586** | Cass Scenic Skeleton Log Car 3-pack, *07* | | 170 | ___ |
| **27587** | Birch Valley Lumber Skeleton Log Car 3-pack, *07* | | 170 | ___ |
| **27594** | Wabash PS-4 Flatcar with stakes (std O), *08–09* | | 65 | ___ |
| **27600** | RI Bay Window Caboose "17070" (std O), *07* | | 90 | ___ |
| **27601** | MILW Extended Vision Caboose "992300" (std O), *07* | | 90 | ___ |
| **27603** | MP UP Heritage Ca-4 Caboose "2891" (std O), *08* | | 95 | ___ |
| **27604** | UP Caboose "3881" (std O), *08* | | 90 | ___ |
| **27605** | Pere Marquette Northeastern Caboose "A986" (std O), *08* | | 90 | ___ |
| **27606** | LL Northeastern Caboose "4679" (std O), *08* | | 90 | ___ |
| **27608** | WM Caboose "1863" (std O), *08* | | 85 | ___ |
| **27609** | B&O Caboose "C-2445" (std O), *07* | | 90 | ___ |
| **27612** | WP Bay Window Caboose "446" (std O), *08* | | 90 | ___ |
| **27615** | NYC Bay Window Caboose "20383" (std O), *07* | | 90 | ___ |
| **27617** | D&H Bay Window Caboose "35725" (std O), *08* | | 90 | ___ |
| **27618** | MKT UP Heritage Ca-4 Caboose "8891" (std O), *08* | | 95 | ___ |
| **27619** | WP UP Heritage Ca-4 Caboose "3891" (std O), *08* | | 95 | ___ |
| **27623** | N&W Northeastern Caboose "500837" (std O), *09* | | 90 | ___ |

Exc  Mint  Cond/S

| | | Exc | Mint | Cond/S |
|---|---|---|---|---|
| 27624 | D&RGW UP Heritage CA-4 Caboose (std O), *09* | | 95 | ____ |
| 27625 | C&NW UP Heritage CA-4 Caboose (std O), *09* | | 95 | ____ |
| 27626 | SP UP Heritage CA-4 Caboose (std O), *09* | | 95 | ____ |
| 27628 | Wabash Northeastern Caboose "02222" (std O), *09–10* | | 90 | ____ |
| 27629 | C&O Northeastern Caboose (std O), *10* | | 90 | ____ |
| 27630 | Virginian NS Heritage CA-4 Caboose (std O), *10* | | 95 | ____ |
| 27631 | NS Heritage CA-4 Caboose (std O), *10* | | 95 | ____ |
| 27633 | UP CA-3 Caboose (std O), *10* | | 95 | ____ |
| 27634 | ATSF Extended Vision Caboose (std O), *10* | | 85 | ____ |
| 27635 | B&O I-12 Caboose (std O), *10* | | 85 | ____ |
| 27636 | NKP Northeastern Caboose (std O), *10* | | 85 | ____ |
| 27638 | Southern NS Heritage CA-4 Caboose (std O), *10* | | 95 | ____ |
| 27639 | N&W NS Heritage CA-4 Caboose (std O), *10* | | 95 | ____ |
| 27640 | Clinchfield Northeastern CA-3 Caboose, *10* | | 90 | ____ |
| 27642 | Postwar "6427" Virginian Scale Caboose, *10* | | 90 | ____ |
| 27702 | Maersk Husky Stack Car 2-pack (std O), *09* | | 225 | ____ |
| 27705 | ATSF Wedge Plow Flatcar "191369" (std O), *09* | | 90 | ____ |
| 27706 | ATSF Idler Flatcar "191852" with load (std O), *09* | | 75 | ____ |
| 27707 | UP Husky Stack Car 2-pack (std O), *09–10* | | 225 | ____ |
| 27710 | No. 6464 Variation Boxcar 2-pack #2, *09* | | 115 | ____ |
| 27800 | B&M Gondola with coke containers, *09–10* | | 80 | ____ |
| 27816 | D&RGW Flatcar "22177" with pipes, *09–10* | | 80 | ____ |
| 27820 | Wabash PS-4 Flatcar with piggyback trailers (std O), *09–10* | | 98 | ____ |
| 27824 | MILW 40' Flatcar with metal pipes (std O), *10* | | 80 | ____ |
| 27826 | CP Skeleton Log Car 2-pack (std O), *10* | | 133 | ____ |
| 27827 | UP Bathtub Gondola "28081" (std O), *10* | | 65 | ____ |
| 27828 | CN Bathtub Gondola "193140" (std O), *10* | | 65 | ____ |
| 27829 | WM Skeleton Log Car 2-pack, *10* | | 133 | ____ |
| 27837 | B&M PS-4 Flatcar with bulkheads (std O), *10* | | 80 | ____ |
| 27838 | PRR PS-4 Flatcar with bulkheads (std O), *10* | | 80 | ____ |
| 27840 | Polar Railroad PS-4 Flatcar with trailers, *10* | | 98 | ____ |
| 27844 | BNSF Bathtub Gondola 3-pack (std O), *10* | | 200 | ____ |
| 27903 | *Sager Place* Observation Car, *09* | | 65 | ____ |
| 27912 | No. 2445 *Elizabeth* Coach, *08* | | 60 | ____ |
| 28000 | C&NW 4-6-4 Hudson Locomotive "3005," *99* | | 205 | ____ |
| 28004 | B&O 4-4-2 E6 Atlantic Locomotive, traditional, *99–00* | | 410 | ____ |
| 28005 | PRR 4-4-2 E6 Atlantic Locomotive, traditional, *99–00* | | 345 | ____ |
| 28006 | ATSF 4-4-2 E6 Atlantic Locomotive, traditional, *99–00* | | 285 | ____ |
| 28007 | NYC 4-6-4 Hudson Locomotive "5406," *99* | | 380 | ____ |
| 28008 | C&O 4-6-4 Hudson Locomotive "306," *99* | | 345 | ____ |
| 28009 | Santa Fe 4-6-4 Hudson Locomotive "3463," *99* | | 330 | ____ |
| 28011 | C&O 2-6-6-6 Allegheny Locomotive "1601," *99* | | 1800 | ____ |
| 28012 | 4-6-4 Commodore Vanderbilt Locomotive, red, *00 u* | | 1700 | ____ |
| 28013 | NH 4-6-2 Pacific Locomotive "1335," *99* | | 325 | ____ |

| No. | Description | Exc | Mint | Cond/$ |
|---|---|---|---|---|
| 28014 | NYC 4-6-2 Pacific Locomotive "4930," 99 | 305 | | ___ |
| 28015 | Santa Fe Pacific 4-6-2 Pacific Locomotive "3449," 99 | 340 | | ___ |
| 28016 | Southern 4-6-2 Pacific Locomotive "1407," 99 | 345 | | ___ |
| 28017 | Case Cutlery 4-6-2 Pacific Locomotive, 99 u | 300 | | ___ |
| 28018 | Reading 4-6-0 Camelback Locomotive "571," CC, 01 | 495 | | ___ |
| 28020 | Lionel Lines 4-6-2 Pacific Locomotive "3344," 99 | 250 | | ___ |
| 28022 | West Side Lumber Shay Locomotive "800," 99 | 810 | | ___ |
| 28023 | PRR K4 4-6-2 Pacific Locomotive "3755," CC, 99 | 375 | | ___ |
| 28024 | 4-6-4 Commodore Vanderbilt Locomotive, blue, 00 u | 1663 | | ___ |
| 28025 | PRR K4 4-6-2 Pacific Locomotive, traditional, 99 | 330 | | ___ |
| 28026 | LL 4-6-2 Pacific Locomotive, CC, 99 | 325 | | ___ |
| 28027 | NYC 4-6-4 Hudson Locomotive "5413," 00 | 590 | | ___ |
| 28028 | Virginian 2-6-6-6 Allegheny Locomotive "1601," 99 | 1318 | | ___ |
| 28029 | UP 4-8-8-4 Big Boy Locomotive "4006," 99–00 | 1500 | | ___ |
| 28030 | NYC 4-6-4 Hudson Locomotive "5450," gray, CC, 00 | 315 | | ___ |
| 28032 | B&O 4-6-2 Pacific Locomotive, CC, 00 | 315 | | ___ |
| 28033 | B&O 4-6-2 Pacific Locomotive, traditional, 00 | 195 | | ___ |
| 28034 | UP 4-6-2 Pacific Locomotive, CC, 00 | 310 | | ___ |
| 28035 | UP 4-6-2 Pacific Locomotive, traditional, 00 | 210 | | ___ |
| 28036 | SP 2-8-0 Consolidation Locomotive "2685," CC, 00–01 | 270 | | ___ |
| 28037 | SP 2-8-0 Consolidation Locomotive "2686," traditional, 00–01 | 295 | | ___ |
| 28038 | UP 2-8-0 Consolidation Locomotive "324," CC, 00–01 | 315 | | ___ |
| 28039 | UP 2-8-0 Consolidation Locomotive "326," traditional, 00–01 | 240 | | ___ |
| 28051 | B&O 2-8-8-4 EM-1 Articulated Locomotive "7617," 00 | 970 | | ___ |
| 28052 | N&W 2-6-6-4 Class A Locomotive "1218," 00 | 870 | | ___ |
| 28055 | GN 4-6-4 Hudson Locomotive "1725," traditional, 00–01 | 170 | | ___ |
| 28057 | Southern 4-8-2 Mountain Locomotive "1491," CC, 00 | 690 | | ___ |
| 28058 | NH 4-8-2 Mountain Locomotive "3310," CC, 00 | 670 | | ___ |
| 27294 | ATSF 57' Mechanical Reefer "3006" (std O), 10 | 85 | | ___ |
| 28059 | WP 4-8-2 Mountain Locomotive "179," CC, 00 | 630 | | ___ |
| 28062 | LL Gold-plated 700E J-1E 4-6-4 Hudson Locomotive, display case, 00 | 1050 | | ___ |
| 28063 | PRR T-1 4-4-4-4 Duplex Locomotive "5511," CC, 00 | 910 | | ___ |
| 28064 | UP Challenger Coal Tender "3985," CC, 00 u | 1350 | 1800 | ___ |
| 28065 | NYC Hudson 4-6-4 Locomotive "5412," RailSounds, 00 | 290 | | ___ |
| 28066 | B&O President Polk 4-6-2 Locomotive, CC, 01 | 750 | | ___ |

| | | Exc | Mint | Cond/$ |
|---|---|---|---|---|
| 28067 | Erie 4-6-2 Locomotive "2934," CC, *01* | 570 | |
| 28068 | D&RGW 4-6-4 Hudson Locomotive, traditional, *01 u* | 300 | |
| 28070 | SP Daylight 4-4-2 Atlantic Locomotive "3000," CC, *01* | 425 | |
| 28071 | NP 4-4-2 Atlantic Locomotive "604," CC, *01* | 415 | |
| 28072 | NYC 4-6-4 Hudson J3a Locomotive "5444," CC, *01* | 790 | |
| 28074 | NP 2-8-4 Berkshire Locomotive "759," CC, *01* | 640 | |
| 28075 | C&O 2-6-6-2 Locomotive "1521," CC, *01* | 930 | |
| 28076 | NKP 2-6-6-2 Locomotive "921," CC, *01* | 960 | |
| 28077 | UP 4-6-6-4 Challenger Locomotive "3983," CC, *01* | 680 | |
| 28078 | PRR 2-10-4 J1a Locomotive "6496," CC, *01* | 880 | |
| 28079 | C&O 2-10-4 Class T Locomotive "3004," CC, *01* | 882 | |
| 28080 | NYC 0-8-0 Locomotive "7745," CC, *01–02* | 540 | |
| 28081 | C&O 0-8-0 Locomotive "75," CC, *01–02* | 520 | |
| 28084 | NYC Dreyfuss Hudson 4-6-4 Locomotive "5452," CC, *01–02* | 790 | |
| 28085 | N&W 2-8-8-2 Y6b Class Locomotive "2200," CC, *03* | 1207 | |
| 28086 | PRR H9 Consolidation Locomotive "1111," CC, *01* | 480 | |
| 28087 | UP Auxiliary Tender, yellow, CC, *01* | 210 | |
| 28088 | N&W Auxiliary Water Tender, CC, *01–02* | 200 | |
| 28089 | PRR 4-4-4-4 T-1 Duplex Locomotive "5511," 2-rail, *00* | 1150 | |
| 28090 | UP Challenger Oil Tender "3977," 2-rail, *00 u* | 1800 | |
| 28098 | NYC 4-6-0 10-wheel Locomotive "1916," CC, *01–02* | 520 | |
| 28099 | UP Challenger Oil Tender "3977," CC, *00 u* | 1700 | |
| 28200 | D&H U30C Diesel "702," CC (SSS), *02* | 375 | |
| 28201 | UP SD90MAC Diesel "8049," *03* | 345 | |
| 28202 | Conrail SD80MAC Diesel "7203," *03* | 325 | |
| 28203 | CSX SD80MAC Diesel "803," *03* | 325 | |
| 28204 | NS SD80MAC Diesel "7201," *03* | 345 | |
| 28205 | Chessie System SD9 Diesel "1833," CC, *03* | 230 | |
| 28207 | Erie-Lackawanna U33C Diesel "3304," CC, *02* | 355 | |
| 28208 | BN U33C Diesel "5734," CC, *02* | 355 | |
| 28211 | CP SD90MAC Diesel "9107," *03* | 300 | |
| 28213 | Amtrak GE Dash 8 Diesel "516," CC, *02* | 300 | |
| 28214 | BNSF GE Dash 8 Diesel "582," CC, *02* | 325 | |
| 28215 | B&O GP30 Diesel "6939," CC, *02* | 315 | |
| 28216 | Reading GP30 Diesel "5518," CC, *02* | 315 | |
| 28217 | Rio Grande GP30 Diesel "3013," CC, *02* | 315 | |
| 28218 | Lehigh Valley Alco C420 Switcher "407," CC, *04* | 325 | |
| 28219 | Seaboard Alco C420 Switcher "136," CC, *04* | 300 | |
| 28222 | Santa Fe Dash 9 Diesel "605" CC, *05* | 250 | |
| 28223 | BNSF SD70MAC Diesel "9433," CC, *05* | 250 | |

Exc Mint Cond/$

| | | Exc | Mint | Cond/$ |
|---|---|---|---|---|
| 28224 | Jersey Central SD40-2 Diesel "3067," CC, *04* | | 350 | ___ |
| 28225 | SPSF SD40T-2 Diesel "8521," CC, *04–05* | | 430 | ___ |
| 28226 | NS SD80MAC Diesel "7204," CC, *04–05* | | 430 | ___ |
| 28227 | UP SD70MAC Diesel "4979," CC, *04* | | 375 | ___ |
| 28228 | C&NW Dash 9-44CW Diesel "8669," CC, *03* | | 350 | ___ |
| 28229 | SP Dash 9-44CW Diesel "8132," CC, *03* | | 350 | ___ |
| 28230 | Amtrak Dash 8 Diesel "505," CC, *04* | | 295 | ___ |
| 28235 | Great Northern U33C Diesel "2543," CC, *05* | | 455 | ___ |
| 28237 | Reading U30C Diesel "6301," CC, *05* | | 455 | ___ |
| 28239 | Union Pacific SD70 Diesel, TMCC, *04* | | 360 | ___ |
| 28241 | C&NW U30C Diesel "935," CC, *06* | | 455 | ___ |
| 28242 | SP U33C Diesel "8773," CC, *06* | | 475 | ___ |
| 28243 | LIRR Alco C420 Hi-nose Switcher "206," CC, *06* | | 420 | ___ |
| 28244 | N&W Alco C420 Hi-nose Switcher "417," CC, *06–07* | | 420 | ___ |
| 28245 | Chessie System SD40T-2 Diesel "7617," RailSounds, *06* | | 265 | ___ |
| 28246 | Chessie System SD40T-2 Diesel "7618," nonpowered (std O), *06* | | 160 | ___ |
| 28247 | Rio Grande SD40T-2 Diesel "5348," RailSounds, *06* | | 265 | ___ |
| 28248 | Rio Grande SD40T-2 Diesel "5349," nonpowered (std O), *06* | | 160 | ___ |
| 28250 | N&W Alco C420 Hi-nose Switcher "416," nonpowered (std O), *06–07* | | 160 | ___ |
| 28251 | LIRR Alco C420 Hi-nose Switcher "206," nonpowered (std O), *06* | | 160 | ___ |
| 28252 | SP U33C Diesel "8774," nonpowered (std O), *06* | | 160 | ___ |
| 28253 | C&NW U30C Diesel "936," nonpowered (std O), *06* | | 160 | ___ |
| 28255 | UP SD40T-2 Diesel "4551," traditional, CC, *07–08* | | 265 | ___ |
| 28256 | UP SD40T-2 Diesel "4596," nonpowered (std O), *07* | | 170 | ___ |
| 28257 | NS SD40-2 Diesel "3340," CC, *06* | | 430 | ___ |
| 28258 | NS SD40-2 Diesel "3341," nonpowered (std O), *06* | | 170 | ___ |
| 28259 | CN SD40-2 Diesel "5383," CC, *06* | | 430 | ___ |
| 28260 | CN SD40-2 Diesel "5384," nonpowered (std O), *06* | | 170 | ___ |
| 28261 | UP (MP) SD70ACe Diesel "1982," CC, *07* | | 450 | ___ |
| 28262 | UP (WP) SD70ACe Diesel "1983," CC, *07* | | 450 | ___ |
| 28263 | UP (MKT) SD70ACe Diesel "1988," CC, *07* | | 450 | ___ |
| 28264 | UP "Building America" SD70ACe Diesel "8348," CC, *07* | | 450 | ___ |
| 28265 | MILW U30C Diesel "5657," CC, *07* | | 455 | ___ |
| 28266 | MILW U30C Diesel "5657," nonpowered (std O), *07–08* | | 170 | ___ |
| 28267 | Conrail U30C Diesel "6837," CC, *07* | | 455 | ___ |
| 28268 | Conrail U30C Diesel "6838," nonpowered (std O), *07–08* | | 170 | ___ |

Exc Mint Cond/S

| | | Exc | Mint | Cond/S |
|---|---|---|---|---|
| 28269 | ATSF Dash 8-40BW Diesel "562," CC, 08 | 500 | | |
| 28270 | ATSF Dash 8-40CW Diesel "563," nonpowered, 08 | 220 | | |
| 28272 | "I Love USA" SD60 Diesel "1776," traditional, 06 | 250 | | |
| 28279 | UP SD70ACe Diesel "1989," CC, 07 | 450 | | |
| 28280 | UP (C&NW) SD70ACe Diesel "1995," CC, 07 | 450 | | |
| 28281 | UP (SP) SD70ACe Diesel "1996," CC, 07 | 450 | | |
| 28283 | UP "Building America" SD70AC3 Diesel, nonpowered (std O), 07 | 170 | | |
| 28284 | Ferromex SD70ACe Diesel "4011," CC, 08 | 495 | | |
| 28287 | KCS SD70ACe Diesel "4050," CC, 08 | 495 | | |
| 28292 | Chessie System U30C Diesel "3312," CC, 02 | 300 | | |
| 28293 | Santa Fe U28CG Diesel "354," CC, 02 | 375 | | |
| 28295 | Conrail LionMaster SD80MAC Diesel, nonpowered, 08 | 200 | | |
| 28296 | UP AC6000 Diesel "7526," CC, 08 | 660 | | |
| 28297 | SP GP9 Diesel "446," CC, 10 | 390 | | |
| 28298 | CSX AC6000 Diesel "608," CC, 08 | 660 | | |
| 28299 | CSX AC6000 Diesel "609," nonpowered, 08 | 220 | | |
| 28300 | NS Dash 9 Diesel "9607," nonpowered, 08 | 220 | | |
| 28302 | BNSF SD70ACe Diesel "9380," CC, 08 | 495 | | |
| 28305 | CSX AC6000 Diesel "610," nonpowered, RailSounds, 08 | 430 | | |
| 28306 | GE ES44AC Evolution Hybrid Diesel "2010," CC, 09–10 | 1000 | | |
| 28307 | Wabash Train Master Diesel "550," CC, 09–10 | 495 | | |
| 28312 | BN SD60 Diesel "8301," CC, 10 | 500 | | |
| 28314 | UP 3GS21B Genset Switcher "2701," CC, 10 | 675 | | |
| 28316 | PRR NS Heritage SD70ACe Diesel "1854," CC, 10 | 500 | | |
| 28327 | UP AC6000 Diesel "7050," CC, 10 | 700 | | |
| 28328 | UPAC6000 Diesel "7055," nonpowered, CC, 10 | 350 | | |
| 28330 | UP SD70ACe Diesel "8444," CC, 10 | 500 | | |
| 28331 | CSX AC6000 Diesel "618," CC, 10 | 700 | | |
| 28333 | Virginian NS Heritage SD70ACe Diesel, CC, 10 | 500 | | |
| 28334 | NS Heritage SD70ACe Diesel "1982," CC, 10 | 500 | | |
| 28339 | ATSF AC6000 Diesel "9876," CC, 10 | 550 | | |
| 28340 | WP GP7 Diesel "705," CC, 10 | 450 | | |
| 28343 | Amtrak Dash 9 Diesel "519," CC, 10 | 500 | | |
| 28344 | Southern NS Heritage SD70ACe Diesel, CC, 10 | 500 | | |
| 28345 | N&W NS Heritage SD70ACe Diesel "247," CC, 10 | 500 | | |
| 28400 | Amtrak Rail Bonder, 05 | | 65 | |
| 28403 | Pennsylvania Ballast Tamper, traditional, 05–06 | | 105 | |
| 28404 | Maintenance Car, 05 | | 105 | |
| 28405 | Picatinny Arsenal Switcher, CC, 05 | | 290 | |
| 28406 | CSX Rail Bonder "92794," traditional, 05 | | 65 | |
| 28407 | UP Speeder, 05 | | 65 | |
| 28408 | CNJ Speeder "MW840," traditional, 06 | | 70 | |

| | | Exc | Mint | Cond/$ |
|---|---|---|---|---|
| **28409** | Conrail Rail Bonder "X409," traditional, *06* | | 70 | ___ |
| **28411** | U.S. Army Missile Launcher Locomotive, *06–07* | | 300 | ___ |
| **28412** | Santa's Speeder, *06* | | 70 | ___ |
| **28413** | Milwaukee Road Snowplow "X903," traditional, *06* | | 210 | ___ |
| **28414** | Lionel Lines Burro Crane, traditional, *06* | | 160 | ___ |
| **28415** | Third Avenue Trolley "1651," traditional, *06* | | 70 | ___ |
| **28416** | Hobo Handcar, traditional, *06* | | 70 | ___ |
| **28417** | Christmas Rotary Snowplow, *06* | | 180 | ___ |
| **28418** | Christmas Trolley, *06* | | 70 | ___ |
| **28419** | Lionel Lines Speeder, *07–08* | | 70 | ___ |
| **28420** | D&RGW Handcar, *07–08* | | 70 | ___ |
| **28421** | Fort Collins Trolley, *07* | | 73 | ___ |
| **28422** | PRR Burro Crane, *07–08* | | 160 | ___ |
| **28423** | Alaska Rotary Snowplow, *06–07* | | 220 | ___ |
| **28424** | Postwar "51" Navy Switcher, *07* | | 210 | ___ |
| **28425** | *Polar Express* Elf Handcar, *06–10* | | 85 | ___ |
| **28427** | Christmas Snowplow, *08–10* | | 210 | ___ |
| **28428** | Halloween Handcar, *07* | | 70 | ___ |
| **28430** | Wellspring Capital Management Trolley, *06* | | 78 | ___ |
| **28432** | Bethlehem Steel Switcher, traditional, *07* | | 210 | ___ |
| **28434** | Christmas Trolley, *07* | | 70 | ___ |
| **28438** | Portland Birney Trolley, *08–09* | | 65 | ___ |
| **28440** | PRR Inspection Vehicle, *08–09* | | 170 | ___ |
| **28441** | Transylvania Trolley, *08* | | 75 | ___ |
| **28442** | Postwar "50" Gang Car, *08* | | 120 | ___ |
| **28444** | NH Handcar, *08–09* | | 75 | ___ |
| **28446** | Silver Bell Trolley, *09* | | 90 | ___ |
| **28447** | 4850TM Factory Trackmobile, CC, *10* | | 300 | ___ |
| **28448** | CSX 4850TM Trackmobile, CC, *10* | | 300 | ___ |
| **28449** | UP 4850TM Trackmobile, CC, *10* | | 300 | ___ |
| **28451** | Christmas Track Cleaning Car, *10* | | 150 | ___ |
| **28452** | M.O.W. Early Era Inspection Vehicle, *10* | | 130 | ___ |
| **28453** | PRR Early Era Inspection Vehicle, *10* | | 130 | ___ |
| **28454** | SP Early Era Inspection Vehicle, *10* | | 130 | ___ |
| **28456** | Coca-Cola Trolley, *10* | | 90 | ___ |
| **28500** | Mopac GP20 Diesel "2274," *99–00* | | 205 | ___ |
| **28501** | ATSF GP9 Diesel "2924," traditional, *99* | | 200 | ___ |
| **28502** | ATSF GP9 Diesel "2925," CC, *99–00* | | 255 | ___ |
| **28503** | ACL GP7 Diesel, CC, *00* | | 245 | ___ |
| **28504** | ACL GP7 Diesel, traditional, *00* | | 170 | ___ |
| **28505** | Monon Alco C420 Switcher "505," CC, *00–01* | | 230 | ___ |
| **28506** | Monon Alco C420 Switcher "506," traditional, *00–01* | | 170 | ___ |
| **28507** | NH Alco C420 Switcher "2556," CC, *00–01* | | 275 | ___ |
| **28508** | NH Alco C420 Switcher "2557," traditional, *00–01* | | 290 | ___ |
| **28509** | FEC GP7 Diesel Set, *99* | | 560 | ___ |
| **28514** | B&O GP9 Diesel "6590," *00* | | 85 | ___ |

Exc Mint Cond/$

| | | |
|---|---|---|
| 28515 | Lionel Service Station Alco C420 Switcher, CC, 00 | 205 ___ |
| 28516 | Lehigh & Hudson River Alco C420 Diesel, 00 | 160 ___ |
| 28517 | C&NW GP7 Diesel "1518," CC, 00–01 | 275 ___ |
| 28518 | PRR EP-5 Electric Locomotive "2352," CC, 00 | 410 ___ |
| 28519 | NP GP9 Diesel "2349," CC, 01 | 290 ___ |
| 28521 | SP Alco RS11 Switcher "5725," CC, 01–02 | 280 ___ |
| 28522 | MP Alco RS11 Switcher "4611," CC, 01–02 | 305 ___ |
| 28523 | Soo SD40-2 Diesel "6622," CC, 01 | 375 ___ |
| 28524 | Chessie SD40-2 Diesel "7616," CC, 01 | 355 ___ |
| 28527 | AEC GP9 Diesel "2001," CC, 01 | 360 ___ |
| 28529 | Norfolk Southern GP9 Diesel, CC, 02 | 200 ___ |
| 28530 | NP Alco S4 Diesel "722," CC, 02 | 285 ___ |
| 28531 | Santa Fe Alco S2 Switcher "2337," CC, 02 | 285 ___ |
| 28532 | LV Alco S2 Switcher "150," CC, 02 | 280 ___ |
| 28533 | Seaboard Air Line Alco S4 Diesel "1489," CC, 02 | 290 ___ |
| 28536 | Rock Island GP7 Diesel "1274," CC, 02–03 | 230 ___ |
| 28538 | WP Alco S2 Switcher "553," CC, 03 | 340 ___ |
| 28539 | B&O Alco S2 Switcher "9045," CC, 03 | 320 ___ |
| 28540 | UP SD40T-2 Diesel "4455," CC, 03 | 390 ___ |
| 28541 | SP SD40T-2 Diesel "8239," CC, 03 | 400 ___ |
| 28542 | Rio Grande SD40T-2 Diesel "5350," CC, 03 | 400 ___ |
| 28543 | Ontario Northland RS3 Diesel "1308," 03 | 80 ___ |
| 28544 | Pennsylvania Alco RS11 Switcher "8618," CC, 04 | 350 ___ |
| 28545 | NP Alco RS11 Switcher "900," CC, 03 | 325 ___ |
| 28548 | Chessie System S4 Diesel "9009," CC, 05 | 400 ___ |
| 28553 | PRR Alco RS11 Switcher "8620," traditional, 07–08 | 285 ___ |
| 28554 | Pennsylvania Alco RS11 Switcher "8618," nonpowered, CC, 07 | 170 ___ |
| 28554 | PRR RS11 Diesel "8621," nonpowered, 08 | 170 ___ |
| 28555 | Alaska GP38-2 Diesel "2001," CC, 06 | 400 ___ |
| 28556 | Alaska GP38-2 Diesel "2002," nonpowered (std O), 06 | 160 ___ |
| 28557 | CP GP30 Diesel "5000," CC, 06–07 | 400 ___ |
| 28558 | CP GP30 Diesel "5001," nonpowered (std O), 06–07 | 150 ___ |
| 28559 | Chessie System GP30 Diesel "3044," CC, 06–07 | 400 ___ |
| 28560 | Chessie System GP30 Diesel "3045," nonpowered (std O), 06–07 | 150 ___ |
| 28561 | NYC GP7 Diesel "5628," CC, 07–08 | 340 ___ |
| 28562 | NYC GP7 Diesel "5629," nonpowered (std O), 07 | 170 ___ |
| 28563 | GN GP7 Diesel "626," CC, 07 | 400 ___ |
| 28564 | GN GP7 Diesel "627," nonpowered (std O), 07 | 170 ___ |
| 28565 | RI GP7 Diesel "1265," CC, 07 | 400 ___ |
| 28566 | RI GP7 Diesel "1266," nonpowered (std O), 07 | 170 ___ |
| 28567 | UP GP7 Diesel "105," CC, 07 | 400 ___ |

| | | Exc | Mint | Cond/$ |
|---|---|---|---|---|
| 28568 | UP GP7 Diesel "106," nonpowered (std O), 07 | | 170 | ___ |
| 28570 | D&RGW GP7 Diesel "5101," CC, 08 | | 440 | ___ |
| 28573 | PRR GP7 Diesel "8512," CC, 08 | | 440 | ___ |
| 28578 | D&H GP38-2 Diesel "7307," CC, 08 | | 440 | ___ |
| 28587 | PRR GP7 Diesel "8510," CC, 10 | | 450 | ___ |
| 28592 | N&W GP7 Diesel "2446," CC, 09 | | 500 | ___ |
| 28594 | White Pass & Yukon NW2 Diesel Switcher, traditional, 09–10 | | 300 | ___ |
| 28595 | ATSF SD40 Diesel "5004," CC, 09 | | 380 | ___ |
| 28598 | ATSF GP7 Diesel "2791," CC, 10 | | 450 | ___ |
| 28599 | Erie GP9 Diesel "1261," CC, 10 | | 390 | ___ |
| 28612 | WP 4-4-2 Atlantic Locomotive, traditional, 02 | | 80 | ___ |
| 28613 | Reading 0-6-0 Dockside Switcher "1251," traditional, 04 | | 100 | ___ |
| 28615 | B&O 4-6-4 Hudson Locomotive, traditional, 02 | | 225 | ___ |
| 28616 | Nickel Plate 2-8-4 Berkshire Locomotive, traditional, 02 | | 190 | ___ |
| 28617 | Southern 2-8-4 Berkshire Locomotive, traditional, 02 | | 235 | ___ |
| 28624 | Santa Fe 0-6-0 Dockside Switcher "2174," traditional, 04 | | 175 | ___ |
| 28625 | Wabash 4-4-2 Atlantic Locomotive "8625," traditional, 03 | | 85 | ___ |
| 28626 | PRR 4-6-4 Hudson Locomotive "626," traditional, 03 | | 175 | ___ |
| 28627 | C&O 2-8-4 Berkshire Locomotive "2755," traditional, 03 | | 200 | ___ |
| 28628 | L&N 2-8-4 Berkshire Locomotive "1970," traditional, 03 | 150 | 200 | ___ |
| 28636 | D&RGW 4-4-2 Atlantic Locomotive "8636," traditional, 04 | | 95 | ___ |
| 28637 | UP 4-6-4 Hudson Locomotive "673," traditional, 04 | | 160 | ___ |
| 28638 | GN 2-8-4 Berkshire Locomotive "3414," traditional, 04 | | 200 | ___ |
| 28639 | NYC 2-8-4 Berkshire Locomotive "9401," traditional, 04 | | 200 | ___ |
| 28646 | North Pole Central 2-8-4 Berkshire "1900," traditional, 04 | | 230 | ___ |
| 28650 | NYC 0-6-0 Dockside Switcher "X-8688," traditional, 05 | | 80 | ___ |
| 28651 | Bethlehem Steel 0-6-0 Dockside Switcher "72," traditional, 05 | | 80 | ___ |
| 28652 | LL 4-4-2 Locomotive "8652," traditional, 05 | | 105 | ___ |
| 28655 | Erie 2-8-4 Berkshire Locomotive "3338," traditional, 05 | | 240 | ___ |
| 28656 | PRR 2-8-4 Berkshire Locomotive "56," traditional, 05 | | 240 | ___ |
| 28660 | North Pole Central 0-6-0 Dockside Switcher "25," traditional, 05 | | 105 | ___ |
| 28661 | Santa Fe 0-4-0 Locomotive "2300" traditional, 05 | | 160 | ___ |
| 28662 | C&O 0-4-0 Locomotive "39," traditional, 05 | | 160 | ___ |

Exc  Mint  Cond/$

| | | Exc | Mint | Cond/$ |
|---|---|---|---|---|
| 28674 | C&O 0-6-0 Dockside Switcher "67," traditional, 06–07 | | 110 | ___ |
| 28675 | SP 0-6-0 Dockside Switcher "675," traditional, 06–07 | | 110 | ___ |
| 28676 | U.S. Steel 0-6-0 Dockside Switcher "76," traditional, 06–07 | | 110 | ___ |
| 28677 | WM 4-4-2 Atlantic Locomotive "103," traditional, 06 | | 110 | ___ |
| 28678 | Rio Grande 0-4-0 Locomotive "55," traditional, 06–07 | | 170 | ___ |
| 28679 | U.S. Army Transportation Corps 0-4-0 Locomotive "40," traditional, 06 | | 170 | ___ |
| 28680 | Reading 0-4-0 Locomotive "1152," traditional, 06 | | 170 | ___ |
| 28681 | Virginian 2-8-4 Berkshire Locomotive "509," traditional, 06 | | 260 | ___ |
| 28683 | B&O 2-8-2 Mikado Locomotive "1520," TrainSounds, 06–07 | | 260 | ___ |
| 28684 | UP 2-8-2 Mikado Locomotive "2498," TrainSounds, 06–07 | | 260 | ___ |
| 28693 | B&O 4-4-2 Locomotive "28," traditional, 05 | | 105 | ___ |
| 28694 | NYC 4-4-2 Atlantic Locomotive "8637," traditional, 06 | | 100 | ___ |
| 28695 | Halloween 0-6-0 Dockside Switcher "X-131," traditional, 06–07 | | 85 | ___ |
| 28699 | Holiday 2-8-2 Mikado Locomotive "25," red, RailSounds, 08 | | 260 | ___ |
| 28700 | CB&Q 0-8-0 Locomotive "543," RailSounds, 05 | | 650 | ___ |
| 28701 | NP 0-8-0 Locomotive "1178," RailSounds, 05 | | 650 | ___ |
| 28702 | Boston & Albany 0-8-0 Locomotive "53," RailSounds, 05 | | 650 | ___ |
| 28704 | PRR 4-4-2 Atlantic Locomotive "68," CC, 05 | | 550 | ___ |
| 28706 | PRR Reading Seashore 4-4-2 Atlantic Locomotive "6064," CC, 05 | | 550 | ___ |
| 28742 | B&O 4-6-0 Camelback Locomotive "1630," CC, 03 | | 335 | ___ |
| 28743 | B&O 4-6-0 Camelback Locomotive "1632," traditional, 03 | | 300 | ___ |
| 28744 | D&H 4-6-0 Camelback Locomotive "548," CC, 03 | | 325 | ___ |
| 28745 | D&H 4-6-0 Camelback Locomotive "555," traditional, 03 | | 300 | ___ |
| 28746 | Erie 4-6-0 Camelback Locomotive "860," CC, 03 | | 375 | ___ |
| 28747 | Erie 4-6-0 Camelback Locomotive "878," traditional, 03 | | 300 | ___ |
| 28748 | Jersey Central 4-6-0 Camelback Locomotive "772," CC, 03 | | 300 | ___ |
| 28749 | Jersey Central 4-6-0 Camelback Locomotive "773," traditional, 03 | | 300 | ___ |
| 28750 | Lackawanna 4-6-0 Camelback Locomotive "690," CC, 03 | | 375 | ___ |
| 28751 | Lackawanna 4-6-0 Camelback Locomotive "1031," traditional, 03 | | 300 | ___ |

| | | Exc | Mint | Cond/$ |
|---|---|---|---|---|
| 28752 | LIRR 4-6-0 Camelback Locomotive "126," CC, *03* | | 300 | ___ |
| 28753 | LIRR 4-6-0 Camelback Locomotive "127," traditional, *03* | | 300 | ___ |
| 28754 | NYO&W 4-6-0 Camelback Locomotive "249," CC, *03* | | 300 | ___ |
| 28755 | NYO&W 4-6-0 Camelback "253" Locomotive, traditional, *03* | | 300 | ___ |
| 28756 | PRR Reading Seashore 4-6-0 Camelback Locomotive "6000," CC, *03* | | 325 | ___ |
| 28757 | PRR Reading Seashore 4-6-0 Camelback Locomotive "6001," traditional, *03* | | 300 | ___ |
| 28758 | Susquehanna 4-6-0 Camelback Locomotive "30," CC, *03* | | 305 | ___ |
| 28759 | Susquehanna 4-6-0 Camelback Locomotive "36," traditional, *03* | | 300 | ___ |
| 28800 | N&W GP7 Diesel "507," *99–00* | | 80 | ___ |
| 28801 | Lionel Lines 44-ton Switcher, *99* | | 135 | ___ |
| 28806 | Jersey Central FM H16-44 Diesel "1516," CC, *01* | | 335 | ___ |
| 28811 | Santa Fe FM H16-44 Diesel "3003," CC, *01* | | 290 | ___ |
| 28813 | Milwaukee Road FM H16-44 Diesel "406," CC, *01* | | 280 | ___ |
| 28815 | B&O GP30 Diesel "6935," CC, *02* | | 295 | ___ |
| 28817 | Reading GP30 Diesel "5513," CC, *02* | | 310 | ___ |
| 28819 | Rio Grande GP30 Diesel "3013," CC, *02* | | 310 | ___ |
| 28821 | GT GP7 Diesel "4438," *01* | | 100 | ___ |
| 28822 | Southern RS3 Diesel "2127," *01* | | 70 | ___ |
| 28823 | Virginian Electric Locomotive "234," *01* | | 122 | ___ |
| 28826 | Pioneer Seed GP7 Diesel "2001," traditional, *00 u* | | NRS | ___ |
| 28827 | Chessie GP38 Diesel, traditional, *01* | | 100 | ___ |
| 28830 | Soo Line GP9 Diesel, traditional, *01 u* | | NRS | ___ |
| 28831 | Conrail U36B Diesel "2971," traditional, *02* | | 100 | ___ |
| 28832 | Santa Fe RS3 Diesel "2099," traditional, *02* | | 70 | ___ |
| 28836 | NYC FM H-16-44 Diesel "7000," CC, *02* | | 330 | ___ |
| 28837 | NH FM H-16-44 Diesel "591," CC, *02* | | 325 | ___ |
| 28838 | UP FM H-16-44 Diesel "1340," CC, *02* | | 325 | ___ |
| 28839 | Alaska GP 30 Diesel "2000," CC, *04* | | 315 | ___ |
| 28840 | Burlington GP30 Diesel "945," CC, *03* | | 325 | ___ |
| 28841 | Seaboard GP30 Diesel "1315," CC, *03* | | 220 | ___ |
| 28842 | C&O GP9 Diesel, horn, *04* | | 160 | ___ |
| 28843 | Southern GP38 Diesel, horn, *04* | | 140 | ___ |
| 28845 | Amtrak RS3 Diesel "106," *03* | | 70 | ___ |
| 28846 | Western Pacific U36B Diesel "3067," traditional, *04* | | 100 | ___ |
| 28847 | DM & IR GP38 Diesel "203," traditional, *04* | | 170 | ___ |
| 28848 | JCPenney Santa Fe GP38 Diesel, *04* | | 125 | ___ |
| 28849 | Western Maryland GP7 Diesel, horn, *04* | | 185 | ___ |
| 28850 | NYC GP30 Diesel "6115" CC, *04* | | 360 | ___ |
| 28851 | Pennsylvania RS3 Diesel, *04* | | 75 | ___ |

Exc Mint Cond/$

| No. | Description | Exc | Mint | Cond/$ |
|---|---|---|---|---|
| 28852 | CSX U36B Diesel "1976," traditional, 05 | | 140 | ___ |
| 28853 | Santa Fe GP38 Diesel "2371," traditional, 05 | | 210 | ___ |
| 28859 | Pennsylvania GP30 Diesel "2206," nonpowered, 06 | | 160 | ___ |
| 28314 | UP 3GS21B Genset Switcher "2701," CC, 09 | | 800 | ___ |
| 28860 | UP GP30 Diesel "844," CC, 06 | | 360 | ___ |
| 28861 | UP GP30 Diesel "845," nonpowered (std O), 06 | | 150 | ___ |
| 28862 | CSX GP30 Diesel "4249," CC, 06 | | 400 | ___ |
| 28863 | CSX GP30 Diesel "4250," nonpowered (std O), 06 | | 150 | ___ |
| 28864 | UP RS3 Diesel "1195," traditional, 06 | | 85 | ___ |
| 28865 | GN GP9 Diesel "688," traditional, 06 | | 210 | ___ |
| 28866 | NYC GP20 Diesel "6110," traditional, 06 | | 140 | ___ |
| 28873 | NYC RS3 Diesel "8226," traditional, 06 | | 85 | ___ |
| 28874 | UP GP9 Diesel "178," traditional, 06–07 | | 210 | ___ |
| 28875 | Santa Fe GP20 "1107," traditional, 06 | | 140 | ___ |
| 28876 | GN FT Diesel "418," traditional, 07–08 | | 245 | ___ |
| 28879 | UPS Centennial GP38 Diesel, traditional, 06 | | 210 | ___ |
| 28881 | Conrail GP20 Diesel "2107," traditional, 07 | | 140 | ___ |
| 28882 | Alaska RS3 Diesel "1079," traditional, 07 | | 85 | ___ |
| 28883 | Diesel, 07–09 | | 120 | ___ |
| 28884 | PRR GP38 Diesel "2389," traditional, 08–09 | | 210 | ___ |
| 28886 | RI RS3 Diesel "492," traditional, 08 | | 95 | ___ |
| 28887 | Southern RS3 Diesel "2028," traditional, 08 | | 95 | ___ |
| 28890 | CN GP9 Diesel "4573," traditional, 08 | | 210 | ___ |
| 28897 | Seaboard U36B Diesel "1762," traditional, 08 | | 140 | ___ |
| 28900 | Iron 'Arry and Iron Bert 2-pack, 08–09 | | 240 | ___ |
| 28905 | ATSF FT Diesel "160," nonpowered, 09–10 | | 120 | ___ |
| 29000 | PRR Caleb Strong Madison Coach "2622," 99 | | 80 | ___ |
| 29001 | PRR Villa Royal Madison Coach "2621," 99 | | 80 | ___ |
| 29002 | PRR Philadelphia Madison Coach "2624," 99 | 30 | 80 | ___ |
| 29003 | PRR Madison Car 4-pack, 98 | | 220 | ___ |
| 29004 | NYC Heavyweight Passenger Car 2-pack, 99 | | 170 | ___ |
| 29007 | NYC Pullman Passenger Car 2-pack, 98 u | | 95 | ___ |
| 29008 | NYC Heavyweight Diner "383," 98 | | 95 | ___ |
| 29009 | NYC Van Twiller Heavyweight Combination Car, 98 | | 95 | ___ |
| 29010 | C&O Heavyweight Passenger Car 2-pack, 99 | | 150 | ___ |
| 29039 | Lionel Lines Recovery Combination Car "9501," 99 | | NRS | ___ |
| 29041 | Alaska Streamliner Car 4-pack, 99–00 | | 230 | ___ |
| 29042 | Alaska Streamliner Baggage Car "6310," 99–00 | | 50 | ___ |
| 29043 | Alaska Streamliner Coach "5408," 99–00 | | 65 | ___ |
| 29044 | Alaska Streamliner Vista Dome Car "7014," 99–00 | | 65 | ___ |
| 29046 | B&O Streamliner Car 4-pack, 99–00 | | 165 | ___ |
| 29047 | B&O Streamliner Baggage Car, 99–00 | | 35 | ___ |
| 29048 | B&O Streamliner Coach, 99–00 | | 50 | ___ |
| 29049 | B&O Streamliner Vista Dome Car, 99–00 | | 50 | ___ |

Exc Mint Cond/$

| | | Exc | Mint | Cond/$ |
|---|---|---|---|---|
| **29050** | B&O Streamliner Observation Car, *99–00* | 40 | | ___ |
| **29051** | ATSF Streamliner Car 4-pack, *99–00* | 200 | | ___ |
| **29052** | ATSF Streamliner Baggage Car, *99–00* | 40 | | ___ |
| **29053** | ATSF Streamliner Coach, *99–00* | 60 | | ___ |
| **29054** | ATSF Streamliner Vista Dome Car, *99–00* | 60 | | ___ |
| **29055** | ATSF Streamliner Observation Car, *99–00* | 40 | | ___ |
| **29056** | NYC Streamliner Car 4-pack, *99–00* | 180 | | ___ |
| **29057** | NYC Streamliner Baggage Car, *99–00* | 40 | | ___ |
| **29058** | NYC Streamliner Coach, *99–00* | 50 | | ___ |
| **29059** | NYC Streamliner Vista Dome Car, *99–00* | 50 | | ___ |
| **29060** | NYC Streamliner Observation Car, *99–00* | 45 | | ___ |
| **29061** | PRR Madison Passenger Car 4-pack, *99–00* | 190 | | ___ |
| **29062** | PRR *Indian Point* Madison Baggage Car, *99–00* | 50 | | ___ |
| **29063** | PRR *Christopher Columbus* Madison Coach, *99–00* | 50 | | ___ |
| **29064** | PRR *Andrew Jackson* Madison Coach, *99–00* | 50 | | ___ |
| **29065** | PRR *Broussard* Madison Observation Car, *99–00* | 50 | | ___ |
| **29066** | CNJ Madison Passenger Car 4-pack, *99–00* | 210 | | ___ |
| **29067** | CNJ Madison Baggage Car "420," *99–00* | 50 | | ___ |
| **29068** | CNJ *Beachcomber* Madison Coach, *99–00* | 50 | | ___ |
| **29069** | CNJ *Echo Lake* Madison Coach, *99–00* | 50 | | ___ |
| **29070** | CNJ Madison Observation Car "1178," *99–00* | 50 | | ___ |
| **29071** | NYC Baby Madison Car 4-pack, *00* | 155 | | ___ |
| **29072** | NYC Baby Madison Baggage Car "1001," *00* | 50 | | ___ |
| **29073** | NYC Baby Madison Coach "1005," *00* | 50 | | ___ |
| **29074** | NYC Baby Madison Coach "1006," *00* | 50 | | ___ |
| **29075** | NYC *Detroit* Baby Madison Observation Car "1019," *00* | 40 | | ___ |
| **29076** | Southern Baby Madison Car 4-pack, *00* | 155 | | ___ |
| **29077** | Southern *Delaware* Madison Baggage Car "702," *00* | 30 | | ___ |
| **29078** | Southern *North Carolina* Madison Coach "800," *00* | 50 | | ___ |
| **29079** | Southern *Maryland* Madison Coach "801," *00* | 50 | | ___ |
| **29080** | Southern Madison Observation Car "1100," *00* | 40 | | ___ |
| **29081** | ATSF Baby Madison Car 4-pack, *00* | 160 | | ___ |
| **29082** | ATSF Baby Madison Baggage Car "1765," *00* | 30 | | ___ |
| **29083** | ATSF Baby Madison Coach "3040," *00* | 50 | | ___ |
| **29084** | ATSF Baby Madison Coach "1535," *00* | 50 | | ___ |
| **29085** | ATSF Baby Madison Observation Car "10," *00* | 45 | | ___ |
| **29086** | Madison Car 3-pack, *99* | 280 | | ___ |
| **29090** | Lionel Liontech Madison Car "2656," *99* | 75 | | ___ |
| **29091** | *Lawrence Cowen* Lionel Legends Madison Coach "2657," *99–00* | 75 | | ___ |
| **29105** | PRR *Trail Blazer* Aluminum Passenger Car 4-pack, *04–05* | 550 | | ___ |
| **29108** | Searchlight Car, *00* | 30 | | ___ |
| **29110** | B&O *Columbian* Aluminum Passenger Car 4-pack, *04* | 425 | | ___ |

Exc Mint Cond/$

| | | Exc | Mint | Cond/$ |
|---|---|---|---|---|
| 29115 | SP Daylight Aluminum Passenger Car 4-pack, 04–05 | | 550 | ___ |
| 29122 | Erie-Lack. F3 Diesel AB Passenger Set, 99 | | 840 | ___ |
| 29123 | Erie-Lack. Aluminum Coach/Baggage Car "203," 99 | | 100 | ___ |
| 29124 | Erie-Lack. Aluminum Coach/Diner "770," 99 | | 100 | ___ |
| 29125 | Erie-Lack. Eleanor Lord Aluminum Coach, 99 | | 100 | ___ |
| 29126 | Erie-Lack. Tavern Lounge Aluminum Observation Car "789," 99 | | 125 | ___ |
| 29127 | ACL Aluminum Baggage Car "152," 99 | | NRS | ___ |
| 29128 | ACL North Hampton Aluminum Coach, 99 | | NRS | ___ |
| 29129 | Texas Special Passenger Car 4-pack, 99 | 650 | 700 | ___ |
| 29130 | Texas Special Edward Burleson Aluminum Coach "1200," 99 | | 115 | ___ |
| 29131 | Texas Special David G. Burnett Aluminum Coach "1201," 99 | | 115 | ___ |
| 29132 | Texas Special J. Pinckney Henderson Aluminum Coach "1202," 99 | | 115 | ___ |
| 29133 | Texas Special Stephen F. Austin Aluminum Observation Car "1203," 99 | | 100 | ___ |
| 29135 | California Zephyr Silver Poplar Aluminum Vista Dome Car, 99 | | 150 | ___ |
| 29136 | California Zephyr Silver Palm Aluminum Vista Dome Car, 99 | | 150 | ___ |
| 29137 | California Zephyr Silver Tavern Aluminum Vista Dome Car, 99 | | 150 | ___ |
| 29138 | California Zephyr Silver Planet Aluminum Vista Dome Car, 99 | | 150 | ___ |
| 29139 | Kughn Lionel Legends Madison Car "2655," 99 | | 113 | ___ |
| 29140 | NYC Castleton Bridge Aluminum Sleeper Car, 99 | | 120 | ___ |
| 29141 | NYC Martin Van Buren Aluminum Combination Car, 99 | | 120 | ___ |
| 29142 | CP Skyline Aluminum Vista Dome Car "596," 99 | | 125 | ___ |
| 29143 | CP Banff Park Aluminum Observation Car, 99 | | 125 | ___ |
| 29144 | Santa Fe El Capitan Aluminum Passenger Car 4-pack, 04 | | 400 | ___ |
| 29149 | CB&Q California Zephyr Aluminum Passenger Car 2-pack, 03 | | 300 | ___ |
| 29152 | Santa Fe Super Chief Aluminum Passenger Car 2-pack, 03 | | 190 | ___ |
| 29155 | D&H Aluminum Passenger Car 2-pack, 03 | | 190 | ___ |
| 29158 | Southern Aluminum Passenger Car 2-pack, 03 | | 205 | ___ |
| 29165 | Amtrak Superliner Passenger Car 2-pack, Phase IV, 04 | | 195 | ___ |
| 29168 | Amtrak Superliner Diner, StationSounds, Phase IV, 04 | | 200 | ___ |
| 29169 | Alaska Superliner Passenger Car 2-pack, 04 | | 200 | ___ |
| 29172 | Alaska Superliner Diner, StationSounds, 04 | | 200 | ___ |
| 29182 | N&W Powhatan Arrow Aluminum Passenger Car 4-pack (std O), 05 | | 550 | ___ |
| 29187 | N&W Powhatan Arrow Aluminum Passenger Car 2-pack (std O), 05 | | 290 | ___ |

Exc Mint Cond/$

| | | Exc | Mint | Cond/$ |
|---|---|---|---|---|
| 29190 | N&W *Powhatan Arrow* Aluminum Diner, StationSounds, *05* | | 290 | ___ |
| 29191 | MILW *Hiawatha* Passenger Car 4-pack, *06* | | 370 | ___ |
| 29196 | MILW *Hiawatha* Passenger Car 2-pack, *06* | | 190 | ___ |
| 29199 | MILW *Hiawatha* Diner, StationSounds, *06* | | 190 | ___ |
| 29202 | Santa Fe Map Boxcar "6464," *97 u* | | 53 | ___ |
| 29203 | Maine Central Boxcar "6464-597," *97 u* | | 35 | ___ |
| 29205 | Mickey Mouse Hi-Cube Boxcar "9555," *97* | | 65 | ___ |
| 29206 | Vapor Records Boxcar #1, *97* | | 75 | ___ |
| 29209 | Postwar "6464" Boxcar Series VII, 3 cars, *98* | | 87 | ___ |
| 29210 | GN Boxcar "6464-450," *98* | | 33 | ___ |
| 29211 | B&M Boxcar "6464-475," *98* | | 27 | ___ |
| 29212 | Timken Boxcar "6464-500," *98* | | 28 | ___ |
| 29213 | ATSF Grand Canyon Route 6464 Boxcar "6464-198," *98* | | 26 | ___ |
| 29214 | Southern 6464 Boxcar "6464-298," *98* | | 27 | ___ |
| 29215 | Canadian Pacific 6464 Boxcar "6464-398," *98* | | 26 | ___ |
| 29217 | 1997 Toy Fair Airex Boxcar, *97* | | 75 | ___ |
| 29218 | Vapor Records Boxcar "6464-496," *97 u* | | 67 | ___ |
| 29220 | Lionel Centennial Series Hi-Cube Boxcar Set, 4 cars, *97* | | 190 | ___ |
| 29221 | Centennial Series Hi-Cube Boxcar "9697-1," *97* | | 43 | ___ |
| 29222 | Centennial Series Hi-Cube Boxcar "9697-2," *97* | | 54 | ___ |
| 29223 | Centennial Series Hi-Cube Boxcar "9697-3," *97* | | 49 | ___ |
| 29224 | Centennial Series Hi-Cube Boxcar "9697-4," *97* | | 54 | ___ |
| 29225 | H.O.R.D.E. Music Festival Boxcar, *97* | 48 | 49 | ___ |
| 29229 | Vapor Records Holiday Car, *98* | | 143 | ___ |
| 29231 | Halloween Animated Boxcar, *98* | | 42 | ___ |
| 29233 | Conrail PC Overstamped Boxcar "6464-598," *98* | | 38 | ___ |
| 29234 | Conrail Erie Overstamped Boxcar "6464-698," *98* | | 32 | ___ |
| 29235 | NYC Boxcar "6464-510," *99* | | 47 | ___ |
| 29236 | MKT Boxcar "6464-515," *99* | | 40 | ___ |
| 29237 | M&StL Boxcar "6464-525," *99* | | 25 | ___ |
| 29247 | Mainline Classic Street Lamps, 3 pieces, *08–10* | | 35 | ___ |
| 29250 | Phoebe Snow Boxcar "6464-199," *99* | | 41 | ___ |
| 29251 | BN Boxcar "6464-299," *99* | | 31 | ___ |
| 29252 | CP Boxcar "6464-399," *99* | | 33 | ___ |
| 29253 | B&M Boxcar "76032," *99* | | 50 | ___ |
| 29254 | B&M Boxcar "76033," *99* | | 50 | ___ |
| 29255 | B&M Boxcar "76034," *99* | | 50 | ___ |
| 29256 | B&M Boxcar "76035," *99* | | 50 | ___ |
| 29257 | Southern Boxcar "9464-199," *99* | | 38 | ___ |
| 29258 | Reading Boxcar "9464-299," *99* | | 36 | ___ |
| 29259 | NP Bicentennial Boxcar "9464-399," *99* | | 34 | ___ |
| 29265 | Maine Central Boxcar "8661," *99* | | 36 | ___ |
| 29266 | Frisco Boxcar "8722," *99* | | 36 | ___ |
| 29267 | Postwar "6464" Boxcar Series VIII, 3 cars, *99* | | 105 | ___ |
| 29268 | Rio Grande Boxcar "63067," *99* | | 40 | ___ |
| 29271 | Lionel Cola Tractor and Trailer, *98* | | 12 | ___ |

Exc Mint Cond/$

| | | Exc | Mint | Cond/$ |
|---|---|---|---|---|
| 29279 | Conrail Jersey Central Overstamped Boxcar "6464-28X," 99 | | 40 | ___ |
| 29280 | Conrail Lehigh Valley Overstamped Boxcar "6464-31X," 99 | | 41 | ___ |
| 29281 | Conrail Overstamped Boxcar 2-pack, 99 | | 70 | ___ |
| 29282 | Postwar "6464" Boxcar 3-pack, 99 | | 130 | ___ |
| 29283 | NYC Boxcar, 99 | | 55 | ___ |
| 29284 | GN Boxcar, 99 | | 40 | ___ |
| 29285 | Seaboard Boxcar, 99 | | 36 | ___ |
| 29286 | Overstamped Boxcar 2-pack, 99 | | 65 | ___ |
| 29287 | NH PC Overstamped Boxcar "6464-29X," 99 | 18 | 34 | ___ |
| 29288 | Conrail Reading Overstamped Boxcar "6464-32X," 99 | | 38 | ___ |
| 29289 | Postwar "6464" Series IX, 3 cars, 99–00 | | 70 | ___ |
| 29290 | D&RGW Boxcar "6464-650," 00 | | 41 | ___ |
| 29291 | ATSF Boxcar "6464-700," 00 | | 38 | ___ |
| 29292 | NH Boxcar "6464-725," 00 | | 39 | ___ |
| 29293 | NH Boxcar "6464-425," 99 | | 95 | ___ |
| 29294 | Hell Gate Bridge Boxcar "1900-2000," 99 u | | 38 | ___ |
| 29295 | PRR "Don't Stand Me Still" Boxcar "24018," 99–00 | | 65 | ___ |
| 29296 | PRR "Merchandise" Boxcar "29296," 99–00 | | 65 | ___ |
| 29297 | PRR "No Damage" Boxcar "47158," 99–00 | | 65 | ___ |
| 29298 | Lionel Boxcar "6464-2000," 00 | | 46 | ___ |
| 29300 | 50th Anniversary Clear Shell Aquarium Car, 10 | | 85 | ___ |
| 29302 | Christmas Music Reefer, 10 | | 75 | ___ |
| 29303 | North Pole Central Crane Car, 10 | | 65 | ___ |
| 29306 | PRR Hi-Cube Lighted Garland Boxcar, 10 | | 70 | ___ |
| 29400 | Bethlehem Steel Slag Car 3-pack (std O), 03 | | 185 | ___ |
| 29404 | Bethlehem Steel Hot Metal Car 3-pack (std O), 03 | | 210 | ___ |
| 29408 | PRR Coil Car, 01 | | 40 | ___ |
| 29411 | Sherwin-Williams Vat Car, 02 | | 34 | ___ |
| 29412 | Tabasco Brand Vat Car, 02 | | 35 | ___ |
| 29413 | Airex Boat Loader Car "29413," 02 | | 42 | ___ |
| 29414 | PRR Evans Auto Loader "480123," 01 | | 56 | ___ |
| 29415 | WM Skeleton Log Car 3-pack #2 (std O), 02 | | 90 | ___ |
| 29419 | West Side Lumber Skeleton Log Car 3-pack #2 (std O), 02 | | 90 | ___ |
| 29423 | Wellspring Capital Management Happy Holidays Vat Car, 03 u | | 245 | ___ |
| 29424 | Meadow River Lumber Skeleton Log Car 3-pack (std O), 03 | | 90 | ___ |
| 29429 | Campbell's Soup Vat Car "29429," 03 | | 38 | ___ |
| 29430 | Meadow River Lumber Skeleton Log Car 3-pack #2 (std O), 03 | | 90 | ___ |
| 29434 | Weyerhauser Skeleton Log Car 3-pack, 05 | | 100 | ___ |
| 29438 | Trailer Train Flatcar with 2 UP trailers, 03 | | 60 | ___ |
| 29439 | Postwar "6414" Evans Auto Loader, 02 | | 43 | ___ |
| 29441 | UP Flatcar "53471" with grader, 02 | | 43 | ___ |

Exc Mint Cond/$

| | | Exc | Mint | Cond/$ |
|---|---|---|---|---|
| 29442 | CSX Flatcar "600513" with backhoe, *02* | | 43 | ___ |
| 29453 | Elk River Lumber Skeleton Log Car 3-pack #2 (std O), *03* | | 90 | ___ |
| 29457 | NS Flatcar "157590" with Caterpillar loader, *03* | | 42 | ___ |
| 29458 | BNSF Flatcar "922268" with Caterpillar truck, *03* | | 44 | ___ |
| 29459 | Water Barrel Car "1878," Archive Collection, *03* | | 40 | ___ |
| 29460 | LL Flatcar "3460" with trailers, Archive Collection, *03* | | 39 | ___ |
| 29461 | Postwar "6500" Flatcar with red-and-white airplane, *03* | | 32 | ___ |
| 29462 | Postwar "6500" Flatcar with white-and-red airplane, *03* | | 31 | ___ |
| 29463 | Postwar "6414" Evans Auto Loader, *03* | | 30 | ___ |
| 29464 | U.S. Army Vat Car "29464," *04* | | 35 | ___ |
| 29465 | U.S. Steel Slag Car 3-pack (std O), *04–05* | | 160 | ___ |
| 29469 | U.S. Steel Hot Metal Car 3-pack (std O), *04–05* | | 190 | ___ |
| 29473 | Youngstown Sheet & Tube Slag Car 3-pack (std O), *03* | | 150 | ___ |
| 29477 | Youngstown Sheet & Tube Hot Metal Car 3-pack (std O), *03* | | 170 | ___ |
| 29481 | Cass Scenic Railroad Skeleton Log Car 3-pack (std O), *03* | | 80 | ___ |
| 29487 | Boat-loader with 4 boats, *04* | | 65 | ___ |
| 29488 | Cass Scenic Railroad Skeleton Log Car 3-pack #2 (std O), *04* | | 90 | ___ |
| 29492 | Pickering Lumber Skeleton Log Car 3-pack #1 (std O), *04* | | 100 | ___ |
| 29496 | Pickering Lumber Skeleton Log Car 3-pack #2 (std O), *04* | | 90 | ___ |
| 29602 | Celanese Chemicals 1-D Tank Car, *05* | | 45 | ___ |
| 29603 | Comet 1-D Tank Car, traditional, *05* | | 53 | ___ |
| 29604 | Meadow Brook Molasses 1-D Tank Car, traditional, *05* | | 53 | ___ |
| 29606 | Elvis Presley Gold Record Transport Car, *04* | | 120 | ___ |
| 29607 | Las Vegas Mint Car, traditional, *05* | | 58 | ___ |
| 29609 | Alien Suspension Car, *06* | | 60 | ___ |
| 29610 | Dixie Honey 1-D Tank Car, *06* | | 60 | ___ |
| 29611 | Sunoco 1-D Tank Car, *06* | | 60 | ___ |
| 29612 | Las Vegas Poker Chip Car, *06* | | 40 | ___ |
| 29613 | Postwar "6463" Rocket Fuel 2-D Tank Car, *06* | | 75 | ___ |
| 29617 | Cities Service Tank Car, *06–07* | | 48 | ___ |
| 29618 | Hooker Chemicals 3-D Tank Car, *07* | | 60 | ___ |
| 29619 | Grave's Formaldehyde 1-D Tank Car, *07* | | 60 | ___ |
| 29622 | Fort Knox Mint Car, lilac, Archive Collection, *07* | | 60 | ___ |
| 29624 | Monopoly Mint Car with money, *08* | | 65 | ___ |
| 29626 | "Case Closed" Mint Car with shredded documents, *08* | | 108 | ___ |
| 29628 | Poinsettia Mint Car, *09* | | 70 | ___ |
| 29629 | AEC Glow-in-the-Dark Tank Car, *09–10* | | 50 | ___ |
| 29633 | Christmas Ornament Lighted Mint Car, *10* | | 70 | ___ |

Exc Mint Cond/$

| | | Exc | Mint | Cond/$ |
|---|---|---|---|---|
| 29634 | Federal Reserve Bailout Mint Car, *10* | | 70 | |
| 29635 | Monopoly "Go To Jail" Mint Car, *10* | | 70 | |
| 29636 | Vampire Transport Mint Car, *10* | | 70 | |
| 29637 | Candy Cane 2-D Tank Car, *10* | | 55 | |
| 29640 | Coca-Cola Tank Car, *10* | | 55 | |
| 29703 | PRR Porthole Caboose, *01* | | 45 | |
| 29708 | C&O Bay Window Caboose "8315," *04* | | 45 | |
| 29709 | Pennsylvania N5c Caboose "477938," *04* | | 40 | |
| 29711 | Santa Fe Bay Window Caboose, *05* | | 60 | |
| 29712 | Postwar "2420" Searchlight Caboose, *04* | | 50 | |
| 29718 | N&W Work Caboose, *06* | | 48 | |
| 29719 | Santa Fe Caboose "6427," Archive Collection, *06* | | 48 | |
| 29726 | Virginian Caboose "6427," Archive Collection, *06–07* | | 50 | |
| 29727 | "I Love U.S.A." Bay Window Caboose "1985," *06* | | 60 | |
| 29729 | Bethlehem Steel Searchlight Caboose, *06* | | 90 | |
| 29732 | PRR Caboose "477871," *08* | | 45 | |
| 29733 | White Pass & Yukon Extended Vision Caboose, *09–10* | | 90 | |
| 29734 | PRR NS Heritage CA-4 Caboose (std O), *10* | | 95 | |
| 29735 | Conrail NS Heritage CA-4 Caboose (std O), *10* | | 95 | |
| 29737 | ATSF Bay-Window Caboose, traditional, *10* | | 70 | |
| 29800 | M.O.W. Crane Car, TMCC, *04* | | 250 | |
| 29804 | UP Crane Car "JPX 250," CC, *05* | | 320 | |
| 29805 | Conrail Crane Car "50202," CC, *05* | | 320 | |
| 29806 | Weyerhaeuser Log Dump Car, *05* | | 75 | |
| 29807 | DM&IR Coal Dump Car, *05* | | 75 | |
| 29808 | Candy Cane Dump Car, *05* | | 55 | |
| 29809 | Dump Car with presents, *05* | | 60 | |
| 29810 | Operating Egg Nog Car with platform, *05* | | 140 | |
| 29811 | Merchant's Despatch Transit Hot Box Reefer "12425," *05* | | 85 | |
| 29812 | Santa Fe Hot Box Reefer "20699," *05* | | 90 | |
| 29813 | Santa Fe Boom Car "19144," Crane Sounds, *05* | | 210 | |
| 29814 | Pennsylvania Boom Car "491063," Crane Sounds, *05* | | 210 | |
| 29815 | NYC Boom Car "X923," Crane Sounds, *05* | | 210 | |
| 29816 | M.O.W. Boom Car "X-816," Crane Sounds, *05* | | 210 | |
| 29817 | UP Boom Car "909438," Crane Sounds, *05* | | 210 | |
| 29818 | Conrail Boom Car, Crane Sounds, *05* | | 210 | |
| 29821 | Postwar "2460" Lionel Lines Crane Car, gray cab, *05* | | 43 | |
| 29822 | Postwar "773W" NYC Tender, whistle, *05* | | 48 | |
| 29823 | Postwar "3484" Pennsylvania Operating Boxcar, *05* | | 38 | |
| 29827 | Postwar "3419" Helicopter Launching Car, *06* | | 49 | |
| 29828 | Postwar "3666" Minuteman Car with cannon, *06* | | 85 | |
| 29829 | Postwar "6905" Radioactive Waste Car, *06* | | 85 | |

Exc Mint Cond/$

| | | Exc | Mint | Cond/$ |
|---|---|---|---|---|
| 29830 | PFE Hot Box Reefer "5890" (std O), *06* | 105 | | |
| 29831 | Swift Hot Box Reefer "15342" (std O), *06* | 150 | | |
| 29832 | Chessie System Crane Car "940504," CC, *06* | 320 | | |
| 29833 | Chessie System Boom Car "940561," CC, *06* | 210 | | |
| 29834 | LL Bay Window Caboose "834," TrainSounds (std O), *06–07* | 110 | | |
| 29835 | SP Bay Window Caboose "4667," TrainSounds (std O), *06–07* | 160 | | |
| 29839 | Cherry Picker Car, *06* | 63 | | |
| 29849 | Lionel Lines Crane Car, silver cab, *06* | 60 | | |
| 29850 | N&W J Class Tender, air whistle, *06–07* | 70 | | |
| 29853 | Postwar "6651" Big John Cannon Car, *08* | 75 | | |
| 29854 | Satellite Launching Car, *07* | 70 | | |
| 29855 | Lionel Lines Operating Milk Car with platform, *07* | 140 | | |
| 29856 | Monon Operating Boxcar, *06–07* | 65 | | |
| 29857 | Lionel Lines Boom Car, *06–07* | 55 | | |
| 29858 | CP Rail Crane Car "414475," CC, *07* | 320 | | |
| 29859 | CP Rail Boom Car "412567," CC, *07* | 210 | | |
| 29865 | Southern Operating Barrel Car, *07–08* | 75 | | |
| 29866 | Pirates Aquarium Car, *07* | 75 | | |
| 29867 | NYC Jet Snow Blower "X27207," *07* | 120 | | |
| 29868 | Alaska Jet Snow Blower, *07* | 120 | | |
| 29869 | Bethlehem Steel Crane Car, *06* | 60 | | |
| 29870 | M.O.W. Jet Snow Blower "MWX-16," *07* | 120 | | |
| 29877 | Southern Crane Car "D76," CC, *08* | 350 | | |
| 29882 | Witches Operating Brew Car, *08* | 150 | | |
| 29884 | CNJ Twin Dump Car, *08* | 85 | | |
| 29885 | BN Crane Car "S-104," CC, *10* | 340 | | |
| 29886 | BN Boom Car "S-1040," CC, *10* | 220 | | |
| 29888 | Postwar "3494-625" Soo Lines Operating Boxcar, *08* | 70 | | |
| 29893 | PRR Operating Stock Car "129893," RailSounds, *09* | 150 | | |
| 29894 | Christmas Chase Gondola, *09* | 65 | | |
| 29895 | Christmas Operating Snow Globe Car, *10* | 75 | | |
| 29900 | "I Love Wisconsin" Boxcar, *01* | 35 | | |
| 29901 | "I Love Kentucky" Boxcar, *01* | 30 | | |
| 29902 | "I Love Iowa" Boxcar, *01* | 31 | | |
| 29903 | "I Love Missouri" Boxcar, *01* | 31 | | |
| 29904 | 2002 Toy Fair Boxcar, *02* | 22 | | |
| 29906 | "I Love Connecticut" Boxcar, *02* | 33 | | |
| 29907 | "I Love West Virginia" Boxcar, *02* | 33 | | |
| 29908 | "I Love Delaware" Boxcar, *02* | 33 | | |
| 29909 | "I Love Maryland" Boxcar, *02* | 65 | | |
| 29910 | Toy Fair Centennial Boxcar, *03* | 40 | | |
| 29912 | "I Love Alabama" Boxcar, *03* | 30 | | |
| 29913 | "I Love Mississippi" Boxcar, *03* | 35 | | |
| 29914 | "I Love Louisiana" Boxcar, *03* | 35 | | |

| | | Exc | Mint | Cond/S |
|---|---|---|---|---|
| 29915 | "I Love Arkansas" Boxcar, *03* | | 30 | ___ |
| 29918 | 2003 Toy Fair Boxcar, *03* | | 48 | ___ |
| 29919 | 2004 Toy Fair Boxcar, *04* | | 37 | ___ |
| 29920 | "I Love North Dakota" Boxcar, *03* | | 35 | ___ |
| 29921 | "I Love South Dakota" Boxcar, *03* | | 40 | ___ |
| 29922 | "I Love Nebraska" Boxcar, *03* | | 30 | ___ |
| 29923 | "I Love Kansas" Boxcar, *03* | | 30 | ___ |
| 29925 | Toy Fair *Polar Express* Boxcar, *05* | | 250 | ___ |
| 29927 | "I Love Washington" Boxcar, *05* | | 45 | ___ |
| 29928 | "I Love Oregon" Boxcar, *05* | | 40 | ___ |
| 29929 | "I Love Idaho" Boxcar, *05* | | 45 | ___ |
| 29930 | "I Love Utah" Boxcar, *05* | | 45 | ___ |
| 29932 | "I Love Oklahoma" Boxcar, *06* | | 45 | ___ |
| 29933 | "I Love New Mexico" Boxcar, *06* | | 45 | ___ |
| 29934 | "I Love Hawaii" Boxcar, *06* | | 45 | ___ |
| 29935 | "I Love Alaska" Boxcar, *06* | | 45 | ___ |
| 29936 | "I Love Wyoming" Boxcar, *06* | | 45 | ___ |
| 29937 | 2006 Toy Fair Boxcar, *06* | | 38 | ___ |
| 29942 | Santa Fe Railroad Art Boxcar, *06* | | 50 | ___ |
| 29943 | *Texas Special* Railroad Art Boxcar, *06* | | 50 | ___ |
| 29944 | 1957 Lionel Art Boxcar, *06* | | 50 | ___ |
| 29945 | 1947 Lionel Art Boxcar, *06* | | 50 | ___ |
| 29949 | Weyerhaeuser Timber Skeleton Log Car 3-pack #2 (std O), *03* | | 90 | ___ |
| 29950 | 1948 Lionel Art Boxcar, *08* | | 50 | ___ |
| 29951 | 1954 Lionel Art Boxcar, *08* | | 50 | ___ |
| 29952 | GN Art Boxcar, *08* | | 50 | ___ |
| 29953 | SP Art Boxcar, *08* | | 50 | ___ |
| 29954 | Dealer Christmas Boxcar, *07* | | 75 | ___ |
| 29955 | Dealer Boxcar, *08* | | 75 | ___ |
| 29959 | 1952 Lionel Art Boxcar, *09* | | 58 | ___ |
| 29960 | Rock Island Art Boxcar, *09–10* | | 58 | ___ |
| 29961 | Meet the Beatles Boxcar 2-pack, *10* | | 130 | ___ |
| 29965 | Lionel Art Boxcar 2-pack, *10* | | 116 | ___ |
| 30000 | PRR Keystone Super Freight Steam Train, TMCC, *05* | | 450 | ___ |
| 30001 | Santa Fe *El Capitan* Passenger Set, TrainSounds, *05–10* | | 370 | ___ |
| 30002 | Neil Young's Greendale Diesel Freight Set, *04* | | 420 | ___ |
| 30003 | Pennsylvania Flyer Operating Freight Expansion Pack, *05* | | 99 | ___ |
| 30004 | Pennsylvania Flyer Passenger Expansion Pack, *05–08* | | 120 | ___ |
| 30007 | NYC Flyer Operating Freight Expansion Pack, *05* | | 99 | ___ |
| 30008 | NYC Flyer Passenger Expansion Pack, *05–08* | | 120 | ___ |
| 30011 | Holiday Expansion Pack, *05* | | 100 | ___ |
| 30012 | Thomas the Tank Engine Expansion Pack, *05–10* | | 120 | ___ |
| 30016 | NYC Flyer Steam Freight Set, *06–08* | | 290 | ___ |

| | | Exc | Mint | Cond/$ |
|---|---|---|---|---|
| **30018** | Pennsylvania Flyer Steam Freight Set, *06–07* | | 200 | ___ |
| **30020** | North Pole Central Christmas Steam Train, *06–07* | | 220 | ___ |
| **30021** | Cascade Range Steam Logging Train, *06–08* | | 190 | ___ |
| **30022** | Southwest Diesel Freight Set, TrainSounds, *06* | | 295 | ___ |
| **30024** | UP Fast Freight Steam Set, TrainSounds, *06–07* | | 340 | ___ |
| **30025** | Chesapeake Super Freight Steam Set, TMCC, *06–07* | | 475 | ___ |
| **30026** | CP Diesel Freight Set, TMCC, *06* | | 540 | ___ |
| **30034** | Great Western Train Set with Lincoln Logs, *07–09* | | 230 | ___ |
| **30035** | Sodor Freight Expansion Pack, *06–09* | | 120 | ___ |
| **30036** | Great Western Expansion Pack, *07–08* | | 120 | ___ |
| **30037** | Pennsylvania Flyer Operating Freight Expansion Pack, *06–08* | | 120 | ___ |
| **30038** | NYC Flyer Operating Freight Expansion Pack, *06–08* | | 120 | ___ |
| **30039** | North Pole Central Passenger Expansion Pack, *06–10* | | 110 | ___ |
| **30040** | North Pole Central Freight Expansion Pack, *06–10* | | 110 | ___ |
| **30041** | Southwest Diesel Freight Expansion Pack, *06* | | 110 | ___ |
| **30042** | Cascade Range Expansion Pack, *06* | | 110 | ___ |
| **30044** | NYC Empire Builder Steam Freight Set, TMCC, *06* | | 2800 | ___ |
| **30045** | Alaska Steam Work Train, *07–09* | | 270 | ___ |
| **30046** | Alaska Work Train Expansion Pack, *07–08* | | 110 | ___ |
| **30047** | Northwest Special Diesel Freight Set, TrainSounds, *07–08* | | 295 | ___ |
| **30048** | Northwest Special Freight Expansion Pack, *07–08* | | 110 | ___ |
| **30049** | D&RGW Fast Freight Set, TrainSounds, *08–09* | | 320 | ___ |
| **30050** | Pennsylvania Super Freight Set, CC, *08* | | 450 | ___ |
| **30051** | UP Diesel Freight Set, TMCC, *07* | | 500 | ___ |
| **30056** | Halloween Steam Freight Set, *07–10* | | 220 | ___ |
| **30061** | UPS Centennial Stream Freight Set, *07–08* | | 230 | ___ |
| **30064** | Pennsylvania Speeder Set, traditional, K-Line, *06* | | 75 | ___ |
| **30066/67** | C&O Empire Builder Steam Freight Set, CC, *07–09* | | 2700 | ___ |
| **30068** | North Pole Central Christmas Freight Set, *08* | | 220 | ___ |
| **30069** | Thomas & Friends Passenger Train, *08–10* | | 170 | ___ |
| **30081** | UP Merger Special GP38 Freight Set, *08* | | 300 | ___ |
| **30082** | UP Heritage Freight Car 3-pack, *08* | | 100 | ___ |
| **30084** | British Great Western Shakespeare Express Passenger Train, *08* | | 300 | ___ |
| **30085** | MTA Metro-North M-7 Commuter Car Set, *07–08* | | 280 | ___ |
| **30087** | Alien Spaceship Recovery Freight Set, *08–09* | | 230 | ___ |
| **30088** | *John Bull* Passenger Train, *08* | | 430 | ___ |
| **30089** | Pennsylvania Flyer Freight Set, *08–10* | | 200 | ___ |

| | | Exc | Mint | Cond/$ |
|---|---|---|---|---|
| 30091 | ATSF Steam Freight Set, *08–09* | | 270 | ___ |
| 30094 | Chicago & North Western Passenger Set, *08* | | 150 | ___ |
| 30096 | Pennsylvania Keystone Special Steam Freight Set, *09* | | 260 | ___ |
| 30103 | NYC 0-8-0 Steam Freight Set, *09–10* | | 300 | ___ |
| 30108 | American Fire and Rescue GP20 Freight Set, *09–10* | | 400 | ___ |
| 30109 | Nutcracker Route Christmas Train Set, *10* | | 270 | ___ |
| 30111 | Pullman Passenger Expansion Pack, *09–10* | | 138 | ___ |
| 30112 | Eastern Freight Expansion Pack, *09–10* | | 138 | ___ |
| 30114 | MTA LIRR M-7 Commuter Set, *09* | | 320 | ___ |
| 30116 | Lone Ranger Wild West Freight Set, *09–10* | | 400 | ___ |
| 30118 | *A Christmas Story* Steam Freight Set, *09–10* | | 330 | ___ |
| 30120 | Menards C&NW Steam Passenger Set, *09* | | 250 | ___ |
| 30121 | ATSF Baby Madison Car 3-pack, *10* | | 190 | ___ |
| 30122 | *Wizard of Oz* Steam Freight Set, *10* | | 310 | ___ |
| 30123 | Boy Scouts of America Steam Freight Set, *10* | | 300 | ___ |
| 30124 | Thunder Valley Quarry Steam Freight Set, *10* | | 300 | ___ |
| 30125 | D&RGW Ski Train, TrainSounds, *10* | | 340 | ___ |
| 30126 | Pennsylvania Flyer Steam Freight Set, *10* | | 230 | ___ |
| 30127 | Scout Steam Freight Set, *10* | | 200 | ___ |
| 30128 | Western Freight Expansion Pack, *10* | | 138 | ___ |
| 30131 | Chessie System Merger Diesel Freight Set, *10* | | 300 | ___ |
| 30133 | Strasburg Steam Passenger Set, *10* | | 330 | ___ |
| 30136 | Thunder Valley Quarry Freight Car Add-on 2-pack, *10* | | 110 | ___ |
| 30138 | Chessie System Merger Freight Car Add-on 2-pack, *10* | | 120 | ___ |
| 30139 | Santa Fe Flyer Steam Freight Set, *10* | | 270 | ___ |
| 30141 | Sodor Tank and Wagon Expansion Pack, *10* | | 138 | ___ |
| 30142 | *Texas Special* Freight Set, TrainSounds, *10* | | 700 | ___ |
| 30144 | Operation Eagle Justice Diesel Freight Set, *10* | | 500 | ___ |
| 30145 | Maple Leaf Diesel Freight Set, *10* | | 550 | ___ |
| 31569 | Western & Atlantic Passenger Car 2-pack, *08* | | 100 | ___ |
| 31700 | Postwar Girls Freight Set, *01* | | 570 | ___ |
| 31701 | Postwar Boys Freight Set, *02* | | 345 | ___ |
| 31704 | *Alton Limited* Steam Passenger Set, *02* | | 870 | ___ |
| 31705 | 50th Anniversary Hudson Passenger Set, *02* | | 900 | ___ |
| 31706 | UP Burro Crane Set, *02* | | 210 | ___ |
| 31707 | C&O Diesel Freight Set, *03* | | 280 | ___ |
| 31708 | Postwar "1805" Marines Missile Launch Train, *03* | | 400 | ___ |
| 31710 | BN Diesel Coal Train, RailSounds, *03* | | 690 | ___ |
| 31711 | Postwar "1563W" Wabash Diesel Freight Set, RailSounds, *03* | | 570 | ___ |
| 31712 | UP Alco PA Diesel Passenger Set, RailSounds, *03* | | 1495 | ___ |
| 31713 | Southern *Crescent Limited* Steam Passenger Set, RailSounds, *03* | | 1195 | ___ |

Exc Mint Cond/$

| | | Exc Mint | Cond/$ |
|---|---|---|---|
| 31714 | Amtrak Acela Diesel Passenger Set, RailSounds, *04–05* | 2000 | ____ |
| 31715 | Fire Rescue Steam Freight Set, *02* | 293 | ____ |
| 31716 | Fire Rescue Steam Freight Set, *03* | 275 | ____ |
| 31717 | CP Rail Snow Removal Train, *03* | 255 | ____ |
| 31718 | SP "Oil Can" TankTrain Freight Set, *03* | 1600 | ____ |
| 31719 | Western Maryland Fireball Diesel Freight Set, *04* | 290 | ____ |
| 31720 | FEC *Champion* Diesel Passenger Set, RailSounds, *04* | 900 | ____ |
| 31721 | Postwar "13138" Majestic Electric Freight Set, RailSounds, *04* | 580 | ____ |
| 31724 | Nabisco 3-Car Passenger Set, *03* | 110 | ____ |
| 31727 | Postwar "2291W" Rio Grande Diesel Freight Set, RailSounds, *04* | 640 | ____ |
| 31728 | Elvis "He Dared to Rock" Steam Freight Set, *04* | 325 | ____ |
| 31730 | Norman Rockwell Boxcar 4-pack, *05* | 95 | ____ |
| 31733 | Jones & Laughlin Steel Slag Train, *05* | 250 | ____ |
| 31734 | Chessie Steam Special Passenger Set, TMCC, *05* | 405 | ____ |
| 31735 | Chessie Diesel Freight Set, TMCC, *05–06* | 670 | ____ |
| 31736 | CP Diesel Grain Train, TMCC, *05* | 700 | ____ |
| 31737 | Napa Valley Wine Train, TMCC, *05* | 900 | ____ |
| 31739 | Postwar "13150" Hudson Steam Freight Set, Super O, *05* | 940 | ____ |
| 31740 | Postwar "2519W" Virginian Diesel Freight Set, TMCC, *05–07* | 620 | ____ |
| 31742 | Postwar "2544W" Santa Fe *Super Chief* Diesel Passenger Set, *05* | 700 | ____ |
| 31747 | Pennsylvania Electric Ballast Train, TMCC, *06* | 550 | ____ |
| 31748 | Santa Fe U28CG Diesel Freight Set (std O), TMCC, *06–07* | 770 | ____ |
| 31749 | Pennsylvania Diesel Coal Train, TMCC, *06* | 770 | ____ |
| 31750 | NYC Hotbox Reefer Steam Freight Set, TMCC, *06–07* | 530 | ____ |
| 31751 | New York City Transit Authority R27 Subway Train, CC, *07* | 700 | ____ |
| 31752 | B&O Diesel Freight Set, TMCC, *06–07* | 740 | ____ |
| 31753 | GN Diesel Freight Set, TMCC, *06–08* | 740 | ____ |
| 31754 | Postwar "2545WS" N&W Space Freight Set, TMCC, *06–07* | 960 | ____ |
| 31755 | *Texas Special* Diesel Passenger Set, CC, *07–08* | 1280 | ____ |
| 31757 | Postwar "2289WS" Berkshire Freight Set, CC, *07* | 750 | ____ |
| 31758 | Postwar "2270W" Jersey Central Diesel Passenger Car Set, CC, *08* | 750 | ____ |
| 31760 | CSX SD40-2 Diesel Husky Stack Car Set, CC, *07–08* | 770 | ____ |
| 31765 | Postwar "11268" C&O Diesel Freight Set, *08* | 580 | ____ |
| 31767 | Bethlehem Steel Rolling Stock Set, K-Line, *06* | 100 | ____ |
| 31768 | B&O Rolling Stock Set, K-Line, *06* | 100 | ____ |

Exc Mint Cond/S

| | | Exc | Mint | Cond/S |
|---|---|---|---|---|
| 31772 | Conrail LionMaster Diesel Freight Set, CC, 08–09 | 535 | | |
| 31773 | NS Dash 9 Diesel TankTrain Set, CC, 08 | 785 | | |
| 31774 | AEC Burro Crane Set, traditional, 09–10 | 260 | | |
| 31775 | "1562" Burlington GP Passenger Set, 08 | 470 | | |
| 31777 | "2124W" GG1 Passenger Set, 08 | 470 | | |
| 31778 | "1484WS" Steam Passenger Set, 08 | 610 | | |
| 31779 | Amtrak HHP-8 Amfleet Passenger Set, CC, 09 | 500 | | |
| 31782 | ATSF Crane Car and Boom Car, CC (std O), 09–10 | 560 | | |
| 31783 | BNSF Ice Cold Express Diesel Freight Set, CC, 10 | 1000 | | |
| 31784 | No. 1593 UP Work Train Set, 09 | 470 | | |
| 31787 | CN SD70M-2 Diesel Coal Train, CC, 09 | 800 | | |
| 31790 | PRR GG1 Passenger Set, 10 | 500 | | |
| 31791 | NYC LionMaster Diesel Freight Set, CC, 10 | 700 | | |
| 31793 | White Pass & Yukon Freight Car Add-on 3-pack, 10 | 195 | | |
| 31795 | Pere Marquette Freight Car 3-pack (std O), 10 | 210 | | |
| 31796 | Feather Route Freight Car 3-pack (std O), 10 | 210 | | |
| 31797 | New York City Transit R16 Subway Set, CC, 10 | 800 | | |
| 31799 | GN Empire Steam Freight Express Set, 10 | 430 | | |
| 31901 | Christmas Steam Freight Set, 02 | 145 | | |
| 31902 | PRR K4 Freight Set, 01–02 | 580 | | |
| 31904 | C&O Steam Freight Set, RailSounds, 01 | 400 | | |
| 31905 | NH Diesel Freight Set, CC, 01 | 660 | | |
| 31907 | PRR Atlantic Freight Set, 01 u | 400 | | |
| 31908 | Reading Hobo Express Freight Set, 01 u | 365 | | |
| 31909 | Santa Fe Shell Tank Car Freight Set, 01 u | 320 | | |
| 31910 | Soo Line Diesel Freight Set, 01 u | 350 | | |
| 31911 | Snap-On Anniversary Steam Freight Set, 00 u | 540 | | |
| 31913 | PRR Flyer Steam Freight Set, 01 | 145 | | |
| 31914 | NYC Flyer Steam Freight Set, RailSounds, 01–02 | 170 | | |
| 31915 | Chessie GP38 Diesel Freight Set, 01–02 | 155 | | |
| 31916 | Santa Fe Steam Freight Set, 01 | 300 | | |
| 31918 | C&O Steam Freight Set, SignalSounds, 01 | 315 | | |
| 31919 | T&P Steam Passenger Set, RailSounds, 01 | 210 | | |
| 31920 | L.L. Bean Freight Set, 01 u | 240 | | |
| 31922 | Snap-On Tool Diesel Freight Set, 01 u | 345 | | |
| 31923 | PRR Flyer Freight Set, 01 u | 130 | | |
| 31924 | Union Pacific RS3 Diesel Freight Set, 02 | 95 | | |
| 31926 | Area 51 FA Diesel Freight Set, 02 | 160 | | |
| 37928 | Great Train Robbery Set, 02 | 180 | | |
| 31931 | Ballyhoo Brothers Circus Train, 02 | 190 | | |
| 31932 | NYC Limited Passenger Set, RailSounds, 02 | 285 | | |
| 31933 | Santa Fe Steam Freight Set, RailSounds, 02 | 320 | | |
| 31934 | Lionel 20th Century Express Steam Freight Set, 00 u | 275 | | |
| 31936 | Pennsylvania Flyer Steam Freight Set, 03–05 | 190 | | |

Exc Mint Cond/$

| No. | Description | Exc | Mint | Cond/$ |
|---|---|---|---|---|
| 31938 | Southern Diesel Freight Set, *03–04* | | 160 | ___ |
| 31939 | Great Train Robbery Steam Freight Set, *03* | | 185 | ___ |
| 31940 | NYC Flyer Steam Freight Set, RailSounds, *03* | | 225 | ___ |
| 31941 | Winter Wonderland Railroad Christmas Train, *03* | | 150 | ___ |
| 31942 | Norman Rockwell Christmas Train, *03* | | 330 | ___ |
| 31944 | NYC Limited Diesel Passenger Set, RailSounds, *03* | | 250 | ___ |
| 31945 | Santa Fe Steam Super Freight Set, RailSounds, *03* | | 350 | ___ |
| 31946 | Disney Christmas Steam Train, *04–05* | | 300 | ___ |
| 31947 | World of Disney Steam Freight Set, *03* | | 215 | ___ |
| 31950 | Kraft Holiday UP RS3 Diesel Freight Set, *02 u* | | 149 | ___ |
| 31952 | Great Northern Glacier Route Diesel Freight Set, *03–04* | | 110 | ___ |
| 31953 | "Riding the Rails" Hobo Train Set, *03–04* | | 225 | ___ |
| 31956 | Thomas the Tank Engine Set, *04–07* | | 195 | ___ |
| 31958 | Santa Fe Flyer Steam Freight Set, RailSounds, *04* | | 205 | ___ |
| 31960 | *Polar Express* Steam Passenger Set, *04–10* | | 235 | ___ |
| 31961 | Bloomingdale's Pennsylvania Flyer Steam Freight Set, *02 u* | | 158 | ___ |
| 31962 | Nickel Plate Road Super Freight Set, RailSounds, *04* | | 350 | ___ |
| 31963 | Southern Pacific Overnight Steam Freight Set, *04* | | 340 | ___ |
| 31966 | Holiday Tradition Steam Freight Set, *04–05* | | 210 | ___ |
| 31969 | NYC Flyer Steam Freight Set, RailSounds, *04* | | 205 | ___ |
| 31976 | Yukon Special Diesel Freight Set, *05* | | 225 | ___ |
| 31977 | New York Central Flyer Steam Freight Set, *05* | | 250 | ___ |
| 31985 | Santa Fe Steam Fast Freight Set, TrainSounds, *05* | | 320 | ___ |
| 31989 | UP Overland Freight Express Set, *04* | | 880 | ___ |
| 31990 | Copper Range Steam Freight Mine Set, *05* | | 175 | ___ |
| 31993 | NS Black Diamond Diesel Freight Set, TMCC, *05* | | 500 | ___ |
| 32900 | DC Billboard, *99* | | 24 | ___ |
| 32902 | Construction Zone Signs, set of 6, *99–10* | | 8 | ___ |
| 32904 | Hell Gate Bridge, *99* | 235 | 415 | ___ |
| 32905 | Irvington Factory, *99–00* | | 295 | ___ |
| 32910 | Rotary Coal Tipple with bathtub gondola, *02* | | 442 | ___ |
| 32919 | Animated Maiden Rescue, *99* | | 65 | ___ |
| 32920 | Animated Pylon with airplane, *99* | | 130 | ___ |
| 32921 | Electric Coaling Station, *99–01* | | 125 | ___ |
| 32922 | Highway Barrels, set of 6, *99–10* | | 8 | ___ |
| 32923 | Accessory Transformer, *99–03, 06–10* | | 40 | ___ |
| 32929 | Icing Station with Santa, *99* | | 90 | ___ |
| 32930 | Power Supply Set with ZW controller and 2 power supplies, *99–02, 06–09* | | 425 | ___ |
| 32933 | Christmas Stocking Hanger Set, 4-piece, *99–00* | | 50 | ___ |
| 32934 | Stocking Hanger, gondola, *99–00* | | 15 | ___ |

Exc Mint Cond/S

| | | Exc | Mint | Cond/S |
|---|---|---|---|---|
| 32935 | Stocking Hanger, boxcar, *99–00* | | 15 | ___ |
| 32960 | Hindenburger Cafe, *99* | | 195 | ___ |
| 32961 | Route 66 UFO Cafe, *99* | | 200 | ___ |
| 32987 | Hobo Campfire, *99–00* | 25 | 45 | ___ |
| 32988 | Postwar "192" Railroad Control Tower, *99–00* | | 75 | ___ |
| 32989 | Postwar "464" Sawmill, *99–00* | | 75 | ___ |
| 32990 | Linex Oil Derrick, *99–00* | | 55 | ___ |
| 32991 | WLLC Radio Station, *99* | | 65 | ___ |
| 32996 | Postwar "362" Barrel Loader, *00* | | 125 | ___ |
| 32997 | Aluminum Rico Station, *00* | | 300 | ___ |
| 32998 | Hobby Shop, *99–00* | | 300 | ___ |
| 32999 | Hell Gate Bridge, *99–00* | | 350 | ___ |
| 33000 | GP9 Diesel "3000," RailScope video camera system, *88–90* | 125 | 170 | ___ |
| 33002 | RailScope Television Monitor, *88–90* | 45 | 70 | ___ |
| 34102 | Amtrak Shelter, *04–08* | | 25 | ___ |
| 34108 | Lionelville Suburban House, *03* | | 20 | ___ |
| 34109 | Lionelville Large Suburban House, *03* | | 15 | ___ |
| 34110 | Lionelville Estate House, *03* | | 30 | ___ |
| 34111 | Lionelville Deluxe Fieldstone House, *03* | | 17 | ___ |
| 34112 | Lionelville Fieldstone House, *03* | | 17 | ___ |
| 34113 | Lionelville Large Suburban House, *03* | | 17 | ___ |
| 34114 | Late Illuminated Station and Terrace, red trim, *03* | | 475 | ___ |
| 34117 | Early Illuminated Station and Terrace, green trim, *03* | | 475 | ___ |
| 34120 | TMCC Direct Lockon, *04–10* | | 45 | ___ |
| 34121 | Lionelville Bungalow, *04* | | 20 | ___ |
| 34122 | Lionelville Bungalow with garage, *04* | | 20 | ___ |
| 34123 | Lionelville Bungalow with addition, *04* | | 20 | ___ |
| 34124 | Lionelville Anastasia's Bakery, *04* | | 20 | ___ |
| 34125 | Lionelville Cotton's Candy, *04* | | 20 | ___ |
| 34126 | Lionelville Market, *04* | | 20 | ___ |
| 34127 | Lionelville O'Grady's Tavern, *04* | | 22 | ___ |
| 34128 | Lionelville Pharmacy, *04* | | 15 | ___ |
| 34129 | Lionelville Kiddie City Toy Store, *04* | | 20 | ___ |
| 34130 | Lionelville Jim's 5&10, *04* | | 25 | ___ |
| 34131 | Lionelville Al's Hardware, *04* | | 30 | ___ |
| 34144 | Santa Fe Scrap Yard, *05–06* | | 80 | ___ |
| 34145 | New Haven Scrap Yard, *06* | | 100 | ___ |
| 34149 | Sly Fox and the Hunter, *05–07* | | 80 | ___ |
| 34150 | Reading Room, *05–06* | | 70 | ___ |
| 34158 | Ring Toss Midway Game, *05–06* | | 20 | ___ |
| 34159 | Camel Race Midway Game, *05–06* | | 20 | ___ |
| 34162 | Operating Oil Pump, *04–09* | | 53 | ___ |
| 34163 | Speeder Shed, *04–06* | | 30 | ___ |
| 34164 | Nutcracker Operating Gateman, *05–08* | | 80 | ___ |
| 34190 | Carousel, *04–06* | | 165 | ___ |
| 34191 | Hobo Depot, *04–05* | | 70 | ___ |

| | | Exc | Mint | Cond/S |
|---|---|---|---|---|
| **34192** | Operating Lumberjacks, *04–06* | 60 | | ___ |
| **34193** | UPS Animated Billboard, *04* | 30 | | ___ |
| **34194** | UPS Package Station, *05* | 120 | | ___ |
| **34195** | UPS People Pack, *06–09* | 27 | | ___ |
| **34210** | TMCC Direct Lockon, *09* | 52 | | ___ |
| **34500** | Rio Grande FT Diesel "5484," traditional, *06* | 245 | | ___ |
| **34501** | Southern FT Diesel "4102," traditional, *06* | 400 | | ___ |
| **34504** | B&O F3 Diesel A Unit "2368," nonpowered, *06–07* | 200 | | ___ |
| **34505** | B&O E7 Diesel AA Set, CC, *07* | 700 | | ___ |
| **34508** | PRR E7 Diesel AA Set, CC, *07* | 700 | | ___ |
| **34509** | PRR E7 Diesel B Unit, nonpowered (std O), *07* | 170 | | ___ |
| **34510** | PRR E7 Diesel B Unit, powered, CC, *07* | 300 | | ___ |
| **34511** | NYC F7 Diesel ABA Set, CC, *07–08* | 900 | | ___ |
| **34512** | NYC F7 Diesel B Unit "2439," powered, CC, *07–08* | 300 | | ___ |
| **34513** | WP F7 Diesel ABA Set, CC, *07–08* | 900 | | ___ |
| **34514** | WP F7 Diesel B Unit "918C," powered, CC, *07–08* | 300 | | ___ |
| **34515** | NYC F7 Diesel Breakdown B Unit "2440," RailSounds, *07* | 270 | | ___ |
| **34518** | PRR E7 Diesel Breakdown B Unit, RailSounds, *07* | 270 | | ___ |
| **34519** | NYC Sharknose RF-16 Diesel AA Set, CC, *07–08* | 630 | | ___ |
| **34520** | NYC Sharknose Diesel B Unit "3818," nonpowered (std O), *07–08* | 160 | | ___ |
| **34521** | Santa Fe F3 Diesel A Unit "17," traditional, *07* | 265 | | ___ |
| **34522** | Santa Fe F3 Diesel B Unit "17," nonpowered (std O), *07* | 150 | | ___ |
| **34544** | ATSF F3 Diesel B Unit, CC, *08* | 270 | | ___ |
| **34545** | D&RGW F3 Diesel B Unit, CC, *08* | 270 | | ___ |
| **34546** | Southern F3 Diesel B Unit, CC, *08* | 270 | | ___ |
| **34547** | *Texas Special* F3 Diesel B Unit, CC, *08* | 270 | | ___ |
| **34559** | Archive New Haven F3 Diesel AA Set, *10* | 500 | | ___ |
| **34564** | SP Alco PA Diesel AA Set, CC, *10* | 750 | | ___ |
| **34567** | SP Alco PB B Unit, CC, *10* | 400 | | ___ |
| **34570** | B&O FA Diesel AA Set, CC, *10* | 650 | | ___ |
| **34581** | Postwar "2331" Virginian Train Master Diesel, CC, *10* | 495 | | ___ |
| **34582** | Postwar "2373" CP F3 Diesel AA Set, CC, *10* | 700 | | ___ |
| **34585** | Postwar "2375" CP F3 B Unit, CC, *10* | 380 | | ___ |
| **34586** | Postwar "2378" MILW F3 Diesel AB Set, CC, *10* | 700 | | ___ |
| **34589** | Postwar "2377" MILW F3 A, powered, CC, *10* | 425 | | ___ |
| **35100** | NYC Vista Dome Car "7012," *07–09* | 45 | | ___ |
| **35101** | NYC Baggage Car "5028," *07* | 40 | | ___ |
| **35102** | Santa Fe *El Capitan* Streamliner Diner, *07* | 65 | | ___ |
| **35124** | *Alton Limited* Madison Passenger Car 4-pack, *08–10* | 240 | | ___ |
| **35128** | ATSF *El Capitan* Baggage Car "2103," *08* | 70 | | ___ |

Exc Mint Cond/$

| | | Exc | Mint | Cond/$ |
|---|---|---|---|---|
| 35129 | ATSF *El Capitan* Vista Dome Car "3153," *08* | | 70 | ___ |
| 35130 | *Polar Express* Disappearing Hobo Car, *08–10* | | 65 | ___ |
| 35133 | MTA Metro-North RR M-7 Commuter Add-on 2-pack, *07–08* | | 85 | ___ |
| 35134 | North Pole Central Vista Dome Car, *08* | | 45 | ___ |
| 35135 | North Pole Central Diner, *08–10* | | 45 | ___ |
| 35167 | PRR Diner "2044," *10* | | 52 | ___ |
| 35168 | PRR Coach "4046," *09* | | 52 | ___ |
| 35173 | North Pole Central Blitzen Coach, *09* | | 45 | ___ |
| 35174 | MTA LIRR M-7 Add-on 2-pack, *09* | | 98 | ___ |
| 35184 | Western & Atlantic Baggage Car, *09* | | 60 | ___ |
| 35185 | Great Western Passenger Car 2-pack, *09* | | 100 | ___ |
| 35193 | PRR Streamliner 4-pack, *10* | | 250 | ___ |
| 35200 | Strasburg Observation Car, *10* | | 60 | ___ |
| 35205 | D&RGW *Pikes Peak* Add-on Coach, *10* | | 70 | ___ |
| 35211 | Strasburg Passenger Car Add-on 2-pack, *10* | | 100 | ___ |
| 35403 | NYC *20th Century Limited* 18" Aluminum Passenger Car 4-pack (std O), *08* | | 625 | ___ |
| 35408 | NYC *20th Century Limited* 18" Aluminum Passenger Car 2-pack (std O), *08* | | 325 | ___ |
| 35411 | NYC *20th Century Limited* Diner, StationSounds (std O), *08* | | 325 | ___ |
| 35412 | Lenny Dean Passenger Coach, *08* | | 100 | ___ |
| 35413 | LL Streamliner Car 2-pack, *08* | | 270 | ___ |
| 35415 | UP 18" Streamliner Car 4-pack (std O), *08* | | 625 | ___ |
| 35423 | UP 18" Streamliner Car 2-pack (std O), *08* | | 325 | ___ |
| 35433 | Amfleet Phase IVB Coach 2-pack (std O), *10* | | 140 | ___ |
| 35454 | Amfleet Cab Control End Car (std O), *10* | | 90 | ___ |
| 35473 | Amfleet Capstone Coach 3-pack (std O), *10* | | 180 | ___ |
| 36000 | Route 66 Flatcar with 2 red sedans, *98* | | 44 | ___ |
| 36001 | Route 66 Flatcar with 2 wagons, *98* | | 42 | ___ |
| 36002 | Pratt's Hollow Passenger Car 4-pack, *98* | | 445 | ___ |
| 36006 | Uranium Flatcar "6508," *99* | | 60 | ___ |
| 36016 | Flatcar with propellers, *98* | | 45 | ___ |
| 36020 | Flatcar "TT-6424" with auto frames, *99* | | 32 | ___ |
| 36021 | Alaska Flatcar "6424" with airplane, *99* | | 44 | ___ |
| 36024 | J.B. Hunt Flatcar "64245" with trailer, *99* | | 44 | ___ |
| 36025 | J.B. Hunt Flatcar "64246" with trailer, *99* | | 50 | ___ |
| 36026 | Flatcar with J.B. Hunt trailers 2-pack, *99* | | 85 | ___ |
| 36027 | Tredegar Iron Works Flatcar with cannon, *99* | | 45 | ___ |
| 36028 | Heavy Artillery Flatcar with cannon, *99* | | 45 | ___ |
| 36029 | SP Auto Carrier "516712," *99* | | 44 | ___ |
| 36030 | Troublesome Truck #1, *99* | | 35 | ___ |
| 36031 | Troublesome Truck #2, *99* | | 35 | ___ |
| 36032 | Christmas Gondola "6462" with presents, *99* | | 35 | ___ |
| 36036 | C&O Gondola, *99* | | 20 | ___ |
| 36038 | Construction Zone Gondola, *99 u* | | NRS | ___ |
| 36040 | Bethlehem Flatcar with block (SSS), *99* | | 75 | ___ |
| 36041 | Bethlehem Ore Car (SSS), *99* | | 40 | ___ |

Exc Mint Cond/$

| | | Exc | Mint | Cond/$ |
|---|---|---|---|---|
| 36043 | Custom Consist Flatcar with pickup truck, *99* | | 40 | ___ |
| 36044 | Custom Consist Flatcar with dragster, *99* | | 40 | ___ |
| 36045 | Flatcar with dragster, *04* | | 30 | ___ |
| 36046 | Flatcar with custom truck, *04* | | 30 | ___ |
| 36047 | Construction Zone Gondola, *99 u* | | NRS | ___ |
| 36048 | Construction Zone Gondola, *99 u* | | NRS | ___ |
| 36054 | Archaeological Expedition Gondola with eggs, *00 u* | | 55 | ___ |
| 36055 | Flatcar with dragster, *01 u* | | 30 | ___ |
| 36056 | Flatcar with roadster, *01 u* | | 30 | ___ |
| 36059 | "Season's Greetings" Gondola, *99 u* | | 50 | ___ |
| 36062 | NYC 6462 Gondola, *99–00* | | 22 | ___ |
| 36063 | Conrail Gondola "604768," *99–00* | | 20 | ___ |
| 36064 | Billboard Flatcar "6424," *00* | | 41 | ___ |
| 36065 | Wabash Flatcar "25536" with trailer, *00* | | 35 | ___ |
| 36066 | Christmas Gondola with presents, *00* | | 32 | ___ |
| 36067 | King Auto Sales Flatcar "6424" with pink Cadillac, *00* | | 40 | ___ |
| 36068 | Pine Peak Tree Transport Gondola, *00* | | NRS | ___ |
| 36079 | Service Station Ltd. Flatcar with trailer, *00* | | 34 | ___ |
| 36082 | Whirlpool Flatcar with trailer, *00 u* | | NRS | ___ |
| 36083 | Santa Fe Gondola "168998," *01* | | 17 | ___ |
| 36084 | Grand Trunk Western Coil Car, *00* | | 32 | ___ |
| 36085 | FEC Coil Car, *00* | | 29 | ___ |
| 36086 | SP Flatcar with trailer, *01* | 34 | 35 | ___ |
| 36087 | Flatcar "6424" with wooden whistle, *01* | | 25 | ___ |
| 36088 | Allis Chalmers Condenser Car "6519," *00* | | 43 | ___ |
| 36089 | Frisco Flatcar with airplane, *00* | | 35 | ___ |
| 36090 | TT Flatcar "6424" with Pepsi truck, *01* | | 44 | ___ |
| 36091 | Maersk Flatcar "250129" with die-cast tractors, *00* | | 55 | ___ |
| 36092 | Maersk Flatcar "250130" with die-cast frames, *00* | | 55 | ___ |
| 36093 | Soo TT Auto Carrier "906760," *00* | | 49 | ___ |
| 36094 | PC F9 Well Car "768122," *01* | | 41 | ___ |
| 36095 | Christmas Chase Gondola, *01* | | 37 | ___ |
| 36098 | PRR Gondola "385186," *01* | | 20 | ___ |
| 36099 | NYC Flatcar with stakes and bulkheads, *01* | | 25 | ___ |
| 36104 | Area 51 3-D Tank Car, *07* | | 60 | ___ |
| 36108 | Candy Cane 1-D Tank Car, *07* | | 60 | ___ |
| 36112 | NP 3-D Tank Car, *08* | | 35 | ___ |
| 36113 | IC 1-D Tank Car, *08* | | 35 | ___ |
| 36114 | ART Wood-sided Reefer, *08* | | 35 | ___ |
| 36117 | Lionel Lines 2-D Tank Car, *08* | | 50 | ___ |
| 36118 | NYC Pastel Stock Car "63561," *08–09* | | 55 | ___ |
| 36128 | Texas & Pacific 3-D Tank Car, *09* | | 40 | ___ |
| 36129 | British Columbia 1-D Tank Car, *09* | | 40 | ___ |
| 36131 | Lackawanna Wood-sided Reefer "7000," *09–10* | | 40 | ___ |

Exc Mint Cond/$

| | | Exc | Mint | Cond/$ |
|---|---|---|---|---|
| 36145 | Philadelphia Quartz 3-D Tank Car "606," *10* | | 40 | ___ |
| 36146 | Cities Service 1-D Tank Car "11800," *10* | | 40 | ___ |
| 36149 | Strasburg Wood-sided Reefer "105," *10* | | 55 | ___ |
| 36151 | Grave's Blood Bank Tank Car, *10* | | 50 | ___ |
| 36200 | Quaker Life Cereal Boxcar, *00* | 400 | 420 | ___ |
| 36203 | Whirlpool Boxcar, *00 u* | | 110 | ___ |
| 36205 | eBay Boxcar, *00* | | 213 | ___ |
| 36206 | REA Boxcar, *01* | | 25 | ___ |
| 36207 | Vapor Records Christmas Boxcar, *01* | | 38 | ___ |
| 36208 | Father's Day Boxcar, *00* | | 35 | ___ |
| 36210 | Burlington Hi-Cube Boxcar "19825," *01* | | 40 | ___ |
| 36211 | NP Hi-Cube Boxcar "659999," *01* | | 33 | ___ |
| 36212 | Lionel Employee Christmas Boxcar, *00 u* | | 400 | ___ |
| 36213 | Vapor Records Christmas Boxcar, *00* | | 39 | ___ |
| 36215 | Train Station 25th Anniversary Boxcar, *00 u* | | 48 | ___ |
| 36218 | Snap-On Boxcar, *00 u* | | 115 | ___ |
| 36219 | UP Boxcar "183518," *02* | | 78 | ___ |
| 36220 | Pioneer Seed Boxcar, *00 u* | | NRS | ___ |
| 36221 | PRR Boxcar "569356," *01* | | 20 | ___ |
| 36222 | NYC Boxcar "162440," *01* | | 20 | ___ |
| 36223 | Chessie System Boxcar, *01* | | 20 | ___ |
| 36224 | Santa Fe Boxcar "16263," *01* | | 20 | ___ |
| 36225 | C&O Boxcar "250549," *01* | | 20 | ___ |
| 36226 | E-Hobbies Boxcar, *01 u* | | 179 | ___ |
| 36227 | Monopoly Community Chest Boxcar, *00 u* | | 50 | ___ |
| 36228 | Lionel Visitor Center Boxcar, *01 u* | | 34 | ___ |
| 36229 | Island Trains 20th Anniversary Boxcar, *01 u* | | 29 | ___ |
| 36232 | Farmall Boxcar, *01 u* | | NRS | ___ |
| 36236 | TM Books "I Love Lionel" Boxcar "7474-1," *01 u* | | 43 | ___ |
| 36238 | Snap-On Tool Team ASE Racing Boxcar, *01 u* | | NRS | ___ |
| 36239 | L.L. Bean Boxcar, *01 u* | | 110 | ___ |
| 36240 | Do It Best Boxcar, *01 u* | | 100 | ___ |
| 36242 | Erie-Lackawanna Boxcar "73113," *02* | | 24 | ___ |
| 36243 | Christmas Boxcar "2002," *02* | | 31 | ___ |
| 36244 | Teddy Bear Centennial Boxcar, *02* | | 36 | ___ |
| 36245 | Lionel 20th Century Boxcar "1900-1925," *00 u* | | 30 | ___ |
| 36246 | Lionel 20th Century Boxcar "1926-1950," *00 u* | | 30 | ___ |
| 36247 | Lionel 20th Century Boxcar "1951-1975," *00 u* | | 30 | ___ |
| 36248 | Lionel 20th Century Boxcar "1976-2000," *00 u* | | 30 | ___ |
| 36253 | Christmas Boxcar (O), *03* | | 32 | ___ |
| 36254 | Goofy Hi-Cube Boxcar, *03* | | 37 | ___ |
| 36255 | Donald Duck Hi-Cube Boxcar, *03* | | 40 | ___ |
| 36256 | GN Boxcar "6341," *03* | | 23 | ___ |
| 36264 | Santa Fe Boxcar "600196, *02* | | 18 | ___ |
| 36265 | Angela Trotta Thomas "Window Wishing" Boxcar, *02* | | 38 | ___ |
| 36267 | Mickey Mouse Hi-Cube Boxcar, *03* | | 50 | ___ |

Exc Mint Cond/$

| | | Exc | Mint | Cond/$ |
|---|---|---|---|---|
| 36270 | Angela Trotta Thomas "Home for the Holidays" Boxcar, *02–03* | | 30 | ___ |
| 36272 | New Haven Boxcar "6501," *04* | | 20 | ___ |
| 36273 | Railbox Hi-Cube Boxcar "15000," *04* | | 21 | ___ |
| 36275 | Christmas Boxcar, *04* | | 35 | ___ |
| 36276 | Angela Trotta Thomas "Tis the Season" Boxcar, *04* | | 34 | ___ |
| 36277 | Pluto Hi-Cube Boxcar, *04–05* | | 50 | ___ |
| 36278 | Winnie the Pooh Hi-Cube Boxcar, *04–05* | | 50 | ___ |
| 36291 | *Simpsons* Boxcar, *04–05* | | 44 | ___ |
| 36294 | UP Hi-Cube Boxcar, traditional, *05* | | 27 | ___ |
| 36295 | CN Boxcar, traditional, *05* | | 27 | ___ |
| 36296 | 2005 Holiday Boxcar, *05* | | 48 | ___ |
| 36297 | Angela Trotta Thomas "Christmas Eve" Boxcar, *05* | | 48 | ___ |
| 36305 | eBay Boxcar, *00 u* | | 100 | ___ |
| 36500 | Western Pacific Caboose "36500," *04* | | 23 | ___ |
| 36501 | D&RGW Caboose "36501," *04* | | 22 | ___ |
| 36502 | Reading Caboose "36502," *04* | | 25 | ___ |
| 36515 | North Pole Central Lines Caboose "36515," *04* | | 36 | ___ |
| 36519 | Lionel Lines Caboose, *04* | | 22 | ___ |
| 36520 | Santa Fe Caboose "36520," *04* | | 22 | ___ |
| 36525 | CSX Work Caboose, lighted, *05* | | 35 | ___ |
| 36526 | Pennsylvania Work Caboose, traditional, *05* | | 27 | ___ |
| 36527 | Santa Fe Work Caboose, traditional, *05* | | 28 | ___ |
| 36528 | Chesapeake & Ohio Work Caboose, traditional, *05* | | 40 | ___ |
| 36529 | North Pole Central Work Caboose with presents, traditional, *05* | | 38 | ___ |
| 36530 | Pennsylvania Caboose, traditional, *05* | | 33 | ___ |
| 36531 | Erie Caboose "C150," traditional, *05* | | 33 | ___ |
| 36532 | SP Caboose "1097," traditional, *05* | | 48 | ___ |
| 36533 | Reading Caboose "92803," traditional, *05* | | 33 | ___ |
| 36534 | NYC Center Cupola Caboose, traditional, *05* | | 40 | ___ |
| 36535 | LL Center Cupola Caboose, traditional, *05* | | 28 | ___ |
| 36536 | Southern Center Cupola Caboose, traditional, *05* | | 40 | ___ |
| 36547 | Bethlehem Steel Transfer Caboose, traditional, *05* | | 40 | ___ |
| 36548 | Transylvania RR Work Caboose, traditional, *05* | | 45 | ___ |
| 36550 | Halloween Transfer Caboose, traditional, *06–07* | | 45 | ___ |
| 36551 | Christmas Caboose, *06* | | 45 | ___ |
| 36552 | U.S. Steel Work Caboose, traditional, *06–07* | | 45 | ___ |
| 36554 | SP Work Caboose, traditional, *06* | | 45 | ___ |
| 36555 | Pennsylvania Transfer Caboose, *06* | | 45 | ___ |
| 36556 | Lionel Lines Work Caboose, *06–07* | | 30 | ___ |
| 36557 | Rio Grande Work Caboose, traditional, *06* | | 29 | ___ |
| 36558 | Virginian Center Cupola Caboose "316," traditional, *06* | | 45 | ___ |
| 36559 | WM Center Cupola Caboose "1863," traditional, *06* | | 45 | ___ |

| | | Exc | Mint | Cond/S |
|---|---|---|---|---|
| 36560 | C&O Center Cupola Caboose "90876," traditional, 06 | | 45 | ___ |
| 36562 | Army Transportation Work Caboose, traditional, 06 | | 45 | ___ |
| 36563 | Reading Work Caboose, traditional, 06 | | 45 | ___ |
| 36565 | UP SP-type Caboose, traditional, 06 | | 48 | ___ |
| 36566 | NYC SP-type Caboose, traditional, 06 | | 48 | ___ |
| 36567 | GN SP-type Caboose, traditional, 06 | | 48 | ___ |
| 36580 | B&O Center Cupola Caboose "C2047," traditional, 05 | | 40 | ___ |
| 36582 | C&O Caboose, 05 | | 22 | ___ |
| 36583 | Holiday Caboose, 07 | | 50 | ___ |
| 36587 | SP Caboose "1121," 07–09 | | 40 | ___ |
| 36589 | PRR Work Caboose, 07 | | 40 | ___ |
| 36590 | UP Work Caboose, 07 | | 45 | ___ |
| 36591 | Southern Caboose "X99," 08 | | 45 | ___ |
| 36592 | Santa Fe Caboose "999471," 06 | | 48 | ___ |
| 36593 | NYC Caboose, 06 | | 48 | ___ |
| 36601 | UP Caboose, 06 | | 48 | ___ |
| 36602 | UPS Centennial Caboose, 06 | | 45 | ___ |
| 36604 | Pennsylvania Caboose, 06 | | 25 | ___ |
| 36607 | K-Line Caboose, 06 | | 40 | ___ |
| 36611 | Conrail Caboose "19674," 07 | | 40 | ___ |
| 36612 | Alaska Caboose "1080," 07 | | 40 | ___ |
| 36613 | NYC Caboose, 07 | | 30 | ___ |
| 36622 | C&O Caboose "C-1838," 08–09 | | 40 | ___ |
| 36623 | ATSF Caboose, 07–09 | | 40 | ___ |
| 36624 | Lionel Lines Caboose, 08–09 | | 40 | ___ |
| 36625 | B&M Caboose, 08 | | 50 | ___ |
| 36626 | Erie Caboose "C101," 08–09 | | 45 | ___ |
| 36634 | Holiday Porthole Caboose, green, 08 | | 50 | ___ |
| 36646 | Monopoly Caboose, 10 | | 48 | ___ |
| 36647 | Strasburg Caboose, 10 | | 48 | ___ |
| 36649 | Pennsylvania Power & Light Work Caboose, 10 | | 45 | ___ |
| 36657 | Western & Atlantic Caboose, 10 | | 48 | ___ |
| 36701 | Baldwin Locomotive Works Operating Welding Car "36701," 02 | | 60 | ___ |
| 36702 | Bosco Operating Milk Car with platform, 02 | | 115 | ___ |
| 36703 | Circus Horse Car with corral, 06 | | 150 | ___ |
| 36704 | Animated Reindeer Stock Car and Corral, 02 | | 145 | ___ |
| 36718 | AEC Security Caboose, 02 | | 42 | ___ |
| 36719 | Lionel Lion Bobbing Head Car, 02 | | 20 | ___ |
| 36720 | Aladdin Aquarium Car, 03 | | 40 | ___ |
| 36721 | 101 Dalmatians Animated Gondola, 03 | | 45 | ___ |
| 36722 | Peter Pan Bobbing Head Boxcar, 03 | | 45 | ___ |
| 36726 | Santa Fe Searchlight Car "36726," 03 | | 50 | ___ |
| 36727 | Weyerhaeuser Moe & Joe Flatcar, 03 | | 65 | ___ |
| 36728 | SP Walking Brakeman Boxcar 163143," 03 | | 42 | ___ |
| 36729 | Lionel Lines Animated Caboose, 04–05 | | 75 | ___ |

Exc Mint Cond/$

| | | Exc | Mint | Cond/$ |
|---|---|---|---|---|
| **36730** | U.S. Army Missile Launch Sound Car "44," *03* | | 175 | ___ |
| **36731** | Motorized Aquarium Car "3435," *03* | | 83 | ___ |
| **36732** | C&NW Jumping Hobo Car, *03* | | 41 | ___ |
| **36733** | Christmas Music Boxcar, *03* | | 45 | ___ |
| **36734** | Santa Fe Operating Searchlight Car "20611," *02* | | 25 | ___ |
| **36735** | WP Ice Car "7045," *02* | | 55 | ___ |
| **36736** | D&RGW Stock Car "39268," RailSounds, *04* | | 45 | ___ |
| **36738** | T&P Poultry Dispatch Car "36738," *02* | | 50 | ___ |
| **36739** | Postwar "3461" Lionel Lines Log Dump Car, *03* | | 50 | ___ |
| **36740** | Postwar "3469" Lionel Lines Coal Dump Car, *03* | | 49 | ___ |
| **36743** | Santa Claus Bobbing Head Boxcar, *03* | | 40 | ___ |
| **36744** | *Little Mermaid* Aquarium Car, *03* | | 55 | ___ |
| **36745** | *Toy Story* Animated Gondola, *03* | | 70 | ___ |
| **36753** | LFD Firecar with ladder, *02* | | 60 | ___ |
| **36757** | Southern Searchlight Car, *03–04* | | NRS | ___ |
| **36758** | Patriotic Lighted Boxcar, *02* | | 60 | ___ |
| **36760** | B&O Sentinel Operating Brakeman Boxcar "3424," Archive Collection, *02* | | 65 | ___ |
| **36761** | Wellspring Capital Management Lighted Boxcar, *02 u* | | 210 | ___ |
| **36764** | West Side Lumber Log Dump Car "36764," *03* | | 55 | ___ |
| **36765** | Alaska Coal Dump Car "401," *03* | | 50 | ___ |
| **36767** | Santa's Radar Tracking Car, *03* | | 40 | ___ |
| **36769** | Fourth of July Lighted Boxcar, *03* | | 70 | ___ |
| **36770** | American Refrigerator Transit Ice Car "23701," *04* | | 42 | ___ |
| **36771** | CN Barrel Car "74208," *04* | | 48 | ___ |
| **36772** | Spokane, Portland & Seattle Log Dump Car "36772," *04* | | 46 | ___ |
| **36773** | Jersey Central Coal Dump Car "92926," *04* | | 45 | ___ |
| **36774** | PRR Moe & Joe Lumber Flatcar, *04* | | 50 | ___ |
| **36775** | Santa Fe Animated Caboose "999010," *05* | | 75 | ___ |
| **36776** | Santa Fe Walking Brakeman Car "19938," *04* | | 43 | ___ |
| **36778** | C&O Searchlight Car "216614," *04* | | 30 | ___ |
| **36780** | Sea-Monkeys Motorized Aquarium Car, *04* | | 45 | ___ |
| **36781** | *Finding Nemo* Aquarium Car, *04* | | 50 | ___ |
| **36782** | Goofy and Pete Jumping Boxcar, *05* | | 70 | ___ |
| **36783** | Disney Operating Boxcar, *04–05* | | 65 | ___ |
| **36784** | *Monsters Inc.* Bobbing Head Boxcar, *04* | | 40 | ___ |
| **36786** | Postwar "3494-150" MP Operating Boxcar, *03* | | 40 | ___ |
| **36787** | M.O.W. Remote Control Searchlight Car, *04* | | 45 | ___ |
| **36788** | Lionel Lines Tender, TrainSounds, *04* | | 75 | ___ |
| **36789** | Railbox Boxcar, TrainSounds, *04–05* | | 105 | ___ |
| **36790** | Christmas Music Boxcar, *04* | | 70 | ___ |
| **36793** | Pennsylvania Derrick Car, *03* | | 22 | ___ |
| **36794** | NYC Log Dump Car, *03* | | 25 | ___ |
| **36795** | Southern Coal Dump Car, *03* | | 25 | ___ |
| **36796** | GN Searchlight Car, *03* | | 24 | ___ |
| **36797** | "Operation Iraqi Freedom" Minuteman Car, *03* | | 45 | ___ |

| | | Exc | Mint | Cond/S |
|---|---|---|---|---|
| 36803 | Santa Animated Caboose, *06* | | 8 | ___ |
| 36804 | Candy Cane Dump Car, *06* | | 80 | ___ |
| 36805 | Reindeer Jumping Boxcar, *06* | | 70 | ___ |
| 36809 | NYC Derrick Car, *07–08* | | 35 | ___ |
| 36810 | PRR Searchlight Car, *07* | | 35 | ___ |
| 36811 | UP Dump Coal Dump Car, *07* | | 35 | ___ |
| 36812 | British Columbia Log Dump Car, *07–08* | | 35 | ___ |
| 36813 | State of Maine Brakeman Car, *08* | | 80 | ___ |
| 36814 | D&RGW Animated Caboose "01415," *07–09* | | 80 | ___ |
| 36815 | Santa Fe Moe & Joe Flatcar, *07–08* | | 80 | ___ |
| 36816 | Virginian Coal Dump Car, *08* | | 80 | ___ |
| 36818 | U.S. Steel Searchlight Car, *07–08* | | 75 | ___ |
| 36821 | "Naughty or Nice" Dump Car, *07* | | 80 | ___ |
| 36823 | Halloween SpookySmoke Boxcar, *07* | | 110 | ___ |
| 36824 | AlienSmoke Boxcar, *07* | | 110 | ___ |
| 36829 | Alien Radioactive Car, *07* | | 70 | ___ |
| 36830 | Trick or Treat Aquarium Car, *07* | | 75 | ___ |
| 36831 | M.O.W. Welding Car, *07–08* | | 75 | ___ |
| 36833 | Christmas Music Boxcar, *07* | | 65 | ___ |
| 36834 | Santa Fe Transparent Instruction Car, *07–08* | | 65 | ___ |
| 36838 | Lionel Power Co. Voltmeter Car, K-Line, *06* | | 75 | ___ |
| 36839 | Operating Milk Car with platform, K-Line, *06* | | 140 | ___ |
| 36841 | Visitor Center 15th Anniversary Lighted Boxcar, *06* | | 70 | ___ |
| 36847 | *Polar Express* Tender, TrainSounds, *08–10* | | 115 | ___ |
| 36848 | Candy Cane Dump Car, *07* | | 80 | ___ |
| 36849 | Tell-Tale Reindeer Car, *07* | | 53 | ___ |
| 36850 | Santa and Snowman Boxcar, *07* | | 75 | ___ |
| 36851 | Generator Car with Christmas tree, *07* | | 75 | ___ |
| 36853 | U.S. Army Exploding Boxcar, *08* | | 60 | ___ |
| 36855 | GW Horse Car and Corral, *08* | | 160 | ___ |
| 36856 | W&ARR Sheriff and Outlaw Car, *08* | | 75 | ___ |
| 36857 | Bobbing Ghost Boxcar, *08* | | 65 | ___ |
| 36859 | Lionel Lines Aquarium Car, *08* | | 80 | ___ |
| 36861 | PRR Poultry Dispatch Car, *08–09* | | 80 | ___ |
| 36863 | Alien Security Car, *08* | | 80 | ___ |
| 36864 | Bethlehem Steel Searchlight Car, *08* | | 40 | ___ |
| 36866 | WP Coal Dump Car "52369," *08* | | 40 | ___ |
| 36868 | NH Barrel Ramp Car, *08* | | 40 | ___ |
| 36869 | Bobbing Santa Boxcar, *08* | | 65 | ___ |
| 36870 | Postwar "6812" Track Maintenance Car, *08* | | 65 | ___ |
| 36875 | *Polar Express* Coach, sound, *08–10* | | 115 | ___ |
| 36878 | NYC Track Cleaning Car, *08* | | 150 | ___ |
| 36879 | REA Ice Car "1221," *08* | | 65 | ___ |
| 36880 | Koi Fish Aquarium Car, *10* | | 75 | ___ |
| 36881 | Christmas Music Boxcar, *08* | | 70 | ___ |
| 36887 | Great Western Animated Gondola, *08–09* | | 65 | ___ |
| 36888 | Casper Aquarium Car, *09–10* | | 90 | ___ |

Exc  Mint  Cond/$

| | | Exc | Mint | Cond/$ |
|---|---|---|---|---|
| 36889 | PRR Barrel Ramp Car, *09–10* | | 46 | ____ |
| 36893 | UP Transparent Instruction Car "195220," *09–10* | | 75 | ____ |
| 36897 | Pennsylvania Power & Light Coal Dump Car, *09–10* | | 46 | ____ |
| 36896 | Christmas Music Boxcar, *09* | | 80 | ____ |
| 36898 | Wisconsin Central Log Dump Car, *09* | | 46 | ____ |
| 36900 | Depressed Center Flatcar with backshop load, *99* | | 115 | ____ |
| 36913 | Allied Chemical 1-D Tank Car 2-pack, *00* | | 150 | ____ |
| 36914 | Allied Chemical 1-D Tank Car "68075," die-cast, white, *00* | | 90 | ____ |
| 36915 | Allied Chemical 1-D Tank Car "68076," die-cast, white, *00* | | 90 | ____ |
| 36916 | Allied Chemical 1-D Tank Car 2-pack, *00* | | 175 | ____ |
| 36917 | Allied Chemical 1-D Tank Car "65124," die-cast, black, *00* | | 95 | ____ |
| 36918 | Allied Chemical 1-D Tank Car "65125," die-cast, black, *00* | | 90 | ____ |
| 36927 | B&O DC Hopper 6-pack, "435040-45," *01* | | 520 | ____ |
| 36935 | Maersk Maxi-Stack Car 2-pack, "250131-32," *00* | | 135 | ____ |
| 36937 | SP Maxi-Stack Car "513957," *02* | | 65 | ____ |
| 37001 | No. 3444 Erie Animated Gondola, *09* | | 70 | ____ |
| 37002 | Operating Plutonium Car 2-pack, *10* | | 140 | ____ |
| 37003 | PRR Jet Snow Blower "491252," *09–10* | | 138 | ____ |
| 37004 | Area 51 Searchlight Car, *09* | | 46 | ____ |
| 37006 | Lionel Flatcar with operating LCD billboard, *09* | | 180 | ____ |
| 37009 | Smoking Mount St. Helens Boxcar, *10* | | 125 | ____ |
| 37010 | Pennsylvania Power & Light Searchlight Car, *10* | | 46 | ____ |
| 37011 | B&M Operating Milk Car with platform, *10* | | 155 | ____ |
| 37012 | GN Jumping Hobo Boxcar, *10* | | 75 | ____ |
| 37807 | Station Platform, *10* | | 21 | ____ |
| 37808 | Sunoco Spherical Oil Tank, *10* | | 100 | ____ |
| 37810 | Curved O Gauge Tunnel, *10* | | 40 | ____ |
| 37813 | Christmas Tractor and Trailer with trees, *10* | | 27 | ____ |
| 37814 | Christmas Crossing Shanty, *10* | | 23 | ____ |
| 37900 | Silver Truss Bridge, *10* | | 70 | ____ |
| 37901 | Lehigh Valley Tugboat, *10* | | 270 | ____ |
| 37902 | Illuminated Barge, *10* | | 180 | ____ |
| 37903 | Cell Tower, *10* | | 60 | ____ |
| 37904 | Boy Scouts Billboard Set, *10* | | 13 | ____ |
| 37907 | Christmas Street Lamps with wreaths, *10* | | 30 | ____ |
| 37910 | Operating Lighthouse, *10* | | 180 | ____ |
| 37911 | D&RGW Blinking Light Water Tower, *10* | | 30 | ____ |
| 37912 | Lighted Coaling Tower, *10* | | 180 | ____ |
| 37913 | Hopper Shed, *10* | | 35 | ____ |
| 37914 | Work House, *10* | | 28 | ____ |
| 37916 | Beige Brick Suburban House, *10* | | 80 | ____ |
| 37917 | Red Brick Suburban House, *10* | | 80 | ____ |

| | | Exc | Mint | Cond/$ |
|---|---|---|---|---|
| 37919 | Operating Sawmill, *10* | | 130 | ___ |
| 37920 | Bascule Bridge, *10* | | 350 | ___ |
| 37992 | Coca-Cola Blinking Light Billboard, *10* | | 28 | ___ |
| 38004 | Virginian 4-6-0 10-wheel Locomotive "203," CC, *01–02* | | 570 | ___ |
| 38005 | Long Island 4-6-0 10-wheel Locomotive "138," CC, *01–02* | | 510 | ___ |
| 38007 | UP Auxiliary tender, black, CC, *01* | | 200 | ___ |
| 38008 | UP Auxiliary tender, gray, CC, *01* | | 205 | ___ |
| 38009 | D&RGW 4-6-6-4 Challenger Locomotive "3803," CC, *01* | | 1550 | ___ |
| 38010 | Clinchfield 4-6-6-4 Challenger Locomotive "673," CC, *01* | | 1400 | ___ |
| 38012 | Wheeling & Lake Erie 2-6-6-2 Locomotive "8005," CC, *01* | | 610 | ___ |
| 38013 | D&H 4-6-6-4 Challenger Locomotive "1527," CC, *01* | | 720 | ___ |
| 38014 | D&RGW 4-6-6-4 Challenger Locomotive "3800," CC, *01* | | 710 | ___ |
| 38015 | NYC 4-6-4 Hudson Locomotive "773," CC, *01* | | 900 | ___ |
| 38016 | Southern 0-8-0 Yard Goat Locomotive "6536," CC, *01–02, 05* | | 530 | ___ |
| 38017 | CN 2-6-0 Mogul Locomotive "86," CC, *03, 05* | | 600 | ___ |
| 38018 | Wabash 2-6-0 Mogul Locomotive "826," CC, *03* | | 485 | ___ |
| 38019 | B&M 2-6-0 Mogul Locomotive "1455," CC, *03, 05* | | 600 | ___ |
| 38020 | PRR 4-4-4-4 T1 Duplex Locomotive "5514," *02–03* | | 630 | ___ |
| 38021 | WP 4-6-6-4 Challenger Locomotive "402," CC, *02* | | 650 | ___ |
| 38022 | WM 4-6-6-4 Challenger Locomotive "1206," CC, *02* | | 690 | ___ |
| 38023 | UP 4-6-6-4 Challenger Locomotive "3976," CC, *02* | | 620 | ___ |
| 38024 | PRR 6-4-4-6 S-1 Duplex Locomotive "6100," TMCC, *03* | | 1000 | ___ |
| 38025 | PRR 4-6-2 K4 Pacific Locomotive "1361," CC, *02* | | 950 | ___ |
| 38026 | N&W 4-8-4 J Class Northern Locomotive "606," CC, *02* | | 1450 | ___ |
| 38027 | Meadow River Lumber Heisler Geared Locomotive "6," CC, *03* | | 880 | ___ |
| 38028 | PRR 6-8-6 S2 Steam Turbine Locomotive, *01* | | 650 | ___ |
| 38029 | UP 4-12-2 Locomotive "9000," CC, *03* | | 570 | ___ |
| 38030 | Santa Fe 2-8-8-2 Locomotive "1795," CC, *03* | | 920 | ___ |
| 38031 | SP 2-8-8-4 AC-9 Locomotive "3809," CC, *04* | | 1100 | ___ |
| 38032 | Virginian 2-8-8-2 Locomotive "741," CC, *03* | | 928 | ___ |
| 38036 | Long Island 2-8-0 Consolidation Locomotive, *01* | | 500 | ___ |
| 38037 | PRR Reading Seashore 2-8-0 Consolidation Locomotive "6072," CC, *01* | | 495 | ___ |
| 38038 | D&RGW Auxiliary Water Tender, *01* | | 230 | ___ |
| 38039 | Clinchfield Auxiliary Water Tender, *01* | | 220 | ___ |

Exc Mint Cond/$

| | | Exc | Mint | Cond/$ |
|---|---|---|---|---|
| 38040 | LV 4-6-0 Camelback Locomotive, *01* | | 405 | ___ |
| 38042 | C&NW 4-6-0 10-wheel Locomotive "361," CC, *02* | | 450 | ___ |
| 38043 | Frisco 4-6-0 10-wheel Locomotive "719," CC, *02* | | 525 | ___ |
| 38044 | PRR 4-6-2 K4 Pacific Locomotive "5385," CC, *02* | | 920 | ___ |
| 38045 | NYC Hudson J-3a 4-6-4 Locomotive "5418," CC, *03* | | 495 | ___ |
| 38046 | GN 0-8-0 Locomotive "815," CC, *02* | | 530 | ___ |
| 38047 | N&W 0-8-0 Locomotive "266," CC, *02* | | 550 | ___ |
| 38048 | NPR 0-8-0 Locomotive "303," CC, *02* | | 530 | ___ |
| 38049 | N&W 2-6-6-4 Locomotive "1234," CC, *02* | | 690 | ___ |
| 38050 | Nickel Plate 2-8-4 Berkshire Locomotive "779," CC, *03* | | 925 | ___ |
| 38051 | Erie 2-8-4 Berkshire Locomotive "3315," CC, *03* | | 810 | ___ |
| 38052 | Pere Marquette 2-8-4 Berkshire Locomotive "1225," CC, *03* | | 1000 | ___ |
| 38053 | NYC 4-8-2 Mohawk L-2a Locomotive "2793," CC, *03* | | 915 | ___ |
| 38055 | Santa Fe 4-8-4 Northern Locomotive "3751" CC, *04* | | 1100 | ___ |
| 38056 | PRR 4-8-2 Mountain M1a Locomotive "6759," CC, *03* | | 850 | ___ |
| 38057 | Weyerhaeuser Shay Locomotive, CC, *03* | | 1000 | ___ |
| 38058 | C&O 2-8-8-2 H7 Locomotive "1580," CC, *04* | | 1200 | ___ |
| 38060 | UP 2-8-8-2 H7 Locomotive "3590," CC, *04* | | 1200 | ___ |
| 38061 | Cass Scenic Heisler Geared Locomotive "6," CC, *03* | | 940 | ___ |
| 38062 | Lionel Lines 4-6-2 Pacific Locomotive "8062," CC, *02–03* | | 275 | ___ |
| 38065 | UP 2-8-8-2 Mallet Locomotive "3672," CC, *02* | | 1002 | ___ |
| 38066 | Elk River Shay Locomotive, CC, *03* | | 1000 | ___ |
| 38067 | MILW 4-6-2 Pacific Locomotive "6316," CC, *03* | | 300 | ___ |
| 38068 | WM 4-6-2 Pacific Locomotive "204," CC, *03* | | 300 | ___ |
| 38069 | Erie Hudson Locomotive, whistle, *05* | | 150 | ___ |
| 38070 | C&O 4-6-2 Pacific Locomotive "489," CC, *04* | | 300 | ___ |
| 38071 | SP Cab Forward AC-12 Locomotive "4294," CC, *05* | | 1550 | ___ |
| 38075 | UP 4-8-8-4 Big Boy Locomotive "4024," LionMaster, *03* | | 800 | ___ |
| 38076 | C&O 2-8-4 Berkshire Locomotive "2699," CC, *04* | | 860 | ___ |
| 38077 | Virginian 2-8-4 Berkshire Locomotive "508," CC, *04* | | 1000 | ___ |
| 38079 | SP 4-8-4 Northern GS-2 Locomotive "4410" CC, *04* | | 980 | ___ |
| 38080 | WP 4-8-4 Northern GS-64 Locomotive "485" CC, *04* | | 1000 | ___ |
| 38081 | C&O 2-6-6-6 Allegheny Locomotive "1650," CC, *05–07* | | 1700 | ___ |

Exc Mint Cond/S

| | | Exc | Mint | Cond/S |
|---|---|---|---|---|
| 38082 | Pennsylvania 2-8-8-2 Y3 Locomotive "374," CC, 04 | | 1000 | ___ |
| 38083 | N&W 2-8-8-2 Y3 Locomotive "2009," CC, 04 | | 910 | ___ |
| 38085 | NYC 4-6-4 Hudson J-3a Locomotive 5422," CC, 03 | | 495 | ___ |
| 38086 | B&A 4-6-4 Hudson Locomotive "607," CC, 03 | | 495 | ___ |
| 38087 | Nickel Plate 2-8-4 Berkshire Locomotive, RailSounds, 05 | | 190 | ___ |
| 38088 | NYC 2-6-0 Mogul Locomotive "1924," CC, 03, 05 | | 600 | ___ |
| 38089 | Pennsylvania 4-6-2 Pacific Locomotive "3678," CC, 04 | | 300 | ___ |
| 38090 | Clinchfield 4-6-6-4 Challenger Locomotive "672" CC, 04 | | 640 | ___ |
| 38091 | NP 4-6-6-4 Challenger Locomotive "5121" CC, 04 | | 660 | ___ |
| 38092 | Pickering Lumber Heisler Locomotive "5," CC, 04 | | 1000 | ___ |
| 38093 | UP 4-6-6-4 Challenger Locomotive "3980," CC, 04 | | 700 | ___ |
| 38094 | MILW *Hiawatha* 4-4-2 Atlantic Locomotive, CC, 06 | | 950 | ___ |
| 38095 | N&W 4-8-4 J Class Locomotive "611," CC, 05–06 | | 1250 | ___ |
| 38100 | *Texas Special* F3 Diesel AB Set, 99 | 860 | 930 | ___ |
| 38103 | *Texas Special* F3 Diesel "2245," 99 | 435 | 510 | ___ |
| 38114 | ATSF FT Diesel B Unit, 99–00 | | 170 | ___ |
| 38115 | NYC FT Diesel B Unit "2403," nonpowered, 99–00 | | 130 | ___ |
| 38116 | B&O FT Diesel B Unit, 99–00 | | 130 | ___ |
| 38144 | C&O F3 Diesel AA Set "7019, 7021," 00 | | 700 | ___ |
| 38147 | GN Alco FA2 AA Diesel Set, CC, 02 | | 405 | ___ |
| 38150 | Platinum Ghost "2333," 99 | | 495 | ___ |
| 38153 | "Spirit of the Century" F3 Diesel AA Set, 99 | | 800 | ___ |
| 38160 | Pennsylvania Alco FB2 Diesel, 02 | | 125 | ___ |
| 38161 | MKT Alco FB2 Diesel, 02 | | 125 | ___ |
| 38162 | Burlington FT Diesel B Unit, 01 | | NRS | ___ |
| 38167 | Burlington FT Diesel AA Set, 01 | | 225 | ___ |
| 38176 | Pennsylvania Alco FA2 AA Diesel Set, CC, 02 | | 405 | ___ |
| 38182 | MKT Alco FA2 AA Diesel Set, CC, 02 | | 360 | ___ |
| 38188 | Southern F3 Diesel ABA Set, 00 | | 557 | ___ |
| 38194 | GN Alco FB2 Diesel, 02 | | 125 | ___ |
| 38196 | Santa Fe FT Diesel A Unit "171," 00 | | NRS | ___ |
| 38197 | SP F3 Diesel ABA Set, 00 | | 640 | ___ |
| 38202 | Wild West Handcar, 10 | | 75 | ___ |
| 38203 | Holly Jolly Trolley 2-car Set, 10 | | 160 | ___ |
| 38204 | ATSF FT B Unit, nonpowered, 10 | | 120 | ___ |
| 38210 | PRR Alco Diesel AA Set, CC, 10 | | 400 | ___ |
| 38215 | ATSF FT Diesel "165," RailSounds, 10 | | 280 | ___ |
| 38300 | Postwar "2331" Virginian Train Master Diesel, 08 | | 210 | ___ |
| 38303 | Postwar "2340" GG1 Electric Locomotive, 08 | | 280 | ___ |

| | | Exc | Mint | Cond/S |
|---|---|---|---|---|
| 38305 | Postwar "2338" Milwaukee Road GP7 Diesel, *08* | | 220 | ___ |
| 38310 | "2185W" NYC F3 Diesel Freight Set, *09* | | 600 | ___ |
| 38311 | "2276W" B&O RDC Commuter Set, *09* | | 470 | ___ |
| 38312 | "2343" Santa Fe F3 Diesel AA Set, *09* | | 500 | ___ |
| 38313 | B&O Budd RDC 2-pack, *09* | | 350 | ___ |
| 38323 | Postwar "2348" M&StL GP9 Diesel, CC, *10* | | 390 | ___ |
| 38324 | Postwar 2507W NH F3 Diesel Freight Set, *10* | | 600 | ___ |
| 38328 | Postwar 1623W NP GP9 Diesel Freight Set, *10* | | 750 | ___ |
| 38329 | Postwar 2261W Freight Hauler Set, *10* | | 610 | ___ |
| 38334 | Postwar 11288 Orbitor Diesel Freight Set, *10* | | 500 | ___ |
| 38339 | Postwar 2505W Virginian Rectifier Freight Set, *10* | | 470 | ___ |
| 38340 | Postwar 1587S Girl's Steam Freight Set, *10* | | 580 | ___ |
| 38342 | Postwar 1619W Santa Fe Freight Set, *10* | | 470 | ___ |
| 38401 | NYC M-497 Jet-Powered Rail Car, *10* | | 300 | ___ |
| 38402 | Amtrak HHP-8 Electric Locomotive, RailSounds, *10* | | 400 | ___ |
| 38600 | UP 0-6-0 Dockside Switcher "87," traditional, *07–09* | | 110 | ___ |
| 38601 | Lionel Lines 0-6-0 Dockside Switcher, traditional, *07–09* | | 110 | ___ |
| 38605 | PRR 0-4-0 Locomotive "94," traditional, *07* | | 170 | ___ |
| 38606 | SP 0-4-0 Locomotive "71," traditional, *07–08* | | 170 | ___ |
| 38607 | Southern 2-8-4 Berkshire Locomotive "2718," RailSounds, *07–08* | | 260 | ___ |
| 38608 | LL 2-8-2 Mikado Locomotive "57," RailSounds, *07* | | 260 | ___ |
| 38609 | NYC 2-8-2 Mikado Locomotive "1843," CC, *07* | | 370 | ___ |
| 38610 | NKP 2-8-4 Berkshire Locomotive "779," CC, *07–08* | | 370 | ___ |
| 38619 | Santa Fe 4-6-2 Pacific Locomotive "2037," traditional, K-Line, *06* | | 260 | ___ |
| 38620 | B&O Porter Locomotive "16," traditional, K-Line, *06* | | 100 | ___ |
| 38621 | 4-6-2 Pacific Locomotive, traditional, K-Line, *06* | | 260 | ___ |
| 38626 | Holiday 2-8-2 Mikado Locomotive "25," green, RailSounds, *08* | | 260 | ___ |
| 38627 | GN 4-4-2 Atlantic Locomotive "1702," traditional, *08–09* | | 110 | ___ |
| 38630 | U.S. Army 0-6-0 Dockside Switcher "486," traditional, *08–09* | | 110 | ___ |
| 38634 | NYC 4-6-4 Hudson Locomotive "5417," TrainSounds, *07* | | 200 | ___ |
| 38635 | C&O 4-6-4 Hudson Locomotive "309," TrainSounds, *08* | | 200 | ___ |
| 38636 | ATSF 4-6-4 Hudson Locomotive "3459," TrainSounds, *07* | | 200 | ___ |
| 38637 | LL 4-6-4 Hudson Locomotive "5242," TrainSounds, *08* | | 200 | ___ |
| 38638 | UP 4-6-2 Pacific Locomotive "2888," RailSounds, *08* | | 300 | ___ |

Exc Mint Cond/$

| No. | Description | Exc | Mint | Cond/$ |
|---|---|---|---|---|
| 38639 | Erie 4-6-2 Pacific Locomotive "2939," RailSounds, 08 | | 300 | ___ |
| 38640 | Southern 4-6-2 Pacific Locomotive "1317," RailSounds, 08 | | 300 | ___ |
| 38641 | B&M 4-6-2 Pacific Locomotive "3713," RailSounds, 08 | | 300 | ___ |
| 38642 | PRR 4-6-2 Pacific Locomotive "5385," RailSounds, 08 | | 300 | ___ |
| 38643 | Alaska Mikado 2-8-2 Locomotive "701," CC, 08–09 | | 280 | ___ |
| 38644 | T&P Mikado 2-8-2 Locomotive "810," CC, 08–09 | | 400 | ___ |
| 38649 | Christmas 4-6-4 Hudson Locomotive, traditional, 08 | | 220 | ___ |
| 38651 | Lionel Lines 0-8-0 Locomotive "100," traditional, 08–09 | | 120 | ___ |
| 38654 | Bethlehem Steel 0-4-0 Locomotive, traditional, 08–09 | | 170 | ___ |
| 38657 | Alton Limited Pacific 4-6-2 Locomotive "659," traditional, 08 | | 300 | ___ |
| 38658 | W&ARR 4-4-0 General "1892," TrainSounds, 08–09 | | 165 | ___ |
| 38664 | LL 4-4-2 Atlantic Locomotive "1058," traditional, 08–09 | | 110 | ___ |
| 38671 | Santa Flyer 4-6-0 Locomotive, 09 | | 200 | ___ |
| 38677 | Strasburg 0-6-0 Dockside Switcher "1252," 10 | | 130 | ___ |
| 38678 | Monopoly Hudson Locomotive, TrainSounds, 10 | | 240 | ___ |
| 38679 | ATSF 0-4-0 Switcher "1387," 10 | | 190 | ___ |
| 38684 | Pennsylvania Power & Light Docksider Switcher, 10 | | 110 | ___ |
| 38687 | Western & Atlantic 0-4-0 Locomotive "1897," 10 | | 190 | ___ |
| 38691 | North Pole Central Santa Flyer "2," 10 | | 190 | ___ |
| 38692 | Angela Trotta Thomas Signature Express, 10 | | 190 | ___ |
| 39008 | PRR Heavyweight Passenger Car 4-pack, 00 | | 225 | ___ |
| 39009 | PRR Indian Rock Heavyweight Combination Car, 00 | | 50 | ___ |
| 39010 | PRR Andrew Carnegie Heavyweight Passenger Coach, 00 | | 60 | ___ |
| 39011 | PRR Solomon P. Chase Heavyweight Passenger Coach, 00 | | 60 | ___ |
| 39012 | PRR Skyline View Heavyweight Observation Car, 00 | | 50 | ___ |
| 39013 | B&O Heavyweight Passenger Car 4-pack, 00 | | 400 | ___ |
| 39016 | B&O Heavyweight Passenger Car 4-pack, 00 | | 200 | ___ |
| 39017 | B&O Harper's Ferry Heavyweight Combination Car, 00 | | 50 | ___ |
| 39018 | B&O Youngstown Heavyweight Passenger Coach, 00 | | 50 | ___ |
| 39019 | B&O New Castle Heavyweight Passenger Coach, 00 | | 50 | ___ |
| 39020 | B&O Chicago Heavyweight Observation Car, 00 | | 50 | ___ |
| 39028 | LL Heavyweight Passenger Car 3-pack, 00 | | 195 | ___ |
| 39029 | LL Irvington Heavyweight Coach "2625," 00 | | 60 | ___ |

Exc Mint Cond/S

| | | Exc | Mint | Cond/S |
|---|---|---|---|---|
| 39030 | LL *Madison* Heavyweight Coach "2627," *00* | | 60 | |
| 39031 | LL *Manhattan* Heavyweight Coach "2628," *00* | | 60 | |
| 39032 | UP Madison Passenger Car 4-pack, *00* | | 275 | |
| 39038 | SP Madison Baggage Car "6015," *01* | | NRS | |
| 39039 | SP Madison Coach Car "1978," *01* | | NRS | |
| 39040 | SP Madison Coach Car "1975," *01* | | NRS | |
| 39041 | SP Madison Observation Car "2951," *01* | | NRS | |
| 39042 | N&W Heavyweight Passenger Car 4-pack, *00* | | 325 | |
| 39047 | B&O Heavyweight Passenger Car 2-pack, *01* | | 160 | |
| 39050 | PRR Heavyweight Passenger Car 2-pack, *01* | | 215 | |
| 39053 | Alaska Streamliner Car 2-pack, *01* | | 90 | |
| 39056 | NYC Streamliner Car 2-pack, *01* | | 75 | |
| 39059 | Santa Fe Streamliner Car 2-pack, *01* | | 100 | |
| 39062 | B&O Streamliner Car 2-pack, *01* | | 75 | |
| 39065 | PRR Streamliner Car 4-pack, *01* | | 165 | |
| 39082 | *Blue Comet* Heavyweight Passenger Car 2-pack, *02* | | 325 | |
| 39085 | "Freedom Train" Heavyweight Passenger Car 3-pack, *03* | | 260 | |
| 39092 | PRR Streamliner Car 2-pack, *01* | | 70 | |
| 39099 | *Alton Limited* Heavyweight Passenger Car 2-pack, *03* | | 230 | |
| 39100 | *William Penn* Congressional Coach, *00* | | 115 | |
| 39101 | *Molly Pitcher* Congressional Coach, *00* | | 100 | |
| 39102 | *Betsy Ross* Congressional Vista Dome Car, *00* | | 100 | |
| 39103 | *Alexander Hamilton* Congressional Observation Car, *00* | | 100 | |
| 39104 | Phoebe Snow Car, StationSounds, *99* | | 255 | |
| 39105 | Milwaukee Road *Hiawatha* Car, StationSounds, *99* | | 235 | |
| 39106 | CP Aluminum Passenger Car 2-pack, *00* | | 185 | |
| 39107 | CP *Blair Manor* Aluminum Passenger Coach "2553," *00* | | 115 | |
| 39108 | CP *Craig Manor* Aluminum Passenger Coach "2554," *00* | | 110 | |
| 39109 | "Spirit of the Century" Aluminum Passenger Car 4-pack, *99* | | 520 | |
| 39110 | "Spirit of the Century" Full Vista Dome Car, *99–00* | | 100 | |
| 39111 | "Spirit of the Century" Full Vista Dome Car, *99–00* | | 100 | |
| 39112 | "Spirit of the Century" Full Vista Dome Car, *99–00* | | 100 | |
| 39113 | "Spirit of the Century" Skytop Observation Car, *99–00* | | 100 | |
| 39118 | Texas Special *Garland* Aluminum Passenger Coach "1203," StationSounds, *99–00* | | 220 | |
| 39119 | Southern Aluminum Passenger Car 4-pack, *00* | | 350 | |
| 39120 | Southern *Grand Junction* Aluminum Passenger/ Baggage Car, *00* | | 280 | |
| 39121 | Southern *Charlottesville* Aluminum Passenger Coach "812," *00* | | 90 | |

| | | Exc | Mint | Cond/$ |
|---|---|---|---|---|
| 39122 | Southern *Roanoke* Aluminum Passenger Coach "814," *00* | | 250 | ____ |
| 39123 | Southern *Memphis* Aluminum Observation Car "1152," *00* | | 90 | ____ |
| 39124 | Amtrak Superliner Aluminum Passenger Car 4-pack, *02* | | 405 | ____ |
| 39129 | Santa Fe Superliner Aluminum Passenger Car 4-pack, *02* | | 305 | ____ |
| 39141 | RI Aluminum Passenger Car 4-pack, *01* | | 400 | ____ |
| 39146 | UP Aluminum Passenger Car 4-pack, *01* | | 285 | ____ |
| 39151 | CP Aluminum Passenger Car 2-pack, *01* | | 315 | ____ |
| 39154 | PRR Congressional Aluminum Passenger Car 2-pack, *02* | | 195 | ____ |
| 39155 | PRR Congressional Baggage Car, *02* | | 105 | ____ |
| 39156 | PRR *Robert Morris* Congressional Coach, *02* | | 100 | ____ |
| 39157 | Southern Aluminum Passenger Car 2-pack, *01* | | 290 | ____ |
| 39160 | KCS Aluminum Passenger Car 2-pack, *01* | 200 | 260 | ____ |
| 39163 | Erie-Lack. Aluminum Passenger Car 2-pack, *01* | | 230 | ____ |
| 39166 | *Texas Special* Aluminum Passenger Car 2-pack, *01* | 300 | 430 | ____ |
| 39169 | ACL Aluminum Passenger Car 4-pack, *01* | | 360 | ____ |
| 39179 | NP Aluminum Passenger Car 2-pack, *02* | | 305 | ____ |
| 39182 | WP Aluminum Passenger Car 2-pack, *02* | | 280 | ____ |
| 39185 | Rio Grande Aluminum Passenger Car 2-pack, *02* | | 290 | ____ |
| 39194 | UP Aluminum Passenger Car 2-pack, *02* | | 220 | ____ |
| 39197 | CP Aluminum Passenger Coach, StationSounds, *02* | | 225 | ____ |
| 39198 | PRR Aluminum Passenger Coach, StationSounds, *02* | | 210 | ____ |
| 39200 | Hell Gate Bridge Boxcar #2 "1900-2000," *00 u* | | 55 | ____ |
| 39202 | Lionel Centennial Boxcar "1900-2000," *00* | | 46 | ____ |
| 39203 | Postwar "6464" Series X, 3 cars, *01* | | 115 | ____ |
| 39204 | New Haven Boxcar "6464-725," *01* | | 44 | ____ |
| 39205 | Alaska Boxcar "6464-825," *01* | | 55 | ____ |
| 39206 | NYC Boxcar "6464-900," *01* | | 40 | ____ |
| 39207 | UP Boxcar "508500," red, *00* | | 50 | ____ |
| 39208 | UP Boxcar "903658," silver, *00* | | 42 | ____ |
| 39209 | UP Boxcar "500200," yellow, *00* | | 40 | ____ |
| 39210 | 6530 Fire Fighting Car, *00* | | 37 | ____ |
| 39211 | Postwar "6464" Boxcar 3-pack #2, *00* | | 85 | ____ |
| 39212 | Postwar "6464" SP&S Boxcar, *00* | | NRS | ____ |
| 39213 | Postwar "6464" Wabash Boxcar, *00* | | NRS | ____ |
| 39214 | Postwar "6464" Kansas, Oklahoma & Gulf Boxcar, *00* | | NRS | ____ |
| 39216 | PRR DD Boxcar "47211," *01* | | 46 | ____ |
| 39220 | B&LE Heavyweight Boxcar "82101," *01* | | 41 | ____ |
| 39221 | L&N Heavyweight Boxcar "109829," *01* | | 41 | ____ |
| 39222 | Conrail Heavyweight Boxcar "269198," *01* | | 44 | ____ |
| 39223 | Postwar "6464" Archive Boxcar Set, 3-pack, *02* | | 125 | ____ |

| | | Exc | Mint | Cond/$ |
|---|---|---|---|---|
| **39227** | Postwar "6468" Automobile Boxcar 3-pack, *01* | | 95 | ____ |
| **39236** | WP Boxcar "6464-250," *01* | | 55 | ____ |
| **39238** | Elvis Boxcar, *03* | | 36 | ____ |
| **39239** | P&LE Boxcar "22300, *02* | | 35 | ____ |
| **39240** | Pennsylvania Boxcar "118747," *02* | | 32 | ____ |
| **39241** | PC Boxcar "252455," *02* | | 28 | ____ |
| **39242** | Postwar "6464" Boxcar 3-pack #1, Archive Collection, *03–04* | | 80 | ____ |
| **39247** | NYC DD Boxcar "6468," *02–03* | | 32 | ____ |
| **39250** | Campbell's Kids Centennial Boxcar, *03–04* | | 40 | ____ |
| **39252** | Lenny Dean 60th Anniversary Boxcar, *04* | | 38 | ____ |
| **39253** | Postwar "6464" Boxcar 3-pack #2, Archive Collection, *04* | | 100 | ____ |
| **39257** | WP Boxcar "6464-100," boys set add-on, *03* | | 50 | ____ |
| **39258** | Elvis Presley "All Shook Up" Boxcar, *03–04* | | 40 | ____ |
| **39259** | Buick Centennial Boxcar, *03* | | 35 | ____ |
| **39260** | New Haven Boxcar, *04* | | 40 | ____ |
| **39262** | Elvis Presley "Elvis Has Left the Building" Boxcar, *04* | | 38 | ____ |
| **39263** | M&StL Boxcar, Postwar Celebration Series, *05* | | 35 | ____ |
| **39267** | Postwar "6464" Boxcar 3-pack #3, Archive Collection, *05* | | 120 | ____ |
| **39271** | State of Maine Boxcar, *04* | | 35 | ____ |
| **39273** | Postwar "6464" Boxcar 3-pack #4, Archive Collection, *06* | | 120 | ____ |
| **39281** | Florida State University Boxcar, *07* | | 45 | ____ |
| **39282** | Purdue University Boxcar, *08* | | 50 | ____ |
| **39283** | University of Virginia Boxcar, *08* | | 50 | ____ |
| **39284** | Penn State University Boxcar, *06–07* | | 45 | ____ |
| **39285** | U.S. Military Academy at West Point Boxcar, *08* | | 50 | ____ |
| **39286** | University of Illinois Boxcar, *06–07* | | 45 | ____ |
| **39287** | University of Alabama Boxcar, *06–07* | | 45 | ____ |
| **39289** | University of Oklahoma Boxcar, *06–08* | | 50 | ____ |
| **39290** | Postwar "6464" Boxcar 2-pack, rare variations, *08* | | 100 | ____ |
| **39291** | University of Michigan Boxcar, *06–07* | | 45 | ____ |
| **39292** | Monopoly Boxcar 3-pack, *08* | | 135 | ____ |
| **39296** | UPS Centennial Boxcar #3, *08–09* | | 55 | ____ |
| **39299** | Lenny Dean Commemorative Boxcar, *08* | | 50 | ____ |
| **39298** | Monopoly Boxcar 3-pack #2, *08* | | 135 | ____ |
| **39302** | University of Maryland Boxcar, *08* | | 50 | ____ |
| **39303** | Villanova University Boxcar, *08* | | 50 | ____ |
| **39304** | Auburn University Boxcar, *08* | | 50 | ____ |
| **39308** | CP Rail "6565" Boxcar "58700," *08–10* | | 55 | ____ |
| **39310** | Monopoly Boxcar 3-pack #3, *09–10* | | 165 | ____ |
| **39316** | New Haven Automobile Boxcar, *09–10* | | 60 | ____ |
| **39317** | *Wizard of Oz* Boxcar #1, *09–10* | | 60 | ____ |
| **39318** | *Wizard of Oz* Boxcar #2, *09–10* | | 60 | ____ |
| **39319** | Boy Scouts "Scout Law" Add-on Boxcar, *10* | | 60 | ____ |
| **39321** | Lionel Art Boxcar 2-pack, *10* | | 116 | ____ |

| | | Exc | Mint | Cond/$ |
|---|---|---|---|---|
| 39326 | UPS Centennial Boxcar #4, *10* | | 60 | |
| 39328 | Monopoly Boxcar 3-pack #4, *10* | | 165 | |
| 39332 | Holiday Boxcar, *10* | | 60 | |
| 39334 | Coca-Cola Christmas Boxcar, *10* | | 65 | |
| 39335 | Thomas Kinkade Boxcar, *10* | | 60 | |
| 39336 | Angela Trotta Thomas "My Turn Yet, Dad?" Boxcar, *10* | | 60 | |
| 39400 | Republic Steel Slag Car 3-pack (std O), *04* | | 100 | |
| 39404 | Republic Steel Hot Metal Car 3-pack (std O), *04* | | 130 | |
| 39411 | Jones & Laughline Hot Metal Car 3-pack (std O), *05* | | 190 | |
| 39423 | Postwar "3460" LL Flatcar with trailers, *05* | | 45 | |
| 39424 | U.S. Steel 16-wheel Flatcar with girders, *05* | | 70 | |
| 39425 | Hood's Flatcar with milk container, traditional, *05* | | 55 | |
| 39426 | Nestle Nesquik Flatcar with milk container, traditional, *05* | | 55 | |
| 39428 | Bethlehem Steel Slag Car #4 (std O), *05* | | 60 | |
| 39429 | Bethlehem Steel Hot Metal Car #8 (std O), *05* | | 70 | |
| 39430 | Youngstown Sheet & Tube Slag Car #7 (std O), *05* | | 60 | |
| 39431 | Youngstown Sheet & Tube Hot Metal Car #11 (std O), *05* | | 70 | |
| 39435 | Postwar "6477" Flatcar with pipes, *06* | | 50 | |
| 39436 | Postwar "6262" Wheel Car, *06* | | 50 | |
| 39437 | Supplee Flatcar with milk container, *06* | | 60 | |
| 39443 | U.S. Steel Slag Car 3-pack #2 (std O), *06* | | 170 | |
| 39447 | Postwar "6561" LL Cable Reel Car, Archive Collection, *06–07* | | 55 | |
| 39450 | Postwar "6414" Evans Auto Loader, Archive Collection, *06* | | 70 | |
| 39452 | White Bros. Flatcar with milk container, *07* | | 60 | |
| 39457 | Postwar "6175" Flatcar with rocket, *08* | | 55 | |
| 39458 | Postwar "6844" Flatcar with missiles, *08* | | 55 | |
| 39463 | Postwar "6430" Flatcar with trailers, *08* | | 55 | |
| 39468 | Allis-Chalmers Car "52369," *08–09* | | 60 | |
| 39469 | Christmas Egg Nog Barrel Car, *08* | | 50 | |
| 39470 | UP Well Car "147128," *08* | | 65 | |
| 39471 | Postwar "6264" Flatcar, *08* | | 60 | |
| 39472 | ATSF Culvert Gondola, *08* | | 60 | |
| 39473 | Play-Doh Vat Car, *08* | | 55 | |
| 39475 | UPS Flatcar with trailer, *08* | | 65 | |
| 39476 | Bethlehem Steel 16-wheel Flatcar, *08* | | 75 | |
| 39477 | Christmas Flatcar with reindeer trailers, *08* | | 60 | |
| 39478 | Postwar "6475" Pickles Vat Car, *08* | | 55 | |
| 39479 | Postwar "6404" Flatcar with brown automobile, *08* | | 50 | |
| 39480 | Western & Atlantic Cannon Flatcar, *09* | | 60 | |
| 39484 | Cocoa Marsh Vat Car, *10* | | 60 | |
| 39488 | Reese's Vat Car, *10* | | 60 | |
| 39490 | Western & Atlantic Cannonball Flatcar, *10* | | 55 | |

Exc Mint Cond/$

| | | Exc | Mint | Cond/$ |
|---|---|---|---|---|
| **39497** | Christmas Reindeer Stock Car, *10* | | 60 | ___ |
| **51008** | Burlington *Pioneer Zephyr* Diesel Passenger Set, RailSounds, *04* | | 875 | ___ |
| **51009** | Prewar "269E" Steam Freight Set, TrainSounds, *06* | | 630 | ___ |
| **51010** | Prewar "246E" Steam Passenger Set, TrainSounds, *07–08* | | 630 | ___ |
| **51012** | Christmas Tinplate Freight Set, *08* | | 675 | ___ |
| **51014** | Prewar "291W" Red Comet Passenger Car Set, *08* | | 675 | ___ |
| **51220** | NYC *Imperial Castle* Passenger Coach, *93 u* | | 500 | ___ |
| **51221** | NYC *Niagara County* Passenger Coach, *93 u* | | 500 | ___ |
| **51222** | NYC *Cascade Glory* Passenger Coach, *93 u* | | 500 | ___ |
| **51223** | NYC *City of Detroit* Passenger Coach, *93 u* | | 500 | ___ |
| **51224** | NYC *Imperial Falls* Passenger Coach, *93 u* | | 500 | ___ |
| **51225** | NYC *Westchester County* Passenger Coach, *93 u* | | 500 | ___ |
| **51226** | NYC *Cascade Grotto* Passenger Coach, *93 u* | | 500 | ___ |
| **51227** | NYC *City of Indianapolis* Passenger Coach, *93 u* | | 500 | ___ |
| **51228** | NYC *Manhattan Island* Observation Car, *93 u* | | 500 | ___ |
| **51229** | NYC Diner "680," *93 u* | | 500 | ___ |
| **51230** | NYC Baggage Car "5017," *93 u* | | 500 | ___ |
| **51231** | NYC *Century Club* Passenger Coach, *93 u* | | 500 | ___ |
| **51232** | NYC *Thousand Islands* Observation Car, *93 u* | | 500 | ___ |
| **51233** | NYC Diner "684," *93 u* | | 500 | ___ |
| **51234** | NYC Baggage Car "5020," *93 u* | | 500 | ___ |
| **51235** | NYC *Century Tavern* Passenger Coach, *93 u* | | 500 | ___ |
| **51236** | NYC *City of Toledo* Passenger Coach, *93 u* | | 500 | ___ |
| **51237** | NYC *Imperial Mansion* Passenger Coach, *93 u* | | 500 | ___ |
| **51238** | NYC *Imperial Palace* Passenger Coach, *93 u* | | 500 | ___ |
| **51239** | NYC *Cascade Spirit* Passenger Coach, *93 u* | | 500 | ___ |
| **51240** | NYC Diner "681," *93 u* | | 500 | ___ |
| **51241** | NYC *City of Chicago* Passenger Coach, *93 u* | | 500 | ___ |
| **51242** | NYC *Imperial Garden* Passenger Coach, *93 u* | | 500 | ___ |
| **51243** | NYC *Imperial Fountain* Passenger Coach, *93 u* | | 500 | ___ |
| **51244** | NYC *Cascade Valley* Passenger Coach, *93 u* | | 500 | ___ |
| **51245** | NYC Diner "685," *93 u* | | 500 | ___ |
| **51300** | Shell Semi-Scale 1-D Tank Car "8124," *91* | 50 | 170 | ___ |
| **51301** | Lackawanna Semi-Scale Reefer "7000," *92* | 138 | 196 | ___ |
| **51401** | PRR Semi-Scale Boxcar "100800," *91* | 118 | 155 | ___ |
| **51402** | C&O Semi-Scale Stock Car "95250," *92* | 125 | 151 | ___ |
| **51501** | B&O Semi-Scale Hopper "532000," *91* | 105 | 115 | ___ |
| **51502** | LL Steel Die-cast Ore Car "6486-3" (SSS), *96* | | 80 | ___ |
| **51503** | LL Steel Die-cast Ore Car "6486-1" (SSS), *96* | | 80 | ___ |
| **51504** | LL Steel Die-cast Ore Car "6486-2" (SSS), *96* | | 70 | ___ |
| **51600** | NYC Depressed Center Flatcar with transformer "6418," *96* | | 105 | ___ |
| **51701** | NYC Semi-Scale Caboose "19400," *91* | 118 | 145 | ___ |
| **51702** | PRR N-8 Caboose "478039," *91–92* | 300 | 385 | ___ |
| **52054** | Carail Boxcar, *94 u* | | 280 | ___ |

Exc Mint Cond/S

| | | Exc | Mint | Cond/S |
|---|---|---|---|---|
| **52066** | Trainmaster Tractor and Trailer, *94 u* | | 93 | ___ |
| **52069** | Carail Tractor and Trailer, *94 u* | | 60 | ___ |
| **52070** | Knoebel's Boxcar #1, *95 u* | | 60 | ___ |
| **52075** | United Auto Workers Boxcar, *95 u* | | 90 | ___ |
| **52082** | Steamtown Lackawanna Boxcar, *95 u* | | 90 | ___ |
| **52132** | Knoebel's Boxcar #2, *99 u* | | 69 | ___ |
| **52133** | Knoebel's Boxcar #3, *98 u* | | 86 | ___ |
| **52134** | Knoebel's Boxcar #4, *00 u* | | 86 | ___ |
| **52136A** | Christmas Special Tractor and Trailer, *97* | | NRS | ___ |
| **52136B** | Frisco Special Tractor and Trailer, *98* | | NRS | ___ |
| **52137** | Red Wing Shoes Boot Oil Tank Car, *98* | | 58 | ___ |
| **52141** | Zep Manufacturing Boxcar, *96* | | 79 | ___ |
| **52158** | Monopoly Mint Car "M-0539," *98* | | 330 | ___ |
| **52159** | Monopoly Depressed Center Flatcar with transformer, *98* | | 95 | ___ |
| **52160** | Monopoly Water Works Tank Car, *98* | | 105 | ___ |
| **52161** | Monopoly SP-type Caboose "M-1006," *98* | | 55 | ___ |
| **52168** | Carail Flatcar with Trailer "17455," *99 u* | | 95 | ___ |
| **52169** | Zep Manufacturing Flatcar with trailer "62734," *99 u* | | 55 | ___ |
| **52174** | REA Baggage Car "0083," *00 u* | | 400 | ___ |
| **52181** | Monopoly Set #2, 4-pack, *99* | | 295 | ___ |
| **52182** | Monopoly Railroads Boxcar "M0636," *99 u* | | 78 | ___ |
| **52183** | Monopoly Jail Car "M-1131," *99* | | 75 | ___ |
| **52184** | Monopoly Free Parking Flatcar with 2 autos, *99* | | 60 | ___ |
| **52185** | Monopoly Chance Gondola "M-0893," *99* | | 50 | ___ |
| **52187** | Madison Hardware Flatcar with 2 trailers, *99* | | 98 | ___ |
| **52188** | Carail Aquarium with 2 autos, 25th Anniversary, *99* | | 95 | ___ |
| **52189** | Monopoly 4-6-4 Hudson Locomotive, *99* | | 540 | ___ |
| **52207** | Lionel Lines SD40 Diesel, traditional, *00* | | 600 | ___ |
| **52208** | Lionel Lines Extended Vision Caboose, *00 u* | | 200 | ___ |
| **52209** | World's Fair Sleeper/Roomette Car "0183," *01 u* | | 170 | ___ |
| **52218** | Monopoly 4-4-2 Steam Freight Set, *00 u* | | 380 | ___ |
| **52219** | Monopoly 4-6-4 Hudson Locomotive, bronze, *00 u* | | 530 | ___ |
| **52224A** | SP Flatcar with Navajo tractor and trailer, *01* | | 25 | ___ |
| **52224B** | SP Flatcar with Trailer Flatcar Service tractor and trailer, *01* | | 25 | ___ |
| **52225** | Monopoly 4-6-4 Hudson Locomotive, pewter, *01 u* | | 495 | ___ |
| **52231** | British Columbia 1-D Tank Car, *00 u* | | 65 | ___ |
| **52235** | World's Fair Vista Dome Car "0283," *02 u* | | NRS | ___ |
| **52249** | Knoebel's Amusement Park 75th Anniversary Boxcar, *01 u* | | 85 | ___ |
| **52253** | San Pedro Boxcar, *02* | | NRS | ___ |
| **52262** | Plasticville Boxcar, *01 u* | | 120 | ___ |
| **52263** | World's Fair Combination Car "0383," *02* | | NRS | ___ |
| **52279** | Dragoon & Northern Ore Car, *02* | | 25 | ___ |

Exc Mint Cond/$

| | | Exc | Mint | Cond/$ |
|---|---|---|---|---|
| 52282 | Western Pacific Feather Boxcar, red, *03* | 365 | | |
| 52315/20 | PRR FM Diesel and Caboose, *04 u* | 440 | | |
| 52336 | U.S. Army Flatcar with tractor trailer, *04 u* | 115 | | |
| 52371 | NYC Flatcar with tanker trailer, *05 u* | 150 | | |
| 62162 | Postwar "262" Automatic Crossing Gate and Signal, *99–10* | 27 | | |
| 62180 | Railroad Signs, set of 14, *99–04, 08–10* | 4 | | |
| 62181 | Telephone Pole Set, *99–04, 08–10* | 5 | | |
| 62283 | Die-cast Illuminated Bumpers, *99–10* | 23 | | |
| 62709 | Rico Station Kit, *99–00* | 46 | | |
| 62716 | Short Extension Bridge, *99–03, 07–10* | 7 | | |
| 62900 | Lockon, *99–10* | 3 | | |
| 62901 | Ives Track Clips, 12 pieces (027), *99–10* | 5 | | |
| 62905 | Lockon with wires, *99–10* | 7 | | |
| 62909 | Smoke Fluid, *99–10* | 7 | | |
| 62927 | Lubrication/Maintenance Set, *99–10* | 19 | | |
| 62985 | The Lionel Train Book, *99–03* | 12 | | |
| 65014 | Half Curved Track (027), *99–10* | 1 | | |
| 65019 | Half-Straight Track (027), *99–10* | 1 | | |
| 65020 | 90-degree Crossover (027), *99–10* | 11 | | |
| 65021 | 27" Manual Switch, left hand (027), *99–10* | 17 | | |
| 65022 | 27" Manual Switch, right hand (027), *99–10* | 18 | | |
| 65023 | 45-degree Crossover (027), *99–10* | 11 | | |
| 65024 | 35" Straight Track (027), *99–10* | 5 | | |
| 65033 | 27" Diameter Curved Track (027), *99–10* | 2 | | |
| 65038 | 9" Straight Track (027), *99–10* | 2 | | |
| 65041 | Insulator Pins, dozen (027), *99–04, 06–10* | 3 | | |
| 65042 | Steel Pins, dozen (027), *99–04, 06–09* | 3 | | |
| 65049 | 42" Diameter Curved Track (027), *99–10* | 3 | | |
| 65113 | 54" Diameter Curved Track (027), *99–10* | 3 | | |
| 65121 | 27" Path Remote Switch, left hand (027), *99–10* | 43 | | |
| 65122 | 27" Path Remote Switch, right hand (027), *99–10* | 43 | | |
| 65149 | Uncoupling Track (027), *99–10* | 12 | | |
| 65165 | 72" Path Remote Switch, right hand (0), *99–10* | 125 | | |
| 65166 | 72" Path Remote Switch, left hand (0), *99–10* | 125 | | |
| 65167 | 72" Remote Switch, right hand (027), *99–10* | 25 | | |
| 65168 | 42" Remote Switch, left hand (027), *99–10* | 25 | | |
| 65500 | 10" Straight Track (0), *99–10* | 2 | | |
| 65501 | 31" Diameter Curved Track (0), *99–10* | 2 | | |
| 65504 | Half Curved Track (0), *99–10* | 2 | | |
| 65505 | Half Straight Track (0), *99–10* | 2 | | |
| 65514 | Half Curved Track (027), *99–03* | 3 | | |
| 65523 | 40" Straight Track (0), *99–10* | 7 | | |
| 65530 | Remote Control Track (0), *99–10* | 38 | | |
| 65540 | 90-degree Crossover (0), *99–10* | 16 | | |
| 65543 | Insulator Pins, dozen (0), *99–10* | 3 | | |
| 65545 | 45-degree Crossover (0), *99–10* | 27 | | |

## MODERN ERA 1970-2011

| No. | Description | Exc | Mint | Cond/$ |
|---|---|---|---|---|
| 65551 | Steel Pins, dozen (O), *99–10* | | 3 | ___ |
| 65554 | 54" Diameter Curved Track (O), *99–10* | | 4 | ___ |
| 65572 | 72" Diameter Curved Track (O), *99–10* | | 5 | ___ |
| 81024 | Christmas Train Set, *02–04* | | 150 | ___ |
| 81027 | Thomas the Tank Engine Set, *01–04* | | 120 | ___ |
| 99000 | Keebler Elf Express Steam Freight Set, *99 u* | | 980 | ___ |
| 99001 | Mickey's Holiday Express Freight Set, *99 u* | | 245 | ___ |
| 99002 | Looney Tunes Square Window Caboose, *99 u* | | NRS | ___ |
| 99006 | Keebler Bulkhead Flatcar, *99 u* | | NRS | ___ |
| 99007 | Smuckers Fudge 1-D Tank Car, *99 u* | | 80 | ___ |
| 99008 | Mickey's Merry Christmas Boxcar, *99 u* | | NRS | ___ |
| 99009 | Mickey's Holiday Express Square Window Caboose, *99 u* | | NRS | ___ |
| 99013 | Case Cutlery Tank Car "1889," *00 u* | | NRS | ___ |
| 99014 | Case Cutlery Gondola "1889," *00 u* | | NRS | ___ |
| 99015 | Case Cutlery Boxcar "1889," *00 u* | | NRS | ___ |
| 99018 | Case Cutlery Rolling Stock 3-pack, *00 u* | | 200 | ___ |
| 79C95204C | Sears Santa Fe Diesel Freight Set, *71 u* | 150 | 165 | ___ |
| 79C9715C | Sears 4-unit Diesel Freight Set, *75 u* | 50 | 65 | ___ |
| 79C9717C | Sears 7-unit Steam Freight Set, *75 u* | 150 | 165 | ___ |
| 79N95223C | Sears 6-unit Diesel Freight Set, *74 u* | 150 | 165 | ___ |
| 79N9552C | Sears 6-unit Steam Freight Set, *72 u* | 150 | 165 | ___ |
| 79N9553C | Sears 6-unit Diesel Freight Set, *72 u* | 150 | 165 | ___ |
| 79N96178C | Sears 4-unit Steam Freight Set, *74 u* | 50 | 65 | ___ |
| 79N97082C | Sears Steam Freight Set, *70 u* | | NRS | ___ |
| 79N97101C | Sears 5-unit Steam Freight Set, *72 u* | 150 | 165 | ___ |
| 79N98765C | Sears Logging Empire Set, *78 u* | 100 | 115 | ___ |
| UCS | Remote Control Track (O), *70* | 4 | 7 | ___ |

### Unnumbered Items

| Description | Exc | Mint | Cond/$ |
|---|---|---|---|
| Amtrak Passenger Car Set, *89, 89 u* | 640 | 770 | ___ |
| B&A Hudson and Standard O Car Set, *86 u* | 1500 | 1700 | ___ |
| Baltimore & Ohio Set, *94, 96* | | NRS | ___ |
| Black Cave Flyer Playmat, *82* | | 8 | ___ |
| *Blue Comet* Set, *78–80, 87 u* | 560 | 620 | ___ |
| Burlington *Texas Zephyr* Set, *80, 80 u* | 980 | 1150 | ___ |
| C&NW Passenger Car Set, *93* | 385 | 460 | ___ |
| Cannonball Freight Playmat, *81–82* | | 8 | ___ |
| Chesapeake & Ohio Set, *95–96* | | NRS | ___ |
| Chessie System Special Set, *80, 86 u* | 560 | 620 | ___ |
| Chicago & Alton Limited Set, *81, 86 u* | 560 | 620 | ___ |
| Commando Assault Train Playmat, *83–84* | | 8 | ___ |
| D&RGW *California Zephyr* Set, *92, 93* | | 900 | ___ |
| Erie Set (FF 7), *93* | 385 | 460 | ___ |
| Erie-Lackawanna Passenger Car Set, *93, 94* | 940 | 980 | ___ |
| Favorite Food Freight Set, *81–82* | 248 | 338 | ___ |
| Frisco Set (FF 5), *91* | 405 | 425 | ___ |
| The *General* Set, *77–80* | 240 | 285 | ___ |

| | Exc | Mint | Cond/$ |
|---|---|---|---|
| GN *Empire Builder* Set, *92, 93* | 620 | 730 | ____ |
| Great Northern Set (FARR 3), *81, 81 u* | 620 | 690 | ____ |
| IC *City of New Orleans* Set, *85, 87, 93* | 885 | 1045 | ____ |
| Illinois Central Set, *91–92, 95* | 255 | 285 | ____ |
| Jersey Central Set, *86* | 345 | 370 | ____ |
| Joshua Lionel Cowen Set, *80, 80 u, 82* | 540 | 580 | ____ |
| L.A.S.E.R. Playmat, *81–82* | | 8 | ____ |
| Lionel Lines Madison Car Set, *91, 93* | 560 | 620 | ____ |
| Lionel Lines Set, *82–84 u, 86, 86–87 u, 94–95* | 530 | 620 | ____ |
| Mickey Mouse Express Set, *77–78, 78 u* | 995 | 1663 | ____ |
| Milwaukee Road Set (FF 2), *87, 90 u* | 380 | 405 | ____ |
| Mint Set, *79 u, 80–83, 84 u, 86 u, 87, 91 u, 93* | 940 | 1050 | ____ |
| Missouri Pacific Set, *95* | | 390 | ____ |
| N&W *Powhatan Arrow* Passenger Car Set, *95* | 370 | 445 | ____ |
| N&W *Powhatan Arrow* Set, *81, 81 u, 82 u, 91 u* | 1450 | 1700 | ____ |
| New Haven Set, *94–95* | | 400 | ____ |
| New York Central Set, *89, 91* | 240 | 270 | ____ |
| Nickel Plate Road Set (FF 6), *92* | 385 | 460 | ____ |
| Northern Pacific Set, *90–92* | 190 | 250 | ____ |
| NYC *20th Century Limited* Set, *83, 83 u, 95* | 980 | 1150 | ____ |
| Pennsylvania Set, *79–80, 79–80 u, 81 u, 83 u* | 1200 | 1350 | ____ |
| Pennsylvania Set, *87–90, 95* | 240 | 270 | ____ |
| Pennsylvania Set (FARR 5), *84–85, 89 u* | 600 | 660 | ____ |
| Pere Marquette Set, *93* | 720 | 770 | ____ |
| Rock Island & Peoria Set, *80–82* | 240 | 315 | ____ |
| Rocky Mountain Platform, *83–84* | | 8 | ____ |
| Santa Fe *Super Chief* Set, *91, 91 u, 92 u, 93, 95* | 1400 | 1700 | ____ |
| Santa Fe Set (FARR 1), *79, 79 u* | 460 | 580 | ____ |
| Southern *Crescent Limited* Set, *77–78, 87 u* | 540 | 650 | ____ |
| Southern Pacific Daylight Diesel Set, *82–83, 82–83 u, 90 u* | 2150 | 2300 | ____ |
| Southern Set (FARR 4), *83, 83 u* | 620 | 690 | ____ |
| SP Daylight Steam Set, *90, 92, 93* | 790 | 940 | ____ |
| Spirit of '76 Set, *74–76* | 570 | 690 | ____ |
| Station Platform, *83–84* | | 8 | ____ |
| Toys "R" Us Thunderball Freight Set, *75 u* | | NRS | ____ |
| Union Pacific Set, *94* | 430 | 500 | ____ |
| Union Pacific Set (FARR 2), *80, 80 u* | 540 | 580 | ____ |
| UP Overland Route Set, *84, 92 u* | 770 | 840 | ____ |
| Wabash Set (FF 1), *86, 87* | 755 | 905 | ____ |
| Western Maryland Set (FF 4), *89* | 345 | 405 | ____ |

## Section 4
# MODERN TINPLATE

Mint  Cond/$

## O Gauge Classics

| | | | |
|---|---|---|---|
| **1-263E** | Lionel Lines *Blue Comet* 2-4-2 Locomotive | NRS | ___ |
| **350E** | Lionel Lines *Hiawatha* 4-4-2 Locomotive | NRS | ___ |
| **882** | Lionel Lines Combination Car | NRS | ___ |
| **883** | Lionel Lines Passenger Car | NRS | ___ |
| **884** | Lionel Lines Observation Car | NRS | ___ |
| **1612** | Lionel Lines Passenger Car | NRS | ___ |
| **1613** | Lionel Lines Passenger Car | NRS | ___ |
| **1614** | Lionel Lines Baggage Car | NRS | ___ |
| **1615** | Lionel Lines Observation Car | NRS | ___ |
| **51000** | Milwaukee Road *Hiawatha* Set, *88 u* | 882 | ___ |
| **51001** | Lionel No. 44 Freight Special Set, *89* | 600 | ___ |
| **51004** | *Blue Comet* Set, *91* | 1600 | ___ |
| **51100** | Lionel Lines Electric Locomotive "44E," *89* | NRS | ___ |
| **51201** | *Rail Chief* Passenger Cars, set of 4, *90* | 458 | ___ |
| **51202** | Lionel Lines Combination Car "892" | NRS | ___ |
| **51203** | Lionel Lines Passenger Car "893" | NRS | ___ |
| **51204** | Lionel Lines Passenger Car "894" | NRS | ___ |
| **51205** | Lionel Lines Observation Car "895" | NRS | ___ |
| **51400** | Lionel Lines Boxcar "8814," *89* | NRS | ___ |
| **51500** | Lionel Lines Hopper "8816," *89* | NRS | ___ |
| **51700** | Lionel Lines Caboose "8817," *89* | NRS | ___ |
| **51800** | Lionel Lines Searchlight Car "8820," *89* | NRS | ___ |

## Standard Gauge Classics

| | | | |
|---|---|---|---|
| **1-318E** | Lionel Lines Electric Locomotive | NRS | ___ |
| **1-4390** | American Flyer *West Point* Baggage Car | NRS | ___ |
| **1-4391** | American Flyer *Academy* Passenger Car | NRS | ___ |
| **1-4392** | American Flyer *Army/Navy* Observation Car | NRS | ___ |
| **5130** | Lionel Lines Flatcar with lumber | NRS | ___ |
| **5140** | Lionel Lines Reefer | NRS | ___ |
| **5150** | Lionel Lines Shell Tank Car | NRS | ___ |
| **5160** | Lionel Lines Caboose | NRS | ___ |
| **13001** | 1-318E Freight Express Train Set, *90–91* | 960 | ___ |
| **13002** | *Fireball Express* Set, *90 u* | 1600 | ___ |
| **13003** | American Flyer *Mayflower* Passenger Car Set, *92* | 2000 | ___ |
| **13004** | Milwaukee Road *Hiawatha* Passenger Set, *01–02* | 2000 | ___ |
| **13008** | NYC Commodore Vanderbilt Passenger Set, *02* | 1600 | ___ |
| **13100** | Lionel Lines 2-4-2 Locomotive "1-390E," *88 u* | 610 | ___ |
| **13101** | Lionel Lines 2-4-0 Locomotive "1-384E," *89 u* | 650 | ___ |
| **13102** | Lionel Lines Electric Locomotive "1-381E," *89 u* | 880 | ___ |

| | | Mint | Cond/$ |
|---|---|---|---|
| 13103 | Lionel Lines *Blue Comet* 4-4-4 Locomotive, *90* | 1350 | ___ |
| 13104 | Lionel Lines "Old #7" 4-4-0 Locomotive, *90* | 900 | ___ |
| 13106 | Lionel Lines *Fireball Express* 2-4-2 Locomotive | NRS | ___ |
| 13107 | Lionel Lines Electric Locomotive "1-408E," *91* | 880 | ___ |
| 13108 | Lionel Lines 4-4-4 Locomotive "2-400E," gray, *91* | 1100 | ___ |
| 13109 | American Flyer *Mayflower* Electric Locomotive, *92* | 2500 | ___ |
| 13200 | Lionel Lines Searchlight Car "1520," *89 u* | 110 | ___ |
| 13300 | Lionel Lines Gondola "1512," *89 u* | 75 | ___ |
| 13303 | Lionel Lines Sunoco Tank Car "1-215," *92* | 135 | ___ |
| 13400 | Lionel Lines Baggage Car "323," *88 u* | 155 | ___ |
| 13401 | Lionel Lines Passenger Car "324," *88 u* | 135 | ___ |
| 13402 | Lionel Lines Observation Car "325," *88 u* | 135 | ___ |
| 13403 | Lionel Lines State Passenger Car Set, *89 u* | 1100 | ___ |
| 13404 | Lionel Lines *California* Passenger Car "1412" | NRS | ___ |
| 13405 | Lionel Lines *Colorado* Passenger Car "1413" | NRS | ___ |
| 13406 | Lionel Lines *New York* Observation Car "1416" | NRS | ___ |
| 13407 | Lionel Lines *Illinois* Passenger Car "1414," *90* | 450 | ___ |
| 13408 | Lionel Lines *Blue Comet* Passenger Car Set, *90* | 1500 | ___ |
| 13409 | Lionel Lines *Faye* Passenger Car "1420" | NRS | ___ |
| 13410 | Lionel Lines *Westphal* Passenger Car "1421" | NRS | ___ |
| 13411 | Lionel Lines *Tempel* Observation Car "1422" | NRS | ___ |
| 13412 | Lionel Lines "Old #7" Passenger Car Set, *90* | 800 | ___ |
| 13413 | Lionel Lines Combination Car "183" | NRS | ___ |
| 13414 | Lionel Lines Passenger Car "184" | NRS | ___ |
| 13415 | Lionel Lines Observation Car "185" | NRS | ___ |
| 13416 | Lionel Lines *New Jersey* Baggage Car "326" | NRS | ___ |
| 13417 | Lionel Lines *Connecticut* Passenger Car "327" | NRS | ___ |
| 13418 | Lionel Lines *New York* Observation Car "328" | NRS | ___ |
| 13420 | Lionel Lines State Passenger Car Set, *91* | 1300 | ___ |
| 13421 | Lionel Lines *California* Passenger Car "2412" | NRS | ___ |
| 13422 | Lionel Lines *Colorado* Passenger Car "2413" | NRS | ___ |
| 13423 | Lionel Lines *Illinois* Passenger Car "2414," *92 u* | 817 | ___ |
| 13424 | Lionel Lines *New York* Observation Car "2416" | NRS | ___ |
| 13425 | Lionel Lines *Barnard* Passenger Car "1423," *91 u* | 1350 | ___ |
| 13600 | Lionel Lines Cattle Car "1513," *89 u* | 90 | ___ |
| 13601 | "Season's Greetings" Boxcar, *89 u* | 105 | ___ |
| 13602 | "Season's Greetings" Boxcar, *90 u* | 100 | ___ |
| 13604 | "Season's Greetings" Boxcar, *91 u* | 110 | ___ |
| 13605 | Lionel Lines Boxcar "1-214," *92* | 155 | ___ |
| 13700 | Lionel Lines Caboose "1517," *89 u* | 105 | ___ |
| 13702 | Lionel Lines Caboose "1217," *91* | 115 | ___ |
| 13800 | Lionelville Passenger Station, *88 u* | 390 | ___ |
| 13801 | Lionelville Station "126," *89 u* | 290 | ___ |
| 13804 | Lionelville Switch Tower "437," *91* | 400 | ___ |
| 13900 | Electric Rapid Transit Trolley "200," *89 u* | 290 | ___ |
| 13901 | Electric Rapid Transit Trolley Trailer "201," *89 u* | 150 | ___ |
| 51900 | Signal Bridge and Control Panel, *89 u* | 399 | ___ |

|  |  | Exc | Mint | Cond/$ |
|---|---|---|---|---|

## Artrain

| | | Exc | Mint | Cond/$ |
|---|---|---|---|---|
| **9486** | GTW "I Love Michigan" Boxcar, *87* | | 305 | ___ |
| **17885** | 1-D Tank Car, *90* | 55 | 65 | ___ |
| **17891** | GTW 20th Anniversary Boxcar, *91* | 70 | 75 | ___ |
| **19425** | CSX Flatcar with "Art in Celebration" trailer, *96* | | 80 | ___ |
| **52013** | Norfolk Southern Flatcar with trailer, *92* | 160 | 228 | ___ |
| **52024** | Conrail Auto Carrier, *93* | 80 | 90 | ___ |
| **52049** | BN Gondola with coil covers, *94* | 50 | 56 | ___ |
| **52097** | Chessie System Reefer, *95* | | 34 | ___ |
| **52140** | Union Pacific Bunk Car, *97* | | 37 | ___ |
| **52165** | SP Caboose "6256," *98* | | 60 | ___ |
| **52197** | Santa Fe GP38 Diesel, *99* | | 243 | ___ |
| **52227** | "Artistry in Space" Boxcar, *00* | | 75 | ___ |
| **52255** | 30th Anniversary Flatcar with billboard, *01* | | 100 | ___ |
| **52283** | Paint Vat Car, *02* | | 59 | ___ |
| **52331** | Flatcar with "America's Railways" trailer, *03* | | 150 | ___ |
| **52349** | Hometown Art Museum Hopper, purple, *04* | | 35 | ___ |
| **52350** | "Native Views" 3-bay Hopper, *04* | | 65 | ___ |
| **52411** | "35 Years" 1-D Tank Car, *06* | | 35 | ___ |

## Carnegie Science Center

| | | Exc | Mint | Cond/$ |
|---|---|---|---|---|
| **26750** | Great Miniature Railroad & Village Boxcar, *99* | | 78 | ___ |
| **36202** | Great Miniature Railroad 80th Anniversary Boxcar, *00* | | 110 | ___ |
| **36234** | Great Miniature Railroad & Village Boxcar, *01* | | 50 | ___ |
| **52277** | Carnegie Science Center 10th Anniversary Boxcar, *02* | | 60 | ___ |
| **52332** | Miniature Railroad & Village Boxcar, *03* | | 58 | ___ |
| **52362** | Miniature Railroad & Village 50th Anniversary Boxcar, *04* | | 50 | ___ |
| **52399** | MRR&V Express Boxcar, *05* | | 50 | ___ |
| **52432** | Miniature Railroad & Village Boxcar, *06* | | 50 | ___ |
| **52510** | Miniature Railroad & Village Caboose, *08* | | 50 | ___ |
| **25085** | Miniature Railroad & Village Boxcar, *09* | | 50 | ___ |

## Chicagoland Railroad Club

| | | Exc | Mint | Cond/$ |
|---|---|---|---|---|
| **52081** | C&NW Boxcar "6464-555," *96* | 40 | 68 | ___ |
| **52101** | BN Maxi-Stack Flatcar "64287" with containers, *97* | | 82 | ___ |
| **52102** | SF Extended Vision Caboose, red roof, *96* | | 75 | ___ |
| **52103** | SF Extended Vision Caboose, black roof, *96* | | 75 | ___ |

## CLUB CARS AND SPECIAL PRODUCTION

| | | Exc | Mint | Cond/$ |
|---|---|---|---|---|
| 52120 | Shedd Aquarium Car "3435-557," 98 | | 100 | ____ |
| 52148 | REA/Santa Fe Operating Boxcar, 99 | | 70 | ____ |
| 52170 | SP Operating Boxcar "52170-561," 99 | | 65 | ____ |
| 52171 | UP Operating Boxcar "52171-561," 99 | | 65 | ____ |
| 52178 | Burlington Operating Boxcar "52178-559," 00 | | 70 | ____ |
| 52179 | ACL Operating Boxcar "52179-560," 00 | | 73 | ____ |
| 52215 | C&NW 3-bay Cylindrical Hopper, 01 | | 60 | ____ |
| 52216 | C&NW Cylindrical Hopper, 02 | | 60 | ____ |
| 52223 | REA/Santa Fe Centennial Operating Boxcar, 00 | | 65 | ____ |
| 52251 | PRR Express Car, green, 01 | | 67 | ____ |
| 52259 | MP GP20 Diesel, traditional, 01 | | 250 | ____ |
| 52292 | PRR Express Car, tuscan red, 02 | | 50 | ____ |
| 52327 | City of Los Angeles Express Car, 04 | | 65 | ____ |
| 52328 | City of New Haven Express Car, 04 | | 55 | ____ |
| 52363 | City of New Orleans Express Car, 04 | | 55 | ____ |
| 52364 | City of New York Express Car, 04 | | 65 | ____ |
| 52388 | Great Northern Tool Car, 06 | | 48 | ____ |
| 52389 | Great Northern Crew Car, 06 | | 48 | ____ |
| 52390 | Great Northern Welding Caboose, 06 | | 78 | ____ |
| 52391 | Great Northern Racing Crew Car, 06 | | 48 | ____ |
| 52426 | City of San Francisco Express Car, 07 | | 55 | ____ |
| 52427 | Rock Island Rocket Express Car, 07 | | 55 | ____ |
| 52475 | Western Pacific UP Heritage Boxcar, 07 | | 60 | ____ |

## Classic Toy Trains

| | | Exc | Mint | Cond/$ |
|---|---|---|---|---|
| 52126 | MILW Boxcar "21027" with CTT Logo, 97 | | 50 | ____ |

## Dept. 56

| | | Exc | Mint | Cond/$ |
|---|---|---|---|---|
| 16270 | Heritage Village Boxcar "9796", 96 | | 56 | ____ |
| 52096 | Snow Village Boxcar "9756," 95 | | 85 | ____ |
| 52139 | Square Window Caboose "6256," 97 | | 72 | ____ |
| 52157 | Holly Brothers 3-D Tank Car, 98 | | 85 | ____ |
| 52175 | 4-6-4 Hudson Locomotive, CC, 99 | | 350 | ____ |
| 52199 | 4-bay Hopper "6756," 00 | | 53 | ____ |
| 52254 | "Happy Holidays" Gondola, 01 | | 35 | ____ |

## Eastwood Automobilia

| | | Exc | Mint | Cond/$ |
|---|---|---|---|---|
| 16275 | Radio Flyer Boxcar "16275," 96 | | 50 | ____ |
| 16757 | Johnny Lightning Auto Carrier "3435," 96 | | 90 | ____ |
| 16985 | Flatcar with 2 Ford vans, 97 | | 49 | ____ |
| 52044 | Vat Car, 95 | | 30 | ____ |
| 52083 | PRR Flatcar "21697" with tanker, 95 | | 41 | ____ |
| 52130 | Flatcar with Hot Wheels tanker, 97 | | 60 | ____ |

# Houston Tinplate Operators Society

| | | Exc | Mint | Cond/$ |
|---|---|---|---|---|
| 8900 | Sam Houston Mint Car, *00* | | 120 | ___ |
| 8901 | Miracle Petroleum 1-D Tank Car, *01* | | 100 | ___ |
| 8902 | *USS Houston* Submarine Car, *02* | | 100 | ___ |
| 8903 | Railway Express Boxcar, *03* | | 100 | ___ |
| 8904 | Lone Star Bay Window Caboose, *04* | | 100 | ___ |
| 8999 | Lone Star Aquarium Car, mermaid or trout, *99* | | 100 | ___ |

# Inland Empire Train Collectors Association

| | | Exc | Mint | Cond/$ |
|---|---|---|---|---|
| 1979 | Boxcar, *79* | | 15 | ___ |
| 1980 | SP-type Caboose, *80* | | 14 | ___ |
| 1981 | Quad Hopper, *81* | | 14 | ___ |
| 1982 | 3-D Tank Car, *82* | | 14 | ___ |
| 1983 | Reefer, *83* | | 14 | ___ |
| 1986 | Bunk Car, *86* | | 14 | ___ |
| 7518 | Carson City Mint Car, *84* | 36 | 43 | ___ |

# Lionel Central Operating Lines

| | | Exc | Mint | Cond/$ |
|---|---|---|---|---|
| 1981 | Boxcar, *81* | | 23 | ___ |
| 1986 | Work Caboose, shell only, *86* | | 14 | ___ |
| 5724 | Pennsylvania Bunk Car, *84* | 30 | 39 | ___ |
| 6508 | Canadian Pacific Crane Car, *83* | | 40 | ___ |
| 6907 | NYC Wood-sided Caboose, *97* | | 50 | ___ |
| 9184 | Erie Bay Window Caboose, *82* | 17 | 21 | ___ |
| 9475 | D&H "I Love NY" Boxcar, *85* | | 34 | ___ |
| 16342 | CSX Gondola with coil covers, *92* | | 20 | ___ |
| 17221 | NYC Boxcar, *95* | | 30 | ___ |

# Lionel Collectors Association of Canada

| | | Exc | Mint | Cond/$ |
|---|---|---|---|---|
| 5710 | Canadian Pacific Reefer, *83* | | 215 | ___ |
| 5714 | Michigan Central Reefer, *85* | 120 | 150 | ___ |
| 6100 | Ontario Northland Covered Quad Hopper, *82* | | 250 | ___ |
| 8103 | Toronto, Hamilton & Buffalo Boxcar, *81* | | 150 | ___ |
| 8204 | Algoma Central Boxcar, *82* | | 150 | ___ |
| 8507/08 | Canadian National F3 Diesel AA, shells only, *85* | | 400 | ___ |
| 8912 | Canada Southern Operating Hopper, *89* | | 95 | ___ |
| 9413 | Napierville Junction Boxcar, *80* | | 10 | ___ |
| 9718 | Canadian National Boxcar, *79* | | 20 | ___ |
| 17893 | BAOC 1-D Tank Car "914," *91* | | 120 | ___ |
| 52004 | Algoma Central Gondola "9215" with coil covers, *92* | 70 | 90 | ___ |
| 52005 | Canadian National F3 Diesel B Unit "9517," *93* | | 30 | ___ |
| 52006 | Canadian Pacific Boxcar "930016" (std 0), *93* | | 108 | ___ |

| | | Exc | Mint | Cond/$ |
|---|---|---|---|---|
| **52115** | Wabash Lake Railway 2-tier Auto Carrier "9519," *98* | | 100 | ____ |
| **52125** | TH&B Gondola 2-pack, *99* | | 90 | ____ |
| **86009** | Canadian National Bunk Car, *86* | | 115 | ____ |
| **87010** | Canadian National Express Reefer, *87* | | 115 | ____ |
| **88011** | Canadian National Caboose (std O), *88* | | 500 | ____ |
| **830005** | Canadian National Boxcar, *83* | | 300 | ____ |
| **840006** | Canadian Wheat Board Covered Quad Hopper, *84* | | 165 | ____ |
| **900013** | Canadian National Flatcar with trailers, *90* | | 225 | ____ |

# Lionel Collectors Club of America

## LCCA National Convention Cars

| | | Exc | Mint | Cond/$ |
|---|---|---|---|---|
| **6112** | Commonwealth Edison Quad Hopper with coal, *83* | 49 | 78 | ____ |
| **6323** | Virginia Chemicals 1-D Tank Car, *86* | 47 | 63 | ____ |
| **6567** | Illinois Central Gulf Crane Car "100408," *85* | 55 | 63 | ____ |
| **7403** | LNAC Boxcar, *84* | 21 | 24 | ____ |
| **9118** | Corning Covered Quad Hopper, *74* | 65 | 92 | ____ |
| **9155** | Monsanto 1-D Tank Car, *75* | 38 | 47 | ____ |
| **9212** | Seaboard Coast Line Flatcar with trailers, *76* | 22 | 31 | ____ |
| **9259** | Southern Bay Window Caboose, *77* | 31 | 41 | ____ |
| **9358** | "Sands of Iowa" Covered Quad Hopper, *80* | 24 | 33 | ____ |
| **9435** | Central of Georgia Boxcar, *81* | 25 | 29 | ____ |
| **9460** | D&TS Automobile Boxcar, *82* | 25 | 34 | ____ |
| **9701** | Baltimore & Ohio Automobile Boxcar, *72* | | 170 | ____ |
| **9727** | TA&G Boxcar, *73* | 105 | 134 | ____ |
| **9728** | Union Pacific Stock Car, *78* | 23 | 26 | ____ |
| **9733** | Airco Boxcar with tank car body, *79* | 37 | 50 | ____ |
| **17870** | East Camden & Highland Boxcar (std O), *87* | 29 | 33 | ____ |
| **17873** | Ashland Oil 3-D Tank Car, *88* | 55 | 70 | ____ |
| **17876** | Columbia, Newberry & Laurens Boxcar (std O), *89* | 32 | 40 | ____ |
| **17880** | D&RGW Wood-sided Caboose (std O), *90* | 43 | 55 | ____ |
| **17887** | Conrail Flatcar with Armstrong Tile trailer (std O), *91* | 30 | 49 | ____ |
| **17888** | Conrail Flatcar with Ford trailer (std O), *91* | 42 | 80 | ____ |
| **17892** | Conrail Flatcar with Armstrong and Ford Trailers (std O), *91* | | 140 | ____ |
| **17899** | NASA Tank Car "190" (std O), *92* | 45 | 51 | ____ |
| **27019** | Imco PS-2 Covered Hopper, *09* | | 50 | ____ |
| **52023** | D&TS 2-bay ACF Hopper "2601" (std O), *93* | 35 | 40 | ____ |
| **52038** | Southern Hopper "360794" with coal (std O), *94* | 38 | 46 | ____ |
| **52074** | Iowa Beef Packers Reefer "197095" (std O), *95* | | 32 | ____ |

## CLUB CARS AND SPECIAL PRODUCTION

| | | Exc | Mint | Cond/S |
|---|---|---|---|---|
| **52090** | Pere Marquette DD Boxcar "71996" (std O), *96* | | 52 | _____ |
| **52110** | CStPM&O Boxcar "71997" (std O), *97* | 18 | 52 | _____ |
| **52151** | Amtrak Express Baggage Boxcar "71998" (std O), *98* | | 64 | _____ |
| **52176** | Fort Worth & Denver Boxcar "8277" (std O), *99* | | 55 | _____ |
| **52195** | Double-stack Car with 2 containers, *00* | | 100 | _____ |
| **52244** | Louisville & Nashville Horse Car "2001," *01* | | 50 | _____ |
| **52266** | PRR "Coal Goes To War" Hopper "707025," *02* | | 86 | _____ |
| **52267** | PRR "Coal Goes To War" Hopper "707026," *02* | | 92 | _____ |
| **52299** | Las Vegas Mint Car, *03* | | 80 | _____ |
| **52343** | MILW Milk Car, orange, *04* | | 160 | _____ |
| **52344** | MILW Milk Car, blue, *04* | | 205 | _____ |
| **52393** | MKT Speeder, yellow, nonpowered, *05* | | 20 | _____ |
| **52394** | Frisco Speeder, red, powered, *05* | | 25 | _____ |
| **52395** | Frisco Flatcar, silver, *05* | | 25 | _____ |
| **52396** | Frisco Flatcar with 2 speeders, *05* | | 125 | _____ |
| **52412** | UP Auxiliary Power Car, *06* | | 55 | _____ |
| **52455** | C&NW/UP Tank Car, *07* | | 110 | _____ |
| **52491** | PS-2 Covered Hopper 2-pack, *08* | | 140 | _____ |
| **52507** | NYC Water Tower, *08* | | 83 | _____ |
| **52514** | ATSF Mint Car with Gold, *09* | | 245 | _____ |
| **52543** | BNSF Mechanical Reefer, *09* | | 140 | _____ |
| | UP Cylindrical Hopper, *10* | | 80 | _____ |

### LCCA Meet Specials

| | | Exc | Mint | Cond/S |
|---|---|---|---|---|
| **1130** | Tender, *76* | | 15 | _____ |
| **6014-900** | Frisco Boxcar (O27), *75* | 17 | 30 | _____ |
| **6483** | Jersey Central SP-type Caboose, *82* | 24 | 28 | _____ |
| **9016** | Chessie System Hopper (O27), *79* | 16 | 20 | _____ |
| **9036** | Mobilgas 1-D Tank Car (O27), *78* | 20 | 22 | _____ |
| **9142** | Republic Steel Gondola, green or blue, with canisters, *77* | 15 | 23 | _____ |

### Other LCCA Production

| | | Exc | Mint | Cond/S |
|---|---|---|---|---|
| **4001** | RJ Corman Boxcar, *99* | | 80 | _____ |
| **4002** | RJ Corman Boxcar, *99* | | 40 | _____ |
| **6464-2002** | Maddox Retirement Boxcar, *02* | | 100 | _____ |
| **8068** | Rock Island GP20 Diesel, *80* | 85 | 120 | _____ |
| **9739** | D&RGW Boxcar, *78* | 17 | 25 | _____ |
| **9771** | Norfolk & Western Boxcar, *77* | | 32 | _____ |
| **14154** | Water Tower with LCCA plaque, *04* | | 90 | _____ |
| **17174** | Great Northern 3-bay Hopper, *03* | | 25 | _____ |
| **17234** | Port Huron & Detroit Boxcar, *00* | | 45 | _____ |
| **17377** | American Railway Express Reefer "302," *06* | | 48 | _____ |

## CLUB CARS AND SPECIAL PRODUCTION

| | | Exc | Mint | Cond/$ |
|---|---|---|---|---|
| **17412** | Gondola, blue, *02* | | 28 | ____ |
| **17895** | LCCA Tractor, *91* | 13 | 21 | ____ |
| **17896** | Lancaster Lines Tractor, *91* | 22 | 30 | ____ |
| **18090** | D&RGW 4-6-2 Locomotive and Tender, *90* | 230 | 303 | ____ |
| **18483** | C&O Ballast Tamper, *07* | | 73 | ____ |
| **18490** | UP Ballast Tamper, yellow, *06* | | 125 | ____ |
| **19998** | "Seasons Greetings" Boxcar, *03* | | 40 | ____ |
| **26023** | Flatcar with bulldozer, *04* | | 53 | ____ |
| **26024** | Flatcar with scraper, *04* | | 63 | ____ |
| **26049** | Speedboat Willie Flatcar with boat, *05* | | 45 | ____ |
| **26132** | UP 1-D Tank Car, *06* | | 27 | ____ |
| **26780** | Operating Giraffe Car, green or pink, *05* | | 70 | ____ |
| **26791** | UP Chase Gondola, red, *03* | | 32 | ____ |
| **26791** | Rio Grande Chase Gondola, black, *06* | | 32 | ____ |
| **26795** | Mrs. O'Leary's Dairy Farm Stock Car, *07* | | 100 | ____ |
| **26834** | "La Cosa Nostra Railway" Operating Ice Car, *07* | 25 | 75 | ____ |
| **29232** | Lenny the Lion Hi-Cube, signed by Lenny Dean, *98* | | 63 | ____ |
| **52025** | Madison Hardware Tractor and Trailer, *93* | 13 | 18 | ____ |
| **52039** | "Track 29" Bumper, *94* | | 23 | ____ |
| **52055** | SOVEX Tractor and Trailer, *94* | 15 | 22 | ____ |
| **52056** | Southern Tractor and Trailer, *94* | 17 | 23 | ____ |
| **52091** | Lenox Tractor and Trailer, *95* | | 14 | ____ |
| **52092** | Iowa Interstate Tractor and Trailer, *95* | | 20 | ____ |
| **52100** | Grand Rapids Station Platform, *98* | | 23 | ____ |
| **52107** | On-track Pickup, orange, *96* | | 50 | ____ |
| **52108** | On-track Van, blue, *96* | | 35 | ____ |
| **52131** | Beechcraft Airplane, blue, *97* | | 25 | ____ |
| **52138** | Beechcraft Airplane, orange, *97* | | 25 | ____ |
| **52152** | Ben Franklin and Liberty Bell Reefer, *98* | | 120 | ____ |
| **52153** | 6414 Auto Set, 4-pack, *98* | | 72 | ____ |
| **52206** | SD40 Diesel and Extended Vision Caboose, *00* | | 650 | ____ |
| **52257** | "Season's Greetings" Gondola, *01* | | 36 | ____ |
| **52273** | Flatcar with submarine, *02* | | 219 | ____ |
| **52300** | Halloween General Train, *04* | | 360 | ____ |
| **52348** | Halloween General Sheriff and Outlaw Car, *04* | | 115 | ____ |
| **52405** | Halloween General Add-on Cars, *06* | | 160 | ____ |
| **52406** | Halloween General Cannon, *08* | | 135 | ____ |
| **52423** | New Haven Alco Diesel Passenger Set, *09* | | 510 | ____ |
| **52468** | Postwar "2434" Passenger Coach, *09* | | 75 | ____ |
| **52469** | Postwar "2432" Passenger Coach, *09* | | 75 | ____ |

# Lionel Operating Train Society

## LOTS National Convention Cars

| | | Exc | Mint | Cond/$ |
|---|---|---|---|---|
| 303 | Stauffer Chemical 1-D Tank Car, 85 | 85 | 210 | ___ |
| 3764 | Kahn's Brine Tank Reefer, 81 | 70 | 85 | ___ |
| 6111 | L&N Covered Quad Hopper, 83 | 37 | 42 | ___ |
| 6211 | C&O Gondola with canisters, 86 | 60 | 90 | ___ |
| 9414 | Cotton Belt Boxcar, 80 | 39 | 55 | ___ |
| 16812 | Grand Trunk 2-bay ACF Hopper (std O), 96 | | 60 | ___ |
| 16813 | Pennsylvania Power & Light Hopper with coal (std O), 97 | | 78 | ___ |
| 17874 | Milwaukee Road Log Dump Car "59629," 88 | 90 | 148 | ___ |
| 17875 | Port Huron & Detroit Boxcar "1289," 89 | 40 | 48 | ___ |
| 17882 | B&O DD Boxcar "298011" with ETD, 90 | 55 | 65 | ___ |
| 17890 | CSX Auto Carrier "151161," 91 | 75 | 80 | ___ |
| 18890 | Union Pacific RS3 Diesel "8805," 89 | 120 | 145 | ___ |
| 19960 | Western Pacific Boxcar "1953" (std O), 92 | 47 | 66 | ___ |
| 38356 | Dow Chemical 3-D Tank Car, 87 | 85 | 125 | ___ |
| 52014 | BN TTUX Flatcar Set with N&W trailers, 93 | 165 | 205 | ___ |
| 52041 | BN TTUX Flatcar Set with Conrail trailers, 94 | 60 | 85 | ___ |
| 52067 | Burlington Operating Ice Car "50240," 95 | | 60 | ___ |
| 52135 | ATSF Reefer "22739," 98 | | 55 | ___ |
| 52162 | Gulf Mobile & Ohio DD Boxcar "24580," 99 | | 65 | ___ |
| 52196 | CP Maxi-Stack Flatcar "524115" with 2 containers, 00 | | 95 | ___ |
| 52234 | WM Well Car with transformer, 01 | | 60 | ___ |
| 52261 | Schlitz Beer Reefer "92132," 02 | | 60 | ___ |
| 52281 | PRR Operating Boxcar, 03 | | 55 | ___ |
| 52342 | Southern Stock Car, sound, 04 | | 57 | ___ |
| 52346 | D&H PS-2 Cement Hopper, 06 | | 65 | ___ |
| 52347 | SF SD80 MAC Diesel, TMCC, 04 | | 350 | ___ |
| 52380/81 | Virginian Coal Hopper, 05 | | 50 | ___ |
| 52382 | SF Extended View Caboose, 05 | | 325 | ___ |
| 52425 | SP&S Boxcar (std O), 07 | | 90 | ___ |
| 52474 | NYC Evans Auto Loader with 4 Studebakers, 08 | | 82 | ___ |
| 52550 | NC&StL Dixieland Boxcar, 09 | | 73 | ___ |
| 52553 | Tennessee Aquarium Car, 09 | 15 | 52 | ___ |
| 52566 | NH State of Maine Boxcar, 10 | | 62 | ___ |
| 80948 | Michigan Central Boxcar, 82 | 145 | 230 | ___ |
| 121315 | Pennsylvania Hi-Cube Boxcar, 84 | 125 | 343 | ___ |

## LOTS Meet Specials

| | | Exc | Mint | Cond/$ |
|---|---|---|---|---|
| 52413 | Saratoga Brewery Reefer, 06 | | 60 | ___ |
| 52456 | Alpenrose Dairy Milk Car, 07 | | 95 | ___ |
| 52506 | Studebaker Automobile Parts Boxcar, 08 | | 75 | ___ |
| 52552 | Radioactive Waste Removal Car, 09 | | 86 | ___ |

## CLUB CARS AND SPECIAL PRODUCTION

| | | Exc | Mint | Cond/$ |
|---|---|---|---|---|

### Other LOTS Production

| | | Exc | Mint | Cond/$ |
|---|---|---|---|---|
| 1223 | Seattle & North Coast Hi-Cube Boxcar, 86 | 150 | 200 | ____ |
| 52042 | BN TTUX Flatcar "637500C" with CN trailer, 94 | 50 | 60 | ____ |
| 52048 | Canadian National Tractor and Trailer "197993," 94 | 28 | 33 | ____ |
| 52129 | Lighted Billboard with Angela Trotta Thomas art, 97 | | 28 | ____ |
| 52217 | LOTS/LCCA 2000 Convention Billboard, 00 | | 10 | ____ |
| 52260 | National Aquarium in Baltimore Car, 01 | | 110 | ____ |
| 52280 | "More Precious than Gold" Mint Car, 02 | | 90 | ____ |
| 52309 | Patriotic Tank Car, 03 | | 68 | ____ |
| 52359 | Silver Anniversary Ore Car "1979," 04 | | 40 | ____ |
| 52360 | Silver Anniversary Ore Car "2004," 04 | | 40 | ____ |
| 52419 | Touring Layout Aquarium Car, 05 | | 90 | ____ |
| 52523 | Santa Fe Flatcar with trailer and tractor, 08 | | 88 | ____ |

### Lionel Century Club

| | | Exc | Mint | Cond/$ |
|---|---|---|---|---|
| 14532 | PRR Sharknose Diesel AA Set, LCC II, 00 | | 690 | ____ |
| 18053 | 2-8-4 Berkshire Locomotive "726," 97 | | 705 | ____ |
| 18057 | 6-8-6PRR S2 Steam Turbine Locomotive "671," 98 | 320 | 568 | ____ |
| 18058 | 4-6-4 Hudson Locomotive "773," 97 | | 734 | ____ |
| 18068 | Tender for PRR Steam Turbine Locomotive "773," 99 | | 210 | ____ |
| 18135 | NYC F3 Diesel AA Set, 99 | | 650 | ____ |
| 18178 | NYC F3 Diesel B Unit, 99 | | 230 | ____ |
| 18314 | PRR GG1 Electric "2332," 97 | 490 | 560 | ____ |
| 18340 | FM Train Master Set, LCC II, 00 | | 900 | ____ |
| 24510 | PRR Sharknose Diesel B Unit, LCC II, 00 | | 200 | ____ |
| 28069 | NYC 4-8-6 Niagara Locomotive "6024," CC, LCC II, 00 | | 920 | ____ |
| 29173 | Empire State Express Passenger Car 4-pack, LCC II, 02 | | 350 | ____ |
| 29178 | Empire State Express Passenger Car 2-pack, LCC II, 02 | | 175 | ____ |
| 29181 | Empire State Express Diner, LCC II, 02 | | 190 | ____ |
| 29204 | Boxcar "1900-2000," 96 | | 331 | ____ |
| 29226 | Berkshire Boxcar, 97 | 115 | 145 | ____ |
| 29227 | GG1 Boxcar, 98 | | 55 | ____ |
| 29228 | PRR Turbine Boxcar "671," 99 | | 60 | ____ |
| 29248 | F3 Boxcar "2333," 99 | | 67 | ____ |
| 31716 | Niagara Milk Train Set, LCC II, 00 | | 300 | ____ |
| 31726 | PRR Sharknose Coal Train Set, LCC II, 00 | | 180 | ____ |
| 31731 | Train Master Freight Train Set, LCC II, 00 | | 180 | ____ |
| 38000 | NYC 4-6-4 Hudson Empire State Locomotive, LCC II, 02 | | 990 | ____ |

| | | Exc | Mint | Cond/$ |
|---|---|---|---|---|
| 38195 | Santa Fe FT Diesel A Unit "170," 00 | | NRS | ___ |
| 39201 | Hudson Boxcar "773," 00 | | 58 | ___ |
| 39215 | Niagara Boxcar, LCC II, 01 | | 48 | ___ |
| 39217 | Boxcar, LCC II, 00 | | 60 | ___ |
| 39218 | Gold Boxcar, LCC II, 00 | | 85 | ___ |
| 39237 | M-10000 Boxcar, LCC II, 00 | | 70 | ___ |
| 39246 | PRR Sharknose Boxcar, LCC II, 00 | | 55 | ___ |
| 39249 | Christmas Boxcar, 03 | | 30 | ___ |
| 39265 | Fairbanks-Morse Train Master Boxcar, LCC II, 00 | | 60 | ___ |
| 39266 | Empire State Boxcar, LCC II, 00 | | 40 | ___ |
| 51007 | UP M-10000 4-car Passenger Set, LCC II, 00 | 600 | 970 | ___ |
| 51249 | UP Overland Route Sleeper Car, LCC II, 02 | | 120 | ___ |

## Lionel Railroader Club

| | | Exc | Mint | Cond/$ |
|---|---|---|---|---|
| 780 | Boxcar, 82 | 55 | 67 | ___ |
| 781 | Flatcar with trailers, 83 | 40 | 50 | ___ |
| 782 | 1-D Tank Car, 85 | 40 | 43 | ___ |
| 784 | Covered Quad Hopper, 84 | 50 | 60 | ___ |
| 12875 | Tractor and Trailer, 94 | 13 | 18 | ___ |
| 12921 | Illuminated Station Platform, 95 | 19 | 22 | ___ |
| 14274 | Water Tower, 07 | | 20 | ___ |
| 16800 | Ore Car, yellow, 86 | 60 | 69 | ___ |
| 16801 | Bunk Car, blue, 88 | 20 | 33 | ___ |
| 16802 | Tool Car, 89 | 24 | 35 | ___ |
| 16803 | Searchlight Car, 90 | 23 | 27 | ___ |
| 16804 | Bay Window Caboose, 91 | 25 | 30 | ___ |
| 18680 | 4-6-4 Hudson Locomotive, 00 | | 300 | ___ |
| 18684 | 4-6-2 Pacific Locomotive, 99 | | 220 | ___ |
| 18818 | GP38-2 Diesel, 92 | 100 | 117 | ___ |
| 19437 | Flatcar with trailer, 97 | | 55 | ___ |
| 19473 | Operating Log Dump Car "3351," 99 | | 38 | ___ |
| 19685 | Western Union Dining Car, 02 | | 47 | ___ |
| 19695 | Western Union 1-D Tank Car, 03 | | 22 | ___ |
| 19774 | Porthole Caboose, 99 | | 49 | ___ |
| 19775 | Stock Car, 99 | | 51 | ___ |
| 19924 | Boxcar, 93 | 18 | 22 | ___ |
| 19930 | Quad Hopper with coal, 94 | 14 | 20 | ___ |
| 19935 | 1-D Tank Car, 95 | 19 | 24 | ___ |
| 19940 | Vat Car, 96 | | 32 | ___ |
| 19953 | 6464 Boxcar, 97 | | 35 | ___ |
| 19965 | Aquarium Car "3435," 99 | | 56 | ___ |
| 19966 | Gondola "9820" (std O), 98 | 18 | 32 | ___ |
| 19978 | Gold Membership Boxcar, 99 | | 46 | ___ |
| 19991 | Gold Membership Boxcar, 00 | | 65 | ___ |

## CLUB CARS AND SPECIAL PRODUCTION

| | | Exc | Mint | Cond/$ |
|---|---|---|---|---|
| **19992** | Western Union Tool Car "3550," 00 | | 50 | ____ |
| **19993** | Gold Membership Boxcar, 01 | | 65 | ____ |
| **19994** | Western Union Passenger Car "1307," 01 | | 60 | ____ |
| **19995** | 25th Anniversary Boxcar (std O), 01 | | 49 | ____ |
| **24217** | Animated Billboard, 08 | | 25 | ____ |
| **26089** | Western Union Gondola with handcar, 05 | | 65 | ____ |
| **26165** | Western Union Reefer, 04 | | 30 | ____ |
| **26382** | Flatcar with tractor and tanker, 08 | | 60 | ____ |
| **26413** | Commemorative 4-bay Hopper, 08 | | 68 | ____ |
| **28062** | 4-6-4 Hudson Locomotive, 00 | | 1150 | ____ |
| **28571** | GP9 Diesel, CC | | 250 | ____ |
| **28665** | Western Union 2-8-4 Berkshire Locomotive "665," 05 | | 175 | ____ |
| **29200** | Lionel Boxcar "9700," 96 | | 38 | ____ |
| **29931** | Holiday Boxcar, 05 | | 25 | ____ |
| **29939** | 30th Anniversary Boxcar, 06 | | 50 | ____ |
| **29941** | Holiday Boxcar, 06 | | 25 | ____ |
| **29946** | Holiday Boxcar, 07 | | 25 | ____ |
| **29947** | Commemorative Boxcar, 07 | | 25 | ____ |
| **36521** | Western Union Searchlight Caboose, 05 | | 32 | ____ |
| **36769** | 4th of July Lighted Boxcar, 03 | | 70 | ____ |
| **39249** | Holiday Boxcar, 03 | | 22 | ____ |
| **39264** | Holiday Boxcar, 04 | | 50 | ____ |
| **39496** | "6475" 50th Anniversary Vat Car, 10 | | 60 | ____ |

## Lionel Railroad Club Milwaukee

| | | Exc | Mint | Cond/$ |
|---|---|---|---|---|
| **52116** | MILW Flatcar "194797," black, with tractor and trailer, 97 | | 76 | ____ |
| **52163** | CMStP&P "Hiawatha" DD Automobile Boxcar, 98 | | 60 | ____ |
| **52180** | MILW Flatcar "194799," tuscan, with trailer, 99 | | 75 | ____ |
| **52228** | CMStP&P 1-D Water Tank Car "908309," 00 | | 50 | ____ |
| **52229** | MILW 1-D Diesel Fuel Tank Car "907797," 00 | | 50 | ____ |
| **52230** | 1-D Tank Car 2-pack, 00 | | 142 | ____ |
| **52246** | CMStP&P "Olympian" Boxcar "194701," 01 | | 67 | ____ |
| **52265** | MILW/Zoological Society Aquarium Car "4701," orange, 02 | | 55 | ____ |
| **52278** | MILW/Zoological Society Aquarium Car "4702," blue, 03 | | 95 | ____ |
| **52297** | MILW Reefer "194703," yellow, 03 | | 67 | ____ |
| **52298** | MILW Flatcar "194704" with orange trailer, 04 | | 115 | ____ |
| **52337** | MILW/Zoological Society Motorized Aquarium Car, 04 | | 90 | ____ |
| **52368** | MILW Flatcar "472004," black, 05 | | 65 | ____ |
| **52369** | MILW Trailer Train Auto Carrier "194705," 05 | | 85 | ____ |
| **52370** | CMStP&P Milk Car "364," tan, 05 | | 81 | ____ |
| **52387** | CMStP&P Flatcar "194706," gray, 06 | | 50 | ____ |

| | | Exc | Mint | Cond/$ |
|---|---|---|---|---|
| 52400 | MILW PS-2 2-bay Hopper "99607," orange, 06 | | 85 | ____ |
| 52401 | MILW PS-2 2-bay Hopper "98809," yellow, 06 | | 65 | ____ |
| 52402 | CMStP&P URTX Operating Ice Car "4706," 06 | | 85 | ____ |
| 52428 | CMStP&P 0-4-0 Switcher and Caboose Set, 60th Anniversary, 06 | | 275 | ____ |
| 52429 | CMStP&P 0-4-0 Switcher, 06 | | 200 | ____ |
| 52430 | CMStP&P Offset Cupola Caboose, 06 | | 70 | ____ |
| 52458 | MILW Stock Car "102721" (std O), 07 | | 67 | ____ |
| 52466 | CMStP&P Stock Car "105254" (std O), 07 | | 67 | ____ |
| 52551 | MILW "Big M" DD Boxcar "200947," yellow, 09 | | 60 | ____ |

# Nassau Lionel Operating Engineers

| | | Exc | Mint | Cond/$ |
|---|---|---|---|---|
| 8389 | Long Island Boxcar, 89 | 70 | 100 | ____ |
| 8390 | Long Island Covered Quad Hopper, 90 | 70 | 100 | ____ |
| 8391A | Long Island Bunk Car, 91 | 70 | 90 | ____ |
| 8391B | Long Island Tool Car, 91 | 70 | 90 | ____ |
| 8392 | Long Island 1-D Tank Car, 92 | 80 | 105 | ____ |
| 52007 | Long Island RS3 Diesel "1552," 93 | 120 | 250 | ____ |
| 52019 | Long Island Boxcar, 93 | 39 | 65 | ____ |
| 52020 | Long Island Bay Window Caboose, 93 | 65 | 95 | ____ |
| 52026 | Long Island Flatcar "8394" with Grumman trailer, 94 | 275 | 465 | ____ |
| 52061 | Long Island Stern's Pickle Products Vat Car "8395," 95 | | 200 | ____ |
| 52072 | Grumman Tractor, 94 | | 75 | ____ |
| 52076 | Long Island Observation Car "8396," 96 | | 350 | ____ |
| 52112 | Long Island Ronkonkoma Vista Dome Car "9783," 97 | | 300 | ____ |
| 52122 | Meenan Oil 1-D Tank Car "8397" (std O), 97 | | 60 | ____ |
| 52123 | Long Island Hicksville Diner Car "9883," 98 | | 300 | ____ |
| 52144 | Long Island Flatcar with Grumman van, 99 | | 94 | ____ |
| 52145 | Long Island Jamaica Passenger Coach, 99 | | 300 | ____ |
| 52145 | Long Island Penn Station Passenger Coach, 99 | | 300 | ____ |
| 52166 | Long Island Flatcar "8398" with Grumman trailer, 98 | | 77 | ____ |
| 52186 | Grucci Fireworks Boxcar, 00 | | 72 | ____ |
| 52232 | Central RR of Long Island Boxcar, 01 | | 60 | ____ |
| 52256 | New York & Atlantic Boxcar "8302," 02 | | 58 | ____ |
| 52296 | Long Island Flatcar with Republic tanker, 03 | | 78 | ____ |
| 52329 | New York & Atlantic Caboose, 04 | | 80 | ____ |
| 52341 | Long Island Flatcar with Pan Am trailer, 05 | | 85 | ____ |
| 52365 | Long Island Flatcar with Lilco transformer, 04 | | 135 | ____ |
| 52420 | Long Island 80th Anniversary Boxcar, 06 | | 45 | ____ |
| 52480 | Long Island Flatcar with pipes, 08 | | 50 | ____ |
| 52489 | Long Island Flatcar with P.C. Richard & Son trailer, 07 | | 67 | ____ |

| | | Exc | Mint | Cond/$ |
|---|---|---|---|---|
| 52555 | Martha Clara Vineyards Vat Car, 09 | | 58 | ___ |
| 52568 | Flatcar with NY Islanders refrigerated trailer, 10 | | 62 | ___ |

## Railroad Museum of Long Island

| | | Exc | Mint | Cond/$ |
|---|---|---|---|---|
| 52416 | RMLI 15th Anniversary LIRR Boxcar, 05 | | 113 | ___ |
| 52433 | Atlantis Marine World Aquarium Car, 06 | | 114 | ___ |
| 52453 | North Fork Bank Mint Car, 07 | | 84 | ___ |
| 52497 | LIRR Flatcar with Entenmann's trailer and tractor, 08 | | 88 | ___ |
| 52498 | Boeing Fairchild Container Car, 10 | | 63 | ___ |
| 52548 | RMLI "Celebrating 175 Years of Railroading" Boxcar, 09 | | 83 | ___ |
| 52557 | Entenmann's Operating Boxcar, 10 | | 65 | ___ |
| 52570 | Riverhead Building Supply Boxcar, 11 | | 55 | ___ |
| 52571 | Riverhead Visitor's Center Boxcar, 11 | | 55 | ___ |

## St. Louis Lionel Railroad Club

| | | Exc | Mint | Cond/$ |
|---|---|---|---|---|
| 52099 | MP Flatcar with St. Louis trailer, 96 | | 65 | ___ |
| 52104 | St. Louis tractor and trailer, 96 | | 20 | ___ |
| 52117 | Wabash Flatcar with REA tractor and trailer, 97 | | 65 | ___ |
| 52136A | Christmas Tractor and Trailer, 97 | | NRS | ___ |
| 52136B | Frisco Tractor and Trailer, 98 | | NRS | ___ |
| 52147 | Frisco Campbell TOFC Flatcar, 98 | | 75 | ___ |
| 52150 | Frisco Campbell TOFC Flatcar, 98 | | 130 | ___ |
| 52167 | ATSF Flatcar "831999" with Navajo trailer, 99 | | 75 | ___ |
| 52190 | IC Flatcar with trailers, 00 | | 80 | ___ |
| 52222 | Cotton Belt Flatcar with SP tractor and trailer, 01 | | 50 | ___ |
| 52224A | SP Flatcar with Navajo tractor and trailer, 01 | | 25 | ___ |
| 52224B | SP Flatcar with service tractor and trailer, 01 | | 25 | ___ |
| 52258 | UP Flatcar with UP tractor and trailer, 02 | | 55 | ___ |
| 52290 | UP Flatcar with tractor trailer, 03 | | 75 | ___ |
| 52392 | PRR Flatcar with Hood's Milk tractor and tank, 06 | | 100 | ___ |

## Train Collectors Association

### TCA National Convention Cars

| | | Exc | Mint | Cond/$ |
|---|---|---|---|---|
| 511 | St. Louis Baggage Car, 81 | 36 | 41 | ___ |
| 2671-1968 | TCA Tender, shell only, 68 | 10 | 54 | ___ |
| 5734 | REA Reefer, 85 | 42 | 51 | ___ |
| 6315 | Pittsburgh 1-D Tank Car, 72 | 55 | 60 | ___ |
| 6436-1969 | Open Quad Hopper, red, 69 | 35 | 65 | ___ |
| 6464-1965 | Pittsburgh Boxcar, blue, 65 | 35 | 163 | ___ |

## CLUB CARS AND SPECIAL PRODUCTION

| | | Exc | Mint | Cond/$ |
|---|---|---|---|---|
| 6464-1970 | Chicago Boxcar, *70* | 69 | 116 | ____ |
| 6464-1971 | Disneyland Boxcar, *71* | 210 | 240 | ____ |
| 6517-1966 | Bay Window Caboose, *66* | 58 | 288 | ____ |
| 6926 | New Orleans Extended Vision Caboose, *86* | 27 | 39 | ____ |
| 7205 | Denver Combination Car, *82* | 37 | 50 | ____ |
| 7206 | Louisville Passenger Car, *83* | 40 | 55 | ____ |
| 7212 | Pittsburgh Passenger Car, *84* | 41 | 50 | ____ |
| 7812 | Houston Stock Car, *77* | 12 | 25 | ____ |
| 8476 | 4-6-4 Locomotive "5484," *85* | 255 | 310 | ____ |
| 9123 | Dearborn 3-tier Auto Carrier, *73* | 25 | 36 | ____ |
| 9319 | "Silver Jubilee" Mint Car, *79* | 105 | 130 | ____ |
| 9544 | Chicago Observation Car, *80* | | 50 | ____ |
| 9611 | Boston Hi-Cube Boxcar, *78* | 21 | 26 | ____ |
| 9774 | Orlando "Southern Belle" Boxcar, *75* | 27 | 35 | ____ |
| 9779 | Philadelphia Boxcar "9700-1976," *76* | 26 | 34 | ____ |
| 9864 | Seattle Reefer, *74* | 37 | 52 | ____ |
| 11737 | TCA 40th Anniversary F3 Diesel ABA Set, *93* | 460 | 528 | ____ |
| 17879 | *Valley Forge* Dining Car, *89* | | 60 | ____ |
| 17883 | *New Georgia* Passenger Car, *90* | 52 | 64 | ____ |
| 17898 | Wabash Reefer "21596," *92* | 41 | 44 | ____ |
| 19211 | Vermont Railway Flatcars (2) with 4 trailers, *08* | | 160 | ____ |
| 52008 | Bucyrus Erie Crane Car, *93* | 44 | 49 | ____ |
| 52035 | Yorkrail GP9 Diesel "1750," shell only, *94* | 44 | 55 | ____ |
| 52036 | TCA 40th Anniversary Bay Window Caboose, *94* | 35 | 40 | ____ |
| 52037 | Yorkrail GP9 Diesel "1754," *94* | 125 | 150 | ____ |
| 52062 | Skytop Observation Car, *95* | 210 | 360 | ____ |
| 52085 | Full Vista Dome Car, *96* | | 115 | ____ |
| 52106 | *City of Phoenix* Diner, *97* | | 100 | ____ |
| 52142 | Massachusetts Central Maxi-Stack Flatcar "5100-01," *98* | | 120 | ____ |
| 52143 | *City of Providence* Passenger Car, *98* | | 140 | ____ |
| 52146 | Ocean Spray Reefer, *98* | | 235 | ____ |
| 52155 | *City of San Francisco* Baggage Car, *99* | | 140 | ____ |
| 52191 | *City of Grand Rapids* Aluminum Passenger Car, *00* | | 135 | ____ |
| 52210 | Rico Station, *00* | | 29 | ____ |
| 52220 | *City of Chattanooga* Vista Dome Car, *01* | | 140 | ____ |
| 52221 | Norfolk Southern Boxcar, *01* | | 50 | ____ |
| 52237 | Lionel Gondola, yellow, *01* | | 110 | ____ |
| 52238 | Lionel Gondola, red, *01* | | 110 | ____ |
| 52239 | Lionel Gondola, silver, *01* | | 110 | ____ |
| 52240 | Lionel Gondola 3-pack, *01* | | 110 | ____ |
| 52241 | Lionel Gondola, black, *02* | | 15 | ____ |
| 52242 | Lionel Gondola, blue, *02* | | 35 | ____ |

## CLUB CARS AND SPECIAL PRODUCTION

| | | Exc | Mint | Cond/$ |
|---|---|---|---|---|
| 52250 | *City of Chicago* Combination Car, *02* | | 130 | _____ |
| 52272 | Lionel Gondola, gold, *02* | | 80 | _____ |
| 52276 | California Gold Mint Car, *03* | | 65 | _____ |
| 52333 | Harmony Dairy Milk Car, *04* | | 90 | _____ |
| 52338 | Lionel 50th Anniversary Mint Car, *04* | | 75 | _____ |
| 52339 | 50th Anniversary Convention Banquet Car with coin, *04* | | 360 | _____ |
| 52340 | Train Order Building, *04* | | 90 | _____ |
| 52373 | Montana Rail Link 2-car Set, *05* | | 90 | _____ |
| 52374 | Montana Rail Link 2-bay Hopper, *05* | | 50 | _____ |
| 52375 | Montana Rail Link Flatcar with pulp-wood logs, *05* | | 50 | _____ |
| 52376 | GN Reefer, *05* | | 60 | _____ |
| 52403 | T&P Stock Car (std O), *06* | | 75 | _____ |
| 52414 | Flatcar with 3 snowmobiles, *07* | | 80 | _____ |
| 52481 | Ben & Jerry's Reefer, *08* | | 95 | _____ |

### TCA Museum-Related and Other Cars

| | | Exc | Mint | Cond/$ |
|---|---|---|---|---|
| 1018-1979 | Mortgage Burning Hi-Cube Boxcar, *79* | 32 | 37 | _____ |
| 5731 | L&N Reefer, *90* | | 95 | _____ |
| 7780 | TCA Museum Boxcar, *80* | | 26 | _____ |
| 7781 | Hafner Boxcar, *81* | | 26 | _____ |
| 7782 | Carlisle & Finch Boxcar, *82* | | 26 | _____ |
| 7783 | Ives Boxcar, *83* | | 26 | _____ |
| 7784 | Voltamp Boxcar, *84* | | 23 | _____ |
| 7785 | Hoge Boxcar, *85* | | 23 | _____ |
| 9771 | Norfolk & Western Boxcar, *77* | 24 | 31 | _____ |
| 16811 | Rutland Boxcar "5477096," *96* | | 34 | _____ |
| 52045 | Pennsylvania Dutch Milk Car "61052," *94* | | 90 | _____ |
| 52051 | Baltimore & Ohio Sentinel Boxcar "6464095," *95* | 36 | 42 | _____ |
| 52052 | TCA 40th Anniversary Boxcar, *94* | | 90 | _____ |
| 52063 | NYC Pacemaker Boxcar "6464125," *95* | | 345 | _____ |
| 52064 | Missouri Pacific Boxcar "6464150," *95* | | 370 | _____ |
| 52065 | Pennsylvania Dutch Grain Operating Boxcar "9208," *96* | | 100 | _____ |
| 52118 | Rio Grande Boxcar "5477097," *97* | | 53 | _____ |
| 52119 | TCA Museum 20th Anniversary Boxcar, *97* | | 70 | _____ |
| 52128 | Pennsylvania Dutch Pretzels Boxcar, *99* | | 80 | _____ |
| 52172 | L&N "Share the Freedom" Boxcar "5477099," *99* | | 56 | _____ |
| 52198 | Frisco Boxcar "5477000," *00* | | 43 | _____ |
| 52215 | Museum Work Train Gondola with pipes, *03* | | 53 | _____ |
| 52226 | Angela Trotta Thomas Boxcar "2000," *01* | | 100 | _____ |
| 52243 | Museum Work Train 1-D Tank Car, *01* | | 50 | _____ |
| 52271 | Museum Work Train Flatcar with wheel load, *02* | | 20 | _____ |

## CLUB CARS AND SPECIAL PRODUCTION

|  |  | Exc | Mint | Cond/$ |
|---|---|---|---|---|
| **52289** | National Toy Train Museum 25th Anniversary Bullion Car, *02* | | 75 | ___ |
| **52295** | National Toy Train Museum Gondola with pipes, *03* | | 16 | ___ |
| **52310** | Museum Work Train Boxcar, *04* | | 53 | ___ |
| **52311** | 50th Anniversary Golden Express Freight Set, *04* | | 450 | ___ |
| **52372** | Museum Work Train Baggage Car, *05* | | 70 | ___ |
| **52408** | N&W Caboose, *06* | | 55 | ___ |
| **52409** | Museum Work Train Idler Caboose, *06* | | 68 | ___ |
| **52437** | Museum Work Train Crane Car, *07* | | 78 | ___ |

### TCA Bicentennial Special Set

|  |  | Exc | Mint | Cond/$ |
|---|---|---|---|---|
| **1973** | Bicentennial Observation Car, *76* | 34 | 50 | ___ |
| **1974** | Bicentennial Passenger Car, *76* | 34 | 50 | ___ |
| **1975** | Bicentennial Passenger Car, *76* | 34 | 50 | ___ |
| **1976** | Bicentennial U36B Diesel, *76* | 140 | 185 | ___ |

### Atlantic Division

|  |  | Exc | Mint | Cond/$ |
|---|---|---|---|---|
| **1980** | Atlantic Division Flatcar with trailers, *80* | 28 | 34 | ___ |
| **6101** | Burlington Northern Covered Quad Hopper, *82* | 21 | 34 | ___ |
| **9186** | Conrail N5c Caboose, *79* | 22 | 30 | ___ |
| **9193** | Budweiser Vat Car, *84* | 80 | 110 | ___ |
| **9466** | Wanamaker Boxcar, *83* | 105 | 135 | ___ |
| **9788** | Lehigh Valley Boxcar, *78* | 19 | 24 | ___ |

### Desert Division

|  |  | Exc | Mint | Cond/$ |
|---|---|---|---|---|
| **52088** | Desert Division 25th Anniversary On-track Step Van, *96* | | 120 | ___ |
| **52105** | Superstition Mountain Operating Gondola "61997," *97* | | 80 | ___ |
| **52442** | Verde Canyon Boxcar, *07* | | 55 | ___ |
| **52443** | Grand Canyon Boxcar, *07* | | 55 | ___ |

### Dixie Division

|  |  | Exc | Mint | Cond/$ |
|---|---|---|---|---|
| **27007/87** | Dixie Division 20th Anniversary PS-1 Boxcar, *06* | | 80 | ___ |
| **52127** | Dixie Division 10th Anniversary Southern 3-bay Hopper, *98* | | 70 | ___ |

### Eastern Division

|  |  | Exc | Mint | Cond/$ |
|---|---|---|---|---|
| **52059** | Clinchfield Quad Hopper "16413" with coal, *94* | 85 | 110 | ___ |

### Eastern Division: Washington, Baltimore & Annapolis Chapter

|  |  | Exc | Mint | Cond/$ |
|---|---|---|---|---|
| **9412** | Richmond, Fredericksburg & Potomac Boxcar, *79* | | 26 | ___ |

| | | Exc | Mint | Cond/S |
|---|---|---|---|---|
| 9740 | Chessie System Boxcar, *76* | | 23 | ___ |
| 9771 | Norfolk & Western Boxcar, *78* | | 30 | ___ |
| 9783 | B&O Time-Saver Boxcar, *77* | | 30 | ___ |

### Fort Pitt Division

| | | Exc | Mint | Cond/S |
|---|---|---|---|---|
| 9984-30X | Heinz Ketchup Boxcar, *84* | | 500 | ___ |

### Great Lakes Division

| | | Exc | Mint | Cond/S |
|---|---|---|---|---|
| 9983 | Churchill Downs Boxcar, *83* | | 200 | ___ |
| 9983 | Churchill Downs Reefer, *83* | | 250 | ___ |
| 9740 | Chessie System Boxcar, *76* | | 23 | ___ |

### Great Lakes Division: Detroit-Toledo Chapter

| | | Exc | Mint | Cond/S |
|---|---|---|---|---|
| 8957 | Burlington Northern GP20 Diesel, *80* | | 230 | ___ |
| 8958 | Burlington Northern GP20 Diesel Dummy Unit, *80* | | 150 | ___ |
| 9119 | Detroit & Mackinac Covered Quad Hopper, *77* | 19 | 22 | ___ |
| 9272 | New Haven Bay Window Caboose, *79* | 19 | 22 | ___ |
| 9401 | Great Northern Boxcar, *78* | | 23 | ___ |
| 9730 | CP Rail Boxcar, *76* | | 27 | ___ |
| 52000 | Detroit-Toledo Division Flatcar with trailer, *92* | 70 | 85 | ___ |

### Great Lakes Division: Three Rivers Chapter

| | | Exc | Mint | Cond/S |
|---|---|---|---|---|
| 9113 | Norfolk & Western Quad Hopper, *76* | 27 | 30 | ___ |

### Great Lakes Division: Western Michigan Chapter

| | | Exc | Mint | Cond/S |
|---|---|---|---|---|
| 9730 | CP Rail Boxcar, *74* | | 25 | ___ |

### Lake & Pines Division

| | | Exc | Mint | Cond/S |
|---|---|---|---|---|
| 52018 | 3-M Boxcar, *93* | | 450 | ___ |

### Lone Star Division

| | | Exc | Mint | Cond/S |
|---|---|---|---|---|
| 7522 | New Orleans Mint Car with coin, *86* | | 420 | ___ |
| 52093 | Lone Star Division Boxcar "6464696," *96* | | 32 | ___ |

### Lone Star Division: North Texas Chapter

| | | Exc | Mint | Cond/S |
|---|---|---|---|---|
| 9739 | D&RGW Boxcar, *76* | | 20 | ___ |

### METCA

| | | Exc | Mint | Cond/S |
|---|---|---|---|---|
| 10 | Jersey Central F3 A Unit, shell only, *71* | | 25 | ___ |
| 9272 | New Haven Bay Window Caboose, *79* | 21 | 25 | ___ |
| 9754 | New York Central Pacemaker Boxcar, *76* | | 31 | ___ |
| 52485 | New York Central Mint Car with copper load, *08* | | 120 | ___ |
| 52486 | Pennsylvania Mint Car, green, *09* | | 125 | ___ |

## CLUB CARS AND SPECIAL PRODUCTION

| | | Exc | Mint | Cond/$ |
|---|---|---|---|---|
| 52487 | Pennsylvania Mint Car, tuscan, *09* | | 125 | ____ |
| 52488 | NYC Lightning Stripe Mint Car, *10* | | 60 | ____ |

### Midwest Division

| | | | | |
|---|---|---|---|---|
| 4 | C&NW F3 Diesel A Unit, shell only, *77* | | 80 | ____ |
| 5 | Midwest Division Covered Quad Hopper, *78* | | 43 | ____ |
| 1287 | C&NW Reefer, *84* | | NRS | ____ |
| 7600 | Frisco "Spirit of '76" N5c Caboose "00003," *76* | | 38 | ____ |
| 9872 | PFE Reefer "00006," *79* | | 410 | ____ |

### Midwest Division: Museum Express

| | | | | |
|---|---|---|---|---|
| 9264 | ICG Covered Quad Hopper, *78* | 22 | 26 | ____ |
| 9289 | C&NW N5c Caboose, *80* | 37 | 44 | ____ |
| 9785 | Conrail Boxcar, *77* | | 35 | ____ |
| 9786 | C&NW Boxcar, *79* | | 20 | ____ |

### NETCA

| | | | | |
|---|---|---|---|---|
| 1203 | Boston & Maine NW2 Diesel, shell only, *72* | | 65 | ____ |
| 5710 | Canadian Pacific Reefer, *82* | 38 | 45 | ____ |
| 5716 | Vermont Central Reefer, *83* | 25 | 30 | ____ |
| 6124 | Delaware & Hudson Covered Quad Hopper, *84* | 25 | 30 | ____ |
| 8051 | Hood's Milk Boxcar, *86* | 44 | 75 | ____ |
| 9181 | Boston & Maine N5c Caboose, *77* | 23 | 35 | ____ |
| 9400 | Conrail Boxcar, tuscan or blue, *78* | 23 | 27 | ____ |
| 9415 | Providence & Worcester Boxcar, *79* | 28 | 34 | ____ |
| 9423 | NYNH&H Boxcar, *80* | 25 | 30 | ____ |
| 9445 | Vermont Northern Boxcar, *81* | 29 | 39 | ____ |
| 9753 | Maine Central Boxcar, *75* | 24 | 34 | ____ |
| 9768 | Boston & Maine Boxcar, *76* | 32 | 39 | ____ |
| 9785 | Conrail Boxcar, *78* | 22 | 26 | ____ |
| 16911 | B&M Flatcar with trailer, *95* | | 150 | ____ |
| 22677 | B&M Baked Beans Boxcar, *10* | | 45 | ____ |
| 52001 | B&M Quad Hopper with coal, *92* | 50 | 75 | ____ |
| 52016 | B&M Gondola with coil covers, *93* | 55 | 65 | ____ |
| 52043 | L.L. Bean Boxcar, *94* | 110 | 210 | ____ |
| 52080 | B&M Flatcar "91095" with trailer, *95* | | 215 | ____ |
| 52111 | Ben & Jerry's Flatcar with trailer, *96* | | 313 | ____ |
| 52212 | Berkshire Brewing Reefer, *00* | | 155 | ____ |
| 52236 | Moxie Boxcar, *01* | | 160 | ____ |
| 52270 | Jenney Manufacturing Tank Car, *02* | | 150 | ____ |
| 52306 | NH Flatcar with New England Transportation trailer, *03* | | 150 | ____ |
| 52352 | Poland Spring Boxcar, *04* | | 131 | ____ |
| 52379 | CP Rail with W.B. Mason trailer, *05* | | 75 | ____ |
| 52383 | Fisk Tire Boxcar, *05* | | 108 | ____ |

## CLUB CARS AND SPECIAL PRODUCTION

| | | Exc | Mint | Cond/$ |
|---|---|---|---|---|
| 52397 | D&H Flatcar with Vermont Railway trailer, 06 | | 90 | ___ |
| 52418 | Indian Motocycle Boxcar, 06 | | 190 | ___ |
| 52434 | New England Central Flatcar with Cabot's trailer, 07 | | 95 | ___ |
| 52448 | Oilzum Tanker 2-car Set, 08 | | 105 | ___ |
| 52457 | Cape Cod Potato Chip Boxcar, 07 | | 93 | ___ |
| 52484A | Cabot's Reefer, 08 | 100 | 250 | ___ |
| 52484B | Bay State Beer Reefer, 09 | | 90 | ___ |

### Ozark Division: Gateway Chapter

| | | Exc | Mint | Cond/$ |
|---|---|---|---|---|
| 5700 | Oppenheimer Reefer, 81 | 55 | 110 | ___ |
| 9068 | Reading Bobber Caboose, 76 | | 20 | ___ |
| 9601 | Illinois Central Gulf Hi-Cube Boxcar, 77 | | 21 | ___ |
| 9767 | Railbox Boxcar, 78 | | 20 | ___ |
| 52003 | "Meet Me In St. Louis" Flatcar with trailer, 92 | | 520 | ___ |

### Pacific Northwest Division

| | | Exc | Mint | Cond/$ |
|---|---|---|---|---|
| 52077 | Great Northern Hi-Cube Boxcar "9695," 95 | | 460 | ___ |

### Rocky Mountain Division

| | | Exc | Mint | Cond/$ |
|---|---|---|---|---|
| 1971-1976 | Rocky Mountain Division Reefer, 76 | | 75 | ___ |

### Sacramento Sierra Chapter

| | | Exc | Mint | Cond/$ |
|---|---|---|---|---|
| 6401 | Virginian Bay Window Caboose, 84 | | 35 | ___ |
| 9301 | U.S. Mail Operating Boxcar, 76 | 26 | 38 | ___ |
| 9414 | Cotton Belt Boxcar, 80 | | 35 | ___ |
| 9427 | Bay Line Boxcar, 81 | | 30 | ___ |
| 9444 | Louisiana Midland Boxcar, 82 | | 35 | ___ |
| 9452 | Western Pacific Boxcar, 83 | | 35 | ___ |
| 9705 | D&RGW Boxcar, 75 | | 38 | ___ |
| 9723 | Western Pacific Boxcar, 73 | | 29 | ___ |
| 9726 | Erie-Lackawanna Boxcar, 79 | | 23 | ___ |
| 9730 | CP Rail Boxcar, 77 | | 30 | ___ |
| 9785 | Conrail Boxcar, 78 | | 22 | ___ |

### Southern Division

| | | Exc | Mint | Cond/$ |
|---|---|---|---|---|
| 1976 | FEC F3 Diesel ABA, shells only, 76 | | 275 | ___ |
| 1986 | Southern Division Bunk Car, 86 | | 30 | ___ |
| 6111 | L&N Covered Quad Hopper, 83 | 20 | 22 | ___ |
| 9287 | Southern N5c Caboose, 77 | 15 | 22 | ___ |
| 9352 | Trailer Train Flatcar with circus trailers, 80 | 29 | 55 | ___ |
| 9403 | Seaboard Coast Line Boxcar, 78 | | 18 | ___ |
| 9405 | Chattahoochie Boxcar, 79 | | 21 | ___ |
| 9443 | Florida East Coast Boxcar, 81 | | 23 | ___ |
| 9471 | ACL Boxcar, 84 | | 23 | ___ |

| | | Exc | Mint | Cond/$ |
|---|---|---|---|---|
| **9482** | Norfolk & Southern Boxcar, *85* | | 23 | ____ |
| **16606** | Southern Searchlight Car, *88* | 17 | 24 | ____ |
| **19942** | Southern Division 30th Anniversary Boxcar, *96* | | 20 | ____ |

### Western Division

| | | Exc | Mint | Cond/$ |
|---|---|---|---|---|
| **52275** | Western Pacific Boxcar, *03* | | 105 | ____ |

# Toy Train Operating Society

## TTOS National Convention Cars

| | | Exc | Mint | Cond/$ |
|---|---|---|---|---|
| **1984** | Sacramento Northern Boxcar, *84* | 65 | 85 | ____ |
| **1985** | Snowbird Covered Quad Hopper, *85* | 42 | 55 | ____ |
| **6076** | Santa Fe Hopper (027), *70* | | 85 | ____ |
| **6167-1967** | Hopper, olive drab with gold lettering, *67* | 25 | 85 | ____ |
| **6476-1** | LV Hopper, gray, *69* | | 50 | ____ |
| **6582** | Portland Flatcar with wood, *86* | 44 | 55 | ____ |
| **9326** | Burlington Northern Bay Window Caboose, *82* | | 25 | ____ |
| **9347** | Niagara Falls 3-D Tank Car, *79* | 38 | 46 | ____ |
| **9355** | Delaware & Hudson Bay Window Caboose, *82* | | 50 | ____ |
| **9361** | C&NW Bay Window Caboose, *82* | 47 | 55 | ____ |
| **9382** | Florida East Coast Bay Window Caboose, *82* | | 70 | ____ |
| **9512** | Summerdale Junction Passenger Car, *74* | 38 | 53 | ____ |
| **9520** | Phoenix Combination Car, *75* | 29 | 33 | ____ |
| **9526** | Snowbird Observation Car, *76* | 36 | 51 | ____ |
| **9535** | Columbus Baggage Car, *77* | 33 | 51 | ____ |
| **9678** | Hollywood Hi-Cube Boxcar, *78* | 25 | 32 | ____ |
| **9868** | Oklahoma City Reefer, *80* | 36 | 44 | ____ |
| **9883** | Phoenix Reefer, *83* | | 50 | ____ |
| **17871** | NYC Flatcar "81487" with Kodak and Xerox trailers, *87* | 185 | 217 | ____ |
| **17872** | Anaconda Ore Car "81988," *88* | 60 | 72 | ____ |
| **17877** | MKT 1-D Tank Car "3739469," *89* | 55 | 70 | ____ |
| **17884** | Columbus & Dayton Terminal Boxcar (std 0), *90* | 32 | 41 | ____ |
| **17889** | SP Flatcar "15791" (std 0) with trailer, *91* | 43 | 63 | ____ |
| **19963** | Union Equity 3-bay ACF Hopper "86892" (std 0), *92* | 30 | 38 | ____ |
| **52010** | Weyerhaeuser DD Boxcar "838593" (std 0), *93* | 20 | 40 | ____ |
| **52029** | Ford 1-D Tank Car "12" (027), *94* | 33 | 40 | ____ |
| **52030** | Ford Gondola "4023," *94* | 23 | 29 | ____ |
| **52031** | Ford Hopper "1458" (027), *94* | 28 | 33 | ____ |
| **52057** | Western Pacific Boxcar, *95* | 45 | 48 | ____ |
| **52087** | New Mexico Central Boxcar, *96* | | 55 | ____ |
| **52114** | NYC Flatcar with Gleason and SASIB trailers, *97* | | 58 | ____ |

# CLUB CARS AND SPECIAL PRODUCTION

| | | Exc | Mint | Cond/$ |
|---|---|---|---|---|
| 52149 | Conrail Flatcar with Blum coal shovel, 98 | | 60 | ___ |
| 52192 | SP Crane and Gondola Set, 00 | | 75 | ___ |
| 52193 | SP Gondola "6060," 00 | | 50 | ___ |
| 52194 | SP Crane Car "7111," 00 | | 35 | ___ |
| 52231 | British Columbia 1-D Tank Car, 01 | | 25 | ___ |
| 52288 | D&RGW Cookie Boxcar, 03 | | 20 | ___ |
| 52293 | D&RGW 1-D Tank Car, 03 | | 40 | ___ |
| 52378 | Las Vegas & Tonopah Boxcar, 05 | | 70 | ___ |
| 52410 | SP Flatcar with 2 trailers, 06 | | 70 | ___ |
| 52441 | Pennsylvania Operating Hopper, 07 | | 60 | ___ |
| 52445 | Pennsylvania Boxcar, 07 | | 68 | ___ |
| 52545 | Erie "6464" Boxcar, 09 | | 50 | ___ |

## TTOS Division Cars

| | | Exc | Mint | Cond/$ |
|---|---|---|---|---|
| 52009 | Sacramento Valley Division WP Boxcar, 93 | 34 | 44 | ___ |
| 52040 | Wolverine Division GTW Flatcar with tractor and trailer, 94 | 42 | 51 | ___ |
| 52058 | Central California Division Santa Fe Boxcar, 95 | 32 | 42 | ___ |
| 52086 | Canadian Division Pacific Great Eastern Boxcar, 96 | | 50 | ___ |
| 52113 | Northeastern Division Genesee & Wyoming 3-bay Hopper, 97 | | 34 | ___ |
| 52264 | New Mexico Division Durango & Silverton Operating Hopper, 02 | | 55 | ___ |

## Southwest Division: Cal-Stewart

| | | Exc | Mint | Cond/$ |
|---|---|---|---|---|
| 19962 | Southern Pacific 3-bay ACF Hopper "496035" (std O), 92 | 50 | 65 | ___ |
| 52047 | Cotton Belt Wood-sided Caboose (std O), smoke, 93–94 | 60 | 68 | ___ |
| 52073 | Pacific Fruit Express Reefer "459402" (std O), 95 | | 65 | ___ |
| 52098 | National Bureau of Standards Boxcar (std O), 96 | | 47 | ___ |
| 52121 | Mobilgas Tank Car "238" (std O), 97 | | 75 | ___ |
| 52154 | Pacific Fruit Express Reefer "459403" (std O), 98 | | 53 | ___ |
| 52205 | SP Overnight Merchandise Service Boxcar 5-pack, 00 | | 185 | ___ |
| 52287 | Operating MX Missile Car, 02 | | 55 | ___ |
| 52385 | Ward Kimball Boxcar, 05 | | 55 | ___ |
| 52431 | Operating MX Missile Car, 06 | | 60 | ___ |
| 52476 | Life Savers Tank Car, 07 | | 85 | ___ |
| 52515 | Life Savers Wild Cherry Tank Car, 08 | | 77 | ___ |
| 52565 | Life Savers Pep-O-Mint Tank Car, 09 | | 60 | ___ |

## Other TTOS Production

| | | Exc | Mint | Cond/S |
|---|---|---|---|---|
| **1983** | Phoenix 3-D Tank Car, *83* | | 100 | ____ |
| **17894** | Southern Pacific Tractor, *91* | 17 | 21 | ____ |
| **27148** | BNSF "4427" PS2 Hopper, *06* | | 50 | ____ |
| **52021** | Weyerhaeuser Tractor and Trailer, *93* | 24 | 31 | ____ |
| **52022** | Union Pacific Boxcar, *93* | | 400 | ____ |
| **52032** | Ford 1-D Tank Car (O27) with Kughn inscription, *94* | 70 | 95 | ____ |
| **52046** | ACL Boxcar "16247," *94* | | 110 | ____ |
| **52053** | Carail Boxcar, *94* | 50 | 55 | ____ |
| **52068** | Toy Train Parade Contadina Boxcar "16245," *94* | | 55 | ____ |
| **52078** | Southern Pacific SD9 Diesel "5366," *96* | | 235 | ____ |
| **52079** | Southern Pacific Bay Window Caboose, *96* | 45 | 55 | ____ |
| **52084** | Union Pacific I-Beam Flatcar "16380" with load, *95* | | 155 | ____ |
| **52384** | Transparent Damage Control Boxcar, *03* | | 71 | ____ |
| **52451** | Pennsylvania "X2454" Boxcar, *07* | | 175 | ____ |
| **52505** | Forest Service/Smokey Bear Flatcar with airplane, *08* | | 45 | ____ |
| **52525** | SP "X6454" Boxcar, *08* | | 45 | ____ |
| **52526** | SP "X6454" Boxcar, *08* | | 90 | ____ |

## TTOS Gadsden Pacific Ore Cars

| | | Exc | Mint | Cond/S |
|---|---|---|---|---|
| **17878** | Magma Ore Car, *89* | 45 | 55 | ____ |
| **17881** | Phelps-Dodge Ore Car, *90* | 36 | 40 | ____ |
| **17886** | Cyprus Ore Car, *91* | 26 | 31 | ____ |
| **19961** | Inspiration Consolidated Copper Ore Car, *92* | 23 | 30 | ____ |
| **52011** | Tucson, Cornelia & Gila Bend Ore Car, *93* | 20 | 29 | ____ |
| **52027** | Pinto Valley Mine Ore Car, *94* | 20 | 29 | ____ |
| **52071** | Copper Basin Railway Ore Car, *95* | | 30 | ____ |
| **52089** | SMARRCO Ore Car, *96* | | 26 | ____ |
| **52124** | EPSW Ore Car, *97* | | 40 | ____ |
| **52164** | SP Ore Car, *98* | | 35 | ____ |
| **52177** | Arizona Southern Ore Car, *99* | | 35 | ____ |
| **52213** | BHP Copper Ore Car, *00* | | 29 | ____ |
| **52248** | Tombstone & Western RR Ore Car, *01* | | 40 | ____ |

# Virginia Train Collectors

| | | Exc | Mint | Cond/$ |
|---|---|---|---|---|
| **7679** | Boxcar, *79* | | 17 | ____ |
| **7681** | N5c Caboose, *81* | | 23 | ____ |
| **7682** | Covered Quad Hopper, *82* | | 26 | ____ |
| **7683** | Virginia Fruit Express Reefer, *83* | | 26 | ____ |
| **7684** | Vitraco 3-D Tank Car, *84* | | 26 | ____ |
| **7685** | Boxcar, *85* | | 27 | ____ |
| **7686** | GP7 Diesel, *86* | | 100 | ____ |
| **7692-1** | Baggage Car (O27), *92* | 35 | 45 | ____ |
| **7692-2** | Combination Car (O27), *92* | 35 | 45 | ____ |
| **7692-3** | Dining Car (O27), *92* | 35 | 45 | ____ |
| **7692-4** | Passenger Car (O27), *92* | 35 | 45 | ____ |
| **7692-5** | Vista Dome Car (O27), *92* | 35 | 45 | ____ |
| **7692-6** | Passenger Car (O27), *92* | 35 | 45 | ____ |
| **7692-7** | Observation Car (O27), *92* | 35 | 45 | ____ |
| **52060** | Tender "7694" with whistle, *94* | | 70 | ____ |

For more information on determining the condition of a box and a description of box types, see pages 11 and 12.

| | | Good (P-5) | Exc (P-7) | Cond/$ |
|---|---|---|---|---|
| 022A | Remote Control Switches, pair (with both inserts) | 23 | 63 | ____ |
| 30 | Water Tower | 18 | 40 | ____ |
| 38 | Operating Water Tower | 15 | 100 | ____ |
| 40 | Hookup Wire, 8 reels (dealer box) | 35 | 125 | ____ |
| 42 | Picatinny Arsenal Switcher | 25 | 75 | ____ |
| 44 | U.S. Army Mobile Launcher | 30 | 98 | ____ |
| 48 | Super O Insulated Straight Track, 6 pieces (dealer box) | 15 | 50 | ____ |
| 49 | Super O Insulated Curved Track, 6 pieces (dealer box) | 15 | 50 | ____ |
| 50 | Section Gang Car | 5 | 21 | ____ |
| 51 | Navy Yard Switcher | 20 | 72 | ____ |
| 52 | Fire Car | 25 | 110 | ____ |
| 53 | Rio Grande Snowplow | 50 | 133 | ____ |
| 54 | Ballast Tamper | 15 | 50 | ____ |
| 55 | PRR Tie-Jector Car | 15 | 50 | ____ |
| 57 | AEC Switcher | | 185 | ____ |
| 58 | Lamp Post | | 10 | ____ |
| 59 | Minuteman Switcher | 90 | 333 | ____ |
| 60 | Lionelville Rapid Transit Trolley (classic) | 5 | 25 | ____ |
| 60 | Lionelville Rapid Transit Trolley (brown corrugated) | 15 | 60 | ____ |
| 65 | Handcar | | 100 | ____ |
| 68 | Executive Inspection Car | 10 | 70 | ____ |
| 69 | Maintenance Car | 15 | 60 | ____ |
| 71 | Lamp Post | 3 | 8 | ____ |
| 76 | Boulevard Street Lamps | 5 | 68 | ____ |
| 89 | Flagpole | 10 | 40 | ____ |
| 97 | Coal Elevator | 10 | 35 | ____ |
| 110 | Graduated Trestle Set | 1 | 5 | ____ |
| 111 | Elevated Trestle Set | 1 | 5 | ____ |
| 112LH | Remote Control Super O Switch, left-hand | 10 | 50 | ____ |
| 112RH | Remote Control Super O Switch, right-hand | 10 | 50 | ____ |
| 114 | Newsstand with horn | 5 | 25 | ____ |
| 118 | Newsstand with whistle | 10 | 48 | ____ |
| 123 | Lamp Assortment | | 75 | ____ |
| 125 | Whistle Shack | 5 | 20 | ____ |
| 128 | Animated Newsstand | | 40 | ____ |
| 132 | Passenger Station | 10 | 35 | ____ |
| 133 | Passenger Station | 10 | 40 | ____ |
| 145 | Automatic Gateman (brown corrugated) | 5 | 27 | ____ |
| 145 | Automatic Gateman, *66* (cellophane) | 30 | 80 | ____ |
| 148 | Dwarf Trackside Signal | 5 | 20 | ____ |

## BOXES

| | | Good (P-5) | Exc (P-7) | Cond/S |
|---|---|---|---|---|
| 153 | Automatic Block Control Signal | 13 | 35 | ____ |
| 154 | Automatic Highway Signal (cellophane) | 5 | 15 | ____ |
| 154 | Automatic Highway Signal (all other boxes) | 1 | 5 | ____ |
| 156 | Station Platform | 15 | 60 | ____ |
| 160 | Unloading Bin | 23 | 94 | ____ |
| 163 | Single Target Block Signal (white box) | 20 | 65 | ____ |
| 164 | Log Loader | 23 | 80 | ____ |
| 182 | Magnetic Crane | | 78 | ____ |
| 192 | Operating Control Tower | | 100 | ____ |
| 197 | Rotating Radar Antenna | 5 | 35 | ____ |
| 204 | Santa Fe Alco AA Set (master carton) | 60 | 200 | ____ |
| 204 | Santa Fe Alco AA Set (P and T boxes) | | 120 | ____ |
| 208 | Santa Fe Alco AA Set (P and T boxes) | | 120 | ____ |
| 209 | New Haven Alco AA Set (P and T boxes) | | 280 | ____ |
| 210 | *Texas Special* Alco AA Set (P and T boxes) | | 50 | ____ |
| 211 | *Texas Special* Alco AA Set (P and T boxes) | | 300 | ____ |
| 214 | Plate Girder Bridge (classic) | 2 | 18 | ____ |
| 214 | Plate Girder Bridge (Hillside orange picture) | 10 | 40 | ____ |
| 217 | B&M Alco AB Set (C and P boxes) | | 225 | ____ |
| 217-16 | Sleeve for 217 and 218 outer boxes | | 60 | ____ |
| 218 | Santa Fe Alco AA Set (master carton) | | 60 | ____ |
| 218 | Santa Fe Alco AA Set (P and T boxes) | 15 | 65 | ____ |
| 220 | Santa Fe Alco AA Set (P and T boxes) | | 105 | ____ |
| 223P | Santa Fe Alco A Unit | 15 | 60 | ____ |
| 224 | U.S. Navy Alco AB Set (C and P boxes) | | 200 | ____ |
| 228P | Canadian National Alco A Unit | 20 | 65 | ____ |
| 231P | Rock Island Alco A Unit | | 38 | ____ |
| 235 | 2-4-2 Scout Locomotive | 25 | 100 | ____ |
| 244T | Tender (overstamped 1625T box) | 25 | 90 | ____ |
| 246 | 2-4-2 Scout Locomotive | | 45 | ____ |
| 247 | 2-4-2 Scout Locomotive | 10 | 40 | ____ |
| 247T | Tender | 5 | 20 | ____ |
| 248 | 2-4-2 Scout Locomotive | | 45 | ____ |
| 250 | 2-4-2 Scout Locomotive | 10 | 30 | ____ |
| 250T | Tender | 3 | 15 | ____ |
| 256 | Illuminated Freight Station | 5 | 20 | ____ |
| 257 | Freight Station with diesel horn | 10 | 30 | ____ |
| 260 | Bumper (Hagerstown checkerboard) | 8 | 35 | ____ |
| 260 | Bumper (all other boxes) | 6 | 25 | ____ |
| 282 | Gantry Crane | 20 | 65 | ____ |
| 313 | Bascule Bridge | 40 | 130 | ____ |
| 315 | Trestle Bridge | 45 | 250 | ____ |
| 316 | Trestle Bridge | 5 | 15 | ____ |
| 317 | Trestle Bridge | 5 | 15 | ____ |
| 350 | Engine Transfer Table | | 40 | ____ |
| 350-50 | Transfer Table Extension | | 40 | ____ |
| 356 | Operating Freight Station | 10 | 40 | ____ |
| 362 | Barrel Loader | 5 | 34 | ____ |
| 364 | Conveyor Lumber Loader | 3 | 10 | ____ |
| 375 | Turntable | | 25 | ____ |
| 400 | B&O Passenger Rail Diesel Car | 15 | 50 | ____ |

| BOXES | | Good (P-5) | Exc (P-7) | Cond/$ |
|---|---|---|---|---|
| 404 | B&O Baggage-Mail Rail Diesel Car | 30 | 108 | _____ |
| 415 | Diesel Fueling Station | 10 | 105 | _____ |
| 419 | Heliport Control Tower | | 125 | _____ |
| 445 | Switch Tower | | 15 | _____ |
| 456 | Coal Ramp | | 35 | _____ |
| 460 | Piggyback Transportation Set | 12 | 42 | _____ |
| 460-150 | Two Trailers | 65 | 163 | _____ |
| 462 | Derrick Platform Set | 60 | 200 | _____ |
| 600 | MKT NW2 Switcher | | 250 | _____ |
| 601 | Seaboard NW2 Switcher | 25 | 128 | _____ |
| 602 | Seaboard NW2 Switcher | 25 | 70 | _____ |
| 610 | Erie NW2 Switcher | | 175 | _____ |
| 616 | Santa Fe NW2 Switcher | 25 | 105 | _____ |
| 617 | Santa Fe NW2 Switcher | 30 | 155 | _____ |
| 621 | Jersey Central NW2 Switcher | | 90 | _____ |
| 622 | Santa Fe NW2 Switcher | 60 | 125 | _____ |
| 623 | Santa Fe NW2 Switcher | | 70 | _____ |
| 624 | C&O NW2 Switcher | 20 | 75 | _____ |
| 626 | B&O GE 44-ton Switcher | | 145 | _____ |
| 628 | Northern Pacific GE 44-ton Switcher | 20 | 163 | _____ |
| 629 | Burlington GE 44-ton Switcher | | 180 | _____ |
| 634 | Santa Fe NW2 Switcher | | 250 | _____ |
| 637 | 2-6-4 Locomotive | | 75 | _____ |
| 637LTS | 2-6-4 Locomotive and Tender (master carton) | 75 | 170 | _____ |
| 646 | 4-6-4 Locomotive | | 80 | _____ |
| 665 | 4-6-4 Locomotive | | 55 | _____ |
| 671 | 6-8-6 Steam Turbine Locomotive | | 75 | _____ |
| 675 | 2-6-2 Locomotive, *47–49* | | 125 | _____ |
| 682 | 6-8-6 Steam Turbine Locomotive | 35 | 203 | _____ |
| 685 | 4-6-4 Hudson Locomotive | | 60 | _____ |
| 726 | 2-8-4 Berkshire Locomotive | 60 | 125 | _____ |
| 726RR | 2-8-4 Berkshire Locomotive | | 80 | _____ |
| 736 | 2-8-4 Berkshire Locomotive | 20 | 57 | _____ |
| 736W | Pennsylvania Tender | 10 | 45 | _____ |
| 746 | N&W 4-8-4 Locomotive | | 180 | _____ |
| 746W | Tender with short stripe | | 185 | _____ |
| 773 | 4-6-4 Hudson Locomotive, *50* | | 480 | _____ |
| 773LTS | 4-6-4 Hudson Locomotive and Tender, *50* (master carton) | | 450 | _____ |
| 773 | 4-6-4 Hudson Locomotive, *64–66* | 60 | 167 | _____ |
| 773LTS | 4-6-4 Hudson and Whistle Tender, *64–66* (master carton) | | 140 | _____ |
| 773W | NYC Tender | | 45 | _____ |
| 810 | Milwaukee Road Freight Set | | 850 | _____ |
| 959 | Barn Set | | 60 | _____ |
| 969 | Construction Set | | 55 | _____ |
| 981 | Freight Yard Set | | 40 | _____ |
| 984 | Railroad Set | | 90 | _____ |
| 986 | Farm Set | | 150 | _____ |
| 1047 | Operating Switchman | 25 | 100 | _____ |
| 1060 | 2-4-2 Locomotive (brown corrugated) | 25 | 150 | _____ |
| 1121LH | 027 Remote Control Switch, left-hand | 10 | 55 | _____ |

## BOXES

| | | Good (P-5) | Exc (P-7) | Cond/$ |
|---|---|---|---|---|
| 1121RH | 027 Remote Control Switch, right-hand | 10 | 55 | ____ |
| 1122 | 027 Remote Control Switches, pair | 10 | 25 | ____ |
| 1130T | Tender | 3 | 15 | ____ |
| 1130T-500 | Tender, pink, from Girls Set | | 180 | ____ |
| 1407B | Steam Switcher Work Set | | 400 | ____ |
| 1425B | Steam Switcher Freight Set | | 190 | ____ |
| 1447WS | Turbine Locomotive Set | | 150 | ____ |
| 1457B | Santa Fe Freight Set | | 200 | ____ |
| 1467W | Union Pacific Freight Set | 30 | 90 | ____ |
| 1469WS | Steam Freight Set | | 50 | ____ |
| 1479WS | Steam Freight Set | 10 | 35 | ____ |
| 1502WS | Steam Freight Set | | 600 | ____ |
| 1519WS | Steam Freight Set | | 170 | ____ |
| 1520W | *Texas Special* Passenger Set | | 675 | ____ |
| 1529 | Pennsylvania Diesel Freight Set | | 250 | ____ |
| 1534W | Burlington Diesel Passenger Set | | 363 | ____ |
| 1538WS | Hudson Passenger Set | | 500 | ____ |
| 1539W | Santa Fe Diesel Freight Set | | 250 | ____ |
| 1543 | Lehigh Valley Freight Set | | 30 | ____ |
| 1578S | Steam Passenger Set | | 500 | ____ |
| 1581 | Jersey Central Mixed Set | | 75 | ____ |
| 1583WS | Steam Freight Set | | 70 | ____ |
| 1587S | Girls Train Set | | 1500 | ____ |
| 1591 | USMC Military Set | | 1500 | ____ |
| 1599W | *Texas Special* Freight Set | 50 | | ____ |
| 1601W | Wabash GP7 Diesel Set | | 200 | ____ |
| 1608W | New Haven Passenger Set | | 1500 | ____ |
| 1615LT | 0-4-0 Locomotive and Tender (master carton) | 15 | 75 | ____ |
| 1615T | Tender | | 100 | ____ |
| 1865 | Western & Atlantic Coach | | 30 | ____ |
| 1866 | Western & Atlantic Mail-Baggage Car | 10 | 40 | ____ |
| 1872 | 4-4-0 Civil War *General* Locomotive | 30 | 100 | ____ |
| 1872T | Tender | 5 | 43 | ____ |
| 1875 | Western & Atlantic Coach | 35 | 140 | ____ |
| 1875W | Western & Atlantic Coach, whistle | 15 | 75 | ____ |
| 1876 | Western & Atlantic Baggage Car | 15 | 60 | ____ |
| 1877 | Flatcar with fence and horses | 5 | 30 | ____ |
| 2016 | 2-6-4 Locomotive | | 25 | ____ |
| 2020W | Tender | 10 | 40 | ____ |
| 2023 | Union Pacific Alco AA Set (master carton) | 25 | 100 | ____ |
| 2028 | Pennsylvania GP7 Diesel | 20 | 110 | ____ |
| 2029 | 2-6-4 Locomotive | 10 | 70 | ____ |
| 2031 | Rock Island Alco AA Set (master carton) | 50 | 118 | ____ |
| 2032 | Erie Alco AA Set (master carton) | 20 | 65 | ____ |
| 2033 | Uinion Pacific Alco AA Set (master carton) | 25 | 80 | ____ |
| 2034 | 2-4-2 Scout Locomotive | | 110 | ____ |
| 2037 | 2-6-4 Locomotive (brown corrugated) | | 30 | ____ |
| 2037-500 | 2-6-4 Locomotive, pink, from Girls Set | | 250 | ____ |
| 2046 | 4-6-4 Locomotive | | 55 | ____ |
| 2046T | Lionel Lines Tender, for export | 25 | 75 | ____ |
| 2046W | Lionel Lines Tender | 10 | 35 | ____ |

## BOXES

| | | Good (P-5) | Exc (P-7) | Cond/$ |
|---|---|---|---|---|
| 2046W-50 | Pennsylvania Tender | 10 | 40 | ____ |
| 2056 | 4-6-4 Locomotive | | 50 | ____ |
| 2124W | GG1 Passenger Set | | 900 | ____ |
| 2126WS | Steam Turbine Passenger Set | | 1000 | ____ |
| 2139 | GG1 Freight Set | | 1250 | ____ |
| 2140WS | Steam Turbine Passenger Set | | 1000 | ____ |
| 2148WS | Hudson Passenger Set | | 3000 | ____ |
| 2151W | F3 Freight Set | | 280 | ____ |
| 2155WS | Berkshire Freight Set | | 75 | ____ |
| 2159W | GG1 Freight Set | 350 | 650 | ____ |
| 2161W | Santa Fe Twin Diesel Freight Set | | 160 | ____ |
| 2175W | Santa Fe Diesel Freight Set | | 150 | ____ |
| 2217WS | Steam Turbine Freight Set | | 200 | ____ |
| 2222WS | Hudson Passenger Set | | 450 | ____ |
| 2223W | Lackawanna FM Freight Set | | 625 | ____ |
| 2227W | Santa Fe Diesel Freight Set | | 300 | ____ |
| 2234W | Santa Fe Passenger Set | | 330 | ____ |
| 2235W | Milwaukee Road Diesel Freight Set | | 175 | ____ |
| 2239W | Illinois Central Freight Set | | 350 | ____ |
| 2240 | Wabash F3 AB Set (C and P boxes) | | 270 | ____ |
| 2242 | New Haven F3 AB Set (C and P boxes) | | 500 | ____ |
| 2243 | Santa Fe F3 AB Set (master carton) | 30 | 130 | ____ |
| 2243 | Santa Fe F3 AB Set (C and P boxes) | | 105 | ____ |
| 2243W | Lackawanna Freight Set | | 350 | ____ |
| 2244W | Wabash Passenger Set | | 1500 | ____ |
| 2245 | *Texas Special* F3 AB Set (C and P boxes) | | 350 | ____ |
| 2254W | Pennsylvania GG1 Passenger Set, *55* | | 1000 | ____ |
| 2257 | SP-type Caboose | 1 | 5 | ____ |
| 2257WS | Steam Freight Set | | 85 | ____ |
| 2259W | New Haven Electric Freight Set | | 195 | ____ |
| 2263W | New Haven Freight Set | | 250 | ____ |
| 2269W | B&O Diesel Freight Set | | 425 | ____ |
| 2270W | Jersey Central Passenger Set | | 700 | ____ |
| 2271W | Pennsylvania GG1 Freight Set | | 275 | ____ |
| 2273W | Milwaukee Road Diesel Freight Set | | 900 | ____ |
| 2276W | Budd Passenger Set | | 200 | ____ |
| 2283W | Steam Freight Set | | 125 | ____ |
| 2289WS | Berkshire Super O Freight Set | | 210 | ____ |
| 2291W | Rio Grande Diesel Freight Set | | 400 | ____ |
| 2292WS | Steam Passenger Set | | 975 | ____ |
| 2293W | Pennsylvania GG1 Freight Set | | 1150 | ____ |
| 2295WS | N&W Steam Freight Set | | 1200 | ____ |
| 2296W | Canadian Pacific Passenger Set | | 1000 | ____ |
| 2297WS | N&W Steam Freight Set | | 600 | ____ |
| 2321 | Lackawanna FM Train Master Diesel | 20 | 75 | ____ |
| 2322 | Virginian FM Train Master Diesel | | 120 | ____ |
| 2328 | Burlington GP7 Diesel | 35 | 85 | ____ |
| 2329 | Virginian Electric Locomotive | | 175 | ____ |
| 2330 | Pennsylvania GG1 Electric Locomotive | | 210 | ____ |
| 2331 | Virginian FM Train Master Diesel | | 210 | ____ |
| 2332 | Pennsylvania GG1 Electric Locomotive | | 105 | ____ |

# BOXES

| | | Good (P-5) | Exc (P-7) | Cond/$ |
|---|---|---|---|---|
| 2332-275 | Pennsylvania GG1 Electric Locomotive | | 270 | _____ |
| 2333 | NYC F3 AA Set (P and T boxes) | 35 | 145 | _____ |
| 2333 | Santa Fe F3 AA Set (master carton) | 40 | 175 | _____ |
| 2338 | MILW GP7 Diesel (classic) | 10 | 58 | _____ |
| 2338 | MILW GP7 Diesel (brown corrugated) | 10 | 50 | _____ |
| 2338 | MILW GP7 Diesel (brown corrugated marked "2338X") | 30 | 120 | _____ |
| 2339 | Wabash GP7 Diesel | | 135 | _____ |
| 2340-10 | Pennsylvania GG1 Electric, tuscan | | 225 | _____ |
| 2340-25 | Pennsylvania GG1 Electric, green, gold stripes | | 125 | _____ |
| 2340-27 | Pennsylvania GG1 Electric, green, green stripes | | 160 | _____ |
| 2341 | Jersey Central FM Train Master Diesel | | 1000 | _____ |
| 2343 | Santa Fe F3 AA Set (master carton) | 75 | 120 | _____ |
| 2343 | Santa Fe F3 AA Set (P and T boxes) | 40 | 205 | _____ |
| 2343C | Santa Fe F3 B Unit | 20 | 70 | _____ |
| 2344 | NYC F3 AA Set (P and T boxes) | 60 | 210 | _____ |
| 2344C | NYC B Unit | 20 | 75 | _____ |
| 2344T | NYC F3 Dummy Unit | 40 | 93 | _____ |
| 2346 | B&M GP9 Diesel | | 200 | _____ |
| 2348 | M&StL GP9 Diesel | | 200 | _____ |
| 2349 | Northern Pacific GP9 Diesel | | 175 | _____ |
| 2350 | New Haven EP-5 Electric Locomotive | | 150 | _____ |
| 2351 | Milwaukee Road EP-5 Electric Locomotive | | 150 | _____ |
| 2352 | Pennsylvania EP-5 Electric Locomotive | | 250 | _____ |
| 2353 | Santa Fe F3 AA Set (master carton) | 125 | 250 | _____ |
| 2353 | Santa Fe F3 AA Set (P and T boxes) | 40 | 125 | _____ |
| 2354P | NYC F3 A Unit (brown corrugated) | 95 | 228 | _____ |
| 2355 | Western Pacific F3 AA Set (P and T boxes) | | 375 | _____ |
| 2356 | Southern F3 AA Set (master carton) | | 400 | _____ |
| 2356C | Southern F3 B Unit | | 375 | _____ |
| 2356P | Southern F3 A Unit | | 125 | _____ |
| 2356T | Southern F3 Dummy Unit | | 275 | _____ |
| 2357 | SP-type Caboose | 5 | 15 | _____ |
| 2358 | Great Northern EP-5 Electric Locomotive | | 325 | _____ |
| 2359 | Boston & Maine GP9 Diesel | | 95 | _____ |
| 2360-10 | Pennsylvania GG1 Electric Locomotive, tuscan | | 210 | _____ |
| 2360-25 | Pennsylvania GG1 Electric Locomotive, green | | 200 | _____ |
| 2363 | Illinois Central F3 AB Set (C and P boxes) | 175 | 450 | _____ |
| 2365 | C&O GP7 Diesel | 15 | 50 | _____ |
| 2367C | Wabash F3 B Unit | | 175 | _____ |
| 2367P | Wabash F3 A Unit | | 125 | _____ |
| 2368C | B&O F3 B Unit | | 450 | _____ |
| 2368P | B&O F3 A Unit | | 125 | _____ |
| 2373 | CP F3 AA Set (P and T boxes) | | 450 | _____ |
| 2378C | Milwaukee Road F3 B Unit | | 300 | _____ |
| 2378P | Milwaukee Road F3 A Unit | | 205 | _____ |
| 2379C | Rio Grande F3 B Unit | 70 | 335 | _____ |
| 2379P | Rio Grande F3 A Unit | 140 | 250 | _____ |
| 2383P | Santa Fe F3 Powered Unit | | 100 | _____ |
| 2383T | Santa Fe F3 Dummy Unit | | 125 | _____ |
| 2400 | *Maplewood* Pullman Car | 10 | 40 | _____ |
| 2401 | *Hillside* Observation Car | 10 | 50 | _____ |

| | | Good (P-5) | Exc (P-7) | Cond/$ |
|---|---|---|---|---|
| 2402 | *Chatham* Pullman Car | 10 | 50 | ____ |
| 2403B | Tender with bell | 20 | 75 | ____ |
| 2404 | Santa Fe Vista Dome Car | 15 | 68 | ____ |
| 2405 | Santa Fe Pullman Car | 15 | 68 | ____ |
| 2406 | Santa Fe Observation Car | 15 | 50 | ____ |
| 2408 | Santa Fe Vista Dome Car | 15 | 50 | ____ |
| 2409 | Santa Fe Pullman Car | 15 | 50 | ____ |
| 2410 | Santa Fe Observation Car | 15 | 50 | ____ |
| 2411 | Lionel Lines Flatcar | 15 | 85 | ____ |
| 2412 | Santa Fe Vista Dome Car | 10 | 40 | ____ |
| 2414 | Santa Fe Pullman Car | 10 | 40 | ____ |
| 2416 | Santa Fe Observation Car | 10 | 40 | ____ |
| 2419 | DL&W Work Caboose | | 70 | ____ |
| 2420 | DL&W Work Caboose with searchlight | 23 | 55 | ____ |
| 2421 | *Maplewood* Pullman Car | | 45 | ____ |
| 2422 | *Chatham* Pullman Car | | 20 | ____ |
| 2423 | *Hillside* Observation Car | | 20 | ____ |
| 2426W | Hudson Tender (early classic) | 35 | 175 | ____ |
| 2426W | Hudson Tender (middle classic) | 35 | 175 | ____ |
| 2432 | *Clifton* Vista Dome Car | 10 | 35 | ____ |
| 2434 | *Newark* Pullman Car | 10 | 35 | ____ |
| 2435 | *Elizabeth* Pullman Car | 10 | 35 | ____ |
| 2436 | *Mooseheart* Observation Car | 10 | 35 | ____ |
| 2440 | Pullman Car, green | 5 | | ____ |
| 2442 | Pullman Car, brown | 5 | | ____ |
| 2442 | *Clifton* Vista Dome Car | 20 | 60 | ____ |
| 2444 | *Newark* Pullman Car | 20 | 68 | ____ |
| 2445 | *Elizabeth* Pullman Car | 35 | 150 | ____ |
| 2445 | *Elizabeth* Pullman Car, separate sale, *56* | | 230 | ____ |
| 2446 | *Summit* Observation Car | 20 | 68 | ____ |
| 2452 | Pennsylvania Gondola | | 30 | ____ |
| X2454 | Pennsylvania Boxcar (marked "Box Car") | 4 | 15 | ____ |
| X2454 | Pennsylvania Boxcar (marked "Merchandise Car") | 6 | 25 | ____ |
| 2456 | Lehigh Valley Hopper | 10 | 25 | ____ |
| 2457 | Pennsylvania N5-type Caboose | 5 | 20 | ____ |
| X2458 | Pennsylvania Automobile Boxcar | 5 | 30 | ____ |
| 2460 | Bucyrus Erie Crane Car (box with toy logo) | 10 | 40 | ____ |
| 2460 | Bucyrus Erie Crane Car (box without toy logo) | 15 | 60 | ____ |
| 2481 | *Plainfield* Pullman Car | 30 | 100 | ____ |
| 2482 | *Westfield* Pullman Car | 30 | 100 | ____ |
| 2483 | *Livingston* Observation Car | 30 | 100 | ____ |
| 2501W | M&StL Diesel Freight Set | | 190 | ____ |
| 2507W | New Haven Diesel Freight Set | | 850 | ____ |
| 2509WS | Super O Steam Freight Set | | 250 | ____ |
| 2511W | Pennsylvania Electric Work Set | 80 | 360 | ____ |
| 2513W | Virginian Rectifier Set | | 450 | ____ |
| 2518W | Pennsylvania Electric Passenger Set | | 1300 | ____ |
| 2519W | Virginian Train Master Super O Freight Set | | 400 | ____ |
| 2521 | *President McKinley* Observation Car | | 60 | ____ |
| 2522 | *President Harrison* Vista Dome Car | | 75 | ____ |
| 2523 | *President Garfield* Pullman Car | | 75 | ____ |

# BOXES

| | | Good (P-5) | Exc (P-7) | Cond/$ |
|---|---|---|---|---|
| 2523W | Santa Fe Super O Freight Set | | 300 | _____ |
| 2526W | Santa Fe Passenger Set | | 735 | _____ |
| 2530 | REA Baggage Car | | 85 | _____ |
| 2531 | *Silver Dawn* Observation Car | | 55 | _____ |
| 2532 | *Silver Range* Vista Dome Car | | 55 | _____ |
| 2533 | *Silver Cloud* Pullman Car | | 160 | _____ |
| 2534 | *Silver Bluff* Pullman Car | | 60 | _____ |
| 2537W | New Haven Freight Set | | 600 | _____ |
| 2541 | *Alexander Hamilton* Observation Car | | 140 | _____ |
| 2541W | Santa Fe Super O Freight Set | | 650 | _____ |
| 2542 | *Betsy Ross* Vista Dome Car | | 130 | _____ |
| 2543 | *William Penn* Pullman Car | | 125 | _____ |
| 2543WS | Berkshire Freight Set | | 250 | _____ |
| 2544 | *Molly Pitcher* Pullman Car | 35 | 115 | _____ |
| 2544W | Santa Fe Passenger Set | | 1100 | _____ |
| 2550 | B&O Baggage-Mail Rail Diesel Car | 75 | 180 | _____ |
| 2551 | *Banff Park* Observation Car | 20 | 82 | _____ |
| 2551W | GN Electric Set | 120 | 400 | _____ |
| 2552 | *Skyline 500* Vista Dome Car | 20 | 78 | _____ |
| 2553 | *Blair Manor* Pullman Car | 60 | 163 | _____ |
| 2553WS | Berkshire Freight Set | 70 | 290 | _____ |
| 2554 | *Craig Manor* Pullman Car | 140 | 235 | _____ |
| 2555 | Sunoco 1-D Tank Car (overstamped 2755 box) | | 140 | _____ |
| 2559 | B&O Passenger Rail Diesel Car | 30 | 128 | _____ |
| 2560 | Lionel Lines Crane Car | 10 | 35 | _____ |
| 2563 | *Indian Falls* Pullman Car | | 130 | _____ |
| 2572 | Boston & Maine Military Set | | 160 | _____ |
| 2574 | Santa Fe Military Set | | 450 | _____ |
| 2625 | *Irvington* Pullman Car | | 190 | _____ |
| 2627 | *Madison* Pullman Car | | 200 | _____ |
| 2628 | *Manhattan* Pullman Car | | 170 | _____ |
| 2671T | Pennsylvania Tender, for export | 25 | 75 | _____ |
| 2855 | Sunoco 1-D Tank Car | 25 | 148 | _____ |
| 3330 | Flatcar with submarine kit | | 110 | _____ |
| 3330-100 | Operating Submarine Kit, separate sale | 75 | 250 | _____ |
| 3356 | Operating Horse Car and Corral Set (classic) | 10 | 40 | _____ |
| 3356 | Operating Horse Car and Corral Set (orange picture) | 18 | 59 | _____ |
| 3356-2 | Horse Car | 68 | 363 | _____ |
| 3356-2 | Horse Car, separate sale | 85 | 350 | _____ |
| 3356-100 | Black Horses (classic) | 3 | 10 | _____ |
| 3356-100 | Black Horses (white box) | 5 | 25 | _____ |
| 3356-150 | Horse Car Corral | | 1200 | _____ |
| 3359 | Lionel Lines Twin-bin Coal Dump Car | | 27 | _____ |
| 3361X | Operating Log Dump Car | 5 | 70 | _____ |
| 3362 | Helium Tank Unloading Car | 15 | 50 | _____ |
| 3366 | Circus Car Corral Set | | 250 | _____ |
| 3366-100 | White Horses | 5 | 25 | _____ |
| 3376-160 | Bronx Zoo Car, green | 10 | 35 | _____ |
| 3413 | Mercury Capsule Car | 10 | 35 | _____ |
| 3419 | Helicopter Car | 5 | 25 | _____ |

| BOXES | | Good (P-5) | Exc (P-7) | Cond/$ |
|---|---|---|---|---|
| **3424-75** | Low Bridge Signal (marked "3424-75" or overstamped on 3424-100 box) | | 400 | _____ |
| **3424-100** | Low Bridge Signal | 5 | | _____ |
| **3435** | Traveling Aquarium Car | 25 | 210 | _____ |
| **3454** | PRR Operating Merchandise Car | 10 | 60 | _____ |
| **3461X-25** | Lionel Lines Operating Log Car, green | 10 | 30 | _____ |
| **X3464** | ATSF or NYC Operating Boxcar | 3 | 10 | _____ |
| **3470** | Target Launching Car | 30 | 58 | _____ |
| **3474** | Western Pacific Operating Boxcar | | 35 | _____ |
| **3482** | Automatic Milk Car | 15 | 25 | _____ |
| **3484** | Pennsylvania Operating Boxcar | | 29 | _____ |
| **3484-25** | ATSF Operating Boxcar | 5 | 20 | _____ |
| **3494-1** | NYC Operating Boxcar | 40 | 65 | _____ |
| **3494-150** | Missouri Pacific Operating Boxcar | 5 | 25 | _____ |
| **3494-550** | Monon Operating Boxcar | 60 | 200 | _____ |
| **3494-625** | Soo Operating Boxcar | 60 | 225 | _____ |
| **3509** | Satellite Launching Car | 15 | 50 | _____ |
| **3512** | Fireman and Ladder Car | 21 | 52 | _____ |
| **3520** | Searchlight Car | 3 | 15 | _____ |
| **3530** | GM Generator Car | 15 | 58 | _____ |
| **3530-50** | Searchlight with pole and base, separate sale | 15 | 50 | _____ |
| **3535** | Security Car with searchlight | | 55 | _____ |
| **3559** | Operating Coal Dump Car | 10 | 40 | _____ |
| **3562-1** | ATSF Operating Barrel Car | 30 | 93 | _____ |
| **3562-25** | ATSF Operating Barrel Car, gray | 23 | 63 | _____ |
| **3562-50** | ATSF Operating Barrel Car, yellow | 16 | 60 | _____ |
| **3562-75** | ATSF Operating Barrel Car, orange | 20 | 55 | _____ |
| **3620** | Searchlight Car | 3 | 15 | _____ |
| **3650** | Extension Searchlight Car | 5 | 20 | _____ |
| **3656** | Stockyard with cattle (set box with car box) | 10 | 50 | _____ |
| **3656-9** | Cattle (marked "3656" on 4 sides, unnumbered tuck flaps) | 10 | 25 | _____ |
| **3656-9** | Cattle (marked "3656" on 4 sides, "3656-44" on 1 tuck flap) | 2 | 10 | _____ |
| **3656-9** | Cattle (marked "3656-34" on 4 sides, "3656-44" on 1 tuck flap) | 2 | 10 | _____ |
| **3656-9** | Cattle (marked "3656" on 4 sides, "3656-44" on 1 tuck flap, OPS markings) | 10 | 25 | _____ |
| **3656-9** | Cattle (unnumbered sides, marked "3656-44" on 1 tuck flap) | 10 | 25 | _____ |
| **3656-9** | Cattle (unnumbered sides, marked "3656-34" on 1 tuck flap) | 15 | 40 | _____ |
| **3656-150** | Corral Platform, separate sale | 263 | 1050 | _____ |
| **3662** | Automatic Milk Car, *55* (classic) | 10 | 40 | _____ |
| **3662** | Automatic Milk Car, *64* (orange picture) | 10 | 40 | _____ |
| **3662** | Automatic Milk Car, *66* (white box) | 15 | 50 | _____ |
| **3830** | Operating Submarine Car | | 30 | _____ |
| **4357** | SP-type Caboose, electronic | 25 | 75 | _____ |
| **4452** | PRR Gondola, electronic | 15 | 60 | _____ |
| **4671W** | Tender | | 25 | _____ |
| **6014-60** | Frisco Boxcar, flat white | 5 | 15 | _____ |
| **6014-85** | Bosco or Frisco Boxcar, orange (classic) | 5 | 30 | _____ |

## BOXES

| | | Good (P-5) | Exc (P-7) | Cond/$ |
|---|---|---|---|---|
| 6014-410 | Frisco Boxcar, glossy white | 20 | 115 | ___ |
| 6015 | Sunoco 1-D Tank Car | 5 | 20 | ___ |
| 6017 | Lionel Lines SP-type Caboose | 1 | 8 | ___ |
| 6017-85 | Lionel Lines SP-type Caboose, gray | 10 | 30 | ___ |
| 6017-100 | B&M SP-type Caboose | 10 | 57 | ___ |
| 6017-185 | ATSF SP-type Caboose | 3 | 15 | ___ |
| 6020W | Tender | | 50 | ___ |
| 6024-60 | RCA Whirlpool Boxcar | 15 | 60 | ___ |
| 6025 | Gulf 1-D Tank Car (classic) | 20 | 40 | ___ |
| 6025-60 | Gulf 1-D Tank Car | 3 | 10 | ___ |
| 6025-60 | Gulf 1-D Tank Car (classic, overstamped 6024 box) | | 60 | ___ |
| 6025-85 | Gulf 1-D Tank Car (classic) | | 60 | ___ |
| 6026W | Lionel Lines Tender | 5 | 25 | ___ |
| 6050 | Lionel Savings Bank Boxcar | 10 | 35 | ___ |
| 6062 | NYC Gondola | 15 | | ___ |
| 6066T | Tender | 10 | 20 | ___ |
| 6111 | Flatcar with logs | 10 | 40 | ___ |
| 6112-85 | Short Gondola (marked "Canister Car") | | 35 | ___ |
| 6112-135 | Short Gondola (marked "Canister Car") | | 60 | ___ |
| 6119 | DL&W Work Caboose, red | 5 | 20 | ___ |
| 6119-25 | DL&W Work Caboose, orange | 5 | 25 | ___ |
| 6119-50 | DL&W Work Caboose, brown | 5 | 25 | ___ |
| 6119-75 | DL&W Work Caboose | 10 | 30 | ___ |
| 6119-100 | DL&W Work Caboose | 5 | 20 | ___ |
| 6121 | Flatcar with pipes | 10 | 53 | ___ |
| 6121-60 | Flatcar with pipes | 10 | 65 | ___ |
| 6130 | ATSF Work Caboose (cellophane) | 10 | 35 | ___ |
| 6130 | ATSF Work Caboose (all other boxes) | 5 | 25 | ___ |
| 6151 | Flatcar with patrol truck | 10 | 48 | ___ |
| 6162-110 | NYC Gondola, blue (orange picture) | 17 | 68 | ___ |
| 6162-110 | NYC Gondola, red, separate sale (orange picture with label) | 30 | 125 | ___ |
| 6175 | Flatcar with rocket | 10 | 42 | ___ |
| 6250 | Seaboard NW2 Switcher | 38 | 78 | ___ |
| 6257 | SP-type Caboose | | 8 | ___ |
| 6257X | SP-type Caboose | 10 | 45 | ___ |
| 6262 | Flatcar with wheel load | 5 | 20 | ___ |
| 6264 | Flatcar with lumber, separate sale | 43 | 150 | ___ |
| 6311 | Flatcar with pipes | 12 | 88 | ___ |
| 6315 | Gulf 1-D Chemical Tank Car (classic) | 20 | 43 | ___ |
| 6315 | Gulf 1-D Chemical Tank Car (Hagerstown checkerboard) | 30 | 53 | ___ |
| 6315-60 | Gulf 1-D Chemical Tank Car (orange picture) | 5 | 25 | ___ |
| 6356 | NYC Stock Car | | 35 | ___ |
| 6357 | SP-type Caboose | | 14 | ___ |
| 6357-50 | ATSF SP-type Caboose | 88 | 338 | ___ |
| 6401 | Flatcar, gray | 25 | 100 | ___ |
| 6414 | Evans Auto Loader | 28 | 60 | ___ |
| 6414 | Evans Auto Loader (orange picture) | 40 | 150 | ___ |
| 6414 | Evans Auto Loader (orange picture, overstamped 6416 box) | | 200 | ___ |

## BOXES

| | | Good (P-5) | Exc (P-7) | Cond/$ |
|---|---|---|---|---|
| 6414 | Evans Auto Loader, *59* (orange perforated) | | 80 | ___ |
| 6414 | Evans Auto Loader, *66* (cellophane) | 20 | 75 | ___ |
| 6414-25 | Four Automobiles | 200 | 800 | ___ |
| 6415 | Sunoco 3-D Tank Car (orange picture) | 30 | 40 | ___ |
| 6415 | Sunoco 3-D Tank Car (cellophane) | 40 | | ___ |
| 6415 | Sunoco 3-D Tank Car (Hillside checkerboard) | 40 | | ___ |
| 6415 | Sunoco 3-D Tank Car (orange picture with label) | 100 | 200 | ___ |
| 6416 | Boat Transport Car | 25 | 80 | ___ |
| 6417 | PRR N5c Porthole Caboose | 4 | 15 | ___ |
| 6417-1 | PRR N5c Porthole Caboose, without "New York Zone" | 8 | 35 | ___ |
| 6417-50 | Lehigh Valley N5c Porthole Caboose | 25 | 110 | ___ |
| 6419 | DL&W Work Caboose | 5 | 20 | ___ |
| 6419-25 | DL&W Work Caboose | 5 | 20 | ___ |
| 6419-50 | DL&W Work Caboose | 10 | 40 | ___ |
| 6419-100 | N&W Work Caboose | 20 | 60 | ___ |
| 6420 | DL&W Work Caboose with searchlight | 10 | 35 | ___ |
| 6424-85 | Twin Auto Flatcar | | 85 | ___ |
| 6424-110 | Twin Auto Flatcar | | 130 | ___ |
| 6425 | Gulf 3-D Tank Car | 10 | | ___ |
| 6427 | Lionel Lines N5c Porthole Caboose | | 22 | ___ |
| 6427-60 | Virginian N5c Porthole Caboose | 40 | 130 | ___ |
| 6427-500 | PRR N5c Porthole Caboose, sky blue, from Girls Set | 35 | 125 | ___ |
| 6428 | U.S. Mail Boxcar | 10 | 105 | ___ |
| 6429 | DL&W Work Caboose | 50 | 175 | ___ |
| 6430 | Flatcar with trailers | 8 | 38 | ___ |
| 6431 | Flatcar with vans and tractor, *66* (cellophane) | 50 | 175 | ___ |
| 6436-500 | Lehigh Valley Open Quad Hopper, lilac, from Girls Set | 30 | 130 | ___ |
| 6440 | Flatcar with vans | | 20 | ___ |
| 6446-25 | N&W Covered Quad Hopper | | 38 | ___ |
| 6446-60 | Lehigh Valley Covered Quad Hopper | 125 | 400 | ___ |
| 6447 | PRR N5c Porthole Caboose | 50 | 225 | ___ |
| 6448 | Exploding Target Range Boxcar | 8 | 35 | ___ |
| 6452 | Pennsylvania Gondola | | 45 | ___ |
| X6454 | Santa Fe, NYC, or Baby Ruth Boxcar | 5 | 27 | ___ |
| X6454 | PRR Boxcar | 10 | 35 | ___ |
| X6454 | PRR Boxcar (classic, overstamped 3464 box) | 10 | 35 | ___ |
| X6454 | SP Boxcar | 10 | 35 | ___ |
| X6454 | Erie Boxcar | 10 | 35 | ___ |
| 6456 | Lehigh Valley Short Hopper | | 10 | ___ |
| 6456-75 | Lehigh Valley Short Hopper | 25 | 100 | ___ |
| 6460 | Bucyrus Erie Crane Car | 10 | | ___ |
| 6462-25 | NYC Gondola, green | | 30 | ___ |
| 6462-500 | NYC Gondola, pink, from Girls Set | 30 | 110 | ___ |
| 6463 | Rocket Fuel 2-D Tank Car | 20 | 35 | ___ |
| 6464-1 | Western Pacific Boxcar | | 65 | ___ |
| 6464-25 | Great Northern Boxcar | 5 | 45 | ___ |
| 6464-50 | M&StL Boxcar | | 25 | ___ |
| 6464-100 | Western Pacific Boxcar | 15 | 65 | ___ |

## BOXES

| | | Good (P-5) | Exc (P-7) | Cond/$ |
|---|---|---|---|---|
| 6464-125 | NYC Pacemaker Boxcar | 15 | 63 | _____ |
| 6464-150 | Missouri Pacific Boxcar | 10 | 40 | _____ |
| 6464-175 | Rock Island Boxcar | | 90 | _____ |
| 6464-200 | Pennsylvania Boxcar | | 55 | _____ |
| 6464-250 | Western Pacific Boxcar (orange picture with label) | 63 | 315 | _____ |
| 6464-250 | Western Pacific Boxcar, *54* (orange picture for 6464-100) | 50 | 150 | _____ |
| 6464-250 | Western Pacific Boxcar (cellophane) | 25 | 110 | _____ |
| 6464-300 | Rutland Boxcar, *55* | 24 | 165 | _____ |
| 6464-325 | B&O Sentinel Boxcar | | 200 | _____ |
| 6464-425 | New Haven Boxcar | 5 | 20 | _____ |
| 6464-450 | Great Northern Boxcar | 15 | 53 | _____ |
| 6464-475 | B&M Boxcar | 5 | 62 | _____ |
| 6464-500 | Timken Boxcar | 5 | 33 | _____ |
| 6464-510 | NYC Pacemaker Boxcar | 80 | 275 | _____ |
| 6464-515 | MKT Boxcar | | 250 | _____ |
| 6464-650 | D&RGW Boxcar (cellophane) | 15 | 39 | _____ |
| 6464-725 | New Haven Boxcar (Hagerstown checkerboard) | 25 | 80 | _____ |
| 6464-825 | Alaska Boxcar | 90 | 300 | _____ |
| 6464-900 | NYC Boxcar | 7 | 30 | _____ |
| 6465 | Gulf 2-D Tank Car, black (classic) | 10 | 40 | _____ |
| 6465-60 | Gulf 2-D Tank Car, gray | 5 | 15 | _____ |
| 6465-110 | Cities Service 2-D Tank Car (orange perforated) | 20 | 93 | _____ |
| 6465-160 | Lionel Lines Tank Car (orange picture) | 188 | 250 | _____ |
| 6465 | Sunoco 2-D Tank Car (classic, overstamped 2465 box) | 25 | | _____ |
| 6465 | Sunoco 2-D Tank Car (classic, overstamped 6555 box) | 20 | | _____ |
| 6465 | Sunoco 2-D Tank Car (orange picture, 6464-900 label) | 100 | | _____ |
| 6465-60 | Sunoco 2-D Tank Car (classic) | 30 | | _____ |
| 6465-85 | Lionel Lines 2-D Tank Car (orange perforated) | 50 | 80 | _____ |
| 6466W | Lionel Lines Tender | 8 | 25 | _____ |
| 6468 | B&O Auto Boxcar, tuscan (marked "X") | 35 | 103 | _____ |
| 6472 | Refrigerator Car | 5 | 15 | _____ |
| 6475 | Pickles Vat Car (orange picture) | | 83 | _____ |
| 6476 | Lehigh Valley Short Hopper | | 15 | _____ |
| 6476-85 | Lehigh Valley Short Hopper | 20 | 70 | _____ |
| 6482 | Refrigerator Car | 5 | 55 | _____ |
| 6500 | Flatcar with Bonanza airplane | 50 | 175 | _____ |
| 6517 | Lionel Lines Bay Window Caboose | 10 | 50 | _____ |
| 6517-75 | Erie Bay Window Caboose | 35 | 108 | _____ |
| 6517-1966 | Bay Window Caboose (TCA) | 20 | 75 | _____ |
| 6518 | Transformer Car | 17 | 56 | _____ |
| 6519 | Allis-Chalmers Flatcar (classic) | 25 | 50 | _____ |
| 6519 | Allis-Chalmers Flatcar (orange perforated) | 20 | 118 | _____ |
| 6520 | Searchlight Car | 10 | 50 | _____ |
| 6530 | Firefighting Instruction Car | 10 | 50 | _____ |
| 6536 | M&StL Open Quad Hopper | | 40 | _____ |
| 6544 | Missile Firing Car | 20 | 58 | _____ |

## BOXES

| | | Good<br>(P-5) | Exc<br>(P-7) | Cond/$ |
|---|---|---|---|---|
| 6555 | Sunoco 1-D Tank Car | | 25 | ___ |
| 6556 | MKT Stock Car | 50 | 275 | ___ |
| 6557 | SP-type Caboose | 15 | 68 | ___ |
| 6560-25 | Bucyrus Erie Crane Car (Hagerstown checkerboard) | 14 | 55 | ___ |
| 6560-25 | Bucyrus Erie Crane Car (all other boxes) | 12 | 40 | ___ |
| 6562-1 | NYC Gondola, gray | 8 | 23 | ___ |
| 6562-25 | NYC Gondola, red | 5 | 20 | ___ |
| 6562-50 | NYC Gondola, black | 10 | 40 | ___ |
| 6572 | REA Reefer (classic) | | 55 | ___ |
| 6572 | REA Reefer (orange picture) | 5 | 25 | ___ |
| 6646 | Lionel Lines Stock Car | 5 | 26 | ___ |
| 6657 | Rio Grande SP-type Caboose | 25 | 175 | ___ |
| 6660 | Boom Car | | 65 | ___ |
| 6736 | Detroit & Mackinac Open Quad Hopper | 30 | 150 | ___ |
| 6800 | Flatcar with airplane | 33 | 88 | ___ |
| 6800-60 | Airplane, separate sale | 100 | 225 | ___ |
| 6801-60 | Boat, separate sale | 30 | 100 | ___ |
| 6803 | Flatcar with USMC tank and sound truck | | 95 | ___ |
| 6804 | Flatcar with USMC trucks | | 80 | ___ |
| 6805 | Atomic Energy Disposal Flatcar | 30 | 130 | ___ |
| 6806 | Flatcar with USMC trucks | | 173 | ___ |
| 6809 | Flatcar with USMC trucks | | 75 | ___ |
| 6814 | Rescue Caboose | 20 | 124 | ___ |
| 6816 | Flatcar with Allis-Chalmers bulldozer | 50 | 185 | ___ |
| 6816-100 | Allis-Chalmers bulldozer | 125 | 400 | ___ |
| 6817 | Flatcar with Allis-Chalmers motor scraper | 50 | 208 | ___ |
| 6822 | Searchlight Car | 5 | 25 | ___ |
| 6823 | Flatcar with IRBM missiles | 15 | 50 | ___ |
| 6826 | Flatcar with Christmas trees | | 60 | ___ |
| 6827 | Flatcar with Harnischfeger power shovel | | 130 | ___ |
| 6828 | Flatcar with Harnischfeger crane (cellophane, no crane kit box) | 50 | 170 | ___ |
| 6828 | Flatcar with Harnischfeger crane (orange picture, no crane kit box) | 10 | 40 | ___ |
| 6828-100 | Harnischfeger Crane, separate sale | 10 | 50 | ___ |
| 6844 | Missile Carrying Car | 20 | 48 | ___ |
| 11268 | Military Set | | 120 | ___ |
| 11560 | *Texas Special* Set | 15 | | ___ |
| 12760 | Berkshire Freight Set | | 400 | ___ |
| 12780 | Santa Fe Passenger Set | | 500 | ___ |
| 12820 | Virginian Train Master Freight Set | | 280 | ___ |
| 13008 | Super O Introductory Set | | 60 | ___ |
| 13018 | Santa Fe Space-age Military Set | | 1200 | ___ |
| 13058 | Santa Fe Space-age Military Set | | 400 | ___ |
| 13088 | Santa Fe Passenger Set | | 1500 | ___ |
| 13098 | Steam Freight Set | | 300 | ___ |
| 13118 | Berkshire Freight Set | | 250 | ___ |
| 13128 | Santa Fe Space-age Military Set | | 650 | ___ |
| 13150 | Hudson Freight Set | | 900 | ___ |

# ABBREVIATIONS

## Descriptions

| | |
|---|---|
| **AAR** | Association of American Railroads (truck type) |
| **AEC** | Atomic Energy Commission |
| **CC** | Command Control |
| **DD** | Double-door |
| **EMD** | Electro-Motive Division |
| **ETD** | End-of-train device |
| **FARR** | Famous American Railroad Series |
| **FF** | Fallen Flag Series |
| **FM** | Fairbanks-Morse |
| **GE** | General Electric |
| **LL** | Lionel Lines |
| **M.O.W.** | Maintenance-of-way |
| **MU** | Multiple unit (commuter cars) |
| **O** | Lionel gauge (1¼" between outside rails) |
| **OO** | Lionel gauge (¾" between outside rails) |
| **PFE** | Pacific Fruit Express |
| **REA** | Railway Express Agency |
| **SSS** | Service Station Special |
| **std** | Standard gauge (2⅛" between outside rails) |
| **std O** | Standard O (scale length and dimension) |
| **TMCC** | TrainMaster Command Control |
| **USMC** | United States Marine Corps |
| **1-D** | One dome |
| **2-D** | Two dome |
| **3-D** | Three dome |

# ABBREVIATIONS

## Railroad names

| | |
|---|---|
| **ACL** | Atlantic Coast Line |
| **ATSF** | Atchison, Topeka & Santa Fe |
| **B&A** | Boston & Albany |
| **BAR** | Bangor & Aroostook |
| **B&LE** | Bessemer & Lake Erie |
| **B&M** | Boston & Maine |
| **BN** | Burlington Northern |
| **BNSF** | Burlington Northern Santa Fe |
| **B&O** | Baltimore & Ohio |
| **C&IM** | Chicago & Illinois Midland |
| **C&EI** | Chicago & Eastern Illinois |
| **CB&Q** | Chicago, Burlington & Quincy |
| **CMStP&P** | Chicago, Milwaukee, St. Paul & Pacific |
| **CN** | Canadian National |
| **CNJ** | Central of New Jersey |
| **C&IM** | Chicago & Illinois Midland |
| **C&NW** | Chicago & North Western |
| **C&O** | Chesapeake & Ohio |
| **CP** | Canadian Pacific |
| **D&H** | Delaware & Hudson |
| **DL&W** | Delaware, Lackawanna & Western |
| **DM&IR** | Duluth, Missabe & Iron Range |
| **D&RGW** | Denver & Rio Grande Western |
| **D&TS** | Detroit & Toledo Shore Line |
| **DT&I** | Detroit, Toledo & Ironton |
| **EJ&E** | Elgin, Joliet & Eastern |
| **Erie-Lack.** | Erie-Lackawanna |
| **FEC** | Florida East Coast |
| **GM&O** | Gulf, Mobile & Ohio |
| **GN** | Great Northern |
| **GTW** | Grand Trunk Western |
| **IC** | Illinois Central |
| **ICG** | Illinois Central Gulf |
| **KCS** | Kansas City Southern |
| **L&N** | Louisville & Nashville |
| **LIRR** | Long Island Railroad |
| **LNAC** | Louisville, New Albany & Corydon |